Anna Laetitia Barbauld

Bathsua Makin

Mary Robinson

Anne, Lady Fanshawe

"Ephelia"

Charlotte Smith

Catherine Macaulay

Elizabeth Carter

Elizabeth Nihell

A Dictionary of
British and American
Women Writers
1660–1800

A Dictionary of British and American Women Writers 1660–1800

Edited by

JANET TODD

Rowman & Allanheld
PUBLISHERS

For Betty Rizzo

ROWMAN & ALLANHELD

Published in the United States of America in 1985
by Rowman & Allanheld, Publishers
(A division of Littlefield, Adams & Company)
81 Adams Drive, Totowa, New Jersey 07512

Library of Congress Cataloging in Publication Data
Main entry under title:
A Dictionary of British and American women writers, 1660–
   1800.

   Includes index.
   1. Women authors, English—18th century—Biography.
2. Women authors, English—Early modern, 1500–1700—Biography.   3. Women authors, American—Colonial period,
ca. 1600–1775—Biography.   4. Women authors, American—
1783–1850—Biography.   5. English literature—Women
authors—Bio-bibliography.   6. English literature—Women
authors—History and criticism.   7. American literature—
Women authors—Bio-bibliography.   8. American literature—
Women authors—History and criticism.   I. Todd, Janet M.,
1942–
PR113.D5   1984   820′.9′9287   [B]   84-2123
ISBN 0-8476-7125-9

85 86 87 / 10 9 8 7 6 5 4 3 2 1
Printed in the United States of America

Contents

Preface and Acknowledgments

The Dictionary aims to stimulate research into female literary history and to indicate the wealth and abundance of female writing. A study of older reference works, such as the *Dictionary of National Biography* or the *Dictionary of American Biography*, would lead one to conclude that women did not become writers until the Victorian era. This conclusion is reinforced by most histories of 18th-century literature in English, for the emphasis on the Augustan tradition—of Pope, Swift, Johnson, and Fielding—has obscured the fact that large numbers of women were writing plays, poems, and novels primarily in the opposing "sentimental" mode. In the same way, the religious concentration on Anglican divines has tended to hide the activities of Quakers and other nonconformists who encouraged women to become publicly polemical. This volume focuses on the years 1660 to 1800, a period during which authorship changed from an indication of loose moral character into an economically viable and respected occupation for women.

Some of the authors treated here, such as Fanny Burney and Ann Radcliffe, are well known; others, for instance Helen Maria Williams and Anna Seward, are less so; still others, famous in their time if one can judge by their numerous titles and editions, exist only in catalogues and closed shelves. The two major purposes of this book are to illuminate the forgotten writers—aristocratic, middle, and working class—and to re-present the major or accepted ones in the light not only of new scholarship but of new consciousness. The witty and gracious Elizabeth Thomas needs to be remembered other than as the slut and dunce of Pope's presentation; Mary Wollstonecraft, listed in the *DNB* as Mrs. Godwin

despite her bearing the title for only a few months out of her 38 years, should receive better treatment than the wish "that her love-affairs had been more delicate"; while the skillful memoirist Laetitia Pilkington deserves rescue from Swift's label of "the most profligate whore in either Kingdom."

The number of women who wrote during the Restoration and 18th century was enormous; some are listed in bibliographies and catalogues, and more are hidden in manuscript collections and in anonymity. Originally this book was to have been in two parts: the first, descriptive entries on the major and representative authors; the second, a list of all other writers, including those whose works were difficult or impossible to obtain and whose life stories were unknown. The new *Eighteenth-Century Short Title Catalogue*, however, makes isolation of women writers—at least those who can boast title pages—a relatively easy matter, so the list has been omitted here. At the same time, it seemed important to include, however briefly, many obscure women whose desultory writing could not claim literary importance, but whose very existence enlarged the conception of the writing woman, her achievements and peculiar difficulties. The book has thus grown to considerable inclusiveness.

The names of women given entries have been taken from many sources; for example, from the National Union Catalogue and the catalogues of the British, Bodleian, Cambridge University, Princeton University, New York Public, and Beinecke libraries. They also come from reference works such as the *Dictionary of National Biography*, the *Dictionary of American Biography*, the *Oxford Companion to American Literature, Notable American Women*

1607–1950, American Women Writers, Charles Evans's *American Bibliography,* Dorothy Blakey's list of Minerva Press authors, Robert Watt's *Biblitheca Britannica* (a listing of books before 1827), Collier's *Great Historical Dictionary,* the catalogue of the Buxton Forman book collection (1867; British Library), Averil Mackenzie-Grieve's *The Great Accomplishment,* concerning colonizing women, Sarah Tytler and J.L. Watson's *Songstresses of Scotland,* Pattie Cowell's *Women Poets in Pre-Revolutionary America,* and the recent *Eighteenth-Century British Books—An Author Union Catalogue.* Some have come from contemporary compilations; for example from George Ballard's *Memoirs of Several Ladies of Great Britain, Who Have Been Celebrated for Their Writings or Skill in the Learned Languages Arts and Sciences* (1752), which listed 63 intellectual women, John Duncombe's *Feminiad* (1754), and the useful sketch in the *Gentleman's Magazine,* in which, through means of a dream, the author argues that there are "female publications, on every subject, sufficient for a female perusal" and provides a handy catalogue as evidence. All bibliographies and catalogues are, however, limited; the modern ones include mainly women who wrote pieces lengthy enough to appear with title sheets and omit those who contributed the odd poem to journals, perhaps with initials only or under the coy sign of "by a lady." Contemporary lists have less concern for publication but they tend to concentrate on the genteel; Ballard's ladies include no Quaker pamphleteers, however doctrinally learned.

The criteria for inclusion here are difficult to formulate. Usually a reference book follows scholarship; in this area, however, there has been relatively little criticism, and the vast majority of 18-century writers has therefore demanded primary decisions. All compilers would, I imagine, include Lady Mary Wortley Montagu or Ann Yearsley, but to select from Methodist letter writers or Dissenting spiritual autobiographers is more difficult. Actual publication between 1660 and 1800 would seem to be an essential qualification, since publication by the authors or by their friends or relatives before 1800 would suggest that they were indeed regarded as authors in their own time or shortly afterward. But, in fact, publication is a less useful guide for women writers than for men, since certain exalted ladies felt a disgrace in publication, and delicacy sometimes kept the middle-class woman out of print. And since publication tended to come from women in accepted roles, as a criterion it gave disproportionate importance to authors of religious works aiming to present the pious wife or mother and to elevate the reader. Discouraged from many literary genres, such as the philosophical tract, the picaresque novel, or the epic, women excelled in the very ones least represented in print, especially the personal letter, and a case might be made for finding women's greatest literary achievement in this private genre. It is of course private only to a degree since, quite frequently, an unpublished Bluestocking letter would pass through as many hands as a printed miscellany of poems. So the published and unpublished are included: Mary Delany and Frances Boscawen with their witty, entertaining, or gossipy letters; Anna Green Winslow with her personal diary; and professional writers like Charlotte Smith or Delarivière Manley.

Dates too are problematic. The arbitrary boundaries of 1660 to 1800, more appropriate for Britain than for America, have meant the elimination of women from groups with which they are normally associated. So Jane Austen, who wrote in the 1790s but did not at that time put her work in final form, is eliminated, but Maria Edgeworth is included, since she published significant works before and after 1800. The dates also divide certain groups, such as the gothic novelists associated with William Lane's Minerva Press, which was at the height of its popularity in 1800.

Of women who wrote, published or unpublished, between 1660 and 1800, I have tried to include examples from all geographic areas and genres, sufficient for informed sociological and literary generalizations to be made. Inevitably, then, a kind of affirmative action has operated; a higher proportion of minorities than of majorities is represented, of Americans than of the far more numerous British, and of peasant poets than of middle-class sentimental writers. I have included the very few women authors on science, cooking, and childbirth. The first show that in exceptional circumstances, usually the existence of a scientific male relative, women could enter the scientific community, while the last two show that women were recognized as both audience and mentor in certain "female" areas. I have included no foreign language writers, other than the influential Dutch scholar

Anna Maria van Schurman, reputedly the most accomplished woman of 17th-century Europe and correspondent of Bathsua Makin, whom she greatly impressed. I have included translators only when their works were important: Mary Collyer with her influential Richardsonian rendering of Marivaux, and not Catherine Collignon, who translated a French biographical dictionary. Also omitted are functional writers, such as catalogue compilers for libraries and estates, and women testifying in divorce cases.

The main problems in selection have come with the largest groupings. The many Quaker pamphleteers who are omitted, for example, are of great interest to a student of family or piety, but the points they make are repeated by the writers who are included, and the general circumstances (particular ones are usually hidden) are duplicated again and again. So the pitiful Alice Curwen with her *Relation of the Labour, Travail and Suffering of That Faithful Servant . . .* (1680) is left out, as is the more robust Hannah Allen, with her *Satan His Methods and Malice Baffled. A Narrative of God's Gracious Dealings with That Choice Christian Mrs. Hannah Allen. (Afterwards Married to Mr. Hatt)* (1683), along with the many fulminators against unhallowed British towns and their inadequate inhabitants. As representatives of these women I have included Judith Boulbie, who takes Ireland to task, especially Londonderry, and who participated in the important publication from the women's meetings in York; Ann Docwra, whose six works discover Satan in Cambridge and the established Church and give love and good advice to old Friends; Rebecca Travers, who argued doctrine and preached the Inner Light; Elizabeth Hooten, one of George Fox's first converts; Mary Pennyman, who tumbled over the accepted edge into idiosyncrasy; and Margaret Fell, the most influential Quaker woman of her time. From the Minerva novelists writing before 1800 I have selected the most successful in terms of art or popularity, the imitators of Ann Radcliffe's moody scenery, such as Emily Clark, Elizabeth Helme, and Mary Charlton, and of the Radcliffean mingling of sensationalism and morality, such as Regina Maria Roche and the conveniently named Mary Anne Radcliffe. The prolific are also included: Eliza Parsons, who wrote one of Jane Austen's "horrid" novels, and Anna Maria Mackenzie, with her reputed 28 volumes. Most of such novelists ring the changes on conventions, but each has some distinction of emphasis—Mrs. Burke's languishing heroines, Maria Hunter's Burney-like satirical vignettes, Ann Ker's neurotic characters, or Mary Meeke's Cinderella plots, beloved of Thomas Babbington Macaulay.

The Minerva Press exemplifies many of the scholarly problems with ascription and identification in the 18th century, which are exaggerated in the case of women. Some publishers, including William Lane, had unscrupulous methods whereby, for example, a book might be issued under several title pages so that an author at first glance appears more copious than she was. Novels similarly titled might be ascribed to several authors, and book-dealers could capitalize on similarities in names. The fame of Ann Radcliffe tempted the publisher to allow Mary Anne Radcliffe to be confused with her, a confusion intensified by the existence of the polemical Mary Ann Radcliffe, apparently distinct from both. Editions were often postdated so that a work might remain "novel" longer, a practice noted by the *Critical Review* in the 1780s, while later editions were often sold before early ones to signify a bogus popularity. Copyright chaos adds to the problem; toward the end of the 18th century when demand for fiction grew exponentially, books were pirated among England, America, and Ireland. Rearrangements, revisions, and translations were published with impunity as new works; in 1772 the *Monthly Review* exposed three examples of "the shameless plunder of superannuated and worthless novels."

By the 1790s most books were signed, although women novelists frequently preferred to remain unidentified, and this female propensity to anonymity is one of the trials of 18th-century scholarship. Sometimes women *were* careful to identify themselves through the various translations, especially when they stressed misery. So *The Old Maid* of 1771, written in the distress following a husband's abandonment, is clearly labeled "by Mrs. Skinn, late Miss Masterman of York"; but even her works have been concealed, for her obituary mentions other novels now unknown. Fanny Burney, Frances Brooke, and Clara Reeve all published anonymously at first, although they later acknowledged their works; Laetitia Hawkins, however, claimed she wrote many volumes of novels but, since she did not publicly own up to them by name, they are now difficult to trace, while Anna Maria

Mackenzie, who may be pursued through pseudonyms, has had only 16 of her 28 volumes positively identified. As well as evasion, anonymity might be achieved by a plethora of names, whereby one woman was touted by a publisher as several authors.

Not only novelists constitute the problem. In the Restoration, "Ariadne" the dramatist, who perhaps authored several plays, has not been identified. Her reticence might have shared the motives of Mariana Starke nearly a century later who, in the preface to *The Sword of Peace* (1789), justified anonymity by the assumption that a public reputation for wit destroyed a woman's social standing. Even earlier than "Ariadne" the playwright Elizabeth Polwhele perhaps intended no concealment; yet she has only now emerged with the ascription to her of *The Faithful Virgins* in the Bodleian Library and the discovery of *The Frolicks* (1671). Dorothy Jordan, songwriter and long-time mistress of the Duke of Clarence, concealed her verses so well that it is still difficult to find them; the responsible governess Jane Warton in the 1780s published her quietly rebellious advice books with the utmost discretion; and Charlotte Forman, a professional author of the 1760s and 1770s, withheld her name from her translations and political writings.

Sometimes men appropriated women either through names or works. The scandalous lives of the Restoration Mary Carleton and the actress Sophia Baddeley may have been written by men for gain or blackmail. Since women writers were all the rage by the end of the century, since the fiction public was regarded as largely female, and since notices were felt to be more lenient for the "fair sex," men may have written under female pseudonyms—certainly reviewers suspected this to be the case. Undoubtedly, though, women lost more works than they gained by subterfuge. The extremely popular 17th-century book *The Whole Duty of Man* was once ascribed to Lady Pakington, who clearly had the ability to write it, the cultured circumstances to provoke it, and all the appearance of having authored it, since her daughter showed witnesses the original manuscript; yet 19th-century scholars, perhaps uneasy at so notable a book from a female pen, judged her to be merely the copyist of another's work and claimed the book for men. Hetty Wright's poems may have been ascribed to her father by her brother, John Wesley, while Ann Eden's verse on *Werther* was once

attributed to John Armstrong. Despite the *DNB*'s attempts to dematerialize her, Elizabeth Steele is proved no male ghost-writer's fantasy. Often, false attribution was due to women's insouciance: the poet Judith Madan cared much about her writing but nothing about its publication, and allowed Pope to associate her works with whomever he willed.

Some of the problems of authorship I have tried to solve. I have endeavored to keep out transvestites, thus omitting authors about whose female identity there is considerable doubt; for example, the supposedly Amerindian princess Unca Eliza Winkfield, whose autobiography, published first in England in 1767, is typical more of that country's sentimental fiction than of the American captivity narrative it professes to be. I have, however, included Esther Burr despite the spurious nature of many of her writings. I have tried to disentangle the several Bowdlers, Plumptres, Charltons, and scandalous duchesses; Philippina Burton has, I hope, been distinguished from Elizabeth Rolt, despite the similarity in their book titles, now confused in libraries, including Yale's. Some errors undoubtedly remain, and many women may still be attenuated or fragmented. Charlotte MacCarthy and Charlotte Forman may or may not be the public and private aspects of one Anglo-Irishwoman.

The Entries

Writers are listed under their most commonly used names or titles or the name they employed professionally, and then cross-referenced from their married or family names, if these were also used in their literary lives. At the cost of marrying women prematurely or keeping them protractedly single, I have retained one name throughout an entry. Fanny Burney is treated as Burney in the main entry and listed also as D'Arblay. For consistency, aristocrats are mainly given their titles and cross-referenced for surnames, if these were employed. Margaret Cavendish, Duchess of Newcastle, appears, first, as Newcastle and also under Cavendish. Since women tended to keep their most august title despite later, less illustrious marriages, the primary reference is to that title. An example is the Duchess of Leinster, who appeared to remain so after wedding Mr. Ogilvie, her sons' tutor. Since common American practice is to retain the family name as a middle one after marriage, I have kept both when evidence suggests they were used. The practice was far less common among the British; I have initially listed only a single British surname, although in both cases I have added in square brackets all other names and variants used by the writer and not mentioned in the text. I have departed from British usage for British women only when a writer was well known under two names, and when confusion might arise from the dropping of one: Hester Thrale Piozzi and Hester Mulso Chapone are examples. Although it is frequently difficult in this period to separate British and American writers, I have labeled "American" those who have a very substantial experience of America; unmarked writers are British.

Each entry consists of biographical detail where available, culled from biographies, other reference works such as the *Dictionary of National Biography* and *A Biographical Dictionary of Actors, Actresses, Musicians, Dancers, Managers & Other Stage Personnel in London 1660–1800*, being edited by Philip H. Highfill, Jr., Kalman A. Burnim and Edward A. Langhans, and materials like *Horace Walpole's Correspondence* (1965–80); but mainly it derives from the women's writing itself, especially from prefaces, and from obituaries and critical notices. Entries list all or most of the known works of the author and usually provide exemplification of style, together with a short assessment of the work and a statement of themes and major genres. To keep the book at manageable length and since works are mentioned in the texts, no final bibliography is given. No reference is made to 20th-century studies because, while most of the writers here are not mentioned at all in modern times, the ones who are, mainly novelists, figure in a few compendious works, for example, J.M.S. Tompkins's *The Popular Novel in English 1770–1800* (1932), E.A. Baker's *History of the English Novel* vol. V (1932), Philippe Séjourné's *Aspects généraux du roman féminin en Angleterre de 1740 à 1800* (1966), and Pierre Fauchery's *La Destinée féminine dans le roman européen du dix-huitième siècle 1713–1807* (1972). Bibliographies of some women are readily available in *An Annotated Bibliography of Twentieth-Century Critical Studies of Women and Literature, 1660–1800* (1977), by Paula Backscheider, Felicity Nussbaum, and Philip B. Anderson. Critical comment from the period is included here, especially from the major journals such as the *Monthly Review*, the *Critical Review*, the *Gentleman's Magazine*, and the *Analytical Review*. Certain works turn women into examples of womanly types, and these works have also been mentioned in the appropriate entries; satiric examples are *The Unsex'd Females* by Richard Polwhele (1798) and "The Vision of Liberty" from the *Anti-Jacobin Review* (1801), while eulogistic ones include Duncombe's *Feminiad* and George Ballard's *Memoirs* of learned ladies.

I should like to thank all the contributors, especially those who, like Margaret Patterson, Lynne Friedli, the students of Robert Mahony at the Catholic University of Washington, D.L. Lantz, Robin Jarvis, and the obliging and thorough contributors from City College, New York, have taken on, with considerable haste, the investigation of little-known women. I must thank, too, Barbara Brandon Schnorrenberg for her wealth of advice on minor writers; Ra Foxton and Gayle Trusdel Pendleton for graciously providing much information on 17th-century religious writers and late 18th-century political ones, respectively; Mary Anne Bendixen and Patricia Addis for invaluable help on content; Maureen Mulvihill, who argued persuasively for the inclusion of Anna Maria van Schurman; and Joyce Fullard, Germaine Greer, and the Tulsa Center for the Study of Women's Literature (T.C.S.W.L.), who shared research on many minor poets. I feel particular gratitude to the John Simon Guggenheim Foundation, which allowed me a productive year in Cambridge in 1981–82, when I worked on part of the book. I am extremely grateful also to the secretaries of the English departments of Douglass College, Rutgers University, and of the University of Southampton, who kindly typed and retyped a seemingly endless supply of entries and lists. My main debt in terms of support, interest, and scholarship in this occasionally overwhelming project cannot easily be contained in a sentence and is acknowledged in the dedication.

PHOTO CREDITS

Contributors

Patricia Addis
Sandra Adickes
Halima Akhtar

Paula R. Backscheider
Marleen Barr
Fredrica K. Bartz
Gillian Beer
Mary Anne Bendixen
June Bobb
Francis J. Bosha
Gayle Boss-Koopman
Sylvia Bowerbank
Gae Brack
Donna Brodie
Marilyn Butler

C. Clark
Grace Isobel Clark
Kathleen Conahan
Nancy Cotton
Pattie Cowell
David M. Craig
Carmen Cramer

Marlies K. Danziger
Mary De Jong
Kathryn Zabelle Derounian
Margaret Duggan

Ann Willardson Engar
Julia L. Epstein
William H. Epstein

Robin Riley Fast
Moira Ferguson
Ra Foxton
Kevin Franklin
Lynne Friedli
Joyce Fullard

G. Douglas Gaddy
Elaine Ginsberg
John A. Godkin
Jane C. Gold

José Gonzales
Deborah Schneider Greenhut
Joseph P. Grome
Phyllis J. Guskin

Patrick Hanafee
Jocelyn Harris

Robin Jarvis
Janet Jones

Judith C. Kohl

D.L. Lantz
Patricia D. Lenihan
Dusky Loebel
Irma S. Lustig

Joseph P. McCallus
William McCarthy
Phyllis Black MacDonald
Ruth MacDonald
Lorraine McMullen
Mark Magnani
Leo M.J. Manglaviti
Marilyn Mason
David W. Meredith
Steven Meyers
Warren Mild
Maureen Mulvihill
Mildred Myree

Allan Nelson
Elizabeth Nelson

Margeret Patterson
Pamela Pelton
Gayle Trusdel Pendleton
Ruth Perry

J.E. Riehl
Betty Rizzo
Jennifer Rizzo
Renata Rizzo
Katharine Rogers
Ruth Rosenberg

Cora Rosenkrantz
Jill Rubenstein

William St. Clair
Ruth Salvaggio
Migdalia Sanchez
Rose Sasso
Kathryn Shevelow
Barbara Brandon Schnorrenberg
Ann B. Shteir
Margarette Smith
Jane Spencer
T.R. Steiner
Sallie M. Strange

Nancy E. Sydnor

David Temes
Janice Thaddeus
Eufemia Thompson
Janet Todd
Tulsa Center for the Study of Women's
   Literature

John A. Vance

Corintha Walker
Amelia Whitehead
Benjamin B. Williams

Linda Yoder

Introduction

Women writers were never the majority of authors in the 18th century, although disgruntled male reviewers and novelists affected to believe them so, but they did represent a substantial minority. Writing for publication, especially fiction, was one of the few growth industries at a time when more traditional female occupations from millinery to midwifery were being appropriated by men.

Women's arrival in literature was frequently seen as a threat to male hegemony: "In former times," wrote Samuel Johnson in an essay of 1753, "the pen like the sword, was considered as consigned by nature to the hands of men. . . . the revolution of years has now produced a generation of Amazons of the pen, who with the spirit of their predecessors have set masculine tyranny at defiance."

The explosion of female writing and female demand for writing had many causes, one being the growth of a rudimentary education for an increasing number of leisured women. During the 18th century the standard of living improved for the middle class in England, and women, barred from much economic activity, grew more moneyed and marginal. Traditions of female education were not strong, and convent female learning was alien; yet the Protestant emphasis on the vernacular and the importance of the individual soul, male or female, meant that women could embrace education when offered, without necessarily trespassing on the manly preserve of Latin. Enlightenment theories did little directly for women, but they did give some spirit to most subordinate groups, and the Lockean emphasis on the mind as a blank sheet suggested that female intellectual equality might be achieved with education.

Facilitating women's entry into literature as consumers and producers was the increase in magazines and newspapers, presses and circulating libraries. In the 1760s, the 14-year-old Charlotte Smith was dispatching her work to the *Lady's Magazine,* while in the 1780s and 1790s Anna Seward, Helen Maria Williams, and Jane Warton were three of the many female poets writing for periodicals. In America, where publishing outlets were much fewer than in England—Bathsheba Bowers noted the difficulty of finding a publisher—magazines played an even greater role, as the careers of Hannah Webster Foster and Sarah Wentworth Morton demonstrate.

In Britain toward the end of the century, circulating libraries demanding pulp fiction became women's primary professional lifeline, and the need for multi-volumed light gothic and sentimental fiction kept many a woman-headed household from want. Fanny Burney made £250 from *Cecilia* in 1782, but in 1796, with careful marketing, she received £2,000 for *Camilla.* Ann Radcliffe was said to have received £900 for *The Italian.* Yet Radcliffe and Burney were exceptional, and many women made only five or ten guineas from a novel; the bookseller Tom Lowndes, "the dullest rude niggardly fellow that the muses ever made to sell their works," was reported at his death in 1784 never to have given "more for a novel than one guinea" (*Cornhill Magazine,* January–June 1868).

As a commercial business for women, writing gained propriety only slowly: the playwrights and scandal romancers of the Restoration and early 18th century were often viewed as scribbling trollops, and the irregular personal lives of Aphra Behn, Susanna Centlivre, Eliza Haywood, and Delarivière Manley associated literature with licentiousness in some minds. By the end of the 18th century, authorship was respectable, if combined with delicacy of tone and life: to write for money, especially when it was needed for the care of infant children or aged parents, was a sad but entirely praiseworthy pursuit. The change meant greater professionalism, particularly for novelists, whose craft much improved, but it also implied increasing duplicity, as indicated by the endless prefaces denying literary ambition or skill.

Women were identified with their works; virtue on the page required virtue off it, and prefaces made domestic motives shape the art. Life histories in this period therefore deserve examination, and the data established here is copious enough to allow some general biographical inferences to be drawn.

Class

Class status is a problematic factor and, while it is worth noting the proportionate decline of aristocrats in literature as time passed or the intrusion of working women into middle-class letters, the experience of patriarchy uniting all women also needs emphasis. Undoubtedly it was easier for the Duchess of Newcastle to pick up her pen than for the washerwoman Mary Collier, but both bore the male label "an additional Part of the Species," and both wrote in a literary code they had little part in formulating.

Aristocrats are well represented in this *Dictionary,* for they usually enjoyed exceptional educational advantages—Lady Anne Barnard, Countess Cowper, the daughters of the Duke of Richmond, or Mary Delany, to name only a few. Apart from the Duchess of Newcastle and Lady Mary Wortley Montagu, who were regarded as deeply eccentric and embarrassing by their contemporaries, most of these ladies did not stray from the private verse or ballad, the book of instructions to daughters, and the familiar letter of friendship. Together with the women of the gentry, such as Elizabeth Montagu, they had no need to publish for money, although often, like Elizabeth Carter, they enjoyed being pressed into publication, and their lively letters were frequently printed.

The 18th-century vogue of the untrained poet and primitive songster, predicated on sentimental theories of natural goodness and spontaneous art, allowed poor women to flourish briefly—British peasants like Elizabeth Bentley, daughter of a cordwainer and later a hawker, and the milkwomen Janet Little and Ann Yearsley, as well as the two American slaves Phillis Wheatley and Lucy Terry. Since they were inspirational, hymns and songs were felt suitable for the untutored, and Susanna Harrison, a domestic servant in the 1780s, and the Scottish ballad-singer Jean Glover each had a short fashion. The sense of being not only a peasant poet but a woman marks the otherwise conventional verse of the washerwoman Mary Collier, writing to the thresher poet Stephen Duck. His life, she suggests, is an improvement on her own, with its double oppressions of gender and class. Peasant women poets were often patronized as novelties and ignored when they palled; many of their lives provide sad reading. Ann Candler, a Suffolk poet, found her hard-won education made more intolerable the illiterate society of the workhouse, where she spent many of her years, and Ann Yearsley grew sour and embittered when spurned by her patron, Hannah More. As a lower-class novelty, it was prudent to die young: Mary Leapor, the daughter of a gardener, became a cook-maid and took to writing poetry in the 1740s; she enjoyed some success and died before she could lose it or grow tiresome to her sponsors. Occasionally there were rises through writing, but not usually of poets. During the Restoration, Jane Wiseman grew from a servant into a playwright, using the profits from her heroic drama to help establish a tavern. Daughter of a grocer, Agnes Maria Bennett became a slopseller, then an admiral's mistress, and finally a popular novelist, providing her audience with exactly what it desired.

As one would expect, the majority of writers in Britain and America had middle-class backgrounds. Some came from the lower reaches, such as Hannah Brand, the daughter of a tanner; Constantia Grierson, apprenticed to learn midwifery and married to a book-seller; or Mary Latter, who kept a linen draper's and millinery business and spent time in debtors' prison. To most writers, it was the fact of femaleness that caused prefatory humility, but the novelist Jane West in the 1790s was also much embarrassed by her lower-middle-class roots.

From the higher reaches of the middle class came some of the Bluestocking ladies—Hester Mulso Chapone, daughter of a gentleman farmer, and Hester Thrale Piozzi, wife of a rich brewer. The learned

Laetitia Hawkins was the daughter of a wealthy lawyer, and the equally scholarly Elizabeth Smith, of a banker who went bankrupt. An extremely large number of writing women, such as Frances Brooke and Mary Pix, were connected with the clergy as wives or daughters. It is clear that such women must have benefited from the habits of literature that clergymen might be presumed to have possessed, while their middling status would frequently demand that they be prepared to use their literacy for a living.

Location

It is difficult to distinguish entirely between British and American writers. Most early women labeled American were born in England: Frances Brooke, from Lincolnshire, wrote one of the earliest Canadian novels, and Susanna Haswell Rowson left England to become America's first best-selling fiction writer. Elizabeth Scott, a hymnist, began life in Norwich and ended it in Connecticut, while Mary Fisher, from Yorkshire, died in Charleston. The women traveled to America variously: Elizabeth Ashbridge arrived as an indentured servant, while Hannah Penn came as the wife of a major landowner; after being whipped in Britain, the Quaker Mary Fisher set out for America with her message of the Inner Light, only to meet similar abuse in the New World.

Yet some distinctions can be made in the literature produced on the two continents. Denied access to European metropolitan culture, the Americans tended to write in a religious mode after it had ceased to dominate in England, and much of American poetry appears doggerel compared to the sophisticated verse of educated British ladies. It is interesting that a sense of Americanness appeared early and increased considerably during the revolutionary period. So Eliza Lucas Pinckney, journeying from South Carolina to London in 1752, approved the familial image of British royalty but was amazed at its etiquette, while Abigail Adams in 1784 was appalled at English frivolity after American seriousness.

One American problem was isolation, such as Ann Bleecker's in rural New York, for example, but there were small centers of writing women, especially in Boston and Philadelphia. In the 1760s and 1770s Elizabeth Graeme Ferguson provided a meeting place for the literary, and in the 1790s Sarah Wentworth Morton gathered around her a literary and political circle. But America produced nothing like the clusters of English writing women. London was inevitably the major center, with its theaters and publishing houses, but large pockets of literary ladies appeared in the provinces as well, especially in Bath, Bristol, Norwich, or Ipswich, where, for example, Priscilla Wakefield, Elizabeth Cobbold, and Clara Reeve all became acquainted. Only Scotland produced few women authors, except for songwriters, possibly because of the greater prejudice against them there. At the end of the 18th century Elizabeth Hamilton, writing fiction in England, was still conscious of a "dangerous distinction of authorship" in the north.

Education

Apart from untutored poets, most writing women tended to have a privileged educational background. Very few benefited from organized schools, which stressed fashionable accomplishments over learning, although the children's writer Mary Martha Sherwood attended, to some purpose, the French emigré school of the St. Quintons in Reading, and Elizabeth Benger was sent to a boys' school to learn Latin. All higher institutions of learning were, of course, closed to women. The scholarly education they received usually came from male relatives or friends: the peculiarly privileged Lady Masham was the daughter of the Cambridge Platonist Ralph Cudworth, and received her philosophical instruction from John Locke, while Viscountess Conway had her brother's tutor, Henry More, as teacher and the scientist Van Helmont as guest.

Usually clergymen relatives were responsible for the instruction. Ann Francis and Elizabeth Carter were educated by their fathers in Latin, Greek, and Hebrew, and Mary Mollineux in languages and mathematics. The Whig historian Catherine Macaulay learned the history of Roman and Greek republics from her father, and Mary Astell was probably tutored by her uncle in philosophy, logic, and mathematics; Hannah More's domineering parent, knowing he could not afford dowries, trained his daughters as teachers, but stopped when he found Hannah too apt at Latin and mathematics for a female. Laetitia Hawkins was carefully brought up by her father, who forbade her speaking unless she could solve a problem or add a pertinent fact to the conversation.

Many women were autodidacts. At the end of the 18th century Matilda Betham achieved her education from her father's well-stocked library when her formal schooling was, in her view, designed to teach "sewing, and prevent a too strict application to books." Although she attended school, Sarah Fielding learned Greek and Latin through private study. Many professional writing women, needing money from translations, telescoped a linguistic education; so Mary Wollstonecraft, no prodigy of learning, acquired dictionaries and set about translating for publication from the French, Dutch, and German. Others of definite learning mastered an impressive array of languages and sciences for their own sakes: in the closing years of the 18th century Elizabeth Smith, deprived in her short peripatetic life of any fixed library, became competent in Hebrew, Arabic, and Persian, as well as mathematics.

Many women were aware of the pitfalls of self-teaching and grumbled about their inadequate instruction and the absence of system, which they assumed was delivered only by institutional learning. Widely read in Enlightenment authors, Abigail Adams still stressed her neglected education, and women from Aphra Behn onward felt keenly their lack of the masculine scholarship of Latin and its rhetorical codes of writing.

The main forbidden area of learning for females was natural science, into which only a few women of extraordinary opportunity ventured, although in *The Female Advocate* Mary Scott urged others to follow. Caroline Herschel, sister of an astronomer, was tutored by him to become his assistant, and she proceeded, in deep humility, to discover several nebulae and comets; Anna Blackburne became a botanist and correspondent of Linnaeus because her father had been a famous naturalist before her. Something of an anomaly, Margaret Bryan seems to have taught herself astronomy and natural philosophy, which she used to the traditional female end of educating the young. In the Restoration the Duchess of Newcastle suffered mockery—even from the equally learned and inquisitive Viscountess Conway—as she grew competent in natural science, but she was allowed to attend a meeting of the Royal Society only because of her husband's social position.

Despite their small numbers among learned ladies, whose usual competence was, as George Ballard's collection indicates, in classics and theology, the female scientists bore the brunt of male ridicule, especially in the Restoration and early 18th century. Thomas Wright mocks them loudly in his play *The Female Virtuoso's* (1693), and James Miller in *The Humours of Oxford* (1730) has his Lady Science duped, tricked, and humbled: "I am justly made a Fool for aiming to . . . move into a sphere that did not belong to me"; the hero considers women's province to be "the Dressing Room," not the study. Even a female playwright, Susanna Centlivre, while more sympathetic to the woman scientist in her *Basset Table* (1705), still fails entirely to endorse her.

Beyond specific mockery was a general antagonism to learning in ladies, as Mary Astell noted at the beginning of the 18th century: if girls managed to get an education, they were "stared upon as Monsters, censur'd, envied, and every way discouraged." Lady Mary Wortley Montagu, who well knew the difficulties of women scholars—"We are permitted no Books but such as tend to the weakening and Effeminateing the Mind, our Natural Deffects are every way indulg'd, and tis look'd upon as in a degree Criminal to improve our Reason, or fancy we have any" she wrote—yet felt compelled to echo male scorn of learned women. By mid-century it was the fashion to preach that females, if they had any learning, should conceal it; in 1750 Lady Hervey was praised by Lord Chesterfield for prudently hiding her knowledge of Latin.

One factor that influenced the amount of formal female education was religious background. Although individual clergymen fathers tutored their daughters, the Anglican Church itself did not especially stress women's education. The liberal Quakers, however, encouraged even the lower class to study the Bible and publish their views; consequently, a large group of writing women in England and America were Quakers. With their emphasis on self-scrutiny, Methodists, too, stressed the writing of spiritual records and their publication when they appeared exemplary.

But only the older established Dissenters emphasized education tending to a life of letters beyond religious polemics and autobiography; in the early part of the century, the poets Elizabeth Rowe and Mary Chandler came from Dissenting families, while in the later period Anna Laetitia Barbauld, Helen Maria Williams, Mary Hays, Amelia Opie, Maria Defleury, and Mary Wollstonecraft all benefited from Dissenting communities which helped educate them and patronized their writings.

Politics

A Dissenting background often discriminated among women in another area—political persuasion—since the struggle for Dissenting rights cradled much political reform, especially toward the last part of the 18th century. To make a political generalization about the earlier period, when politics was so much a matter of families and personalities, is difficult, but royalism and feminist leanings seem to have been loosely linked.

The early women were shadowed by the Civil War and its aftermath: Lady Fanshawe experienced poverty with her royalist family, then flourished under the favor of Charles II; Lucy Hutchinson and Celia Fiennes followed the fortunes of the defeated Puritans. In the Restoration, Aphra Behn, the midwife Elizabeth Cellier, Mary Astell, and the Countess of Winchilsea were all more or less zealous royalists; Lady Halkett gained a pension from James II, and Elinor James spent time in Newgate for her pamphlets in support of the deposed King. As the Civil War receded and Jacobitism became an issue, a similar preponderance of women were on the high royalist side: Jane Barker lamented the passing of the Stuarts, while Lady Grissel Baillie helped an imprisoned Jacobite. In the opposing camp, the intrepid Jean Elliot hoodwinked Jacobites to allow her Hanoverian father to escape to safety.

As Whigs and Tories, women were equally divided. The playwright Susanna Centlivre wrote as an ardent Whig attacking Tory corruption, and Delarivière Manley supported Tory nostalgic conservatism, suggesting that, as in the days of Aphra Behn, the court might prove the best cushion for personal irregularity. By the mid- to late 1700s, the connection of royalism and liberation seems to have broken, and most outspoken political women took to reform, allying, like Catherine Macaulay and Maria Weylar, with John Wilkes, who proposed the extension of the suffrage and supported the American cause, or with Charles James Fox, for whom Anne Damer and Georgiana, Duchess of Devonshire, canvassed.

In the later 18th century it is almost possible to distinguish political affiliation along modern lines, especially in the few years of relatively open expression between the fall of the Bastille and the British re-pressive reaction. At this time Hannah More, Fanny Burney, Hester Thrale Piozzi, Clara Reeve, Jane West, Ann Francis, Priscilla Wakefield, and Lady Wallace, who threatened the British aristocracy with a French fate if they failed to reform, could all be termed conservative in stance, since they defended the status quo and the British constitution, while deploring the effects of the French Revolution. But their views are not monolithic, and Hannah More, preaching the danger of atheism and radicalism to the poor, could stand for the new reactionary conservatism, while the older Hester Thrale Piozzi might be said to represent the Augustan Johnsonian worldview, distrusting innovation and individualism. In the years following the Reign of Terror, more liberal women veered toward conservatism. Harriet Lee was sympathetic with the moderate side of the Revolution only, while Anna Seward, a liberal Whig, and Charlotte Smith, supporter of the earlier American Revolution, approved French politics until the Jacobin bloodletting.

"The most sensible women," wrote George Dyer in 1792," are more uniformly on the side of liberty than the other sex; witness a Macaulay, a Wollstonecraft, a Barbauld, a Jebb, a Williams, and a Smith." To this list of liberal-to-radical women might be added Mary Hays, Elizabeth Inchbald, Maria Defleury, Anna Plumptre, and possibly Mary Robinson and Amelia Opie. All saw the need for British reform, and all, with various qualifications, supported the Revolution—Mary Wollstonecraft most assertively when, in her *Vindication of the Rights of Men* (1790), she took on Burke's sentimental reverence for the old regime. Along with Mary Hays, Mary Robinson, and Helen Maria Williams, Wollstonecraft led what the conventional regarded as an irregular life; for many years thereafter she riveted feminism, radicalism, and immorality in the public mind.

The backgrounds of the various political groupings were similar. Most of the women were provincial in origin although living as adults in the capital, but a larger proportion of liberals than conservatives was London-based and came from Dissenting homes. All the groups were predominantly middle class, although upper- and upper-middle-class women were more represented among the conservatives. The struggle to earn a living through writing seems to have made women dwell on the struggle for livelihood in general, and on the impediments to the advancement of both women and the poor.

It is easier to align American writers and, with some loyalist exceptions such as Janet Schaw and Helena Wells, American women generally embraced the revolutionary struggle. Hannah Griffitts paralleled America and Rome, urging her countrymen to achieve self-reliance and eschew English tea, a plea made earlier by the Quaker Milcah Martha Moore. Some highly placed ladies, such as Abigail Adams and Mercy Otis Warren, took part in debates with politically active men, although, unlike the French revolutionary women, they acted and wrote little on their own behalf. In the post-revolutionary and pragmatic period, women tended to become the conscience of the Republic and a few moved their religious exemplary role into politics: in the 1790s Sarah Porter still held to a concept of America as the New Israel, while Judith Sargent Murray urged her readers to a true Americanism that did not look to Europe.

The two revolutions, American and French, disrupted the lives of women as well as influencing their writings. The American War of Independence bankrupted Elizabeth Smith's father in the west of England and removed her only settled home, and it reduced to poverty the family of the novelist Eliza Parsons. In America its effect was more dramatic. Sometimes the distress was not especially onerous: Margaret Coghlan suffered a genteel imprisonment as a loyalist in New Jersey, and Eliza Jonge Wilkinson, trying to capture the enormity of war, complained of little more than a tight squeeze of her arm; Sally Wister in her diary shows how a young girl adapted to revolutionary disruption. But others felt more closely the effects of combat. Annis Boudinot Stockton's husband, betrayed by loyalists, was imprisoned and impoverished; Susanna Anthony suffered hardship from the British garrisoning of Newport, as well as being pained by military profanity. Eliza Lucas Pinckney in South Carolina tasted poverty for the first time in her affluent life, and the Quaker Elizabeth Sandwich Drinker records both the harrassment of Quakers and the upheaval of war. Perhaps the most distressing case was Ann Bleecker, whose life was utterly disrupted when she had to flee, her mind scarred with visions of dying relatives; at the end of the war, she grew deeply depressed and died.

The French Revolution directly affected only Mary Wollstonecraft and Helen Maria Williams, who were actually in Paris during the upheavals and were caught in the anti-British measures. Before leaving for France in 1792 Wollstonecraft was turned from a genteel writer of children's books into a political polemicist. Helen Maria Williams, translated in British eyes from a sentimental Bluestocking poet into a blood-obsessed "trollop," to use Horace Walpole's description, suffered imprisonment in Paris as a foreigner and was watched throughout the revolutionary period as a spy.

Marriage

Greatly overshadowing any civil upheavals were the domestic disasters that affected women and drove them into print for vindication or money. As the century and a half wore on, spinsters grew in number, especially after 1780, and Elizabeth Hamilton, Charlotte Brooke, and Lady Mary Coke all seem to have chosen the single life, so longingly imaged by Richardson's Clarissa. Certainly it had many advantages when coupled with the affluence Jane Austen knew to be essential for the unmarried; Lady Louisa Stuart, although not rich, maintained her own establishment and seems to have enjoyed her life.

Some women no doubt had spinsterhood thrust upon them through the role of dutiful daughter: Charlotte Brooke devoted herself to her ailing novelist father; blind Priscilla Poynton was subjected to an aged parent and deprived of books; while Hester Thrale Piozzi pitied Ellis Cornelia Knight's life with her strange old drunken mother. For some women the single life represented freedom—Jane Elizabeth Moore in 1796 lamented being "obligated to any man breathing"—while Catherine Talbot complained of the appearance without the reality of being free that spinsterhood gave to the genteel woman.

The majority of women married at some time in their lives, and some of the unions, especially the childless ones like those of the Duchess of Newcastle and the Countess of Winchilsea, were fulfilling. The domestic letters of Richard and Elizabeth Griffith charmed the contemporary public, as the short, experimental marriage of Mary Wollstonecraft and William Godwin did a later age. But the possibility of women suffering in an institution legally almost the equivalent of slavery was immense.

As Wollstonecraft depicted in *The Wrongs of Woman,* power and property were male, and any breakdown of marriage usually left the woman socially ostracized and destitute. At the same time, sentimental thought was valorizing bourgeois marriage, giving women expectations of companionship and love beyond the implications of earlier mercenary unions and beyond anything the sexual matches of youth could deliver. Writing women, especially professional ones, no doubt represented a higher incidence of failed marriages than the population as a whole; otherwise, marriage could almost be said to have broken down.

Many women, miserably matched, feared the horrors of a single existence. In 1682 the unhappily married Anne Wharton was dissuaded from leaving her husband by Bishop Burnet. Nearly a century later, Hester Thrale Piozzi stayed with her unwanted brewer, although she felt bartered, and Mary Delany, given at 17 to a drunkard of nearly 60, suffered for seven miserable years of his life. After an elopement attempt, cultured Hetty Wright was forced to marry a drunken plumber and stay with him for life.

Other women married but did not remain so. Some, like Elizabeth Montagu, were left to manage estates as affluent widows; others, like Bathsua Makin, found poverty with widowhood. A very large number separated, sometimes with considerable flamboyance, especially in the upper classes. In a few cases the wife left—few because a wife had no right of maintenance unless she had suffered intolerable cruelty, and divorce with right to remarry needed an act of Parliament and was actually feasible only for husbands of adulterous wives. Lady Elizabeth Craven left her husband and wandered scandalously around Europe in the 1780s, while Margaret Coghlan abandoned a brutal spouse to become a whore of considerable renown. In 1721 Jane Brereton left her husband because of his violent temper and compensated for this lapse by a lifetime of philanthropic activity. Against her will Susanna Cibber was married to Theophilus Cibber, whose infidelity and collusion in her seduction she had to endure; when she tried for a legal separation, he milked the situation, endeavoring to destroy her lover with suits and his wife through scandals that threatened her singing career.

The majority of separated women were ejected or abandoned, often with numerous children to support. Elizabeth Gooch was deserted in France and was imprisoned for debt. After an affluent childhood, Ann Eme-linda Skinn was left in extreme poverty and had to turn to novel writing, needlework, and teaching for support; when her husband deserted her, Ann Candler ended in the workhouse with her children. Separated from her bankrupt husband, Eliza Fenwick spent much of her sad life writing and teaching to support herself, her children, and her grandchildren; Charlotte Smith, working at translations and poetry to keep her shiftless husband and ten children, after their separation turned to novels to support her eight remaining dependents. Mary Ann Radcliffe, who wrote a pamphlet on the difficulties of unprotected middle-class women, saw her wealth squandered by her husband before they parted; she was left to provide for eight children. In America, after a dismal childhood, Margaretta Faugeres married an adventurer who wasted her fortune and left her and her daughter destitute.

Women went beyond the pale in other ways besides broken marriages. One route was a second marriage deemed inappropriate by society. Many of their friends never forgave Fanny Burney and Hester Thrale for indecorously snatching happiness from unions with foreigners, while Catherine Macaulay lost her considerable reputation as an historian by marrying a man much her junior, a mistake also made by the actress Ann Barry and by Lady Charlotte Bury, who, like Hester Thrale, upset her children with her second match. The Duchess of Leinster so riled society with her anticipated marriage that she, her fiancé, and her children all escaped to France and remained there until the scandal faded.

Other women lost respectability through seduction and scandal. The actress Dorothy Jordan was seduced by her manager. She then lived with many men including, for 20 years, the Duke of Clarence, later William IV; she died destitute. Mary Robinson as "Perdita" caught the eye of the young Prince of Wales, briefly became his mistress, and never lived it down, despite paralysis and a harsh life supporting her daughter and widowed mother. Sometimes women welcomed the gratifying or financially remunerative image scandal gave them. After her alleged seduction, possibly by Lord Chesterfield, Teresia Constantia Phillips became a courtesan and vindicated herself in print, making a substantial profit, while Viscountess Vane was eager to intrude her scandalous self into Smollett's *Peregrine Pickle.*

Different periods recoiled more or less strenuously from female irregularities. In the Restoration and early 18th century, the naughty lives of Aphra Behn, with her lovers, or Delarivière Manley, abandoned after being fooled by her cousin into a bigamous marriage, were not accepted, but neither were they shrilly condemned. For a short time in the 1790s it was possible to be sexually eccentric. Margaret Coghlan flaunted her lovers, and Mary Wollstonecraft intentionally avoided wedlock while bearing an illegitimate child. Mary Hays published a novel full of her own love letters to a man who spurned her, and Helen Maria Williams openly consorted with the traitorous John Hurford Stone. None of these women had the approval of the majority, but their very existence as a group would have been almost inconceivable in 1760.

Motives for Authorship

The marital difficulties of so many women writers provided strong inducement for writing. Several wrote for money when they became the main support of households, while others became authors to vindicate themselves when society shunned their conduct. Still others wrote because they enjoyed writing and knew themselves to be gifted poets or novelists; but very few dared give enjoyment and ambition as reasons for publication, and the prefaces almost invariably declare sad necessity of one sort or another.

The vindicating ladies were concerned to present themselves suitably, to set records aright, and to attract readers to their new images. The Restoration Lady Halkett, Henrietta Knight, and the Margravine of Anspach all wrote in this way to justify themselves. Sometimes the tone is contrite, but it often turns aggressive in theatrical memoirs. George Anne Bellamy and Charlotte Charke desired to display themselves and accuse their persecutors, as well as to vindicate conduct, while the anonymous Miss F. wrote to promote her singing career and to embarrass, perhaps to blackmail, the nobleman who had plagued her. In the 1760s Lady Pennington, admitting social but not moral sins, wrote to restore her lost reputation, and her advice book of conventional wisdom is made poignant by her earlier inability to heed it. Before turning to fiction for money, Elizabeth Gooch wrote *Appeal to the Public* (1788) from debtors' prison, telling a pathetic tale of abandonment and distress.

A more numerous band of women wrote for money. In the Restoration and early 18th century, they tended to do so with little fuss, like Aphra Behn, Jane Barker, and Delarivière Manley. But, as the sentimental passive stance grew essential for women, in their prefaces they pleaded circumstances to prevent criticism and apologize for the act of writing. Many (including Charlotte Smith, Eliza Fenwick, and Charlotte Lennox) gave children as the excuse, while others blamed a "sick husband" or "ancient" relative. Mary Latter wrote when her millinery business failed; the American Judith Sargent Murray collected her essays and plays in 1798 to make money when her husband's finances declined; and Priscilla Wakefield started her writing career at 40 when both husband and sons were in need.

Almost all the commercial writers mitigated the effrontery of authorship with a domestic image. The American novelist Sally Wood wrote to support herself in her penurious widowhood, but stressed that her writing had never intruded on "one social, or domestic duty," and Fanny Burney insisted she would sacrifice authorship to her womanly image. Jane West declared that domestic duties always preceded writing, while Samuel Johnson said admiringly of the immensely scholarly Elizabeth Carter that she could "make a pudding as well as translate Epictetus."

Allied to the urge of subordinating commercial writing to domesticity was the need to denigrate the most lucrative genre, the novel. So Sarah Green in the 1790s, supposedly the author of twelve novels, condemned her form, and Eliza Parsons, who embarked on an enormous fictional series when fire destroyed her husband's property, declared her disinclination to novelwriting. Even good writers felt obligated to protest: Elizabeth Inchbald complained of being forced to authorship, Charlotte Smith bitterly resented her dependence on her pen, and Sarah Fielding claimed she wrote because of "Distress" in her circumstances.

In 1712, the American Cotton Mather noted that, although several women wrote, "they have been patterns of humility. They have made no noise; they have sought no fame." Yet many women clearly did write for aesthetic gratification or fame. Although she later aimed at money, Fanny Burney obviously penned *Evelina* because she wanted to, and Ann Radcliffe, undoubtedly happy to pocket £500 for *The Mysteries of Udolpho,* began by writing to amuse herself.

Sentimental poets, scholars, and letter writers, like Anna Seward and Elizabeth Carter, enjoyed writing and, feeling it improper to display anxiety about publication, also enjoyed being pressed into print by friends. Delicacy prevented Lady Mary Wortley Montagu from admitting she wanted her letters published, but she failed to conceal the fact. A few robust souls said that they sought fame: the Duchess of Newcastle saw writing as the only route for ambitious women, who were denied heroism on the battlefield and power through politics. Judith Sargent Murray exhibited rare candor when she stated flatly, "I love the paths of fame."

Occupations

To swell the earnings of authorship many women took other work. Some were actresses and singers and wrote plays and songs as vehicles for themselves, like Sarah Gardner or Charlotte Charke. Susanna Cibber and Catherine Clive were primarily singers and actresses, while Maria Hunter and Mary Robinson turned to the novel when their acting careers foundered. The prudent Elizabeth Inchbald learned French while she acted and so was ready, when the stage failed her, to turn translator—which she did with considerable success. Although denied access to Anglican, Dissenting, and Methodist pulpits, women could become Quaker preachers; Elizabeth Hooten, Mary Fisher, Rebecca Travers, and Anne Camm all preached in the Restoration, as did Jane Hoskens, ordered by the Lord to Pennsylvania in 1712.

One new professional opportunity for women sprang from the proliferation of magazines needing editors and reviewers. In 1711 Delarivière Manley succeeded Swift as editor of *The Examiner,* while from 1737 to 1738 Lady Mary Wortley Montagu wrote a weekly essay pamphlet on politics, *The Nonsense of Common Sense.* Eliza Haywood ran her *Female Spectator* from 1744 to 1746, and from 1749 to the 1760s Isabella Griffith was an editor and probably a reviewer for her husband's *Monthly Review;* she was much reviled as an "antiquated female critic." Frances Brooke edited a weekly periodical—*The Old Maid*—for eight months in 1755–56; from 1760 to 1761 Charlotte Lennox worked on the *Lady's Museum,* a most valuable women's peri-odical containing serialized novels and scientific articles. Sarah Trimmer published, from 1788 to 1789, her *Family Magazine,* aimed at cottagers and servants, which abridged sermons and preached contentment. In the late 1780s Mary Wollstonecraft mistakenly thought herself the first of a new genus when she joined the *Analytical Review* as editorial assistant and later reviewer. Mary Hays wrote for the *Monthly Magazine,* and Elizabeth Inchbald became the first professional woman drama critic.

As they became more accepted as professional literary workers, women also found employment cataloguing, compiling, anthologizing, and editing. Learned ladies instigated the catalogues which formed part of the early debate on female intellectual capability. These ranged from the *Essay* in 1673 of Bathsua Makin to Mary Scott's *The Female Geniad* more than a century later. Together with the biographical dictionaries compiled by Mathilda Betham, Mary Hays, and Ann Thicknesse, they suggest an enjoyment of female achievement.

As editors, women mainly worked on family papers or friends' letters, but a few gained fame by meddling in men's affairs. The most notorious was Eugenia Stanhope, who edited the letters of her father-in-law, the Earl of Chesterfield, with their emphasis on gallantry and discretion over morality. She was much abused for their publication, which was felt to be against the late Earl's wishes, and also for allowing such pernicious views onto the market; Courtney Melmoth ironically dedicated to Stanhope his *Pupil of Pleasure,* in which a student of Chesterfield comes to a miserable end. Mary Berry more quietly edited the letters of her friend and correspondent Horace Walpole.

As well as journalism and miscellaneous literary activity, another intriguing minority occupation for writers appears to have been espionage. By the nature of the job, it is difficult to identify practitioners, but Aphra Behn and Mary Tonkin were spies, and possibly Helen Maria Williams, as well; certainly Napoleon thought so.

The majority of women seeking a profession, from Bathsua Makin in the Restoration to Mary Wollstonecraft at the close of the 18th century, fell back on the great female duty of educating the young. Many combined pedagogy with authorship of instructional treatises and manuals of advice. Some women were merely teachers, like Anna Maria Mackenzie, an assistant at a ladies' boarding school, until writing became profitable; Helena Wells, who emigrated from America, found it harder than she had expected to establish herself in teaching. Others were successful school entrepreneurs, like Bathsua Makin or the enterprising Hannah Woolley, who in the 1660s was servant, governess, schoolteacher, maker and seller of medicines, and operator of a registry and training-school for servants. In the 1750s and 1760s Hannah More and her sisters were proprietors of a successful school in Bath, as were Sophia and Harriet Lee from 1781 to 1803.

Although education was always a standby, other traditional occupations such as midwifery and millinery were dwindling. In 1798 Priscilla Wakefield noted how women were being squeezed from previously female areas like hairdressing, and in the following year Mary Ann Radcliffe remarked how few remunerative alternatives to prostitution were left for the uneducated, unsupported woman. She knew of what she spoke since, to provide for her children, she herself had been a lady's companion, governess, pastry-shop keeper, and seller of patent medicines and shoes.

For more affluent and leisured ladies, there remained the business of philanthropy. This was combined with writing by Jane Bowdler, who published her poems to benefit the Bath hospital, or by Mrs. Hale, who had her poetry printed to help a clergyman's family. Mary Astell opened a school for the poor daughters of the outpatients of the Chelsea Hospital; and Hannah More, Sarah Trimmer, and Mary Martha Sherwood all busied themselves with the Sunday school movement. When she was able, Isabella Graham, who knew poverty intimately, relieved the poor and mentally sick.

Female Groups

Much of women's philanthropy in the 18th century was aimed at other women. In addition, female friendship and networks of relationships were often a support to middle-class ladies in distress. In literature, women provided markets for each other, and the Bluestockings in particular exerted an immense power of patronage on behalf of their sex.

Many women were linked through major male writers, who gathered clusters of female authors. Swift provided a focus for Esther Johnson, Mary Barber, Mary Davys, the learned Constantia Grierson, Delarivière Manley, and Laetitia Pilkington; Samuel Richardson, much mocked for his circle of intellectual ladies with whom he visited and corresponded and whom he advised and consulted, knew Susanna Highmore and her daughter Susanna Duncombe, Hester Mulso Chapone, and Charlotte Lennox. Samuel Johnson appears to have known everyone, from aristocratic ladies like the Duchess of Devonshire, to young, aspiring writers like Fanny Burney, Hannah More, and Helen Maria Williams. Smaller groups were centered around John Wesley, who corresponded with the Countess of Huntingdon, Hannah Ball, and Anne Dutton, and around William Godwin, who knew Mary Wollstonecraft, Elizabeth Inchbald, Mary Hays, Mary Robinson, Amelia Opie, Eliza Fenwick, and Harriet Lee.

Major groupings were, however, women-generated, both provincial and metropolitan. They formed around strong female personalities such as Hannah More, Anna Laetitia Barbauld, or Anna Seward, "Swan of Lichfield," whose resolute literary image slightly appalled the young Mary Martha Sherwood. Or they settled around major hostesses such as Helen Maria Williams in Paris, or the much mocked Lady Miller holding poetical court at Batheaston, attended by Fanny Burney, Anna Seward, Mary Delany, and Hester Thrale Piozzi. In America smaller clusters of corresponding and visiting women emerged. Hannah Griffitts, Susanna Wright, Deborah Logan, and Elizabeth Graeme Ferguson wrote to each other about their poetry; Abigail Adams and Mercy Otis Warren discussed politics; and Sarah Osborn and Susanna Anthony exchanged lugubrious spiritual notes in Rhode Island.

One large group, especially in the Restoration, is of Quaker women organized into meetings through the encouragement of George Fox, who was eager to give women a forum where they could uninhibitedly express themselves. By the end of the 17th century, women's Quaker groups supervised charitable activities and, from 1668, they collectively composed records. Often these meetings were extremely large: one document was signed on behalf of 150 London women, while a gathering in Barbados was said to have had 187 women present. Yet Quaker women, although they preached and suffered persecution, were always less important than their male colleagues, and the power of women's meetings was in the main channeled into social matters and away from the theology and politics of the movement.

The primary female literary and social network of the age was undoubtedly the Bluestocking one, and its existence stressed the relative isolation of earlier women, such as Lady Mary Wortley Montagu, while highlighting the importance of friends over kin. The network was formed around the major hostesses—Mrs. Montagu, Mrs. Boscawen, Mrs. Vesey and, to a lesser extent, Hester Thrale Piozzi—all highly placed ladies. Equivalent in some ways to the earlier French salon hostesses and frequenters, Bluestockings were more women-directed and, in fact, seem to have been remarkably free of tribulations associated with men. Hannah More and Elizabeth Carter were single, while Elizabeth Montagu was first married to a well-meaning older man and then affluently widowed, with no wish to remarry.

In their houses Bluestocking ladies provided the equivalent of male clubs, to which women were denied access; instead of cards they encouraged serious conversation among men and women, and they corresponded copiously among themselves on all intellectual matters. Aiming to raise the tone of society in general, they were careful to keep their private lives impeccable and so were harsh on Hester Thrale when she planned to remarry imprudently. They did not wish to endanger their tenuous gains, so they steered away from radical expression and from a claim of equality with men, although they implied it through the intellectual sureness of their writing. Instead of combating female curbs, they elevated them into a proof of a kind of superiority. They flourished partly because of the sentimental 18th-century view of the civilizing role of pure womanhood, but their achievement is nonetheless immense, and the growth of nonfictional female literature must in some part be attributable to them.

Like Samuel Johnson, Elizabeth Montagu, "Queen of the Blues," knew everyone: Mary Delany, Lady Craven, Ellis Cornelia Knight, Helen Maria Williams, Fanny Burney (who satirized the Blues in her play "The Witlings"), and Hannah More (who poked fun at them in "The Bas Bleu"). She was a good friend of the scholar Elizabeth Carter, and knew Catherine Talbot, the novelist Sarah Fielding, Frances Boscawen, Hester Mulso Chapone, and Anna Laetitia Barbauld. As a child, Ann Radcliffe (who probably attended the school of Sophia and Harriet Lee) was taken to meet Mrs. Montagu, whose fame even spread across the Atlantic, where Mercy Otis Warren addressed her poetically.

The Bluestockings had an enormous network of patronage, used especially for scholars and poets. Novelists they largely ignored but, toward the end of the century with expanding markets, these managed quite well on their own and did not need the influence exerted for the translator of Epictetus. Elizabeth Montagu was thanked in the prefaces to numerous translations and in a host of sentimental poems. She patronized Hannah More and the young Helen Maria Williams when she was a refined poet, not a revolutionary chronicler; she helped toward the income of the translator and poet Anna Williams and the novelist Sarah Fielding, and she settled an annuity on Elizabeth Carter. In addition, she took seriously her role of encourager to literary women in general, and her letters reveal her reading, sometimes with reluctance, learned female works; she praised women authors of all sorts, from the novelist Charlotte Lennox to the playwright Joanna Baillie and the historian Catherine Macaulay.

Other networks pale beside the Bluestocking one, but are worth noting. In the early 1700s, Susanna Centlivre, Jane Wiseman, Delarivière Manley, Catharine Trotter, Mary Pix, Lady Piers, Martha Fowke, and Eliza Haywood knew each other, while Mary Astell was a friend of Elizabeth Thomas, Lady Chudleigh, and Lady Mary Wortley Montagu. Often women showed great kindness to each other: Delarivière Manley befriended many women, including Mary Hearne, who dedicated her 1718 tale to her; Mary Hays was a source of strength to Eliza Fenwick through her domestic turmoil; Laetitia Hawkins went out of her way to attribute the irregular life of Mary Robinson to poverty.

But jealousy also erupted, and in one famous outburst in 1779 Hannah Cowley attacked Hannah More for alleged plagiarism; More retaliated with public grumbling in the newspapers. Hannah More also provoked the resentment of her protégée Ann Yearsley, who accused her patron of ruining her poems and overly controlling the money she earned from them. In 1786 Anna Seward and Clara Reeve exchanged acrimonious opinions on Richardson's novels, while many years earlier Delarivière Manley and Susanna Centlivre had rained political blows on each other.

Literature often appears to have run in families, with daughters emulating mothers, and nieces, aunts. In households of literary women, writing presumably was encouraged and the oddity of the intellectual female mitigated. Maria Cowper must have been encouraged by her gifted mother, Judith Madan; Lady Gethin by her mother, Lady Frances Norton; the novelist Elizabeth Plunkett by both her aunt, Margaret Minifie, and her mother, Susannah Gunning, whose posthumous novel she revised and published; Lady Louisa Stuart by her grandmother, Lady Mary Wortley Montagu, and by her strange first cousin once removed, Lady Mary Coke, whose single life she echoed and whose biography she wrote; Susanna Duncombe by her mother, Susanna Highmore; and the Bowdler sisters by their mother, Elizabeth. In America, Elizabeth Graeme Ferguson was an example for her niece, Anna Young Smith, and Ann Bleecker for her daughter, Margaretta Faugeres. Sisters such as the Kings, Kilners, Falconars, Lees, and Plumptres collaborated and inspired each other, while Fanny Burney's success must have helped her half-sister, Sarah Harriet Burney.

Beyond blood families were literary ones, female traditions formed through grateful emulation and experience of similar restrictions. The dramatist Aphra Behn was the progenitor of many professional playwrights, including the unidentified "Ariadne," Catharine Trotter, and Mary Pix, all of whom saw themselves as her literary daughters. In poetry, Elizabeth Rowe provided a model for devotional women; she was celebrated by the Countess of Hertford, and admired throughout the century by, for example, Jane Turell in the 1720s and Elizabeth Harrison in the 1750s. In gothic fiction Ann Radcliffe dominated—although Clara Reeve and Sophia Lee had eased the way for her—and her formulae were imitated by countless novelists; by the beginning of the 19th century Maria Edgeworth could acknowledge debts to Fanny Burney, Elizabeth Inchbald, and Anna Laetitia Barbauld. Among polemical writers, Mary Astell as defender of her sex inspired female intellectuals of her day, such as Elizabeth Thomas, Lady Chudleigh, and Lady Mary Wortley Montagu; Mary Wollstonecraft's personality and writings greatly affected women in the 1790s, especially Mary Hays, while she herself acknowledged her debt to Catherine Macaulay in *A Vindication of the Rights of Woman.*

Working-class women poets rarely saw themselves as a group and were in constant need of patronage from the middle class, not always forthcoming. Until the relationship soured, Hannah More supported the milkwoman Ann Yearsley, while Hester Mulso Chapone and Elizabeth Carter encouraged Elizabeth Bentley. Elizabeth Cobbold edited the poems of Ann Candler to help her escape the workhouse; in 1773, when she came to England, Phillis Wheatley was patronized by the Countess of Huntingdon.

In other spheres, too, were chains of patronage. The Duchess of York supported the grateful novelist and poet Mary Julia Young, and the wealthy Mrs. Crespigny was thanked in prefaces by the playwright Mariana Stark and the biographer Ann Thicknesse. Lady Elizabeth Hastings, taught by Bathsua Makin, was patron of the Anglo-Saxon scholar Elizabeth Elstob and, with Lady Mary Wortley Montagu, sympathized with Mary Astell's project for a female college. Later, Elstob was rescued from penury by an assortment of benevolent ladies: Hester Mulso Chapone's mother-in-law, Queen Caroline, and Mary Delany. Literary aid was further provided among women through subscriptions. Thus Elizabeth Scott and Anna Seward subscribed to Elizabeth Smith's poems, and Mary Delany and Elizabeth Carter to Mary Whateley. The subscription list to Elstob's Anglo-Saxon work in 1709 was almost half female.

More subtle help came from the habit of mentioning and including women in literary works. In Jane Austen's *Northanger Abbey* the heroine reads from Ann Radcliffe and Eliza Parsons, while the author alludes favorably to Fanny Burney. Clara Reeve included Susannah Dobson's *Life of Petrarch* among books on medieval romance and declared herself proud of a "writer of my own sex." Charlotte Smith put Henrietta O'Neil's poems in her own novel, and the Falconar sisters included Mary Blackett's verse in a preface. Henrietta Maria Bowdler published the writings of the scholar Elizabeth Smith after her early death; she also wrote a life in which Smith, despite her belief in female inferiority, became a useful intellectual exemplar for her sex. Elizabeth Benger wrote a biography of Elizabeth Hamilton, and Joanna Baillie made of Lady Grissel Baillie an heroic figure—while she herself was eulogized by Anne Bannerman as "priestess of the tragic muse." Aphra Behn, who published the poems of Mrs.

Taylor in her 1685 *Miscellany,* was much eulogized by proper and improper women alike: Delarivière Manley commended her along with Trotter and Pix in *The Royal Mischief* (1696), while Mary Astell in the same year praised the "incomparable Mrs. Behn."

Genres

The genres in which women chose to write depended on the times, although there was always a stress on autobiographical writings and more informal modes. Many professional women wrote across genres: Helen Maria Williams was a poet, translator, and novelist, Elizabeth Helme was all three and children's author as well. In the Restoration, private female writing mainly took the form of poetry and spiritual autobiography, while the professional woman turned to comic drama; later came satire and the racy or romantic tale, followed in the mid-18th century by the novel and poem of sensibility. Toward the end of the period, gothic fiction dominated professional writing, but women were also busy publishing polemics, travel narratives, plays, educational manuals, translations and, as always, books of poems, less devotional in England than in earlier times, but still bleached and decorous.

Drama: Playwriting is the first literary area in which women earned a living. While the theaters were closed, the Duchess of Newcastle, "Mad Madge," wrote closet drama; later Katherine Philips and the Countess of Winchilsea tried their hand at heroic blank-verse plays. But with the reopening of the theater under Charles II, a new breed of nonaristocratic professional women appeared. In the 1660s and early 1670s a demand arose for traditional tragedies and comedies of manner, fed by adaptations of French plays and English classics. The shadowy Frances Boothby in about 1669 wrote an old-fashioned tragi-comedy, and Elizabeth Polwhele composed a rhymed tragedy. By the late 1670s more sensational fare was wanted, turning on cuckoldry and ribald wit, while heroic plays such as Aphra Behn's *Abdelazar* tended to flop. Aphra Behn cleverly responded to the new appetite for bawdy slapstick, as did Elizabeth Polwhele with her light confection, *The Frolicks.*

Another intrusion of women into the theater occurred around 1695, as direction changed once more. Under the influence of the growing sentimental and moral movement, rakes reformed and married, and satiric butts grew less frivolous. Catharine Trotter's first tragedy appeared in 1695 and was well received; the unidentified "Ariadne" wrote a comedy in 1696, aware of herself in the line of Aphra Behn and needing to purify the image of the female playwright. Susanna Centlivre's irregular life, however, echoed Behn's, and in a few of her fast-paced comedies she caught the public mood for sentiment, audience-exploitation, and light satire.

The cluster of Restoration and early 18th-century women playwrights is not repeated in the remainder of the years, but most decades find some women busy in drama. In the 1730s Elizabeth Cooper wrote a successful comedy in which she herself acted, and in 1753 Catherine Clive in her *Rehearsal* depicted a character based on herself waiting for the arrival of herself as author of the play. In the 1750s Frances Brooke wrote worthy heroic female tragedies but was more successful with her comic pieces in the 1780s. In the 1760s several of Elizabeth Griffith's plays had some success, as did the witty comedies of manners of Frances Sheridan. In the 1770s Mercy Otis Warren in America allowed her "satirical propensity" to enter her political dramas, and in the 1780s the eccentric Lady Wallace was "emulous of attaining the fame of Mrs. Behn and of Mrs. Centlivre."

In the same period Elizabeth Inchbald skillfully and dramatically adapted French and German plays for the British stage, and Hannah Cowley had considerable success with her moral comedies. In 1799 Elizabeth Boyd tried an odd mixture, a ballad opera mingling comedy and masque, while about the same time Joanna Baillie, the major female dramatist of her day, began her series of wooden plays for each passion, designed to return decent moral drama to a debilitated stage.

Poetry: Poetry accounts for a large portion of women's literary output, forming with letters the major part of the unpublished material. In quality it varies enormously; some of it, like the poetry of the American Elizabeth Bradford or Jane Dunlap, approaches doggerel, while the epithet-ridden sentimental effusions of most British ladies, often popular in their time, have lost appeal for modern ears, more open to the light, amusing verse of Countess Temple or the Popean couplets of Judith Madan. The division tends to be along class lines, since mainly aristocrats wrote in the latter styles; lower-middle- and working-class women tended toward melancholic musings, partly no doubt because their lives justified the mode.

The Restoration exhibits great poetic variety, from the mnemonic doctrinal pieces of Quakers, such as Ann Docwra, to the evocative nature descriptions of the Countess of Winchilsea, the frank erotic verse of Aphra Behn and Mrs. Taylor, and the burlesque of Alicia D'Anvers and Mary Evelyn. Soon the last two types dwindled, and pious Anne Wharton was reprimanded by Bishop Burnet for exchanging verses with the notorious Behn.

As the 18th century wore on, poetry increased its sentimental content and style. Elizabeth Rowe, publishing verse of love and friendship in the 1690s, grew more pious through the early 1700s, until by 1758 she was writing rapturous religious poetry, the Protestant equivalent of Catholic mystical verse so popular with Dissenters. By the mid to late 1800s, titles often became variations on *Effusions of the Heart* (published in 1798 by Mary Stockdale), with its typical mixture of pastorals, sonnets, occasional poems, and gothic tales, and its authorial portrait of the pious, solitary, and sensitive lady. Mary Robinson, Maria Madan, Charlotte Smith, and Helen Maria Williams, much admired by the young William Wordsworth, all exemplify the melancholic, graveyard kind of poetry in vogue throughout the years and thought peculiarly suitable for the female pen. Yet a few women continued to use poetry satirically: Margaret Ogle wrote a crude attack on Robert Walpole in 1742, and Henrietta Battier and Mary O'Brien each composed humorous political verse. But by the end of the century Mary Blackett's mockery of courtiers and Ann Murry's satire on the modish lady seem distinctly out of date.

In America, poetry at first appeared dangerous: a 17th-century Massachusetts minister wrote forthrightly to his sister that her "printing of a book beyond the custom of your sex doth rankly smell." Later, verse writing was encouraged, and while most of it was written in the prevailing British melancholic mode—even by the slave Phillis Wheatley—its subjects tended to be slightly different: religious themes dominated longer than in Britain, and in the revolutionary decades poetry grew patriotic.

Almost all verse forms were attempted by women. Elizabeth Ryves and Ann Francis wrote odes; Susanna Pearson and Anna Seward composed the still unpopular sonnet. Lady Sophia Burrell in 1794 unsuccessfully tried an epic, mindful of her inappropriate femaleness. Some, like Elizabeth Cobbold, wrote sentimental elegies in Ossianic style, and in isolated America Ann Bleecker turned to pastorals. Hymns were written by British and American poets: often by literary ladies, such as Hannah More, or Helen Maria Williams composing also in other genres, and often by illiterates like Lucy Allen. England produced one substantial congregational hymn writer, Anna Steele; America had no equivalent, although Anna Beeman was represented in late 18th-century hymn anthologies, and Phoebe Hensdale Brown's verses, not published until the 19th century, were then widely sung.

Women were represented, too, in the ballad revival; indeed, Lady Wardlaw in the early 1700s may have helped to originate it with a poem she declared to be a discovery but which she perhaps partially composed. Her ballad versions appear in Percy's *Reliques.* Between this influential volume and the *Lyrical Ballads,* Hannah More and R. Roberts prove the continuing female interest.

In Scotland, the ballad or patriotic song became a vehicle for aristocratic ladies such as Lady Grissel Baillie and Lady Anne Barnard, and for peasants such as Jean Glover. Alicia Cockburn, Jean Elliot, and Anne Hunter all wrote words to "The Flowers of the Forest," exploiting the vogue for nostalgic Jacobitism and helping to create the romantic image of literary Scotland.

Autobiography and Biography: Turning to prose, one finds a major genre throughout the period in autobiography, especially the spiritual type. This can be movingly detailed but also highly stylized, since several sects encouraged self-scrutiny in print, almost provided formulae for it, or demanded life-assessments for church admission. Sometimes the effect on the modern reader differs from that assumed by the writer; thus the Methodist diary of Elizabeth Johnson captures her self-hatred and sexual longing, and Arabella Davies depicts her religious fear as well as her faith. Journals came close to autobiographies when organized, often posthumously by men, into uplifting patterns. An example is the life of Susanna Anthony, used by her minister to edify the congregation. Quaker autobiographies span the period, beginning with Restoration examples, like Elizabeth Hooten's descriptions of the horrors of persecution and prison. In 1709 Bathsheba Bowers recorded an experience far from the vicissitudes of the early converts—she describes how her faith made her relinquish finery and take up gardening.

On both continents a great change occurred between the tone of 17th-century spiritual autobiographies and those written during the evangelical movement. The early Sarah Fiske, in her *Confession of Faith,* reveals her knowledge of theological doctrine, and her odyssey is mainly intellectual. By the 1730s and '40s in America, the Great Awakening had arrived and the emphasis was on emotion. Sarah Haggar Osborn and Elizabeth Hull wrote of the heart, not the intellect, while Susanna Anthony described the heights and depths of religious turmoil in the context of a physically painful life.

Secular autobiographies are a difficult genre to define. The formal and ordered Gibbon autobiography or the confessional Rousseauian type had no female equivalent, although the first life-histories seem to point that way. The Duchess of Newcastle published an early female autobiography in 1656, describing her own family, including her capable widowed mother; in 1677–78 Lady Halkett wove her own experiences into political events. Later secular autobiographies tended to sensationalize or vindicate, occasionally the motive in religious autobiographies also, as when Agnes Beaumont felt called to explain her scandalous climb up onto John Bunyan's horse. They vary enormously in quality: Laetitia Hawkins's works are rambling and disorganized, and no real picture of the author emerges; Margaret Coghlan's racy life as an adventurer carries her narrative along. On a different level, the skillful, vindictive memoir of Laetitia Pilkington recorded not merely her justification, but also her growth into writing and her construction of the image of learned lady.

Two subgroups of autobiographies deserve noting: the Indian captivity narrative, and the private writings of women colonists. The first, a peculiarly American type, quickly established itself as a genre speaking to the fears of early Americans and carrying their spiritual myths. Since some of the women captured were illiterate the accounts were transcribed by others, and much editorial embroidery was possible.

The first book-length record of a single captivity was that of Mary Rowlandson in 1682. A victim of the Indian upheaval known as King Philip's War, Rowlandson, like Elizabeth Hanson in 1726, was clearly writing a Puritan spiritual autobiography, in plain style, giving events a providential framework and the spiritual and physical drama an exemplary tone. Subsequent accounts move toward sentiment, fiction, and propaganda. The first process is at work with Mercy Harbison, whose crude, first-person narrative of 1792 is sentimentalized so that an editor can highlight both Indian horrors and the author's present sad plight. In *The History of Maria Kittle* (1779) Ann Bleecker fictionalized the suffering of the French and Indian wars to sadly comic effect: the stock sentimental terms jar with real horrors when a "laughing" babe is dashed to the floor and when Ceres presides over fields of screaming Indians. Propagandist purpose was inserted into Jemima Howe's story, which grew into an anti-Indian attack, while she herself was turned into an Englishwoman so the barbaric Americans could also be assailed.

Among the colonists, Anna Maria Falconbridge laconically caught the early chaotic development of Sierra Leone; the more highly placed Elizabeth Simcoe captured in her prose something of primitive Canada, as well as her own intrepidity as she sketched and embroidered in damp forest clearings. The extraordinary adaptability of such women makes credible the seemingly bizarre habits of Ann Radcliffe's heroine, who sets out her library and sketching equipment in the most menacing Italian castles.

Early biographies are written about husbands. The Duchess of Newcastle created a loyal nobleman through war and exile, an ideal aristocrat; on the other side, Lucy Hutchinson made of her spouse an exemplary Puritan, while allowing the fervor of courtship and her own personal love to shine through her prose. Among early Quakers, Anne Camm wrote a tribute to her first husband, John Audland, describing their devoted and God-centered relationship.

In the 18th century one finds fewer biographical examples: in 1790 pious Sarah Young published the life of her friend Mrs. Scudamore as Christian exemplar, and in 1786 Hester Thrale Piozzi published her frank, unsentimental anecdotes of Samuel Johnson. In tribute, Margaretta Faugeres wrote a short memoir of her suffering and war-ravaged mother, Ann Bleecker.

Journals and Letters: Often merging with autobiography, journals and letters include some of the best female writing: the diary of Fanny Burney, for example, pictures life at the end of the 18th century—the public world of Bluestockings, the court, and Samuel Johnson's circle, and the private one of marital fears and mastectomy. Women's letters are almost always more satisfying than their other works, and they were often written in proto-fictional style by writers who scorned the novel. They catch female lives and emotions, chatting of people, towns, events, and ideas and, if the writer were highly placed, like Abigail Adams or Lady Louisa Stuart, of politics as well.

Especially in America, letters expressed individual spiritual anguish and its comfort in a general way, and these pious, often self-pitying missives were passed around for inspiration. In England, they frequently conveyed friendship through gossip and confidences, like the elegant correspondence of the Countesses of Pomfret and Hertford in the 1730s and '40s, or the more intellectual and sentimental one of the Bluestockings Elizabeth Carter and Catherine Talbot.

Even the malicious and abrasive person could entertain by post: writing in journal letters to her sister in 1764, the waspish Lady Mary Coke declared, "Miss Chudleigh is going to wash herself in the Bathes of Bohemia. They will be very famous if they can cleanse her from all her disorders. She sets out in february, and has, as the Town says, left the Duke of Kingston a Milliner that She found in Cranbourn Alley to supply her place during her Absence." Other writers still impress by capturing a particular despair in the conventional language of the time. Mary Wollstonecraft did so when she wrote in 1795, "I expect nothing from you, or any human being: my die is cast! I have fortitude enough to determine to do my duty; yet I cannot raise my depressed spirits, or calm my trembling heart." Her letters were addressed to her faithless lover, Gilbert Imlay, but they moved a later one, William Godwin.

From established colonies letters gossip of social life: Anne Brodbelt, writing from the West Indies, saw the great martial upheavals of the age in terms of delayed dresses and missing partners. From the unestablished colony of Australia, Elizabeth Macarthur revealed the adaptability of the pioneering woman, together with the growing snobbery of the rooted colonist who found newer arrivals inadequate.

With leisure, skill, and a network of correspondents, aristocratic and upper-middle-class English women were supreme letter writers: Lady Mary Wortley Montagu with her wit and passion, the sprightly and socially aware daughters of the Duke of Richmond, Hester Thrale Piozzi, Mary Delany, and Frances Boscawen. All are lively, amusing, gracious, and malicious by turns; all are psychologically astute, inquiring, and articulate, wry about their own difficulties as intelligent women in a patriarchal society, but accepting of human limitations. "Tis my firm persuasion," wrote Lady Caroline Holland, "that a too prudent foresight in us shortsighted mortals is the most imprudent way of acting for one's own happiness."

Didactic Prose: With the concept of specifically female culture and spheres of activity went nonfictional prose genres, such as advice works on education and decorous behavior. This type began with the devotional manuals of the Restoration and early 18th century, those of Lady Halkett and Susanna Hopton, written primarily for private use but possibly also with an eye to publication.

By the mid- to late 18th century, the middle classes were avid for advice. On domestic matters women had been counseling each other since the Restoration, when the versatile Hannah Woolley dispensed household wisdom and recipes to prepare genteel women for a possible life in service. But she did not achieve the popularity of Elizabeth Moxon (1749) or Hannah Glasse, whose famous work on cookery (1747) taught how to prepare food and set a newly affluent table.

Above all, women seemed to want guidance on educating children, especially daughters. A spate of guidebooks for parents, instructions for young people, and children's books entered the market from the 1770s. Usually the advice was conservative, not subversive—although some independence might be modestly intruded—and commonsensical in its acceptance (and understanding) of the patriarchal reality. Most educational authors considered themselves to be righting the balance tipped by fiction toward sentiment by stressing reason and by countering the novelist's predilection for romance. With their emphasis on early education, Locke and Rousseau were great influences, although the Rousseauian picture of the contingent Sophie in *Emile* was firmly eschewed by an outraged Mary Wollstonecraft.

Advice books *for* young people were even more popular than works *about* them, and they spoke to the growing prominence of children in late 18th-century England. The message was usually subordination and patience. Hester Mulso Chapone preached the conservative way in 1773, although she lightened it with touches of realism. In 1781 Mary Deverell counseled submission in marriage while she implied that a girl should enjoy courtship, her only period of power. In 1776 Ann Murry began her popular *Mentoria* books, in which a governess answers her pupils' questions; the subjects allowed are gender-dependent, with geometry rigorously excluded for girls. In her form, Murry shows the influence of Rousseau's *Emile,* which taught through fictional conversations with children and gave the impression that learning was natural, not systematic. The form was used by Wollstonecraft to give harsh moral lessons in *Original Stories* and by Margaret Bryan to give simple scientific ones. It was also employed by the very popular Anna Laetitia Barbauld, whose moral dialogues of 1778 preached obedience by easy stages.

Travel, History, and Translation: Borrowing much in style from familiar letters, travel narratives also fed the 18th-century hunger for knowledge, while allowing writers to display themselves. The works covered a large proportion of the world. In about 1700 the intrepid Celia Fiennes wrote crude accounts of her tours through Britain in the 1680s, confounding details of religion and food with gusto, and entirely avoiding the sentimental effusions so prevalent in later travelogues. In Puritan America Sarah Kemble Knight gave a rare secular description, of the route from Boston to New York in 1704. Lady Mary Wortley Montagu wrote dazzlingly of Turkey; and Elizabeth Hamilton and the Hon. Mrs. Murray less so of the Scottish Highlands. Mrs. Piozzi chatted of France, Italy, and Germany, and Ann Radcliffe informed about Germany and Holland. Mariana Stark was unremittingly British in her guidebooks to France and Italy in peace and war, while Lady Mary Coke specialized in Continental courts and courtiers. Janet Schaw wrote of North Carolina, Lady Anne Barnard of South Africa, Jemima Kindersley of Brazil and India, and Mary Ann Parker of her world voyage. Maria Riddell made practical observations in the West Indies; the Margravine of Anspach, on an amazing journey through the Crimea to Constantinople, mainly noted other people's responses to her. Helen Maria Williams wrote of Switzerland in political turmoil, and Mary Wollstonecraft trailed her baby and wounded heart through the wilds of Scandinavia.

Formal history by women was much rarer than informal anecdote. The Duchess of Newcastle considered that women should eschew political history altogether and write on particular figures instead, staying in her view, within "the circumference of truth." Yet some women in the late 18th century did try their hand at the "masculine" mode of formal history, especially Catherine Macaulay, who studied parliamentary debates and pamphlets in the British Museum. Mercy Otis Warren, a close friend whom Macaulay visited in America, suggested that Macaulay write a history of the American Revolution; engrossed in her educational work, Macaulay refused, so Warren took on the task with the scholarly care Macaulay had shown. Her judgments were based on her findings and were given even when they opposed her interests, as when she criticized her friend John Adams. In 1799 Hannah Adams followed history from the Mayflower to the federal Constitution, seeing it as the providential narrative of America.

During the Jacobin period of the French Revolution, Mary Wollstonecraft wrote a history of its moderate beginnings, informed with her knowledge of later troubling events. Although much was derived from English periodicals, its main thesis, that revolutions should come when people's minds are prepared for them, was influential both on John Adams and Percy Bysshe Shelley. Late in life Hester Thrale Piozzi attempted to answer Gibbon's whiggish and unchristian history, but she was felt by most to have overstepped female limits, and her work was mocked as "history in dimity."

More informal history, thought suitable for women, occurs in biographies of the Duchess of Newcastle and Lucy Hutchinson, in diaries like Lady Northumberland's which chronicles for posterity great events such as the arrival and wedding of Queen Charlotte, in gossipy court journals like that attributed to Lady Charlotte Bury, and in letters like those on the Revolutionary War by Eliza Yonge Wilkinson, who was keenly aware of the impropriety of a woman's writing of such matters. In public letters, Helen Maria Williams chronicled the whole course of French events from the beginning of the Revolution in 1790 to the Restoration of Louis-Philippe; although in sentimental impressionistic style, the letters were quoted extensively as history, since they provided one of the few eyewitness accounts of the bloody period of the Revolution. Yet Williams, too, was taken to task by Laetitia Hawkins for failing to understand the inappropriateness of a lady's intruding into the male territory of politics.

Women undertook translation for pleasure and money. Sometimes they invaded the scholarly languages, regarded as peculiarly male. Susanna Dobson, Mary Arundell, and Lucy Hutchinson translated from Latin, the last working in a room full of noisy children. Elizabeth Carter was widely renowned for translating Epictetus and for providing clear scholarly notes and introduction, while Elizabeth Smith and Ann Francis translated from Hebrew to some acclaim. Even more esoteric was Anglo-Saxon: Elizabeth Elstob found a market for her first Anglo-Saxon work through subscription but could not do so for others, and she remained a linguistic oddity.

Female translations were predominantly of contemporary European works. Penelope Aubin translated from French in the 1720s; Mary Collyer took on Marivaux; R. Roberts, Mme. de Graffigny and Marmontel; and Jemima Kindersley, the feminist work of Antoine Leonard Thomas. Ellis Cornelia Knight and Mary Wollstonecraft translated from German; most important, Anna Plumptre and Elizabeth Inchbald made German drama accessible to an English audience, especially the works of Kotzebue—including *Lovers' Vows,* which caused such havoc in the billiard-room of Mansfield Park. By translating from the Irish and Welsh, Charlotte Brooke and Anne Penny helped the vogue for ancient British poetry.

The Novel: Mostly women wrote fiction, regarded as a lesser genre and therefore suitable for the second sex. In the novel they could write in the familiar style perfected in informal letters and use their own experience and consciousness as material. With his female-centered, sentimental fiction, Samuel Richardson was a dominant influence (while Fielding, with his picaresque form and realistic description, was viewed as a proper masculine example in an age sure that style and content should be gender-marked). But although Clara Reeve acknowledged the female debt to him, Richardson was already a part of a tradition formed from the novels of many early women, of Delarivière Manley, Eliza Haywood, and Penelope Aubin, to name only a few.

The works of these early women vary enormously in merit and aim. The awkward novellas of Jane Barker include touches of intriguing psychology—a deserted wife cleaves to her husband's mistress, and an unmarried woman wonders why she keeps avoiding matrimony. The schematic moral romances of Penelope Aubin and Mary Davys encourage "Virtue" but make dull reading, while much of Manley and Haywood could be classed as scandal. By the 1730s and '40s, the cult of sensibility forced almost all women into the moral path, and Eliza Haywood forsook her naughty novels and adapted to the market; in Clara Reeve's phrase, she "repented of her faults."

Gaining momentum in the 1740s, the female novel became a flood in the 1780s and 1790s. The characters were on the whole generalized and stylized, although the sentimental component increased as the century progressed. So Sarah Fielding in the 1740s and '50s could combine picaresque and sentiment and reveal both the necessity of virtue and the suffering usually attendant on it. In the 1760s Frances Brooke and Elizabeth Griffith still allowed wit to the approved character, although the "sudden sense of right," in Hannah More's phrase, was usually the source of goodness.

By the 1770s instinctive virtue had largely carried the day and characters were exemplars of sentimental theory. Women lost any touch of the lusty lovers of Behn and Manley and instead became mothers, friends, and maidens—almost invariably beautiful, always chaste, in need both of receiving male social guidance and of giving spiritual inspiration. Heroes were often "feminized" men and displayed the attributes of gentleness and sensitivity associated with women. If they failed in these qualities, they were harshly treated: affirming the sacredness of womanhood, Mrs. Woodfin reformed erring females but rigorously punished erring men. Marriage and parenting were turned from comic necessities for cuckoldry and rebellion, as in the Restoration, into sentimental relationships conveyed through emotional tableaux of dying parents and reunited spouses. The society described was rarely below the aristocratic, although the heroine herself might be bourgeois and achieve union with the upper class through virtue and stamina. This marriage myth of the aristocratic spouse was most distressingly caught in the popular novels of the Minifie sisters, where, in Mary Wollstonecraft's contemptuous phrase, virtue was invariably rewarded by a coach and six.

The last part of the century was heavily gothic. One exception was Fanny Burney's single-view novel with the subject of social embarrassment and adaptation, so influential on Jane Austen. Others were the political writers, Mary Wollstonecraft, Mary Hays, and Elizabeth Inchbald, who tried to use fiction to counter social abuse. But they were few compared to the gothic novelists, and even these writers reveal the effect of the emotional orgy in which their sister-writers were indulging.

The gothic form originated with Horace Walpole and Tobias Smollett earlier in the century, but it achieved popularity only in later years. In 1778 Clara Reeve tried to domesticate it in *The Old English Baron;* more important for the future, Sophia Lee in *The Recess* (1783–85) added dramatic horrors and a sense of fear. In 1787 Anne Fuller tried an historical gothic work with a precise setting. But not until Ann Radcliffe's potent combination of sentimental womanhood, familial tableaux, picturesque setting, and masculine villainy did the gothic become for the nation both a fantasy of fidelity, power, and grandeur and a nightmare of impotence and persecution. Most female gothic writers—Anna Maria Mackenzie, Elizabeth Helme, and Mary Charlton—adopted Radcliffe's formulae but exaggerated the sensational rendering of emotion; perhaps only Harriet Lee made any worthy innovation when she explored the bizarre psychology of Kruitzner.

The new departure in the novel that would take it into the next century did not come from gothic fiction or the political works, but probably from Maria Edgeworth. Her *Castle Rackrent* (1800) used realistic dialect, which had been attempted to some extent by the Minifies in the 1760s and by Elizabeth Blower in the 1780s, but on the whole had been little exploited. Edgeworth combined an awareness of class and regional dialect with social content to indicate an important direction of Victorian female fiction.

America experienced nothing resembling the fictional explosion in England, and the few novels produced there seem rather old-fashioned. Hannah Webster Foster in 1797 wrote the very popular seduction novel *The Coquette,* and Susanna Rowson had great success with a similarly Richardsonian concoction, *Charlotte Temple.*

A brief consideration of genres shows how difficult it is to group women writers into traditional classifications. Perhaps new terminology is needed to name the public letter or the scandal novel aimed at female display. But the exercise does indicate where female strengths and weaknesses tend to be found and where women's experience pushes against forms and expectations. It also reveals the sad spectacle of women conforming to genres and styles temperamentally alien to them—perhaps some of the headaches that pepper the letters of writing women derived in part from the struggle. Laetitia Hawkins, for instance, almost seems suffocated in the genre she felt she must choose—the sentimental novel—when she showed most skill at sharp, realistic sketches. Talented at slight, lively tales like *Perourou,* Helen Maria Williams instead wrote sentimental stories and rambling histories. Mary Latter expended effort on effusions of self-pity, although her strength lay in social satire and realistic description, while Hannah More felt herself cheapened by her shrewd, practical stories and considered repetitive moralizing more appropriate for her pen.

Themes

The Sentimental Female Image: As writers and subjects, women were the prime bearers of the cult of sensibility in the 18th century, and their consciousness became both exploited and exemplary. Stressing those qualities considered feminine by the sexual psychology of the time—intuitive sympathy, passivity, and emotionalism—the movement simultaneously glorified and debased women.

To many early writers, the sentimental emphasis appeared to be an advance on the harsh reviling of the Restoration period and its lusty image of women, as well as on the misogyny of Pope and Swift—although Swift, in particular, warned of the subordination implied by the idea of sexual qualities. Giving women centrality in the context of their inferiority, the cult brought female consciousness under investigation and permitted women to express a restricted desire. In sentimental literature women could complain obliquely, refashion the structures of power they inhabited, recreate their own images, and reform men. Through writing, repression turned into expression, and the passivity of the ideal was modified by a creative act of literature that could not be passive. By the mid-18th century, women writers had turned the sentimental ideology to use, and their plots had become the main vehicle for the collective female wish-fulfillment of compensatory moral superiority and powerful passivity.

Male writers depicting female exemplars appreciated the faithful wife—the Pamela image of Richardson or Fielding's Amelia, who was married to a generous rake. In 1714 an early popularizer of the sentimental route, *The Spectator,* announced of a woman: "All she has to do in this World, is contained within the Duties of a Daughter, a Sister, a Wife, and a Mother." It considered that "a right Woman . . . should have gentle Softness, tender Fear, and all those parts of Life, which distinguish her from the other Sex; with some Subordination to it, but such an Inferiority that makes her more lovely," and it put these words into the mouth of the ideal wife: "I . . . have no other Concern but to please the Man I love: he is the End of every Care I have."

Woman writers usually paid lip-service to this extraordinary wifely ideal, but in mid-century they tended to glorify the mother to whom, with the pure maiden, they gave wonderful power, especially over men, who came by the end of the tale to approach her with almost religious reverence. Sophia Lee created men who vowed to cater to every whim of her chaste passive heroines, and the Minifie sisters made sacred the very hem on the gown of their fictive mothers. The switch to motherhood was a clever move for women since the mother, unlike the wife, could be exalted without intrusive subordination, and the passivity with which she influenced could become not a contingent quality, but strong and manipulative.

The powerful passivity of the pure maiden was less easy to promote, and it revealed a large element of female fantasy. Lady Echlin could not accept that the virtuous passivity of Richardson's Clarissa was powerless and that in the last resort she would be raped; so she deleted the violence Richardson had written and closed her revision of the book with the rake reformed by "Clarissas virtuous conversation." This ending, she declared, was more in keeping with "womanly pride."

The development of the sentimental image can be demonstrated by citing three semifictional autobiographical works of distinct periods, written to vindicate conduct. They exist because literature provided women with a receptive public, denied them in law and government, and a marketplace to sell their image. "I have discovered," wrote James Boswell, "that we may be in some degree whatever character we choose," and the vindicating ladies support this discovery by having chosen their roles, if not their fates. The characters each created conformed with her time's stereotypes, and the available stereotypes were few. A degree of duplicity was involved in each portrait beyond any consideration of truth or falsehood, for any writing woman denies the spontaneity, innocence, and passivity on which she must insist. When Laetitia Pilkington wrote "Poor I, have been for many years a Noun Substantive, obliged to stand alone," she obscured her own act of writing, at the heart of the image of self she was covertly peddling. She was a witty, active woman, far from the undeclinable femininity she lamented.

In 1663, Mary Carleton, the daughter of a Canterbury fiddler, set herself up as a German princess, de Wolway, with the aid of forged letters, linguistic ability, and fake jewels. Soon she entrapped a lord, only to discover—foreshadowing Moll Flanders—that he was as much a fraud as herself. Unfortunately the advantage was his, since he was Mary Carleton's third husband, and all her previous spouses were alive. She was ineptly tried for bigamy and freed. She then wrote a literary version of her fraud, an account of her life that was both appealing and alluring, asserting aristocracy and feminine worth and attracting men through the portrait of a witty and seductive lady who was stripped naughtily of her clothes and jewels and maligned from Wolway to Vulva. Her ambiguous image was suitable for the Restoration, but was unlikely to have carried much weight a century later. It is not suprising that Carleton, a few years after its creation, was acting herself on the stage in the story of her own fraud.

By the 1760s female purity was far more in vogue than in the Restoration, although a dash of spiritedness could remain. In a pamphlet Miss F. wrote to vindicate herself, she assumed entire innocence although she could still prove herself energetic under her wrongs and could titillate with hidden names. *A Letter from Miss F. addressed to a Person of Distinction* aimed to remove the prejudice of the public and allow its author a singing career, despite the opposition of the elderly lord who had designs on her virtue. She was all naive girlhood, Pamela imposed upon by a scheming aristocrat who would label her mistress or whore before he would let her work as a singer. Yet he had allowed her to perform at his own gatherings; when controlled by a man her actions are proper, she noted, but when she alone pocketed the proceeds, they were not. Like Mary Carleton, Miss F. was well aware of the power of the word to display without impurity and to entertain with profit.

By 1790 Susannah Gunning, writing in images created in the sentimental and gothic fiction of the 1770s and 1780s, made a portrait of sensibility, and absolute purity was assumed. The threat and power of writing are still there, but energy is denied. Susannah was writing to vindicate her "angel" daughter, her "innocent" and "glorious child," and herself as "A HAPPY MOTHER" against the charges that her daughter had forged letters to make a match between herself and her noble cousin, the Marquis of Lorne. The villain of the piece was the gothic general, the father, a mixture of Lovelace and Manfred. Susannah Gunning created her daughter in the hyperbolic prose she had used in her early novels as Miss Minifie. She appealed to the heart of the reader, setting up sentimental tableaux of sacred motherhood and filial piety. Since her daughter did not die as a sentimentalist might have expected—although she did fall ill—Mrs. Gunning could only imagine that at her death, she would have "grieved like a mother." As in most sentimental literature, susceptibility to the image became the test of sensibility in the reader. "Terrific is the Picture I am forced to exhibit—it must be a mere body indeed who can look upon it unmoved."

In the 1660s the eye that looked and the money that bought were clearly male. Mary Carleton knew she must sell herself as heroic female, but she spiced her portrait with sexuality. Her scandalous self-display was not allowed to Miss F., who might laugh a little but still remain energetically naive. Knowing her largely female fiction audience, Mrs. Gunning abolished the risqué woman and capitalized on the mother; energy and spiritedness fell before self-pity and passivity. Yet she was as aware of using female strategies as her predecessors, for she, like them, was going to market in and for herself.

Despite gothic uses of it and some effort on the part of Charlotte Smith to return to the 1740s mixture of sentiment and intelligence in heroines, sensibility had by the 1790s provoked a decided reaction. Many women had come to see that, in its glorification of female qualities, it was extolling female victimization. Novels like those of Eliza Parsons revealed the extreme vulnerability of women trained in dependence and passivity, while their plots seemed fantasy substitutes for effort in real life. So sensibility was attacked by radicals who saw it as escapist self-indulgence, and by conservatives who saw it as anti-Christian and relativistic; both groups however frequently used its powerful devices to make their antagonistic points.

A series of novels descended from Charlotte Lennox's 1752 work, *The Female Quixote,* including the American Tabitha Tenney's *Female Quixotism,* mocked female expectation from novel-reading. Without fictional aid, Anna Laetitia Barbauld in her 50-volume British Novelists series exposed the exploitative attitudes beneath sensibility and deplored the sentimental novel's tendency to center on love. Jane West as "Prudentia Homespun" in 1796 pitted excessive sensibility against virtue, insisting on the everyday world over the febrile creation of fiction. Titles became variations on delusion and deceit, on "the curse of sentiment"; by the end of the century it was almost a must to rail at sensibility as that "most fatal poison."

Causes: Women took stands on all the issues and ideas of their day. Religion was treated politically, intellectually, and emotionally, the dominant style depending on the decade. The 17th-century Quakers, writing both terrorist tracts and staid argument, opposed the alliance of church and state, attacked the hierarchical Church of England, and urged religious tolerance, often promising divine wrath if it was not delivered. Judith Boulbie counseled and cautioned magistrates to use their power sparingly in religious matters, and Ann Docwra and the later Sophia Hume explored the gray area where the law impinged on religion. On the other side of the question, Mary Astell wrote in favor of the Occasional Conformity Bill barring Dissenters and asserting established authority in religion.

There is little of this kind of activity later in the 18th century although, following her husband's lead, Ann Jebb in the 1770s wrote against the mandatory subscription to the Anglican Thirty-Nine Articles, and Mary Hays went into print for the first time to defend the public communal worship of the Dissenters. In *A Vindication of the Rights of Men,* the nominally Anglican Mary Wollstonecraft echoed the Quakers in opposing the established Church, "this national religion, this ideal consecration of a state."

Theological polemic begins with the learned Damaris Masham attacking the theories of the Cambridge Platonist John Norris in 1696; she put forward her Lockean view that reason could combine with faith and that earthly life had its own intrinsic, nonsymbolic merit. Accepting Norris's ideas, Mary Astell wrote of loving God through loving the Creation. In the same period, the Puritan Sarah Fiske investigated doctrine and, after a flirtation with Roman Catholicism, Susanna Hopton defended the Protestant route.

With the Great Awakening in America and the evangelical movements of Whitefield and the Wesleys in England in the 1740s, emotion and faith came to the fore. Through sentimental poetry Sarah Parsons Moorhead opposed the religious excess which the Awakening's emotional emphasis allowed. Her point is well illustrated by Martha Brewster, who in a poem of 1757 depicted the terrors of Judgment Day, and by the Prince sisters of Boston in their fearful abasement and sense of sin.

Defended vigorously by the Countess of Huntingdon, the Methodists were attacked in England by Charlotte MacCarthy, who attributed the country's low moral state to the Methodist emphasis on faith over good works. In the 1750s, the Quaker Catharine Phillips argued against the Methodist refusal of women ministers, while at the end of the period the rationalist Mary Wollstonecraft reviled the sect as emotional and self-indulgent.

Women entered philosophical controversy less often than religious, but in the late 17th century they vigorously joined in the argument over John Locke's theories. Mary Astell applied his antiauthoritarian views to the family and sexual relationships, although in religion she argued against his thinking, which tended toward skepticism. In 1698 Catharine Trotter wrote an essay defending Locke, while Damaris Masham, whose tutor he had been, used his theories to defend women's right to reason. She educated her children on his principles, as did Eliza Lucas Pinckney in South Carolina many years later. Locke remained a force in women's writing throughout the period, and Mary Wollstonecraft used his views in her early education manual; Hannah More, her ideological opposite in many ways, suggested that girls read his *Essay Concerning Human Understanding.*

The sentimental movement led to concern for victimized groups. Toward the end of the century antislavery opinion became a vogue among conservatives and liberals, lending itself to polemic and fiction, as it had to a limited extent in the times of Aphra Behn and the Countess of Hertford, both of whom romanticized its misery. Mary Locke, Helen Maria Williams, Anna Maria Mackenzie, and Hannah More all wrote antislavery poetry which, in many ways, mocked the problem by resolving it through idealizing particular slaves or through individual humanitarian action. In America, Margaretta Faugeres wrote an essay on slavery, and Abigail Adams discussed it in letters, while from Sierra Leone Anna Maria Falconbridge at first opposed its horrors, then came to see them as preferable to free life in Africa. Emotive tableaux, like those drawn for slavery, were employed by Mariana Stark in her poem "The Poor Soldier" to expose the sad treatment of wounded men returning from the American war.

Other causes tended to have autobiographical resonance. Bathsua Makin, whose brother may have been imprisoned for debt, stressed the social stupidity of jailing people for misfortune, a point made more than a century later from debtors' prison by Maria Barrell, who noted that the harsh treatment of debtors surpassed that of criminals.

Midwifery was an issue throughout the age, with women championing their right to the profession and both sexes mythologizing their contribution. The agitation had occurred since at least 1616, when women midwives tried, but failed, to become incorporated. In the Restoration, the debate concerned male intrusion into midwifery and its transformation into scientific obstetrics, a process seen by men as a progress from female darkness to scientific male light, and by women as male exploitation and appropriation of a female preserve. On this debate, which continues today, Jane Sharp, the first noted Englishwoman to publish on midwifery, Elizabeth Cellier, and Elizabeth Nihell all joined. The number of women giving their view was necessarily small since contemporary opinion discouraged female medical writing, and since midwives, who were expected to be mature women with their own children, found it difficult to keep abreast of discoveries and theories. By the end of the 18th century the battle was more or less lost, and men and their implements had entered the profession. Mary Wollstonecraft mourned the passing of the midwife, while Martha Mears accepted the situation, working to upgrade the image of the medical woman by gaining for her an entry into male medical study.

Relationships: Love was a theme in poetry, plays, and polemics. In the Restoration and early 18th century it was often frankly erotic, with Aphra Behn and Mrs. Taylor discoursing on the joys of sex, and Manley's heroine in *The Fair Hypocrite* remaining both lusty and lucky. Eroticism of a kind entered the devotional poetry of Elizabeth Rowe, becoming a part of female religious vocabulary, although it had to be divorced from sexual content: when Ann Francis in 1801 published her poetical translation of *The Song of Solomon,* she was at pains to make its obvious and voluptuous eroticism allegorical.

Sentimentalism caused a polarizing of love into its spiritual and domestic aspects associated with women, and its sexual ones entering only with the male villain and seducer. Passion was not directly expressed, although the concentration on physiological details sometimes hinted at its presence. Female sexual desire was largely silenced, conveyed more in deathbed tremors and melancholic languishings than in direct response; in the brief period of the 1790s, however, Mary Wollstonecraft and Mary Hays tried to convey its idea, if not its reality, in their novels, *The Wrongs of Woman* and *Emma Courtney.* But in *A Vindication of the Rights of Woman,* and indeed in *The Wrongs of Woman* to some extent, passion was labeled a trap for women, and rational friendship, better for everyone, was substituted for it. In similar fashion in the early 1700s, Mary Davys argued for friendship with men over romantic love, and Lady Wallace roundly condemned passion as a menace to society.

Until the last decade of the century, prostitution and adultery, often seen as crimes of passion, were rarely treated with understanding, although in 1745 Charlotte MacCarthy included the rehabilitation of a fallen woman in her novel *The Fair Moralist.* In the 1770s, R. Roberts defended fallen women in *Sermons Written by a Lady,* and Charlotte Smith's *Emmeline* (1788) showed some feeling for an adul-

teress. In 1796 Elizabeth Inchbald's *Nature and Art* was compassionate about the plight of women seduced and abandoned to prostitution, and in Harriet Lee's *Canterbury Tales,* from the closing years of the century, are pleas for an unwed mother and the young erring wife of an old man. The major treatment is, however, Mary Wollstonecraft's: in *The Rights of Woman* she pleaded for social and economic responsibility from seducers, and in *The Wrongs of Woman* she created the first sympathetic picture of a working-class prostitute.

Much mocked by men from the fictional Lovelace onward, female friendship is one of the great themes of women's literature in England and America. In the 17th century Mary Mollineux wrote in its praise, as did Sarah Egerton, "Ephelia," and the rapturous Katherine Philips. The true rhapsodic period, however, came with sentimentalism—in the letters of Elizabeth Carter and Catherine Talbot, in the poems of Mary Whately, Ann Yearsley, Anna Seward, and Hannah Brand, and in the novels of Sarah Fielding, Elizabeth Griffith, and Elizabeth Sophia Tomlins. Eliza Tuite found friendship a comfort in sorrow, and Harriet Lee and Charlotte Lennox created fictional women sustained in loveless matches by female friends. Occasionally it is anatomized, as in the crude but psychologically interesting *Mary, A Fiction* (1788) by Wollstonecraft, which analyzes her own difficult relationship with her friend; and sometimes it is generalized into female utopias, the semi-satiric one of Delarivière Manley in *New Atalantis,* or the idyllic philanthropic society of Sarah Scott and Barbara Montagu.

Women's Rights: Almost every female author considered the state of her sex and, however conservative, in some way disturbed patriarchal assumptions—necessarily so since her very existence as a writing subject challenged the prevailing ideology of female marginality. Consideration ranged from the outright attacks of Mary Astell or Mary Wollstonecraft to the fantasies of the Duchess of Newcastle and the modest grumblings of countless women about their stunted education; even Hannah Woolley in her cookery book managed to lament its neglect. Sometimes feminist expression seems at odds with the stated message. So Fanny Burney, eschewing outright protest, allowed secondary characters to express feminist views. In *A Simple Story* Elizabeth Inchbald set up a conventional female ideal over her independent spirited woman, but the superior artistry lavished on the latter betrayed a different partiality.

Marriage was much debated. In the Restoration and early 18th century, the arranged marriage focused hostility in the farces and plays of Aphra Behn, Elizabeth Polwhele, and Mary Pix; in 1716 Mary Davys railed against materialistic unions, and in 1732 Elizabeth Boyd described the misery of the loveless arranged match. One strain peculiar to this period is the argument against matrimony of any kind and for female celibacy. In *Some Reflections upon Marriage* (1700) Astell called marriage the most potentially tyrannical of relationships, and she advocated spinsterhood for women and fulfilling female relationships within a female community (although, if they were so foolhardy as to marry, they should please their parents and obey their husbands). Lady Mary Wortley Montagu fancied Astell's female monastery, while Mary Davys thought women might indeed do better to avoid matrimony. "Ephelia" and Sarah Egerton opposed marriage and celebrated women's freedom from sexual and romantic love; Mary, Lady Chudleigh, in her poetical version of Astell's doctrines, urged women to scorn altogether "the wretched state."

The advocacy of celibacy largely disappeared from feminist writing at the end of the 18th century, although marriage was much reviled—by Mary Wollstonecraft and Margaret Coghlan, for example, using variations of the common phrase "legal prostitution." Novelists often avoided the misery of matrimony for their characters by fantastical endings, whereby feckless husbands were killed (Charlotte Smith) or banished to castle corners to repent, while the wife managed the property (Agnes Maria Bennett). In Charlotte Lennox's novel, the wife received a legacy preventing her financial dependence on an unworthy husband.

Wollstonecraft's *Wrongs of Woman* illustrates the male tyranny implied in marriage and, following French revolutionary policy, argues for the right of divorce, although the novel provides no fantasy picture of liberation. In the face of the enormous legal and economic power marriage gave to men, most women could only advocate fortitude, like Jane Warton, well aware that power makes tyranny and that women will suffer.

Specific female rights were pursued at different periods; Restoration Quakers like Margaret Fell campaigned against men's refusal to allow female speech at meetings, and Ann Docwra and Elizabeth Bathurst argued for women's participation in church matters, there being no male and female in Christ. From a slightly different perspective, the Philadelphian Jane Lead in the 1680s insisted on the androgyny of the ideal being, and on the female as well as male attributes of God. At the end of the 18th century the mystic Joanna Southcott, identifying herself as "the Woman clothed with the Sun," appealed mainly to women, especially single ones who were encouraged to believe themselves brides of the Spirit. Confounding the patriarchal theological scheme, she taught that, while a woman brought death, she would also deliver liberation; women were thus freed from the burden of having initiated Adam's fall and were emancipated into theological feminism.

In the early 1700s Catharine Trotter championed the female right to earn an independent living. Almost a century later Mary Ann Radcliffe argued for more professional opportunities for women, otherwise forced into prostitution; she urged them to patronize each other, so forcing men from areas into which they had unfairly trespassed. Priscilla Wakefield also wanted more working possibilities—although she still believed that gender and class should determine occupation—and she proposed a teachers' college for women.

In 1718 Anne Long expressed her sense of women's exclusion from law-making, and "Sophia" in 1739 argued, as Wollstonecraft was to do many years later, that women could hold public office if not deprived of training. No feminist in many areas, Abigail Adams made her famous plea "Remember the Ladies" to her husband John Adams, who was engaged in drawing up the American Declaration of Independence.

At the beginning and end of the period, the double sexual standard, accepted and valorized in the high sentimental years, was attacked: by "Ephelia," who scorned the concept of sexual virtue; Manley, who noted the injustice of the unreasonable expectations for women; and by the Countess of Winchilsea, who felt women ought to be free to express sexual passion. Bitter at the endless harping on female chastity, Lady Mary Wortley Montagu lashed out at the absurd cruelty of putting men's "precious honour" in female hands and then obliging women "to prove a negative for the preservation of it." While depicting the reality of repression, Wollstonecraft argued that men and women should be bound to similar standards, since sexual desire crossed genders; the much-mocked Mary Hays claimed for women the power of initiation and sexual choice.

The main feminist statements came with the demand for educational parity and for the right to prove intellectual equality. They arrived in two clusters—at the beginning of the period, with Bathsua Makin, Mary, Lady Chudleigh, Mary Astell, "Sophia," Lady Masham, and Delarivière Manley, and at the end, with Catherine Macaulay, Charlotte Smith, Mary Wollstonecraft, and Mary Hays. The early cluster is in the tradition of the Dutch scholar Anna Maria van Schurman, who in 1641 directly argued for women's share in education and public life, and indirectly made a plea with her own immense learning. She influenced Makin who, in 1673, appealed for a rigorous education for women, while definite proposals for institutions and learning came from Mary Astell.

In the mid- and late 18th century, women seemed to retreat from assertion and demand. Although she wanted education for women, Sarah Fielding did not insist on it, while Viscountess Irwin, answering Pope's misogyny, noted only how women were trained in foolishness. Although agreeing with Astell in her early life, Lady Mary Wortley Montagu by mid-century seemed cut off from women, muddled in a way by her own female passion which Astell's formulation ignored; she shied away from asserting female equality with men. In the 1750s Elizabeth Tollet could only lament through her character of Hypatia the fate of being born female and clever in a male world. Elizabeth Griffith noted bitterly the difficulties of the uneducated woman writer, bound always to flatter the male ego.

The feminism of the 1790s—of Mary Wollstonecraft, Catherine Macaulay and Mary Hays—attacked the patriarchal prison of sensibility and believed rational education to be the only exit from "the magic circle" of repression, passivity, and marginality into which women had been placed and had placed themselves. As the early protest was predicated partially on the Restoration Enlightenment, of Locke in particular, so the later one was influenced by the radicalism of the revolutionary period, of Paine and Godwin, although radical men showed little concern for women's rights and requirements, and the French revolutionary leadership listened with scant attention for only a few months.

The women of the 1790s seemed unaware of their sisters almost a century earlier, although they echoed many of their arguments. But Wollstonecraft went beyond Makin or Astell in seeing the need for entire social reform to accommodate the changes demanded for women. In addition, she veered from Astell in appreciating women's need both for rational and emotional fulfillment. But her pleas for sexual and emotional freedom were ill-timed and served to discredit all her theories; so Wollstonecraft was vilified in a way experienced by none of the early women—except possibly the equally irregular Manley—through focus on her unconventional loves and misery.

In the conservative reaction that followed the Revolution's violent stage, the Anglo-French hostilities, and the repressive political measures in England, even liberal women shunned Wollstonecraft's insights: Mary Hays, ridiculed by Elizabeth Hamilton in *Memoirs of Modern Philosophers,* still preached the crippling effect of subordination and unmitigated obedience, but she retreated from the rationalism of *The Rights of Woman* to restate the sentimental view of women's primary role in loving and caring; sympathetic to Wollstonecraft's marital ideas, Amelia Opie in *Adeline Mowbray* nonetheless sent her heroine to a sentimental death. In the early years of the 19th century, Lady Louisa Stuart worried over the feminist issues raised years earlier, but felt she could accommodate herself to female dependence and social limitation. The future lay not with Wollstonecraft's passionate polemics and demand for entire societal change, but with the prudent and chaste feminism of more respectable women like Fanny Burney or Maria Edgeworth.

The women in the *Dictionary* are little read now, even those most famous in their times, such as Ann Radcliffe and Catherine Macaulay. A few, like Mary Wollstonecraft, have gained a new relevance through the feminism of the 1970s and are again in print. But it is rare to find even a student of literature who has heard of more than half a dozen of them. This book is a plea for notice.

Probably no undiscovered masterpieces are embedded in the material, and even the concept of the masterpiece seems inappropriate for women's literature of that era, which failed to conform to established critical hierarchies or to the classification of genres. Far more than male texts, female ones always have a subtext which marks them: the justification, even vindication, of their own existence and of their authors.

The criteria for judgment are also problematic. On what grounds do we discriminate between Minerva novels or spiritual autobiographies of illiterate captives, self-doubting Quakers, and devotional Anglicans? In sentimentalism, women's major vehicle, which delivered for the first time female centrality, tragedy and comedy are confounded, and the demands of naturalism, the privileged fictional mode, are ignored. The distance between text and reader and between author and text, so prized by modern criticism, is actively frustrated, and the reader is taken into the work almost as a character. How can we judge sentimental writing? We are ill-attuned to it; we want wit and raciness, not effusive posturing, and collision with ideology, not collusion with it.

Yet, by modern critical standards there is aesthetic and rhetorical development in female writing in the period. From the beginning to the end there was growth in ease of writing, which reveals women's increasing sureness in the role of author. The awkwardness of Polwhele or Behn was not duplicated in the less outspoken but more polished plays of the late 18th century, and the crude style of Celia Fiennes would have been unthinkable for the Bluestockings. By the end of the century, even the most conventional and dull novelist could handle plot with a dexterity far beyond Eliza Haywood or Jane Barker. By any standards there was considerable achievement. Perhaps it is most obvious, however, in the form in which women are least marginalized and which is little regarded by critics and historians of literature, the familiar public and private letter, written by Bluestockings and radicals alike, the "desultory" form in which, as Mary Wollstonecraft admitted, "I could not avoid being continually the first person."

J.T.

A

ADAMS, Abigail (1744–1818), American letter writer, was born in Weymouth, Mass., into the cultured and politically aware family of a minister, William, and his wife, Elizabeth Quincy Smith. Sickly in youth, AA read widely in the Bible and in Enlightenment figures such as Locke, although she later insisted that her education had been neglected. In 1764 she married the lawyer John Adams and settled in Braintree. She bore five children, one of whom died in infancy, while another, John Quincy Adams, became the sixth president. During the American War of Independence, when Adams was much involved in politics and often absent, AA was left to manage the family and farm. In 1784 she accompanied him to London and Paris, where she was initially appalled by the frivolity, although in time she grew more tolerant of alien ways. In 1789 John Adams became vice president and in 1797 president of the US. Since her health was delicate, AA spent most of these years at their home, but she did pass some time between 1797 and 1801 in the new capital of Washington, where she complained of discomforts and noted her husband's political disappointments. Just before her death, AA mocked the idea that her correspondence might be collected and published; where John Adams was concerned to preserve his letters, she often expressed the wish that hers might be burnt.

AA's letters chart her life and the course of American history during an important 40 years, from the 1760s to Adams's retirement from public life; for the reader they convey both the political excitement of the revolutionary years and the demanding clutter of a women's life. Other correspondents include MERCY OTIS WARREN, to whom she wrote warmly and high-mindedly of family affairs and patriotism, her sister, and CATHERINE MACAULAY, whose support for the American cause she praised in 1774. The letters to Adams, published in *Adams Family Correspondence* (1963) begin with the courtship with its loving upheavals. AA's tone is forthright and the style sometimes pithy; during Adams's illness she warned: "Still be careful, good folks are scarce." She is often playful; in April 1764 she wrote, "I think I write to you every Day. Shall not I make my Letters very cheep; don't you light your pipe with them?" After her marriage, her letters continue loving and lighthearted— her first girl is "the dear Image of her still Dearer Pappa"—although she writes also of her loneliness without Adams. In December 1773 she lamented, "Alass! How many snow banks devide thee and me and my warmest wishes to see thee will not melt one of them." Love and sadness at separation are constant themes. In July 1775, while she recognized Adams's proper immersion in politics, she complains, "I want some sentimental Effusions of the Heart," but she is entirely satisfied with his next "longest and better Letter." A May 1776 note ends, "I bid you good night. O that I could annihilate Space." AA dreads the war in which she knows that her husband cannot be "an inactive Spectator": "If the Sword be drawn I bid adieu to all domestick felicity, and look forward to that Country where there is neither wars nor rumors of War." AA writes much of domestic calamities; in 1774 she describes the drought, lightly in terms of politics: "My poor Cows will certainly prefer a petition to you, setting forth their Greavances and informing you that they have been deprived of their ancient privilages." As hostilities begin, she is upset to experience the selfishness of neighbors refusing to help refugees: "It would make your heart ake to see what difficulties and distresses the poor Boston people are driven to" (July 1775). By September 1775 she is entirely engrossed by an epidemic of dysentery: "As to politics I know nothing about them. The distresses of my own family are so great that I have not thought about them." She graphically describes the horrors of the disease, the necessary cleansing of the house with hot vinegar and the dying of the servant who, as a "putrid mass," becomes the "most gastly object my Eyes ever beheld." In extremity AA turns to religion finding comfort in the fact that all is from God and can be borne. In July 1776, fearing smallpox, she and the children are innoculated and AA records their symptoms and anxiety.

Political events sometimes press as heavily on AA as domestic ones. She respects Adams as a public man but offers her advice freely, accepting her patriotic part: "I have felt for my Country and her sons, I have bled with them, and for them." Although she laments the disruption of war—"All domestick pleasures and enjoyments are absorbed in the great and important duty you owe your Country," she writes to Adams (May 1776)—she is firm in her own loyalty, and in November 1775 she castigates "debauched patriots" who cannot be kept "in the visionary chains of Decency." In the political sphere AA is most famous for her defense of women and slaves. In 1774 she wishes "most sincerely there was not a slave in the province" and she hopes that the chaos of the Revolution will give to slaves and other deprived groups those rights which the republican ideology of freedom seems to promise. In April 1776 she pleads: "in the new Code of Laws which I suppose it will be necessary for you to make I desire you would Remember the Ladies, and be more generous to them than your ancestors." Commenting that "all Men would be tyrants if they could," she notes the contradictions in men's emancipating nations while "retaining absolute power over Wives." If women are not listened to, she declares, they will "foment a Rebellion, and will not hold ourselves bound by any Laws in which we have no voice, or Representative." When Adams responds to her arguments with a laugh, declaring "We know better than to repeal our Masculine systems," AA writes indignantly of the treatment to Mercy Otis Warren, complaining of Adams's idea that

women have power through charming; yet her reply to Adams accepts the claim, although she still winces at the "absolute power" men retain over wives.

As this skirmish shows, AA is not, on the whole, revolutionary in her views; she reveals an acceptance of, even enthusiasm for, the role of dependent wife, while a firm Christian faith allows her to deflect suffering and anger into belief in a compensatory afterlife. If she insists on any particular principle in politics and society, it is that great power should be avoided in anyone, president or husband. AA confesses that her letters are not "moddles" of form; spelling and punctuation are often crude. Nonetheless, they greatly appeal with their detail, common sense, and lack of squeamishness. For example, she writes of the ailments following dysentery that she "took a puke which has relieved me" (November 1775). She can be pointed as often as diffuse: "I am more and more convinced that Man is a dangerous creature, and that power whether vested in many or a few is ever grasping, and like the grave cries give, give." Her assessment of personalities is succinct: Washington is much approved—"Dignity with ease, and complacency, the Gentleman and Soldier look agreably blended in him"— while General Lee comes off less well— "The Elegance of his pen far exceeds that of his person."   J.T.

ADAMS, Hannah (1755–1831), American historian and compiler, was the first professional woman writer in the US. She was born in Medfield, Mass., a distant cousin of President John Adams. She inherited her father's passion for knowledge and because of her frailty studied at home in Greek, Latin, geography, and logic. Her father's business failure plunged the family from wealth into near poverty, and HA pursued a literary career as the only means of support available. Despite critical and commercial success, her income was substantially reduced by poor business deals, ill health, and failing eyesight, incurred by years of painstaking research. Yet her warmth, simplicity, and perseverance won her many influential friends, including Abbé Grégoire, with whom she corresponded on her history of the Jews, and William Shaw, who granted her access to the Boston Athenaeum. Remaining near Boston, she spent her final years in comfort, supported by an annuity raised by friends and sustained by companionship, literature, and a devout belief in God.

Since HA chose her subjects for their "public utility," not for her own enjoyment, her works are usually theological, or historical with theological overtones. Outstanding for its candor and impartiality, *An Alphabetical Compendium* (1784) (retitled *A View of Religions* for later editions) is a comprehensive survey of the various religions of the world, offering arguments for the principal sects. *Summary History of New England* (1799) was the first history to extend from the Mayflower voyage to the acceptance of the federal Constitution; while HA views the Puritans with historical detachment as products of their age, she also reflects throughout on "the wonders of divine Providence, rising conspicuously on every scene." Her *Abridgement* (1805?) of this work for school use is more didactic, highlighting the specific moral behind each historical episode. *The Truth and Excellence of the Christian Religion Exhibited* (1804) contains biographical sketches of 60 eminent laymen since 1600 who exemplified the Christian spirit, with excerpts from their writings as "evidence" in defense of Christianity. HA's monumental *History of the Jews from the Destruction of Jerusalem to the Nineteenth Century* (1812) represents one of the earliest Jewish histories written with sympathy and admiration; nevertheless, her sympathy is tempered by her belief that the countless miseries suffered by the Jews were "the just judgment of heaven," prophesied by Christ when they rejected him. *Letters on the Gospels* (1824) includes 30 letters addressed to her nieces, intended to make the New Testament appealing to youth for their improvement and pleasure. Additional works include her *Narrative of the Controversy* (1814) between herself and Rev. Jedidiah Morse, who preempted the design for her abridgement and issued a cheaper edition before her; *A Concise Account of the London Society for Promoting Christianity Amongst the Jews* (1816); and her *Memoir* (1832), a brief and modest account of her life and hardships, frequently disparaging of her own work. Generally HA strove to remain unbiased, and critics repeatedly praised her objectivity, clarity of style, depth of research, and judicious use of sources. Although she considered herself merely a "compiler" of historical information, not an original thinker, her works remain impressive for the prodigious knowledge and meticulous scholarship they reveal and for the sensitive and open-minded treatment of subjects regardless of HA's personal sentiment.   J.C.G.

ADAM[S], Jean (1710–65), poet, was born in Crawfordsdyke in Renfrewshire, Scotland, the daughter of a shipmaster. Orphaned young, she worked as maid and nurse in the house of Mr. Turner of Greenock, a minister, whose library she used to educate herself. Her poems were published by Mrs. Drummond as *Miscellany Poems,* by Mrs. Jane Adams, in Crawfordsdyke; the volume had 154 subscribers. Later JA set up a girls' school, where she was known for her dramatic Shakespeare readings to her pupils. Much impressed with Samuel Richardson's novels, she is said to have closed her school for six weeks to walk to London to visit the author. In time her school failed and JA became a vagrant, earning a precarious living as a hawker. In 1765 she was admitted to Glasgow poorhouse as "a poor woman in distress"; there she died the next day. The preface to *Miscellany Poems* by Archibald Crawford announces that the book is in two parts, one in "meeter" and one in "blank verse in imitation of Milton"; an example from the latter is "Adam's Reflections upon his Soul": "'Tis not my Regularity of Shape, / My florid hue, nor yet my graceful Mien / I boast, nor yet the Organs of my Sense: / For these in some Degree the Brutes can boast, / But hallowed Reason's Fire within my Breast / My Soul with Love and Gratitude inspire." Although they interest as the productions of a self-taught working woman, the poems are on the whole pious and dull, given to extended metaphor and sometimes to childish sing-song rhythms. In 1771 Robert Burns heard in the streets the song "There's nae luck aboot the house" which many ascribed to JA. It presents a devoted wife considering her absent husband, concluding with the conventional advice: "Do everything to pleasure them, / nor ne'er begin a strife; / Be obedient to their just commands, / it well becomes a wife." A parodic companion piece, possibly by the same author, is the complaint of a man who has lost his spouse and is unable to perform domestic chores or sleep because of fleas, which would normally feed on his wife.   J.T.

ALCOCK, Mrs. Mary (?–1798), poet, was the daughter of Denison Cumberland, who taught at Trinity College, Cambridge, and later became Bishop of Clonfert and Kilmore. Her mother was Joanna Bentley, daughter of the celebrated critic and orator Richard Bentley, who became the object of satire in Swift's *Battle of the Books*. Her brother, Richard Cumberland, was a scholar and man of letters. MA probably had some part in her brother's literary life and may even have known his friends—Garrick, Reynolds, Goldsmith, Foote, Sheridan, and Lord Sackville. Surrounded by well-educated, well-published, and well-known relatives, MA yet wrote only two books: a seven-page poem, *The Air-Balloon; or, The Flying Mortal* (1784), and a collection of poems, *Poetical Writer* (1799), edited by Joanna Hughes and published a year after MA's death.   M.P.

ALLEN, Lucy (fl. 1784–88), American poet, wrote 26 hymns that were reprinted in Windsor, Vt., in 1795. According to the preface of this volume, she was a devout Baptist who could neither read nor write but was moved to compose verse by "accidents, and other occurrences" of her life in the mid-1780s. One of these was the death of her daughter by David Allen. A versifier of Calvinist doctrines, LA offers "the elect" solace and exhortation to rejoice in the "sweets of Communion with Jesus." Unbelievers, especially the young, are warned about Satan's wiles and told, "if you don't believe in Christ, / He'll send you down to hell." All people must realize that they deserve damnation. But their fear will be relieved when they are washed in Jesus's blood; thereafter, even when they go astray, Christians are secure in divine love. Four of LA's hymns are elegies. She speaks of her mission to comfort mourners. At first she rebelled when her own daughter was dying, but was "call'd . . . up before [God's] throne" and assured that the child's soul would be saved. She then sat beside the deathbed and "gloried in the cross"—as she now exhorts bereaved saints on earth to do. *Hymns, on Various Subjects* displays the poet's familiarity with the Bible, traditional Christian metaphors, and the popular meters for hymns. Her most personal hymns, the narratives about the "Shaking Quakers" and her child's death, illustrate her simple piety and view of herself as a moral teacher; her own experiences are treated as exemplary. LA is less polemical and sophisticated than other contemporary Baptist poets such as ANNA BEEMAN or JENNY FENNO.   M.D.J.

ANSPACH, Lady Elizabeth Craven, Mar-

gravine of (1750–1828), memoirist, travel diarist, dramatist, and poet, is best labeled an autobiographer because every work she undertook became a pulpit for her personal and often eccentric concerns. She was the daughter of Augustus, fourth Earl of Berkeley. In 1767 she married William Craven, later the Earl of Craven, to whom she bore seven children, three sons and four daughters. Despite her busy household, M of A became a social celebrity. Her charming conversation and open personality gained her association with Horace Walpole, who called her "*infinitamente* indiscreet," Dr. Johnson, Garrick, Reynolds, and ELIZABETH MONTAGU. During 1781–82, the Cravens' marriage deteriorated as a consequence of both their extramarital transgressions. Accounts vary as to the degree of M of A's culpability—she claims to be the injured party—but she became a wanderer, leaving the children except for the youngest, Keppel, with their father to ensure their economic future, relying for herself upon the hospitality of friends. M of A journeyed through Versailles, Madrid, Lisbon, Vienna, Berlin, Constantinople, Warsaw, St. Petersburg, Rome, Florence, Naples, and finally Anspach, where she came under the protection of the Margrave, Christian Frederick Charles Alexander, a nephew of Frederick the Great. At first M of A was welcomed as his "adopted sister" but, upon the nearly simultaneous deaths of their spouses, she married the Margrave, who exchanged his land-holdings in Prussia for a pension so they might reside in England. They were not, however, welcomed at Court as nobility. Their new residence at Hammersmith, Brandenburgh House, included a theater, which afforded M of A the much-coveted center stage in her own home. After the Margrave's death in 1806, M of A devoted herself to projects, including a scheme for paving the streets, and to several naturalist treatises. She left most of her property to her son Keppel.

Published works include *The Sleepwalker* (1778, trans. drama), *Modern Anecdotes of the Family of Kinkverankotsprackengotchern* (1780), *The Miniature Portrait* (1780, drama), *A Fashionable Day* (1780, etiquette), *The Silver Tankard* (1781, drama), *Journey Through The Crimea to Constantinople* (1789, letters), *Correspondence* (1789), *The Georgian Princess* (1799, drama), *The Robbers* (1799, trans. drama), *Treatise on the art of pruning fruit trees* (1806), and *Autobiography* (1825). The

Strawberry Hill Press published much of her poetry during the 1770s, and numerous selections from her dramatic works were also published. Although prodigious in her output, M of A did not win the respect of her literary colleagues or of her biographers who wished, at least privately, that she had written as engagingly as she conversed. M of A's observations are generally too self-preoccupied to be interesting because she refuses to describe any scene with emotional detachment. In her *Journey*, she records people's responses to herself, as, for example, when she descended into the grotto of Antiparos and the Greek peasant women took "her to be a supernatural being." She cannot resist some self-serving criticism of English society in her plays: "by our asiatick customs, it is the Husband enobles the wife" (*The Georgian Princess*).   D.S.G.

ANTHONY, Susanna (1726–91), American devotional writer, was born in Newport, R.I., one of seven daughters of a Quaker goldsmith. She was sickly and lived all her life with her family, supporting herself at times with needlework. Deeply religious from childhood, she was influenced by the Evangelical preacher George Whitefield. After much spiritual wrestling SA made a written covenant at age 14; at 15 she forsook the Quakers to join the first Congregationalist church in Newport, where she attended weekly women's devotional meetings. SA decided that she could best serve God in prayer: "In the year 1744, in September, I came to a fixed resolution to spend some days in a year to seek God's favor to a miserable world." She made prayer "the grand pursuit" of her life, although deeply fearful of the sinful pride that might be involved in the decision. From 1743 she kept a diary in which she repeatedly worried over the sacrifice religion demanded of "all that the world calls delightful" and investigated her own state, which vacillated dramatically between assurance of salvation and fear of damnation. During the War of American Independence, she traveled to various communities, noting in her letter their piety or spiritual problems; she also taught in a family and kept a small school. She was in Newport when it was garrisoned by British troops, whose profanity she deplored. In 1791 she attended her youngest sister in an illness, caught the disease, and died.

SA left diaries and letters recording her life and devotion, her frequent depressions, and her ill health; some of these writings were included by Samuel Hopkins, the pastor of her church in Newport, in *The Life and Character of Miss Susanna Anthony, who died in Newport, Rhode-Island, June 23, 1791 in the sixty-fifth year of her age.* A later edition of 1802 has a dedication by Dr. Ryland, Mr. Fuller and Mr. Sutcliffe, presenting SA as a humble example of female excellence, of "pure, practical christianity" and of "the powerful influence of evangelical principles upon the heart and life." The documents records SA's spiritual turmoil, her near-suicidal depressions and her "extacy of love and wonder," and reveal a deep longing for death as union with Christ and release from bodily suffering. SA's letters to SARAH OSBORN, published in 1807 as *Familiar Letters Written by Mrs. Sarah Osborn and Miss Susanna Anthony, late of Newport, Rhode-Island*, were written between 1740 and 1779; they again describe religious raptures and fears, and also reveal the deep and supportive friendship of the two women. SA tends to be more ecstatically religious than Osborn; she exhorts her friend to greater faith and often breaks up her letters with exclamations such as "O infinite grace, and love!" When Osborn grieves that her only child is dying, SA comforts her by envying the child's flight "to the blessed Jesus."   J.T.

"ARIADNE" (fl. 1696), playwright, remains unidentified except as the author of *She Ventures and He Wins*, a comedy staged at Lincoln's Inn Fields, Sept. 1695, and published (1696) as the work of "a Young Lady." In the preface to this play, the first by a woman after APHRA BEHN, "Ariadne" noted that her "Muse," barely restrained in Behn's time from "shewing her Impertinence," has, since Behn's death, "claim'd a kind of Privilege; and, in spite of me, broke from her Confinement." Her further comment that this play is "the first I ever made Publick by appearing on the Stage" also suggests some earlier unrevealed works. Although self-deprecatory, asserting that "the best Apology I can make for my Self and Play, is, that "tis the Error of a weak Woman's Pen," "Ariadne" claimed literary succession both to Behn and to KATHERINE PHILIPS. The play's epilogue, by Motteux, attributes the author's (reluctant) pseudonymity to fear of criticism from "Beaux" and "Wits," and "Ariadne" herself suggested that a favorable reception for this play and her next might make her "ambitious enough to be known." This next play was probably the anonymous *The Un-*

natural Mother, staged at Lincoln's Inn Fields in Sept. 1697 and published in 1698. Its prologue, which states that "A Woman now comes to reform the Stage, / Who once has stood the brunt of this unthinking Age," is clearly intended to improve the contemporary image of the woman playwright by the adoption of a high moral tone. Its author's anonymity is again explained as a necessary defense against criticism: "Nor shall you know, harsh Men, at whom you rail."   R.F.

ARUNDEL[L], Mary (?–1691), translator, was the daughter of Sir John Arundell and Catherine Stowe. She married Robert Radcliff, Earl of Essex, and then Henry, Earl of Arundel. MA was known as a learned lady and was included in George Ballard's collection of celebrated women. She translated from the Latin, and her works included the "Sayings and Doings of the Emperor Severus," dedicated to her father, and "Select Sentences of the Seven Wise Men of Greece." Her manuscripts are preserved at Windsor and in the British Library.   J.J.

ASHBRIDGE, Elizabeth (1713–55), American autobiographer, came to America as an indentured servant and, more as an accommodation than out of interest, began to attend Quaker meetings. She soon took an active part, was converted, and eventually became well known as an accomplished preacher. She and her husband were school teachers in different schools in New Jersey. She died while on a religious mission in Ireland. EA produced nothing for publication during her lifetime, but she kept a record of her activities and thoughts. It was published long after she died and went through many editions under various titles. The title of the 58-page manuscript reads *Some account of the fore part of the life of Elizabeth Ashbridge, who died in truth's service at the house of Robert Lecky at Kilnock in the county of Carlow in Ireland on 16 May 1755* (1761?). The first 48 pages are the composition of EA, but the manuscript is all in one hand; a note explains that it was "continued by her third husband."   M.P.

ASTELL, Mary (1666–1731), polemicist and feminist, was born into a Newcastle coal merchant's family. Her father, Peter Astell, was a leading member of the coal Hostmen; her mother, Mary Errington, was also from a prosperous Newcastle coal-mining family.

She is thought to have been educated when very young in philosophy, logic, and mathematics by her uncle Ralph Astell, her father's bachelor brother, a graduate of Cambridge University and a curate in St. Nicholas Cathedral. At the age of 22, at the time of the Glorious Revolution, MA went to London, where she had great difficulty finding a means of providing for herself. Archbishop Sancroft came to her aid "when even my Kinsfolk had failed, and my familiar Friends had forgotten me." By 1692, thanks to his and / or others' charity, she had settled in Chelsea—where she was to remain the rest of her life—and had begun to correspond with the Rev. John Norris of Bemerton, the last of the so-called Cambridge Platonists. For ten months they discussed in their letters how one owed one's love to God rather than to His creatures, how to respond to the misfortune and pain dispensed by Divine Providence, and other claims of the spirit as they might contradict the claims of the flesh. Norris wanted to publish their correspondence; while he was negotiating this, MA anonymously published her first book, *A Serious Proposal To the Ladies* (1694), which, together with the correspondence with Norris published the following year under the title of *Letters Concerning the Love of God* (1695), established her reputation as an intellectual and a writer.

In *A Serious Proposal To the Ladies*, MA suggested that wealthy women who did not intend to marry use their dowries to finance residential women's colleges—protestant nunneries—to provide the recommended education for upper- and middle-class women and to serve as living quarters for "hunted heiresses" or decayed gentlewomen. The book was followed by *A Serious Proposal To the Ladies Part II* (1697), whose purpose was to provide the rules for rational thought, a distillation of the Port Royal logic and Descartes' method, for women who were still unprovided with an institution of higher learning. These books were subsequently published together. Her next book may be the most clearly feminist in emphasis. *Some Reflections on Marriage* (1700) discusses the obedience that a wife owes her husband and concludes that, since it is the most potentially tyrannical of relationships, no woman ought to undertake this slavery lightly, and that the morally responsible nature of one's husband-to-be is his most important qualification to consider. The preface added to the 1706 edition is an excellent early example of 17th-century liberal, political rhetoric applied to the issue of women's rights. MA writes wittily, sometimes sarcastically, exhorting women to rise above the petty concerns of dress and flirtation, and to be worthy of their natures as creatures of a divine being. "You may be as ambitious as you please, so you can aspire to the best things. . . . Remember, I pray you, the famous Women of former Ages . . . and blush to think how much is now and will hereafter be said of them, when you your selves . . . must be buried in silence and forgetfulness! . . . Let us learn to pride our selves in something more excellent than the invention of a Fashion, and not entertain such a degrading thought of our own *worth* as to imagine that our Souls were given us only for the service of our Bodies, and that the best improvement we can make of these is to attract the Eyes of Men."

In 1704, the Whigs and Tories of Parliament continued to polarize on the issue of the Occasional Conformity Bill, a bill designed to bar Dissenters from holding public office by making it illegal for them to qualify by occasionally conforming, or taking the Anglican communion. Politically a conservative Tory, MA was concerned over the Church of England's struggles to maintain political power in England. She published three political works that year: two of them, *Moderation Truly Stated* and *A Fair Way With Dissenters and Their Patrons*, argued in favor of the Occasional Conformity Bill and were much appreciated by religious conservatives. The third, *An Impartial Enquiry Into The Causes of Rebellion and Civil War*, a royalist manifesto, argued that the subversive, individualistic element in Whig and Dissenting ideology had led to the war. MA's conservative religious convictions were as well developed and central to her intellectual system as her political or feminist views. Throughout her life she campaigned for conservative Anglicanism as the necessary basis for personal morality and national politics as well as spiritual understanding. She followed the Tory Atterbury's debates with Dr. Hoadley over the doctrine of Divine Right and passive obedience (the degree to which subjects ought to submit passively to their rulers), and offered Atterbury advice on his rebuttal of Hoadley's *The Measures of Submission to the Civil Magistrate Considered* (1705). She worked with John Walker on his polemical *The Sufferings of the Clergy* (1714)

and collected and transcribed for him the information on the persecutions of the Anglican clergyman Dr. Squire. In 1705 MA published her religious manifesto, *The Christian Religion As Profess'd By a Daughter of the Church*, in which she seeks to establish the philosophical principles of her religion—her own version of the Cartesian sequence from the existence of reason to a belief in God—and to refute the materialistic thinking of her own day—like Locke's—which led to skepticism. Her last book was an attempt to bolster up 17th-century religious piety before the onslaughts of a tolerant, latitudinarian individualism: *Bart'lemy Fair: or, An Inquiry After Wit* (1709) was written as an answer to Lord Shaftesbury's *Letter Concerning Enthusiasm*, the first treatise of his *Characteristics*. In it, MA scorns "this Blessed Age of Liberty! which has made us so much Wiser than our Fathers," and notes that never before was it "thought a Service to the Public to expose the Establish'd Religion, no not when it was ever so false and ridiculous in it self, to the Contempt of the People." She wrote a new preface to *Bart'lemy Fair* in 1722, and issued new editions of *Letters Concerning the Love of God*, and *Some Reflections Upon Marriage* in 1730 just before she died. Her style in her religious works is less vivacious than in her feminist ones and tends toward the rhapsodic or lugubrious.

MA's importance as the first widely read, expressly feminist polemicist is incalculable. She was perhaps the first respectable woman prose writer in England, the prototype for the Bluestockings of the next generation. She inspired many of the women intellectuals of her own time: ELIZABETH THOMAS, LADY CHUDLEIGH, ELIZABETH ELSTOB, and LADY MARY WORTLEY MONTAGU. She was satirized in *The Tatler* for her otherworldly Platonism, but her ideas—and often her language—were picked up and imitated by the leading male authors of the day. Defoe, Steele, and Richardson all make reference to *A Serious Proposal To The Ladies*: Defoe in *Essay on Projects* (1697), Richardson in volume II of *Sir Charles Grandison* (1753–54), and Steele, who actually uses more than 100 pages of it verbatim, without attribution, in his *The Ladies Library* (1714). The fact that MA's active role in the public realm did not damage her reputation is probably due to the extreme conservatism of her political and religious views, her unimpeachably pious and ascetic habits, and the wealth and social standing of her particular friends, the pious and philanthropic Lady Elizabeth Hastings, the COUNTESS OF COVENTRY, and Lady Catherine Jones. Through these women MA came to know the famous scholars, antiquarians, and clergymen who sought their patronage and, with their backing, she opened a school for the poor daughters of out-pensioners at the Royal Hospital in 1729. MA died after an operation for a breast tumor and was buried in the churchyard at Chelsea. R.P.

AUBIN, Penelope (1679–1731), novelist, translator, playwright, and lay preacher, was born in London probably of French émigré parents; her family may have been Catholic. References in her novels to locations in southwest England and Wales indicate that she spent part of her life there, perhaps as a child or a young married woman. Her husband's circumstances are not known, but the 13-year gap between her first published poems (1708) and the beginning of her major career as a novelist (1721) suggests that this was the period of her marriage. Financial difficulties—probably connected with the death of her husband (who died some time before 1722) and perhaps related to the collapse of the South Sea Bubble— forced her to turn to writing to support herself. For the remainder of her life, PA lived in London. By 1729 she was preaching to popular acclaim in her own oratory in the York buildings near Charing Cross. Presumably she died in London.

PA wrote three poems, seven novels, one play, four translations from the French, and two "editions" of French works she took over after the death of her friend, Thomas Mornington Gibbs. The poems are Pindaric imitations: "The Stuarts" (1707), "The Extasy" (1708; presented to Queen Anne by the Duchess of Ormonde), and "The Well-come: A Poem to his Grace the Duke of Marlborough" (1708). Her novels are *The Strange Adventures of the Count de Vinevil and His Family* (1721), *The Life of Madam de Beaumont* (1721), *The Nobel Slaves* (1722), *The Life and Amorous Adventures of Lucinda* (1722), *The Life of Carlotta DuPont* (1723), *The Life and Adventures of the Lady Lucy* (1726), and *The Life and Adventures of the Young Count Albertus* (1728). She translated Robert Challes' *The Illustrious French Lovers* (1720), Petis de la Croix's *The History of Genghizcan the Great* (1722), Mme. de Beaucour's *The Life of the Countess de Gondez* and *The Adventures of the Prince of Clermont and Madam de Ravezan* (both 1722). She edited Sieur de Gomberville's *Moral Virtue Delineated in 103 short lectures* and his *The Doctrine of Morality* (both 1721). Her last work was a play, *The Humours of the Masqueraders*, which was staged but not successful, ending its short run in December 1730; an edition was published in 1733.

PA's career as a preacher is not inconsistent with her career as an author of romances for, unlike her contemporary ELIZA HAYWOOD, PA's intention in her work is clearly to instruct as well as entertain, "to encourage Virtue, and excite us to heroic Actions." Although, after her death, she was attacked by the Abbé Prévost (on literary, not moral, grounds), her novels were popular, most going into second editions during the first year. PA is the major inheritor of the technique used by Defoe of combining, to often bizarre geographical effect, elements of the travelogue and romance: love, accident, separation/reunion, exotic settings, and coincidences. Unlike other romance writers, however, PA is consistent in her emphasis upon morality: unusually large numbers of her characters are married, and moral considerations determine their behavior as they undergo the various adventures dictated by her form. K.S.

B

BAILLIE, Lady Grissel [Grizel] (1665–1746), Scottish poet, was born at Redbraes Castle, Berwickshire. Her father, Sir Patrick Hume, employed "Little Grizel" to deliver secret messages to the imprisoned Jacobite Robert Baillie of Jerviswood; she also contrived secretly to convey food to her father in hiding when the family properties were confiscated. GB's youthful romantic heroics became legendary in Scottish literature, and they are recounted in JOANNA BAILLIE'S *Metrical Legends of Exalted Characters* (1821). After managing the family during their exile in Holland, GB refused the post of maid of honor to the Princess of Orange, returning instead to Scotland to marry Robert Baillie's son, George. The couple's seasons in London attracted the best company and GB was part of the circle of LADY HERVEY. Sir Thomas Burnet wrote GB's monumental inscription, praising her "dignity of mind, good breeding, good humour, good sense." GB's Scottish songs appeared anonymously in collections such as Allan Ramsay's *The Tea-Table Miscellany* (1723–40). One of her songs, "And werena my heart licht I wad dee," has become a favorite in Scottish literature. Allan Cunningham (1784–1842) says that it is "very original, very characteristic, and very irregular." Poetic fragments were left in a notebook possessed by her daughter, Lady Murray, whose *Memoirs* of her parents was published in 1822. GB also left voluminous memoranda and account books preserving valuable records of domestic history, especially three folio-size "Day Books" covering 1692–1733 (selections published as *Household Book,* Edinburgh, 1911).   G.B.

BAILLIE, Joanna (1762–1851), poet and dramatist, was born in Lanarkshire. After the death of her Presbyterian clergyman father, her uncle William Hunter, one of two famous Scots physician-surgeon brothers who practiced in London, undertook responsibility for the family. In 1784 JB, her mother, and sister moved to London, living first in Windmill Street and then in Hampstead. After their mother's death in 1806, the sisters continued to live together. At Hampstead JB was visited by many admirers; among her friends and correspondents were ANNA LAETITIA BARBAULD, MARY BERRY, Walter Scott, and Lady Noel Byron.

JB's first work (published anonymously) was *Fugitive Verse* (1790). It reflects conventional late 18th-century subject matter and diction. Her later verse, *The Family Legend* (1810) and *Metrical Legends of Exalted Characters* (1821), was influenced by her renewed acquaintance with Scotland, her friendship with Scott, and the ballads of Robert Burns. Her primary concern was drama. The first volume of *A Series of Plays, in which it is attempted to Deliniate the Stronger Passions of the Mind; each Passion being the Subject of Tragedy and a Comedy* (usually known as *Plays on the Passions*) appeared anonymously in 1798, the second in 1802, and the third in 1812. She published volumes of *Miscellaneous Plays* in 1804 and 1836, individual plays in 1810 and 1826. *A View of the General Tenor of the New Testament* (1831) was a Unitarian tract. JB's most important work is *Plays on the Passions.* In a long "Introductory Discourse" she explained her objectives and method. Other dramatists "made use of the passions to mark their several characters, and animate their scenes, rather than to open to our view the nature and portraitures of those great disturbers of the human breast." She proposed to write a blank-verse tragedy and a comedy in Shakespearean style on each passion (hatred, love, jealousy, etc.), concentrating only on that emotion without distracting "bustles of plot, brilliancy of dialogue, and even the bold and striking in character." Tragedy would show the dangers of unbridled passion, comedy the moral value of passion restrained. Although this plan pointed her moral, it did little for the dramatic quality of the works. Only a few of these plays were produced; the performances were generally failures. *De Monfort* was the best known of the *Plays on the Passions.* Sarah Siddons appeared as Jane in its first production, but even she could do little with such exchanges as: *De Monfort:* "I'll tell thee all—but, oh! thou wilt despise me. / For in my breast a raging passion burns, / To which thy soul no sympathy will own— / A passion which hath made my nightly couch / A place of torment; and the light of day, / With the gay intercourse of social man, / Feel like th' oppressive airless pestilence. / O Jane! thou wilt despise me."*Jane:* "Say not so: / I never can despise thee, gentle brother. / A lover's jealousy and hopeless pangs / No kindly heart contemns." *De M:* "A lover, sayst thou? / No, it is hate! black, lasting, deadly hate!" Her other plays were less elevated and some had a modest success on the stage. JB attempted to write serious moral plays when dramatic writing in England was at a low point, and *Plays on the Passions* was generally well received as reading matter, so that through the first half of the 19th century she was acknowledged as Britain's foremost female dramatist. Several critics attributed the work to Scott, and the discovery that the author was a woman caused considerable amazement, for there seemed to be nothing "feminine" about its subject matter or style.   B.B.S.

BALL, Hannah (1733?–1792), diarist and letter-writer, lived in High Wycombe. She became engaged to a man whose faith did not agree with her own and, on the advice of John Wesley, broke off the match. By 1759 she was living with her brother; when his wife died, she cared for the children. In 1762 she described her religious conversion: "Horribly caught and compassed round in the midnight of my grief and fear, Mercy, divine Mercy, came to my relief, and graciously disposed me to resign myself up into the hands of the Lord." Later she became a Methodist and in 1766 began a

diary of her spiritual life, recording her temptations and the vicissitudes of her faith. She also described her bodily suffering, her domestic trials, and her own character failings: "I this day felt a distant, unloving spirit haunting my soul: but even this gives a fresh gust to prayer." In 1769 she started a Sunday school, which was continued by her sister after her death. HB corresponded copiously with John Wesley, who warned her against a tendency toward mysticism, and with many pious women, to whom she addressed exhortations and comforting letters. By 1790 she was ill, regarding herself as "yet the Lord's prisoner; but my soul still hungers and thirsts after righteousness." The last entry of her diary records "I am very low, but quite resigned to the Lord." After her death, some of her letters to Wesley and parts of her diary were arranged as *Memoirs of Miss Hannah Ball, with extracts from her Diary and Correspondence.* This was originally compiled by the Rev. Joseph Cole and published at York in 1796; a revised, enlarged edition appeared in 1839.   J.T.

BANNERMAN, Anne (?–1829), poet, was left destitute and without living relatives after the deaths of her mother and brother in 1803. She had already published *Poems* (Edinburgh, 1800) and *Tales of Superstition and Chivalry* (London, 1802). After her friend, Dr. Robert Anderson, failed in his efforts to obtain a government annuity for her support, she raised some money by selling subscriptions to a combined edition of her earlier publications. This appeared as *Poems . . . A New Edition* (Edinburgh, 1807). In 1807 AB went to Exeter as governess to Lady Frances Beresford's daughter, but it is not known how long she stayed with the family; she died in Scotland. Apparently she wrote nothing for publication during the last 22 years of her life. AB appears to have read widely and been greatly influenced by the "Sturm und Drang" movement. Most of her poems are filled with images of rocky coasts, tempests, and shipwrecks, which convey a mood of romantic melancholy. *Poems* includes translations from French and Italian as well as original works. One of the latter, "To Miss Baillie. On the Publication of Her First Volume of Plays on the Passions," praises JOANNA BAILLIE as "priestess of the tragic muse." The original poems also include a sequence of ten "Sonnets From Werter," based on Goethe's novel and described in AB's notes as an attempt to remedy "the capital defect of the sonnet . . . the tedium and monotony attending the perusal of a numerous collection of small unconnected pieces of fourteen lines." In the long narratives that comprise the *Tales,* AB demonstrates her ability, in poems such as "The Dark Ladie" and "The Penitent's Confession," to tell a story involving a situation of rising suspense. In his correspondence with Bishop Percy about AB's situation in 1804, Dr. Anderson wrote: "Her literary powers, eminent as they are, do not seem, from any of her efforts hitherto, to be of ready or popular application. They are, perhaps, better qualified to acquire fame than profit." J.F.

BARBAULD, Anna Laetitia (1743–1825), poet and essayist, was the only daughter of a prominent nonconformist clergyman and educator, Dr. Aikin. She was born in Leicestershire and was educated by her father, along with her younger brothers. Her early prowess at reading English, French, and Italian persuaded her father to allow her to learn Latin and Greek, although he disapproved in principle of females being so educated. In 1758 the family moved to Warrington, Lancs., where Dr. Aikin became one of the teachers at the newly established Dissenting academy. ALB's acquaintance there broadened to include Joseph Priestley and other leading Dissenting intellectuals. In 1774 ALB married the Rev. Rochemont Barbauld of a Huguenot refugee family. His father, a Church of England cleric, had sent Rochemont to Warrington, where he received probably the best education available in England at the time, but where he was also converted to nonconformity. The couple moved to Palgrave, Suffolk, where Barbauld ministered to a congregation and established a boys' school. The school became mainly the province of ALB and was a great success. Barbauld, never a very stable personality, gave up the Suffolk place in 1785. The couple traveled on the Continent for about a year and then settled in Hampstead, where Barbauld again had a congregation. ALB usually taught a few female students, some resident in her house and some day students. Her friends included such literary figures as ELIZABETH MONTAGU, Dr. Johnson, Richardson, the publisher Joseph Johnson, JOANNA BAILLIE, HANNAH MORE, and FANNY BURNEY, as well as leading Dissenters and political liberals. In 1802 the Barbaulds moved to Stoke Newington, where ALB's brother John, a physician and writer, lived.

Barbauld's health collapsed; he died insane in 1808. The couple had no children but adopted one of ALB's nephews, Charles Rochemont Aikin.

ALB's first works were published in 1773 at the urging of her brother John. They were *Poems* and *Miscellaneous Pieces in Prose,* the latter written jointly by brother and sister. She composed several devotional and instructional works for children while living in Suffolk, but her major works began to appear after she settled in Hampstead. Several of these responded to the current situation; ALB was a strong proponent of the abolition of slavery and the repeal of civil prohibitions limiting political participation of Dissenters. Her works on these subjects were *Address to the Opposers of the Repeal of the Corporation and Test Acts* (1790); *Epistle to William Wilberforce* (1791), a poem against those who rejected the bill to abolish the slave trade; *Letter to John Bull* (1792), a satiric attack on those who regarded as disloyal any criticism of country and constitution; and *Remarks on Mr. Gilbert Wakefield's Enquiry* (1793), about freedom of public worship. Her most serious topical work was her last, *Eighteen Hundred and Eleven,* a long poem criticizing contemporary society. Other works included short essays on devotional and instructive topics and occasional poems. She contributed a number of essays to her brother's *Evenings at Home* (1792). Her main later work was as an editor. In 1804 she edited the *Correspondence of Samuel Richardson* in six volumes with a long biographical and critical introduction, and in 1810 she edited *The British Novelists* in 50 volumes. *The Female Speaker* (1811) was a widely used selection of the best British poetry and prose for use in educating girls. Her *Works,* which included all the poetry and shorter prose pieces as well as some correspondence and a memoir, were edited in two volumes in 1825 by her niece Lucy Aikin.

ALB is one of the most neglected writers of her day. A far better poet than ANNA SEWARD, she offers imaginative subjects, often portrayed with much humor. Although written within the conventions of late 18th-century verse, her poems are seldom labored in diction or rhyme. A charming example is *The Mouse's Petition,* for a mouse caught in a trap in one of Priestley's experiments: "If e're thy breast with freedom glowed / And spurned a tyrant's chain, / Let not thy strong oppressive force / A free-born mouse detain." A quieter mood can be found in *Verses written in an Alcove,* which begins: "Now the moonbeam's trembling lustre, / Silvers o'er the dewy green, / And in soft and shadowy colours, / Sweetly paints the chequer'd scene." One of her hymns, "Praise to God, immortal praise, / For the love that crowns our days," has appeared in many hymnals since 1812. Although highly educated at her own insistence, ALB never paraded her learning, and did not believe that girls in general should be so educated. According to her niece, ELIZABETH MONTAGU and others proposed that ALB start a school for girls, but she replied that girls should be educated at home, for they needed "only to have such a general tincture of knowledge as to make them agreeable companions to a man of sense." Nonetheless, ALB's essays and editions and her teaching methods for both boys and girls showed that scholarship and being female were not mutually exclusive.   B.B.S.

BARBER, Mary [Sapphira] (1690–1757), poet, was married to a Dublin tailor/clothier by whom she had at least three children. Her close friends included Dr. Delany, Matthew and LAETITIA PILKINGTON, CONSTANTIA GRIERSON, and Swift. She also knew Arbuthnot and was a patient of the famous Dr. Mead. Lady Carteret and the Earl of Orrery were also influential friends and patrons. MB made several visits to Bath for medical treatment before finally settling in England. On a 1733 visit she was arrested for carrying into the country Swift's manuscripts of "Epistle to a Lady" and "On Poetry: A Rapsody," both in reality attacks on Walpole's administration; however, she was quickly released without having to face trial. Her only publication, *Poems on Several Occasions* (1734) was planned as a money-raising effort. Dedicated to the Earl of Orrery and including a letter from Swift to the Earl, its subscription list reads like a social and literary register of the day. In 1736, when she was again badly in need of money and apparently receiving little financial support from her husband, she asked Swift to give her the manuscript of his *Polite Conversations.* He willingly did so, and she reaped the proceeds from its successful publication in 1738.

In addition to MB's work, *Poems* includes verses by CONSTANTIA GRIERSON and ELIZABETH ROWE. MB's verses are mostly occasional poems addressed to particular individuals, plus a few fables and epigrams. Many criticize the habits of the wealthy, especially the socialites of Bath, with whose selfishness MB was well acquainted. Several comment on society's views of intellectual women. In one of these, "The Conclusion of a Letter to the Rev. Mr. C- - -," MB imagines the dismay of her correspondent if he should receive a letter in verse: "May I have a Wife, that will dust her own Floor; . . . She has wisdom enough, that keeps out the Dirt, / And can make a good *Pudding,* and cut out a *Shirt.*" Later in the poem, MB advises her son to marry "a Woman of Wisdom, as well as good Breeding, / With a Turn, at least no Aversion, to Reading: / In the Care of her Person, exact and refin'd; / Yet still, let her principal Care be her Mind." Swift said of JB's poems: "They generally contain something new and useful, tending to the Reproof of some Vice or Folly, or recommending some Virtue. . . . In short she seemeth to have a true poetical Genius, better cultivated than could well be expected, either from her Sex, or the Scene she hath acted in, as the Wife of a Citizen" (*Poems,* vi–vii).   J.F.

BARKER, Jane (fl. 1688–1726), novelist and poet, was a Catholic spinster from a Royalist family. She spent most of her life in rural Lincolnshire, although she lived in France for a time after the reign of James II and in London during part of the reign of George I. Her father fought in the Royalist cause, an uncle fought for James II against William, and another uncle died at Sedgemoor, fighting against Monmouth. Several of her poems praise Charles I (one describes him as the "compleat Mirrour of Christianitie"), and her novels leave no doubt about her strong antipathy toward Monmouth and equally passionate loyalty to the Stuarts (one character dies of grief shortly after Charles II's death, which "put a stop to the Wheel of all Joy and Happiness in England"). A manuscript, *A Collection of Poems Refering to the Times* (1700), attacks William and laments a number of specific political events in England. In *Poetical Recreations* (1688) JB addresses the themes of female friendship, lost love, religious faith in hard times, the dangers of strong emotions, and the desire for fame and praise. The collection shows considerable experimentation; the poems written in heroic couplets and the odes are generally better than the ballads, songs, and sonnets. *Poetical Recreations* includes some poems written by literary friends of JB's youth. Some of these men seem friends primarily of her brother, who studied medicine at Cambridge and Leyden and whose early death was a grief from which JB never fully recovered. A poem addressed to JB and printed in the second section of *Poetical Recreations* proves that in the 1680s she was working on parts of her first fiction work, *Exilius* (1715). *Love Intrigues* (1713), JB's first publication for Edmund Curll, had four editions by 1750; and *Entertaining Novels* (1715), two by 1719 and a third in 1736. *Entertaining Novels* included her *Exilius* and *Love Intrigues* and nine previously unpublished tales with such titles as *Piso: Or, The Lewd Courtier* and *The Happy Recluse: Or, The Charms of Liberty*. In 1718 she published a translation of Fénélon's *The Christian Pilgrimage* to which she added "An Hymn on the Ascension" and 14 psalms. *A Patch-work Screen* (1723) and *The Lining for the Patch-work Screen* (1726) show considerable influence from the developing English novel and have a decidedly pessimistic turn. In her last years JB became blind and employed an amanuensis.

JB's novels often have intriguing psychology. In one, the heroine, and the reader, cannot tell if modesty, the man's uncertainties and indecisiveness, or circumstances doom a relationship. In another, a wife deserts her husband to live in poverty with his mistress, and in yet another the heroine ponders what metamorphosed the regicides from law-makers to law-confounders. JB presents her situations simply and clearly, captures the facets of the psychological puzzles, and recreates the resulting experience of confusion and frustration without trapping herself in the need to provide answers for her readers. Her later works, suffering from her usual stylistic infelicities and faults in consistency, are darker than her earlier. Narrators describe their unabated grief over the deaths of relatives and friends and recount bizarre tales of near-marriages to men who were hanged, of people driven to suicide by lovers, and of unmarried mothers escaping parish officers by scrambling over rooftops. Some of the anecdotes might come from Defoe's social pamphlets and conduct books (a debauched country girl begins again on a colonial plantation; an Irish woman saves her destitute family by selling boiled wheat and running a bartering service in London). While her early poems and novels reflect a happy, intelligent girl who loved the outdoors, was betrayed by a suitor, and became

a woman acquainted with the mundane hardships and petty cruelties of the middle classes, JB's later work portrays a growing ambivalence about the roles of women. Sometimes she praises learning as fulfillment and solace; at other times she describes it as "being neither of Use nor Ornament to our Sex" or as ridiculous as paint and washes would be for men. She satirizes the daily occupations of women devastatingly: "I was not capable to distinguish which Dress became which Face, or whether the *Italian, Spanish,* or *Portugal* Red, best suited such or such Feature." She can conclude, however, that the unmarried life "frustrate[s] the End of our Creation."

JB was a popular fiction writer in her time. She combined the oldest narrative structures characteristic of many 17th-century novellas—the old-fashioned interwoven romantic tales and the framework plan—with surprisingly modern attention to realistic detail and subtle character creation. She is an early example of the didactic, even pious, novelist whose themes of patience, virtue, submission to Providence, and endurance would come to dominate English fiction.   P.R.B.

BARNARD, Lady Anne [Lindsay] (1750–1825), poet and diarist, was one of 11 children of James, fifth Earl of Balcarres; she was raised in Fifeshire. In her late teens she became a member of the Edinburgh circle, which included David Hume, Lord Monboddo, and Henry Mackenzie. After the death of AB's father in 1768, she and her sister Margaret, widow of Alexander Fordyce, moved to London. They lived first in Manchester Square, then in a house AB purchased in Berkeley Square. AB became friends with the Prince of Wales and his mistress, Mrs. Fitzherbert. In 1773 she was introduced to Dr. Johnson when he visited Edinburgh. Friends in London included William Pitt, Horace Mann, Edmund Burke, the Marquess of Abercorn, and the Duke of Queensbury. AB visited revolutionary Paris, returning to London in 1791. After two abortive courtships by Henry Dundas, afterward Lord Melville, and the statesman William Windham, AB, when aged 42, married Andrew Barnard, the son of Thomas, Bishop of Limerick. Barnard, only 30 at the time, accepted a post as colonial secretary under Lord Macartney at the Cape of Good Hope, where AB accompanied him. AB's "Journals and Notes" about her travels, illustrated with her own sketches and drawings, are printed in A.W.C. Lindsay's

Lives of the Lindsays, vol. III (1849). They vividly recount the two-and-a-half month voyage, conversations with generals, soldiers, and civilians, social and political affairs in a country torn by tribal dissention, and AB's own good-humored attempts to introduce a degree of civilization and to master local history and geography. "This place," she lamented, "is not wholly to be governed by wisdom, ability, or elevation of mind." After her husband's death in 1807, AB moved back to London where she lived again with her sister and was visited by Richard Sheridan and the Prince of Wales. In her later years AB wrote a journal and memoirs, which she left to her nephew, the Earl of Crawford and Balcarres, with an interdiction against their publication. Some letters from this collection were published in 1924 by Dorothea Fairbridge in *Lady Anne Barnard at the Cape of Good Hope.*

AB is remembered for the ballad "Auld Robin Gray," written in 1772 when she was 22. Published anonymously, the ballad was claimed by her two years before her death. In a letter to Sir Walter Scott (1823), AB related the history of the poem's creation: "Robin Gray, so called from its being the name of the old herd at Balcarres, was *born* soon after the close of the year 1771. . . . I was melancholy, and endeavoured to amuse myself by attempting a few poetical trifles. There was an English-Scotch melody of which I was passionately fond. Sophy Johnstone . . . used to sing it to us at Balcarres. She did not object to its having improper words, though I did. I longed to sing old Sophy's air to different words, and give its plaintive tones some little history of virtuous distress in humble life, such as might suit it." The tune to which the ballad was set is "The Bride-groom greets when the sun gaes doun." Scott published the ballad in a revised version, with two continuations by AB, in 1824. The continuations were not as good as the original ballad, which is striking for the stoicism of its female point of view: "My father couldna wark, my mither couldna spin; / I toil'd day and nicht, but their bread I couldna win: / Auld Rob maintain'd them baith, and wi' tears in his e'e, / Said, 'Jeanie, for their sakes, will ye marry me?' / . . . My father urged me sair, my mither didna speak, / But she looked in my face till my heart was like to break. / They gied him my hand—my heart was at the sea; / Sae auld Robin Gray, he was gudeman to me." T.C.S.W.L. and G.B.

BARRELL, Maria (fl. 1788–90), poet, dramatist, and polemicist, was probably the wife, and later the widow, of a British soldier who fought in America and then was imprisoned for debt. In 1788 she published *British Liberty Vindicated,* pleading the right of debtors and the stupidity of imprisoning them at the whim of creditors, thus placing them in situations which they could never improve. She called her pamphlet "A Delineation of the King's Bench," in which prison presumably she was confined. Claiming to be the author of *Reveries du Coeur,* MB describes herself as an "unfortunate loyalist," a woman "oppressed by fortune," facing "perpetual imprisonment." After the argument, a poem follows, praising British liberty but noting its incompatibility with the treatment of debtors. Two years later, MB published her play, *The Captive* (1790), and gave her address again as the King's Bench. Describing herself as writing from "the gloomy walls of a prison," she dedicates her work to the Prince of Wales. Noting that she has been in her situation for five years, she writes of her "mind wounded by disappointment, and harrassed by scenes of sorrow almost incredible"; she asks leniency from the critics for her play because of the "severity" of her plight. A preface notes how the British have been horrified at the French Bastille and yet can treat debtors inhumanly, and it begs readers to petition Parliament for reform, so that debtors can work to repay what they owe: "where is the utility of inhumation, depriving society of its useful members, and filling our miserable receptuals of wretched penury, with the wives and children of the unhappy insolvent." Railing against the separation of husband and wife caused by imprisonment, she also stresses the corruption of long confinement, after which a person finds it hard to work again. The short play, *The Captive,* follows, its prologue depicting the author as "a captive stranger in her native land, / While by her widow'd side two Orphans wait." The play presents sentimental tableaux, the central ones being the husband dying in prison, the virtuous wife in distress, and the faithful servant. The message is reiterated throughout, that insolvency, which derives from ill luck, is punished in England as if it were the worst of crimes, thus confounding misfortune and guilt: "O! savage laws that laid my Heartly low, and is insolvency so great a crime that man must die, because he is in debt?" J.T.

BATHURST, Elizabeth (fl. 1678–83), polemical writer, went with her sister Anne to a Sunday service conducted by Samuel Ansley some time in 1678. As worship was ending, EB began to preach to the congregation, trying to provoke them to listen to the voice of Jesus in their own hearts. They responded by throwing the two women out. Shortly afterward, EB wrote to her persecutors her seven-page autobiographical *An Expostulatory Appeal to the professors of Christianity, Joined in Community with Samuel Ansley,* in which she relates what little we know of her life. Her story is at once unique and typical of the young women who became disillusioned with formal professions of religion and sought what they called "experimental knowledge" of spiritual truth. EB could find no personal satisfaction in public worship; she did not experience God when reading Scripture: "Although I daily read the Reports which his Ancient Primitive Servants have left there upon record, concerning how they witnessed him . . . but what was this to me? whilst I knew him not myself." Since this spirit "but what was this to me?" permeates her writings, it is not surprising that EB joined the Quaker movement, which propagated George Fox's teaching of the Inner Light. And, like many other spiritually radical women, EB felt called publicly to defend freedom of conscience. In *Truth's Vindication or a Gentle Stroke to Wipe off the Foul Aspirations, False Accusations, and Misrepresentations cast upon Quakers* (1679), EB argues from two grounds of authority—that of inspired Scripture and that of inspired self—which cannot contradict one another. Her skill in exegesis is nowhere more evident than in her demonstration of the "heresy" that humans are free to reform and perfect themselves and hence that the effects of original sin can be overcome on earth. Because she saw the experiences of her own heart as the strongest evidence, EB spoke out defiantly as a witness to the Spirit operating in the world and transforming it heart by heart. Yet her self-effacement as a writer, but not as a witness, is characteristic not only of her writing, but of other Quaker women; for example, "Neither have I fondly desired to get my Name in Print; for 'tis not an Inky Character can make a Saint." *The Sayings of Women* (1683) is a collection from Scripture. S.B.

BATTIER, Henrietta (1751?–1813), poet, wrote voluminously, even before her husband died and left her to support two daughters. She was considered in her day to be an Irish Bluestocking, and she produced poetry that was politically astute and satirical. She collected her poems under the titles *Protected Fugitives* (1791) and *The Gibbonade* (1793–94), and published many others individually, such as "Marriage Ode, after the Manner of Dryden," "The Kirwanade," "An Address on the Subject of the Projected Union," "The Lemon," "Bitter Orange," and "An Irregular Ode to Edward Byrne." Although she died poor and was quickly forgotten, HB was during her lifetime respected in literary circles; even Londoners like Sir Joshua Reynolds, Dr. Johnson, Samuel Whyte, and Benjamin West paid "British Shillings" for her printed poetry. Her popularity was due to her ability to sling words on a page with power and wit: "Was is for these illegal offers, / That Dalkey's gold has fill'd thy coffers? / Was it for this we were so glad, / When you no more ostensibly were mad. . . . / What time Count Baker's marble miss'd you, / And all the naughty boys had hiss'd you, / Before your carriage landed" (from "An Address on the Subject of the Proposed Union"). HB did not hesitate to state her patriotic mind, and most of her verse deals with politicians and topical issues. Her favorite form, the ode, fits her subjects and allows her satiric intellect to display itself. Her wit is illustrated well by her primary pseudonym: Patt. Pindar, who disavows "any knowledge of that filthy production, called a SERMON." C.C.

BAYNARD, Ann (1672–97), learned lady and poet, was born in Preston, the daughter of Edward Baynard, a physician who sometimes versified his medical advice. She visited Bath and later lived in London and Barnes. Her father educated her in mathematics, physics, astronomy, philosophy, and the classics, and she became noted, when still young, for her learning, as well as for her religious devotion. She wrote several satires in Latin against atheists and libertines, and she urged her female friends to abandon "visits, vanity, and toys" and instead embrace "study and thinking." Much of her short life was spent in meditation and in charitable works. AB is mentioned in Ballard's *Memoirs of Learned Ladies* as famous for her classical learning, especially Greek, and for her piety. J.J.

BEAUMONT, Agnes (1652?–1720), autobiographer, was, in the early 1670s, living in the village of Edworth, Beds., with her widowed farmer father, John Beaumont. In November 1672, AB was received into the Bedford Baptist congregation; her name is inscribed on the church roll in the hand of the pastor, John Bunyan. At one time her father had found Bunyan's nonconformist teachings moving, but, probably influenced by malicious gossip, he turned against Bunyan and only reluctantly allowed his zealous daughter to continue to hear Bunyan preach. On one fatal Sunday, AB managed to beg a ride with an unwilling Bunyan, who happened to pass by on his way to services. The enraged father saw them ride off together. AB's "Life," which has been published as *The Narrative of the Persecution of Agnes Beaumont in 1674,* relates the events of a few weeks from that Sunday to the death of her father. It includes the attempts of Bunyan's enemies and a rejected suitor of AB's to slander AB and Bunyan not only as fornicators, but also as murderers of her father. In the fifth edition of his *Grace Abounding* (1680), Bunyan added a well-known passage that is taken to be his denial of the slanders connecting him with AB: "But that which was reported with the boldest confidence, was, that I had my Misses, my Whores, my Bastards, yet two Wives at once, and the like." AB's *Narrative* is her self-vindication. AB lived on to marry two husbands, the second of which was a Mr. Story, a prosperous merchant at Highgate. She is buried beside the Tilehouse Street Baptist Chapel in Hitchin. On the back wall of the chapel a tablet was erected in 1812 to commemorate her story.

Unfortunately, *Narrative* has been remembered mainly as an appendix to John Bunyan's biography and as a minor devotional work in Baptist circles, but it deserves more attention. In general, it has the conventional theme of a spiritual testimony: how the Spirit's love helped AB to overcome the trials and persecutions she faced at the time of her father's death. But, in detail, *Narrative* is remarkable for its insightful and concise description of a young woman's struggle to reconcile the demands of her inner spiritual life with her duty to an overbearing father who was loving only when obeyed. Every detail included is relevant and vivid, and the style seems artless and candid, as in this passage in which she describes her misguided exultation when riding behind Bunyan: "I had not ridden far, before my heart began to be lifted up with pride, at the thoughts of riding behind this servant of the Lord, and was pleased if any looked after us. . . . My pride soon had a fall; for, in coming to Gamlingay, we were met by a clergyman who knew us both. He looked very hard at us as we rode along, and soon after raised a vile scandal upon us." Best of all are the colorful anecdotes AB selects to characterize the playful, prayerful, and tearful strategies she uses, in the end successfully, to "incline the heart" of her father to her wishes. In one of the skirmishes after her ride with Bunyan, the old man slams the door, almost crushing her leg in order to keep her out of his house. She boldly steals the key and he pursues her and grabs hold of her shouting, "Hussy, give me the key quickly, or else I will throw you into the pond." She obediently resigns the key "with silence and sadness" and goes off to try prayer. S.B.

BEEMAN, Anna (1739?–?), American hymn writer and religious polemicist, identifies herself in an acrostic poem as the wife of Park Beeman of Warren, Conn. She bore nine children to her husband, named as one of Warren's tithingmen in 1792. Her *Hymns on Various Subjects* (1792) deals with God's boundless love and man's responsibility to prepare himself for grace. Sometimes doubting her salvation, AB rejoices in the assurance that Christ redeems the faithful. Nine of the 31 hymns justify adult baptism; a few are concerned with women's role in marriage and the church. "The Author's feelings towards her children" expresses the hope that her unregenerate offspring will repent—but if they do not, "She sure will say, Amen" when they are damned. The refrain of Hymn XXV, which recounts Christ's earthly sufferings, epitomizes the collection: "In his sweet example O pray let us come, / Each bearing his cross as dear Jesus hath done." As early as 1791 two of AB's hymns were included in Joshua Smith's *Divine Hymns, or Spiritual Songs.* In *Three Letters to a Lady in Opposition to the Baptist Plan* (1794) AB examines pedobaptist arguments which had been current since the mid-17th century. Scripture, she maintains, supports neither sprinkling nor infant baptism; gentiles do not partake of God's covenant with Abraham—rather "by faith we become heirs of the promise." She presents herself as a "poor old woman," expert in neither theology nor translation, but moved to say that those who reject Baptist doctrines endanger their souls. M.D.J.

BEHN, Aphra (1640–89), playwright, novelist, poet, and translator, was probably the daughter of Bartholomew and Elizabeth Johnson (he a yeoman) in Kent. In her early twenties, AB went to Surinam with her parents, brother, sister, and some servants. Evidently her father died on the voyage. AB stayed at Sir Robert Harley's plantation in Surinam for several months, during which time she became involved in an uprising of slaves led by Oroono and became intimate with William Scott. Scott then left Surinam for Rotterdam; shortly afterward AB and her family returned to England. Apparently AB married a tradesman in London who died in the plague of 1664. In 1666 she was sent as a spy to Antwerp, where she contacted Scott. After nine months of passing on information fed to her by Scott, AB returned to London, in debt, and was briefly imprisoned. Then, in 1670, she set about earning her living as a playwright: sixteen of her plays were printed and produced over the next 19 years. During this time her patrons were Sir Thomas Gower, the Duke of Buckingham, Henry Howard, and James II, while she numbered the Duke of Rochester and the Earl of Salisbury among her friends. Dryden encouraged and supported her efforts at the beginning of her writing career. Other friends, connected mainly with the theater, included Edward Ravenscroft, Henry Neville Payne, Thomas Otway, Thomas Killigrew, Elizabeth Barry, Emily Price, and former actress Nell Gwynn. She corresponded with ANNE WHARTON. In her late thirties, she entered a passionate and painful affair with the lawyer John Hoyle, a notorious rake and bisexual. Not until ten years later could she write of him dispassionately as "Honest Hoyle." During her last years she suffered from severe arthritis. AB was buried in Westminster Abbey under a black marble stone, with an epitaph attributed to Hoyle: "Here lies a proof that wit can never be / Defence enough against mortality."

Her plays include *The Forc'd Marriage* (1670), *The Amorous Prince* (1671), *The Dutch Lover* (1673), *Abdelazar* (1676), *Sir Timothy Tawdry* (1676), presumably *The Rover* (1677), *Sir Patient Fancy* (1678), *The Feign'd Curtezans* (1679), *The Rover, Part II* (1681), *The False Count* (1682), *The Roundheads* (1682), *Like Father, Like Son* (a flop, never published), *The City Heiress* (1682), *The Young King* (1679–83), *The Lucky Chance* (1686), *The Emperor of the Moon* (1686), *The History of the Nun* (1688), and *The History of Bacon in Virginia* (1689). Plays attributed to AB are *The Debauchee* (1677), *The Counterfeit Bridegroom* (1677), and *The Revenge* (1680). In her first three plays, AB was finding her voice as a writer of the fast-paced, witty, bawdy plays that characterized Restoration drama, but her stance is already bold. In the prologue to *The Forc'd Marriage,* she writes that each masked woman in the audience is her "spy on purpose sent, / To hold you in wanton compliment; / That so you may not censure what she's writ / Which done they face you down 'twas full of wit." In the preface to *The Dutch Lover,* she defends her ability as a playwright by emphasizing the non-intellectual nature of plays: "I'll only say as I have touch'd before, that plays have no great room for that which is men's great advantage over women, that is learning. . . . I dare to say . . . that a woman may well hope to reach their greatest heights." *Abdelazar* was a tragedy, not her forte. But with *Sir Timothy Tawdry, Sir Patient Fancy,* and *The Feign'd Curtezan* (dedicated to Nell Gwynn) she found her form and her voice. These are comedies of intrigue where the witty dialogue is used for furthering the plot, not for embellishing the fun. AB was determined to speak out on the joy of sex, which is crippled by a forced marriage in which a wife is no better than a prostitute and a husband is expected to be unfaithful. In addition, AB believed that love was blind to social classes (*The Forc'd Marriage, The False Count,* and *The History of Bacon*). She saw the Whig emphasis on property and narrow morality *(The False Count* and *The Roundheads)* as further crippling love. The delights of sexuality *(The Rover; The Rover, Part II; The City Heiress)* led her to incorporate in the character Wilmore the wildness and vitality of Rochester and John Hoyle. But AB wanted to move the suitor to constancy—to make the ecstacy of sexual union permanent. Her belief in the beauty of sexuality led her to be tolerant and even accepting of the bisexuality of Hoyle; in a poem "To the fair Clarinda, who made love to me, imagined more than a woman," AB writes: "In pity to our sex sure thou wer't sent / That we might love, and yet be innocent: / For sure no crime with thee we can commit; / Or if we should—thy form excuses it." She dedicated *The History of the Nun* to Hortense Mancini, the bisexual mistress of Charles II.

As can be surmised from her patrons and her criticism of the Whig emphasis on property, AB was a royalist. In 1685 she wrote three long poems: *A Pindaric on the Death of our Late Sovereign, A Poem . . . to . . . Catherine Queen Dowager,* and *A Pindaric Poem on the Happy Coronation.* The last is elaborately descriptive, as the toilet of Mary suggests: "And now the nymphs ply all their female arts / To dress her for her victory of hearts; / A thousand little loves descend! / Young waiting cupids with officious care / In smiling order all attend; / This decks her snowy neck, and that her ebon hair." In the year of her death, AB rallied to write *A Congratulatory Poem to . . . Queen Mary,* in which she defends the Queen (to AB, the true successor) as warm, and by inference attacks William's coldness: "Through all no formal nicitye's seen, / But free and generous your majestic mien, / In every motion, every part a queen." AB also wrote songs, epitaphs, and elegies. That she felt her lack of education keenly is seen in her "imitation" of Ovid, which Dryden included in his volume of 1680 and for which he praised her. But his statement that she did not understand "Latine" must have galled. In 1682 she wrote a poem in thanks to Creech, whose translation of Lucretius allows the "Divine mysteries" concealed from uneducated women to be perused. In 1688, AB showed her scholarship by translating Fontenelle's *The History of the Oracles* and *A Discovery of the New Worlds.* In her introduction, she acknowledges that she is only "a *woman* who is not supposed to be well versed in the terms of philosophy [but is already] so much of a philosopher as to despise what the world says of it." AB, however, believes that preaching and studying the sciences are not outside a woman's province, comments on the French language as compared with the English, and defends Copernicus's theory by pointing out that the Bible can only be read allegorically.

AB's *Love Letters Between a Nobleman and His Sister,* a 200,000-word epistolary novel, was published in three installments (1684–87). It was based on a real scandal, in which Forde Grey, Lord Grey of Werke (Philander), eloped with his sister-in-law Lady Henriette Berkeley (Sylvia). Other people—Monmouth, Lady Wentworth, etc.—appear under thinly disguised names. It is set in France, and Philander is being taken to the Bastille, not the Tower, when he escapes. AB's novel was immensely popular, running into at least 16 editions during the next 100 years. The posthumously published *Court of King Bantam,* is a short prose narrative set in the Christmas season, probably written in 1682 and inspired by the Bantam ambassador's visit to England in that year. It deals with dowry and love. *The Fair Jilt* (1688) concerns two sisters: Miranda, who "had a great deal of wit, read much, and retain'd all that served her purpose," and Alcidiana, a pleasure-seeking, unintellectual young woman who would be left powerless when her "vast fortune" was gone. AB translated a romantic story entitled *Agnes de Castro* (1688). AB's prose narrative, *Oroonoko* (1688), is based on the slave uprising she had witnessed in Surinam. Oroonoko, a well-educated African prince who had been separated from his love Imoinda, is a slave in the British colony where he again meets Imoinda and takes her as his wife. Oroonoko leads a rebellion and is beaten to near death by the overseers, while Imoinda and her unborn child are removed from the scene so that she won't miscarry. When they both escape and meet again, Oroonoko kills Imoinda to save her and the child from further humiliation. Later he kills himself. The novel praises the true nobility of the educated Oroonoko and the constancy of Imoinda, which can only flourish in "the first State of Innocence, before *Man* knew how to sin." Religion destroys "that Tranquillity"; Laws "wou'd but teach 'em to know Offence." Above all, it is the notion of property that puts one man (an inferior one) over another (a superior one), and this notion destroys trust, love, and beauty.   S.M.S.

BELLAMY, George Anne (1731?–1788), actress and autobiographer, the daughter of a married actress, Mrs. Bellamy, and her lover, James O'Hara, second Baron of Tyrawley, was probably born at Fingal, Ireland. She was educated in Boulogne until the age of 11 and then enjoyed the companionship and support of her father in London. After a few minor appearances on the stage, she made her debut at Covent Garden in 1744. A year later, she proved her potential at the Smock Alley Theatre in Dublin, where she knew Thomas Sheridan and David Garrick. In 1748 she returned to London and Covent Garden, where she enjoyed great success. She eloped in mid-season with George Montgomery Metham and had by him a son, George. In 1750 she went to Drury Lane under Garrick's management and stayed until 1753. She agreed to marry

John Calcraft but instead eloped again with Metham before returning to Covent Garden. In February 1754 she gave birth to Caroline Elizabeth, a child of Calcraft, who supported GAB in grand style. About three years later she bore Calcraft a son, Henry. They parted when Calcraft, married to another, tired of GAB's extravagance. GAB returned to Dublin; she appeared to be aging and her performance had little success. In 1763 she supposedly married her lover, the actor West Digges, in Scotland, where they both appeared on the stage until her return to Covent Garden the next year. In 1770 she retired from the stage because of ill health and failing beauty. She lived with another actor-lover, Henry Woodward, who, upon his death in 1777, left her a large part of his moderate estate. For the next 11 years she lived modestly and then penuriously.

An Apology for the Life of George Anne Bellamy, late of Covent Garden Theatre, written by herself was published in 1785. Although claimed by GAB, the book was undoubtedly written by another with facts and sentiments supplied by GAB. It is quite long, about 300,000 words, and uses the epistolary format; all letters are from "Mrs. Bellamy to the Hon. Miss- - -" and are undated. She looks back even into her mother's youth. The tone is stilted, and the facts are presented barely: "I was born on St. George's day, 1733, some months too soon for Captain Bellamy to claim any degree of consanguinity with me. As soon as Lord Tyrawley had gained intelligence . . . of the place of her destination . . . he wrote to his adjutant . . . to request, if she should prove pregnant in time to conclude it was the effect of her visit to his lordship" that GAB would be put in the care of a wet nurse. GAB gives her justification of her life and presents herself as duped, manipulated, cheated, and wronged. The work is a tedious account of a successful actress and an unsuccessful woman.   S.M.S.

BENGER, Elizabeth Ogilvy (1778–1827), biographer, poet, and novelist, was born at Wells, Somerset. Her father, a naval purser, noting her early appetite for books, sent her to a boys' school to learn Latin at the age of 12. The next year she published *The Female Geniad,* a poem in praise of women scholars. When her father died in 1796, she was much reduced in means and remained quite poor for most of the rest of her life. Between 1800 and 1809 she tried to cultivate friendships among the writers of the time. She was unsuccessful with the Lambs, because of Charles Lamb's ill will toward the circle of ANNA LAETITIA BARBAULD, of which EB was a member. She was on the whole well liked and a good conversationalist, but her last days were spent in poverty; her works never had large sales.

EB produced two novels, *Marian* and *The Heart and the Fancy,* a poem "On the Abolition of the Slave Trade," and biographies of ELIZABETH HAMILTON, the playwright John Tobin, Anne Boleyn, Mary Queen of Scots, and Elizabeth of Bohemia. The works generally show a concern for the victims of society, for people hurt not by individual evil, but by the evil of a system. In the biography of Mary, EB comments that both Mary and Elizabeth I were victims: "If Elizabeth hated Mary, she abhorred the puritans by whom she had been persecuted, and grudged them the triumph they were eager to obtain over her catholic rival. Much has been said of female jealousy, and much attributed to petty malice; but, in reality, Mary was herself aware that the ministers of the English Queen were more inimical than their mistress to her preservation." In EB's earlier poem on the slave trade, she was unreservedly sympathetic to the slaves: "Thy school was suffering, and thy teacher scorn: / Thine was the orphan's desolated state, / The strife of rapine, and the curse of hate / Woe was thy portion, by oppression seal'd / Wrongs unrevenged, dishonour unrepeal'd: / Who should protect thee? thou wast poor and low." EB's biographies are sensitive, her poetry undistinguished but pleasant, her histories carefully researched. In everything she wrote, her style was vigorous, thoughtful, and controlled. Her political sympathies were progressive, but she stirred no controversies and attracted little attention.   J.E.R.

BENNETT, Agnes Maria [Evans] (?–1808), novelist, appears to have been born in Bristol, where her father was a grocer. After a brief marriage to Mr. Bennett, probably a tanner at Brecon, AMB found work in London as a slop-seller. Her early financial struggles are reflected in her virtuous but lowly-born heroines, who consistently display moral superiority to those more highly placed. While working at a chandler's shop, AMB met Admiral Sir Thomas Pye, who had been reinstated as Commander-in-chief at Plymouth following a well-publicized court-martial for "negligence of duty." AMB was soon installed as housekeeper in Pye's home in Surrey, and bore by Pye several of her many children, including the acclaimed actress Harriet Esten, noted for her beautiful features (not inherited from her "ungainly" father, whose nickname was "Nose-y"). Esten's stage debut was arranged by her mother in 1785; AMB continued to manage Esten's career aggressively even after her own began to flourish. She died at Brighton and was buried in London; a large crowd of admirers attended her funeral.

AMB's first novel, *Anna; or Memoirs of a Welch Heiress*, was published anonymously in 1785, the year of Pye's death. It is her most lively, realistically drawn novel; it sold out on its first day of issue since readers hoped for a *roman à clef*. They were probably disappointed to find a strictly moral tale. *Juvenile Indiscretions* was published in 1786, again anonymously, and was first attributed to FANNY BURNEY, to whom AMB bears a stylistic resemblance. *Agnes-de-Courci, a domestic tale* (Bath 1789), an epistolary tragedy, appears to be a reworking of Richardson's *Clarissa*; it was followed in 1794 by *Ellen, Countess of Castle Howel*. AMB was haunted by her humble origins and clearly projected herself into the impecunious heroine of *The Beggar Girl and her Benefactors* (1797) who exclaims complacently, "They despise me for my poverty . . . while I pity them for the want of talent, candour, sentiment and charity which heaven has given to me and which I feel for them." *De Valcourt* appeared in Dublin in 1800. AMB's popularity continued to rise until it peaked in 1806 with her last completed novel, *Vicissitudes Abroad; or, The Ghost of my Father*, which sold 2,000 copies on its publication day. Her novels are long and sprawling. They lack original ideas and perceptions, but are lively and occasionally witty. The importance of financial reversals in the plots reveals a basic understanding of economic realities which is strongly felt but superficially considered. The *Monthly Review* found *Agnes* "well-wrought," but noted that "character, that almost indispensable requisite in all such performances, is seldom to be found." AMB's collected novels read like a compendium of 18th-century literary tendencies, ranging from the sentimental and gothic, to the psychological and satiric; they suggest a desire to please, which accounts for her popularity as well as for its short duration.   D.T.

BENTLEY, Elizabeth (1767–1839), poet, was born in Norwich, the only child of Daniel Bentley and his wife, the daughter of a cooper. EB's father, whom she describes as "having received a good education," was a journeyman cordwainer until a disabling stroke reduced him to hawking garden produce. A few months before his death in 1783 he was appointed bookkeeper for a coach line. Her father taught EB reading, spelling, and writing. She enjoyed reading "such books as were in the house; which were chiefly a spelling-book, fable-book, dictionary, and books of arithmetic; and such little pamphlets as I could borrow of my neighbors." After her father's death she purchased a grammar book to learn how to express herself correctly. This brief description of her education, taken from her autobiographical account, does not seem sufficient to explain her knowledge of contemporary politics, the great English poets, and the classics. About the age of 17, two years after her father's death, EB began writing verses. Her mother brought her efforts to the attention of acquaintances, who encouraged her. Within two years she had produced a sufficient quantity of passable verse for the Rev. John Walker of Norwich to sponsor a subscription to publish a volume of her poetry, the proceeds being applied to purchase an annuity for EB and her mother. The initial edition attracted subscriptions for 1,935 copies. The patrons came from all political persuasions and included gentry and peers, and the literati—ELIZABETH CARTER, HESTER CHAPONE, William Cowper, John Bowdler, and some of the future staff of the *British Critic. Genuine Poetical Compositions on Various Subjects* appeared in 1791, dedicated by permission to William Drake, Jr. The portrait affixed to it shows a modestly dressed girl with a strong, pleasant face and pug nose. The work was followed in 1805 by a short ode to Nelson after the Battle of Trafalgar. EB's compositions are derivative lyric poems, showing the influences of the masters she herself acknowledges—Pope, Gray, Thomson, Shakespeare, and Milton. The topics include the seasons and the classical virtues, and occasionally national and local political issues treated from a moderately liberal point of view. Her poems are unforced and correct, showing imagination but lacking great force or originality. Some of her lines are pleasing, as these from "On a Summer Morning": "Awake! my muse, expand thy gentle wing, / And in thy flight the Morn's bright beauties scan." Or, from "On a Winter Evening":

"Clad in a fog, dim Evening draws around, / Adieu, thou cold, short space, a winter's day." G.T.P.

BERKELEY, Eliza (1734–1800), memoir writer, was born in the vicarage of White Waltham in Windsor Forest. Her mother was co-heiress with two sisters to the considerable fortune of her father, Francis Cherry of Shottesbrook House, Berks. EB's father was the Rev. Henry Frinsham, M.A., who declined further preferment in the Church to preserve his principles. When she was 11, this precocious, pious child wrote two sermons and was sent, with her sister Anne, to Mrs. Sheele's school, Queen Square, London, where she remained for a year until her father's death. In 1761 she married the Rev. George Berkeley, son of the famous bishop. EB was small in stature, near-sighted, and an avid reader. She spoke French, read Hebrew and Spanish, and always carried a Spanish prayerbook to church. She knew ELIZABETH CARTER, ELIZABETH MONTAGU, Lord Lyttelton, and was a close friend of CATHERINE TALBOT, who, unsuspected by EB, had been attached from an early age to the Rev. George Berkeley. During the first ten years of their marriage, her husband's livings were at Bray, Acton, and Cookham, at each of which EB was known for good works and also for being a busybody. After their birth, the education of her two sons, George Monck (b. 1763) and George Robert (b. 1766), occupied most of her attention. The family moved to Canterbury when Berkeley became prebendary there in 1771. Their younger son died in 1775, after which EB became extraordinarily watchful over her remaining son. After he finished at Eton, the Berkeleys resided in St. Andrews during the three and a half years the young man spent at the university there. This son, after years of delicate health, died in 1793. EB's husband died in 1795, and her sister in 1797. After their deaths EB became decidedly eccentric. Along with SUSANNA DUNCOMBE, she ruled the circle of wives and widows in the Canterbury Cathedral precincts, earning a reputation for loquacity and waspishness. EB died in Kensington and, after a funeral procession through Oxford, was interred in the vault in Cheltenham where George Monck was buried.

After their deaths, EB decided to publish her son's poems and her husband's sermons. *The Poems of George Monck Berkeley* appeared in 1797 in a quarto volume beautifully printed by Nichols. What public there was for the book viewed it as an absurd production, containing as it did 178 pages of poetry and 630 pages of a rambling preface, with another 30 pages of postscript. The preface is more a life and opinions of EB than an introduction to her son's poems, and the tone is often sharp and uncharitable. It is, however, a rich storehouse of gossip, reflecting social life in the Cathedral precincts during the final decade of the century. As the writer of her obituary (probably Mrs. Duncombe) commented, "The Preface, had it been intitled Memoirs, Anecdotes, and Apology . . . to excuse the multifarious ingredients which compose it, would have been acceptable, as it affords great entertainment, real information, and useful instruction" (*Gentleman's Magazine,* November 1800). In 1799 EB published a volume of her husband's sermons, of which she had just 200 copies printed by a country printer of handbills, who disappointed her with an ugly job. She was a frequent contributor to *GM,* always with rambling digressions and an infallible capacity for antagonizing readers with her eccentric opinions. W.M.

BERRY, Mary (1763–1852), journal writer and editor, was born in Yorkshire; except for periods of residence in France, she made her home in London. Her mother died when MB was very young; her father, who trained for but never practiced the profession of law, was a man of liberal politics and easy, indolent ways, and so neglectful of his own and his children's interests that he allowed a younger brother to supplant him as the principal heir to the fortune of his uncle, a wealthy Scottish merchant. MB was deeply embittered by the loss of a great inheritance and the privation she and her younger sister, Agnes, experienced in their youth and young womanhood. Yet displacement from what she regarded as her true estate did not prevent her from maintaining a solid, lifelong identification with the upper classes. In 1783, MB made the first of many trips to Europe; there she began the journal she continued throughout her life. A friendship with Horace Walpole, begun in 1788, brought MB into contact with the distinguished people she had longed to know, and at Walpole's death in 1797 she and her sister were left some money and property. In 1795, MB became engaged to General Charles O'Hara, but her claim that family obligations would prevent her from accompanying O'Hara as his wife when he was appointed governor of Gibraltar caused the relationship to dwindle, leaving MB in rueful spinsterhood. Nevertheless, there were compensations. MB received prominent visitors from England and France in her London home; she enjoyed long friendships with Madame de Staël and JOANNA BAILLIE. In her later years, MB's bitterness faded in the glow of her celebrity as a writer and hostess.

MB edited *Horace Walpole's Works*, 1798; wrote a play, "The Fashionable Friends," in 1801; edited *Letters of Madame du Deffand to Horace Walpole* (1810), and *Letters of Rachel, Lady Russell* (1819); and wrote *A Comparative View of Social Life in England and France* in 1828, vol 2 in 1831 (the two volumes were published together in 1844). *Journals and Correspondence of Miss Berry* was edited by Lady Theresa Lewis in 1865; *The Berry Papers*, edited by Lewis Melville, appeared in 1914. MB was principally and narrowly concerned with chronicling the grand and petty activities of the upper classes of England and France. Her long witness of the turbulent events of the French Revolution brought her from her original detestation to a more moderate view. In her well-regarded major work, *A Comparative View*, she deplored revolutionary violence, "the wild visions of impossible freedom," but, like HELEN MARIA WILLIAMS and MARY WOLLSTONECRAFT, she affirmed the inevitability of the event: through all the stages of the French Revolution, the universal intention of the nation was "a general participation in the political, as well as the social excellence of the country—a deliverance from all monopoly, and all privilege, and security against all great concentrations either of power or property."　S.A.

BETHAM, [Mary] Matilda (1776–1852), poet, diarist and compiler, was the eldest of 14 children of the Rev. William Betham of Stonham in Suffolk, compiler of genealogical tables of world sovereigns and English aristocrats; her mother was Mary Damant. As a child, MB had access to her father's well-stocked library and she became especially knowledgeable in history. Her formal school education was intended to teach "sewing, and prevent a too strict application to books." MB taught herself the art of miniature painting, at which she became fairly successful. In 1794 she began a diary in which she recorded her friendships, especially with Charlotte Jerningham. In 1794 she visited her uncle in London and noted the festivities for Admiral Howe's victory, and in 1796 she was in Cambridge learning

Italian. In 1797 appeared her *Elegies and Other Small Poems*, dedicated to Lady Jerningham, with poems dated between 1794 and 1797. The following year she was exchanging verses with friends, claiming for women a superiority through the rules of gallantry: "He claims alone the privilege of war, / But 'tis our smiles that must reward the scar!" MB worried about her failure to marry and about her competence to earn a living. In London, her portraits were exhibited and she gave Shakespearean readings. Clearly a popular woman, she was considered a good conversationalist and companion, although a trifle eccentric; in 1801 Lady Bedingfield commented: "You are just the sort of person my dear Matilda to lose your place in a stage coach." She became friends with Coleridge, Southey, ANNA LAETITIA BARBAULD, and Charles and Mary Lamb. She knew the Ladies of Llangollen, Sarah Ponsonby and Lady Eleanor Butler, HANNAH MORE, and Madame de Staël, whose discourse she described as "like the flow of a beautiful and rapid river." In 1804 MB published *A Biographical Dictionary of Celebrated Women of Every Age and Country* and in 1808 a further book of poems. In 1814 she was searching for a profitable literary project when Southey advised her to adapt an old play for the stage or to versify a popular tale. She chose to write in verse the story of Marie, "an Anglo-Norman Minstrel of the thirteenth century." This appeared, to some acclaim, in 1816 as *The Lay of Marie: A Poem*; it had two appendices providing historical information about Marie and giving versions of her lays. MB's poetry was much praised by Southey and much read by the Lambs.

MB's early verses are mainly translations or typical sentimental pieces exploiting the vogue for British historical subjects. For example, one poem is set against a background of Druid religion, another against the Norman Conquest. A few deal with contemporary matters; one is addressed amusingly to a friend who wants to be called Anna: "Be what you will with all mankind, / But *Nancy* still with me." *The Lay* is an heroic and sentimental poem in rhyming tetrameter; it makes high claims for poetry: "I brought the pallid lip to smile, / Clear'd the maz'd thought for ampler scope, / Sustain'd the flagging wings of hope." In 1818 Coleridge quotes some comic verse of MB describing a search for love: "Poor Damon bit his nails and sigh'd, /

But still he was not satisfied"; in the end he realizes he has "vex'd my brains in looking round / For that which never could be found." On the whole MB's verse is mediocre and it rarely achieves distinction; one can only assume that the author's personal charm recommended it. The letters and diaries contain shrewd observations and reveal a relish for society and friendship. J.T.

BEVERLEY, Charlotte (fl. 1792), poet, wrote *Poems on Miscellaneous Subjects* (1792). The works are mainly on familiar themes; many are occasional and pastoral. The light poems are generally more successful than the serious ones, which are inert and stylized. Several are concerned with the poor, destitute and outcast—for example, "The Dying Prostitute": "Who now beholds, but loathes my faded face, / So wan, and sallow, chang'd with sin and care? / Or who can any former beauty trace, / In eyes so sunk with famine and despair?" There is also a curious sequence of "enigmas," of which the following is representative: "Take half an ancient poetess, / And half the produce of distress; / With two fifths of what we shun, / Makes up one colour—and soon is done." Answers are not provided. R.J.

BLACKBURNE, Anna (?–1794), botanist, was one of several children of the former Miss Atherton and John Blackburne of Orford near Warrington, who was famous for his garden of exotic plants. *Gentleman's Magazine* (1787) claims he was "the second gentleman in England who cultivated that delicious fruit . . . the Pine Apple." AB inherited her father's taste for botany and added an interest in natural history in general, collecting specimens from America and elsewhere for her museum. She was a correspondent of Linnaeus. She died at Fairfield near Warrington. J.J.

BLACKETT, Mary [Dawes] (fl. 1780–91), poet, lived in London during the last part of her life, and she appears to have had a wide range of acquaintances, including the poet Thomas Chatterton. In one poem she includes a brief reference to having lost a brother at sea: "For whose lov'd sake I gave my remnant store, / And only griev'd that I could give no more!" In the opening lines of a later poem, "To Miss H. Falconar," she refers to her loneliness and her widowhood: "Forsook by Fortune, and opprest by Fate, / Far from the haunts of pleasure

and the great; / A lonely widow in an humble cell, / With resignation and the Muse I dwell." This short poem is included in the prefatory material of MARIA and HARRIET FALCONAR's *Poetic Laurels* (London, 1791). MB's works include *The Antichamber: A Poem in Three Cantos. Canto I* (London, 1786). This first canto, 158 lines in heroic couplets, was apparently the only part published. A satire on courtiers, it seems to reflect MB's own experience, "From day to day attending, doom'd to wait / An humble suppliant to th' unreal great." The poem is of interest because of the author's comments on some eminent contemporaries, including James Mansfield, Charles Pratt, and Lord Thurlow. Another work in heroic couplets, *Suicide; A Poem* (London, 1789), has 402 lines; it is inscribed to Richard Cosway, principal painter to the Prince of Wales. In a preface MB condemns the indiscriminate use of the death penalty and suggests that frequent public executions lead many depressed individuals to view the taking of life with equanimity. She then notes that of the six suicides she describes, all involved "instances which have passed under my own knowledge, and characters with all of whom I had some degree of personal acquaintance, except the Earl of Caithness." After urging fortitude in adversity, MB concludes her poem with the example of a young woman who resisted the urge to end an unhappy life; she then asks, "Say then, shall lordly man retreat, and yield / To female courage the contested field?" MB also published *The Monitress, or, The Economy of Female Life, in a Series of Letters from M.D. Blackett to her Daughter* (1791). J.F.

BLACKWELL, Elizabeth (1700?–1758), naturalist, was the daughter of an Aberdeen merchant; she eloped to London with Alexander Blackwell, who fell into debt and was thrown into prison. To raise funds for his release, EB published her two-volume herbal in 1737 and 1739. Afterward Alexander went to Stockholm and, because of an alleged involvement in a plot against the Swedish government, was executed in July 1747. EB took four years to complete *A Curious Herbal containing Five Hundred Cuts of the most useful Plants which are now used in the Practice of Physick*. She copied the flowers and plants from the botanical gardens at Chelsea, made copper engravings, and colored all 500 plates herself. The text was taken and abridged by her husband from Joseph Miller's *Botan-*

icum Officinale (1722). EB's *Curious Herbal* was admired and endorsed by leading members of the College of Physicians, as EB makes clear in her opening dedications. The following address to Dr. Mead, curator of the Chelsea gardens, reveals her characteristic modesty: "As the world is indebted to the encouragers of every publick good, if the following shou'd prove such, it is but justice to declare who have been the chief promoters of it; and as you was the first who advised its publication and honoured it with your name, give me leave to tell its readers how much they are in your debt for this work." *Curious Herbal* proved to be one of the most popular herbals of the century; it was enlarged and republished in five volumes with a Latin text in Nuremberg, 1750–73.   S.B.

BLAMIRE, Susannah (1747–94), poet, called "the Muse of Cumberland," was born at Cardew Hall, about six miles from Carlisle, the youngest of William Blamire's children by his first wife, Isabella Simpson. When she died in 1754, SB and the other children, William, Richmond, and Sarah, were cared for by their aunt, Mrs. Simpson of Thackwood. The school at Raughton Head they attended for a shilling a quarter probably provided all the formal education SB received. Nor had she any encouragement to write poetry until her sister married Colonel Graham of Gartmore, and she found an appreciative audience among her in-laws. Several of SB's poems deal with ill-fated love, and possibly a "scion of a noble house" proposed marriage but his family opposed the match—the theme of the hermit story in one poem, "Stoklewath." Patrick Maxwell, who published her works, is the source of the only physical description of SB: "She had a graceful form, somewhat above the middle size, and a countenance—though slightly marked with smallpox—beaming with good nature; her dark eyes sparkled with animation and won every heart at first introduction. She was called by her countrymen 'a bonny and a verra lish young lass'" (Maxwell, Memoir in *The Poetical Works*). She had some knowledge of herbal medicine and often doctored her poorer neighbors. SB was attended in her last illness by her brother, Dr. William Blamire, and is buried at Raughton Head.

SB's half-sister, Bridget Brown, was the most diligent collector of her work, which eventually passed into Maxwell's hands and was published in Edinburgh in 1842 as *The Poetical Works of Miss Susannah Blamire.*

The 85 poems include "Stoklewath," which has been compared with Goldsmith's *The Deserted Village* but owes more to Thomson's *The Seasons*, as well as lyrics, epistles, elegies, and ballads. The earliest, "Written in a Country Churchyard" (1766), is clearly influenced by Gray's *Elegy*; another of SB's poems contains a reference to Ramsey's "The Gentle Shepherd," and she clearly knew the work of Milton, Collins, and Prior. She is best known for the freshness and authenticity of her poems of Cumbrian life, often written in a humorous or flyting vein, with the poet assuming the persona of one of her characters. "Wey, Ned, Man," written for Lord Tankerville, takes the form of a conversation between two farmers. "The Nabob" is the lament of a traveler on his return to England. In "Dear Nancy" she warns a friend against marriage ties: "Dear Nancy, since men have all made their own laws, / Which oppress the poor women, whatever's the cause; / Since by hardness of reason or hardness of fist / All wrong must be right if they choose to persist; / I'd have you with caution in wedlock engage, / For if once you are caught you're a bird in a cage, / That may for dear liberty flutter the wing / As you hop round the perch, but 'tis chance if you sing." Most of SB's poems are light in tone, but a few dwell on darker themes, such as the imminence of death, and are described as written "after the illness." Her battle with rheumatism is alluded to in an "Epistle to her Friends at Gartmore," written to her sister and her two sisters-in-law, describing her daily routine and celebrating the values of friendship. Her chosen themes, the serenity of rural life, the blessing of health, the faithlessness of frivolous love, the dangers of marriage, social injustice, and contempt for pomp and ostentation, are typical of the traditional Augustan worldview.   T.C.S.W.L.

BLAND, Elizabeth (fl. 1681–1712), Hebrew scholar, was the daughter of Robert Fisher of Long Acre. In 1681 she married Nathaniel Bland, a London merchant; in 1692 she became lord of the manor in Beeston, Yorkshire, where the couple lived. They had six children, two of whom survived infancy; both were taught Hebrew by their mother. EB is mentioned by George Ballard as a learned lady and by Ralph Thoresby in his *Ducatus Leodiensis* of 1715. She was the composer of a phylactery in Hebrew, four sentences on a scroll presented to the Royal Society, and of a Turkish Commission on "thick and smooth" paper with a very large seal. Both objects are listed as curiosities from the area of Leeds by Thoresby, who terms EB "that learned Gentlewoman." J.T.

BLEECKER, Ann Eliza (1752–83), American poet, short-story writer, and correspondent, was born in New York City to Brandt Schuyler and Margareta Van Wyck. Given the educational advantages of a well-to-do merchant family, AEB began writing even as a child, although she did not save her work until after her marriage to the lawyer John J. Bleecker in 1769. After two years in Poughkeepsie, the Bleeckers moved to Tomhanick, 18 miles north of Albany, a rural setting about which urban-bred AEB had mixed feelings. Several of her poems detail her attraction to pastoral life, but "To Mr. L- - -" and her later letters emphasize the isolation of this frontier community. Compounding the difficulties of isolation, the Revolutionary War forced AEB and her two small daughters to flee Tomhanick in 1777 on foot. The younger died of dysentery in the ensuing hardships, and AEB's mother and sister died soon after. Although the Bleeckers returned to their home after Burgoyne's defeat, they were again forced to Albany in 1779, and in 1781 John Bleecker was captured by Loyalists. Although he was rescued soon after, AEB was near nervous collapse; the baby she carried was stillborn. She died in Tomhanick just weeks after the signing of the Treaty of Paris officially ended the American Revolution.

AEB's manuscripts have apparently been lost, but her daughter, MARGARETTA FAUGERES, gathered 36 poems, two stories and several letters in *The Posthumous Works of Ann Eliza Bleecker . . .* (1793). Fourteen of these poems and the fictionalized "History of Maria Kittle" had already appeared in the *New-York Magazine* (1790–91); the "History" was later reissued as a separate publication (1797). If read in chronological order, *Posthumous Works* traces the heavy personal toll of the American Revolution. The earlier poems, influenced by Dryden, Pope, and Gray, are often playful, although not free from melancholy. AEB teases her friends or invites them to visit; she describes her gardens and characterizes her neighbors. Written in 1779, "The History of Maria Kittle" fictionalizes the sufferings of captives during the French and Indian War. Her poem "Written in the Retreat from Burgoyne" responds to the death of her daughter Abella: "Nor shall the mollifying

hand of time, / Which wipes off common sorrows, cancel mine." She reacts "On Reading Dryden's Virgil" by paralleling her experiences to that of Aeneas: "Like him I lost my fair one in my flight / From cruel foes—and in the dead of night." But finally even Aeneas's plight cannot compare to her own: "*He* held his way o'er the Cerulian Main, / But *I* return'd to hostile fields again." A letter written during a period of relative calm summarizes AEB's reaction to the war most clearly: "think not I dislike my situation here; on the contrary, I am charmed with the lovely scene the spring opens around me.—Alas! the wilderness is within: I muse so long on the dead until I am unfit for the company of the living." P.C.

BLOWER, Elizabeth (1763–?), novelist about whose life little is known, was born in Worcester. Her father, a gentleman, unfortunately involved in local politics, was attached to a politically unsuccessful candidate for Parliament. Whether because of his political activities or for other reasons, his family became needy, and EB turned to writing novels to contribute to their support. She wrote all of her four novels between the ages of 17 and 25. Her financial situation must then have altered, perhaps through marriage; she was still alive as late as 1816. The four novels are *The Parsonage House* (1780), *George Bateman* (1782), *Maria* (1785), and *Features from Life; or, A Summer Visit* (1780).

EB is one of the most direct 18th-century predecessors of Jane Austen, although her novels are less restrained and less well constructed than those of her successor. *Features from Life*, for instance, contains domestic tragedy and some sexual acknowledgment: seduction of a virtuous husband by a sophisticated society woman, separation from his wife, repentance and forgiveness, and a deathbed reconciliation. EB's strength lies in the presentation of character-sketches and in vignettes reminiscent of the *Tatler* and foreshadowing Austen's satiric characterization. Mrs. Tonto, of *Maria*, is a stock character with antecedents in Smollett and Fielding, an affected woman whose weak nerves are ostentatiously shaken by even a knock on the door (except those announcing visitors): "This lady's figure was long, dry, and uninteresting; her nose narrow and pinched in at the bottom; her lips were remarkably thin, and her eyes in colour, size, and power of expression, pretty much resembled a couple of black cherries."

EB's novels of manners include both moralizing and romance, but both are always touched with humor and satire. The affectations and hypocrisy of London society are much mocked through eyes of naturally virtuous rural people. Although EB is too prone to authorial interpolations, she writes dialogue well and makes some attempt in *George Bateman* to render the servants' dialect. K.S.

BONHOTE, Elizabeth (1744–1818), novelist and essayist, grew up in Bungay, Suffolk. Little is known of her life other than what she mentions in the introductions to her works. She was married to Daniel Bonhote, a solicitor, and had several children. Her husband died at Bury in 1804; she died at Bungay. EB's first, anonymously published, work was *The Rambles of Mr. Frankly* (1772), a series of observations on morality and town and country life, hung on a thin story line. This was followed by several novels: *The Fashionable Friend* (1773), *Olivia* (1786), *Darnley Vale* (1789), *Ellen Woodley* (1790), and *Bungay Castle* (1796). EB also wrote *The Parental Monitor* (1788), a series of short essays concerning the education of children, and a volume of poetry, *Feeling* (1810). Copies of all her works are now scarce. EB's novels are romantic and gothic. The earlier ones have extremely elaborate plots but very little development of character and no sense of time or place. *Bungay Castle* has the most feeling for atmosphere and setting, perhaps because she laid the story in a place she knew well. The book was dedicated, with permission, to the Duke of Norfolk, the owner of the castle ruins. EB says in the introduction that she had grown up playing in them and hearing local stories about them. The novel is set during the Wars of the Roses; its plot is the usual kind of complex gothic story, including mysterious prisoners, long-lost sons, and wicked uncles. According to the introduction, EB wrote *The Parental Monitor* for her children's guidance, in case she should die before she could personally oversee their upbringing. It is in two volumes, the first directed primarily at girls, the second at boys. The advice is entirely conventional, of the sort to be found in any conduct book of the day. It teaches acceptance of one's lot and complete dependence on adults, especially for girls. B.B.S.

BOOTHBY, Frances (fl. 1669), playwright during the reign of Charles II, claims in the dedication of her only known play to be related to Lady Yate of Harvington, in Worcestershire. Nothing else is known of her life. *Marcelia: or the Treacherous Friend* (1670) is a tragi-comedy that was "performed with some success at the Theatre Royal" in 1669, preceding by a year APHRA BEHN's first play, *The Forced Marriage*. Marcelia, virtuous although tempted by pride to marry a king, is exploited by a duplicitous court favorite, suspected by a jealous lover, and betrayed by a brother, who claims, "I had rather see her live in Fame for Virtue when she's dead, than in a Title." Much conventional jesting about women's wavering resolutions and "unconstant humours" relieves the highly improbable coincidence and exaggerated passion. G.B.

BOOTHBY, Hill (1708–56), letter writer, was the daughter of Brook Boothby of Ashbourne Hall, Derbyshire, and Elizabeth Fitzherbert. In or before 1753 she met Samuel Johnson, with whom she became very friendly. He called her "sweet angel" and declared he had "none other on whom his heart reposes." HB had many women friends, including ANNA SEWARD, with whom she corresponded and who called her a "sublimated Methodist" because of the enthusiastic piety with which she wrote. HB's correspondence with Johnson, published in 1805, runs from 1753 to December 1755, shortly before her death. There is much domestic news, solicitude about Johnson's health, expression of affection and esteem, and discussion of morals. Referring to her own declining health in one letter, she remarks: "I hope, however, to see you the *author of a Great Dictionary* before I go, and to have the pleasure of joining with a whole Nation in your applause: and when you have put into their hands the means of speaking and writing the English language with as much purity and propriety as it is capable of being spoken and wrote, give me leave to recommend to you your future studies and labours—let them all be devoted to the glory of God." The boredom and torpor of HB's day-to-day existence, and hence too the personal urgency of her religious commitment, are conveyed in a remarkable letter to Johnson: "I am abstracted from common life, as you say. What is common life, but a repetition of the same thing over and over? And is it made up of such things, as a thinking, reflecting being can bear the repetition of, over and over, long, without weariness? I have found not;

and therefore my view is turned to the things of that life, which must be begun here, is ever new and increasing, and will be continued eternally hereafter." J.T.

BOSCAWEN, Frances (1719–1805), Bluestocking letter writer, was the daughter of William Evelyn of St. Clere, Kent, who changed his name to Glanville on his marriage in 1718 to FB's mother, Frances Bromehall Glanville (d. 1719). FB grew up rich, good, sensible, and wise. Her portraits show her to have had strong, plain features; her acquaintances found her lively and charming. In 1742 FB married Edward Boscawen (1711–61), already established in a distinguished naval career; he was to become Admiral of the Blue, General of Marines, Lord of the Admiralty, and a principal hero of his time. On FB's side at least the marriage was a love match, and during its 18 years she devoted herself to domestic duties and her husband's interests. Much of her time was absorbed in the country with their five children. In the last domestic years she settled into a new house at Hatchlands, Surrey. With her husband much absent at sea or at the Admiralty in London, she practiced letter writing and management skills later to stand her in good stead. Both to amuse herself and to advance her husband's career, she began to entertain, from the beginning evincing the celebrated skill of attentiveness to each guest of which HANNAH MORE said, "I dare say everybody, when they got home, thought as I did, that they alone had been the immediate object of her attention." Her life was shadowed by the admiral's much-publicized affair, from about 1756, with the actress Jane Lessingham, by whom he was said to have had two sons (for whom FB had to make provision on his sudden death). The admiral died almost without warning in 1761, and at 41, the dedicatee of Edward Young's poem *Resignation*, FB began 44 years of autonomous widowhood. Hannah More considered her life "a continued series of afflictions that may almost bear a parallel with those of the righteous man of Uz," but FB also had her share of felicities. She reopened her old house at 14 South Audley Street and divided her time there and in various country villas, the last Rosedale, between Richmond and Kew, the former home of the poet James Thomson. In 1766 her daughter Elizabeth married the Duke of Beaufort and in 1773 her daughter Frances married the Hon. John Leveson-Gower; in 1769 her son William, in the Navy, was drowned in Jamaica and in 1774 her eldest son, Edward Hugh, died abroad. In 1784 her remaining son, George, now Lord Falmouth, married Miss Crewe, granddaughter of FRANCES GREVILLE. The descendants of her three surviving children turned out to be numerous, gifted, and illustrious. FB was a devoted mother and grandmother, but she also spent the years of widowhood refining her social skills, and she became one of the major Bluestocking hostesses. Elegance was her hallmark. James Boswell said, "Her manners are the most agreeable and her conversation the best of any lady," and Hannah More noted, "She is at once polite, learned, judicious, and humble." By 1770 her evening parties, like those of Mrs. Vesey and ELIZABETH MONTAGU dedicated to conversation rather than cards, were the rage of London. A keen observer of society, FB also had a strong moralistic streak and was privately religious; she left Hannah More a library of 400 volumes, "chiefly Port Royal authors." She was buried in her husband's family vault near Truro.

FB's letters have not yet been collected and published. Some are preserved in the life of Hannah More, some in the correspondence of MARY DELANY. Some letters to Elizabeth Montagu are in *Bluestocking Letters*, ed. R.B. Johnson (1926). Her letters to her husband, preserved in the family, are published in *Admiral's Wife* (1940); later letters appear in the companion volume, *Admiral's Widow* (1943). The early letters to her husband are often in a loving, familiar style. FB keeps him informed of domestic and social events, but the predominant tone is that of an insecure wife bent on asserting her own value. One theme is the immense superiority of her own children to all others; another is her own usefulness as estate manager, decorator, and hostess; a third, the compliments and approval given her by his friends and associates. As rumors of the Lessingham affair grow, she does not challenge directly, but writes, "Sometimes I wish I had beauty to please you. But then, perhaps that beauty might have produced a youth of folly, an old age of cards. Those who are adorned with it often neglect to adorn their mind and their heart. . . . Upon the whole, you see, I would fain pass myself off upon you as a useful and a pleasant appendix to your state in this life" (4 Oct. 1756). Later she almost begs, but maintains her dignity: "*Enfin, mon cher, cher, ayez pitié de votre pauvre solitaire*, for if you spend all your life in London, I shall begin to think that you have found something there, something very unworthy of your interest!" (21 Sept. 1757). FB's one real passion probably died with Edward Boscawen. Her later letters are often carefully and elegantly designed; they were frequently compared with the letters of Mme. de Sevigné although lacking their emotional appeal. FB writes to Mrs. Montagu, "I would not have you guess how cold it is upon these hills; I have just left a very good fire to come up and write to you in my chamber where there is none, and in so doing, *I show my love* which I desire you cordially to accept; it would not be worth a farthing if my heart were not warmer than my hands." Descriptions of nature mingle with social notes: "All the fields are adorned with haycocks, which look as if they had had their full share of wet, and wanted to get dry and go home. . . . Miss Rowley is to marry Sir John Cotton's eldest son. Mrs. Worgan gives them £500 a year *pour aider le ménage*, in consideration of which I forgive her all the gauzes, ribbands and flowers with which she decorates her cadavrous figure." B.R.

BOULBIE, Judith (?—1706), religious polemicist, wrote the fierce pamphlet *A Testimony for Truth against all Hireling-Priests and Deceivers: With a Cry to the Inhabitants of this Nation, to turn to the Lord, before his dreadful Judgments overtake them* (1665?), blaming priests and bishops for their "Ungodly Gaines" and for "eating the Fat, and clothing your selves with the Fleece." She describes Anglican clergy in terms of Cain and Balaam as "Strangers to the Covenant of Promise" and demands that they "leave off . . . Deceit, and keep the People no longer in your dark Forms; but let them have Liberty to Worship God in Spirit and Truth." If the priests do not change, she fears divine wrath will come: "The Lord will turn your Feasting into Fasting, and your Mirth into Lamentation." A poem urges national repentance: "O *England*, wilt thou still forget, / God's Kindness unto thee?" and the end of the pamphlet inveighs against English habits of dicing, drinking, feasting and special keeping of Christmas when all days should be holy. In 1667 JB addressed a pamphlet *To All Justices of Peace, or Other Magistrates to Whom This May Come* and, in 1673, to governors, *A Few Words to the Rulers of the Nation*. In 1679 she warned England in general and Londonderry in particular of their evil ways: *A Warning and La-*

mentation Over England and *A Few Words as a Warning . . . to the Inhabitants of Londonderry*. In 1692 she was associated with the Quaker Women's Meeting in York, and her name appears with those of other women on their annual communication. J.T.

BOWDLER, Elizabeth Stuart (1717?–1797), commentator on the Scriptures, was the second daughter of Sir John Cotton of Conington, Hunts., fifth baronet in direct descent from the famous antiquary Sir Robert Cotton. She married Thomas Bowdler, a gentleman descended from an ancient family of Hope Bowdler, Salop., and lived most of her married life in and around Bath. She studied the Scriptures and probably knew Hebrew. She was the mother of four children, all of whom were authors: JANE BOWDLER (1743–84), John (1746–1823), HENRIETTA MARIA (1754–1830), and Thomas (1754–1825), the editor of *The Family Shakespeare*. John's two sons, Thomas and John, were also writers on religious subjects. EB's husband died in 1785.

The New York Public Library attributes a work entitled *Bible O.T. Song of Solomon* to EB. The title page notes that the work was written in 1775 and published in 1779. In it EB offers both a new translation of the *Song* and a commentary. The poem is literally about Solomon and describes the seven days after his wedding. "But whilst we attend to the literal sense of this poem . . . we must not forget that the whole idea is a symbolic representation of Christ and his Church. Christ is a bridegroom to the body of the Church, but is so likewise to every individual in it, and every humble soul may truly say 'his left hand is under my head and his right does embrace me.'" EB's other work, *Practical Observations on the Revelation of St. John*, also written in 1775, was first published anonymously in 1787. She considered it a duty to show to the young and ignorant the advantage she herself had found in reading the Scriptures. She does not offer a total interpretation of the *Book of Revelation*, but infers from it the doctrine of free will and the consequent necessity of diligent application in life. The *Monthly Review* approved the work as "not rhapsodical, or merely fanciful"; the author appeared to be a man of sense, who had an acquaintance with his subject, and what explanations or hypotheses he advanced were proposed with a becoming modesty and piety. The work was republished, probably by one or more of her children, in 1800 with ESB's name on the title page. C.R.

BOWDLER, Henrietta Maria (1754–1830), known as Harriet, sermon writer and novelist, daughter of ELIZABETH STUART BOWDLER and sister of JANE BOWDLER, was a successful author but apparently published none of her work before 1800. The *DNB* erroneously attributes to her *Poems and Essays* (1786) in two volumes, published at Bath; although she may have edited this work, it is actually the *Poems and Essays by a Lady, lately deceased* of her sister Jane, who died in 1784. The work has probably been confused with *Fragments, in Prose and Verse; by a young lady, deceased* (ELIZABETH SMITH), edited in 1808 by HMB, with a memoir of the author. HMB wrote the vastly successful *Sermons on the Doctrines and Duties of Christianity* (1801), which had reached a 44th edition in 1836. It is said she was offered a benefice on its (anonymous) appearance. A novel, *Pen Tamar, or the History of an Old Maid*, was published posthumously (1830; actually 1831). The British Library catalogue attributes two other possible works to HMB: *Creation and other poems* (1818) and *Essay on the Proper Employment of Time* (1836), the latter attributed only because it was published with an edition of her *Sermons*. C.R.

BOWDLER, Jane (1743–84), poet and essayist, was the eldest child of Thomas and ELIZABETH STUART BOWDLER, and siter of John, Thomas, and HENRIETTA MARIA BOWDLER. Both sisters lived and died unmarried in their parents' house near Bath. In 1759 JB suffered a severe attack of smallpox and never again enjoyed good health. From 1771 until she died she was bed-ridden. Two years after her death *Poems and Essays by a Lady lately deceased* was published anonymously for the benefit of the Bath hospital, with such success that between 1787 and 1800 16 more editions with her name on the title page were published in Bath; others appeared in London, Dublin, and New York (1811). JB's posthumous success may well have been due more to aggressive promotion by the Church than to any inherent merit in her work, which is bland to the point of insipidity, unenlivened by any originality of thought or expression or any suggestion of an independent personality. Perhaps, however,

the correctness of her sentiments may have been the best selling point with her pious readership. JB occasionally contributed verses to LADY MILLER's poetic salon at Batheaston, and the abstract purity of her diction may owe something to its influence. Her "Subject, LOVE. For the vase, at BATH-EASTON VILLA" includes the following lines: "Coquetry here with roving eyes, / Quick darts a thousand arrows round; / She thinks to conquer by surprize— / But ah! those arrows never wound." It is quite probable that Elizabeth, Henrietta Maria and Jane received no income from their literary activities. T.C.S.W.L.

BOWERS, Bathsheba (1672?–1718), American autobiographer, was the daughter of Benanuel and Elizabeth Dunster Bowers, English Quakers who settled in Charlestown, Mass., and later sent their daughter to Philadelphia to escape Puritan persecution. Only one small published volume is known to be by her, but it suggests that she may have written and destroyed others. *An alarm sounded to prepare the inhabitants of the world to meet the Lord in the way of his judgments* (1709) is an immensely detailed autobiographical account of her painful search for understanding and peace with God. It presents her life as a series of tests, a "spiritual Passage" in which she has to overcome her pride, joy, and fear— in friendships, home, preaching, clothing, and publishing, as well as in her attitudes to death, hell, and God. The work describes her conversion when, after a violent fever at the age of 19, she awakened to feel "divine sweetness" and resolved to "leave off my little fineries," to cease reading romances and visiting friends, to take up the "much despised *thee* and *thou* to a single person," and to find delight in gardening and contemplation. It then concentrates on the years of struggles—"overturns" as BB calls them: "Why it pleased the Almighty to bend his bow and set me as a mark for his arrows, not only from my youth, but even from my infancy up, I know not but even so it has been." BB feels that her melancholy and suffering stem from her inability to submit and her lack of faith; this melancholy is well caught in such expressions as "I wore out the day, wishing for the night, and in the night was weary of my bed." She attempts to conceal her condition from friends because "Cries and complaints make but a very ungrateful sound in the ears of those that dwell in ease and pleasure." Finally, in 1703 she fasts and in resignation writes, "Let this time be the time of love, for I can never be brought lower than I am now." She realizes that she has overcome only "in part," but she can now find delight in the company of the poor and in the confines of her own small home. BB eventually became a Quaker preacher and moved to South Carolina.   M.P.

BOYD, Elizabeth ["Louisa"] (fl. 1730–40), poet and novelist, is unknown except for the biographical information published with her single novel, *The Happy Unfortunate; or, The Female Page* (1732). This includes the advertisement in which the author refers to her own long illness and her need to provide for an "ancient, indulgent Mother; whom Age, and the Charge of many Children hath render'd incapable of providing for herself." EB then explains that she will use the profits from the book to open a shop and sell "all Manner of Stationary Goods." Subscribing to the novel, which was reissued in 1737 as *The Female Page*, were 328 people, including 92 members of the nobility. In the preface to the novel, EB states that it was written when she was very young, and ill-health has prevented her from making extensive corrections. Influenced by the Arcadian romance tradition, the story is set in Cyprus, an island said to be "appropriated to Venus and her Son." Throughout the three parts, emphasis is placed upon incident; characters are given little depth or development. The plot centers on the ill-effects of arranged and loveless marriages, a theme expressed by the heroine, Amanda, in a letter to the woman who had tried to arrange her seduction: "A Man must be settled enough to form a certain Judgement, of his own Affections and Inclinations, before in my Opinion he's qualified for either a Husband, a Lover, or a Friend, which three Persons ought to be always blended in one, if Happiness is propos'd in the Connubials."

Prior to 1732, EB had published *Variety: A Poem in Two Cantos . . . By Louisa* (1727) and *Verses . . . to His Majesty King George IId on His Birth-Day* (1730). Her later works include *The Humorous Miscellany; or Riddles for the Beaux* (1733), a short collection of occasional and commemorative verse, riddles, and songs; *The Happy North-Briton* (1737), a poem celebrating the marriage of the Duke of Hamilton; and *Glory to the Highest, a Thanksgiving Poem on the Late Victory at Dettingen* (1743). Another long patriotic poem, *Admiral Haddock; or The Progress of Spain,* was published in 1739 or 1740. In addition to these and other commemorative poems, EB published a ballad opera, *Don Sancho, or The Student's Whim* (1739). Set in Oxford, this strange mixture of comedy, necromancy, and masque depicts the ghosts of Shakespeare and Dryden and a descent of Apollo and Minerva. The cast also includes students, Mercury, attending deities, ethereal spirits, and Lilliputians. As well as offering incense at monuments to the two great poets, the pagan deities sing the praises of other modern authors including Gay, Congreve, Addison, Waller, and Lord Lansdowne, the last being described as the "Glory of his Soil." EB was obviously a partisan of the moderns, and one of her two prologues is addressed to the living modern, Alexander Pope.   J.F.

BRADFORD, Elizabeth (1663?–1731), American poet, was born in London, the daughter of a Quaker printer, Andrew Sowle. She married William Bradford, her father's apprentice, in 1685 and emigrated to America. The couple first lived in Philadelphia and then settled in New York. Bradford published an edition of the Baptist Benjamin Keach's *War with the Devil . . .* (1707), and he and EB wrote prefatory poems for it, which they initialed. EB's is an almost doggerel defense of poetry against blame and calumny, and a claim that it is above other arts because "inspir'd into the heart / By divine means / . . . / for true divinity / Hath with this science great affinity: / Though some through ignorance, do it oppose, / Many do it esteem, far more than prose." EB died in New York.   J.T.

BRAND, Hannah (?–1821), poet and playwright, was born in Norwich, the daughter of a tanner. Her brother was John Brand (d. 1808), a Tory writer on politics and political economy, and her sisters, Mary and Sarah, unmarried school mistresses. HB taught school with Mary in Norwich until she turned to the stage. In 1792, she played the role of Agmunda, with John Kemble, in her own tragedy of *Huniades* with the Drury Lane Company at the King's Theatre, Haymarket (a 1791 MS is in the Larpent Collection at the Univ. of Missouri). The play was withdrawn after one performance and reproduced a month later entitled *Agmunda*, but met with no greater success. She later appeared with Tate Wilkinson's company at the York Theatre in March 1794, playing the role of Lady Townly in *The Provok'd Husband* (Vanbrugh-Cibber). Her stilted movement and provincial dialect were ridiculed by the audiences; she was described as "starched in manner, virtuous in conduct, and resolute in her objections to a low-cut dress" (Tate Wilkinson, *The Wandering Patentee*, iv). She stayed with the Wilkinson company until May 1794, when *Agmunda* again flopped. That summer she performed unsuccessfully in Liverpool. HB left the stage to become a governess, but her behavior was so eccentric that it caused strife between her employers.

In 1798 a set of HB's *Plays and Poems* was published at Norwich, which contained: *Adelinda*, a comedy based on Destouche's *La Force du naturel* (never performed); *The Conflict, or, Love, Honour, and Pride*, an adaptation of Corneille's *Don Sanche d'Arragon* (never performed); *Huniades: or the Siege of Belgrade*; and six poems: "Valentine to Miss Brand" (1786); "The Monk of La Trappe: A Tale" (1787); "Ode to Youth" (1791); "Ode to Adversity" (1795); and "Prayer to the Parcae" (1796). Three of the poems are about her friendship with her sister. Her "Imitation of a French Hymn" (by Des Barreaux, 1795) suggests HB's fervent religious belief: "My Sins bereave my Soul of Hope / To hear, O God! thy pardoning Voice; / In Thy dread power they nought have left / But of my Punishment the choice."   T.C.S.W.L.

BRERETON, Jane (1685–1740), poet, second daughter of Ann Jones and Thomas Hughes of Bryn-Griffith, Wales, married Thomas Brereton, a commoner of Brasenose College, Oxford, in 1711. Of her four children, only two girls survived infancy. The couple separated in 1721, owing to Brereton's wasteful habits and violent temper. He was drowned in 1722. JB's only brother, a wealthy brewer, invited her to Ireland, but she preferred instead to settle in Wrexham, Wales, where she cared for the poor. She was buried in Wrexham Church.

JB's only book-length publication is *Poems on Several Occasions ... with Letters to her Friends and An Account of Her Life* (1744). In the five letters, two of which are addressed to Mrs. M[A]D[A]N, JB expresses her views on some of the issues of the time. She disagrees with Law's judgment concerning the propriety of stage entertainment, stating that she sees drama as a perfectly acceptable diversion: "I would, at least, set Plays upon a level with Dancing, Back-Gammon, or a Game of Cards, etc. tho' in my own Opinion, I prefer a well-wrought Play to them all." In other letters she comments on the works of ELIZABETH ROWE and defends luxury on the grounds that it helps to eliminate poverty through the creation of jobs for the poor. Between 1734 and 1736 JB carried on a verse correspondence in the *Gentleman's Magazine* under the name "Melissa"; the other writer, who turned out to be a man of her acquaintance, called himself "Fido." *Poems* includes these verses and several longer poems. Two of the latter, "Merlin" and "The Royal Hermitage," had been published together in 1735 under the title, *Merlin: A Poem*. The longest work in the collection, "The Dream," is an imitation of parts of Chaucer's *The House of Fame*, a piece which demonstrates JB's ironic humor in its mockery of the conventional dream-vision setting: "Descriptions I must lay aside, / I slept, and dreamt at the Fireside: / Tho' Men in Fields may sleep or roam, / Women had best to nap at Home." Many of MB's poems have physico-theological themes; she praises the scientific progress of the age, especially as exemplified in Newton. Some comment on contemporary attitudes toward women writers and one apostrophizes Queen Caroline as the patron of learning. Her best works are satirical such as "On Mr. Nash's Picture, at full Length, between the Busts of Sir Isaac Newton and Mr. Pope," a poem attributed to the Earl of Chesterfield. Her anonymous biographer in *Poems* comments: "Tho' she liked Wit, she could never bear any Thing that seem'd to her to be scurrilous; and some Things that she wrote, at the Entreaty of her Friends, that were a little Satirical, afterwards gave her great Uneasiness. . . . Her Poetical name of *Melissa* was given by a Gentleman of her Acquaintance, from the Latin Word 'Mell' as bearing some allusion to the Sweetness of her Numbers."   J.F.

BREWSTER, Martha Wadsworth (1710–?), American poet, was born in Lebanon, Conn., to the farm family of Joseph and Lydia Brown Wadsworth. Like most girls, she was probably educated by her parents, although she may have had the unusual advantage of access to two libraries: her father owned a small personal library, and the Congregational church at Goshen, four miles away, opened a modest collection of books to its members in 1734. MB had been admitted to full communion in 1730, just two weeks before the newcomer Oliver Brewster also joined the congregation. Oliver and Martha

Brewster were married in 1732; their children, Ruby and Wadsworth, were born in 1733 and 1737, respectively. Town records note that MB bought and sold land after her marriage, both with her husband and in her own name. Several years after their marriage, the Brewsters resettled seven miles to the north, near present-day Columbia, Conn., perhaps the occasion for "A Farewell to Some of my Christian Friends at Goshen, in Lebanon" (1745). Oliver Brewster moved to Bernardston, Mass., in 1765, although no records survive to indicate whether MB was still alive to accompany him. MB's *Poems on Divers Subjects* (New London, Conn., 1757; repr. Boston, 1758) has a range of forms and themes. The 21 poems include acrostics, eulogies, epithalamiums, verse letters, scriptural paraphrases, a love poem, a quaternion, a verse prayer, and other occasional pieces. In addition to more than 1100 lines of verse, the volume contains a prose summary of a dream-interview with her dead father. Chief among MB 's themes are eschatology, grace, and mortality. Her *Poems* reveal an intense involvement in the "Great Awakening." A committed "new light," she devotes two long poems to the terrors of Judgment Day, but does not neglect the corollary theme of the irresistible grace of the chosen saints. She records the joy and, more often, the mystery of God's working: "There is a Wheel within a Wheel, / Beyond what we descry; / He'll make us feel Sin's deadly Wound, / And then his Blood apply." MB also writes of marriage and love, of "the noble man," and of her ambitions as a poet. "A Funeral Poem, on the Death of . . . Isaac Watts," for example, expresses her wish that "When he Expir'd might I have been his Heir." The tone here is cautious. MB is fully aware of her position as a woman poet: "For rare it is to see a *Female Bard*, / Or that my Sex in Print have e're appear'd." But however muted her expressions of ambition, they recur too often to be ignored, as in the awkward lines: "Let me improve my Talent tho' but small, / And thus it humbly wait upon you shall."   P.C.

BRISCOE, Sophie [or Sophia] (fl. 1771–72), wrote *Miss Melmoth; or, The New Clarissa* (1771). It concerns a heroine who suffers many trials and tribulations through an envious rival. *Critical Review* (July 1771) found the book amusing without being corrupting and considered it suitable for women because it was entertaining and instructive; it was, however, marred by extravagant

characters and unnatural romantic situations. *Monthly Review* (June 1771) noted that the heroine was more fortunate than her namesake, but that the novel was inferior to the original. SB's second work, *The Fine Lady: A Novel* (1772), was an epistolary novel concerning a man's fatal attraction to two women: Harriet, the coquette, and Louisa, who disdains the pursuit of conquests. He expresses his dilemma thus: "My veneration, esteem and tenderness for Louisa is still the same it ever was; and my love and desire towards Harriet, the dear destructive Harriet, hardly knows any bounds." Despite its slightly risqué sexual intrigue, the novel is perfectly representative of the sentimental literature of the time; *CR* (February 1772) judged that the volumes "deserve not to be classed with the lowest, nor to be ranked with the highest productions in this species of writing. . . . it is not easy to read the catastrophe, of which the Fine Lady is the eventual cause, without feeling powerful emotions."   R.J.

BRODBELT, Anne (1751–1827) West Indian letter writer, was born in Jamaica, the daughter of Thomas Penoyre, from a Herefordshire family, and Sarah Gardner, from an established colonial background. She was educated in England; in 1766 her father died and in 1770 she married Dr. Francis Rigby Brodbelt. The couple set up house in some style in Spanish Town and produced three children, Rigby, Nancy, and Jane. All were educated in England. In 1790 AB traveled to England to fetch Nancy home, returning early in 1792. Jane remained in England, while Rigby went for further education to France; he was there when the French war with England broke out. In Jamaica AB's life was also interrupted by the war, as well as by uprisings of the Maroons and by outbreaks of yellow fever. In 1795 Dr. Brodbelt died, leaving considerable property to his wife and children. Jane was instructed to return to Jamaica with relatives, but by the time she arrived AB had decided to live in England for the remainder of her life. AB moved to Chudleigh, where Nancy was married in 1798. In 1799 Jane also married, and settled in Jamaica. When in 1810 Rigby came to live in Batheaston Villa, AB moved to Bath, where she encountered many other West Indian landowners. In 1827, to her great grief, Rigby died, and AB followed him in the same year.

AB's letters and those of Nancy were preserved by Jane; they provide a detailed picture of fashionable life in the West Indies in the late 18th century. Apart from expressions of grief at family loss and some anxiety at the ideas of revolution and abolition, they are unremittingly frivolous, seldom mentioning the major political events of the period except in terms of their effect on dresses and balls. For Nancy the "Horrid Rebellion among the Maroons," as AB termed it, meant an absence of soldiers for partners and, for AB, the French Wars primarily interrupted the shipment of modish gowns from England. The large amount written on dress is indicative of the enormous expense lavished on it. When Jane was to return from England, she was instructed by her mother to bring a large wardrobe with her, together with "some fashionable music, both in the Lesson as well as Sing song way" so that she could impress Jamaican society, "as anything *new* is very taking here." When AB is somewhat depressed by war and pestilence in 1794, she cheers herself by ordering more dresses, "anything in colours which is very fashionable and pretty." She is much concerned to keep up with London modes, but is provincial enough to be shocked by their daring nature. "Surely they have kicked all Delicacy out of doors, or are they in a state of Insanity?" she writes when she hears that English women have ceased to wear handkerchiefs and petticoats. AB's letters, almost devoid of literary reference, convey well the feeling of plantation life, the heat, the ubiquitous slaves, the journeys to the hills, the partying, and the leisured pursuits of embroidery, music, dancing, and gossip. J.T.

BROMLEY, Eliza [Nugent] (fl. 1784–1803), novelist, was an officer's widow who had several other military men in her family. Her two novels reveal a familiarity with life on the Continent, a love of adventure and danger, and a sense of the constant threat of misfortune and death, the temptations of the city, and the problems of lovers. The first, *Laura and Augustus, an authentic story; in a series of letters* (1784), is dedicated to the Dowager Countess Spencer. The story opens with a young seasick girl writing to her friend full accounts of her visits to Madeira, Madras, Antigua, and other exotic places. Her letters are full of impulsive, frivolous girl-talk. She describes town life, quotes Pope, and blushes at the sight of half-naked Portuguese sailors. When she falls in love, a series of letters from her lover to his friend relate his wonder

and ecstasy. Soon, however, the letters lament the abandoned woman and the fatherless child, and the shambles of love and life. They end with melodramatic descriptions of explosions aboard ship that deal out disaster and death for all. The second volume, *The Cave of Cosenza: A Romance of the Eighteenth Century, altered from the Italian* (1803) is dedicated to the Duke of York and opens with an imposing list of subscribers. It is again a romance, but less descriptive and more conversational. The focus is on a fine young gentleman, happily married with a lovely wife and babe in England, who is on a diplomatic mission to the Continent. In Italy he is ensnared by a sultry woman, but resists all temptations and nobly returns to his family. The temptress follows him and throws herself into his arms, forcing him to struggle "between love and reason. The latter was too feeble; and our hero was precipitated into an abyss of misery." The author uses this situation to castigate all things Italian—the life, customs, morals, court, and especially, the woman. The seducer is "cunning": "Money was her duty, and debauchery her element." The seduced can only be miserable, and he finds himself betrayed and abandoned. This novel, too, ends in an explosion and is resolved satisfactorily on the last page, with justice for everyone. M.P.

BROOK, Mary Brotherton (1726–82), polemicist, wrote *Reasons for the Necessity of Silent Waiting, In order to the Solemn Worship of God* (1774). The Quaker tract argues against ceremony and public worship and in favor of a silent submission of soul: "The Influences of the Spirit are not at our Command, circumscribed in our Time, or limited by our Wills, and therefore must be humbly waited for, seeing we can have no Access without it." Her espousal of the Inner Light leads her to criticize with some vigor the mechanical repetition of prayers "whilst the Heart neither feels the Thing the Mouth speaks, nor ever experienced what the Tongue declares." Despite its earnestness the work is restrained in expression and not inelegant in style, and compares favorably with the prose of a fellow Quaker like ABIGAIL FISHER. It was published in London and Dublin and later in New York and Philadelphia. R.J.

BROOKE, Charlotte (1740–83), poet, playwright, biographer, and translator, was born in Rantavan, Co. Cavan. She was one of the youngest of 22 children of the novelist and playwright Henry Brooke (1703–83). While her own circle of friends included MARIA EDGEWORTH and the historian / translator Joseph Walker, it was CB's aged father who introduced her to art and who was undoubtably the major artistic and social influence in her life. She remained unmarried, and devoted herself to her ailing father. When he died at the family estate at Killibegs, Co. Kildare, in 1783, CB, well into her middle years, found herself impecunious. Turning to writing as a means of support, she produced an extensive body of work in the final decade of her life. But despite their being critically acclaimed, her works earned little, and CB died poor and nearly friendless.

While her published works included an unproduced tragedy entitled *Belisorius*, a juvenile piece, *The School for Christians* (1791), and her own poetic rendition of a Gaelic folk-story, *Maon: An Irish Tale* (1789), CB's literary importance lies in her careful translation of traditional Celtic poetry. To what degree she was influenced by Thomas Percy's *Reliques of Ancient Poetry* (1765) or the Ossianic works of James Macpherson cannot be fully ascertained, but her father must have been an influence since he was an avid patriot, who experimented with bardic poetic form; shortly after his death CB produced a number of translated songs by Turlogh O'Carolan, blind harper and last of the Irish bards. Heartened by favorable critical response, she began to work in earnest in the area of Irish-Gaelic poetry, and in 1789 published her most important work, *Reliques of Irish Poetry*. The collection consisted mostly of heroic, sentimental songs, odes, and elegies, popular and marketable in an England still enthralled by fashionable Celtic melancholy: "Rise, might of Erin! rise! / O! Osgur, of the generous soul! / Now, on the foes astonished eyes, / Let thy proud ensigns wave dismay!" While the constant sentimental glorifiation of Irish heroic subjects renders the work tedious, *Reliques* was both popular and critically lauded in its own day. But it has importance now for its numerous scholarly notes which concern traditional Irish history, literature and language, and which shed valuable light on a diminishing culture. As CB's memoirist Aaron Seymour pointed out in 1816, the notes aided in preserving part of her country's heritage

and perhaps helped to inspire an interest in Irish antiquities.   J.P.M.

BROOKE, Frances (1724–89), novelist, dramatist, periodical essayist, and translator, was born in Claypole, Lincs., eldest daughter of the Rev. Thomas Moore and Mary Knowles. Orphaned in childhood, Frances and her sister Sarah were brought up in the Lincolnshire rectories of clerical relations. A younger sister died in childhood. Throughout her life FB remained close to her surviving sister and her Lincolnshire relations and was a staunch advocate of the established Church. In the early 1750s she was living in London and writing poetry and plays. By 1756 she had married the Rev. John Brooke, rector of Norfolk and several Norwich parishes. By this time her theatrical acquaintances included Peg Woffington and her sister Mary (Polly) Cholmondeley, James Quin, Tate Wilkinson, Arthur Murphy, and Henry Woodward. Samuel Johnson, too, was a friend. FB first came to attention with her editorship of a weekly periodical, *The Old Maid*, which appeared from November 1755 to July 1756. In 1756 she published a tragedy, *Virginia*, written some years earlier but rejected by Garrick and never produced. In 1757 her husband sailed for America as a military chaplain. That year their only son, John Moore, was born. Three years later, FB published *Letters from Juliet, Lady Catesby, to her friend, Lady Henrietta Campley*, a translation of Marie-Jeanne Riccoboni's popular novel of sensibility. Her own first novel, *The History of Lady Julia Mandeville*, appeared in 1763; the same year, with her son and her sister, she joined her husband, now military chaplain at Quebec. Here the Brookes participated in the social life around Gov. James Murray and, after 1766, his replacement, Guy Carleton, and here FB wrote *The History of Emily Montague*, the first Canadian novel. Returning to England late in 1768, she translated Nicolas Framéry's sentimental and melodramatic novel, *Mémoires de M. le Marquis de S. Forlaix* (1770) and Abbé Millot's *Elémens de l'histoire d' Angleterre* (1771). From 1773 to 1778 she was comanager with her friend the tragic actress Mary Ann Yates of the Haymarket Opera House, which had been bought by FB's brother-in-law, James, and Mrs. Yates's husband, Richard. In the meantime, the second Canadian novel, *All's Right at Last; or, the History of Miss West*, was published anonymously in 1774; evidence suggests FB as its author. In 1779 she published *The Excursion*. During these years, her acquaintances included the musician Charles Burney and his daughter FANNY BURNEY, the portraitist Catherine Read, the musician William Shield, ANNA SEWARD, and HANNAH MORE. In 1782, Thomas Harris produced her tragedy *The Siege of Sinope* at Covent Garden with Mrs. Yates in the title role, and followed with her two comic operas, *Rosina* in 1783 and *Marian* in 1788. By 1788 FB had moved to Sleaford, Lincs., to live with her son, now vicar of Helpringham and rector of Folkingham. Her last novel, *The History of Charles Mandeville*, appeared the year after her death.

In *The Old Maid*, under the pseudonym Mary Singleton, Spinster, FB writes with lively wit on subjects ranging from courtship to current events, from religion to theater. Her comments on theater mark her as an astute drama critic. She writes as a feminist with a strong sense of decorum. The very popular *Julia Mandeville*, a sentimental novel in the epistolary mode, shows the influence of Richardson and the French novel of sensibility, most directly through Mme. Riccoboni. FB differs from Riccoboni in her creation of a witty, outspoken, independent-minded woman as one of two main letter writers to contrast with the excessively sentimental heroine Julia and her equally sentimental lover, a device used again in the epistolary *Emily Montague*. In the latter, FB expresses feminist views, through a male character as well as a female. Emily's lover says, "Equality is the soul of friendship: marriage, to give delight, must join two minds, not devote a slave to the will of an imperious lord; . . . I have always wished the word obey expung'd from the marriage ceremony," and, "The sex we have so unjustly excluded from power in Europe have a great share in the Huron government." Emily's lively confidante warns her against excessive sensibility: "Take care, my dear Emily, you do not fall into the common error of sensible and delicate minds, that of refining away your happiness." *Emily Montague* depicts life in Canada in the 1760s and exploits the setting in innovative ways to influence actions and mirror events. In *The Excursion*, FB uses an omniscient narrator, a witty, ironic, worldly-wise woman, to tell of a naive young country girl's first encounter with corrupt London society. In her narrator as well as in the mildly picaresque adventures of her heroine, FB recalls Henry Fielding, although in theme the novel resembles Fanny Burney's *Evelina*, published the following year. For contemporary critics, its most notable feature was its lampoon of David Garrick, through an actor-manager who rejects the young protagonist's play, as Garrick had so often rejected FB's work. *Charles Mandeville*, a sequel to *Julia Mandeville*, returns to the epistolary mode with long, chapter-length letters. FB transfers her Eden from pastoral England and primitive Canada to a futuristic world. Of FB's plays, two are heroic tragedies in blank verse in the mode of Dryden. Both have women protagonists. More successful, and more popular, were her two comic operas, both pastorals with simple plots, idyllic rural settings, attractive music by William Shield, and happy endings. Like the novels, they suggest that happiness is found in the simple virtues and pleasures of country life.

FB's theatrical interests contributed to her fictional techniques. She skillfully wove a complex of voices and manipulated her settings to echo emotions. At a time when the novel was excessively sentimental, FB's works combined sensibility with wit and realism and provided astute and witty observations on a woman's world.

For the most part, the press of the day praised her work, and several periodicals reprinted excerpts. The *Critical Review* and the *Monthly Review* regularly reviewed her novels, usually commending their sensibility, their support of contemporary mores, and on occasion their wit and their lively women characters. The excessive sensibility of the lovers in *Julia Mandeville* met with approval, but their tragic end did not. "It has been often . . . wished that the catastrophe had been less melancholy," writes John Nichols, in his *Literary Anecdotes* (1812–15). In France, in a period of anglophilia, FB was among the most popular English novelists. Her books were quickly translated into French and were praised in such widely read periodicals as *Année littéraire* and *Gazette littéraire de l'Europe*. L.M.

BROOKS, Indiana (fl. 1789), novelist, wrote only *Eliza Beaumont and Harriet Osborne* (1789). Nothing is known about her life, but she is sometimes confused with FRANCES BROOKE. The novel episodically and laboriously moves to its predictable conclusion. It has some interest for the modern reader in its occasional comments on contemporary issues. IB congratulates Britain on its women writers: "Happy,

happy nation, whose females possess such find understandings, and whose memories are so retentive as to retain such multifarious learning!" She rails against British imperialism: "It was with regret I observed that such has been our fatally mistaken method of exerting power, that it has reduced the countries around to mere deserts. . . . Is it, let me ask, possible for the honest husbandman to labour, when he is in dread of being plundered by those whose duty, nay, whose interest it is to protect him?" Although the novel was never popular enough for reprints, the *Critical Review* (Dec. 1789) perhaps overgenerously praised it: "The language is . . . clear, natural, and easy. We have read these volumes with some pleasure, and think they rise much beyond the common herd, though we cannot style them excellent." The *English Review*, perhaps more accurately, realized that IB "may have the knack of saying things in a pretty manner, but nature has not blessed her with the faculty of writing to the heart."   M.A.B.

BRYAN, Margaret (fl. 1797–1815), writer on science, was one of the few Englishwomen of her time with extensive knowledge of the physical sciences. Little is known of her background. The frontispieces of her books show a beautiful woman, and in one portrait she is accompanied by two adolescent daughters. MB was apparently largely self-taught; she kept a school for young ladies at various locations in Blackheath and London. Her books are organized as lectures and usually contain a dedication to her pupils, many of whom were of genteel and aristocratic origin. The manuscript of her first book was forwarded to Dr. Charles Hutton, F.R.S., then Professor of Mathematics at the Royal Academy, Woolwich, whom she knew only through a brief introduction. He responded favorably and offered the work "sanction and privilege." In 1797 the book was published by subscription. The list of 388 subscribers was headed by the Archbishop of Canterbury and included Edward Jenner and the Rev. Dr. Nevil Maskelyne, the Astronomer Royal. This work, illustrated with her own sketches and diagrams, was lengthily but accurately entitled *A Compendious System of Astronomy, in a Course of Familiar Lectures; in which the Principles of That Science Are Clearly Elucidated, so as to be Intelligible to Those Who Have Not Studied the Mathematics. Also Trigonometrical and Celestial Problems, with a Key to the Ephemeris, and a Vocabulary of the Terms of Science*

Used in the Lectures; Which Latter Are Explained Agreeably to Their Application in Them. In 1806 it was followed by the *Lectures on Natural Philosophy: The Result of Many Years' Practical Experience of the Facts Elucidated. With an Appendix: Containing, a Great Number and Variety of Astronomical and Geographical Problems; and Some Useful Tables, and a Comprehensive Vocabulary*, also published by subscription, and in 1815 by *An Astronomical and Geographical Class Book for Schools*. Her later prefaces—the second was dedicated "by permission" to the Princess Charlotte of Wales—assume a slightly egotistical air. A number of other works have been ascribed to MB under the name of Jane Marcet, possibly because Marcet's *Conversations on Chemistry* is similar in method to Bryan's and the central figure is a schoolmistress.

MB was a devout Anglican, for whom—like so many 18th-century English thinkers—science served to complement theology. "Natural objects," she wrote, "continually admonish us in the important science of Divine Wisdom." Every lecture began and ended with the devotional implications of the subject matter, although the space dedicated to these homilies decreased after her first book. Her works, written in a more lucid and attractive style than one would guess from the titles, covered optics, astronomy, trigonometry, mechanics, pneumatics, hydrostatics, and electricity. The lectures, rich with experiments, demonstrations, and mathematical proofs, treated the subject matter in a technical rather than popular manner. MB's writings reveal wide reading and intelligent consideration of contemporary scientific issues. Although they relied upon authorities, she was not hesitant to indicate her preferences among competing theories. For example, while her own observations led her to believe that the moon probably had an atmosphere, she preferred to suspend judgment between Ellis's and Franklin's competing theories of electricity, because her experiments did not support either to the exclusion of the other. She took a somewhat liberal position on the theologically sensitive issue of the plurality of worlds, believing that the planets, "regulated by the same laws as our Earth . . . also are the residences of rational creatures, like ourselves, endowed with like sensibilities." While MB was fascinated by balloons and diving bells, she was apparently unfamiliar with the early industrial applications of technology. The form of her works shows the influence of Rousseau's *Emile;* they present conversations with children, intended to suggest that the child is learning naturally. It was a popular method of textbook writing used by, among others, MARY WOLLSTONECRAFT. G.T.P. and J.E.R.

BRYTON, Anne (fl. 1780), poet, published *Richmond: A Pastoral*, a short foray in heroic couplets. It uses the labored conventions of pastoral as the background or excuse for some patriotic and monarchist propaganda. The king and queen are honored in a traditional celebration of the dawn. Political reference is made throughout, alongside rather than through the idiom of pastoral, as in the proud boast of the River Thames: "A Clive decides the fate of eastern kings, / The western world its wealth and honour brings, / Which we to the grand capital convey / In gallant ships, which thro' our sides make way." R.J.

BUNBURY, Lady Sarah [Lennox, Napier] (1745–1826), letter writer, was the fourth surviving daughter of Charles, second Duke of Richmond, and Sarah, daughter of William, Earl Cadogan. Orphaned at five, Lady Sarah was brought up by her sister, the DUCHESS OF LEINSTER, in Ireland, and at 14 was sent to her eldest sister, Lady Caroline Fox (later LADY HOLLAND) in England. She was the most vivacious and charming of four beautiful sisters; her brother-in-law Henry Fox described her: "She had the finest complexion, most beautiful hair, & prettyest person that ever was seen, with a sprightly & fine air, a pretty mouth, & remarkably fine teeth, & excess of bloom in her cheeks, little eyes,—but this is not describing her, for her great beauty was a peculiarity of countenance, that made her at the same time different from & prettyer than any other girl I ever saw." At the age of 14 she had already had several flirtations before the Prince of Wales saw her at court in late 1759, just before he became George III, and fell deeply in love. Henry Fox and Lady Caroline did their best to promote the match but were defeated by the King's mother and the "thoughtless, wild, & giddy spirits" (as she later called them) of SB herself. In 1761 it was announced that the King would marry Princess Charlotte; SB coolly insisted on being a bridesmaid. The following year, she herself married Thomas Bunbury, a man devoted

to the turf; during the marriage she had no children but several lovers, including Lord Carlisle, the Duc de Lauzun, and Lord William Gordon, in 1768 the father of her daughter, Louisa. An elopement with Lord William was followed by 11 years of penitent seclusion at Halnaker, SB's house at Goodwood. In 1781 SB married the handsome but poor Hon. George Napier. They settled eventually at Celbridge, near LADY LOUISA CONOLLY, and raised a family of three daughters and five sons, three of whom became army generals and heroes. After her husband's death in 1804, SB, growing blind, settled in London, where she died. The most individualistic, clever, and observant of the Lennox sisters, SB never lost her wit or charm. Even her first husband continued to love her, and in 1830 her daughter, Emily Napier, married Sir Henry Bunbury, Thomas Bunbury's nephew and heir; later the next Sir Henry married SB's granddaughter Cecilia.

SB's letters are the most sprightly and incisive of the letters in the Leinster correspondence (see the Duchess of Leinster). Some of her letters have been published in *The Life and Letters of Lady Sarah Lennox* (1901). She was an amusing and perceptive observer, even as a girl. In 1760 she writes: "The Prince of Wales is very agreeable and a mighty pretty sort of man, I think. He don't talk nonsense . . . and pester one with music, but talks like other people. In short, I like him vastly, and am more partial to him as Mr. Fox and one or two people tell me he likes me, and that always prejudices one in people's favour, you know." To her cousin and best friend, Lady Susan Strangways, she confided in 1761, "Luckily for me I did not love him, & only liked him, nor did the title weigh anything with me. . . . The thing I am most angry at, is looking so like a fool, as I shall for having gone so often for nothing." In 1779 she relates her reconciliation with Bunbury: "I cannot describe to you how light my heart has felt since this meeting, & *that* will fully convince you that all love is out of the question, for I don't know what effect it may have on others, but love has ever given me a heavy heart. The very friendly manner in which he treated me gives me the most *comfortable* feel." In 1807 approaching blindness forced her to abandon her 50-year correspondence with Lady Susan: "I write to you litterally because I think it the last letter I shall ever *write*. . . . We must for the future only receive letters of a merchantile style, 'Yours is come to hand, all's well,' etc.; for I give all my letters to my girls or anybody present to read for me." And in a witty allusion to the great adventure of the King's advances, which the girls had shared so long before, she adds, "Nor do I *much* dwell on the *charms* of my cataract, tho' it is *just like the King's*." B.R.

BURKE, Mrs. (fl. 1780–1805), novelist, wrote at least four popular novels. *Ela: or, Delusions of the Heart: A Tale, Founded on Fact* was first published serially in *Columbian Magazine* and then went through several editions from 1787 to 1790. It is a romance told in letters to a sister from a young man who is observing the heroine. She is supposedly marrying a dashing military officer, but the letter writer soon discovers that the military lover is actually engaged to marry someone else. Scandal ensues, and tears, lies, fainting, swords and pistols, prisons and chains; the villain dies repentant, forgiven by Ela, who languishes delicately away to her own death. The last chapter makes it clear that the reader should profit from their sad example: "Vice stands exposed in her native deformity. The wisdom of virtue is no less conspicuous." The second novel, *Emilia de St. Aubigne* (1788), varies only the type, not the intensity or frequency, of crises. Here there are storms, orphans, travelers, long-lost friends, shipwrecks, rescues, coincidences, fainting, kidnapping, sorrow, and pain. Although one of the villains is forced to marry the innocent girl and the deserving do inherit a fortune, the heroine dies a lingering death and the novel ends with a bleak "The poets' assertion of 'To be good is to be happy' is not always verified in this world." B's third novel is *Adela Northington* (1796); the title is occasionally misspelled Nerthington and is sometimes confused with B's name, which is not Adele Northington Burke. *The Sorrows of Edith; or, The Hermitage of the Cliffs: A Descriptive Tale, Founded on Facts* (1796) is ascribed to B; it is dedicated to the Duchess of York. B may also have authored *Elliott, or Vicissitudes of Early Life* (1800), which the *London Monthly Review* (1801) calls "a tale of thwarted love and suffering virtue," as well as *Secret of the Cavern: A Novel*, written for Minerva Press in 1805.   M.P.

BURNET, Elizabeth (1661–1709), religious writer, was born near Southampton, the daughter of Sir Richard Blake and Elizabeth Bathurst. In 1678 she married Robert Berkeley of Spetchley, Worcs. In about 1684 the couple settled in The Hague and became admirers of the Prince of Orange; soon after he became William III, they returned to Worcestershire, where they used their wealth charitably on a hospital and a school for poor children. In 1693 Berkeley died. In 1700 EB became the third wife of the Bishop of Salisbury Gilbert Burnet, historian and promoter of broad church views; she had two children who died in infancy. Caring for her step-children, she continued her charitable works. In 1707 she was in Spa for her health; when she died two years later she was buried at Spetchley. EB is mentioned by George Ballard as a learned lady. She read assiduously in the Bible and in theological commentary. After Berkeley's death, she composed *A Method of Devotion*, printed anonymously, although she was later recognized as its author. When she died, the book was reissued with her name on it, and the Archdeacon of Oxford contributed an account of her life. The work went through several editions.

A Method of Devotion, subtitled "Rules for Holy and Devout Living" is a prescriptive guide to conducting one's devotional life and to regulating one's conduct at all times with proper humility and selflessness. It contains many sets of rules, questionnaires for self-assessment, texts from the Scriptures, model prayers, and so on. It covers both special days and the course of a single day. In her "Rules for Conversation," for example, EB advises: "Before you enter on any foreseen Conversation, beg God's Blessing and Direction in some short Ejaculation; and during the Time you are in Company, observe how you keep to your Duty, and mix with your Conversation pious Thoughts and Desires, to do or receive Good; and consider how you may be most useful to those you converse with, to encourage each other in the Search of Truth, Increase of Knowledge, or Practice of some Duty and Christian virtue." In "Some Reflections on Death," she makes the following rather ghoulish suggestions: "Make the frightful Image of a dead Body familiar, by your Meditation, and by a ready attending sick and dying Persons, where desired; consider you lay down your body in the Grave, as you lay off your Cloaths at Night: And why more unwilling to part with one than the other?"   J.T.

BURNEY, Fanny [Frances, d'Arblay]

(1752–1840), diarist and novelist, was born in King's Lynn, the daughter of Charles Burney, author and musician, and his first wife, who died when FB was ten. She was the third of the six children who survived. Burney's second wife, although intelligent and devoted to him, was cordially disliked by his children. She appears in FB's last novel, *The Wanderer*, as the fury Mrs. Ireton, who abuses the heroine, her hired companion, with self-pitying tirades. The Burneys were a remarkably gifted family—all of them charming, witty, and talented in literature and music. FB's father belonged to the highest social and intellectual circles of London, including Samuel Johnson's club. Among many fascinating visitors to his house in London was David Garrick, who used to delight the Burney children with mimicry. FB, who educated herself, early took to voluminous scribbling. In 1768 she began her diary, which soon turned into journal-letters to her favorite sister, Susan, and was continued (less regularly after Susan's death in 1800) to the end of her long life. She also secretly began the novel *Evelina* (published 1778). To maintain anonymity, and thus save herself and the family from disgrace should the book prove a failure, she copied it in a feigned hand, for her own was known by printers from copying her father's manuscripts for the press. (A brother and male cousin negotiated with her publisher.) But the book was a sensational success, and the secret gradually spread; when her father found out, he publicized it everywhere. She was introduced to HESTER THRALE, Johnson, and their friends, and lionized by everyone; but she remained genuinely embarrassed by public recognition as an author. Lively and amusing with her intimates, FB was painfully shy among people she did not know well. She was urged to write a comedy and produced "The Witlings," an unkind but extremely funny satire on pretentious Bluestockings. But her father thought it too personal—he recognized their friend ELIZABETH MONTAGU, the "Queen of the Bluestockings," in the villain Lady Smatter—and persuaded her to suppress it. Because of constant social demands, FB felt she had to "steal" time to write both the play and her next novel, *Cecilia* (1782), which she published without adequate revision and condensation. Nevertheless, it was widely read and admired, although she received only £250 for it (and a mere £20 for *Evelina*). With no prospect of marriage—a young clergyman was most attentive but failed to propose, probably because her family lacked fortune and influence—when the Queen offered her a post at court as Second Keeper of the Robes, she was pressured to accept. She foresaw that this position would entail boring slavery, but she took it (1786), mostly to please her adored father. It meant constant attendance, with almost no time to herself, and separation from family, friends, and congenial company in general. Yet she wrote *Edwy and Elgiva* and two other dreary blank-verse tragedies in her few spare moments, and remained in the position for five years before she worked up courage to ask permission from her father and the Queen to resign.

On a visit to her sister Susan, she met a group of *émigrés* from the French Revolution, including Mme. de Staël and Alexandre d'Arblay, formerly a general under Lafayette. He was a gentle, cultivated, upright man; soon he and FB fell in love. They married (1793), inspite of d'Arblay's being a Roman Catholic Frenchman with no economic prospects in England: their total income would be FB's £100 pension from the Queen and £20 income from the invested profits of *Cecilia*. Nonetheless, they were blissfully happy. *Edwy and Elgiva* was produced but failed ignominiously. Her next effort to support the family was the novel *Camilla* (1796), which, skillfully marketed, brought them £2000. She wrote three lively and presentable comedies, but for various reasons none was produced. (Nor were they printed; the manuscripts, with that of "The Witlings," are in the Berg Collection at the New York Public Library.) When England and France made peace, d'Arblay returned to France to recoup some of his family property. FB followed him in 1802 and, when war broke out again, was trapped there until 1812. She returned to England alone, to be joined by him two years later. She published *The Wanderer* (1814) and made £2000 by it, but it disappointed readers' expectations of a picture of French manners. She devoted her later years to editing the family papers, in 1832 publishing *Memoirs of Dr. Burney*, which was savagely criticized for its pompous style. She suffered from the deaths of her father, brothers, husband, sisters, and son. Alexander, her one child, had been a chronic worry to her: feckless and improvident, although gifted, he could never advance his career in the Church. Despite an imprudent marriage and occasional covert protests against woman's lot, FB was timidly conventional. She thought of introducing "right-minded" politics into *Camilla*, but decided not to on the grounds that even conservative politics "were not a *feminine* subject for discussion." Ever concerned with propriety in her life as well as writings, she said, "A fear of doing wrong has always been the leading principle of my internal guidance."

FB's most lasting and attractive works are perhaps her journals, where she reported experience to her family without feeling the need to censor, moralize, or dignify her style. The journals give fascinating pictures of FB and her social circles. Examples are the diary entries of August 1778, which describe her introduction to Johnson and the Thrales (she portrays a playfulness in Johnson unknown to Boswell); her descriptions of a Bluestocking party at which *Cecilia* was discussed (8 Dec. 1782); her first meeting with King George III (16 Dec. 1785); her mastectomy (30 Sept. 1811); and her near-drowning at Ilfracombe (12 Sept. 1817). Through constant journal writing, FB learned to portray dramatically the characteristic manners of a class or an individual. She developed her ability to characterize quickly, to make individuals reveal themselves in dialogue, and to make the most of incongruities in and comic interplay between people. These gifts, refined by an awareness of social nuances, provide the best part of *Evelina:* the ill-bred wrangling of the Branghtons and upstart complacency of Mr. Smith, played against the equally rude superciliousness of the aristocrats. FB satirizes both the boorish Captain Mirvan, who roars down young women because their opinions are not worth hearing, and the superficially gallant Mr. Lovel, who has "an insuperable aversion to strength, either of body or mind, in a female." The book is also original in presenting the world through the eyes of a 17-year-old girl. Through Evelina, trying to behave correctly on her entrance into society, FB introduces into the novel the social embarrassments and uncertainties of female adolescence. She presents small but real and universal mortifications, such as being coolly looked over by potential partners at a ball or being seen with vulgar relatives by the very aristocratic young man one wants to impress. *Cecilia* is in some ways even better than *Evelina*, although it is overlong and begins to show the verbose circumlocution which was increasingly to weigh down FB's style. It

presents a mature, critical picture of society, as it skillfully satirizes the insipidity of fashionable life, such as "large parties . . . collected . . . without any possible reason why they might not as well be separated." Again, characters such as the pompous aristocrat Mr. Delvile and the equally self-satisfied vulgarian Mr. Briggs are effectively played off against one another. Other effective comic butts in high and low society include Miss Larolles, an empty-headed socialite with a ceaseless flow of meaningless words; Mr. Hobson, a vulgar retired tradesman who never stops congratulating himself; and Mr. Morrice, torn between his desire to ingratiate and his need to draw attention to himself at any cost. In *Camilla*, unfortunately, FB subdued her comic gifts in favor of developing a pretentious moral message; she actually insisted it was not a novel but "sketches of characters and morals put in action." Camilla, an occasionally injudicious but thoroughly virtuous young woman, must abandon her pitifully small stock of spontaneity and independence to acquire propriety and become worthy of the priggish hero, Edgar Mandlebert. It is slightly enlivened by the irreverent Mrs. Arlbery, who, like the mannish Mrs. Selwyn in *Evelina*, can be allowed to express unconventional opinions because FB has firmly condemned her lack of feminine propriety. *The Wanderer* recounts the "Female Difficulties" of a young woman without family or fortune who must make her way in society. It shows how her genteel education has systematically disqualified her from looking after herself and how vital it is to maintain her reputation, which depends not on her own innocence and exertions but on other people's opinions. Hard social reality, not weak self-pity, makes the heroine exclaim: "how insufficient . . . is a female to herself! How utterly dependent upon situation—connections—circumstances! how nameless, how for every fresh-springing are her DIFFICULTIES, when she would owe her existence to her own exertions! Her conduct is criticised, not scrutinized; her character is censured, not examined; her labours are unhonoured, and her qualifications are but lures to ill-will." Society justified disabling women by the myth that they could always depend on men—a well-meaning but foolish old admiral in the book is convinced that no man, nor the world, would leave a woman desolate "who has kept tight to her own duty, and taken a modest care of herself."

But the plot of the novel demonstrates the contrary.

FB's works (except *The Wanderer*) were greatly admired then and now for the humor and realistic depiction of the social scene. Johnson delighted in the liveliness of the low characters of *Evelina*, and Hester Thrale admired the photographic realism of *Cecilia*. The *English Review* praised her characters as originals taken from life (January 1783). But FB's contemporaries were unlike the modern reader in appreciating as well the serious parts of her novels, their pathos and moral teaching. They were deeply affected by Evelina's maudlin reunion with her father and Cecilia's factitious mad scene. They also admired FB's priggish morality. MARY DELANY extolled the moral usefulness of *Cecilia*. The most highly praised part of *Camilla* was the letter in which Camilla's saintly father explains why a woman of delicacy cannot choose her own husband and tells her: "the proper education of a female [is] still a problem beyond human solution; since its refinement, or its negligence, can only prove to her a good or an evil, according to the humour of the husband into whose hands she may fall" (*Monthly Review*, October 1796; *British Critic*, November 1796; *Critical Review*, September 1796). Readers and reviewers treated FB as an important writer. But they may have damaged her work by leading her to misjudge her gifts. Too often she turned from the vivid rendition of life's surface and the humorous social satire she did so well, to shallow conventional moralizing or pathos and passion based on nothing deeper than theatrical rhetoric. K.R.

BURNEY, Sarah Harriet (1770?–1844), novelist, was the daughter of Charles Burney, author and musician, and his second wife, Mrs. Stephen Allen, widow of a wealthy merchant. She was the half-sister of three important people: the noted novelist FANNY BURNEY; James Burney, a captain in the Royal Navy, who accompanied Captain Cook around the world, wrote several books, and later commanded his own ship; and Rev. Dr. Charles Burney, Greek scholar, headmaster, author, professor, and librarian. SB was well educated herself, able to translate the Italian of Ariosto, and to act as interpreter for French émigrés. Her first novel was published anonymously in 1796. *Clarentine* is reported to have been well received and to have been read by the King and Queen. The second edition came out in 1816 and it was printed in Philadelphia in 1818. *Geraldine Fauconberg* (1808) also went into a second edition (1812) and was published in America in 1817. In 1812 *Traits of Nature* sold so well that a second edition was required three months later and a third in 1813; it was also published in Philadelphia and in Paris. *Tales of Fancy* consists of three volumes published between 1816 and 1820, when it immediately went into a second edition. Volume 1, *The Shipwreck*, was dedicated to Lady Crewe and was later published in Germany, in 1821. It focuses on the virtues of the heroine, who, as an obedient, well-trained daughter, is on her way to India to marry someone she has never met. On the voyage she meets the handsome but willful hero who is reformed and uplifted by her excellencies of character. Predictably, the novel ends with the good rewarded and the evil punished. Volumes 2 and 3, *Country Neighbours; or, The Secret*, were dedicated to Princess Elizabeth and published both in Paris under the title *Les Voisins de Campagne, ou Le Secret*, and in New York. At about this time SB moved to Florence, where she lived until 1839. When she returned to England, she published a novel she had been working on in Italy entitled *Romance of Private Life* (1839). Volumes 1 and 2 are titled *The Renunciation* and are dedicated to the Italian singer Niccolini. Volume 3, *The Hermitage*, is dedicated to Lord Crewe. In the first volumes, the heroine is a little apprentice, who is abducted from her kindly protectors to live with a French family, where she is trained to be a lady, poised, accomplished, and gentle in manner. She is not only well informed but also amusing, humble, playful, dutiful, and an interesting conversationalist. In *The Hermitage*, another young maid is introduced to society with yet another set of perilous adventures, this time including murder, but she too eventually marries the noble gentleman. Contemporary reviews comment on the resemblance between SB's characters and situations and those of Fanny Burney, but they note that SB lacks Fanny Burney's raciness of humor and power of painting the varieties of the human species. SB apparently also served as an editor for the publisher T. Tegg in London. M.P.

BURR, Esther Edwards (1732–58), American letter writer, was born and raised in Northampton, Mass. She had seven sisters and three brothers, some of whom died at an early age. Her mother taught her to read and write. Her father, Jonathan Edwards, the famous New England minister, fell out with his congregation and in 1750 removed his family to Stockbridge, Mass. Here the family was in dire financial straits for a time. In 1752 EEB married Aaron Burr, a minister and associate of her father, and moved with him to Newark, N.J. In 1756 they moved to Princeton. Burr was a founder and the second president of the College of New Jersey, now Princeton University. They had two children: Sarah (b. 1754) and Aaron (b. 1756), who was to become the third American vice-president. Her children were a great source of delight to her, but she suffered much anxiety on account of her daughter's poor health. She was devoted to her husband and eagerly entertained his numerous political and religious acquaintances. In spite of this contact, she offered no political views of her own, save to refer to the French as "that popish sect," a phrase which is more indicative of her religious upbringing than her political acumen. EEB was an avid reader and seems to have read much of the literature of her time, including Edward Young, Fielding, and Richardson. Of the last two, she preferred Richardson. She once signed a letter to a friend "Burrissa." She died at Princeton after contracting a fever.

Esther Burr's Journal (1903) by Jeremiah Eames Rankin is a work of fiction, supposedly covering the period from EEB's ninth birthday to her marriage. Even the dates are inaccurate. In an afterword Rankin claims that EEB left a number of manuscripts that were lost after her death. She did keep a journal from 1754–57, now in the Yale Library, which consists of a record of her letters to a friend, Fidelia Prince, who lived in Boston. Miss Prince wrote poetry and sent her attempts to EEB, who expressed her delight with them and gave much encouragement. No actual lines or titles are quoted, however. EEB also mentioned another woman poet several times but only by her first name, Joan. EEB's style in these letters is candid and forthright, but never humorous. She suffered constantly from melancholy and often complains of being "vapory." She used to read Scripture for solace and often quotes it in her letters, but sometimes even this bulwark proved too weak for her nature: "how vain and empty is the world and all its enjoyments—tis enough to make one weary of life and all its charms." P.H.

BURRELL, Lady Sophia [Raymond] (1750?–1802), poet and dramatist, married William Burrell, an M.P., in 1773. The next year, her father was made a baronet, a title which descended to her and her husband. She wrote some minor poetry and, when her husband's health failed, published her *Thymriad* and *Telemachus* (1794). On her husband's death, she married Rev. William Clay and thereafter wrote two tragedies, *Maximian* and *Theodora*, both of which were published; neither was produced.

The Thymriad is based on Xenophon's *Cyropedia*, and it is loosely arranged around an important battle in Cyrus's career. Although its title suggests Homer, it is really in the vein of the Italian romance epic, concerned more with the intrigues of love than with "arms and the man." The story in which SB seems most interested is that of Panthea, a captive who commits suicide in grief over her husband's death. SB does not relate more than the bare events of the story and is little concerned with the character's inner states of mind. The epic is therefore short, seven books in less than a hundred pages. SB apologizes for her work more than once, anticipating that readers would object to an epic written by a woman: "Say Muse! altho' a female pen is made / Most fit for tales of love and times of peace, / Wilt thou not aid thy votary in a theme / Where Cyrus is the subject?" SB's *Telemachus* is adapted from the *Telemachus* of Fénélon. She claims that she has done little more than translate it. In this work, about as long as *The Thymriad* but without its complex plotting, Telemachus visits the island of Calypso with Mentor and there is tangled in a love intrigue; he is saved at the last minute from Calypso's jealousy by Mentor, who pushes him bodily into the sea. Mentor's advice is succinct: "Fly the dang'rous snare—let freedom reign! / And break the bondage of a woman's chain." SB's work was neither popular nor lasting. J.E.R.

BURTON, Phillipina (fl. 1768–87), poet and autobiographer, published *Miscellaneous Poems* anonymously in three volumes (1768); it reveals little of her family and connections, unless we believe, as we are meant to, that *The Memoirs of a Lady Now in the Bloom of Life* (Vol. 3) are PB's. The lady, of a good family and a country upbringing, made a secret marriage with an army recruiting officer. The secrecy compromised the lady's reputation, but the marriage was blissful until the sudden death of the husband, upon which the lady journeyed to Lisle to enter a convent, but had second thoughts. The second volume includes a series of letters describing a tour in France. They reveal PB as a pretty, shallow young woman, intent on little beyond attracting followers. Her account of romantic successes and setbacks at Versailles, where she was briefly countenanced by respectable women, who were subsequently warned off by a calumniating colonel, suggests that the primary purpose of the publication was self-advertisement. The *Monthly Review* complained of the *Memoirs*, "They afford us not a single ray of light to inform us who or what she is, or has been." The expensive volumes sold to subscribers for a guinea, and the list of 83 subscribers included 11 earls, 12 lords, and not one woman; the author addressed her dedication to "My Lords." *MR* noted, "One thing . . . seems . . . evinced by her list of subscribers,—that *she is a person in distress*." From 1770 PB essayed the stage. At the Haymarket she played the principal character in her own play (never published but in the Larpent Collection), "Fashion Display'd," produced for three nights only. That summer in Sheridan's company at the same theater she played the roles of Constance in Shakespeare's *King John*, Elizabeth in Henry Brooke's *The Earl of Essex*, Maria in Arthur Murphy's *The Citizen*, and the eponymous heroine in Nicholas Rowe's *Jane Shore*. On her benefit night she spoke an epilogue she had written herself. PB subsequently married an actor named Hill. In 1787 *The World* reported that Mrs. Hill had lately acted Scrub (in *The Beaux' Stratagem*) at Brighton and written a pamphlet about it. The full title of this pamphlet suggests that at Brighton PB had joined the group around the Prince of Wales.

PB had little talent as an author; her work better exemplifies a new use of the printed word for advertising purposes. She ended Vol. 1 of her 1768 *Miscellaneous Poems* with an exhortation: "You that would animate my muse anew, / Are all intreated to send your names in time, / E're I retire and quit this much-lov'd clime / . . . Annually I'll write if you approve my choice, / Bid me to proceed with one united voice." In 1770 her comedy "Fashion Display'd" was advertised for spring publication but did not appear. Among other works, she published in about 1785 *Portraits, Characters, Pursuits and Amusements of the present fashionable world, interspersed with poetic flights of fancy*, reprinted ca. 1795, and in 1787 *Mrs. Hill's Apology for having*

been induced by particular desire, and the most specious allurements that could tempt female weakness, to appear in the character of Scrub, Beaux Stratagem . . . at Brighthelmstone, last Year, 1786 . . . With an address to Mrs. Fitzherbert. Also, some of Mrs. Hill's Letters to His Royal Highness the Prince of Wales, Mrs. Fitzherbert, and others*. Her 1768 *Miscellaneous Poems* in three volumes, sold by Dodsley, should not be confused with ELIZABETH ROLT's one-volume 1768 *Miscellaneous Poems* sold by N. Turpin and J. Catling.   B.R.

BURY, Lady Charlotte [Campbell] (1775–1861), novelist, was born Lady Charlotte Susan Maria Campbell, youngest child of John Campbell, fifth Duke of Argyll, and Elizabeth Gunning, at Argyll House, London. Owing to her mother's ill health, much of CB's early life was spent in France and Italy, where she gained a knowledge of art, literature, and music. After her mother's death in 1790, she was presented at court, and was much praised for her beauty, manners, and character. She was frequently hostess to literary guests, and introduced Walter Scott to Matthew "Monk" Lewis, to whom she was "Divinity." In 1796, she made a financially inauspicious marriage to her cousin, Colonel Jack Campbell, the youngest of 14 children. In 1809 he died, leaving her with nine children. Within a year she was appointed lady-in-waiting to Princess Caroline, with whom she felt some sympathy. Whether her uneasy financial situation made it necessary for CB to accept the post is not known, but it did lead her to augment her living through writing. In 1814, she resolved to leave the Princess's service but only made the final break in May 1815, the last of the English suite to leave. Although called as a defense witness in the Queen's trial, she had no other contact with her. From that time, CB alternated between the Continent and Britain. In 1818 she displeased her children by marrying again. Rev. Edward John Bury was a clergyman of good birth but with no fortune, 15 years her junior. He had traveled to Italy with her eldest son, and they shared a love of art. Finances were continually troublesome, and she turned again to writing. In May 1832 John Bury died, leaving her with two more daughters. For the next 30 years, she continued to travel and write. She died in Chelsea.

CB's literary outpourings began in 1797 when she published a self-conscious volume, *Poems on Several Occasions*. The verses tended to be conventional, romantic, and somewhat contrived. But the bulk of her work was popular novels of the Minerva school, probably published to solve her financial difficulties. The first, *Self-Indulgence* (1812) CB wrote while in service to the Princess of Wales, but she only returned to writing permanently after her marriage to Bury with *Conduct is Fate* in 1822. From the publication of *Alla Giornata, or the Day* in 1826, she produced 19 books in the next sixteen years, most of them novels: *Flirtation* (1828), *The Separation* (1830), *The Exclusives* (1830), *The Disinherited* and *The Ensnared* (printed together in 1834), *The Devoted* (1836), *The Divorced* (1837), *Love* (1837), *A History of a Flirt* (1840), *Family Records; or the Two Sisters* (1841), *The Manoeuvering Mother* (1842), and *The Willfulness of Woman* (1844). Three later novels were *The Roses* (1853), *The Lady of Fashion* (1856), and the posthumous *The Two Baronets, a novel of Fashionable Life* (1864). Her books sold well, pandering to the desire for romantic novels about high society, and she is said to have obtained as much as £200 for each. CB did not restrict herself to fiction, and published a series of prayers, *Suspirium Sanctorum, or Holy Breathings* in 1826. In memory of Rev. Bury, a volume of verses illustrated by his engravings, *The Three Great Sanctuaries of Tuscany*, was issued in 1833. One critic reckoned that its great value rested in the artwork, not the poetry. She also edited two series of *Journal of the Heart* in 1830 and 1835.

Despite the popularity of her novels, CB was best known for the *Diary Illustrative of the Times of George IV* (1838). It was published anonymously like all her work, but contemporaries immediately attributed it to CB because of its intimate knowledge of Princess Caroline's court, and CB never denied it. It was vehemently criticized because, first, friends felt she had broken a trust by publishing private correspondence, and many refused to meet her; and, second, the scandalous nature of the revelations caused them to be labeled vulgar, untrustworthy, and unreliable. The author herself was contemptuous of the proceedings but sympathetic to the Princess. Catering to the prurient interest of the public, the work was an immediate success, several editions being sold in a few weeks. In the same year an expanded version was edited by J. Galt, and the British Museum copy contains suppressed pages. Its continued popularity stimulated a reissue in 1896 as *The Court of England under George the Fourth* and again in 1908 as *The Diary of a Lady in Waiting*, edited by A. F. Steuart. Twice CB edited the diaries of other women of society with success: *A Marriage in High Life* by Lady Caroline Lucy Scott, in 1828, and *Memoirs of a Peeress* by Catherine Gore, in 1837.   D.L.L.

BURY, Elizabeth (1644–1720), diarist, was born in Clare, Suffolk, one of four children of Captain Adams Lawrence of Lynton, Cambs., and Elizabeth Cutts of Clare. Her father died in 1648, and three years later her mother married the Rev. Nathaniel Bradshaw of Wivelingham, Cambs., and bore six more children. As a child, EB was markedly learned, studying especially divinity, philology, and Hebrew. She was an ardent Dissenter and considered herself converted at the age of nine. Before she was 20, she began a spiritual diary in shorthand, and from 1690 this was written in longhand. It recorded the organization of her day, her falling from the standards she set herself, and her struggles to come to terms with the many physical and mental pains she suffered. In 1667, despite marriage offers from more highly placed men, displeasing because they were members of the Established Church, she married Griffith Lloyd. He died in 1687. In 1697 she married Samuel Bury; there were no children of the marriage. Ailing for some years, she went in 1719 with her husband to Bath and Bristol for her health. She died in Bristol.

An Account of the Life and Death of Mrs. Elizabeth Bury, Who Died May 11th 1720. Aged 76 Chiefly Collected out of her Own Diary. Together with Her Funeral Sermon, Preach'd at Bristol, May 22, 1720. By the Reverend Mr. William Tong . . . (1720) was edited by her husband, who found the Diary "one of the most affecting Things I ever read." Of his wife he wrote, "It was not possible (I think) there should be a more Observant, Tender, Indulgent, and Compassionate *Wife* than she was" and he praised her for her inoffensive way of finding fault with him. EB's Diary is a minute analysis of character, motives, and actions, full of death-longings, spiritual rapture, and self-hatred, expressed sometimes in extreme biblical imagery: "I abhor the Fountain and filthy Streams of my polluted Nature" and sometimes in descriptions of physical debility: "my Head fail'd, my Body fainted, and I could pray but shortly with the Servants." The text frequently breaks off at moments of despair: "My Head is so dull and torpid, I can do little at Heart-Examination," only to be resumed in resignation or exultation. The urgency of the questioning sometimes raises the writing to an almost poetic expressiveness: "peevish, selfish, carnal, unsuitable Frames of Spirit, after such Love purchased, published, tasted to Soul-Ravishment, so oft, after so many turns again to Folly: Lord! what Bowels doth my perverse Heart spurn against?" J.T.

BYROM, Elizabeth (1722–1801), diarist, was the daughter of the hymn writer John Byrom. She wrote a journal which runs from 14 August 1745 to 23 January 1746; it is reprinted in Vol. 2, Part 2 of the *Remains of John Byrom*. The diary describes the Jacobite rebellion, which is observed sympathetically and at close quarters in the north of England, chiefly in and around Manchester and Preston. It is, however, an insubstantial work and frequently rather flat; only occasionally does it convey something of the excitement of living through the rebellion, of being in the thick of events. Among its notable passages is one describing EB's first sight of the Pretender: "his horse had stood an hour in the court without stirring, and as soon as he got on he began a-dancing and capering as if he was proud of the burden, and when he rid out of the court he was received with as much joy and shouting almost as if he had been king without dispute, indeed I think scarce anybody that saw him could dispute it." There is also an excited entry for 9 December 1745: "continual accounts of the highlanders coming; about two o'clock they brought us word that a party of them was come in, and some people had slutched 'em and thrown stones, and so it proved; but the highlanders told them, if they did not give over they must fire amongst them, so they gave over." R.J.

C

CAMM, Anne [Audland] (1627–1705), religious polemicist, was born in Kendal, the daughter of Richard Newby. When aged 13 she was sent for education to an aunt in London, where she became a Puritan. At 20 she returned to Kendal and joined a religious group, in which she met John Audland. She married him and had one son. In 1652, after hearing George Fox, she and her husband joined the Quakers and became preachers. In 1653 she was ill treated and arrested at Banbury on a charge of blasphemy, but was found guilty of only a misdemeanor and acquitted. Unfortunately, the judge refused to liberate her unless she found bond for good behavior. This she refused to give, and was committed to a filthy, partly subterranean prison; she emerged eight months later. She then accompanied her husband on preaching expeditions until his death in 1663 when aged 34. AC married Thomas Camm, a friend of her former husband, and had one daughter; for several years of their marriage Camm was confined in prison for preaching. AC's last public testimony was at Kendal in 1705, where she gave her farewell address; she died the following day, "her remains being accompanied to the ground by many ancient Friends and others from thirteen of the adjacent meetings."

AC was a fervent preacher who believed in the efficacy of prayer and in the power of inspiration. She spoke often of fortitude and the need of faith. "The cross is the only way to the crown immortal; shun it not, therefore, lest you fall short of the crown." In 1684 she wrote *The Admirable and Glorious Appearance of the Eternal God . . . in and through a Child,* but her most popular work with early Quakers was her tribute to her first husband's memory: *Anne Camm, her Testimony concerning John Audland her late Husband* (1681). In it she described their devoted relationship: "by the quickening of his holy power, we were made one in a spiritual and heavenly relation—our hearts being knit together in the unspeakable love of God, which was our job and delight, and made our days together exceedingly comfortable."   J.T.

CANDLER, Ann (1740–1814), poet, was born Ann More in Yoxford, Suffolk, where her father was a glover and her maternal grandfather the surveyor of window-lights. She taught herself to read and write by studying plays, romances, and travelogues. On her marriage to Candler in 1762, she moved to Sproughton, near Ipswich. Candler's drunkenness and enlistment brought AC to the workhouse, together with four of her six children. Twin sons were born and died there, where she herself remained owing to her husband's desertion. In 1803, *Poetical Attempts by Ann Candler, a Suffolk Cottager* was published by subscription. It is prefaced by a letter of AC from the workhouse, dated 1801, in which she reviews her life of misery and considers her love for her uncaring husband: "All I can urge to extenuate, or palliate my folly is, that he was my husband, and the father of my children, and that my affection for him was unbounded." *Poetical Attempts* was published to raise money for AC to furnish a room outside the workhouse, near her married daughter at Copdock near Sproughton, where she could earn her living. The *Ipswich Journal* published AC's poems, "On the Death of a Most Benevolent Gentleman" (1785), "To the Inhabitants of Yoxford" (1787), two spring songs (1789), a paraphrase of part of the Book of Kings, the

"History of Joseph," and the "Life of Elijah the Prophet" (1790 onward). Her other work appears in *Poetical Attempts*. Much is doggerel, but she achieves some pathos in her description of her life in the workhouse: "Within these dreary walls confin'd, / A lone recluse I live, / And, with the dregs of human kind, / A niggard alms receive." Her literary education only makes her situation more painful, and she comments thus on her fellow-sufferers: "Uncultivated, void of sense, / Unsocial, insincere, / Their rude behavior gives offence, / Their language wounds the ear."   J.T. and J.H.

CARLETON, Mary (1634–73), literary self-promoter, was born in Canterbury. She seems to have left her first husband, a shoemaker, in 1658, and married a second in Dover, but escaped punishment for bigamy when her first husband did not appear against her. By 1663 she had left her second husband and moved to London, where she set up as a high-born German lady or princess fleeing from relatives who wished to force her into an unwanted marriage. Aided by forged letters and false jewelry, she imposed successfully on the innkeeper where she lodged and was soon courted by a law student, John Carleton, who pretended to be a lord. They were hurriedly married. A few weeks later, her past was made public in a letter declaring her "an absolute Cheat," and MC was arrested for bigamy. In prison she was visited by a sensation-hungry crowd of "many hundreds"; among them was Samuel Pepys, who thought her innocent. Because of her wit and a bungled prosecution case, MC was freed. She immediately published two pamphlets in her justification, *An Historical Narrative of the German Princess* and *The Case of Madam Mary Carleton* (1663). Subsequently she became poor and took to the stage, acting herself in a satire on her own fraud entitled *The German Princess*. Seven years later, in 1671, she was transported to Jamaica for theft. She escaped, was recaught in 1672, and hanged for theft in 1673. At each stage of her colorful life, MC was the subject of biographical writing, journalistic pamphlets, and scurrilous poems. In 1663 they included "The Man in the Moon" and a pamphlet giving a romanticized picture of the courtroom proceedings, *The Arraignment, Trial, and Examination of Mary Moders, otherwise Stedman, now Carleton, styled the German Princess,* in which she appears a witty heroine of "most courageous spirit and a magnanimous countenance." A further flurry of pamphlets occurred in the year of her death; they included *Memoirs of the Life and Death of the Famous Madam Charlton; commonly stiled the German Princess,* purported to be "from her own Relation" and concentrating on her early life as a petty thief, the daughter of "a jolly Fidler"; *The Life and Character of Mrs. Mary Moders,* which adds information about her confidence tricks and thieving between 1664 and 1671; *The Memoires of Mary Carleton,* which details her scandalous living in Jamaica; and Francis Kirkman's *The Counterfeit Lady Unveiled,* a fuller, more serious, and more imaginative account than the others.

MC's two works in 1663, the second an expansion of the first, show a marked literary skill, and may have been collaborations, although her obvious verbal ability and linguistic proficiency argue at least partial authorship. In *The Case,* dedicated to Prince Rupert, she gives a lively account of her imagined life, describing the two German suitors, her own noble composure at her trial, and the battle of civilities and deception during Carleton's courtship. Her account of her undoing is equally spirited; when caught, she was "divested and stript of all my clothes, and plundered of all my jewels, and my money, my very bodice, and a pair of silk stockings, being also pulled from me." When she generalizes her fall, it is again in terms of clothing: "See the fickleness and vanity of human things, to-day *embellished,* and adorned with all the female Arts of bravery and gallantry, and courted and attended on by the best rank of my sex, who are jealous observers what honour and respect they give among themselves, to a very punctilio; and now disrobed and disfigured in mishapen Garments, and almost left naked, and haled and pulled by Beadles, and such like rude and boisterous fellows, before a Tribunal, like a lewd Criminal." On the whole, MC strikes a dignified pose, presenting herself as an injured innocent, "a foreign and desolate woman." She makes much of her scholarly and linguistic skills extending to Greek, Latin, French, Italian, Spanish, and "the Oriental Tongues." Her accomplishments and noble stance, she feels, refute the "vile and impertinent falsehood, that I am of a most sordid and base extraction." Yet there is a humor in *The Case* that modifies the delicacy she professes; for instance, she calls herself Maria de Wolway, which she admits became the lewd De Vulva and, when she enumerates the coaches and jewels Carleton promised her, she notes that they were charged to her own estate "by a figure of anticipation." At intervals throughout *The Case,* she reveals her discontent with the situation of women. In her dedication she complains of being a *femme couverte* and unable to act legally for herself; later she castigates English law that gives the husband entire power over marital property. Describing her invented childhood, she bewails the lot of girls, kept passive and sedentary, and she wishes she had had the freedom of a boy. J.T.

CARLISLE, Isabella Howard, Countess of (1721–95), author of occasional works, was the daughter of William, fourth Baron Byron, and Frances, daughter of William, Lord Berkeley of Stratton. In 1743 she married Lord Carlisle, a widower near 50; their children were Frederick, the fifth Earl (1748–1825), and four daughters: Anne, Frances, Elizabeth, and Juliana. They lived at Castle Howard. The Earl died in 1758 when C of C was 37 and, said LADY LOUISA STUART, had to that time lived a model life, eschewing both dress and diversion. Now she indulged in both. By 1759 she had taken Sir Thomas Robinson's house in Whitehall, had the gay FRANCES GREVILLE for companion (and a company of rakes) and was indulging, according to LADY HOLLAND, in continual parties and suppers. For the remainder of her life, although aging and plain, C of C was famous for her affairs of gallantry and accounted somewhat of a jest; Lady Holland thought "the poor woman's folly almost incredible." In 1759 C of C married the 24-year-old Sir William Musgrove, proclaiming his age to be 33. This marriage, though no great success, lasted more than ten years, and letters from Sir William in 1767–68 to young Lord Carlisle show that he acted a responsible role in the family. In 1770 C of C left England for Aix to meet a lover; he was side-tracked in Vienna by another amour, but C of C soon consoled herself. Thereafter she became notable for the barons who dangled after her, and LADY MARY COKE once noted the good luck of her age and plainness, for if an opportunity to disgrace herself had presented itself, she could not have resisted. To her four daughters she was not the best guide. In 1767 Lord Aylesbury jilted one daughter; C of C carried his letters to his father, nearly provoking a duel between Lord Aylesbury and her son. In 1768 she publicly encouraged the attachment between another daughter and the married Lord Percy, because he contemplated divorce. In 1771 she was encouraging the imprudent marriage abroad of another daughter; as Lady Mary Coke observed, "She is so indulgent to the passion of Love, that it makes her a bad adviser." At about 70, her wanderings finished; she retired to England and died there.

Horace Walpole admired and collected C of C's etchings, and her watercolors of flowers were celebrated. She was widely considered to be the author of "The Fairy's Answer to Mrs. Greville's Prayer for Indifference." Published in *Elegant Extracts* (1800), these verses were assigned by John Heneage Jesse, editor of the 1882 *George Selwyn and his Contemporaries* (in which several of C of C's letters appear) to C of C's daughter-in-law (b. 1753). Lady Holland, however, seems to refer to both sets of verses in a 1758 letter (see Greville entry). In the verses, the Fairy denies Mrs. Greville's plea for indifference: "Such incense has perfum'd my throne! / Such eloquence my heart has won! / I think I guess the hand: / I know her wit and beauty too; / But why she sends a pray'r so new, / I cannot understand." In 1789, perhaps as an *apologia* on the occasion of her return to England, C of C published *Thoughts in the Form of Maxims, Addressed to Young Ladies on their First Establishment in the World,* a 57-page pamphlet (the subject matter aroused some merriment from her acquaintance.) The form probably derives from the 1756 publication of Frances Greville's husband, *Maxims, Characters, and Reflections.* C of C admits that the path of instruction to the young has been well trod, but it is her intention "to treat of such minute follies and blemishes, on the first entrance of young persons into the great and critical world, as are the less avoidable, as their consequences do not strike at first sight." Her advice to the young is mostly indisputable, for example: "Do not consider, during your youth, the aged as distinct beings from yourself: your journey, if you live, will be more speedy than you imagine to the same period, and tender you equally dependent on the compassion and patience of a younger race"; "In no other light, but that of decency and modesty, at public diversion seek to be conspicuous"; and "Preserve a copy of every letter you write or receive. This exactitude will secure you against future accusations and misinterpretations." C of C's book, which probably represents hard-won experience, was reprinted several times—once, in America, bound with *The Rudiments of Taste,* by Mrs. PEDDLE.   R.R.

CARTER, Elizabeth (1717–1806), poet, translator, essayist, and letter writer, was born in Deal, where she lived for the rest of her life. Her father was Perpetual Curate of Deal Chapel and a preacher at Canterbury Cathedral. The eldest caughter of a large family, EC assumed considerable household duties at an early age. Educated by her father in the same way as her brothers, she was proficient in Latin, Greek, Hebrew, French, Italian, Spanish, and German, and as an adult taught herself Portuguese and Arabic. She was a good musician and a student of astronomy, history, and geography. Tradition says that as a child she ruined her health staying awake to study; she did suffer from severe headaches all her life, but there could be other causes for these, among them dislike of domestic chores. Her mother died when EC was about ten; after her step-mother's death EC took over housekeeping for her father until his death in 1774. She also cared for various siblings, nephews, and nieces. Her father was a friend of Edward Cave, the editor of the *Gentleman's Magazine;* Cave published a riddle by EC in his magazine in 1734. This was followed by various other contributions from her, usually signed "Eliza." Through Cave she met Samuel Johnson and others. Her closest friendship, with CATHERINE TALBOT, began in 1741. She also became a close friend of ELIZABETH MONTAGU, William Pulteney (later Earl of Bath), Elizabeth Vesey, FRANCES BOSCAWEN, and others in the Bluestocking circle. She knew and corresponded with Samuel Richardson, Edmund Burke, Horace Walpole, HANNAH MORE, MARY DELANY, and most of the literary figures of her day. The success of her books and the generosity of her friends (Montagu settled an annuity on her, and both the Earl of Bath and Catherine Talbot's mother left her legacies) enabled her to travel. She visited London every winter, staying first with Talbot and later in lodgings, and in the summer visited at friends' country houses. In 1763 she went with the Montagus and the Earl of Bath to France, the Low Countries, and the Rhineland, and visited France again in 1782. She died in her London lodgings.

Cave published EC's *Poems upon Particular Occasions* in 1738 and in 1739 her translations: *Sir Isaac Newton's Philosophy Explained, for the use of Ladies,* from Algarotti's *Newtonismo per le dame,* and *An Examination of Mr. Pope's Essay on Man,* from J.P. Crousaz's *Examen de l'essay de Monsieur Pope sur l'homme.* These are now quite scarce. She contributed two papers to the *Rambler* (no. 44, 18 August 1750; no. 100, 2 March 1751). They were described by Talbot as efforts to relieve the prevailing melancholy of the paper. Her most famous work was her translation, *All the works of Epictetus,* published by subscription in 1758. In 1762 she published *Poems on Several Occasions.* All her poetry and some shorter prose pieces were published by her nephew and literary heir, Montagu Pennington, in 1808 as the second volume of his *Memoirs of the Life of Mrs. Elizabeth Carter.*

As a poet EC is unexceptional. Some of her verses are translations from Latin and Italian; all are full of classical allusions and conventional 18th-century diction. She wrote verses to her friends and family, for example, to her father: "Thy hand my infant mind to Science form'd, / And gently led it thro' the thorny road: / With love of Wisdom, and of Virtue warm'd, / And turn'd from idle toys to real good." Her best known verse is "Ode to Wisdom," which Richardson included, without acknowledgment, in *Clarissa.* The translation of Epictetus, on which EC's fame largely rests, was not originally intended for publication. Encouraged by Talbot, and also by Bishop Secker who advised and corrected her work, EC labored on it between 1749 and 1752. When it was published, she added notes and a long introduction explaining Stoicism. She had a subscription for the first printing of over a thousand copies at a guinea each; there were three more editions in which she made some alterations. EC's prose is clear and straightforward. The introduction is scrupulously fair to the Stoics, although as a devout, practicing, 18th-century Anglican EC could not really approve of all their ideas. She could not have liked the Greek philosopher's attitude toward women when he observed: "Women from Fourteen Years old are flattered with the Title of Mistresses, by the Men. Therefore, perceiving that they are regarded only as qualified to give the Men Pleasure, they begin to adorn themselves; and in that to place all their Hopes. It is worthwhile, therefore, to fix our Attention on making them sensible, that they are esteemed for nothing else, but the Appearance of a decent, and modest, and discreet Behaviour." Her translation long remained the standard English version of Epictetus. Like most of her friends, EC was an enthusiastic and constant letter writer. Several selections from her letters were printed by Pennington; some are in the first volume of the *Memoirs.* Others are in *Letters from Mrs. Elizabeth Carter, to Mrs. Montagu* (3 vols., 1817) and *A Series of Letters between Mrs. Elizabeth Carter and Miss Catherine Talbot* (4 vols., 1809), which also includes letters to Elizabeth Vesey. The letters told about her travels and friendships. They always commended and encouraged women writers; among those mentioned are CHARLOTTE LENNOX, HESTER MULSO CHAPONE, FANNY BURNEY, Hannah More, ANNA LAETITIA BARBAULD, and JOANNA BAILLIE. She liked CATHERINE MACAULAY's *History* but not her conduct. EC's letters from her travels show an intelligent and well-educated Protestant Englishwoman's reaction to the places she saw and people she met. Well read in history, she was pleased to see the continental cities and buildings, but patriotically disapproved of the governments and customs, especially the religious ones, of the largely Roman Catholic areas she visited. She was an enthusiastic admirer of gothic architecture in England and on the Continent; as she wrote to Montagu, "I have, at least, as much of the Goth as of the Athenian, in my composition." B.B.S.

CARTWRIGHT, H., Mrs. (fl. 1776), educational writer, was the author of *Letters on Female Education Addressed to a Married Lady* (1776), which she dedicated to ELIZABETH MONTAGU. The work is a conservative and fairly typical tract on the accomplishments and virtues necessary for a young girl; it strongly emphasizes the role of the mother in supervising her children's education herself. L.F.

CAVE, Jane [Winscom] (fl. 1786), poet, published a single volume, *Poems on Various Subjects, Entertaining, Elegiac, and Religious* (1783), which reached four editions by 1794 and was supported by a large subscription list. The volume contains poems inspired by commonplace local events—partings, walks, visits, deaths—and people—aunts, brides, clergy, children. But the charm of local color cannot compensate for JC's limited poetic talents: "My soul like a stern oak, inmov'd remains" or "Here,

filled with new ideas, we / Regale us with a dish of tea." Most interesting is her prefatory poem, "The Author's Plea," in which she explains the "numberless impediments," social and domestic, frustrating her early inclination to write: "The Muses seem'd to court me for their friend, / But Fortune would not to their suit attend." G.B.

CELESIA, Dorothea (1738–90), dramatist and poet, daughter of the poet David Mallet, was baptized in Chiswick. After her early marriage to Signor Pietro Paolo Celesia, a Genoese patrician, she left England in 1759 to reside permanently in Genoa, where David Garrick visited her. *Almida* (1771), her tragedy in blank verse based on Voltaire's *Tancrède,* received some revisions and an epilogue by Garrick before its performance at Drury Lane in January 1771. Mrs. Elizabeth Barry, a frequent actress in APHRA BEHN's plays, gave an excellent performance as Almida, so the play had a successful run despite its unnatural plot and versification. The victim of irrational, blind patriotism in ancient Syracuse, Almida is enmeshed in a "labyrinth of woe" and made victim of "The iron dictates of unfeeling minds." DC's poem "Indolence" (1772) celebrates in amateurish heroic couplets the powerful charms of sleep and rest, "By Nature's hand deep grav'd in every breast." G.B.

CELLIER, Elizabeth (fl. 1678–88), pamphleteer and midwife, was characterized by her contemporary, the Whig Bishop Gilbert Burnet, as "a Popish midwife, who had a great share of wit, and was abandoned to lewdness." EC's own *Malice Defeated* (1680) presents a different perspective: EC was a zealous Royalist who converted to Catholicism because of her horror at the excesses of the Civil War. She became active during "the pretended Popish plot" to bring relief to those Catholics suffering in prison because of the machinations of Titus Oates and other Whigs, such as Shaftesbury and Waller. At a hazard to her safety and reputation, she went daily to Newgate to document the torturing of prisoners, which she witnessed. Unfortunately, she became involved with a prisoner named Dangerfield in an obscure intrigue to discredit the Whig party. This abortive Catholic conspiracy is known as the Meal Tub Plot because, as EC tells us, when Dangerfield turned traitor to the Catholics, the evidence implicating

EC and others was found by Waller "between the pewter in my kitchen." In June 1680, when EC appeared in court charged with treason, she successfully challenged the credibility of the notorious Dangerfield as a witness. Shortly afterwards, she wrote and sold from her own house *Malice Defeated*. This led to another arrest for libel because of her accusations about conditions in Newgate. EC was not only fined £1,000 by the court, but also put in the pillory. In a letter of September 1680, LADY RACHEL RUSSELL, wife of the Whig leader who later went to the scaffold for his part in the Rye House Plot of 1683, described the intrepid EC as she stood in the pillory protecting her head with a battledore: "All the stones that were thrown within reach, she took up and put in her pocket." During her trial, EC was charged with lewdness; one witness accused her of telling a bawdy joke. Her defense illustrates her wily humor: "I said, If I did not lose my Hands, I should get Money as long as Men kiss'd their Wives." "And Mistresses," added the witness. But the court decided her quip was "but witty" and "natural to her practice." She insists in *Malice Defeated* that, although many thought her behavior "too masculine," "I preserv'd the Modesty if not the Timorousness common to my Sex." EC was also maligned by her Whig enemies as an agent of the Pope and the Jesuits in numerous pamphlets of the 1680s with such titles as: *The Pope's letter to Madam Cellier, The Scarlet Beast, Stripped Naked, Being the Mystery of the Meal-Tub the Second time unravelled* and *A Whip for Impudence: A Lashing Repartee to a Snarling Midwife*.

EC's best-known pamphlet, *A Scheme for the Foundation of a Royal Hospital . . . and such for the Maintenance of a Corporation of skillful Midwives* (1687), includes a number of practical proposals addressed to James II, who apparently agreed to the establishing of a union of midwives. As we learn from EC's *To Dr.- - -, An Answer to his Queries concerning the College of Midwives* (1688), male physicians were "pretending to teach us midwifery." EC boasts of her success, in spite of Dr.- - -'s ridicule of her methods, in assisting the breeding of Queen Maria of Modena. EC argues that the struggle between physicians and midwives is a recurrent historical phenomenon. For example, she describes a crisis in Athens in which the physicians caused the government to legislate against midwives. EC depicts the heroic Agnodicea, inspired "to pity the miserable condition of her own sex, and hazard her life to help them, which to enable herself to do, she cut off her hair, apparelled herself like a man, and became the scholar of Hyrophilus, the most famous physician of that time." Agnodicea got the unjust law revoked. EC was less fortunate; the fall of James II in 1688 ended her public career. S.B.

CENTLIVRE, Susanna (?–1723), playwright known as "the celebrated Mrs. Centlivre," has been given a fanciful and romantic early life by her biographers. Her frequent trips to Holbeach support the tradition that she was born in that town, although the date and her family name are not known. In spite of the legend of her residence at Cambridge in boy's clothing, nothing is known of her education; her use of French sources in some of her works suggests a knowledge of that language. She first appeared in print in 1700 under the name Susanna Carroll (Carroll apparently being the name of a husband who soon died). At this time she was writing fashionable amatory letters and incidental verse that associate her with a wide circle of literary figures including Tom Brown, Ned Ward, JANE WISEMAN, William Burnaby, George Farquhar, DELARIVIÈRE MANLEY, CATHARINE TROTTER, MARY PIX, and LADY PIERS. During her life she was also acquainted with Richard Steele, Nicholas Rowe, Anne Oldfield, Thomas Baker, Colley Cibber, Nicholas Amhurst, Charles Johnson, Eustace Budgell, and Ambrose Philips. She may also have been associated with ELIZA HAYWOOD, MARTHA FOWKE, and Anthony Hammond. Like many of her friends, she was an ardent Whig, which probably accounts for the barbs directed at her by Pope. In 1707 she married Joseph Centlivre, a widower with a son and a daughter. He was Yeoman of the Mouth to Queen Anne; he had been a royal cook since the reign of King William. In 1713 the Centlivres moved to Buckingham Court, where they lived the rest of their lives. Early in her career as a playwright she encountered hostility because of her sex; her response, at least temporarily, was a feminist stance and the anonymous presentation of several of her plays. Her popular success dispersed the hostility. Her incidental writings suggest a lively, frank, affable personality, supported by a contemporary description (perhaps by John Mottley): "She had much vivacity and good humour; she was remarkably good-natured and benevolent in her temper and ready to do any friendly office."

SC wrote 16 full-length plays and three short farces. She began her career inauspiciously with three failures: a tragicomedy called *The Perjured Husband* (1700) and two comedies, *The Beau's Duel* and *The Stolen Heiress* (both 1702). Her first solid commercial success was *Love's Contrivance* (1703), based on Molière. This fast-paced comedy was acted at intervals through 1706; the last act was often played as an afterpiece, and the full-length play was revived in 1724. Early in 1705 SC produced a smash hit in *The Gamester,* a topical play about a major 18th-century vice. Ostensibly writing sentimental reform comedy, SC actually caters to audience interest in gaming; the hero's penitence is less convincing and less well realized than his obsession. *The Gamester* became a stock piece and was performed regularly for 50 years. *The Basset Table* (1705), written within the year to exploit the formulas of *The Gamester,* unsuccessfully varied the pattern with a female gambler. The play, actually a comedy of love intrigue rather than a gambling exposé, has more talk about than action at cards. SC's next play, *Love at a Venture* (1706), was denied London production by Colley Cibber, who then plagiarized the main intrigue for his highly popular play *The Double Gallant* (1707). Meanwhile, SC wrote another unsuccessful comedy, *The Platonick Lady* (1706). Her next hit was *The Busy Body* (1709), which remained a repertory favorite until the late 19th century. *The Busy Body* is a beautifully proportioned intrigue comedy in which two young couples outwit the two comic old men. The special ingredient is the character of the busybody, Marplot, who, in his impertinent but good-natured eagerness to discover his friends' secrets, repeatedly brings the young lovers to near-disaster. Because they must outwit not only their enemies but also their friend, the audience is kept in anxious hilarity. More light-weight but also pleasant is *The Man's Bewitched* (1709), which occasioned a disagreement between SC and the actors about cuts; the disagreement was magnified into a public quarrel by a story in *The Female Tatler,* probably prompted by the malice of the Tory Delarivière Manley. The disputed scenes pleased at the première and were made into a two-act farce, *The Ghost,* which was performed regularly throughout the second half of the century. *The Man's Bewitched* is also a possible source for

Goldsmith's *She Stoops to Conquer.* The first of SC's three farces is *A Bickerstaff's Burying* (1710), a spoof of protestations of conjugal affection beyond the grave. *A Gotham Election* and *A Wife Well Managed* (both of 1715) are satirical farces. The first is a heavy-handed satire of Tory corruption in a local election, and the second mocks Catholicism in the person of a lustful priest; neither was performed. After SC's death, however, *A Wife Well Managed* was acted as an afterpiece in 1724, and in 1732 was adapted without acknowledgment into a ballad opera called *The Disappointment.* SC's production was uneven: along with hit plays she continued to write failures, among them *Marplot* (1710), a poor sequel to *The Busy Body. Marplot* reproduces the plot structure of the earlier play, but the lovers do not care seriously about the intrigues, and the sunny tone of the earlier play is lost. Only modest success attended *The Perplexed Lovers* (1712), a cloak-and-dagger comedy with a plot in perpetual motion. *The Cruel Gift* (1716) dresses in 18th-century gentility the bloody story of Tancred and Ghismonda. This tragedy is inane, and the blank verse flat. *The Artifice* (1722), a comedy clumsy in characterization and tone, contains more plot material than can be worked out. SC wrote two of her finest comedies late in her career. *The Wonder: A Woman Keeps a Secret* (1714) is a comic masterpiece. The action turns on Violante's promise to protect the secret of her friend Isabella's elopement and romance. Violante keeps her promise, even when every event conspires to make her appear false, to the point of passionate quarrels with her beloved Felix. Believing that true love does not admit of doubt, she insists on Felix's trust as a precondition of unraveling the secret. Their relationship is believable and the best scenes are their irrational quarrels and their fumbling attempts at reconciliation. Providing emotion as well as motion in the plot, Felix and Violante delighted theatergoers for generations, until the end of the 19th century. The role of Felix was one of Garrick's triumphs, and he chose it for his farewell performance in 1776. *A Bold Stroke for a Wife* (1718) is also a comic delight and remained popular for 150 years. The play turns on a single premise: in order to marry Anne Lovely, Colonel Fainwell must gain the consent of four amusingly different guardians—a beau, a virtuoso, a businessman, and a Quaker. He wins the lady by assuming five successive disguises, the last being an impersonation of the real Simon Pure, which added that expression to the English language. The continued success of SC's plays was due to her use of a dramatic mode that suited her talents and the increasing verbal prudery of 18th-century audiences. Characteristically, she writes farcical comedy of intrigue, with the intrigues furthering love and marriage rather than sexual adventure. There are no cuckoldings, those few liaisons alluded to having ended before the plays begin. The romantic hero is usually a blunt soldier rather than a witty beau, a choice perhaps made by SC from political sentiment but which affects the tone and language of the plays. The soldier's suitable dramatic mate is the forthright, sensible heroine; the lovers waste little time in witty sparring, for they are both decided on marriage from the beginning, so that the thrust of the play is toward action rather than verbal wit. SC lacks verbal flash and grace and uses little double entendre; instead she provides wide topical allusions and lively use of jargon, slang, religious cant, dialect, and foreign accents. SC is a superb stage technician, adroit at moving characters on and off stage plausibly, rapidly, comically. Her plays are above all acting vehicles, with dozens of comic roles that remained favorites of such distinguished actors as Garrick and Kitty Clive. Among her many 19th-century admirers was William Hazlitt, who in 1819 wrote of her in *Lectures on the English Comic Writers:* "Her plays have a provoking spirit and volatile salt in them, which still preserves them from decay.... Their interest depends chiefly on the intricate involution and artful *dénouement* of the plot, which has a strong tincture of mischief in it, and the wit is seasoned by the archness of the humour and sly allusion to the most delicate point." N.C.

CHAMBERS, Marianne (fl. 1799–1812) playwright, was the daughter of Charles Chambers, first mate on the Winterton East Indiaman; he died in a shipwreck off Madagascar in August 1792 when MC was apparently very young. She published a novel and two plays; the novel, *He Deceived Himself (a domestic tale),* by subscription in three volumes from Dilly (c. 1799), met with little critical or economic success. The *Monthly Review* (Sept. 1799), noting that the author pleaded extenuating youth and inexperience, added, "It certainly requires some talents to write even a *mediocre* novel; and to such claims we cannot deny Miss

Chambers's right: though she may perhaps *deceive herself.*" MR's plays fared better. *The School for Friends,* a comedy, was performed at Drury Lane in December 1805 and periodically thereafter; it went into at least six editions. The play was perhaps applauded less for its own merits than for the absence of absurdities currently popular on stage. MC displayed, however, a command of dialogue that was often satiric and a convoluted plot in which romance goes awry and comes right only after much misunderstanding caused by malevolent meddling. The characters are Sir Edward and Lady Epsworth, Sir Edward's friend Lord Belmore, and the dissolute Lady Courtland, who shelters the estranged Lady Epsworth as "Mrs. Hamilton." The last one eventually rescues Lord Belmont from Lady Courtland's clutches and, upon receiving her husband's visit of thanks, is recognized and reconciled to him. The *Critical Review* (April 1806) noted that the distinguished success of the play could be attributed more to the morality pervading it than to the *vis comica* "of which it is entirely destitute," but found this first attempt of the authoress highly creditable, giving rise to a hope that she would some day be able to drive the current trash from the theaters. MC's second comedy, *Ourselves,* was produced at the Theatre-Royal Lyceum in 1811 and published in the same year. It has a plot, character, and dialogue similar to those of her first; in it Miss Beaufort soliloquizes in the manner of Congreve's Millamant: "A husband! Fortune forbid!—To have one's actions, words, and even thoughts, scrutinized, to tremble at putting on a new dress, for fear it should not be made to his humour, see him smile on one before company, and bite his lip in anger aside. Know no more of his concerns than one's waiting-woman; and yet be required to regulate our expences by his means, hear him praise every other lady, than the one he vowed to cherish; and to love him just enough to be stung by his scorn, one's heart fluttering with ten thousand jealousies in his absence, and beating high with resentment on his return. Thus to sit day after day, fighting and weeping over these accumulated wrongs, with enlivening reflections of being tied to the creature for life!" K.F.

CHAMPION DE CRESPIGNY, Mary, Lady (1748?–1812), novelist, poet and educational writer, was the only child of Joseph Clarke of Rigton, Yorks. At age 16, she married Claude Champion de Crespigny, heir of a Huguenot family allied with Lord North and connected to the Admiralty. After several months at Bath, where she often conversed with Lord Chesterfield, MCdeC and her husband settled at Champion Lodge, his family's estate in Camberwell, south of London. Her husband soon became Receiver-General of the Droits of Admiralty, a post he held for half a century. Their circle, largely naval, included Admirals Sir Henry Martin and Lord Viscount Keppel; MCdeC also cultivated ecclesiastics, such as Bishop Porteus of London and Archbishop Moore of Canterbury, and knew HESTER THRALE, Claude CdeC's career was crowned by a baronetcy in 1805, a reward for the fête MCdeC gave the Prince of Wales in June 1804. The *Gentleman's Magazine,* remarking that "the pleasure of [MCdeC] is uniformly to render pleasure rational by making it subservient to virtuous sentiment," describes the party: MCdeC led the Prince along the meandering walks of her 30-acre park (which was strewn with gypsies and young ladies dancing or selling articles from booths), and they paused at the grotto dedicated to Contemplation, with glimpses "through the foliage" of "haymakers neatly dressed" making hay the while. MCdeC died at Richmond House, Twickenham, having lived there for two years, evidently without her husband. She was survived by him and by her only child, who succeeded to the baronetcy in 1818.

MCdeC's *Letters of Advice from a Mother to Her Son* was written about 1780 and published in 1803. Like Chesterfield's *Letters,* they address the needs of a young man of position, but the focus differs. *"Trifles* much oftener turn the scales in life than we are accustomed to imagine," MCdeC declares. "I feel an attention to them as necessary as Lord Chesterfield did an attention to the graces." Good conversation, for example, demands "a knowledge of the world, the customs, feelings, and etiquettes of the times, a good memory, a competent knowledge of books, with good judgement, discrimination, and a considerable share of forebearance." Should her son be a guest in a house where there is dancing, he must "ask the lady of the house first, unless . . . she is decidedly past the age of dancing, or of being *asked* to dance—very *different* situations." Equally lucid are the letters devoted to religion. MCdeC advances "the notion of a God" as "the hypothesis that perfectly solves . . . all the appearances in the natural and moral world"; atheistic ideas,

by contrast, "are, like dreams, incoherent, wild, and irrational." *Critical Review* said that "the unsunned snow is not purer than [MCdeC's] morality . . . but sometimes *faire l'agréable* is her motto"; the *Gentleman's Magazine* spoke of "universal approbation." Her novel, *The Pavilion* (1796), gained less praise. "The usual ingredients," sniffed *CR,* "the incidents trite, and the sentiment feeble." It is a just estimate of the tale of Ethelinda, of genteel but mysterious origin, who was raised by cottagers until introduced by a local dowager to society. There all men fall before her, and she returns the love of a lord who is, handily, heir to the selfsame duke whose daughter she at last discovers herself to be. MCdeC always notes whether her women characters are educated; Ethelinda, instructed by the learned local curate, shines in intellect no less than in beauty. MCdeC also wrote *A Monody to the Memory of the Late Lord Collingwood* (1810); her grandson had served under the great admiral. S.M.

CHANDLER, Mary (1687–1745), poet, was born in Malmesbury, Wilts., the eldest daughter of Henry Chandler, a Dissenting minister, who later settled at Bath. Her brothers were raised as doctors and clergymen, but her family could not afford to give her a polite education as well. Despite a crooked spine, MC set up a shop in Bath in about 1705, when still in her teens. Her deformity kept her from social amusement, so she spent her leisure educating herself and composing rhyming riddles and poems to friends. The local gentry requested copies, and she resolved to print a collection, *A Description of Bath.* MARY BARBER was her literary friend, and she was also a friend of ELIZABETH ROWE. When she was 54, a wealthy gentleman of 60, who admired her poems, traveled eighty miles to see her and proposed marriage. She refused the offer, preferring independence, and turned the incident into verse, appended to the sixth edition of her book in 1744.

A Description of Bath went speedily through two editions. A third was issued in 1736, a fourth in 1738, and a fifth in 1741. Written in heroic couplets, the Bath poem is faintly satirical of fashionable society, although MC knew her place, and "would rather chuse to be taken Notice of as one that deals honestly in Trade, and behaves decently in the Relations of Life, than as a writer" (in the dedication). Her other verses, e.g., those praising the country houses of friends who invited her to stay, are written in simple meters, or octosyllabic couplets, and testify to a moderate love of nature. Many contain a personal reference; e.g., when she notes that, since her person was never formed to please, "Friendship's the sweetest joy in human life, / 'Tis *that* I wish—and *not* to be a Wife." Her "Life" in Th. Cibber's *Poets,* vol. V, suggests that such equanimity was not attained without a struggle. Peevish by nature, she consciously cultivated benevolence; recommended to follow a vegetarian diet, she further mortified the flesh by living for long periods on bread and water. Her lines on temperance in her Bath poem are written from experience and, perhaps, necessity: "Think *Virtuous Knowledge* WOMAN'S *truest* Pride." Yet her version of her marriage proposal, "A True Tale," shows she could regard her deformity with humor: "Fourscore long Miles, to buy a crooked Wife! / Old, too! I thought the oddest thing in Life." In youth she had religious doubts, but became committed to rational Christianity, and was engaged in a poem "On the Attributes of God" when she died. Pope commended her Bath poem for its good sense and politeness.   M.S.

CHAPONE, Hester Mulso (1727–1801), essayist and poet, was born at Twywell, Northants., the only surviving daughter of a famously beautiful mother who was a sister of the Rev. Dr. John Thomas, successively bishop of Peterborough, Salisbury, and Winchester. HMC's father was Thomas Mulso, a gentleman farmer. Her three brothers, Thomas, John, and Edward, who also wrote, found preferment in the Church of England. At the age of nine, HMC wrote a short romance, "The Loves of Amoret and Melissa," which aroused the jealousy of her mother, who suppressed any other immediate literary efforts. Upon the early death of her mother, HMC managed her father's household and studied French, Italian, Latin, music, and drawing. Visiting an aunt in Canterbury, she met ELIZABETH CARTER and William Duncombe, the playwright and translator of Horace, who introduced her to Samuel Richardson, Thomas Edwards, and SUSANNA HIGHMORE; both women became members of Richardson's North End circle. HMC appears in the sketch Highmore drew of Richardson reading *Sir Charles Grandison,* which was used as a frontispiece to Richardson's *Correspondence* (1804). Both women wrote poems in praise of Thomas Edwards, who

sometimes confused their literary works, an error compounded by later writers who have given credit to both for HMC's "Story of Fidelia" in *The Adventurer.* HMC gained early notice in *The Feminiad* (1754) as Delia, of whom John Duncombe wrote "that the happiness of her genius is only excell'd by the goodness of her heart." Samuel Johnson said that letting her verses be read too publicly was "the very crime [that] broke the links of amity between Richardson and Miss Mulso after a tenderness and confidence of many years." HMC gained her social position through wit, poise, and talent. Charlotte Burney called her "deadly ugly" and FANNY BURNEY, describing her in later years, noted her "good sense, talents, and conversational power, in defiance of age, infirmities, and uncommon ugliness." MARY DELANY, however, quoted Mrs. Donellan, who admired HMC's sense and her letters, but thought "her only second rate as to politeness of manners"; Richardson modeled his genteel characters on her, which was "the reason they are not so really polished as he thinks them to be" (*Autobiography,* 1861, 3). Elizabeth Carter's judgment was more generous: "She has an uncommon exactness of understanding and a lively agreeable turn of conversation; and her conduct seems to be governed by the best and noblest principles" (August 1752 to Talbot). Richardson introduced HMC to a hard-working young lawyer, John Chapone, as he did her brother Thomas to Miss Prescott, a general's daughter. Both couples wished to marry, but Mr. Mulso put them off for years, perhaps for financial reasons of his own. Then he arranged for both to be married in the same ceremony in December 1760. Chapone's profession took much of his time, leaving HMC to her writing and correspondence. After only ten months of marriage, he caught a fever and died. HMC was taken to her brother Thomas's residence, where for 23 days she also seemed near death. Then she stayed with friends until she recuperated. Contents of her house were auctioned in 1762. With only limited means, which were slightly augmented when her father died in 1763, HMC spent the rest of her life visiting friends and family. Frequently she lived with her uncle who, as Bishop of Winchester, had palatial residences at Farnham Castle and in London. She was at Farnham Castle in 1778 when the King and Queen visited the Bishop, and the Queen complimented HMC on her *Letters on the Improvement of the Mind.* Toward the end of her life she hired a house at Hadley to be near an old friend; her youngest niece lived with her as companion.

HMC's works include letters, tales, and poetry. Johnson used four of her letters in *The Rambler* (no. 10, 21 April 1750). Hawkesworth printed her "Story of Fidelia" in *The Adventurer* (nos. 77–79, July–August 1753), not knowing she was the author. A stanza from "To Stella," addressed to Susanna Highmore, was used by Johnson as the example for *quatrain* in his dictionary, before the poem was published. In 1758, HMC provided an ode for Carter's *Epictetus.* Her most important work is *Letters on the Improvement of the Mind* (1773), written for a niece in Yorkshire. This work became so popular that the 25th edition was published in 1844. Dedicated to ELIZABETH MONTAGU, it speaks of the author's reluctance to publish until pressed by Montagu through "partiality of friendship." Sections concern religion, the regulation of the heart and temper, economy, politeness and accomplishments, and the learning of geography and history. Religion is emphasized throughout and the young girl is warned against fashionable sensibility: "Let a vain young woman be told that tenderness and softness are the peculiar charms of the sex—that even their weakness is lovely, and their fears becoming—and you will presently observe her grow so tender as to be ready to weep for a fly; so fearful, that she starts at a feather; and so weak hearted, that the smallest accident quite overpowers her. . . . Remember, my dear, that our feelings were not given us for our ornament, but to spur us on to right actions." *Miscellanies in Prose and Verse* (1775), a collection of HMC's early works, appeared in a new edition in 1787, which henceforth included *A Letter to a New-Married Lady.* The latter, first published by itself in 1777, appeared in three editions with John Gregory's *A Father's Legacy to his Daughter* in the next century. A Dublin edition of her works (1786) appeared in two volumes. Her family published a four-volume *Works and Life* in 1807, which was reprinted in America. W.M.

CHARKE, Charlotte (1713–60), novelist, playwright, and autobiographer, was born in London to Colley Cibber, actor, playwright, part manager of Drury Lane Theatre, and Katherine Shore, a former actress. The last of 12 children, CC was given three years of schooling and allowed for a time to indulge herself in such outdoor activities as gardening, hunting, and riding. At 17 she married Richard Charke, musician and actor. Ten months later, she gave birth to Katherine, or Kitty, and a month after that was hired as a dancer at Drury Lane. She soon became a regular member of the company and was with them at the time of the actors' secession in 1733 when her brother Theophilus Cibber, injured at not succeeding his father as a patentee of Drury Lane, persuaded the principal actors to secede with him to the New Haymarket. Separated from her husband, CC worked with Fielding's company and, when it was disbanded by the Licensing Act, opened a puppet theater and worked the towns around London with her own and provincial troupes. Interspersed were her forays into the nontheatrical world: as owner of a grocer business, drawer (barmaid) in a pub, owner of a steak and soup shop, valet, sausage seller, etc. During this time, to avoid creditors CC donned male dress and was known as "Mr. Charles." After her husband died in Jamaica, CC took a lover, to whom she considered herself married; later, she did marry John Sacheverelle, whom she left after two months. For eight years, CC, Kitty and CC's friend "Mrs. Brown"—CC was "Mr. Brown"—played with various intinerant troupes in the provinces. Kitty having married a stroller, CC and Mrs. Brown returned to London, where CC wrote three novelettes and an autobiography. She died impoverished.

Her one extant play is *The Art of Management* (1735), an attack on Charles Fleetwood, the manager of Drury Lane who had fired her in 1733. It is full of bombast interspersed with low comedy. *The History of Henry Dumont, Esq; and Miss Charlotte Evelyn* (1756) is a typical novel of the period: it has a central plot of romance between two attractive, noble, and pure people and a subplot involving the gauche family of a country peer. It is unusual only in that it presents a homosexual—and in an unfavorable light. *The Mercer; or Fatal Extravagance* (1755) tells of a man who runs through his fortune and kills himself from guilt shortly before his debts are repaid by an inheritance of which he was unaware. The 40-page *The Lover's Treat; or Unnatural Hatred* (1758) involved a wicked elder brother and his innocent sister, whom he puts into a brothel. She escapes this "prison" and marries a "king of beggars" worth more than £40,000. It purports to be "a true narrative." *The History of Charles and Patty,* a 32-page undated tale, is also attributed to CC. CC's reputation as a writer is based on her autobiography, published in eight installments in 1755. In it, CC tries to explain her life so that her father might take pity on her and leave her some money (he did not). But she was also mindful of entertaining her readers. She jauntily dedicates the book to herself: "I hope, dear Madam, . . . that you and I may ripen our Acquaintance into a perfect Knowledge of each other, that may establish a lasting and social Friendship between us." She narrates her life in sprightly vein, then interrupts it with a discourse on her problems with her father and quotes the letter she sent him: "As I am conscious of my Errors, I thought I could not be too publick in suing for your Blessing and Pardon; and only blush to think, my youthful Follies would draw so strong a Compunction on my Mind . . . which I might have so easily avoided." The juxtaposition of humor and pathos works in this book to present a woman desperately trying to entertain her audience. In 1755 the autobiography was serialized in the *Gentleman's Magazine* and was printed in two editions. S.M.S.

CHARLTON, Mary, (fl. 1794–1830), novelist, poet, and translator, earned through her popularity sixth place on William Lane's 1798 list of "particular and favourite Authors" published by the Minerva Press. Little is known about her life. Her best work well reflects the gothic tendencies of the day. It combines plots of domestic persecution with exotic details and loosely historical background. In *Phedora* (1798), one of MC's earlier and better romances, much of the action takes place in a forest—a setting popularized by ANN RADCLIFFE. The characters include Russian villains and a little boy raised as a wild animal in the woods. In *The Pirate of Naples* (1801), another fairly successful work, the heroine is first imprisoned in a convent and then captured by pirates. MC is always at her best when describing gothic scenes of horror: "Again the words unintelligible to Angela were pronounced, and the coffin on her left hand shook at the sound—the lid rose up—damp and mouldering as it was, it fell against her face, and the tenant of the tomb, habited in black and veiled, quitted the open receptacle." MC also wrote one mild parody of the genre to which she devoted most of her efforts, *Rosella* (1799).

The *Anti-Jacobin Review* comments that in *Rosella* "the very touches of satire tickle rather than wound the feelings of those writers who have deviated beyond nature and propriety." The reviewer clearly enjoyed this story of a mother who, "not cured of the circulating-library *mania* . . . takes her daughter, an unaffected and unconscious girl, [on] a tour into Wales, that castle-bearing country; expecting in every dingle some 'hair-breadth 'scape', at every inn some surprising incident, and in every man some libertine adorer, or prosing swain." Misfortune yields only delight for such heroines: "'You were born to shine in adversity: no—I never yet saw anguish so delightfully attractive! You are quite a heroine—don't wish, my dear, to be a happier one, for distress quite becomes you.'" Other novels by MC, many lengthy and rather dull, include *The Parisian* (1794), *Andronica* (1797) *Ammorvin and Zallida* (1798, apparently lost), *The Wife and the Mistress* (1802), *The Homicide* (1813), *Grandeur and Meanness* (1820), and *Past Events* (1830). Her *Pathetic Poetry for Youth* appeared in 1815. Although *The Life, Adventures, and Vicissitudes, of Mary Charlton, the Welch Orphan* (1817) has been attributed to MC, more likely it is a fabricated account by another, attempting to capitalize on her popularity. MC translated from French and German (and is sometimes inaccurately given credit for writing) three novels: *The Reprobate* (1802), *The Philosophic Kidnapper* (1803), and *The Rake and the Misanthrope* (1804). The reaction of the period is perhaps summed up best by the *Critical Review:* "notwithstanding all this has been related a hundred times before, it is not badly repeated by Mrs. Charlton." M.A.B.

CHILCOT, Harriet [Meziere] (fl. 1783–90), poet and novelist, published a collection of poems, *Elmar and Ethlinda; A Legendary Tale: and Adalba and Ahmora, an Indian Tale: with other pieces* (1783). The poems are in various meters, the title poem being in ballad meter. It tells the story of Ethlinda, whose lover Elmar has gone to war. He is shipwrecked and washed up on a nearby shore; his father, whom he thinks dead (and who thinks him dead), later returns from the war and lusts after Ethlinda. He kills Elmar as a rival, discovers what he has done, and falls on his own sword. Ethlinda dies of shock and grief, as does her father. The poem marshals passions and atmospherics in a heavy-handed way and evidently satisfied the period's taste for the exotic, morbid, and sensational. A familiar undercurrent of melancholy is also apparent: "Great powers of nature—what is man? / His woes—his being scarce an hour, / Stretched to his nature's utmost span, / Alone a short-liv'd with'ring flower." As Mrs. Meziere, HC published the novel *Moreton Abbey* in 1790. R.J.

CHUDLEIGH, Mary, Lady (1656–1710), poet and essayist, was born in Winslade, Devon, to Richard Lee and to a mother referred to as "Philinda" in her elegiac poem "On the Death of My Honoured Mother Mrs. Lee." Nothing is known of her childhood or education. She married a baronet, Sir George Chudleigh of Ashton, Devon, and had three children: George, who succeeded to the title and estate, Thomas, and Eliza Maria, whose early death was a terrible blow. MC wrote a poem about her sorrow—"On the Death of My Dear Daughter Eliza Maria"—in dialogue, in which her fortitude is encouraged by her friendship with "Lucinda." MC was a friend of ELIZABETH THOMAS and a correspondent of John Norris of Bemerton. Through Norris she met MARY ASTELL, whom she admired and wished to emulate as a poet and defender of her sex: "Attracted by the Glory of your Name / To follow you in all the lofty Roads of Fame." She distilled Astell's *Some Reflections Upon Marriage* (1700) into a poem called "To The Ladies": "Wife and Servant are the same, / But only differ in the Name: / For when that fatal Knot is ty'd, / Which nothing, nothing can divide: / When she the word obey has said, / And Man by Law supreme has made, / Then all that's kind is laid aside, / And nothing left but State and Pride . . . / Then shun, oh! shun that wretched State, / And all the fawning Flatt'rers hate: / Value your selves, and Men despise, / You must be proud, if you'll be wise."

MC was best known for her poem in dialogue called *The Ladies Defence: or, The Bride-Woman's Counsellor Answer'd* (1700/01), a response to a sermon preached by the nonconformist minister Mr. Sprint at a wedding in Sherbourne, Dorset, and printed in 1699, about the weak moral nature of women and the necessity for their absolute obedience to their husbands. Her poem is in four voices: Sir John Brute, a tyrannical husband (adapted from Vanbrugh's *The Provok'd Wife*); Sir William Loveall, whose naive chivalry is no help to anyone; a caricature of Mr. Sprint, called "a Parson"; and pert Melissa who speaks

in MC's voice, reminding them all that it is *her* life they are talking about. *The Ladies Defence* was MC's first published work, originally anonymous, although the Epistle Dedicatory was initialed. She subsequently published under her own name a major collection, *Poems on Several Occasions Together with the Song of the Three Children Paraphras'd* (1703), dedicated to Queen Anne. In 1710 *Essays Upon Several Subjects in Prose and Verse* appeared, dedicated to the Princess Sophia, Electress and Duchess Dowager of Brunswick. The preface gives an account of the publishing and pirating of *The Ladies Defence.* In 1722 another edition of the poems was printed. MC appears to have read widely and she refers to classical writers such as Homer, Epictetus, Plutarch, Marcus Aurelius, Virgil, Ovid, and Horace, as well as to philosophers such as Gassendi and Malebranche and their contemporaries. In "To Mr. Dryden on his Translation of Virgil" she eulogizes the poets of the English tradition: Chaucer, Spenser, Waller, Milton, Cowley. George Ballard, in his *Memoirs of Several Ladies* (1752), records that she wrote two tragedies, two operas, a masque, and verse translations of Lucian which, although never printed, were carefully preserved in the family.

MC was apparently part of a small circle of respectable literary-minded women who originally urged her to publish *The Ladies Defence;* after its appearance she enjoyed a wide reputation in London as a writer. Her prose on topics such as pride, death and solitude has the smoothness, apt examples, and epigrammatic construction typical of the Augustan period. Her poetry, which often uses the uneven pindaric stanza form made popular by Cowley, is assured, lively, and polished, with occasional lapses into sentimental piety; as she claims, it gives "a Picture of my Mind, my Sentiments all laid open to their View; they'll sometimes see me cheerful, pleas'd, sedate and quiet; at other times griev'd, complaining, struggling with my Passions, blaming my self, endeavouring to pay a Homage to my Reason." R.P.

CIBBER, Susanna Maria (1714–66), dramatist, oratorio and opera singer, and actress, was the daughter of a Covent Garden upholsterer whom Joseph Addison in the *Tatler* fictionalized as the man who cared more for world affairs than for his own domestic situation. Both SMC and her brother Thomas Arne (the composer) were formally educated until their family resources deteriorated; her musical training continued, much of it supervised by her brother. SMC's personal correspondence at this time reflects this liberal education, which was later relevant to her musical and dramatic performances. In 1734 SMC made an unpropitious marriage to Theophilus Cibber (son of Colley Cibber), a widower "ugly . . . and of extravagant and vicious habits." This ill-advised marriage proved troublesome: after arranging for SMC and Mr. Sloper (a respected friend of the family) to meet and encouraging their friendship, Cibber brought charges of adultery against Sloper, suing for £5,000; the court awarded Cibber £10 in damages. A year later, pressed by creditors, Cibber brought suit against Sloper for "detaining Mrs. Cibber" and engaging her in "criminal conversation." Cibber claimed £10,000; the court awarded him £500. From then on, SMC spent most of her time at Woodhays, the Sloper estate. Fortunately, her professional career was considerably more successful than her marriage. Dr. Burney records her singing debut in Lumpe's *Amelia* (1732): "Miss Arne's performance interested every hearer." When in 1738 she made her debut as a dramatic actress in Hill's *Zaire* she did so with "complete success." In addition to her musical and dramatic achievements, in 1752 SMC's name appeared as one of the dramatists of the one-act comedy *The Oracle* (1741), actually a translation from the French of G.F. Poullain de Saint Foix. Although a minor literary achievement, it does suggest an interest in comedy that is not apparent in SMC's repertory. The following year she joined David Garrick at Drury Lane, an association that lasted until her death. After several years of failing health, she died at her home in Scotland Yard. She was buried in the Cloisters, Westminster Abbey.

Until 1736 her reputation rested primarily on her singing. Handel considered her one of the very best English singers and wrote the contralto parts in the *Messiah* and *Samson* for her. After hearing her perform the *Messiah* in Dublin, a friend of Swift's remarked: "Woman, for this be all thy sins forgiven thee." Dr. Burney thought "She captivated every ear by the sweetness and expression of her voice in singing." Yet her successful dramatic debut in 1736 all but ended her singing career; she devoted the rest of her life to the theater. In his *Memoirs,* Tate Wilkinson admires several roles including Ophelia, and makes particular mention of her "elegance and neatness." In *The Life of Garrick,* Thomas Davies states that SMC rendered her dramatic parts with "sensibility, refinement, and imaginative dreaminess." Charles Churchill paid this poetic tribute: "Mistress of each soft art, with matchless skill . . . / Awake the sigh and teach the tear to flow." Not all critics found SMC's passionate renderings appealing, however. "Her lifting up and down of the arms at almost every period was at once ineffectual and unpleasing." Even Samuel Foote, who greatly admired her, wished she "would not shake her head quite so much." P.B.M.

CLARK, Emily (fl. 1798–1819), novelist, was the granddaughter of Colonel Frederick, who was the son of Theodore, King of Corsica. Her first novel, *Ianthé, or the Flower of Caernarvon,* was dedicated to the Prince of Wales (1798). The plot concerns jealousy between brothers, the younger of whom marries the woman he loves, is wounded, has two children (one of them Ianthé), and is blessed with his retirement in Wales near Mount Snowdon. The descriptions are obviously written by one who loves the Welsh countryside. The book is laden with conventional elements—coincidence, sudden storms, forged letters, kidnapping, perils by boat, warm friendships, faithful servants, and a contrast of peace and happiness in Wales with sorrow and deceit in London. *Ermina Montrose; or, The Cottage of the Vale* (1800) lists MARIA EDGEWORTH as a subscriber. The setting of the novel is a river valley sheltered from "the storms of life." The heroine has just died, and the remainder of the book extols her exemplary life, in which she has been beloved by all and has raised the perfect family (three sons and two daughters) who, as a perfect ending, have been fortunate enough to die "almost together," prepared by religion for a better world. As a young girl, the heroine had been sent to France, where she was rescued from the convent by her father, with whom, after many accidents, life-threatening illnesses, and fortuitous eavesdropping on villainous monks, she returned safely to Wales. There her virtue was again tested before she married the hero. Scenery is described as threatening or protective; the benevolence of nature relates to the benevolence of virtuous people. Other works by EC are *The Banks of the Douro; or, The Maid of Portugal: A Tale* (1805), *Tales at the Fire Side; or, A Father and Mother's Stories* (1817), *The Esquimaux; or Fidelity*

(1819), and *Poems: Consisting principally of ballads* (1810).   M.P.

CLARK, Sylvia [Lewis] (fl. 1788–89), poet, lived in Holt before marrying Robert Clark of Tetbury. In 1788 she published *Poems, Moral and Entertaining* "at the Request of her Husband, for the Benefit of the Infirmary at Gloucester, the Hospital at Bath, and the Sunday Schools at Tetbury." At this time SC had been married "for almost thirty years" and had written the works included in the collection much earlier in her life. Although the publication is noted in the *Monthly Review* (81, 1789), the reviewer declines comment on the merit of the poems on the grounds that publication is for charity.   J.F.

CLIVE, Catherine (1711–85), actress, singer, playwright, and pamphleteer, was one of the large family of William Raftor. Her education seems to have been meager. She was hired at Drury Lane in 1728 and given comic and singing roles, in which she excelled. After the 1733 secession of actors from Drury Lane under Theophilus Cibber's influence, she stayed until her retirement in 1769, except for two years at Covent Garden and a summer in Dublin. In 1735 she got into a public quarrel with Theophilus Cibber, who had maneuvered CC's part of Polly in *The Beggar's Opera* for his wife, SUSANNA CIBBER. CC won the argument. She was chosen by Handel to sing Delilah in *Samson.* In 1743, she joined a theatrical secession from Drury Lane and went to Covent Garden, from which she wrote a pamphlet, "The Case of Mrs. Clive," attacking the management of both theaters and accusing them of forming a cartel. When David Garrick took over the management of Drury Lane in 1747, CC came into conflict with him but eventually called a truce to their squabbles. Her temper flared against the rising young actress Peg Woffington, and once more she became an object of gossip. In 1761 she entered a paper war with Ned Shuter, who had castigated her for translating from the French (anti-Gallic feeling ran high during this period). Many playwrights wrote roles for CC, who was a most successful comedienne. When she retired, her longtime friend Horace Walpole vowed that he would never again attend the theater, and offered her the use of a cottage he owned in Twickenham next to his own house. The friendship between the two deepened and flour-

ished; Walpole's titled friends accepted CC, and she, in turn, enjoyed their company. In 1778 she began to suffer from ill health, from which she was never free until her death seven years later.

CC's *The Rehearsal: or, Bags in Petticoats* (1753) is a short play, an afterpiece, using the format of a play within a play. The author of the play is Mrs. Hazard, as fierce and temperamental as CC was reputed to be, played by CC herself. To complicate this issue of identity, Mrs. Hazard has written a play to be played by Mrs. Clive. When Mrs. Clive doesn't show up for the rehearsal, Mrs. Hazard is persuaded to take her part. Mr. Cross, the prompter, suggests, "If you please to put on Mrs. *Clive's* [clothes], her Dresser is here to attend, as she expected her, and I believe it will fit you exactly, as you're much of her size." To this, Mrs. Hazard replies sarcastically, "O, yes; to be sure it will fit me exactly, because I happen to be a Head taller, and I hope something better made." The play ridicules emptyheaded women in the person of Miss Giggle, and pretentious, educated men, exemplified by Sir Albany. It is clever, but clearly not a work of comic art. The pamphlet, "The Case of Mrs. Clive" (1744), is an effective piece of persuasion. The tone is reasonable, logical, and factual, unlike the tone in most pamphlets of the time, but at the same time the work is psychologically astute: "If any think I treat this matter too seriously, I hope they will remember, that however trifling such Things may appear to them, to me, who am so much concerned in 'em, they are of great Importance, such as my Liberty and Livlihood depend on."   S.M.S.

COBBOLD, Elizabeth (1767–1824), poet and occasional writer, was born Eliza Knipe, in London and lived in Manchester, Liverpool, and Ipswich. Her first husband, William Clarke, died in 1791, six months after they were married. In 1792 she married John Cobbold, a wealthy Ipswich brewer, a widower with 14 children. They had seven children together. EC's circle of friends included CLARA REEVE and PRISCILLA WAKEFIELD. She had a deep interest in natural history and was philanthropically active. In a poetic epistle EC described her daily life in the late 1790s thus: "A botanist one day, or grave antiquarian, / Next morning a sempstress, or abecedarian; / Now making a frock, and now marring a picture, / Next conning a deep philosophical lecture; / At night at the play, or assisting to kill / The time of the idlers with whist or quadrille; / In cares or amusements still taking a part, / Though science and friendship are nearest my heart." Her son Richard Cobbold commemorated her in his novel *The History of Margaret Catchpole: A Suffolk Girl* (1847).

As a young woman, EC wrote *Poems on Various Subjects* (1783) and *Six Narrative Poems* (1787). The latter, dedicated to Sir Joshua Reynolds, contains sentimental evocations of pity, grief, and remorse; for example, "The Return from the Crusade" has Sir Leoline mourning his ancient mansion: "Lo! (sad reverse!) dismantled towers, / Rude grass-grown courts, and mould'ring walls." Her *The Sword; or, Father Bertrand's History of His Own Times* (1791), a romance set in Norman England, seeks to teach the advantages of solitude and serenity over "the busy Scenes of proud Castles, Courts, and Cities." EC's poems on scientific themes include "On the Death of Francesco Borone," a "martyr to the science of Botany" (1798). As Carolina Petty Pasty, EC wrote *The Mince Pye: An Heroic Epistle* (1800), a verse burlesque of *The Sovereign* by C.S. Pybus praising not Emperor Paul of Russia, but rather "the sovereign dainty of a British feast," the plum pudding; EC's own drawing of HANNAH GLASSE, whose cookery book was well known, is on the frontispiece. EC composed poems and short plays for family, social, and charitable purposes, and edited *Poetical Attempts* (1803) by ANN CANDLER, a Suffolk cottager, to assist the needy author. She contributed poems to *The Chaplet* (1807) and to the periodical *Ladies' Fashionable Repository,* and wrote verse valentines to friends over a 20-year period, collected as *Cliff Valentines* (1813, 1814). Her patriotism is displayed in "Ode on the Victory of Waterloo" (1815). The posthumous *Poems* (1825) carries a rhapsodic memoir by Laetitia Jermyn, which highlights EC's "conduct in the faithful discharge of the great and essential duties of social and domestic life" and the "versatility and universality of her genius." Frequent themes in EC's poetry are rural innocence, the superiority of nature over art, and the value of friendship. Her poems with a moral purpose (e.g., the virtue of perseverance) are outnumbered by those that are light and good-humored. A.B.S.

COCKBURN, Alicia [Alison] (1712?–1794), poet, was a daughter of Robert Rutherford of Fernilie, Selkirkshire. In Edinburgh she became celebrated for her beauty and charm. There in 1731 she married Patrick Cockburn, an advocate, who died in 1753. One son died in 1780. Through her mother, AC was related to Sir Walter Scott, who became a close friend. In 1777, when he was still a boy, she noted his genius; "Lines to Mr. Walter Scott," which he found among his mother's papers, was presumed by him to be from AC. During the rebellion of 1745 AC supported the government and wrote a song on the Pretender's manifesto. She became a hostess, noted not for her lavishness but for the good company she provided. She was a stimulating conversationalist and letter writer. In old age she still charmed, and her auburn hair reminded onlookers of Queen Elizabeth. Walter Scott described her thus: "She was one of those persons whose talents for conversation made a stronger impression on her contemporaries than her writings can be expected to produce. . . . She maintained the rank in the society of Edinburgh which French women of talents usually do in that of Paris, and in her little parlour used to assemble a very distinguished and accomplished circle, among whom David Hume, John Horne, Lord Monboddo, and many other men of name were frequently to be found." Three playful and informal letters of AC are published in *Letters of Eminent Persons addressed to David Hume* (1849). All her life she wrote poetry, most of it unpublished. She was known mainly for the lyric "Flowers of the Forest," admired by Robert Burns, whom AC met in 1786, but two other songs of AC's, "A Copy of Verses wrote by Mrs. Cockburn on the back of a picture by Sir Hew Dalrymple" and "All health be round Balcarras board," occur in Johnson's *Scots Musical Museum.* AC's ballad "The Flowers of the Forest" differs from JEAN ELLIOT's more traditional lament in expressing individual feelings of melancholy. One of its four stanzas reads: "I've seen the smiling / Of Fortune beguiling; / I've felt all its favours, and found its decay; / Sweet was its blessing, / Kind its caressing; / But now it is fled—it is fled away." J.T.

COGHLAN, Margaret (1762?–1787), autobiographer, produced one of the 18th-century's more racy autobiographies. She was born in the US, the daughter of Major Thomas Moncrieffe and an English mother, whose maiden name was Margaret Heron. After her mother's early death MC and her brother were sent to boarding school in Dublin. She returned to the American colonies at about the age of nine. Although her father had married into a prominent American family, he remained in British service during the American Revolution. Young MC was for some months a genteel prisoner of war in New Jersey, where she was once pert to General Washington at dinner. Upon returning to her father, MC was persuaded at the age of 14 to marry the British lieutenant John Coghlan. Her husband soon returned to Britain with his wife, apparently treating her so badly— perhaps brutally—during the voyage that she ran away when they landed. She made her way to relatives, then sought protection at the home of Lord Thomas Clinton, who had been intimate with her friends in America. She became his mistress and passed on to a series of lovers that included Charles James Fox (by whom she claimed to have had a daughter), Lord John Augustus Hervey, and the Duke of York. MC died suddenly in 1787, but her *Memoirs* describes adventures in London and Paris until 1794, when she supposedly published them from debtors' prison. By 1795 the *Memoirs of Mrs. Coghlan, (Daughter of the Late Major Moncrieffe) Written by Herself, and Dedicated to the British Nation; Being Interspersed with Anecdotes of the Late American and Present French War; with Remarks Moral and Political* had gone through three British and two American printings. Possibly Charles Pigott, of *The Female Whig Club* fame, edited the *Memoirs* and composed the later chapters, but the sections of the book dealing with MC's lifetime appear to be reasonably authentic. The bitter remarks on the condition of women are consistent with her personal experiences: "My union with Mr. Coghlan I never considered in any other light, than an honourable prostitution, as I really *hated* the man whom they compelled me to marry."   G.T.P.

COKE, Lady Mary (1726–1811), journal writer, was the youngest daughter of John, Duke of Argyll and Greenwich, who had married the coarse and insensitive Jane Warburton. In the education of their daughters, the father took only enough interest to forbid their learning French, since he believed one language sufficient for a girl. Their mother had them taught writing and accounts by the steward, and needlework by a kind of governess. Despite her considerable intelligence, MC lacked education and her temper was spoiled by her father, who encouraged her violent furies; she was good-natured and charitable, but indulged in tantrums all her life and, according to

LADY LOUISA STUART, became such a "study for the observer of human character as a rare plant or animal would be for the naturalist." She had a handsome figure and agreeable smile, but, because of her white skin and lack of eyebrows, resembled a white cat. In 1747 she married the only son of the Earl of Leicester: Edward, Viscount Coke, a profligate who, annoyed by her premarital vanity and scorn, may never have consummated the marriage. His contemptuous neglect in the first year was followed by her virtual incarceration in Norfolk. As Lady Louisa noted, MC wished to be a heroine of high romance like Mary Queen of Scots. In Norfolk she remained in her room for months to emphasize her plight, while rumors of her intended assassination began to circulate. At last her mother obtained a writ of *habeas corpus;* she was produced in London and sued for divorce, eventually winning the suit although having to pay the costs. She retired on her pin money of £500 a year, despite the fortune of £20,000 she had brought her husband. When he died in 1753, she began to receive her jointure of £2,500 a year. The high drama she craved was next provided by her belief that she was loved by the Duke of York (1739–67), the youngest brother of George III. The relationship apparently began in 1756. The couple were friends, but the prince evidently mocked MC's delusions. To this obsession may probably be attributed her interest in history, genealogy, and etiquette. There were rumors that the couple were secretly married, and she displayed great grief on his death. During the rest of her long life MC never married, but retained her reputation as a great but quarrelsome authority on her particular subjects; she traveled much in Europe and was buried in the Argyll vault in the Chapel of Henry VII in Westminster Abbey.

The journals of MC were written as weekly or semiweekly letters to her sisters, Lady Dalkeith and Lady Strafford, from 1766 to 1785, and after Lady Strafford's death, to Lord Strafford from 1785 to 1791. With a few surviving letters of the period, the journals of 1766–74 were privately published by her family in four volumes in 1889; the journals of 1775–91 have not been published. In general MC reserved reverence for herself. On the Duke of York's death, she wrote of her meeting with Princess Amelia (October 1767): "'Wou'd you have married him?' I told H.R.H. that I never wish'd him to do anything that was likely to be to his disadvantage, & upon her insisting upon a more positive answer, I begged Her Royal Highness wou'd not press me any more, that I had never spoke freely upon that subject to any Mortal living." The dashing Miss Chudleigh in 1764 was mocked: "Miss Chudleigh is going to wash herself in the Bathes of Bohemia. They will be very famous if they can cleanse her from all her disorders. She sets out in february, & has, as the Town says, left the Duke of Kingston a Milliner that She found in Cranbourn Ally to supply her place during her Absence; but others say they have quarrel'd & that She leaves England on that account." MC was a close observer of, among others, the daughters of the Duke of Richmond: "They told me LY SARAH BUNBURY was come to Goodwood, & arrived the same day with the Corps of poor Ly Cecilia Lenox. LY HOLLAND said it was lucky for the late Duke & Duchess of Richmond that they cou'd not look out of their graves to see that sight" (Jan. 1770); and "The DUCHESS OF LEINSTER must fall in everyone else's opinion, & in a little time in her own; for however She may be blinded at present by the unhappy passion for an unworthy Object, time must convince her of the terrible impropriety of such a marriage. I pity her children" (Sept. 1774). B.R.

COLLIER, Jane (1709?–1754?), satirist, was born in Salisbury, the daughter of Arthur and Margaret Collier. Her father was a philosopher and rector of Langford Magna; she was the sister of Arthur and MAR-GARET COLLIER. Having lived beyond his means, the Rev. Collier sold his property, leaving his children to make their own way in the world. JC and Margaret were friends of SARAH FIELDING, who, with her brother Henry, invited the sisters to stay in London. The three women became friends and correspondents of Samuel Richardson, JC giving her comments on *Clarissa*. Richardson possibly provided lodgings for the Collier sisters; with him JC composed *An Essay on the Art of Ingeniously Tormenting; with Proper Rules for the Exercise of that Pleasant Art* (1753). With Sarah Fielding, JC wrote *The Cry: A New Dramatic Fable* (1754). According to ANNA LAETITIA BARBAULD (Richardson's *Correspondence*) she died poor.

The *Essay,* an often amusing catalogue of minor cruelties, is an early exercise in black comedy, the principle of which is "remember always to do unto every one, what you would least wish to have done unto yourself." It is divided into advice to those in power (parents, husbands, masters) and advice to those in subordinate positions (children, wives, servants). Among her suggestions to parents is the following: "On no account miss that useful season of the year the summer; in which you may give your children as much fruit as they can cram down their throats: then be sure not to contradict the poor little things, if they should choose to play about, and overheat themselves, in the middle of the day; and afterwards should choose to cool their limbs, by sprawling about on the wet grass, after the dew is fallen." *The Cry* is a piece of pseudo-dramatic prose that treats the conflict between truth and falsehood in a social scenario typical of the sentimental novel. The central characters are Portia, who recounts her life to the opposing ears of Una, a mock-Spenserian representation of Truth, and the Cry, which represents public opinion or people in general and is characterized as delighting in misfortune and scandal, raillery and the distortion of news, etc. Speeches are apportioned in the manner of drama, but extended passages of omniscient narration, which pose as the "chorus," give the work more the appearance of a novel. At one point Portia defines love as "A sympathetic liking, excited by fancy; directed by judgement; and to which is join'd also a most sincere desire of the good and happiness of its object. *Una* with a smile, stamp'd this definition with her own seal, which the *Cry,* by various inventions, vainly endeavour'd first to hinder, and then to make frustrate." Like the *Essay,* this is an unusual, if far from distinguished work. The character sketches suggest Sarah Fielding's style, while the satiric wit probably belongs to JC. *Monthly Review* (X, 1754) criticized *The Cry* for its heavy style and excessive use of narrative, but praised its content: "The sentiments are, generally, just; the passions drawn from nature; and the whole performance contains more . . . good sense, than, a few only excepted, all our modern novels put together. We write this with more pleasure, as we believe we are doing justice to the production of a lady." R.J.

COLLIER, Margaret (fl. 1735–57), letter writer,was the youngest of the children of the Salisbury philosopher the Rev. Arthur Collier and the younger sister of Arthur and JANE COLLIER. In Salisbury after

1732 the Collier family was befriended by the Fieldings when Collier senior died after financial losses. After 1745 Henry Fielding, left responsible for a £400 debt that Arthur Collier the younger refused to pay, hated even his name, but Fielding and SARAH FIELDING continued to befriend the two sisters, who were poor to the point of dependency. With SARAH FIELDING, they had become intimate with Richardson while he was writing *Clarissa* (all three were listed among the 36 examples of superior women which he sent to a friend in 1750), and by 1750 one of the Miss Colliers was living with him. MC's necessities made her artful, ingratiating, accommodating, and expert at arousing in others a sense of obligation. Not unnaturally, her first aim was to be invited to stay, her ultimate one to find a husband. In 1754 she accompanied Fielding, his wife and daughter on his final voyage to Lisbon. At the journey's outset the party stayed in Ryde on the Isle of Wight in an inn run by Mrs. Francis, with whom Fielding found much fault in his *Journal of a Voyage to Lisbon*, published posthumously in 1755. The party was also befriended in Ryde by a lady of substance, a Mrs. Roberts. In Lisbon, according to a letter sent by Fielding to his brother, MC caused him considerable distress by trying to attract a marriage proposal and scheming (when Mrs. Fielding wanted to return home) to fulfill her objective by remaining in Lisbon with Fielding in his wife's place. Fielding's death in October 1754 dashed her hopes. MC had been a witness to his will, is sometimes credited with having cut the paper silhouette that was the basis for Hogarth's drawing of Fielding, and may have assisted the blind John Fielding with the editing of the *Journal*. At about this period Jane Collier died, and MC retired to Ryde because of its cheapness; in her letters she made much of the friendship and patronage of Mrs. Roberts. A letter from Ryde (March 1755) details Mrs. Francis's rebuttal of Fielding's charges in the *Journal;* found among Richardson's papers, it is attributed on the cover to "Peggy Collier" (see *Library,* April 1917). Most disingenuous if MC's work, it betrays resentment against Fielding and no knowledge of his actual stay in Ryde. After 1755 MC lived in Ryde for several years at least.

From Ryde MC exchanged letters with Richardson, some of which are preserved in ANNA LAETITIA BARBAULD's edition of Richardson's correspondence. In October 1755 MC wrote quoting Ariosto, whom she had been reading, and described her lowly situation: "in my very poor house, sitting on my earthen floor, eating my dinner out of a platter, and my poor bedchamber without any door to it, and a little window peeping out from under the thatch, bare walls, and everything suitably poor." She went on: "I was forced to make a great slaughter, and lay about me prodigiously, before I could conquer those bitter enemies to peace and humility called passions; but now I think and hope they all lie dead in heaps at several places in London and elsewhere; and I brought down nothing with me but a bundle of mortifications." She claimed to be annoyed at the attribution of *Voyage to Lisbon* to her in Ryde (one suspects her hints may have contributed to the tale) and thought it due to its falling short of Fielding's usual standards: "If they [women] write well, and very ingeniously, and have a brother, then to be sure—'She could not write so well; it was her brother's, no doubt.'" But if a man wrote poorly, the work was attributed to a woman. MC's letter was designed to compel Richardson to invite her to London for the cold winter. He replied by advising her to conquer the last remnants of impatience in herself, and he sent her five guineas to pay for a bedchamber door. Taking up her remarks on women authors, he suggested that women were themselves to blame "as *degraders* of their own sex" for hiding their talents, by which they confess, indirectly, an inferiority. In reply MC was obliged to indicate spiritual superiority by showing satisfaction in her retreat (December 1755). In a letter of February 1756 MC commented feelingly on the plight of the superior woman: "You say (and truly) that there are little-minded creatures who would be afraid of such talents in their respective wives as would outshine themselves.—and again, ask if such girls would be afraid that *such men* should slight them? Why no, surely.—But O! Mr. Richardson (with a deep sigh I say it) that I never had heard men of real good sense, great parts, and many fine qualities, lower themselves down to these little-minded creatures, . . . and [shew] when they come to marry, that they are as much afraid of rivalship of understanding in their wives, as those men you mention." A final letter of February 1757 suggests that MC had been away from Ryde, perhaps in London. Her life probably continued poor, dependent, and embittered to its end. A.W.

COLLIER, Mary (fl. 1740–60), poet, is

described in the "Advertisement" to her first publication as a "Washer-Woman"; it states: "I think it no Reproach to the Author, whose life is toilsome, and her Wages inconsiderable, to confess honestly, that the view of her putting a small Sum of Money in her Pocket, as well as the Reader's Entertainment, had its Share of Influence upon this Publication." The title of this first work is *The Woman's Labour: An Epistle to Mr. Stephen Duck; In Answer to his late Poem, called The Thresher's Labour. To which are added, The Three Wise Sentences, Taken from The First Book of Esdras, Ch. III and IV* (1739). *The Woman's Labour* is a 246-line poem in which MC describes the daily tasks of women who work in the fields: "when we Home are come, / Alas! we find our Work has just begun." She reminds Duck that in the winter, "While you on easy Beds may lie and sleep," women frequently must rise before dawn to wash and clean in the homes of the wealthy. The thresher is fortunate by comparison: "For us, you see, but little Rest is found; / Our Toil increases as the Year runs round." MC later published *Poems on Several Occasions* (Winchester, 1762) and *The Poems of Mary Collier* (Petersfield, 1765?). Two works, "To a Friend in Affliction" and "Verses Addressed to Mrs. Digby," were included in vol. 2 of *The Lady's Poetical Magazine* (4 vols., 1781–82). J.F.

COLLYER, Mary (?–1763), novelist and translator, was born Mary Mitchell and married Joseph Collyer the elder, an editor and translator. She published a translation of Marivaux's *La vie de Marianne* as *The Virtuous Orphan: or, The Life of Marianne* in 1742; a 1746 edition appeared, with some changes, as *The Life and Adventures of Indiana.* Further editions of *The Virtuous Orphan* were published in 1747 and 1784. The translation often moves the Marivaux text toward the style and sentiments of Samuel Richardson, by whom MC was much influenced. MC also published *Felicia to Charlotte: Being Letters from a Young Lady in the Country, to her Friend in Town* (1744); written in typical sentimental style, it tells of the romantic adventures of Felicia: "Here I was going to fling out of the room, when a sudden glance in a moment dispelled my indignation; while Love, with all its humbling powers, took entire possession of my soul. I saw him with his eyes greedily fixed on me; they overflowed with a melting softness, and at the same time sparkling through the crystal swell with awful dignity,

seemed to express some great, hidden purpose." In the second volume Felicia is a married lady and changes accordingly: "You have no reason to expect any more romantick adventures. I have nothing more to do with the affecting scenes of fond distress, the pangs of jealousy, or the fears of incurring a father's displeasure." In 1761 MC published *The Death of Abel,* a translation of Salomon Gessner's *Der Tod Abels;* this translation had reached its 27th edition by 1786, and at least another 19 editions appeared before 1845. It is a dramatic sentimental rendering of the story of Cain and Abel in which Cain says to Adam: "I promise I will obey thee, and embrace my brother: but—while I breathe my firm soul will never be dissolved to that effeminate weakness, that so endears him to you, and makes your eyes run over with transport. To a softness like this we all owe the curse denounc'd against us, when in Paradise you weakly suffer'd yourself to be overcome by a woman's tears." After the murder Cain becomes a romantic outcast pondering God's motives: "Wherefore not annihilated me? that no traces of me might remain in the creation. Why was I not blasted by his lightnings? Why did not his thunder strike me to the depths of the earth?—But his ire reserves me for perpetual sufferings—torments without end—Detested by my fellow creatures—all nature abhors me—I abhor myself—." Before her death MC had translated part of Klopstock's *Messiah;* her husband completed the work, publishing vols. 1 and 2 late in 1763 and vol. 3 in 1772. J.F. and R. J.

CONOLLY, Lady Louisa (née Lady Louisa Augusta Lennox) (1743–1821), letter writer, was the third surviving daughter of Charles, second Duke of Richmond, descendant of Charles II, and Lady Sarah Cadogan, and one of a family of clever beauties. Orphaned at eight, she lived until she was 15 in Ireland with her sister the DUCHESS OF LEINSTER, and was then by the provision of her father's will to go to her sister Caroline (later LADY HOLLAND) in London for three years. But in Ireland the Duchess took her to visit Thomas Conolly's fine Castletown estate, and at 15 she married Conolly, the richest man in Ireland and grand-nephew of William Conolly, Speaker of the Irish House. The groom's lack of character dismayed his sisters-in-law, who hoped that his wife would not notice it; but if LC was unhappy she did not reveal it, and she faithfully looked after her ailing husband until his death in 1803. The couple, who settled in Ireland, never had children, but in 1784 LC adopted Emily Napier, the daughter of her sister LADY SARAH BUN-BURY. LC spent her life in entertaining at Castletown—in the gallery, where they principally lived, one could dine at one end undisturbed by music or amateur theatricals at the other—in cultivating and looking after her very numerous relatives, and in charities: she supported two industrial schools, one for each sex, in her own grounds, looked after a Female Charter school and a chip-hat manufactory, and was regarded with near-reverence by the local people. MARIA EDGEWORTH described her in 1815 as "the most respectable, amiable, and even at seventy . . . charming person I ever saw or heard."

LC's letters to her sister the Duchess of Leinster (ed. Brian Fitzgerald) were published by the Irish Manuscripts Commission (1957). They reveal at first an enthusiastic, carefree girl of 15 whose tact and forebearance are already apparent: "I must tell you of a thing I'm sure will divert you, and that is that Lady Coventry says she was vastly uneasy till she saw me for fear I should be too handsome; but that when she saw me she lifted up her hands and eyes to Heaven and said 'Well thank God! she is not near so handsome as Lady Kildare!'" By 1769, when the blow of Lady Sarah Bunbury's elopement fell, LC had matured into the family bulwark. "I am one of the most miserable creatures in the world, and my feelings under this misfortune are so different from what I ever felt under others. For where things afflict one by the hand of Providence, one has the satisfaction of knowing that all is for the best . . . But in this unhappy case . . . one has the misery of reflecting that it has all been brought on by human frailty and passion getting the better of every virtue in a disposition formed to be amiable . . . And yet I love her better than ever I did, or at least have discovered how much I love her." LC's reputation for thinking rightly, tolerantly, and independently on every subject is always borne out: "It is said that the King admires Mlle Heinel, and has a mind to have her for his mistress; but the Queen has taken fright about it, and prevailed on him not to go to the opera. The Dukes, his brothers, are angry with the Queen, as they think that the King's treatment of them is owing to her, and therefore are determined, whenever they can, to get him a mistress, to take him from under the Queen's influence. Poor little woman, think how barbarous they are to her! for she doats upon the King. I feel quite sorry at the plot they have against her, and hate them for it; for I should think her happiness with her husband they might let her enjoy, for her situation in other respects is not so very enviable" (1773). Her later letters are filled with her efforts to soothe the trouble ensuing from the Duchess's marriage to William Ogilvie, and to help establish Lady Sarah Bunbury on her remarriage to Col. George Napier. B.R.

CONWAY, Anne Finch, Viscountess (1631–79), philosopher, was born the daughter of Sir Henry Finch, Speaker of the House of Commons, a member of the same distinguished family into which the poet Anne Finch, COUNTESS OF WINCHILSEA, married in 1684. Although little is known of AC's early life, three aspects bear noting: for a girl of her period, she was remarkably learned, especially in philosophy; when aged 12, she began suffering the mysterious headaches that tormented her all her life; and her brother John introduced her to his teacher, the Neo-Platonist Henry More, whose enthusiasm for the Cabbala AC soon came to share. In 1651, at 19, she married and moved to her husband's estate at Ragley Hall, Warwickshire. By that time, her erudition was so marked that her father-in-law, Lord Conway, quipped that "you write like a man." Because of her health, AC lived in retirement, but she attracted to Ragley some of the most celebrated seekers of truth of her age, including More, Francis Mercury Van Helmont and, in her last years, the leading Quakers. The few surviving letters written by AC reveal a discerning, independent intellect. Her correspondence with More, which lasted from 1650 to her death, vividly demonstrates the mutual affection and esteem these two philosophers felt for each other, whether they were evaluating the system of Descartes, disparaging William Harvey's attempts to cure AC's headaches, or laughing at the eccentricity of the DUCHESS OF NEWCASTLE, who sent More a copy of her *Philosophical Letters* (1664) although More's ideas are attacked in it; in a letter to AC, More wishes AC were rid of her pain so that she could answer "this great Philosopher." In 1670, Van Helmont, "the scholar gypsy," came to Ragley to attempt a cure for AC's headaches and, finding a co-seeker of truth, stayed there for the rest of AC's life. Both eventually embraced Quakerism.

In 1690, Van Helmont had AC's notebook translated into Latin and published on the Continent; in 1692 it was retranslated into English and published as *The Principles of the Most Ancient and Modern Philosophy.* . . . In opposition to the mechanists, AC proposes a vitalistic universe in which every creature has an inner motion by which it strives, according to its own degree, toward greater perfection. Given her philosophical orientation, it is no wonder that AC was attracted to the Quaker belief in the Inner Light. *Principles* denies Cartesian dualism, arguing that spirit and body do not differ essentially: "Body is nothing but a fixed and condensed Spirit and a Spirit nothing but a subtile and volative Body." Although AC uses the traditional analogy, at least as old as Aristotle, that the spirit is the active male principle and the body, the passive female one, she transforms the analogy by making the difference a matter of degree (only "more active"), by elevating matter to spirit's partner in seeking perfection, and by emphasizing cooperation, rather than subordination, as the essential characteristic of life (her mother Substance cocreates with God the Father). AC's great admirer, Leibnitz, wrote that his aim closely resembled hers in trying to reconcile Plato and Democritus; like AC, he held that "every thing takes place according to a living principle and according to final causes—all things are full of life and consciousness, contrary to the views of the Atomists." In AC's system, "perfectability of man," a species-centered notion, is replaced by the holistic "perfectability of all creation," or, as AC puts it, reinforcing her reasoning with biblical authority, Jesus says, "God is able of stones to raise up Children of Abraham." S.B.

COOPER, Elizabeth (fl. 1735–40), anthologist and playwright, was married some time before 1735 to Thomas Cooper, who was either an auctioneer or a bookseller, or possibly both, and left a widow. Beyond this, only a few facts are known about her life. She was apparently a well-read, competent researcher, with an unusual and independent taste in poetry, and a vivacious, attractive woman with some knowledge of the stage and some talent for acting. EC's first work was a comedy, *The Rival Widows: or, Fair Libertine.* Staged at Covent Garden in March 1735, it had a successful run of nine nights and was published later in the

year. EC herself, on her benefit night(s?), played the lead role of Lady Bellair, a spirited, sophisticated young widow "capable of thinking for herself and acting on the Principles of Nature and Truth" (according to the preface). The play contains witty dialogue and amusing incidents in a unified plot that sets three pairs of characters against each other; it draws points about moral and social behavior without sentimentalizing. EC's second play, "The Nobleman" (a tragedy), was acted only once, at the Haymarket in May 1736, and was never printed. She is best known for compiling and editing an anthology of English poetry entitled *The Muses' Library* (1737; reissued 1741), a notable scholarly work of about 400 pages presenting poems by English writers from Edward the Confessor and Thomas Langland through the 16th century to Spenser and Daniel. In her preface she declares several aims: to memorialize some worthy but neglected authors, to provide the public with some generally unknown and unavailable works, to trace the progress of English literature, and to record the growth of the English language from its early "Gothique Rudeness." This book, in which she was aided to some extent by the antiquarian William Oldys, expands upon the researches of several other literary biographers such as Edward Phillips, William Winstanley, and Giles Jacob, and correct errors they had made. EC projected further volumes of *The Muses' Library* and also a history of English criticism, but possibly because this first volume met with little financial success, nothing more appeared. It has been credited with influencing Thomas Chatterton in his conception of the poems he attributed to Thomas Rowley. D.W.M.

COVENTRY, Anne, Countess of (1673–1763), religious writer, was the daughter of Henry Somerset, Duke of Beaufort, and his wife Mary, widow of Lord Beauclerk. C of C married Thomas, Earl of Coventry, who died in 1710, followed by their son in 1712. After 1726 she lived in Snittersfield, Warwickshire, where she died, having become notable for her charity and piety. Her friend Richard Jago, vicar of Snittersfield, preached a biographical sermon after her death; it was printed in 1763 and entitled *The Nature of a Christian's Happiness in Death. The Right Hon. Anne, Countess of Coventry's Meditations and Reflections, Moral and Divine,* was published in 1707; it is divided into several short sections and consists of prayers, aphorisms, and pious and philosophical thoughts. Section 1, for example, includes her saying, "Self-conceit is self deceit" and her musings on sin: "The sins of the saints are set down in scripture, not for our warrent, but for our caution; that we may not make too bold with temptation. For the pleasures of sin do appear with such irresistible charm (to them that are deluded by it) that many have been betray'd to do things criminal, which they never thought to have done." Section 59 discusses the ease of controlling speech but the greater difficulty of regulating thoughts: "experience tells us that tis next to impossible to be wholly quit of two sorts of thoughts—the first are, evil imaginations, and all impurities; the second are trifling and idle impertinences." C of C is much concerned with the afterlife and with the world as a preparation for it, and she continually justifies human suffering as necessary to the divine scheme and beneficial to humanity: "It is just from God that great sinners should be great sufferers." Her aim in times of misery is, she asserts, "perfect submission to divine Providence."   J.T.

COWLEY, Hannah (1743–1809), playwright and poet, was born in Tiverton, Devon. Her interest in writing was encouraged by her father, Philip Parkhouse, a bookseller who had been educated for the clergy, and perhaps by the fact that John Gay was a cousin of her paternal grandmother. Nothing is known of her early life. In 1772 she married Thomas Cowley, a newspaper writer and clerk in the Stamp Office, and moved to London, where she bore him at least three children. Probably out of financial necessity, her husband in 1783 went to India with the East India Company and remained there until his death in 1797. Except for a possible visit to India and a year spent in France, HC remained in London, caring for her family and writing for the stage. Her career began in 1776 and continued for 18 years with popular success and moderate financial gain. She is said to have had many friends, not including HANNAH MORE, whom she attacked in print for allegedly plagiarizing from her tragedy *Albina.* In 1801 she retired to Tiverton. In the preface to her *Works,* her biographer emphasizes her religious nature and concern for family, and also makes the incredible claims that she seldom read or attended the theater.

HC wrote 13 plays, 11 of which, corrected during her retirement, appear as volumes I and II of her *Works* (1813). Her comedies excel in witty, effortless dialogue and avoid the sentimental excess characteristic of much comedy of the period. The characters are mannered stereotypes, but she gives them life, especially her spirited, determined young heroines; the plays treat the problems of courtship, satirize affectation, and laud England. They stress the importance of the husband's loving, respecting, and trusting his wife, and of the wife's living up to the image of the fine lady: "She is a creature for whom nature has done much, and education more; she has taste, elegance, spirit, understanding. In her manner she is free, in her morals nice. Her behaviour is undistinguishingly polite to her husband, and all mankind;—her sentiments are for their hours of retirement. [She] is the life of conversation, the spirit of society, the joy of the public!" HCs two tragedies are wooden and tedious period pieces that reward virtue and punish injustice. In addition, HC wrote poetry, most notably several long narrative romances published during her lifetime and collected in volume III of *Works.* Also, as "Anna Matilda" she carried on a poetical correspondence in *The World* with "Della Crusca" (Robert Merry) that was satirized by William Gifford in his *Baviad* and *Maeviad.* Her finest works were her comedies— for example *The Runaway* (her first, 1776), *Who's the Dupe?* (1779), *The Belle's Stratagem* (1780), and *Which Is the Man?* (1782)—which were popular in her own time and beyond, as demonstrated in reviews in *London Magazine, London Review, Critical Review,* and *Westminster Magazine;* they constitute a dramatic oeuvre unmatched before her time by any woman except APHRA BEHN.   D.W.M.

COWPER, Maria Frances Cecilia (1726–97), poet, eldest daughter of JUDITH MADAN and Colonel Martin Madan, Equerry to the Prince of Wales, sister to the Rev. Martin Madan and Spencer Madan, Bishop of Peterborough, was born at Hertingfordbury Park. Because of her weak eyes, she was sent to school to a female oculist at Gravesend. She learned French and acted in Racine's *Athalie* with such success that she longed to be an actress. At home, her father taught her to read Fénélon and Le Sage, while her distinguished mother directed her to worthwhile English literature, like the *Spectator,* the *Guardian,* and ELIZABETH ROWE. MC and her sister Penelope became well-known beauties and toasts of society. In 1749 she married her cousin, Major

William Cowper of the Park House, Hertingfordbury, by whom she had seven children. "Good Maria," as her father called her, became fervently evangelical, corresponding with her poet cousin William Cowper on religious and domestic topics. In 1765 she recorded for posterity one of John Wesley's sermons. Many of her letters survive; her verse was revised by Cowper and published as *Original Poems on Various Occasions* (1792), going through three editions in London, two in Philadelphia, and one in Newark (1808). Her work is like the fervid and melancholy *Night Thoughts* of Edward Young; her themes are bodily affliction, the transitoriness of human life, the pleasures of retirement, and the divine scheme of justice: "Slave to the wretched world's imposing forms, / See Sacharissa deck'd in gold brocade; / She owns that grandeur has no real charms, / And sighs for virtue in the sylvan shade." J.H.

COWPER, Mary, Countess (1685–1723?), court diarist, was born the daughter of John Clavering, Esq., of Chopwell, Co. Durham. She grew up under the influence of her family's strong Jacobite sentiments but apparently abandoned them on her marriage to William, the first Earl Cowper, in 1706. The marriage was kept a secret for several months. For many years MC corresponded with the DUCHESS OF MARLBOROUGH, and with Caroline of Anspach. When the latter went to England as the Princess of Wales, MC was named Lady of the Bedchamber. Her beauty was much admired in the court of George I and she inspired verses written by Earl Rivers in the *History of the Kit Kat Club*. In 1723, after her husband was implicated (apparently erroneously) in a Jacobite conspiracy, MC destroyed parts of her own *Diary*, fearing that her record of court life might prove embarrassing or dangerous. Lady Sarah, her daughter, insisted that MC died of a "broken heart" only four months after her husband's death.

MC began her *Diary* about the time of George I's accession to the throne; it was edited in 1864 by Spencer Cowper. The surviving section of the *Diary* carefully records the period from October 1714 to October 1716 and then breaks off until 1720, when a "rough and fragmentary Document is appended." The *Diary* opens with an explanation of MC's purpose: "The perpetual Lies that One hears have determined me, in spite of my Want of Leisure, to

write down all the Events that are worth remembering whilst I am at *Court;* and although I find it will be impossible for me to do this daily, yet I hope I shall be able to have an Hour or two once a Week: and I intend this only for my own Use, it being a rough Draft only, which, if *God* bless me with Health and Leisure, I intend hereafter to revise and digest into a better Method." The first portion of the *Diary* recounts events at court during the rebellion of 1715. Much of the later part of her *Diary* (which was destroyed) seems to have included information on a quarrel between George I and the Prince of Wales. Although the material is both entertaining and historically valuable, MC never had a chance to revise her *Diary,* and the style remains rough. M.A.B.

CROCKER, Hannah Mather (1752–1829), American memoirist, poet, and polemicist, lived in Boston all her life in the house where she was born. She was the youngest of the seven children of the Rev. Samuel Mather (1706–65), grandson of the famous Puritan Cotton Mather. Hannah (Hutchinson) Mather, her mother, was the sister of the governor of the colony. HMC was given only a limited education. As she wrote later, it was thought adequate at the time "if women could even read and badly write their name." In 1779 she married Joseph Crocker, a Harvard graduate and captain in the army of the Revolution. They raised ten children, and he also lived in the Mather home until he died in 1797.

HMC, a Federalist, was interested in public affairs. In her first publication, in a newspaper of 1810, she defended the Masons against public criticism of their behavior at lodge meetings. She mentioned that she herself had founded a women's lodge in 1778 from a group of friends studying languages, and urged others to form such societies to improve their minds. This tract was published in book form as *A Series of Letters on Free Masonry by a Woman of Boston* (1815). The Rev. Thaddeus Mason Harris, chaplain of the Mass. grand lodge, wrote the preface. HMC maintained that the autumn of one's life, "when child-rearing duties are past," was the time to harvest one's thoughts "for the improvement of the rising generation." With similar didactic intentions, she urged sailors to temperance in *The School of Reform or the Seaman's Safe Pilot to the Cape of Good Hope (1816)*. HMC naively assumed that sailors would reform "if the necessity of a regular course of living was pointed out to them in a pleasant manner by a female." HMC's *Observations on the Real Rights of Women with their appropriate duties, agreeable to Scripture, reason, and common sense* (1818) was dedicated to HANNAH MORE and published by subscription. She mentioned as exemplars of strong women such Americans as MERCY WARREN and SARAH WENTWORTH MORTON. She believed that MARY WOLLSTONECRAFT'S *Vindication* (1792) went too far in its assertion of women's independence, although she felt that it was "replete with fine sentiments." HMC urges equal education for women, but advocates subordinate roles for them: "For the interest of their country, or in the cause of humanity, we shall strictly adhere to the principle and the impropriety of females ever trespassing on masculine ground: as it is morally incorrect and physically improper." Perhaps because of such clumsy prose, the book failed to gain an audience. In her 70s, HMC worked on "Interesting Memoirs and Original Anecdotes of Boston history," now in the New England Historic and Genealogical Society in manuscript. She also penned occasional verse to her friends, which was never published.   R.R.

CROFTS, Jane (fl. 1800), wrote *The History of Jenny Spinner, The Hertfordshire Ghost* (1800). This is ostensibly an autobiography and claims that JC was imprisoned and taken for a ghost by local people. The work is unusual in its account of the life of a young girl in service and in its focus on the sexual pressures exerted on women by upper-class men: "'Oh Jenny,' said Anthony, 'how differently we feel! A prison would be a palace to me if you were to be my gaoler.' 'Oh! the goodness of the best man that ever was born would not make up to me for the loss of my liberty.'"   L.F.

D

DAMER, Anne Seymour (1748–1828), novelist, was the only child of Field Marshal Henry Seymour Conway and his wife, Lady Caroline Campbell. Her childhood was enriched by close contacts with David Hume, whose teasing led her to take up sculpture, and Horace Walpole, who eventually made her his executrix and left her the use of his estate, Strawberry Hill, for life. Her education included lessons in art, sculpture, and anatomy; later in life she learned Latin, Greek, French, and Italian. In 1767 she married John Damer, the eldest son of Lord Milton. Nine years later, after he and his brothers had contracted a debt of £70,000, he killed himself. AD was left with a comfortable jointure of £2,500 a year. Thereafter she devoted herself chiefly to travel, politics, and her sculpture, for which she was best known and which was of museum quality. She assisted the DUCHESS OF DEVONSHIRE in canvassing for Charles James Fox during the famous Westminster election of 1780, and she knew both Napoleon and Admiral Nelson.

AD's three-volume novel *Belmour* was published by Joseph Johnson in 1801, during a period in her life when she produced MARY BERRY'S comedy *Fashionable Friends,* administered Walpole's estate, and visited the First Consul in Paris. Although conventional, the novel's plot and execution are above the average, and some boldly Whiggish political passages and a quantity of French conversations distinguish the work from the ordinary hack publications. The plot deals with star-crossed lovers who eventually overcome all obstacles to obtain happiness. Belmour, the central character, is a young, well-educated aristocrat. He first falls in love with an artful young lady already married to an elderly titled gentleman. When the scales fall from his eyes, he turns to the virtuous Emily. Although Emily returns his affection, she is already betrothed to another and sends Belmour away. Finally, of course, they are free to marry—"a bright example of that reward, which bounteous Heaven can alone bestow on virtue, constancy, and truth." While the novel is not autobiographical, a number of passages appear to reflect AD's own experiences. Her own tragic marriage and considerable record of personal achievement lend sincerity to the urging of "sound principles of religion, virtue, and philosophy." *Belmour*'s praises of Voltaire, Rousseau, and Hume during the height of the anti-Jacobin reaction show the depth of her commitment to the liberal principles of the Enlightenment. AD was not, however, deeply influenced by radical politics or the feminism of MARY WOLLSTONECRAFT, her contemporary; and the novel's emphasis on marital fidelity and control of the passions implicitly combats the new philosophies.   G.T.P.

D'ANVERS, Alicia (possibly a pseudonym) (fl. 1671–93), poet, has left no information about her personal life. It seems likely that for a considerable period she resided in Oxford. Her first effort, *A Poem upon His Sacred Majesty, his Voyage for Holland: by way of Dialogue between Belgia and Britannia,* was published in London in 1671. *Academia: or, The Humours of the University of Oxford. In Burlesque Verse* (1691; republished 1716) is a satire in Hudibrastics; it begins with a mock-serious dedication to "Great Britain's Pride" and declares the author's aim is to raise smiles and please herself. The opening lines of the actual poem declare: "I intend to give you a Relation / As prime as any in the Nation: / The name of the Place is—let me see, / Call'd most an end the 'Versity; / In which same Place, as Story tells, / Liv'd once Nine handsome bonny Girls. . . ." The girls (the Muses) are beaten, mauled, reviled, and pinched: "All these, and twenty more Abuses / Are daily offer'd to the Muses . . . / You may perceive, I'm mightily / Disturb'd, they're us'd so spitefully; / And must confess, there's no denying, / That I can hardly hold from crying; / But that I mayn't be seen to bellow, / Like Girl forsaken by a Fellow . . . / I'll lay aside my Bowels yearning, / And talk of Scholars, and their Learning." Through the eyes of an ingenue in Oxford, AD characterizes various loutish scholars and graceless aspects of the university and blames the frequent "over-dulness" on "over fulness." AD's final poem, *The Oxford-Act,* was published in 1693.   C.R.

DARWALL, Mary [Whateley] (fl. 1764–94), poet, came from a well-known Birmingham family. After her marriage to the Rev. Randle Darwall she lived in Walsall. Although she termed herself a "Stranger to classic Eloquence," having been denied a learned education, she saw her *Original Poems on Several Occasions* published (twice) by Dodsley in 1764; she dedicated the volume to Lady Wrottesly. Lord Dartmouth stood patron for her subscription list, which contains the names of MARY DELANY and ELIZABETH CARTER. MD's *Poems on Several Occasions* appeared in 1794, *The Storm and Other Poems* in 1811, and her "Ode to May" in *London Magazine* for July 1764. A few pieces from *Original Poems* were printed later in *Collection of Poems* in the *Lady's Poetical Magazine.* MD's poems were not written for publication and she had no great ambitions. Themes of "Friendship, Gratitude, and native Freedom of Fancy" result in addresses to her future husband, repudiations of "Female Toys" in favor of "th' immortal Mind," and a tart explanation for the frivolity of women: "Since Woman's Happiness depends on Man; / 'Tis easy to conclude where first began / This Group of Follies, that o'er-spread the Earth: / From our wise *Lords* they first receiv'd their Birth." MD praises rural and contemplative life and insists on the divine in nature, "th' Eternal Cause thro' all his works, / Minutely and magnificently wise." John Langhorne called *Original Poems* "more correct than the literary productions of Ladies in general" and associated the author with ELIZA-

BETH CARTER (*Monthly Review* 30, 1764). William Shenstone, who helped MD publish, thought "many of the pieces written in an excellent and truly classical style; simple, sentimental, harmonious, and more correct than I almost ever saw written by a lady."   J.H. and J.F.

DAVIES, Arabella (1753–87), letter writer and diarist, was the daughter of Richard and Eleanor Jenkinson of Hoxton. Her upbringing nurtured the religion that is central to her writing. Handling her father's correspondence during her early years may have encouraged her interest in writing. In 1774 AD married Edward Davies, the rector of Coychurch, a widower with four children. She died during childbirth. AD's *Letters from a Parent to her Children* (1788), collected after her death by her husband, is concerned almost completely with religious piety. The more interesting *Diary* (1788) is a spiritual autobiography covering a period of about 20 years, beginning at the age of fourteen; it reveals a life spent preparing for death, which AD calls the "great change." Although devout, AD continually agonizes over the uncertainty of salvation: "I now view how great, how vast a thing it is to be a Christian. O the various windings of error, and the constant and deep artifice of Satan! the storms within, and tempests without! O God, teach my soul knowledge. The dulness of the scholar requires the daily severity of the rod. . . . May the most horrid and tormenting trial pain my soul, rather than my grand enemy be suffered to whisper Peace, peace, when the Lord says there is no peace!" When mourning the death of her youngest child, AD writes: "The dread and terror lest our children should live in sin, and be volunteers to Satan, reconcile me to their early departure. Should the Lord spare, to bless with his grace, the enjoyment is great and pleasing." Apparently AD also kept a journal, now lost, in which she recorded journeys taken with her husband.   M.A.B.

DAVYS, Mary (1674–1732), novelist and playwright, was the wife of the Rev. Peter Davys, master of the Free School of St. Patrick's, Dublin; the couple were friends of Swift. After the death of her husband in 1698, MD emigrated to York and then moved to Cambridge, where she established a coffee-house and became part of an intellectual circle.

  MD's first published efforts, *The Amours of Alcippus and Lucippe* (1704) and *The*

Fugitive (1705), were conventional tales of thwarted love, revenge, and poetic justice; they met with little success. Her 1716 play, *The Northern Heiress, or the Humours of York,* was performed three times at Lincoln's Inn Fields. It attacks materialistic marriages and turns upon a stale trick: the heiress pretends to have lost a fortune in order to test her fiancé's devotion. After eight years of silence, MD published *The Reform'd Coquet* (1724); its subscription list included the names of Bishop Burnet, John Gay, and Pope, and it went through seven editions by 1760. The hero disguises himself as an elderly tutor to test the heroine's merit, and the novel combines a series of adventures with a firm focus on the heroine's maturation. In the next year, MD published her two-volume *Works,* which included her earlier pieces and *The Lady's Tale,* an early version of *The Amours; The Cousins,* a love story she would expand into *The False Friend* (1732); *The Modern Poet,* an ironic picture of the poverty-stricken, professionally jealous poet; *The Self-Rival: A Comedy As it should have been Acted at the Theatre Royal in Drury-Lane; The Merry Wanderer,* anecdotes from a series of houses visited; and *Familiar Letters Betwixt a Gentleman and a Lady.* MD insists her novels were intended to "restore the Purity and Empire of Love," and the *Familiar Letters* (and most of the other novels) stress the necessity of friendship and respect preceding romantic love and marriage. Her final original novel, *The Accomplish'd Rake* (1727), satirizes the fashionable pastimes and vices of the London leisure class. MD's plays and novels depend upon the conventional plots, characters, and themes of her time. She was particularly skilled, however, at providing a strong plot to frame didactic or amusing digressions, and she sometimes showed considerable talent for satire. In an incident from *The Merry Wanderer,* which is tantalizingly similar to those involving Swift's Yahoos, a man offers an Irish girl a shilling to show him one of the "wild Irish" who have long tails and are covered with hair. The girl replies, "I was just such a thing as you speak of, and going one day a little farther than I should have done, I was catch'd in a Net with some other Vermin, which the *English* had spread on purpose for us; and when they had me, they cut off my Tail, and scalded me like a Pig, till all my Hair came off." The credulous man asks to see where her tail was cut off, but she declines

"for it would not be decent." In a sterner mode, the character in *The Accomplish'd Rake* takes revenge on Gaylove, the man who has debauched his sister, by tricking him into sleeping with a woman with venereal disease. MD's works draw less from satirists than from Addison, Steele, Congreve, women's periodicals (such as ELIZA HAYWOOD's *The Female Spectator),* and novels made up of tales held loosely together by a love story (such as PENELOPE AUBIN's *The Life of Charlotta Du Pont* and JANE BARKER's *The Patchwork Screen,* both 1723). P.R.B.

DAWE, Anne (fl. 1770), novelist, published *The Younger Sister: or, History of Miss Somerset* (1770), an epistolary social comedy in the sentimental mode. It concerns the fortunes of the heroine, who, under the care of a cruel sister, is given the choice of marrying a man she detests or living with her equally distateful aunt. She chooses the latter, from which decision her trials develop. The characters are stereotypes and the language conventionally inert. The familiar theme of threatened modesty and honor often appears as little more than titillation, as when the heroine's friend tells of an intruder in her bedroom: "After a long time spent in useless disquiet, I began to undress myself, and going to the closet to hang up my gown, I perceived something shine on the floor, when stooping down to see what it was, I perceived a man's foot, which made me give a violent shriek, and instantly Mr. Fenton appeared from behind a heap of gowns, saying, with a loud laugh, Ha! have I frightened you?" Although it found nothing else complimentary to say about the novel, *Critical Review* (Aug. 1770) remarked that "there is *a good deal of business* in it. There is indeed much contrivance discoverable throughout, and the denouement is conducted with no small ingenuity." R.J.

DAY, Eliza (1734?–?), poet, published late in a long life. Her grandfather, Maximilian Crosland, although educated at Eton for the Church, retired to the country to farm at Weybridge. Her father later rented two farms nearby. ED's "Short Sketch of the Former Part of the Author's Life" is a sentimental elegy for her rural childhood. Of the larger part of her life nothing can be discovered, except that she married Thomas Day (d. 1807). In 1789, in her mid-50s, she published *Thoughts Occasioned by the Death* *of Maria; Who Departed this Life, August 8, 1788* and *Serious Reflections on the Death of Johannes, Who was shot by his Friend, July 12, 1789*, two poems in heroic couplets. In 1798 *Poems on Various Subjects* appeared, while a completely new volume of *Poems on Various Subjects, with Several Pieces on the Death of Relatives and Friends, Written During the Last Fifty-Seven Years of the Author's Life*, was published in 1814. In the preface of this last book ED speaks of being in her 80th year, and of the illness which seems to have dogged her in old age. During the later years of her life she appears to have lived in Surrey, to which references abound in her poetry. A Methodist, she declares in 1814 that she is now divided in "nonessentials" from the creed and cannot approve all Wesley's "sentiments." ED's first two poems of 1789 celebrate the divine mercy granted to a penitent sinner. The 1798 volume contains mostly memorial and epistolary verses, odes, and moral-personificatory poems such as "On Friendship": "Love is a transient flame at best, / As vivid lightnings glaring fly; / And must with friendship quickly rest, / Or soon with cold indifference fly." The 1814 *Poems* contains more occasional and lyric pieces, including ten separate poems on "Affliction": "Feeble and faint, and worn by long disease, / No more on earth I'd seek myself to please." The poem "On John Wesley's recovery from a Dangerous Illness" reveals concern for the "starving poor," while her long "Poem on the Proclamation of Peace" (1814) celebrates a providential intervention in history: God's power "hath quell'd the haughty Tyrant's rage, / Who did the nations of the earth engage / In horrid wars." ED's work is well intentioned but lifeless, the imposition of crude metrical form on unimpeachable Christian sentiments.   R.J.

DEFLEURY, Maria (fl. 1781–91), poet and polemicist, participated in Dissenting political and theological controversies and produced a quantity of inspirational prose and poetry. Internal evidence indicates an unmarried woman with deep affection for a brother and a sister (who died young), modest economic circumstances, Baptist religious affiliation, familiarity with the classics, and residence in London. Among her acquaintances were the well-known Dissenting clergymen John Towers and John Ryland, both of whom wrote prefaces for her works. MD's dozen publications range from poetry and pamphlets to a collected volume. Her talents for vigorous and correct verse were

employed in religious polemic, such as the *Unrighteous Abuse Detected and Chastised* (2nd ed. 1781) (directed against the militant Protestant Association), and in conventional inspirational poetry, such as *Henry, or the Triumph of Grace* (1781). A few lines from *Henry* show its quality: "And high enthron'd, from clouds emerg'd the moon, / Walking in brightness through the spangled arch, / Dispers'd the darkness with her lucid rays, / And tipp'd the hills with silver." In the late 1780s MD entered into a lengthy theological controversy with the Rev. William Huntington, S.S., an eccentric evangelical and antinomian, in which she eventually produced five pamphlets. In 1790 she published a poem celebrating the French Revolution, *British Liberty Established, and Gallic Liberty Restored*. Contemporary critics held mixed opinions of MD's efforts. The *Analytical Review* (9, 1791; 12, 1792) and *Critical Review* (1, 1791) considered her controversial prose style overzealous and violent. The *Critical Review* (10, 1794), however, warmly praised her *Divine Poems and Essays* as showing "a fertile and vigorous imagination, and . . . a very considerable portion of poetic expression."   G.T.P.

DELANY, Mary [Pendarves] (1700–88), letter writer, was the daughter of Bernard Granville, of a prominent West Country Tory and royalist family. She was sent to court at an early age, but the death of Queen Anne shattered the family's hopes. Her father was briefly arrested, along with his brother Lord Lansdowne and other office holders from the Queen's last ministry. After his release, Lansdowne settled at Longleat; MD was sent there by her parents, then living in Gloucestershire, to break up what they regarded as an unsuitable romance. Lansdowne arranged for the marriage of his niece to Alexander Pendarves, a wealthy but generally disagreeable Cornish landholder of nearly 60. After the marriage in 1718 the couple lived mostly in Cornwall. Pendarves's temper did not improve; he was, according to MD, extremely jealous of anyone who paid attention to her, and by 1720 he had begun to drink heavily again after two years of relative sobriety. He died suddenly in 1725, leaving his wife with no income but her marriage settlement, but in other respects better off.

MD settled in London where she became a member of court and aristocratic social circles, and where she enjoyed a long flirtation with Lord Baltimore. In the early 1730s she made a protracted visit to Ireland

and met Swift, who became one of her correspondents. In England her friends were drawn from the various aristocratic families with which she was connected, as well as from musical, artistic, and literary circles. Her closest friend was Margaret Cavendish Harley, Duchess of Portland, with whom she frequently stayed at Bulstrode, Berks. The ladies enjoyed all sorts of books, handicrafts, botanizing, and shell and fowl collecting. It was to MD that Mrs. Chapone, an old friend (mother-in-law of HESTER MULSO CHAPONE) appealed when she found ELIZABETH ELSTOB, the Anglo-Saxon scholar, living in poverty. MD persuaded the Duchess to make Elstob governess to the Bentinck children; she died in this position at Bulstrode. In 1743 MD married Dr. Patrick Delany, an Irish Anglican clergyman, widower, and Dean of Down. The marriage was a happy one; the couple lived primarily in Ireland but with long visits to England, where they stayed with family and friends, in lodgings in London, and at Bath. Dr. Delany died at Bath in 1768. MD thereafter established a residence in London, although she continued to spend much time at Bulstrode. In London she and the Duchess of Portland were part of the Bluestocking circle, often visiting the salons of ELIZABETH MONTAGU, FRANCES BOSCAWEN, and others. In this period MD became acquainted with many younger women writers, including FANNY BURNEY and HANNAH MORE. She was an active copier of paintings and also developed her own art form, which she called paper mosaic. She cut, without patterns, parts of flowers and plants from various colored paper and pasted the whole together, to make a lifelike botanic specimen. The manuscript volumes of this work are now in the British Library. Through the Duchess she became well acquainted with the royal family, who often came to Bulstrode for tea. After the Duchess's death in 1785, George III gave MD a pension and a "grace and favour" house at Windsor. She lived there until her death, as intimate a friend of the royal family as court etiquette allowed. Although MD knew almost every major literary figure in London or Ireland from Swift through Edmund Burke, she had no intellectual pretentions or ambitions. By the standards of her day she was well educated; she read French and some Italian, but not Latin. She was acquainted with Handel from the time he came to England; one of her brothers was

his patron. She always attended the performances of his oratorios in London and Dublin; when she was at Windsor, George III had his band play Handel's music for her. Another brother was a patron of Rousseau during his stay in England, although MD did not approve of many of his ideas. She was respected by all who met her for her charm, intelligence, and warm interest.

MD was a constant and superb letter writer, a sort of domestic Horace Walpole, although her letters were not as planned as his. She did not often discuss politics and was always loyal to the government in office. Her primary correspondents were her family, beginning with her sister Ann Dewes. After Ann Dewes's death in 1761, her daughter Mary Port and Mary's daughter (later Mrs. Waddington) were the focus of their aunt's affection and correspondence. She also wrote to a large group of friends of both sexes, describing her life, reading, hobbies, and other matters of largely domestic and personal interest. She often commented on problems faced by young women who were forced to marry, no doubt a reflection of her own earlier experience. For example, in 1752 she wrote: "Happy indeed is the woman who *has* a conscientious and reasonable companion: without truth and virtue there is no real happiness: other desirable accomplishments are additions that are very agreeable, but to be possessed of both the good and the agreeable is an extraordinary share of good fortune. So circumstanced the common casualties of life (in marriage) are supportable, but otherwise intolerable." She was a great admirer of Samuel Richardson's works, but she wrote: "You asked me what I thought of Sir Charles Grandison consenting to have his daughters bred papists? Why I think it the only blot in Sir Charles's character. Had a woman written the story, she would have thought the *daughters of as much consequence as the sons,* and when I see Mr. Richardson I shall call him to account for that fauxpas; but on the whole it is a most excellent book, calculated to please and improve all ages." Some of MD's letters, mainly from her residence at Windsor, were published as *Letters from Mrs. Delany . . . to Mrs. Frances Hamilton* in 1820. Her *Autobiography and Correspondence* was published in six volumes in 1861 and 1862, edited by Lady Llanover, the daughter of Mrs. Waddington.   B.B.S

DEVERELL, Mary (1737?–?), essayist, poet, and sermon writer, was born near Minchin

Hampton, Glouc., into the large family of a clothier. She read voraciously, later earning general admiration for her extensive learning. At the suggestion of friends she began writing individual sermons which were published as a group in 1774. Apparently remaining unmarried, MD spent much time in Gloucestershire, although she probably lived for a period in London. She seems to have been accepted by London society and the literary community. Dr. Johnson, HANNAH MORE, Mrs. Siddons, and HESTER THRALE were numbered among her subscribers, and she found patrons in the Rt. Hon. Edward Stratford and the Duchess of Rutland.

Her collection, *Sermons* (1774), was popular among the gentry and clergy and went through several reprints. *Miscellanies in Prose and Verse* (1781), the product of a long illness, offers a variety of essays and poems "particularly calculated for the improvement of younger minds." Portions of her *Miscellanies* were later reprinted, along with other essays by HANNAH MORE, as *The Ladies' Literary Companion* (1792), a book intended for "American ladies." In "On Marriage" MD offers advice to young women: "To the moment of your marriage it is your reign; your lover is proud to oblige you, watches your smiles, is obedient to your commands, anxious to please you, and careful to avoid every thing you disapprove; but you have no sooner pronounced that harsh word *obey,* than you give up the reins, and it is his turn to rule so long as you live. Then it is that he, very justly expects an adequate return; and the laws of nature, the bonds of society, and the injunctions of religion, now claim your grateful obedience—not to the mandates of a tyrant, but your chearful submission, and pleasing compliance to the soft dictates of a friend, a guardian, and protector." *Mary, Queen of Scots: An Historical Tragedy, or, Dramatic Poem* (1792), her first and only attempt at drama, was apparently unsatisfactory both to MD and her critics. She was repeatedly criticized for not being familiar with the difference between verse and prose. It is not surprising that the play was never acted. *Theodora and Didymus* (1784), an heroic poem in three cantos, praises female heroism and religious strength. The *London Review* perhaps sums up the critical reaction of the period: "[Her] talents, if they are not brilliant, are yet respectable. . . . We [only] wish she had confined herself to epistolary writing, in which she conducts herself with ease, and not inelegantly plays with her subject." Certainly, her *Miscellanies* offers an interesting and readable guide to the moral ideas of the time.   M.A.B.

DEVONSHIRE, Georgiana Cavendish, Duchess of (1757–1806), poet and letter writer, was the eldest daughter of John, first Earl Spencer, and Georgiana Poyntz. She was brought up at Althorp and married the fifth Duke of Devonshire in 1774 when she was 17. She had two daughters and a son. Much admired for her beauty and social manner, she set the fashion in dress, became a notable hostess at Devonshire House and Chatsworth, and associated with some of the most distinguished literary and political figures of the day. She admired Samuel Johnson and Richard Brinsley Sheridan, a constant visitor, while Gibbon declared she was made for something "better than a duchess." She had strong Whig convictions and, with her sister-in-law, the Duchess of Portland, campaigned vigorously for Charles James Fox in the election of 1784, using her lively social manner to engage voters. D of D's name was coupled with many men, including the politician Charles Grey. She was a compulsive gambler and incurred huge debts, which the Duke had to pay. Early in her marriage, she befriended LADY ELIZABETH FOSTER, estranged wife of John Thomas Foster. Lady Elizabeth became part of the Devonshire household and the Duke's mistress, bearing him two children. D of D came to accept the situation and the ménage à trois appears to have been amicable, although deeply shocking to society in general. For the various children, D of D employed as governess Selina Trimmer, daughter of the educationist SARAH TRIMMER; she was a disapproving but stable presence in the eccentric household. D of D died at Devonshire House; on hearing of her death, the Prince of Wales commented, "Then we have lost the most amiable and best-bred woman in England!!!" Some of her letters from 1773 to 1806 appear in Lord Bessborough's *Georgiana, Duchess of Devonshire.*

In poetry D of D is most famous for her "Passage of the Mountain of St. Gothard," reprinted by Lady Elizabeth in 1816. When the poem first appeared in the 1790s, Coleridge wrote an ode to D of D, claiming inspiration from her 24th stanza: "And hail the Chapel! hail the Platform wild! / Where Tell directed the avenging dart, / With well-strung arm, that first preserv'd his child,

/ Then aim'd the arrow at the tyrant's heart." The poem is addressed "To my Children" and ends with an invocation to them: "Hope of my life! dear children of my heart!" Other verses describe current events and personalities. The poetry is decorous and rarely inspired; it was praised after her death for demonstrating "a fanciful imagination, and an elegant taste" (*Gentleman's Magazine,* May 1806). D of D also wrote an epistolary novel, *The Sylph* (1780), describing the marriage of a young woman, Julia, to a libertine. Julia is secretly advised and befriended by the sylph, an earlier lover who watches over her progress through the corruptions and dissipations of London: "I fancy the people in this part of the world esteem reflection an evil and therefore keep continually hurrying from place to place, to leave no room or time for it." As her husband tires of her, she tries various measures to reattract him: "I accommodate myself to what I think his taste; but, owing to my ignorance of mankind, I may be defeating my own purpose." Like her creator, Julia takes refuge in gaming and is warned by the sylph about the results of this "unhappy predilection," since he sees in her a gambling personality: "The triumphant joy which sparkled in your eyes when success crowned your endeavours, plainly indicated you took no common satisfaction in the game." At the end of the novel, her ruined husband commits suicide, so allowing Julia's union with the sylph.

D of D was the subject of much painting and writing, some complimentary and some critical. An example of the latter is *The Calf's Will* (1777) which noted that her name was "so often bandied about in Print, that the Town are almost tired of reading it," and it accused her of valuing social position over prudence and virtue; according to this author, she was "blessed with understanding superiour to most of your Sex. But to figure as the standard of Fashion, has been, and is the rock you split on. Health, Fortune, and Beauty, are sacrificed at the shrine of that Idol." J.T.

DICK, Ann [Annie], Lady (?–1741), poet, was the child of Sir James MacKenzie, a Senator of the College of Justice, who bore the title Lord Royston; her mother was the first Earl of Cromerty's daughter. AD married William Cunyngham, who took the name Dick of Prestonfield in 1728 on the death of his grandfather. The couple had no children. AD was notorious for her way of life, especially her habit of walking about dressed as a man, and for her lampoons and epigrams, which often provoked considerable anger. Two of her poems appear in C. Kirkpatrick-Sharpe's *A Ballad Book* (Edinburgh, 1823). The first, beginning "Oh, wherefor did I cross the Forth, / And leave my love behind me," is the lament of a woman who has gone north with a man who "does not mind" her, when she had more suitable lovers in the south. The careless lover appears to be Sir Patrick Murray of Balmanno, the subject also of the second song, written to protest his attentions to another lady. In the verses, AD reveals that Sir Patrick has venereal disease: "Since that's, alas, thy woful case, / There's none so fit as I; / For ne'er a lass in all the land, / Can boast more mercury." Sharpe considers that a third song, entitled "Mrs. Mitchell and Borlan," is probably by AD; it mocks an indiscreet amour and the lady's fear of detection by her father. J.T.

DIXON, Sarah (fl. 1740), poet, is known only for her *Poems on Several Occasions,* published by subscription in Canterbury in 1740. The subscribers included Pope and ELIZABETH CARTER, but there is no evidence of any actual association. On the inside cover and flyleaves of the British Museum copy, several unpublished poems have been copied in an unidentified hand, together with notes that provide a few clues to her life. Her niece, Elizabeth Bunce, was the wife of John Bunce, Vicar of St. Stephen's, near Canterbury; the notes indicate that the Bunces encouraged SD's literary endeavors, and Bunce himself corrected her work for the press. The anonymous preface states that "Some little Taste of Poetry, improved by some Reading, tempted our Author to try her Talents for her own Amusement, and the Diversion of her Friends, in a Country Solitude." The poems are a mixture of innocuous pastorals and more serious religious verse, yet one is struck by the element of lightheartedness throughout the collection, even in the devotional poems. SD is most adept at light satiric verse, most of which is aimed at the vanities of coquettes and beaux. "Verses left on a Lady's Toilet" expresses her attitude to empty-headed women: "I hate to think that things so vain / As heedless Maids and dirty Men, / A Dish ill-cook'd, a Glass unwash'd, / A Petticoat wrong-cut and slash'd, / Shou'd make good Humour, Wit and Sense / Give Way to their Impertinence." In "On the XXXth of January," she refers to Charles I as "the Christian

Hero perfected." Her Toryism contains a pronounced Anglo-Catholic element; her paraphrase of the Twenty-third Psalm includes the couplet "In Deserts wide thou shalt my Table spread, / And feed my Soul with Eucharistic Bread." A cutting inserted in the back of the British Museum copy of *Poems on Several Occasions* from the *Kentish Gazette,* 30 June 1774, includes a poem celebrating monasticism, "The Ruins of St. Austin's Abbey." A note adds that SD wrote it "after she was seventy-three years old." T.C.S.W.L.

DOBSON, Susannah [Dawson] (?–1795), translator, was born in the south of England and was married to Matthew Dobson, M.D., F.R.S., the author of several medical treatises. Although little is recorded about her life, she was clearly an active scholar, producing a considerable amount of translation during a twenty-year period. Her two outstanding translations were the *Life of Petrarch* (1775), which went through six editions until 1805, and Sainte-Palaye's *Literary History of the Troubadours* (1779), which appeared in a second edition in 1807. She also translated Sainte-Palaye's *Memoirs of Ancient Chivalry* (1784) and Petrarch's *View of Human Life [De Remediis Utriusque Fortunae]* (1791). Two anonymous works have been attributed to her: *Historical Anecdotes of Heraldry and Chivalry* (1795) and *Dialogue on Friendship and Society.* SD's concern for high standards of behavior can be seen not only in the types of work she translated, but in her own commentary. In the preface to Sainte-Palaye's *Memoirs* she writes: "Women, in particular, ought to hold these ancient writers in high esteem, for the deference they paid to modesty, and the fame they so liberally bestowed on virtue. They taught generous firmness, judicious observance of superiors, and constant love, to unite in the same hearts: they taught to honour the valiant, to attend the wounded, to relieve the distressed, and to dispense the sweet solace of chearful and gentle manners to all around them: they taught them to respect themselves, and to prefer others; to be silent, observant, and industrious in youth, graceful and dignified in maturity, venerable in age, and lamented at death." SD's descriptions of chivalry consistently reflect the importance she attached to a life of virtue. In the *Memoirs,* for instance, she carefully traces the life of a knight "from the cradle to the tomb," and in the attributed *Historical Anecdotes* she explains: "When a knight is made, the

brethren first present him with a sword, as an emblem of valour. . . . With the sword he is given three blows, to teach him patiently to suffer: after this they make him wipe the sword, expressing by this action, the purity of life they expect him to observe" (p. 170). SD was a careful scholar, preferring the intellectual demands of her work to the liveliness of society. Although she was interested in becoming a part of HESTER THRALE's circle, she failed to obtain her attention. R.S.

DOCWRA, Ann[e] (1624–1710), polemicist, wrote numerous pamphlets. Some are part of personal controversies, and some argue the Quaker case for religious toleration. For example, *A Looking-Glass of the Recorder and Justices of the Peace, and Grand Juries for the Town and County of Cambridge* (1682) explores the area where the law and religion overlap, informing the legal authorities about past statutes and pointing out that they are allowing the law to meddle too much in what does not concern it, "for forcing Conformity upon any, there can be no service to God in that." Men must not, AD warns, "play the Devil for God's sake." She argues that people are bound to God, not to the opinions of others; thus no law should compel them to conform in worship. She ends her pamphlet with a poem about the crippling effects of persecution on the sufferers: "Great Storms of Persecution blew, / That nipt the bud, and chang'd the hew, / And so, away the Blossoms flew. / What Fruit can then expected be, / From a feared and blasted Tree?" In *An Epistle of Love and Good Advice to my Old Friends & Fellow-Sufferers in the Late Times, the Old Royalists and their Posterity, and to all others that have any sincere Desires towards God* (n.d.), AD again pleads for toleration and an acceptance of Christ in different forms. Religion, she contends, is not a matter of money and priests but of "inward and spiritual Grace"; as she puts it in the poem concluding the pamphlet, "The Mystery of God's love to all / Is Light within." AD also argues for women's participation in the church, pointing out that St. Paul declared there was no male or female in Christ and that, after his resurrection, Christ appeared first to women. AD's *Treatise concerning Enthusiasm, or Inspiration, of the Holy Spirit of God* (1700) again promotes Inner Light and warns against fear of enthusiasm, which to her merely signifies inspiration. Looking back over her long religious life, she notes that the learned, more than the enthusiastic, have obstructed truth, and she reiterates her faith in personal religion and good works.

As well as promoting religious toleration, AD attacked, sometimes inconsiderately, those who she felt had harmed the Quaker cause. In 1683 she published *A Brief Discovery of the Work of the Enemy,* and in *An Apostate Conscience Exposed* (1699), a work approved by her Quaker meeting, she began a pamphlet war with Francis Brigg, an apostate Quaker who argued that Quakerism was "Pernicious to both Church and State." Brigg countered with *Jezebel Withstood, and Her Daughter Anne Docwra, Publickly Reprov'd,* in which he challenged AD to make good her charges. This in turn provoked a reply from AD, *The Second Part of an Apostate Conscience Exposed: Being an Answer to a Scurrilous Pamphlet . . . by F. Brigg, intituled, Jezabel withstood* (1700); in this 36-page pamphlet AD accuses Brigg of being "a Mercenary Agent" and a repetitive author. She claims that she is 75 "and can see without Spectacles still, to read F. Brigg's Lyes and Deceit," and she details the deceptions of Brigg and his family. She also criticizes those who, when others were persecuted, lay "skulking, until the Storm of Persecution was over." The abuse sent Brigg into print again in 1700 with *A Winding-Sheet for Ann Dockwra,* in which he calls her "old," "Crazy," "Crackbrain'd," and "Slanderous" and orders her: "for shame Cover thy Face; wear a Vail, and sit down and mourn for thy Sins." He accuses her of deception and notes her difficulty when she finds herself wrong, since Quakerism has no place for confession. AD used her pamphlets to support as well as to attack. She was a great admirer of George Fox, whom in *An Apostate Conscience* she defends against accusations of luxury by detailing rather crudely his abstemiousness and physical suffering. J.T.

DOUGLAS, Lady Jane [Stewart] (1698–1753), letter writer, was famous for the ill-treatment she received from her brother, Archibald, Duke of Douglas, who disputed the legitimacy of her children and their right to inherit the title. Some of her letters survive. JD was the only daughter of James, second Marquis of Douglas, and Lady Mary Ker. Her father died when she was three, and she was brought up by her mother at Merchiston Castle, then outside Edinburgh. Although a beautiful heiress, when her engagement to the Earl of Dalkeith was broken off in 1720 owing to a false report that he

had been attached to another, JD determined to enter a convent and set off for Paris in male dress. She was followed and brought back. Her brother jealously guarded her. They quarreled and in 1736, after her mother's death, she lived at Drumsheugh House, Edinburgh, on £300 a year from her brother. There she hid Chevalier Johnstone after his escape from Culloden (1746), and there, fearing that her brother would withdraw his allowance, she secretly married Col. (afterward Sir) John Stewart, an impoverished younger son of good family. She traveled abroad and in 1748 gave birth to twin sons at Paris. She informed her brother, who refused to believe the children were hers, and stopped her annuity. When the family returned to England in 1749, her husband was confined to the King's Bench by his creditors. After much hardship, in 1750, JD received an annuity of £300 from the Royal Bounty. In 1752, poverty made her seek a reconciliation with her brother. She journeyed to Edinburgh with her children, Sholto and Archibald, but her brother turned her from his castle gates. She had to return hastily to London on business, and in her absence Sholto died. JD was heart-broken. She returned to Edinburgh, but her illness increased, and she died of cancer of the stomach; her son Archibald was prevented by her brother from attending the funeral. A small volume, *Letters of Lady Jane Douglas,* was published in 1767, compiled from the papers amassed during her son's successful legal battle to become the Duke's heir. These letters are interesting mainly for the insight they give into domestic relations of the time. They also win admiration for JD's strength of character and unshaken piety under humiliating circumstances. M.S.

DRINKER, Elizabeth Sandwich (1734–1807), American diarist, kept a continuous journal consisting of 36 volumes from 1758 to 1787. ESD was the second wife of the Quaker shipping merchant and the mother of nine children, only five of whom survived childhood. Her journal, edited by her great-grandson Cecil K. Drinker in *Not So Long Ago* (1937), gives an intimate view of a prosperous Quaker family in colonial Philadelphia. The entries through the years consist of simple yet fascinating notions and observations on topics such as local gossip, sicknesses, the cesspool problem, and most of all her children. On the servant problem ESD writes in 1784, "little Ned Fifer came upon tryal; his mother is desirous of binding him to us 'till he is, 16 years of Age, he is now between 8 & 9." Later she writes "Peter Wallover came to us a dutch Boy about 12 years of age, purchased from on board a ship." Her diary affords a picture of the current ills and the prescribed cures. She notes in 1807, "Dr. Rush visited my husband he advised another bleeding which was done, 8 ounces was taken by John Uhle he also advis'd rice water, and an injection at going to bed, of flaxceed tea a gill, and 40 drops liquid laudonun." About her daughter's miscarriage she writes, "if she lives the same excruciateing trouble a year the sooner for this loss," and on her son's falling into a lake, she notes, "strip'd him after rubing him well with a coarse towel, put on warm cloaths gave him some Rum & water to drink, and made him jump rope till he sweated." At times ESD is involuntarily funny. She writes that in 1798 the family acquired a shower bath: "I bore it better than I expected, not having been wett all over at once, for 28 years past." In 1777 her entries take a quite different turn and move from ordinary matters to the Revolutionary War. She remarks, "I was awaken'd this morn^g before 5 ° clock by ye lound fireing of Cannon." She gives an eyewitness account of the approaching men and boats, prisoners taken, food shortages, plundering for food, and some actual fighting on the river: "The town illuminated and as great number of windows broken on ye Anniversary of Independence and freedom." Earlier in 1777 her husband was arrested and imprisoned for not supporting the Colonies nor swearing allegiance to the new government. ESD traces her journey with petitions for her husband's release from Philadelphia to Valley Forge to meet General Washington. Her journal also painfully recounts the harassment the Quakers suffered—the hangings, seizures, closing of schools, fines, and taxes extracted in furniture and pewter.   P.P.

DUBOIS, Lady Dorothea (1728–74), poet and playwright, was born in Dublin, the eldest of the three daughters of Ann Simpson, daughter of a prosperous merchant, and the profligate Richard Annesley, who became Earl of Anglesey in 1737. In 1740, Annesley declared his marriage to Simpson spurious and turned her and her daughters out of doors. DD's mother brought charges of cruelty and adultery against him, and although she was awarded alimony by the Ecclesiastical Court in Dublin, Annesley

never paid it. For this he was excommunicated for the rest of his life. In 1752 DD secretly married Dubois, a French musician, with whom she had six children in eight years. In 1760, when DD traveled to Wexford to be reconciled with her ailing father, she was beaten, kidnapped, and forcibly removed to another town at the hands of a hostile mob. She relates the incident in "A True Tale," the first of her *Poems on Several Occasions,* published by subscription in 1764: "Sh' obtained the sight, so earnestly she sought, / But at the Hazard of her Life 'twas bought. / The cruel Father imprecating lay, / Disowning Nature, order'd her away; / . . . A num'rous Throng of Ruffians now surround / The sad *Dorinda* prostrate on the Ground. / His base-born Son, A Pistol e'en presents, / Behind her Head; but watchful Heav'n prevents / The Fiend from executing his Intents. / They pull and drag her, tear her Hands and Cloak, / . . . Force her from Room to Room, then down the Stairs, / Nor heed her piteous Cries, nor flowing Tears." In other poems DD dwells on her father's ill treatment of her mother and sisters, appealing to the country at large, the clergy, and to Annesley himself. Interspersed with these are lavish encomiums to George III and Queen Charlotte and parables and other didactic verse, all of which display a certain facility and ease of expression. Her resentment toward her father is usually cloaked in submissive piety, but in "The Amazonian Gift" she threatens to "take the pistol, sword or gun, / And thus equip'd, live free," while to "degen'rate Man" she would give "That simple thing, a Fan." After her mother's death she published *The Case of Ann, Countess of Anglesey, Lately Deceased* (1766), then *Theodora, a Novel* (1770) on the same theme, and *The Divorce,* a musical entertainment performed at Marylebone in 1772; "The Haunted Grove" was acted in Dublin but never printed. *The Lady's Polite Secretary; or, New Female Letter Writer* has been tentatively dated about 1768. DD died completely destitute in Dublin after a life of poverty.   T.C.S.W.L.

DUNCOMBE, Susanna (1725–1812), poet, illustrator, and member of Samuel Richardson's North End circle, was born at Lincoln's Inn Fields, London. Her mother was SUSANNA HIGHMORE from Effingham, Surrey, and her father the eminent painter and essayist Joseph Highmore, who taught her and her older brother to draw. SD spoke French, Italian, and some Spanish. Her sketch of Richardson reading *Sir Charles Grandison* became a frontispiece to Richardson's *Correspondence* (1804), edited by ANNA LAETITIA BARBAULD. SD's reputation as a poet in her early 20s was based on a now lost allegory, in which Fidelio and Honoria, unable to find the House of Happiness, reside in the House of Content. Her obituary (*Gentleman's Magazine,* November 1812) confuses this poem with HESTER MULSO CHAPONE's story of Fidelia, printed in *The Adventurer* (1753). SD married (in 1761) a lifelong friend, the Rev. John Duncombe, a prolific writer for *GM* and author of *The Feminiad* (1754), in which she appears as Eugenia. They lived in Canterbury, where Duncombe held the united rectories of St. Andrew and St. Mary Bredman and eventually became one of the Six Preachers of the cathedral and vicar of Herne. Of four children, only Anna Maria survived infancy, and she reputedly became a novelist, although none of her works can be found. SD's poetry was published in collections, some edited by her husband. After his unexpected death in 1786, SD and her daughter continued to live on Green Court in the cathedral precincts, where she was a close friend of ELIZA BERKELEY and notorious for keeping cats. She was buried in St. Mary Bredman.

Much of SD's poetry was addressed to friends and had only temporary interest. Eight pieces "By a Lady" appeared in the *Poetical Calendar* (1763), edited by Frances Fawkes and William Woty. "To Aspasia," *Works of Mrs. Chapone,* vol. 4, answers Hester Mulso Chapone's "To Stella," written before 1755. Biographical information and two poems appeared in *Kentish Poets* (1821), for which Rowland Freeman had access to family manuscripts now lost. "To Anna Maria D." written at Herne in 1781 appeared in Duncombe's *The History and Antiquities of Reculver and Herne* (1784). SD drew illustrations for this work, as well as frontispieces for her husband's editions of John Hughes' *Letters* (1773) and Lord Orrery's *Letters from Italy* (1733). She was deeply disappointed by the engravings of her four drawings for Duncombe's *Horace* (1767). Two drawings for Edward Hasted's *History of Kent* (1782) do her credit as an illustrator. Robert Watt, in *Biblitheca Britannica* (1824), erroneously credited her with *The Village Gentleman and the Attorney at Law* (1808), a two-volume romance actually written by Ann Duncombe,

no relation. SD is now important for the literary figures she knew, especially Samuel Richardson, ELIZABETH CARTER, John Hawkesworth, Thomas Edwards, and Hester Mulso Chapone, and for the poetry that was written to her by Thomas Mulso, William Dodd, Christopher Smart, and Bonnell Thornton. Her father wrote a poem about her parrot (*GM,* April 1750). Thomas Edwards, who urged her to publish—("A larger share of fame is but your due, / Who write so well")—wrote an ode to her at Richardson's suggestion when she burned herself with curling irons in 1752 (Nichols, *Select Collection,* vol. 6, 1780). W.M.

DUNLAP, Jane (fl. 1771), American poet, came from Boston. After her husband's death, she lived, she states, in an "obscure station of life." In 1771 she published a few ballad-type works as *Poems Upon Several Sermons Preached by the Rev'd . . . George Whitefield,* asking leniency for her errors and anticipating mockery and ridicule for her book, but asserting at the same time that "those that truly fear the Lord, / They will it not despise." In the poems, Whitefield is much praised: "His worthy deeds, and holy life, / The brightest luster casts, / Upon his worthy name which shall / To endless ages last." Another poem exhorts New England churches to return to their initial piety, expressed when these members first came "after Christ . . . / Into this howling wilderness, / For love of his great name." In one poem JD refers to PHILLIS WHEATLEY's verse on Whitefield's death. J.T.

DUTTON, Anne (1692–1765), poet and writer on religion, was born in Northampton; she survived a nearly fatal childhood illness and underwent a religious education. She married a Mr. Coles at the age of 22, and lived for five years in Warwick and London before being widowed. Her second marriage was to Benjamin Dutton, a clothier, with whom she lived in various East Midland towns before settling at Great Gransden, Hunts. Her husband entered the ministry, and a chapel was built partly at his and his wife's expense. Despite problems with eyesight, AD here produced a vast number of tracts and discourses. She was also a prolific letter writer and corresponded with Wesley, disagreeing with him over the question of Election. Her letters do not always seem to have been answered, however. Her husband went to America in 1747, ostensibly to sell her tracts; she was widowed for the second time when his ship was lost on his return trip. Her complete bibliography runs to 50 titles; it includes *A Narration of the Wonders of Grace, in verse* (1734), *A Discourse upon walking with God; in a letter to a friend* (1735), *A Discourse concerning the New-Birth* (1740), *A Letter to all the Saints on the general duty of Love* (1742), *A letter to the Reverend Mr. John Wesley* (1742), *Letters on spiritual subjects, and divine occasions, sent to relatives and friends* (1748), *A brief account of the gracious dealings of God with a poor, sinful . . . creature* (1750), and *Divine, moral and historical Miscellanies* (1761).

A Narration of the Wonders of Grace, a poem in heroic couplets of some 1500 lines, reviews the whole course of redemption from the standpoint of Calvinist Methodism. Nearly every couplet is bolstered by a marginal reference to the Scriptures. AD writes of those unlucky enough not to be numbered among the Elect: "The Rest, that only were ordain'd, / As Creatures for a lower End; / When they were view'd in th' Guilt of Sin, / And filthy as an unclean Thing; / These then, by just Severity, / Were made for Wrath eternally." It is execrable verse, interesting only as testimony to the mental tilt of a particular kind of zealot. The same can be said of *A Discourse upon walking with God,* a lengthy examination of the "Way of Faith," the "Way of instituted worship," the "Way of Divine Providence," and the "Way of Conversation-Holiness." In a more personal vein AD speaks of "Satan and his Temptations," and without being specific of her "Corruptions" and "innumerable Trials." Despite an undercurrent of self-distrust and even despair, she is confident of her own Election: "He was yet, nevertheless pleas'd in the rich aboundings, and superaboundings of his Grace, to add Abundance of spiritual Sense to my Faith; By giving me frequent Communion, and sweet Fellowship with himself, in his Three glorious Persons." R.J.

E

ECHLIN, Elizabeth, Lady (1704?–1782?), novelist, was the daughter of William Bellingham of Westmoreland. According to her sister, in her youth EE "read divinity, and all grave books . . . and talked like a sage old woman." In 1725 or 1727 she married Sir Robert Echlin (d. 1757) in Dublin, where she subsequently lived and bore a daughter, as well as two sons, who died young. EE's sister Dorothy in 1731 became Lady Bradshaigh and grew intimate with Samuel Richardson; through her sister EE was brought to Richardson's attention, although the two probably never met. Her extant correspondence with him begins in 1753 and continues until just before his death in 1761. EE was a careful reader of *Clarissa*, which she described as "not a faultless peice [sic]"; as a woman she was deeply shocked by the physical violation of the heroine: "I felt Emotions not to be describ'd; and was too much oppresst, or distracted, to admitt a rational sensibility to take place." She was provoked into writing an alternative rapeless version of the ending, not published until 1982 (Swiss Studies in English); it has none of Richardson's psychological acuteness but interests as a contemporary woman's response to the novel and to the subject of rape. A prefatory note to Richardson indicates EE's aim of giving all characters just desserts and of stressing the power of female virtue, since she felt the point of the novel lost "if this accomplish'd Libertine be not reformed by Clarissas virtuous conversation." Consequently in her version Lovelace "renounced his former wicked attachments, became a sincere convert, spent the twelve months he survived Clarissa, in imitating his dear departed; constantly observing her pious way of life." A more commonsensical but physically weaker Cla-

rissa dies of debility but is allowed the beginnings of reconciliation with her parents; Arabella, who clearly outrages EE, ends in the lowest state of poverty, married to "a Lousey Taylor" called "Cabbage." To hammer home the moral point, EE introduces the almost allegorical characters of Doctor Christian and the surgeon Mr. Carefull. Richardson noted EE's changes and her annoyance at his plot, remarking that, since she had spared Lovelace the great crime, she might as well have let Clarissa live to spread universal happiness and sent Lovelace out of the way as "governor of one of the American Colonies."   J.T.

EDEN, Anne (fl. 1790), novelist, wrote *Confidential Letter of Albert; from his first attachment to Charlotte to her death. From the Sorrows of Werter* (1790). The work had previously been ascribed to John Armstrong of Leith, who used the pseudonym "Albert." The "author" of the letters in this novel, based on Goethe's work, is the married Albert who, as the omniscient observer, narrates the life story of Charlotte, the daughter of a friend. He finds in her the perfect woman—artless, vivacious, sensitive, intelligent, and loyal to her brother and father. For her he feels only the affection and concern of a brother until Werter comes to befriend her. Werter, in Albert's view, is an emotional, unsteady man who is desperately in need of reassurance from Albert and Charlotte, but Albert believes he is unworthy of Charlotte's attention. When Werter dies, Albert finds that three women have been in love with him—Albert's wife, his sister, and a stranger at the grave. In seeking understanding and humility, Albert asks, "Where is that being that can command the erring human heart?" and begs,

"Teach me a perfect submission to his wise decree, who guides us through the labyrinth of transitory sufferings, to the realms of eternal rest and felicity." Plot and character studies are slight, and the tone alternates between the evangelical and the melodramatic.   M.P.

EDGEWORTH, Maria (1768–1849), novelist and educational writer, was born at Black Bourton, Oxon., the daughter of the former Anna Maria Elers (1743–73) and Richard Lovell Edgeworth (1744–1817). When Anna Maria Edgeworth died in childbirth, Edgeworth quickly married Honora Sneyd, who was able but severe and exacted reverence rather than love from her stepchildren. R. L. Edgeworth took his family to settle on his estate in Ireland, but his two elder children, a son and ME, proved unmanageable and had to be sent away to school in England. Honora Edgeworth died of tuberculosis in 1780, and after some reluctance, his own and on the part of the Church of England, Edgeworth married her sister Elizabeth, in order, he said, to provide a mother for his children. In 1782 the family went once more to Ireland, ME accompanying them, this time contentedly. For the remainder of her life, apart from tours of a few months' duration to England, Scotland, France, and Switzerland, her home was the family house at Edgeworthstown, Co. Longford, in the Irish Midlands.

Richard Lovell Edgeworth was the emotional and intellectual focus of ME's life. During his second marriage, when she was aged between five and seven, her behavior was disturbed, partly because her father and stepmother were too mutually absorbed to attend to her needs. On her return to Ireland at 15, she trained herself to become her father's amanuensis and assistant in running the estate, with its rental income during her lifetime of between £1600 and £3500 a year; in these roles, she rivaled her new stepmother for his time and attention. Edgeworth was a man with the wide-ranging interests and liberal political sympathies characteristic of the Enlightenment. During his years in England (especially 1764–73), he developed his interest in experimental science, especially mechanics, and became one of the original members of the Lunar Society of Birmingham, along with the industrialists James Watt, Matthew Boulton, and Josiah Wedgwood, the doctor and poet Erasmus Darwin, and the chemist and Unitarian polemicist Joseph Priestley. An even closer friend was the eccentric Thomas Day, with whom Edgeworth shared an interest in education, particularly in the theories of Rousseau. ME became acquainted with her father's friends in childhood, and stayed for some school holidays with Day, who attempted to instruct her in the Rousseauistic ideal of womanhood, which was feminine, passive, and unintellectual.

Once in Ireland, Edgeworth and ME took up this educational work together. Although he had early rejected much of Rousseau's *Emile* (1762) as impractical, Edgeworth retained his interest in current French educational writing, and ME's first literary attempt was a translation of Mme de Genlis's *Adèle et Théodore,* which was completed but recalled before publication in 1783. As child after child was born to his Sneyd wives in the 1770s, 1780s and 1790s, Edgeworth experimented with various teaching methods and kept notes of the children's comments and reactions. By the late 1780s, ME had begun to compose stories for the domestic circle of children, which from the 1790s were gradually published in series such as *The Parent's Assistant* (1796–) and *Early Lessons* (1801–). The theories on which the stories are based, together with the notes, are explained in R. L. Edgeworth and ME's *Practical Education* (2 vols., 1798), a work immediately accepted as important in Napoleonic Europe as well as in Britain.

Meanwhile ME's fiction for adults, which is more independent of her father, began to establish her separate reputation. *Letters for Literary Ladies* (1795) contains three stories with feminist themes, the first a dialogue between two progressive gentlemen (resembling Day and Edgeworth) who differ over whether women should become authors. This was followed in 1800 by the most celebrated of her books, *Castle Rackrent,* supposedly the memoirs of the Irish servant of a family of feckless Anglo-Irish gentry. This brilliant and apparently wholly original book draws richly on ME's domestic experience and family background. The Rackrent dynasty resembles her own forebears, while the tones of the narrator are patterned on the Edgeworths' steward. R. L. Edgeworth's liberal and tolerant attitudes in Irish politics are reflected in *Castle Rackrent*'s well-disposed (if arguably external) treatment of the native Irish. A concern for the dignity of the common man tends increasingly to coincide with an interest in the manners and in the distinctive language of different classes and regions in the era of the American and French revolutions. This egalitarian approach to language is illustrated in the work of the Edgeworth's favorite grammarian, John Horne Tooke (*Diversions of Purley,* 1787–1805), in Wordsworth's Preface to the *Lyrical Ballads* (1800), and in their own further defense of Irish dialect, *Irish Bulls* (1802), where they represent Irish speech-patterns as warm, witty, and eloquent, and of equal dignity with standard English.

During the 1790s, the Edgeworth family were somewhat isolated on their Co. Longford estate, cut off by their liberalism and supposed pro-French sympathies from their Protestant Anglo-Irish neighbors. After the French invasion of Ireland was repelled in 1798 and Ireland's political union with England was engineered in 1800, animosities among the local gentry subsided, and the Edgeworths' social circle widened. Gradually ME's fiction reflects these changed circumstances, becoming richer in observed incident and character, and more conventional in attitude. For 15 years she published unceasingly: two full-length novels, *Belinda* (3 vols., 1801) and *Patronage* (4 vols., 1814) and, more characteristic, novellas and tales— *Popular Tales* (3 vols., 1804), *The Modern Griselda* (1805), *Leonora* (2 vols., 1806), and the six-volume *Tales of Fashionable Life* (1809 and 1812), which contain some of her finest work, with *Ennui* and *Manoeuvring* included in the first issue, and *Vivian, Emilie de Coulanges* and *The Absentee* in the second.

In 1802, during the brief lull in the Napoleonic Wars, Edgeworth took his fourth wife, the former Frances Beaufort, and his two elder unmarried daughters, ME and Charlotte, to Paris. They remained there from October 1802 to March 1803, moving in scientific and intellectual circles which already knew their work in translations carried by the Swiss periodical the *Bibliothèque Britannique.* While in Paris, ME met and considered marrying a Swedish courtier of scientific pursuits, Abraham Niclas Clewburg-Edelcrantz, an experience she recalled with emotion for many years. She gave as her reason for refusing him her reluctance to leave her father and her home.

ME had no comparable experience of London society until her first protracted visit there in 1813. Before that, however, her name attracted fashionable visitors to Edgeworthstown in increasing numbers, and during the first decade of the century she corresponded with fellow-writers and intellectuals such as ANNA LAETITIA BARBAULD, ELIZABETH INCHBALD, Walter Scott, and Etienne Dumont (a friend of Mirabeau and Bentham). Her commanding position as a serious novelist ended when Scott took over her regional subject-matter with *Waverley* in 1814. She wrote one more fine Irish novel, *Ormond,* in 1817, the year her father died. After this she declared that her motive for writing sustained fiction was gone; nevertheless, her last novel of domestic and fashionable life, *Helen* (3 vols., 1834), is probably her best on this theme. In her last 30 years she traveled in Ireland, England, and on the Continent, recording her social encounters in pleasing, amusing letters, while at home she showed toughness and resourcefulness in helping her surviving stepmother to run the Edgeworthstown estate.

ME was undoubtedly the most commercially successful and prestigious novelist of her heyday, 1800–14. The £2,100 she earned from *Patronage* (1814) is three times Scott's £700 for *Waverley* (1814), which Lockhart thought unprecedented, and seven times Jane Austen's £300 for *Emma* (1816). ME calculated that in all she earned £11,062.8.10d from her writing, and this for books which, unlike most other novels, were singled out for full-length and largely favorable reviews by the *Edinburgh Review* and the *Quarterly Review.* No Englishwoman had a comparable literary career before George Eliot's. For contemporary women, the most significant fact about ME may well have been her successful competition with men. Although she used a woman's form, she wrote for both sexes and (notably in *Patronage*) ignored the convention that politics and professional life could be discussed, as they could be experienced, only by men. But while not a doctrinaire feminist like MARY WOLLSTONECRAFT, ME was always consciously a woman writer who identified herself with a women's literary tradition. She acknowledged debts to FANNY BURNEY, Inchbald, Barbauld, de Genlis, and de Staël. Together with her father, she proposed to Barbauld in 1799 that they might combine to inaugurate a politically liberal women's journal, *The Feminead,* an idea scotched by Barbauld because women were ideologically too divided: "Mrs. Hannah More would not write along with you or me, & we should probably hesitate at joining Miss Hayes, or if she were living, Mrs.

Godwin." Like other moderate feminists, ME clearly was embarrassed by Wollstonecraft's sensationally unconventional career; ME's novel *Belinda,* which urges that women should think and act independently, contains a hostile caricature of an ill-conducted, mannish woman, Mrs. Harriott Freke. (Writing even more pointedly in favor of women's self-sufficiency in *The Wanderer* [1814], Fanny Burney also includes an unflattering portrait of a feminist, Elinor Joddrell.) Having prudently disavowed at the outset that she wanted sexual emancipation for women, ME consistently claims equality of treatment for them. Her novels of English fashionable and domestic life portray women rather than men, and counter the contemporary tendency to polarize the sexes by denying that any personal characteristics, except the most foolish ones, are feminine. ME's women sound like women, for she is the first novelist to apply an insight articulated by Wollstonecraft, that women have their own language. But her women vary as much as her men, from the simplistic (Virginia in *Belinda*), to the intellectually pretentious (Olivia in *Leonora*), the manipulative (Mrs. Beaumont in *Manoeuvring*), and the masterful (Lady Delacour in *Belinda,* Lady Davenant in *Helen*). The range of women character-types, which is unprecedented, amounts to a denial of typing. Almost as notable, ME deploys the stereotyped romance-and-marriage plot, but insists that marriage for women is an economic partnership with a man, and leads to a socially responsible task, the education of children. Her handling of plot reassesses the assumptions behind the conventions of the "women's novel," even if she falls well short of Wollstonecraft's wholesale challenge.

ME's interesting position as a woman writer has been overlooked in favor of her more obviously innovatory treatment of Irish common life, in four short novels— *Castle Rackrent* (1800), *Ennui* (1809), *The Absentee* (1812), and *Ormond* (1817). In these works, Edgeworth documents Irish society, from the Anglo-Irish in their great houses to the peasants in their hovels, and she analyzes the relations between classes with a subtlety belied by her didactic tone. The fundamentally liberal concern with the language of different orders and regions has already been defined as characteristic of the late Enlightenment. These were the features of ME's Irish fiction that helped to stimulate Scott's *Waverley,* as he acknowledges in his postscript, and thus to become key formal elements in the 19th-century European realistic novel.

ME's aesthetic assumptions, outside or prior to Romanticism, and her debts to an 18th-century genre, the moral tale, have cast long shadows over her work for the modern reader. Criticism has been overwhelmingly biographical, and crudely inclined to blame R. L. Edgeworth for his supposed appropriation of his daughter's work: Virginia Woolf does this, in a superficial essay in *The Common Reader.* Certainly ME resembles many women writers of her period, including Burney, HESTER THRALE, Barbauld, de Staël and Austen, in seeking a special intimacy with her father, and in viewing her writing as in some sense his. There is virtually no substance in the often-repeated charge that he interferred in the detail of her stories. During her most productive decades, 1795–1814, he probably steered her, consciously and unconsciously, toward more writing on public, masculine, "serious" subjects, less in the accepted feminine mode of what he called "pretty stories and novellettes." In this he acted unlike other patriarchal mentors, and arguably to her advantage. On the other hand, the scale of values he thus communicated may have inhibited her from identifying with her female protagonists, as other women writers were wont to do. The great exception is the novel she wrote without him, *Helen,* a sympathetic study of the conflicting loyalties of two young women caught between patriarchal authority, with its moral absolutes, and their affection for one another. This intelligent and characteristically individual book was admired and imitated (in *Wives and Daughters*) by Elizabeth Gaskell, the Victorian novelist who most resembles ME.   M.B.

EGERTON, Sarah Fyge (1669–1722), poet, was born in London to the Figge family of Winslow, Bucks., landowners. Winslow parish register records identify SFE as the daughter of the "pious and learned Tho. Fyge, Gent.," possibly an apothecary, who died in 1706; SFE's mother died in 1704. SFE was one of six daughters. Accounts of SFE in DELARIVIÈRE MANLEY's *Atalantis* (1709) and *Memoirs of Europe* (1710) and *Gentleman's Magazine* document SFE's banishment from her London home by her father, who was evidently shamed by the success of her *Female Advocate* (1686, 1687), a long, feminist verse-satire which was one of several responses to Robert Gould's scabrous, popular misogynist verse-satire, *Love Given O're* (1682) (see SFE's "Lady Campbell" and "Leaving London," *Poems* [1703], 1706). Also documented are SFE's early engagement to the "Philaster" of her *Poems,* her two marriages (to an attorney Field, the Amintor of *Poems,* and later to a Rev. Thomas Egerton of Aldstock, Bucks., the "wealthy Strephon" of her *Poems*). SFE's inamorato and sealer of her fate is one Alexis (sometime "Exalis"), possibly a legal associate of Field's, who drives SFE to breakdown, as recorded in her long, cautionary (anti)pastoral, "The fond Shepherdess" (*Poems*), self-acknowledged "darling" of her poetic efforts. Field died at the turn of the century and Egerton in 1720. SFE's verse and dedications, as well as commendatory poems to her in her *Poems,* reveal that she enjoyed connections with such men of letters as Dryden, her Restoration antagonist Gould, Joshua Barnes, John Norris, the first Earl of Halifax, dedicatee of her *Advocate* and *Poems,* possibly Matthew Prior, and Congreve, dedicatee of her "Shepherdess." Minor contemporaries who may have been SFE's associates include the poets ELIZABETH THOMAS, John Froud, and Thomas Yalden, and Delarivière Manley. In *Poems,* SFE also mentions Anne Bracegirdle the actress, the portrait-painter Johann Clostermann, and the scientist Robert Boyle. If her 15-page pastoral, the "Shepherdess," is autobiographical, SFE suffered emotional deterioration and stopped writing after the publication of *Poems* in 1703.

Texts attributed to SFE are *The Female Advocate: Or, An Answer To A Late Satyr Against the Pride, Lust and Inconstancy of Woman. Written by a Lady in Vindication of her Sex* (1686, 1687), with a preface signed "S.F."; "An Ode, On the Death of John Dryden, Esq; By a Young Lady," signed "S.F.," printed in *Luctus Britannici* (1700); three elegies to Dryden "By Mrs S.F." as muses "Erato," "Euterpe," and "Terpsichore," printed in *The Nine Muses. Or, Poems Written by Nine Several Ladies Upon the Death of . . . Dryden* (1700), all three elegies reprinted in SFE's *Poems; Poems on Several Occasions, Together with a Pastoral. By Mrs S.F.* (1703), reissued as *A Collection of Poems on several Occasions . . . by Mrs Sarah Fyge Egerton* (1706), with a dedication signed "S.F.E." SFE's verse includes pastoral, elegy, panegyric, song, love lyric, and the irregular or Cowleyan ode. Her *Advocate* exploits features of verse-satire and verse-essay. Features of rural retirement verse exist in her more private, introspective poems. The heroic couplet is her characteristic meter. SFE's best poetry records personal episodes marked by romantic disillusionment, aimless wandering, and brooding self-portraiture (see "Fatality," *Poems*). Thematically, SFE's verse falls into two distinct units: spirited feminist statements and somber self-portraiture. The character of her feminism is assertive and retaliatory. Her *Advocate* is part of the 17th-century "fair-sex debate," wherein one sex asserts superiority over the other. SFE's poem responds to Gould's stinging lines with moderation: "I think when a Man is so extravagant as to Damn all Womankind for the Crimes of a few, he ought to be corrected." Drawing upon historical exempla, SFE demonstrates woman's superiority to man, and concludes that woman is mankind's "only steady and most constant Bliss." The feminism of SFE's *Poems* is shown in a group of antiromantic, cynical poems celebrating woman's freedom from masculine/patriarchal control; conventions attached to courtship, love, and marriage are debunked in "The Fate," "The Emulation," "The Power of Love," and "The Liberty." Anti-marriage sentiment derives from woman's unequal legal status as a *femme coverte:* "The Husband with insulting Tyranny / Can have ill Manners justify'd by Law, / For Men all join to keep the Wife in awe. / Moses first our Freedom did rebuke, / Was marry'd when he writ the Pentateuch" ("The Emulation"). Anti-male portraiture exists in SFE's poems to her "sporting Boys." Her *Poems,* however, is more typically dominated by self-portraiture of poignant despair before her adversary, "Fate." This dark center of her verse, where no human or moral values operate, is represented in "Lady Campbell," "Leaving London," "Leaving S- - -y," "The Gratitude," and "The Fatality" (a linked group). The collection's second poem, "The Exctacy," illustrates the seclusive, inward-pulling movement typical of SFE's best work. Her "Shepherdess" serves as a coda to her *Poems* by telescoping major themes into a composite image of feminine vulnerability in a world of duplicity and caprice. The heroine is abandoned by her lover and, after manifesting symptoms of acute distress, collapses in the arms of a "careful" friend. The poem ends on an elegic note.   M.M.

ELLIOT, Jean [or Jane] (1727–1805), poet,

was the third daughter of a judge, Sir Gilbert Elliot, Lord Minto, and of Helen Stewart of Allanbank. She was born in Teviotdale and was remarkable for her early maturity and intellectual ability. At the age of 19 she cleverly entertained a party of Jacobites while her father, a Hanoverian supporter, escaped. Her father had literary interests, as did her brother, Gilbert Elliot. One brother became the last British governor of New York, while another became a noted admiral. In 1756 JE's words to "The Flowers of the Forest" on the subject of the battle of Flodden were published anonymously. The poem was very successful, and some believed it a genuine relic from the past. On her father's death, JE, her mother, and sisters settled in Edinburgh, where they avoided fashionable society. After her mother's death, JE lived on in Edinburgh, famous for holding to old ways, such as the use of her own sedan chair. In 1804 she returned to the area of her childhood, where she died. Both Robert Burns and Walter Scott thought highly of JE's ballad, "in which," wrote Scott, "the manner of the ancient minstrels is so happily imitated, that it required the most positive evidence to convince me that the song was of modern date." The poem has six stanzas and, unlike ALICIA COCKBURN's one for the same tune, is not a mood poem but a lament over defeat; the first and part of the fifth stanzas are: "I've heard the lilting at our yowe-milking, / Lasses a' lilting before the dawn of day; / But now they are moaning on ilka green loaning— / The Flowers of the Forest are a' wede away / . . . The Flowers of the Forest, that foucht aye the foremost, / The prime o' our land, are cauld in the clay." J.T.

ELSTOB, Elizabeth (1683–1756), Anglo-Saxon scholar, was born at Newcastle-upon-Tyne. Her father, a merchant, died in 1688 and her mother three years later, having given EE the rudiments of an education. Her uncle and guardian then put a stop to her studies, despite her obvious intelligence, because "one tongue was enough for a woman." Later EE gained permission to learn French. Her brother William (b. 1673) was educated at Eton, Cambridge, and Oxford; he was a Saxon scholar and, later, a London clergyman. By 1702 EE was living with him and he encouraged her learning of languages (she had mastered eight by her death). Even before 1702 she may have spent some time with him in Oxford and profited from the learning there. At first

EE assisted in his Saxon studies, then published on her own account, supported by the Old English scholar George Hickes. When William died in 1715, she was unable to find sufficient patronage to enable her to continue her studies. EE retired in debt to Evesham, Worcs., where she set up a school, but the project was not a success, and she barely earned enough to live on. EE fortunately made the acquaintance of Mrs. Chapone, HESTOR MULSO CHAPONE's mother-in-law, who sent a circular letter asking for a subscription on EE's behalf, and this produced an annuity of £21. Queen Caroline sent £100 in 1733 and promised the same amount every five years, but she unfortunately died in 1737. Finally, EE was recommended by MARY DELANY to the Duchess of Portland, who made her governess to her children in 1738, and EE passed the rest of her life in the family.

EE's first published work was a translation of Mme de Scudéry's *Essay on Glory* (1708). In 1709 she published by subscription Aelfric's *An English-Saxon Homily on the Birth-day of St. Gregory . . . translated into modern English, with Notes etc.* At the time of its appearance, the work was considered important with reference to the controversy on the primitive state and doctrines of the Anglo-Saxon church. In the preface, EE defends female education against the charge that it leads women to "neglect their household Affairs," and she hoped that the edition would be particularly useful to women students (almost half the subscribers were women). Also in the preface she refers readers to the discourse on women's learning by ANNA MARIA VAN SCHURMAN. EE undertook later to publish a collection of Aelfric's homilies, which was to consist of about 80 homilies and other tracts, with an English translation and notes. Her brother's death and lack of funds probably prevented the completion of this work, although a copy of the few sheets that were printed remains in the British Library. In 1715, EE published *Rudiments of Grammar for the English Tongue . . . with an Apology for the Study of Northern Antiquities,* part of which appeared in 1712. The Apology comprises a competent defense of the study of Anglo-Saxon against certain critics of the period, including Swift, who dismissed it as a barbarous dialect, unworthy of the attention of men of letters. EE concludes by declaring that, if proved wrong, she would not "involve the whole sex, by pleading woman's frailty," but adds, somewhat ambivalently, that, if she were attacked, "the learned, the candid, and the noble" would protect "a damsel in distress." EE certainly contended with prejudice against female scholarship in her own time, but by the end of the century her achievement was generally recognized.   M.S.

ENGLISH, Harriet, (fl. 1799), children's writer, authored two didactic works; *The Faithful Mirror* and *Conversations and Amusing Tales Offered to the Publick for the Youth of Great Britain* (both 1799). The former consists of six exempla, arranged in pairs corresponding to the three levels of society: royalty, middle classes, and lower classes. In each pair the development of a child for better or worse reflects the standards set and the values displayed by its parents, of whom it is therefore a "faithful mirror." In the upper classes virtue, learning, liberality, and kind-heartedness are among the qualities prized; the middle classes are recommended dutifulness, modesty, and moderation, while the lower classes are praised for honesty and industry. There is little subtlety of approach; of the middle-class Julia, for example, one is told approvingly: "Pleasure she finds within her family; she seeks no joy beyond her home." In the dedication to her *Conversations and Amusing Tales,* HE writes that "Attention to religion and morality, is now almost wholly neglected" in the education of the young, with dire consequences for society. Her work therefore represents "a young family in real life" and aims to "interest and amuse" while conveying some "just notions" to young people. It depicts a series of meetings between a group of children and their sententious aunt, who speaks thus: "Numbers, some of your own particular Friends, have been called from their state of trial within the last year; and life is still spared to you. You are again permitted to see the sun begin its annual course. Hasten, each of you, to improve this mercy." To which her nephew not unreasonably replies: "I should like my aunt a great deal better if she were not so grave."   R.J.

"EPHELIA" (fl. 1679), poet and playwright, wrote *Female Poems On Several Occasions, Written by Ephelia.* Her identity and immediate background are conjectural, but the poetry suggests she was born into a well-connected, upper-class London family, and that both parents died "in their Tender Age" (see "My Fate"). Possibly E is Joan Philips, the only daughter of KATHERINE PHILIPS, "the matchless Orinda," born after 1654, publishing her poetry in her 20s, and marrying Wogan of Pembrokeshire after being jilted by a "J.G.," the Strephon of *Female Poems.* J.G. may be the Gilbert of one of E's acrostics. In "My Fate" and "To one that asked," E implies J.G. was a voyager or entrepreneur "Twice my Age and more." A copy of the first edition of E's *Female Poems,* sold for 4s. at the auction of the library of James Perry in 1822, attributed the work to APHRA BEHN. Other "Ephelias" in 17th-century verse are Lady Vernon (née Mary "Mall" Kirke) of the Ephelia-Bajazet epistles, ascribed to Etherege and Rochester, and Lady Worsley (née Frances Thynne of Longleat), a correspondent of ANNE FINCH, who appears as "Ephelia" in two of Finch's poems. Some evidence of E's life and times comes from verse dedicated to royal or prominent figures: the Epistle Dedicatory to Princess Mary, Duchess of Richmond and Lenox; a panegyric to Charles II on the discovery of the Popish Plot; and an elegy on the death of Gilbert Sheldon, Archbishop of Canterbury. E's literary models and/or associates are documented in "To Madam Bhen" [sic] and "To Madam F[inch?]." Elsewhere, E compliments Katherine Philips, Cowley, and Dryden. *Female Poems* also contains several spurious pieces, since ascribed to Etherege, Rochester, Scroope, Behn, and D'Urfey. Was E a member of their coterie? The misogynist Robert Gould portrays E as a whore and literary parasite (a popular "type" of the publishing woman writer) in his "she-satire," "The Poetess" (*Works,* 1709).

E's unestablished canon consists of *Female Poems* (1679, 1682), and the broadside verse "Advice to his GRACE" (the Duke of Monmouth) signed "Ephelia" (1681). E's apparently unpublished play, "The Royal-Pair of Coxcombs" (1678?), probably a satiric comedy, was performed at a dancing school, unidentified in her poem on the play's unsuccessful debut. Its prologue, epilogue, and first two songs are printed in her *Female Poems.* Poetic forms represented in E's verse include love lyrics and songs cast in the pastoral-urbane mode, acrostics, broadside verse, panegyric, and elegy. She employs the heroic couplet pervasively and vigorously. Unlike ELIZABETH ROWE and SARAH FYGE EGERTON, E does not attempt the ode, probably because her combative feminist stance does not lend itself to the ode's reflective themes. Nor does E draw upon the conceited analogies of "meta-physical" and cavalier poets of her day, possibly because she was not intellectually predisposed as a poet. Her poetic unpretentiousness may derive from her lack of formal education. She often disparages herself ("my Infant Muse," "these untuned Lays"). Romance, friendship, and feminism are E's themes. The dramatic center of her poems is a group of several verses to her lover. She records their courtship and her bitter disillusionment when he abandons her for the wealthy Mopsa ("an ill-lookt Hag"), whom he marries in Tangier. ("Mopsa" may derive from the homely Mopsa of Sidney's *Arcadia,* 1590). Friendship with men is E's alternative to love's merciless tyranny ("To *Phylocles,* inviting him to Friendship"). Woman-friendship, a major theme of 17th- and 18th-century women writers, appears in many of E's verses, but, unlike Katherine Philips, E does not cultivate a "SOCIETY of Friendship." E's feminism is robust and occasionally strident. In misandric portraits of suitors and lovers, she adopts the stance of the satirist and rails at man's callous treatment of her and her women friends: "Thing, call'd a Man! Ambition cheats thy Sense, / Or, thou'rt deceiv'd with too much Impudence." E is the first English feminist poet who could also be a humorist of sex, especially when she deflates mystical and platonic notions. She mocks traditional sexual values for women, like virginity and sexual complaisance, and exploits *libertin* traditions of Restoration verse. More so than Aphra Behn, E explicitly employs sexual themes and imagery, often for comic effect ("The Green-Sickness Cure," "Maidenhead," "Nuptial Song"). E is an important poet because of the early publication date of her verse, her use of 17th-century feminist themes, and her connections with literary and court circles. The poetic merit of her poem lies in her ability to portray and project complex emotional responses to romantic crises. Anticipating the new sentimental values, E's verse displays feeling over argument and reason. Her assertive feminism and cynical romantic attitudes ally her with other subversive feminist poets of her day: Behn, the early JANE BARKER, and the Egerton of *The Female Advocate* (1681). M.M.

EVELYN, Mary (1665–85), poet and devotional writer, was born at Wotton, Surrey, the daughter of diarist John Evelyn and Mary, daughter of Sir Richard Browne. Reasonably educated by contemporary standards, ME had some musical talent, considerable intellectual curiosity, and an "abundance of witt." Her father, anxious that she should direct her life toward religious devotion, in emulation of his spiritual protegée, Margaret Godolphin, provided ME with written "directions for the employment of her time," to which she added her own "Rules for spending my pretious tyme well." After ME's death from smallpox, Evelyn discovered her many manuscript "books, offices and papers" of devotional material, including original prayers and meditations and personal letters. He noted that ME "could compose very happily," and praised both her judgment and her literary style. ME's poem "A Voyage to Maryland: Or, The Ladies Dressing Room" was published anonymously by Evelyn in 1690 as the major part of *Mundus Muliebris* (reprinted three times, 1690, reissued 1700). A long doggerel poem satirizing women's concern for fashions, the "Voyage" and its companion-piece, "The Fop-Dictionary," constitute a pamphlet burlesque on contemporary manners, with an antifeminist tone characteristic of the genre: "Whoever has a mind to abundance of trouble, / Let him furnish himself with a Ship and a Woman, / For no two things will find you more Employment, / If once you begin to rig them out with all their Streamers." Although unpolished, the poems are indicative of a lively "wit" and, with ALICIA D'ANVERS's *Academia* (1691), form one of the few contributions by women to the burlesque genre during this period. R.F.

F

F, Miss (fl. 1761), autobiographer, published *A Letter from Miss F addressed to a Person of Distinction, with a New Ballad to an old tune. Sent to the author by an unknown hand* (1761). The *Letter* describes Miss F's life and the loss of her reputation through the wickedness of Lord - - -. She is publishing her description, she asserts, not from resentment, but from a desire for vindication "to remove the prejudices the public (in whom my dependence now is) have conceived against me." Miss F's version recounts how she met the nobleman at Bath and accepted his friendship, suspecting no further designs because of his great "age and condition." She and her father returned to London, where the neighbors were dazzled by "the parade of a coronet chariot" when the nobleman visited three times a week. Soon he swore "inviolable love" to F and offered her £800 a year, which she refused. Her father ridiculed her for the refusal and the disagreement led to their separation. She claims she had received from the nobleman only an inedible boar's head, "rather an odd, first, and only present, from a L- -d to his beloved mistress." By his calumny and misrepresentation, he has, F charges, prevented her from making a living as a singer and, by his frequent visits, from making a good marriage. When he refused her a subscription for a concert, she wrote her *Letter* for publication, trusting that it would "make good the deficiency of your L-d-p's subscription," and at the same time render her some justice. The ballad, presumably Miss F's as well, mocks the nobleman by telling of an aged and amorous earl pursuing a "lovely maid" and by concluding: "Dishonest love can never bear / True virtue's pride and scorn." Possibly Miss F is ANN [FORD] THICKNESSE

and the "Person of Distinction," William Villiers, Earl of Jersey. At least two sequels of the *Letter* are in existence: "A Dialogue Occasioned by Miss F- - -'s letter to a person of distinction," possibly by someone wishing to profit by the furor, and *A Reply to "A Letter from Miss F- - -, addressed to a person of distinction"* (both 1761). Miss F's original *Letter* went through two editions.   J.T.

FALCONAR, Harriet (1774–?), poet, in collaboration with her sister, Maria, published in London three volumes of poetry: *Poems* (1788; 2nd ed. 1788), *Poems on Slavery* (1788), and *Poetic Laurels* (1791). Both sisters appear to have ceased publishing after 1791. Biographical information is lacking, but it seems probable that the work of such promising young writers could have ended only because of their early deaths; when their first volume was published Maria was 17 and Harriet only 14. Their poems are based on themes popular during the closing decades of the century: the evils of slavery and colonial exploitation, the snares of ambition, neglect of merit in favor of vain pretention, defeat of superstition, and praise of British freedom. Two of these themes occur in the following lines of HF's from *Poems on Slavery*: "Shall Britain view, unmov'd, sad Afric's shore / Delug'd so oft in streams of purple gore! / Britain, where science, peace, and plenty smile, / Virtue's bright seat, and freedom's favour'd isle!" A characteristic of the work of both writers is the association of nature with religious sentiment, although romantic subjectivity is absent. In HF's "Winter," for example, the first four quatrains describe the changes wrought on the winter landscape, and the poem concludes: "Through every change of varying time / My voice shall grateful sing, / And own thy goodness most sublime, / O mercy's gracious King!" The sisters are not always so serious, however, as can be seen from the first piece in *Poetic Laurels*, apparently a joint poem. In this they anticipate the misogynist critics who comment thus: "Sure madness rages now with ev'ry woman, / And when one fav'rite scheme is grown too common, / With matchless art she strikes some novel's plan, / To sooth her pride, and tyrannize o'er man; / Tells an affected sentimental story, / Or prates in senseless rhymes of fame and glory." Each volume of poems by the Falconars received favorable comment in contemporary reviews. One writer (*Critical Review* [65, 1788]) wrote of *Poems*: "They are, in general, easy and correct; and if they have been only revised by the two friendly sisters, display greater accuracy than could be expected in two such juvenile composers." Another critic (*Monthly Review* [79, 1788]) disliked some of the diction in *Poems on Slavery*, especially recommending "the disuse of that vile contraction '*neath*, for *beneath*," but conceded that the authors had "said many good things, in very pleasing numbers." A reviewer (*CR* [2nd ser., 3, [1791]]) of the later publication, *Poetic Laurels*, while speaking favorably of the work, failed to see the improvement claimed in the preface, stating that "on the whole, we cannot perceive any very decided marks of superiority, which these poems afford, over those we have already examined."   J.F.

FALCONBRIDGE, Anna Maria [Dubois] (fl. 1790s), travel writer, was living in Bristol in 1790 when she married a ship's surgeon, Alexander Falconbridge, against her parents' wishes. Falconbridge was an abolitionist associated with William Wilberforce and the Clapham Sect, intellectual opponents of the slave trade. By these men, Falconbridge was sent to collect information from slave captains and in 1791 to Sierra Leone to rebuild a colony for destitute blacks and some poor whites. The St. George's Bay Company was formed to make the colony into a commercial venture. With Falconbridge went his brother and AMF. West Africa was in a very unstable state, with warring colonists and African tribes, but AMF was excited by its novelty and inspired by enormous curiosity for "new objects." While her husband quarreled and drank and coped with the great problem of colonizing with inadequate supplies, AMF

noted the people, customs, insects, and animals. "I cannot stir out with out admiring the beauties or deformities of her creation," she commented. Both were appalled at the condition of the original settlers, who included several white prostitutes "decrepit with disease, and so disguised with filth and dirt that I should never have supposed they were born white." Her brother-in-law died of fever within a few months of landing; shortly thereafter Falconbridge and AMF left for England to report on the colony. They took with them the son of one of the chiefs for education in England. The difficult return voyage, with most of the crew feverish, took 107 days. When the Falconbridges arrived, they learned that the British government wanted to settle in Sierra Leone more than 1,000 loyalist blacks from the American War of Independence. AMF called it a "hair-brained and ill-digested scheme," but nonetheless accompanied her husband to Sierra Leone again, with the promise that, if Falconbridge died, the Company would provide for her. They arrived in early 1792, but Falconbridge no longer had the backing of the Company and was, in AMF's view, unsuited to the mercantile role he was supposed to play. He also discovered he was to be subject to a Council consisting of men "whose heads," according to AMF, "are too shallow to support a little vicissitude and unexpected, imaginary aggrandisement." Food was scarce and in a few months most of the colonists were ill: "Five or seven are dying daily and are buried with as little ceremony as dogs or cats." Meanwhile, Falconbridge grew more drunken under the strain and finally died. AMF said honestly that she could not regret his death for "his conduct to me for more than two years past was so unkind (not to give a harsher term) as long since to wean every spark of affection . . . I ever had for him," although she conceded that "he possessed many virtues." A month after his death, AMF married Isaac Dubois, a colonist expert in building and town planning. The quarrels and misfortunes of the colony continued, exacerbated by the war between Britain and France which involved the African coast. Six months after her new marriage, in mid-1793, AMF and her husband left for the West Indies where she noted a very different colonial situation, more settled and more luxurious but also more precarious, with a few whites dominating a huge slave population. By this time AMF's abolitionist sympathies had waned, and she thought the philanthropists "impelled by too keen notions of humanity." She found slavery benefiting the Africans since, she claimed, three-quarters were more uncomfortably enslaved in their own country and slavery mitigated the "ignorance, superstition and savageness" of the Africans. But she refused a doctrinaire position and proclaimed herself "neither a friend of slavery or wholly an enemy to abolishing the slave trade." Later in 1793 AMF arrived in England where she fought the Company for the balance of Falconbridge's salary and for the land rights of the colonists in Sierra Leone. To help her case, she published an indictment of the colonial policy, insisting on the need to keep faith with the black colonists. By 1794 she had given up her suit against the Company and published *Narrative of Two Voyages to the River Sierra Leone during the Years 1791, 1792, and 1793 . . . in a Series of Letters.*

AMF's accounts present an attractive picture of a curious, hardy, and observant woman. Despite extremely arduous conditions, she expressed little self-pity, concentrating instead on the difficulties of others and her fascination with a new continent. She accepted easily the Africans she met, describing them neither sentimentally nor contemptuously. She gives a shocking description of the slaves she first encountered—"wretched victims chained and parcelled out in circles just satisfying the cravings of nature from a trough of rice placed in the centre of each circle"—and a humorous one of the threadbare majesty of an African chief—"his legs to be sure were *harlequined* by a number of holes in the stockings, through which his black skin appeared." Throughout her account AMF is extremely critical of the impractical idealists in London, "our boasted Philanthropists," who had no experience of the difficulties of colonization, and she blamed them both for the enormous sums wasted on the ill-advised colonial project and for their sending of settlers before there were buildings to receive them. She disapproved too of their providing moral idealists and missionaries for the colony rather than practical workers. AMF's diaries, intended for publication, aim to show the stupidities of the Company's colonial policy and, to some extent, to justify her first husband, but they also convey an intense delight in African society and customs and provide one of the few detailed records of life during the founding of an African colony.   J.T.

FANSHAWE, Anne, Lady (1625–80), memoirist, was born in London to an aristocratic, royalist family, elder daughter and fourth child of Sir John Harrison of Balls, Hertford, and his first cousin Margaret Fanshawe, daughter of Robert Fanshawe. During her youth, AF was instructed by her mother in the domestic arts, French, music, and singing. In her writing, she portrays herself as high-spirited: "what graver people call a hoyting girl." After the death of her mother in 1640, when AF was 15, the family moved from London to Oxford, where they lived with a local baker in relative poverty. Harrison had had a serious falling out with the King over a large financial loan and was subsequently deprived of his property and briefly imprisoned in 1642 by order of Parliament. AF's fortunes improved in 1644 when, at 19, she married her cousin Sir Richard Fanshawe (her "Dicky of Devonshire"), who was to become a prominent diplomat and man of letters. During their 26-year marriage, "fine Mistress Fanshawe" experienced both the comforts of royal favor and serious political and financial misfortune. Of their 14 children (six sons, eight daughters), nine died before their father. Because of Sir Richard's prestigious political posts as Secretary of War, Privy Councillor in 1663, and Ambassador to Portugal and Madrid, AF enjoyed close ties with the court and traveled with her husband to France, Ireland, Portugal, the Scilly Isles, and Spain. In 1667, Sir Richard died in Madrid of an ague at 58. AF wrote her popular *Memoirs* ostensibly for her only surviving son, then ten years old, as tribute and memorial to her deceased spouse and the Fanshawe family.

AF's only published work is entitled *The Memoirs of Ann, Lady Fanshawe, Wife of the Right Honble Sir Richard Fanshawe Bart., 1660–1672. Written in 1676 for her only surviving Son, Sir Richard Fanshawe, 2nd Baronet* (1676). It was first printed in 1829 and reissued in 1830 by Sir N. Harris Nicolas from a transcript made in 1766 by Catherine (Charlotte?) Colman, supposed great-granddaughter of AF. (Other printings of the *Memoirs* appeared in 1905 and 1907). One MS of the *Memoirs* is in the British Library in a bound volume bearing AF's signature and the Fanshawe coat-of-arms on the cover. While it is not in AF's own hand, it does bear her corrections. Her original MS is in the possession of a Mr.

J. G. Fanshawe. In effect a revised journal originally intended for family circulation, AF's *Memoirs* records something of the life of its author, her husband, their marriage, and the political transitions during the Commonwealth and Restoration, particularly as they affected the gentry and aristocracy. Best appreciated as essentially objective reportage of the changing scene, the *Memoirs*' principal strength is its vivid reconstructions of AF's historical past (done solely from a sometimes faulty memory), such as her escape to France in 1658 clad as a common woman; her leave-taking of Charles I at Hampton Court; and her participation in all the gaiety of the Restoration, including sailing with Charles II in May 1660 from the Hague back to England. AF's account of the landing of Queen Catherine at Portsmouth and her impressions of social and domestic manners abroad, as when she visited the court of Henrietta Maria, are also memorable entries. Horace Walpole, reviewing AF's memoirs in 1792, found them too full of "domestic distresses" to be fully entertaining. AF portrays herself primarily in conspicuous public roles as an exemplary wife and bereaved widow. Among several anecdotes is one concerning her early morning visits to Sir Richard during his brief imprisonment after the battle of Worcester in 1651: "And I would go under his window and softly call him. He that after the first time expected me, never failed to put out his head at first call. Thus we talked together; and sometimes I was so wet with rain that it went in at my neck and out at my heels." And in a passage on their happy married life, AF concludes: "Glory be to God we never had but one mind throughout our lives, our souls were wrapped up in each other, our aims and designs one, our loves one, and our resentments one. We so studied one the other that we knew each other's mind by our looks; whatever was real happiness, God gave it me in him." This largely idealized portrait is realistically modified (albeit rarely) when AF reveals more private accounts of their life together, such as an argument with Sir Richard over his refusal to give her access to royal political secrets, and her hostility toward men such as the Earls of Shaftesbury and Clarendon, whom she regarded as responsible for her husband's shifting political fortunes.   M.M

FARRELL, Sarah (fl. 1792), poet, about whom little is recorded, was apparently unhappy in youth. She reveals this in a letter dedicating her only book of poems to the Right Hon. Lady Charlotte Finch, who is thanked for having a heart "so susceptible of every finer feeling of sympathy, and benignity of soul! which led your Ladyship to cast a cheering ray over the very gloomy path I so early trod in life." The book calls SF "Mrs. Farrell," and the letter alludes to her children. SF's works appeared in 1792 as *Charlotte, or a Sequel to the Sorrows of Werter . . . and Other Poems.* The 420-line title poem is of historical interest as one of the large number of British compositions inspired by Goethe's *Sorrows of Young Werther.* Other poems in the collection include "An Epistle from Abelard to Eloisa" and "A Vision, or Evening Walk." Like "Charlotte," both are long narratives in couplet form with little originality of content. Apparently heavily influenced by the graveyard school, in all her pieces SF combines religious precepts with a melancholy sentimentality. Typical are the words of Charlotte as she dies on Werter's grave after believing she has seen his ghost: " 'What!–seize my hand!—thou cold—thou palid shade! / Alas! he drags me to yon darksome glade.' " The only short poem in the collection is the "Sonnet to Harmony," which was printed in the *Critical Review's* notice of the book prefaced by the statement: "Mrs. Farrell's reputation, we fear will not be of a very long duration, as the reader may conjecture from the following Sonnet. We give it without comment, being neither the best nor worst poem in the collection, but the shortest" (Sept. 1792).   J.F.

FAUGÈRES, Margaretta Van Wyck Bleecker (1771–1801), American poet, playwright, and essayist, was born in New York, a descendant of the prominent Schuyler and Van Wyck families, and spent her childhood in Tomhanick, a village north of Albany. Her tranquil family life was disrupted in 1777 by the Revolutionary War. The approach of Burgoyne caused her mother, ANN BLEECKER, to flee with her children, and MBF suffered in sudden succession the deaths of a sister, a grandmother, and an aunt; in 1781 her father was captured and held briefly by Canadian raiders. The shock of these incidents contributed to her mother's subsequent melancholia and death a few years later, and left their mark on the poetic sensibilities of the young MBF. Well-educated and prosperous after the war, with promising social connections, MBF defied her father's wishes and in 1791 married

Dr. Peter Faugères, an adventurer who soon sqandered her family fortune and left her destitute and widowed in 1798. She was forced to become a teacher to support herself and her daughter until her early death.

In 1793, ten years after her mother's death, MBF published a volume in tribute to her entitled *The Posthumous Works of Ann Eliza Bleecker, in Prose and Verse. To which is added, A Collection of Essays, Prose and Poetical*. In addition to her moving "Memoirs of Mrs. Ann Eliza Bleecker," her short essays include an uncharacteristically humorous one on the "Benefits of Scolding" and a heartfelt anti-slavery piece. Her verse, some of which appeared in the *New-York Magazine* (where her mother also published), dates from 1790 to 1793 and is typically replete with personification, natural imagery, and inflated language. She reiterates the conventional religious view that only after death does the soul find eternal bliss, while life on earth is a sorrowful round of separations, deaths, and mourning. Much of her early poetry is awash with tears, for "to rouse my Muse—woe is a ready theme." Night and winter serve as pervasive metaphors, fit settings for "pensive ELLA's weeping lyre." (She sometimes published under the name "Ella.") A certain ghoulish delight is evident in MBF's descriptions of the terrors of a destructive sea, the agonies of war victims, or the horrors of the Bastille. Perhaps the childhood upheavals she experienced contributed to the vividness of the violence she portrays. Her firsthand knowledge of the American Revolution and her secondhand views of the French Revolution (she married a Jacobin sympathizer) are reflected in the fiercely patriotic "A Salute to the Fourteenth Anniversary of American Independence" (1791) and in other poems applauding the export of revolutionary fervor to France. MBF's lengthy poem "The Hudson" (1793), probably her best and most popular work, traces the river from its northern source to the Atlantic, praises its natural beauty, catalogues its flora and agricultural bounty, reenacts the often-bloody historical events along its shores, and celebrates its commercial vitality. In MBF's only play, *Belisarius: A Tragedy*, published by subscription in 1795, plots against the Roman emperor Justinian and counterplots by his vicious, ambitious wife abound; but the faithful general Belisarius, unjustly blinded and exiled, remains incorruptible, rejecting opportunities for vengeance,

wealth, and political power. The author's message, offered as "plain sense," is delivered by another vanquished warrior who, having exchanged royalty for rustic peace, states that he willingly gave up "the follies of the great . . . the emptiness of pomp" and learned "that *men* were *brethern*—that to be humane was to be great." *The Ghost of John Young* (1797) is a short sophisticated monody underlining the moral inconsistency of capital punishment, in which the shade of a confessed murderer rhetorically asks citizens whether cool, deliberate murder by the state restores the first victim's life, deters others, or enables the murderer to prepare his soul for God.   P.A.

FEARON, Jane (fl. 1704–9), Quaker polemicist, recorded few autobiographical facts. She was probably from Cumberland, where many Fearons lived, but subscribed her two works "Shatton" (a small village in Derbyshire or perhaps Seaton, near Cockermouth). Early in 1704 she heard a sermon whose doctrines impelled her to write her first work, *Absolute Predestination not Scriptural: or, Some Questions upon a Doctrine which I Heard Preach'd, 1704, to a People call'd Independents, at Cockermouth in Cumberland*. The 40-page pamphlet was published in London (1705). The author's intention, she says, is to honor God and to manifest her duty and love to her neighbors; it is actually to refute the doctrine of predestination, which presents God "as the Author of all the sin and iniquity of all kinds that have been committed since the foundation of the world." The form of the book is in 48 queries. JF intended even more brevity than she achieved, and her style is plain and clear: "Query 32. Moreover why did the prophet Habakkuk say, 'I will stand upon my watch, and set me upon the tower, and will watch to see what he will say unto me, and what I shall answer, when I am reproved,' Hab. ii. 1. And not rather say, if I be one that is predestinated to life, I need do nothing but what I please, be it good or bad, it cannot alter God's absolute decree; and if I be of that number that is for damnation; let my diligence and seeking be what it will, it will avail me nothing? . . . Query 45. Why should the apostle say, 'Knowing the terror of the Lord, we persuade men;' if he had believed there was no possibility of salvation for the greater part of mankind? For according to this predestination doctrine, it doth appear there was not." JF's queries were refuted, point by point, by a Calvinist named John Atkinson, whereupon JF again, query by query, answered him in a 104-page *Reply to John Atkinson's Pretended Answer to Absolute, Predestination Not Scriptural* (1709). In this refutation, JF recounts the atrocities of Calvinists against Quakers, telling how in Boston in 1659 four Quakers were tormented, with drums beaten to prevent them from speaking and cruelly hanged for their beliefs. JF's first brief work was popular enough to be reprinted in Concord, N.H., in 1813 as *A Plain Refutation of that false and injurious doctrine, so prevalent in the world, which presents God as the author of all sin, or that He hath decreed from all eternity whatsoever comes to pass. Written by way of queries, on Scripture passages, in 1704. By Jane Fearon.*   J.P.G.

FELL, Margaret [Askew] (1614–1702), polemicist, the Mother of Quakerism, was born in Marsh Grange in the parish of Dalton-in-Furness, Lancs. In 1632, she married the lawyer (later Judge) Thomas Fell (d. 1658) and moved to Swarthmore Hall where, 20 years later, she met George Fox (1624–91) and converted to the Quaker belief in the Inner Light. Under MF's direction, the Swarthmore household became the fund-raising base, the spiritual refuge, and the communication center for the itinerant Quakers. That MF shared in the leadership of the early Quaker movement is clear from the fact that, both in person and in letter, she repeatedly represented the Quaker position to various governments from the 1650s to the 1680s. She also suffered persecution, such as spending the years 1664 to 1668 in prison for holding Quaker meetings in her home. In 1669, she married George Fox; both continued their spiritual mission as independently as before, he at large and she at Swarthmore.

MF's writings share the Quaker tendency to apply the spiritually democratic teachings of biblical Christianity to their contemporary social situation. In her *A Declaration . . . to the King* (1660), MF speaks for the thousands in prison asking Charles II for the civil right to freedom of conscience. This letter was the first public statement of the pacifist principle "our weapons are not carnal but spiritual" which we now associate with the Quakers. MF's characteristic "weapon" was the writing of tracts and letters. Her *Women's Speaking Justified . . . by the Scriptures* (1666) uses biblical authority to condemn those men who forbid female witnesses of the Spirit to speak in meetings. From God's perspective (Genesis

I), men and women are created equally "in His own image." She points out the many female spiritual teachers, leaders, and prophetesses mentioned in the Bible. God's grace is strength enough for the supposedly weak vessels of the Spirit He elevates. For example, she cites Mary Magdalene and the women who sat weeping by Christ's tomb after the men had fled. "Mark this, ye despisers of the Weakness of Women, and look upon your selves to be so wise. . . . What had become of the Redemption of the whole Body of Mankind, if they had not cause to believe the Message that the Lord Jesus sent by these Women of and concerning his Resurrection?" This passage is typical of her polemical style. Although she writes from her inner conviction, she invariably fortifies her argument with biblical authority. Modern Christian feminism might dismiss Paul as being blinded by social custom when he condemns women to silence, but MF goes through exegetic acrobatics to show that his remarks apply only to indecent and irreverent women and not to those with prophetic gifts. In her *Epistle against uniform Quaker Costume* (1700), she warns Friends against their increasing preoccupation with outward institutionalized observances and pleads for a return to the guiding inner Spirit of the early movement: "Let us stand fast in that liberty wherewith Christ has made us free." After her death, many of MF's tracts, including her 14-page autobiographical *A Relation of MF*, were brought together in *A Brief Collection of Remarkable Passages* (1710).   S.B.

FENN, Eleanor [Frere], Lady (1743–1813), writer of fiction and reading texts for children, was born in London. Her marriage in 1766 to Sir John Fenn, an antiquarian and first editor of the Paston letters, brought her to live in East Dereham, Norf., where she became known for her philanthropy; she founded Sunday schools and revived the cottage spinning industry in the area. Writing under the pseudonyms "Mrs. Teachwell," "Mrs. Lovechild," and "Solomon Lovechild," EF published works she originally wrote for her nieces and nephews; she herself had no children. John Marshall, her publisher, was keenly aware of the growing competition in the field of children's books and may have encouraged her to use successful examples by others as models for her writing. EF's most long-lived and popular book, *Cobwebs to Catch Flies* (1783), a series of dialogues with progressively more difficult words, appears to be an early experiment of Marshall's to capture the reading text market; the book bears a strong resemblance to ANNA LAETITIA BARBAULD'S *Lessons for Children* in format and conduct. EF's works, including *School Occurrences* (1782), *Fables in Monosyllables* and *Morals to a Set of Fables* (1783), *The Fairy Spectator* (1789), *The Female Guardian* (before 1789), *The Juvenile Tatler* (1788–90), *Lilliputian Spectacle de la Nature* (c. 1789), and *Sketches of Little Boys* (c. 1783), are not very entertaining, although they are consistently manageable by young readers. In all, EF published 15 works, all for children, primarily fables, fairy tales, and dialogues between children and adults. Although she did write fiction and fantasy, her prefaces show her insistence on their value as moralizing agents for the young. In *The Fairy Spectator* she promises the reader, "I will write you a dialogue where the fairy shall converse, and I will give you a moral for your dream" of her. Her favored form of composition was the playlet, or short dialogue, where the child learns always to be obedient to his parents' word and accepting of the parents' interpretation of whatever piece of fiction—fable, short story, or tale—is being examined. Her works are noted for their copious, if inferior, illustration, the large type, and ample use of white space on the page, which make the books particularly appealing to a beginning reader. R.M.

FENNO, Jenny (fl. 1791), American poet and religious writer, published one volume of moral and religious compositions. She was probably a member of Boston's Second Baptist Church. Her writings indicate familiarity with the works of ELIZABETH ROWE, Isaac Watts, Edward Young, and other British poets esteemed in her day. JF's modest and pious preface to *Occasional Compositions in Prose and Verse* (1791) explains why she has made her "private thoughts and reflections" public. Her motive is not pride: God has brought her through a serious illness, which gave her time to finish her book, and she hopes that the "feeble efforts of a young female" will glorify Him and benefit her readers. Most of the poems are in heroic couplets, but there is some metrical variety. She frequently describes nature, sometimes using poetic diction; she attempts to depict the Boston fire of 1787 and the sublimity of the Judgment Day. Several poems incorporate scriptural

paraphrases. Her elegies offer consolation and traditional sentiments; death, always imminent, is seen as "a kind messenger from heav'n." The prose meditations emphasize the sweetness of religion, which is far more delightful than "the trifles of sense." In prose and verse JF reiterates that God is revealed in nature. But the evanescence of "flow'ry nations" and other earthly things should prompt thoughts like these: "we all must shortly die, / And launch into a vast eternity; / Life is the time, Oh may we it improve, / To get an interest in redeeming love." As the only being possessed of an "immortal mind," man is responsible for "serving and glorifying God, and . . . being useful to [his] fellow creatures." JF is at her best when describing landscape and gardens and portraying the change of seasons. In the Puritan tradition, she sees natural phenomena as "monitors" of timeless truths, but she conveys a joy in earth's beauties as well as in God's love. M.D.J.

FENWICK, Eliza (?–1840), novelist and writer for children, married John Fenwick, an editor and translator immortalized for his constant borrowing by Charles Lamb as Ralph Bigod. The couple moved in radical and liberal circles and knew William Godwin, MARY WOLLSTONECRAFT, MARY HAYS, and Francis Place, who called EF "a fine, handsome, sensible, well-educated lady, a good judge of the world, and desirous to be useful in it." She published *Secresy; or, The Ruin on the Rock* "By A Woman" in 1795. In 1797 she was with Mary Wollstonecraft when she died following childbirth, assisted Godwin in notifying his friends of her death, and helped him care for the baby Mary over the next weeks. Her friendship with Mary Hays, probably begun through Wollstonecraft, was carried on in letters until old age. These letters, and those to Crabbe Robinson written between 1798 and 1828, reveal EF's later miserable life, trying to earn a living for herself, her children, and her grandchildren. In 1799 John Fenwick had to flee London to escape debts acquired through endorsing a bill for a friend; EF separated from him in 1800. Accompanied by her son and daughter, she spent part of the summer with MARY ROBINSON. In 1806 she worked for a short time for Godwin, assisting him with his recently founded Juvenile Library; she wrote several educational works for children, including *The Life of Carlo, the famous dog of Drury*

Lane Theatre (1804), *The Class Book; or, three hundred and sixty five reading lessons adapted to the use of schools* (1806), *Infantine Stories* (1810), *Lessons for Children* (1811, intended as a sequel to the celebrated Lessons of ANNA LAETITIA BARBAULD), and *Rays from the Rainbow* (1812). Helped by Thomas Holcroft, EF's daughter became an actress and went on the stage in the West Indies, where she married an actor. Meanwhile, EF worked as a governess in Ireland. When her daughter's drunken husband left her with four children, EF, with her son, went to Barbados to help her daughter and with her set up a school. In 1816, EF's son died of fever. The school deteriorated, and EF and her daughter went to America, where EF worked in a school. After her daughter died in 1828, EF and the grandchildren moved from place to place. The two older boys drowned, a third married and became a farmer, and the remaining granddaughter stayed with EF until she died in Rhode Island.

Secresy, an epistolary novel, is a typical sentimental work warning against excessive sentiment. It centers on two girls and the effect on them of their different educations. One has been separated from the world and confined in a castle. "With such an education," remarks her friend, "unless you had been a mere block without ideas, it was impossible you should not become a romantic enthusiast." She falls in love unwisely and the attachment ends with her death. *Secresy* was well received. *Critical Review* noted that the "characters, sentiments, and reflections, bespeak a more philosophic attention to the phenomenon of the human mind than is generally sought for, or discovered, in this lighter species of literary composition" and the *Monthly Magazine* found the characters created "with great strength." More appealing today than the fictional letters is EF's actual correspondence with Mary Hays, written in an informal style, in which one glimpses the difficulties of women writing for a living: "I cannot write, perpetually surrounded with my family even were I assured that I have talents to make writing profitable & I possess no such confidence." Many letters are self-pitying, begging clothes, patronage or money from friends; they give a moving description of the joys and pains of motherhood and of EF's heroic struggle against ill-health, poverty, and her own defects of character: "On Monday I was sadly disposed to compare the present with the past & make discomfort more uncomfortable, but I soon found crying encreased my headach & I got as fast as possible into a better mood." J.T.

FERGUSON, Elizabeth Graeme (1737–1801), American poet, was born in Philadelphia to Anglican parents, Ann (Diggs) and Thomas Graeme. Her Scottish father was a wealthy physician active in Pennsylvania politics. EGF was raised and educated at their country estate, Graeme Park, near Philadephia. In 1764, suffering from bad health and low spirits (the latter due to a broken engagement with Benjamin Franklin's son William), she traveled to London, where she met Laurence Sterne and other leading literary figures. The next year, during her absence, her mother died, and EGF returned to take care of the estate and her orphaned niece and nephew. Although she had published nothing, she gained a literary reputation based on her correspondence and her home became a gathering place for the literati of the area. Her 1772 marriage to Henry Hugh Ferguson ended in estrangement in the late 1770s. A British loyalist, Ferguson implicated his wife in several incidents which could have been considered treasonous. EGF, however, was sympathetic to the American cause, and hoped the war would end in compromise. Soon after the separation, financial problems forced EGF to sell her estate; yet she refused charity from friends and lived an independent, simple life, turning to religion for support. EGF's first literary work, probably written to distract her from the pain of her early broken engagement, seems to have been a blank verse translation of Fénélon's *Télémarque;* she tried to publish it in 1794 but could not meet the publishing costs. A few poems appeared in *Poems on Several Occasions* (1772) by Nathaniel Evans and in the *American Magazine and Monthly Chronicle for the British Colonies, 1757–58.* She mainly wrote occasional verse, such as "On the Death of N. Evans" and "Hymn on the Charms of Creation." In addition, in her mother's memory, she attempted a metrical version of the Psalms, which she admitted was "dull and lifeless." In contrast, the unpublished journal she kept of her travels in Europe and her correspondence are lively and entertaining. For example, in her humorous poetical letters to Evans she teases the minister: "Of manners gentle, and of temper even, / He jogs his flocks, with easy pace, to heaven. / In Greek and Latin, pious books he keeps; / And, while his clerk sings psalms, he—soundly sleeps." D.L.

FERRAR, Martha (1729–1805), poet, daughter of Edward Ferrar, attorney of Huntingdon, and descendant of the Little Gidding Ferrars, became like her friend E[LIZABETH] PENNINGTON a close friend of Samuel Richardson. About 1752 she married the Rev. Peter Peckard, biographer of Nicholas Ferrar, Dean of Peterborough and Master of Magdalene College, where portraits of them both may be found. MF was not a copious writer. Her epitaph on a parish clerk appears in *Gentleman's Magazine* (2, 1789) and her "Ode to Cynthia" in Dodsley's collection, Richardson's *Correspondence,* and Sir E.S. Brydges's *Censura Literaria.* Her "Ode to Spring," also in Dodsley, was called by Thomas Edwards "a charming piece" which "must do her honour with all judges"; John Duncombe terms her odes "elegant" in *The Feminead.* Despite this praise, MF's verse was slight and conventional; for example, she asks Cynthia to help her find her love: "guide me from thy silver throne, / To steal *her* heart, or *find* my own." J.H.

FIELDING, Sarah (1710–68), novelist and scholar, was born in East Stour, Dorset, to Edmund Fielding, of a well-established landed family, and Sarah Gould, daughter of Sir Henry Gould, a judge. SF's mother died in 1718, and her father remarried in 1719. SF's maternal grandmother obtained management of the East Stour estate and care of SF and her three sisters and two brothers. SF's stepmother, who was said to ill-treat the children, may be the model for several unkind stepmothers portrayed in the novels. SF attended boarding school in Salisbury, but she later learned Greek and Latin and gained her wide knowledge of English literature in private study. SF's small private income could not keep her from poverty and partial dependence on her brother the novelist Henry Fielding; the preface to her first work, *David Simple* (1744), explains that she writes because of financial difficulties. Some publications were profitable: *Familiar Letters* (1747) had 500 subscribers at 10s a copy. Yet SF remained poor, and Ralph Allen, ELIZABETH MONTAGU, and SF's half-brother John Fielding helped her financially in her later years. During the 1740s SF lived in London, sometimes with her sisters, sometimes with Henry. She contributed to some of her brother's works, and he revised *David Simple* for its second edition. A friend of Samuel Richardson, who praised her works and printed three of them, she defended *Clarissa* in an anonymous pamphlet in 1749. SF's acquaintances included SARAH SCOTT, ELIZABETH CARTER, FRANCES SHERIDAN, and Joseph Warton. Arthur, JANE, and MARGARET COLLIER were close friends. Jane Collier collaborated with SF on *The Cry* (1754). SF's three sisters died in 1750 and 1751, and Henry in 1754. In 1758 SF settled near Bath, and stayed there until her death.

SF's works are mainly fictions of various kinds. *David Simple* has a picaresque structure and a sentimental theme. The hero searches through London for a friend, meeting only hypocrites until he finds Cynthia, Valentine, and Camilla. *Familiar Letters,* with letters by characters in *David Simple,* is a collection of short essays and narratives rather than an epistolary novel. *Volume the Last* (1753) is a sequel to *David Simple. The Governess* (1749), one of the earliest children's storybooks, teaches moral lessons through a story about girls at school. In the fantasy world of *The Cry,* the heroine tells her story to Una, who represents truth, and a malicious audience. In *Cleopatra and Octavia* (1757) the protagonists rise from the dead to give their life histories. *The Countess of Dellwyn* (1759) tells of a heroine gradually corrupted by vanity until she becomes an adulteress. In *Ophelia* (1760) Lord Dorchester's abduction and attempted seduction of the heroine end virtuously and happily. SF's last work is *Memoirs of Socrates* (1762), a translation from Xenophon. SF is a sentimentalist and satirist who investigates the virtues and drawbacks of the sentimental attitude to life. In *David Simple, The Cry, Ophelia,* and the life of Octavia, her protagonists are naive innocents in a hostile world. Innocence can comically expose corruption. When Ophelia explains that she did not realize "that to declare I was pleased with the Conversation, and touched with the Affection of one so tenderly attached to me, was an Offence to Decency, if the Person did not wear the same sort of Dress as myself," her ingenuousness becomes a satirical comment on prudishness. Ophelia's innocence protects her, but SF's other protagonists are less fortunate. David Simple's naiveté, which makes him amiable but incompetent, causes him trouble. Octavia is miserable because she is virtuous. In *Volume the Last* SF develops the idea that virtue brings suffering. David's idyllic family life is destroyed by outside forces. He loses his money because of others' greed and cunning. This grieves him for his family's sake, and he becomes dependent on powerful acquaintances, who disappoint him. Nearly all his loved ones die, and his own death is a release, because "neither the Malice of his pretended Friends, nor the Sufferings of his real ones, can ever again rend and torment his honest Heart." The balanced dignity of SF's style here is well suited to the seriousness of her subject. Short, witty comments are also characteristic when she is attacking certain attitudes. The equation of female virtue with virginity is her target in *David Simple* when she describes a man who "had no Idea of *a Woman's being ruin'd any way but one.*" Male dominance is criticized in *The Countess of Dellwyn* when Lord Dellwyn is about "to take to Wife his destined Prey." Feminist ideas are expressed in *David Simple* by Cynthia, who tells of the prejudices against an intelligent girl and describes her comic rejection of a pompous suitor. SF defends learned women by presenting them as gentle, attractive, and dutiful. She compares Cleopatra, who dispraises intellectual women and uses feminine wiles to dominate Antony, with Octavia, an intellectual woman and a tender, obedient wife. Like Richardson, SF attaches great importance to friendship between people with feeling hearts. She is not a skillful creator of realistic characters and settings. Her characters are analytically rather than dramatically presented. Some of her techniques, particularly her use of irony, are similar to Henry Fielding's. Fantasy and allegory enrich her work, and in the introduction to *The Cry* she defends an author's right to "wander in the aerial fields of fancy." Richardson told SF that a judge of writing (probably Johnson) had told him that her knowledge of the human heart was greater than her brother's: "His was but as the knowledge of the outside of a clockwork machine, while your's was that of all the finer springs and movements of the inside." This is a partial comment, but SF is certainly most skillful at examining human motivation. Contemporary reviewers praised her, and in 1762 Arthur Murphy wrote that she was "well known to the literary world" for her "lively and penetrating genius."   J.S.

FIENNES, Celia (1662–1741), travel writer, came from a distinguished Puritan family.

She was born in the manor house at Newton Toney, near Salisbury; her parents were Col. Nathaniel Fiennes and Frances Whitehead, and her grandfather Viscount Saye and Sele, a parliamentary opponent of Charles I. Her three uncles and her five uncles by marriage all fought against the King in the Civil War. Her father's military career was interrupted when he surrendered Bristol, but he later became a parliamentary politician until the Restoration. He died in 1669; her mother lived at Newton Toney until 1691. In about 1687 CF visited Bath and in about 1691 London, where she seems to have been based thereafter, possibly with her sister. She was there for the coronations of James II, of William and Mary, and of Anne. Her travel writings date from 1685 to 1703. In 1697 she took her first large tour of the north and of Kent, but most of the journal that became *Through England on a Side Saddle in the time of William and Mary* (1888) was written from notes in 1702. Although she disclaims any intention of publishing, the foreword suggests she had publication in mind.

CF was a hardy and vigorous traveler, and her account belies her statement that she was traveling primarily for her health: "haile and raine . . . drove fiercely on me but the wind soone dry'd my dust coate." During her journeys she seems to have been accompanied by two servants, and her bed linen was carried with her, although she notes its loss between Durham and Darlington. In the Lake District "noe carriages but very narrow ones like little wheelbarrows" could travel the roads, and her horses slipped and needed reshoeing; in the Fens her horse nearly fell in a dyke, and on the rain-logged clay of Cornwall was "quite down on his nose." Nine miles of Derbyshire needed six hours to travel. CF stayed occasionally with relatives but mostly at the noisy inns, "sometymes . . . so crowded that three must lye in a bed." In Scotland where the inn had no chimney, she was smoked out and she recorded the "dirty blanckets." In Ely she found "froggs and slow-worms and snails in my roome." She was once waylaid by highwaymen and escaped, as so often in her travels, by "speciall providence." Her descriptions are detailed, sometimes long-winded, fresh and naive, varying to include cathedrals and houses, soil and gooseberries. CF travels as conscious tourist, printing her name "severall tymes" in the printing room of the Sheldonian Theatre in Oxford and taking home fragments of moss from Yorkshire.

As a Puritan CF shows anti-Catholic feeling, and she notes the number of Dissenters in the towns she visits. She has a keen sense of propriety, approving the bathing costumes in Bath that do not cling too closely and deploring the immodest pictures in Burghley House. She has an enquiring mind and a taste for detailed documentation. She is unromantic in her view, preferring the modern and spacious to the picturesque, and she has no talent for describing prospects or "vistas"; in nature she is especially enthusiastic about birds. Interested in trade and industry of all kinds, she is fascinated by people at work, the glove-makers in Derby, the shipbuilders in Rochester, and especially miners. She is also very aware of food and its cost, noting that at Beverley she was "offered a large Codfish for a shilling," and she often describes the quality of beer and wine. Approving all signs of bustle and trade, she attributes the poverty of the Scottish borderers to their laziness.

CF's foreword apologizes for "the freedom and easiness I speak and write [with]" as well as for defects in spelling and punctuation. Her style is breathless and her vocabulary limited, but she can surprise with a striking visual image. Salisbury spire is "sharp as a Dagger" and in the Fens the swans "on little hillocks of earth on the wett ground . . . look as if swimming with their nests." In Staffordshire she "went on the side of a high hill below which the River Trent rann and turn'd its silver streame forward and backward into Ss which looked very pleasant circling about the fine meadows in their flourishing tyme—bedecked with hay almost ripe and flowers." J.T.

FISHER, Abigail (fl. 1690–94), Quaker polemicist, published *A Salutation of True Love to all Faithful Friends, Brethren and Sisters, in the Fellowship of the Blessed Truth* (1690), in the dedication to which, in common with many writers of her persuasion, she refers to "various Exercises, in which Time the Enemy was not wanting to discourage me." In 1694 she continued her proselytizing with *A Few Lines in true love to such that frequent the meetings of the People called Quakers, and love to hear the Sound of Truth, but are not yet come to obey the testimony of it, that they may also hear and learn to read at home, etc.* The *Salutation*, written largely in a derivative biblical phraseology and imagery, car-

ries too much mock-afflatus. It attempts a prophetic stance ("For the Lord that has begun a *Work of Reformation*, will yet go on to a further perfecting the same in this our Age") and evinces the author's personal sense of mission: "the Lord hath caused many to rise early, and go forth late to Preach the Everlasting Gospel among you." R.J.

FISHER, Mary (1623?–1697), Quaker preacher and polemicist, became active after George Fox visited Yorkshire in 1652. In the same year, while she was in prison in York Castle for speaking out against priests, MF and six other prisoners, including ELIZABETH HOOTEN, wrote *False Prophets and False Teachers Described*. For her commitment to the Inner Light and her rebellion against external authority, she spent much of 1653–54 in York Castle. In December 1653, MF and Elizabeth Williams felt themselves called to preach against the "cage of unclean birds" at Cambridge and thus provoked the anger of a university crowd. When a magistrate asked their husbands' names, the women said they had no husband but Christ. The magistrate called them whores and had them stripped to the waist and whipped for causing a public disturbance. They sang and rejoiced during their punishment. In 1656 MF and Ann Austin went to Boston with the Quaker message, but were banished after five weeks of inhuman treatment; they continued their work in the West Indies. Between 1658 and 1660, MF made her famous journey to Adrianople to visit Sultan Mahomet IV, who received her and her message with more civility than she met from Christian authorities. In 1662, MF married William Bayley, former sea captain turned Quaker, who died in 1665 and left her with three children. In 1682 she and John Cross, her second husband, emigrated to Charleston, S.C., where she died in 1697. MF's "Testimony," written when Bayley died, is conventional despite her intrepid spirit. She writes that she is resigned to his death because "It is his Joy, though it be my Sorrow; his Gain, though my Loss; and . . . I shall go to him, and he not return to me." S.B.

FISKE, Sarah (1652–92), American spiritual autobiographer, was born in Charlestown, Mass., to a family originally from Bedfordshire, England. Her father was Captain William Symmes, a J.P. In 1672 SF married Moses Fiske, who served as the pastor of the church in Braintree (now Quincy) for 36 years. They had 14 children. Both SF and her husband were from educated, wealthy Protestant families, on both sides of which were outstanding preachers and teachers. SF's educational and religious background accounts for her knowledge of and interest in religious matters, and she must have been encouraged by her husband, a devoted minister who, toward the end of his life, was carried to his church where he preached from a chair.

SF's only published work, *A Confession of Faith* (1704), which she presented upon her admission into the church, was written when she was only 25 and not published until after her death. Her publisher, Benjamin Eliot, stated that it was drawn up without her husband's assistance. The manuscript was shown to Eliot by a friend, who decided it merited publication for "the design of it is to do good, so I hope it will be received with all candor, without any carping or critical reflections, upon anything merely circumstantial, for the main is serious, solid, and no way to be disapproved." The *Confession* is a very rigid piece without the recognition of individual frailty and the struggle to overcome personal transgressions that are found in similar writings of the 17th century. It is patterned after the Creed, with SF discussing the Trinity, divine providence, the creation, and the fall of man. She defines guilt, original sin and actual sin, corporal death and spiritual death, prayer and faith. Faith is "the grace of God, whereby the soul is brought to confide and acquiesce in the Lord Jesus Christ, both for the grace it stands in need of here and for glory hereafter." This statement is reflective of her strong belief in the redemption of mankind. SF's writing displays a knowledge of theology and spiritual subtleties unusual for a woman of her period. Equally unusual is her analysis of the church's worldly and spiritual responsibilities, and these include the administering of the sacraments. She sees the church as a communal body, with each member having a specific function, and this earthly unity as a reflection of the heavenly. "I believe that a viable particular church is a society of faithful ones, with their seed, who are in ecclesiastical confederation with God, and one with an other." After the statement of her religious philosophy and her scheme of church organization, SF concludes with a restatement of the Christian prophetic revelation, the apocalypse. J.B.

FLAXMER, Sarah (fl. 1790s), religious polemicist, wrote one tract, *Satan Revealed; or, the Dragon overcome. With an explanation of the twelfth chapter of the Revelations. And also a testimony that Richard Brothers is a prophet sent from the Lord* (London, 1795?). Richard Brothers was the author of *Prophecies and Times, Explanation of the Trinity* (1795) and other tracts (1798–1802). He believed that God spoke through him, and he called himself "nephew of the Almighty." In 1795 he was judged a criminal lunatic. SF was one of many pamphleteers who wrote in his support. M.P.

FLEMING, Elizabeth (fl. 1756), an Irish immigrant to America, is remembered for her Indian capativity narrative. Although EF's early life remains obscure, it is known that she married William Fleming, a frontier pedlar, in about 1754 and settled in Conalloway Creek, Penna. In November 1755, the Flemings were captured by Captain Jacob and his party of Shawnee and Delaware Indians. Escaping the same night, they became separated and returned to the settlement safely despite bands of marauding Indians. "A Narrative of the Sufferings and Surprizing Deliverance of William and Elizabeth Fleming" (1756) divides into two parts: William Fleming's account and EF's. It is likely that neither was actually written down by the Flemings. EF's story traces her adventures as she dodges roving Indians to return to the settlement. She hides in a gum tree, a forest, a cornfield, and finally a large oven before other settlers find her. EF's account of her escape focuses on the Indians' cruelty (she calls them "Bloodhounds" and "merciless Ravagers"), the enmity of the French, her hardships, and her providential delivery. These factual details are interspersed with sentimentalized observations (probably interpolations) such as, "But I was now forlorn in Wilderness, and had no other Comfort than to sit down on the cold Earth, indulge my usual Reflections, and bathe my bleeding Feet with my Tears." Indian captivity narratives developed from religious documents to anti-French and anti-Indian propaganda. EF's brief work perfectly conforms to the latter type. K.Z.D.

FLETCHER, Bridget Richardson (1726–70), American hymn writer, published *Hymns and Spiritual Songs* in 1773. The poems are in the usual hymn stanza and show little poetic skill. Some seem suitable for congregational singing, but several are more personal statements, especially those concerning BRF's writing. A few hymns are melancholic, but there is emphasis more on the mercy than on the terror of God. Hymn XXXVI elevates women by stressing that Jesus was born of one and asks men, "Did one so high, so dignify, / Those that you treat with scorn?" Hymn LXX on the duty of man and wife, however, insists that marriage requires submission, although according to reason and fitness. The hymns were published after BRF's death; their editor points out BRF's lack of opportunity to revise her work and pleads leniency toward poetry "which may be serviceable and instructive to some, but injurious to none." J.T.

FORMAN, Charlotte (1716–1787), journalist, translator, and political essayist, was probably born in France, the daughter of the Irish Jacobite pamphleteer Charles Forman and his wife, Mary. Forman was first clerk of the English War Office when, during the Stuart uprising of 1715, he delayed orders to General Wills and then fled to France with his wife and two daughters, leaving three sons in Ireland. In 1717 he obtained a pension from the Jacobite court in France, functioned for some time as secretary to John Law, and wrote or translated a variety of political pamphlets. In 1718 he was in Versailles, in 1724 in Amsterdam, and in 1725 in Rotterdam. CF later said that she had been "nursed in the palace of Trianon" and genteelly bred without having been taught a means of supporting herself, but she was probably writing for the newspapers at least by the 1750s. Following their fathers' death in 1739 she was helped by an elder brother until his death in 1764, after which a second brother in the service of Lord Hillsborough introduced her to Meres, printer of the *London Evening Post,* who engaged her to translate the foreign news at 9s a week. CF was now ill, without sufficient food or clothing, and miserably housed in a tiny room in Dean's-Court, Old Bailey, the windows of which were stuffed with rags, the bed without linen or coverlet. In 1766 she was arrested for debt but reprieved through the charity of Mrs. Meres and the publisher John Newbery. In 1767 her brother departed for Ireland without contacting her again. In 1768, having attempted in vain to procure help from Lord Hillsborough, she appealed to a stranger, John Wilkes, then in the King's Bench prison, and asked him to be her patron, describing herself as well-born, with nothing mean about her but her appearance. Wilkes more or less assumed responsibility, and ten of her letters to him survive among his papers in the British Library. In November 1768 Meres' enterprise failed, and in January CF began translating the news for Charles Say of the *Gazetteer.* Say dismissed her at the end of February and failed to remit her earnings until the end of May. In November 1768 she was also translating books for booksellers. CF's last letter to Wilkes is dated April 1770. She was buried at St. Bride's.

CF is a representative professional author of her period; most of her works, consisting of political writings and translations, were anonymously published. Wilkes noted on one of her letters that she was the author of a long series of letters and political essays in the public prints "which continued some years, under the distinguished signature of Probus." Contributions from Probus can be found in the *London Chronicle* of 12 April and 14 May 1757 and 22 July 1758. Verses by Probus, "A Card to John Wilkes," are in the *London Magazine,* September 1768. Politically CF, like Wilkes, was dedicated to liberty, although a devout Christian. Her letters to Wilkes are in a nervous, romantic strain. "If there is such a thing as female fortitude, I believe I have a spice of it. Sometimes I laugh at my fate, and think my case somewhat similar to that of Sisyphus. . . . At other times I compare myself to the poor wretches in Holland, who for certain crimes are let down into a deep hole half full of water, where a cock is turned upon them to let in more; on the other hand, there is a pump, which they are obliged to keep going, in order to escape drowning. So in like manner, as long as I am able to earn a shilling, I may escape drowning, and no longer. . . . I often wish I had been brought up at a green stall, for I have known people get estates that way." B.R.

FOSTER, Lady Elizabeth (Duchess of Devonshire) (1758–1824), editor and patron of the arts, was the daughter of the fourth Earl of Bristol and Bishop of Derry, an eccentric philanthropist concerned more with the problems of Ireland than with those in his own family. She was the granddaughter of LADY HERVEY. Early in life, she married John Thomas Foster, an Irish MP, from whom she separated, leaving behind her two children and putting herself outside respectable society. She became a close friend of Georgiana, DUCHESS OF DEVON-SHIRE, whose household she soon joined, acting occasionally as chaperone to the Duke's illegitimate daughter and soon becoming the Duke's mistress. Both EF and the Duchess had children by the Duke, EF going abroad for her two confinements to avoid scandal. EF was greatly admired for her beauty and manner and inspired much romantic devotion from, for example, Edward Gibbon. In France she became friendly with ANNE DAMER. Her two children by the Duke remained in France until the Revolution, after which they were brought up with those of the Duchess. In 1796 Foster died and EF was reunited with her two sons. The Duchess of Devonshire died in 1806 and EF wrote of her, "She was the only female friend I ever had. Our hearts were united in the closest bonds of confidence and love." In 1809 EF married the Duke. After his death in 1811 she lived in Rome, entertained distinguished society, and patronized the arts, supporting, for example, the excavation of the Forum.

The two outstanding editions she printed were Horace's *Fifth Satire of the First Book* (1816) and Virgil's *Aenead* (1819). Both were lavishly designed. The edition of Horace included engravings by the brothers Ripenhausen and an Italian translation attributed to Molagani. When some errors were found in the translation and printing, she printed another edition in 1819, this one with engravings by Caraccioli. Her two-volume edition of the *Aenead* was prefixed by her own portrait, and included engravings by Marchetti. The two works enjoyed a select audience throughout the Continent and were presented to some of the outstanding libraries. *The Passage of the Mountain of Saint Gothard* (1816) was a handsome bilingual edition by EF of Georgiana's poem, with lithographs by EF and one by the Countess of Bessborough. Notes explain that the poem and drawings grew out of a journey of the two women in 1793. During the last five years of her life, EF planned to publish decorous editions of Cora and Dante, but neither scheme was executed. Several medals illustrative of her printings were struck, and her portrait was painted by Reynolds and Gainsborough. In 1863 EF's papers, letters, and journals were published as *Anecdotes and Biographical Sketches*. These concern people EF met, for example a ferryman at Twickenham who remembered Pope; the Duke of Wellington;

Chateaubriand, who was not approved—"An eloquent writer, but, I believe, a factitious character; extremely vain selfish, and full of ambition"; Constant, found repugnant—"His cold and cynic countenance, designing look, and constrain'd manner, were always peculiarly disagreeable to me"; and Madame de Stael, much admired for her wit and "perfectly natural" manner. Many of EF's letters to her family appeared in *The Two Duchesses . . . 1777–1859*, edited by Vere Foster in 1898; they concern her separation, travels, and affection for her friend, whom her mother called "your dear Duchess."   J.T. and R.S.

FOSTER, E. M. (fl. 1795–1803), novelist, wrote *The Duke of Clarence: An Historical Novel* (1795), *Frederic and Caroline* (1800), and *Light and Shade: A Novel* (1803); title pages refer to other works entitled *Federetta, Rebecca,* and *Miriam. The Duke of Clarence* concerns the decision of Reginald to retire to his ancient castle to educate his daughter Elfrida, and Elfrida's troubled romance with his ward de Montford. The plot eventually hinges on de Montford's discovered royal birth. The novel is set against the Wars of the Roses through the accession of Henry VII. Including creaky coincidences and much historical color, it is basically a historical romance with gothic elements; for example, on Elfrida's abduction to another castle: "after having crossed the bridge, and heard the loud and horrid crash, which it made, as it returned to its fastenings, the sound reverberated to her heart:—it sunk within her; and she feared, she was for ever separated from happiness, as she was from the world." While admitting that the work displayed "some powers of invention," the *Critical Review* dwelt on the implausibility of the narrative links and stated that those "who can be entertained by surprising coincidences, in which the laws of nature and probability are violated without scruple, may beguile a vacant hour, without any hazard to their morals, by the perusal of this novel." *Light and Shade* ventures into a different genre, following the upbringing and social career of Cary Saville. It is written in a light, ironic style, with frequent addresses to the reader, and parades a variety of social types who represent different dispositions of "light" and "shade."   R.J.

FOSTER, Hannah Webster (1758–1840), American novelist who also wrote for magazines and newspapers, was born in Salisbury, Mass., the daughter of a prominent merchant. Little is known of her childhood or education, although historical and literary allusions in her writings indicate that she was well-read. In 1785 she married the Rev. John Foster, minister of the First Church of Brighton, Mass., and became a leader in social and literary activities of his parish; they had six children. After her husband's death, she lived the last years of her life in Montreal with two daughters, also writers.

HWF contributed regularly to magazines and newspapers before the anonymous publication of *The Coquette; or the History of Eliza Wharton* (1797), her best-known work. Subtitled "Founded on Fact," it is based upon the life of a distant cousin of her husband. An epistolary novel, it shares many of the strengths and weaknesses of the genre. The reporting of incidents several times by different people reveals character through a comparison of points of view; many of the letters sound natural and spontaneous. A few letters, however, are excessively long, didactic, and sentimental. Obviously much influenced by the seduction novels of Samuel Richardson (especially *Clarissa*), *The Coquette* introduces two interesting and complex major characters. Eliza is strong-willed and rebellious, a clergyman's daughter who covets wealth and excitement. Major Sanford, in the mold of Richardson's Lovelace, glories in the role of rake and determines to win the coquette Eliza to "avenge [his] sex by retaliating the mischiefs she meditates." Eliza knows Sanford is dangerous but cannot reconcile herself to "the tedious round of domestic duties" until she has "sowed [her] wild oats." Both characters receive appropriate punishment, accompanied by lengthy moral lectures and confessions. *The Coquette* went through thirteen editions in its first 40 years, enjoying its greatest popularity between 1824 and 1828. Not until 1866, however, when it was included in T.B. Peterson and Brothers' "Dollar Series" reprints of popular fiction, was the novel attributed to HWF. Her second book, *The Boarding School; or Lessons of a Preceptress to Her Pupils* (1798), was less successful. Lacking plot, the letters here purport to show how a clergyman's widow educates her female charges to fulfill their future roles as well-bred ladies, wives, and mothers. Needlework, reading, composition, "the sprightly dance," and "the sentimental song" comprise their curriculum.

In thinly disguised lectures, the widow warns against the "dangerous" influence of novels and argues against the accepted maxim that "reformed rakes make the best husbands." She demands greater punishment for seducers and more tolerance for their victims. After the publication of *The Boarding School* HWF wrote only short newspaper articles. E.G.

FOWKE, Martha (fl. 1720), essayist, published only one volume: *The Epistles of Clio and Strephon, being a collection of letters that passed between an English lady, and an English gentleman in France, who took an affection to each other, by reading accidentally one another's occasional compositions both in prose and verse* (1720). The preliminary pages state that it is "A critical essay containing some remarks upon the nature of epistolary and elegiac poetry, by way of letter from Mr. John Porter to his friend Richard Pocock." A second edition was published in 1728, and a third in 1732, when it was given another title, *The Platonic Lovers.* M.P.

FRAMPTON, Mary (1773–1846), diarist and letter writer, was the daughter of the well-to-do James and Phillis Frampton of Moreton, Dorset, where her father had been High Sheriff. Her mother married first Charlton Wollaston, physician to Queen Charlotte; the couple had two children. She then married James Frampton; MF was their second child, born when her mother was 46 and her father 62. As a child MF traveled to London once every two years with her parents and was there when the Gordon Riots occurred, the Warren Hastings trial, the thanksgiving for the recovery of George III in 1789, and the wedding of the Duke of York to the Princess of Prussia in 1791. MF never married, and in about 1786 she and her mother settled in Dorset where they became a center of local society. Many friends admired MF's accomplishments and sociability. *The Journal of Mary Frampton, From the Year 1779, Until the Year 1846* (1885) was edited by MF's niece, Harriet Mundy. It begins in 1803 but starts with memories from 1779. The "Journal" is in a minority: the work consists mainly of letters (of which the vast majority were not written by MF, but by her brother and half-brother), loosely stitched together by passages of documentary narrative. MF's letters contain much society gossip, especially about the court and Princess Charlotte, whose governess was a friend of MF and her mother. The journal entries, conservative in tone, refer detachedly to political upheavals of the time. An entry of 1814 notes: "After the expulsion of Napoleon from Paris, and the first possession of that city by the allied armies, all the great Princes and generals—the Emperor of Russia and King of Prussia setting the fashion—came to England, where the madness to see persons who had become so famous was carried to an extravagant height: people from the most distant parts of England flocking to London to get a peep from a garret window or an area grating at a hero or a Prince as they passed." Among the entries of 1802 are various anecdotes of Paris, derived from a Mr. Churchill, for example of Bonaparte: "His policy in regard to opening *to all*, entirely free of charge, all the fine galleries of pictures, statues, and other monuments of the arts, is admirable [but] the arrestation of the English, on the contrary, was the measure of a light mind swayed by passion, and could not in any light conduce to the glory or advantage of the nation he governs." J.T.

FRANCIS, Ann (1738–1800), scholar and poet, was the daughter of Daniel Gittins, rector of South Stoke, near Arundel, Sussex, who educated her in Latin, Greek, and Hebrew. AF spent most of her adult life in Edgefield near Holt, Norfolk, the wife of Robert Brainsby Francis, the rector.

AF published *A Poetical Translation of the Song of Solomon, From the Original Hebrew, with a Preliminary Discourse, and Notes, Historical, Critical and Explanatory* (1781) dedicated to John Parkhurst, author of a Hebrew lexicon; the translation is remarkable for its use of the Hebrew and for its highly dramatized form. AF divides the speeches between Solomon and two women, the Spouse and the Jewish Queen (Solomon's new and old loves). Thus she transforms the poem into a triangular drama which psychologizes the emotions and legitimizes the switches of mood. She adds such stage directions as "Jewish Queen (to Solomon, signifying her firm resolution of keeping her distance)." Her translation is stately and voluptuous: "Thy lips are like a scarlet thread, / Thy speech enchanting flows! / Behind thy veil, what vivid red / On each soft temple glows! / So glows the gay pomegranate's purple hue, / When the bright sections open to the view." AF feels it necessary to defend her enterprise: it may "be thought an improper undertaking for a woman [because] the learned may imagine it a subject *above* the reach of my *abilities*; while the unlearned may incline to deem it a theme unfit for the exercise of a *female* pen." But, she says, the poem praises married love and its eroticism is allegorical. She emphasizes that her translation is a fresh one in the face of imagined objections that "it is needless for a *woman* to step forth, and expatiate on a subject, which has already been so satisfactorily treated by [learned men]; since no *new* lights can be expected, or hoped for, from the *feeble* efforts of a *female* muse." AF's translation is strengthened by extended citation of material attempting to set the poem in its cultural milieu. For this purpose, she makes great play with LADY MARY WORTLEY MONTAGU's *Letters*. AF's classical education comes into service in her poem *The Obsequies of Demetrius Poliorcetes* (1785), which sometimes has a jabberwocky effect: "Its ample leaves, in part, how green / Virid, 'mid the brumal scene." AF's *Poetical Epistle from Charlotte to Werther* (1788) is in the tradition of heroic epistle with its central insistence on the woman writing rather than on the active hero.

Miscellaneous Poems (1790) includes two more such epistles, "Dido to Iarbas" and "Anna to Aeneas." Most of the poems in this collection, however, are domestic in theme—elegies and poems addressed to a Tame Robin, a Rosebush, and "Don Pedro, a Favourite Spaniel." Some poems give an exact sense of intimacy and have a touchingly playful acceptance of experience, for example the long autobiographical "The Sylph"; in this "The Author, after taking leave of her elder Son, retired to her Closet, with a full heart; but on opening her bureau—a beautiful Pot of Ginger, in full bloom, presented itself: curiosity suspended grief, and the following thoughts occurring, she threw them into the present form; and addressed them to her Son." "The Sylph" also gives an accurate image of AF's own aim and achievement: "Delight a favourite thought to paint, / In number'd lines, with pleasing art / To trace the features, or the heart—/ The task be hers—nor further try / The latent source of harmony." The collection includes some royalist poems, "A Sacred Ode, on his Majesty's Recovery," and "Ode on the Arrival of His Royal Highness Prince William of Gloucester, at the University of Cambridge." *A Plain Address to My Neighbours* (1798) is a broadside ballad offering a lurid tale of what the

French Revolution may bring in its wake for the workers of England: "Could they but land on Britain's coast, / They'd set the *poor man* free! / They'd set him free— alas! from what? / From wife, and children dear; / They'd eat his bread, and burn his cot; / What has he *then* to fear? . . . / 'Tis thus 'The Glorious Rights of Men' / Leave NOTHING—to deplore."   G.B.

FRENCH, Mary (fl. 1703), American poet, was captured by Indians in a raid on Deerfield, Mass., in 1703 and, with others, was taken to the French in Canada. There she was made to accept Roman Catholicism. In 1706 Cotton Mather collected together the writings of the captives in a work entitled *Good Fetch'd Out of Evil.* Among these was MF's 104-line poem to her sister: "A Poem Written By a Captive Damsel, About Sixteen or Seventeen Years of Age, Who Being [Told?] That Her Younger Sister at a Distance From Her [Would?] Be Led Away by the Popish [ ], Address'd Her in these Lines." It is a crude statement of Puritan belief, urging constant attention to death and acceptance of earthly cruelty as the will of God: "That earthly things are fading flow'rs / We by experience see; / And of our years and days and hours / We as observers be . . . / Let us be silent then this day / Under our smarting rod."   J.T.

FULLER, Anne (?–1790), novelist, published two historical romances and perhaps an epistolary novel between 1786 and 1789. Little is known about her life except that she died of consumption near Cork, Ireland. *Alan Fitz-Osborne* (1786), which is set during the reign of Henry III, claims to be a historical novel. But in her "Preface" AF explains: "I mean not to offend the majesty of sacred truth by giving her but a secondary place in the following pages. Necessity, stronger than prudence, obliges me to give fiction the pre-eminence." AF's indebtedness to Walpole is obvious in this gothic tale of usurpation, ghosts, murder, and underground caverns. *The Son of Ethelwolf* (1789), another historical tale written much in the vein of *Alan Fitz-Osborne*, is set during the time of Alfred and is made more interesting by the inclusion of a resourceful female character who, disguised, even fights by Alfred's side in battle. AF's historical novels are superior to those written by her contemporaries. Published anonymously, *The Convent* (1786) is a very different type of work. It consists almost entirely of letters exchanged between two young women who carefully examine the world around them: they make fun of grocers and tallow chandlers who strut about as soldiers, and they satirize women who, "having no ideas of their own, they get a little consequences in the world, by adopting those of other people." Although commonly attributed to AF, *The Convent* is stylistically and thematically different from AF's other works, and its authorship is in doubt.   M.A.B.

G

GARDNER, Sarah [Cheney] (fl. 1763–95), dramatist, first appeared on the stage in 1763, as Miss Prue in *Love for Love* at Drury Lane Theatre. She is reported to have "play'd with spirit,—a very pretty, genteel Figure, but very raw and awkward— got great applause." In the same season she played Rose in George Farquhar's *The Recruiting Officer*, and first appeared at Covent Garden in 1765, as Polly in George Colman the Elder's *Polly Honeycombe*. In the same year she married the minor actor William Gardner. SG moved to the Haymarket in 1767 and until 1777 played leading roles there in such plays as Farquhar's *The Beaux Stratagem*, William Congreve's *The Old Batchelor* and SUSANNAH CENTLIVRE's *The Busy Body,* returning occasionally to Covent Garden, usually to play in benefits or substitute for a regular member of the company. In 1777, SG's comedy "The Advertisement; or, A Bold Stroke for a Husband" was produced once, for her benefit, at the Haymarket. SG spoke the prologue and played the central role of Widow Holdfast. The plot concerns a wealthy, vivacious young widow who advertises for a husband. It is a light, comic play or romantic intrigue, which, of course, ends happily. The contretemps surrounding the production of this play, which was never published and never again acted, is more interesting than the play itself. SG claimed that she submitted her play to Colman and quarreled with him when he wished to postpone production, and that many of the actors, Colman's friends, refused to learn their parts. The *London Chronicle* (August 1777) reported that SG's eagerness to have the play produced for her benefit was due to the necessities of her young family. On the evening of the performance, SG ad-dressed the audience, complaining of the lack of cooperation of some of her colleagues. The audience then hissed those actors who did not know their lines and applauded SG on each appearance and at the conclusion. *London Magazine* (August 1777) reported that the play was "well received." The *Morning Chronicle* (August 1777) absolved Colman of blame, reporting that he had agreed that SG could present her play provided she could persuade the company to learn their parts; that SG would have acted well if she had not been affected by having written the play; as it was, "she spoke, walked, and moved, as if she had lost her senses." After this incident SG did not act in London for five years, during which time she played in Jamaica. In 1782, she appeared once again on the London stage, in Foote's *The Author* and in *The Female Dramatist*, a play sometimes ascribed to her but which Richard Brinsley Peake in his *Memoirs of the Colman Family* insists was written by George Colman the Younger. With the exception of a benefit performance in 1795, SG did not again appear in London. In 1783 she delivered at the Capel Theatre "a course of humorous, entertaining, political, and satyrical Lectures." She is described by the actor John Bernard, who knew her in Dublin, as "a chambermaid actress of great merit" and, "though a married woman, fond of very singular adventures." Bernard describes her eluding her Dublin creditors with a mock illness and funeral. Later in 1783 SG surfaced in Liverpool, once more lecturing. SG returned to the West Indies in 1785; and in 1789 she appeared in Charleston in "a Concert of Vocal and Instrumental Music." In November of that year she was in New York for the first time; in "Fashionable

Raillery; or, the Powers of Eloquence Displayed in a Spirited and Humorous Touch on the Times," a performance she was said to have given 47 times in Dublin and with equal success in Jamaica and Charleston. A month later SG appeared in a benefit at the John Street Theatre, since she had been deceived in Charleston by "a plausible scamp," brought north, "stripped of every penny," and "left helpless." SG's final London performance took place in 1795. She wrote the prelude and played in all of the three pieces presented. The recent discovery of several manuscripts in SG's hand suggests that she was interested in further playwriting: two plays apparently never acted were "The Loyal Subject," a comedy in five acts, and "Charity," a one-act farce. They are unremarkable and would have added nothing to her reputation.   L.M.

GETHIN, Grace, Lady (1676–97), learned lady, daughter of Sir George Norton of Abbot's Leigh, Somerset, acquired considerable learning as a child; she married Sir Richard Gethin, baronet. GG was buried in Westminster Abbey. *Reliquiæ Gethinianæ* (1699) was published posthumously as "A Collection of Choice Discourses, Pleasant Apothegms, and Witty Sentences" thought to be her original compositions. Except for a religious poem written by GG at age 11, however, the book contains not the gleanings of "her overflowing Wit and Fancy," but merely extracts copied from works by Lord Bacon and other writers on such topics as Friendship, Reading, and Charity. William Congreve wrote memorial verses for the third edition, in praise of her learning, intelligence, and beauty, "Some Angel-mind with Female Form endu'd," and "Her Beauteous Looks were join'd / To a no less admir'd Excelling Mind."   G.B.

GIBBES, Phebe (fl. 1764–88) novelist, wrote her books for circulating libraries stressing fashion and sensibility. *The Life and Adventures of Mr. Francis Clive* (1764) possesses a plot resembling *Amelia* but has some scenes set in the East Indies. *The Woman of Fashion* (1767) documents the growth of sensibility. *The American Fugitive: or, Friendship in a Nunnery* (1784) permits the rescue of a young woman from a convent in America and also promises in the title "a full description of the mode of education and living in convent schools . . . , the manners and characters of the nuns; the arts practiced on young minds;

and their baneful effects on society at large." Although the plot is improbable, style and language in the novel "are of a superior order" and some political passages on the American Revolution "would make a capital figure in the most conspicuous column of a republican print" *Critical Review* (Oct. 1778). *The Niece* (1788) exposes an innocent heroine to the machinations of servants. This novel PG claims to have "written on a plan entirely new"; that is, epistolary form gives way to conversation and narrative.   G.B.

GILL, Sarah Prince (1729–71), American devotional writer, in her works represents many currents in colonial culture. Her father, Thomas Prince, was the pastor of Boston's Old South Church and author of the noted *Chronological History of New England*. The Prince children were encouraged to read in the family's unusually good library of divinity and history. Of the several offspring, SPG was the only child to survive her father. Her sister DEBORAH PRINCE died of a fever at 21 in 1744. The two girls experienced religious conversion about the same time, probably as a result of George Whitefield's visit to Boston in 1740, and thereafter both kept records of their spiritual meditations. As an adult SPG moved in Boston's active political circles. She became the first wife of Moses Gill, a Boston merchant who was the brother of John Gill of the radical *Boston Gazette* and a friend of John Adams. (After her death Gill served as a member of the Continental Congress and eventually as lieutenant governor of Massachusetts.) The couple had no children. John Adams once referred to SPG as "a very learned lady," and she corresponded with CATHERINE MACAULAY. Her obituary in the *Boston Evening Post*, 12 August 1771, states: "Nor was her benevolence confined within the narrow limits of *private* connections, but extended to the whole human race. . . . she, to her latest hour, fervently wished and prayed for the liberty of the world in general, and of her own country in particular."

SPG's *Devotional Papers* was first published as an appendix to the Rev. John Hunt's sermon on her death, and was republished (usually in tandem with her sister's writings) in the US in 1773. The work reveals strong Congregational traditions of mysticism and guilt, centering on themes of submission to God, a deep sense of sin, and abasement before the Creator. "God All, and in All!" and "Breathings after

GOD" are typical chapter headings. A particularly striking passage dates from SPG's early adulthood: "I love to serve my friends, but I delight vastly more in feeling my very will intirely subject to God.—Yea, I have found an unspeakable pleasure in having my will cross'd, and my carnal desires denied by him." SPG's deathbed letter returned to the themes of her youth: "I am expecting a call into the invisible world, that unknown region. The prospect is grand, awful, and all important, and sometimes I am all amazement—I have no hope in anything but the value of a Redeemer's blood, and the free mercy of God."   G.T.P.

GLASSE, Hannah (1708–70), writer on housekeeping, was born in London, the daughter of Isaac Allgood, son of the Rev. Major Allgood, rector of Simonsburn; her mother, Hannah, was the daughter of Isaac Clark, a London vintner. HG had at least one brother, Lancelot (1711–82), first sheriff, then MP for Northumberland from 1748 to 1759, who was knighted in 1760. Nothing is known of HG's own life, except that she bore three sons and six daughters to John Glasse, son of an Irishman and a Scotswoman, and that in 1751, the middle of her writing career, she was "Habit Maker to Her Royal Highness the Princess of Wales, in Tavistock Street, Covent Garden." It is possible that she is the "Hannah Glass of St Paul's Co. Garden" named in the May 1754 bankruptcy list in the *Gentleman's Magazine*. HG must have been an active, enterprising woman. Her *Compleat Confectioner* (Dublin, 1742) appeared in at least seven editions in Dublin and London before 1800. It was followed by her most widely known work, *The Art of Cookery Made Plain and Easy*, first published in London in 1747, for which she amassed nearly 200 subscribers. *The Servant's Directory, or House-keeper's Companion* (1760) was in its fourth edition by 1762. Four children's books—*Cato, or Interesting Adventures of a Dog of Sentiment* (1816), *Easy Rhymes for Children From Five to Ten Years of Age* (1825), *The Infant's Friend* (n.d.), and *Little Rhymes for Little Folks* (n.d.)—are also attributed to HG.

   The Art of Cookery, ostensibly intended for the use of servants and written "in so full and plain a manner, that the most ignorant Person, who can read, will know how to do Cookery well," evidently interested many of their mistresses also. By the time of HG's death, it had appeared in at least ten editions. Between 1770 and 1843,

16 more were issued, including one in Edinburgh (1781) and two in America (1805 and 1812). The work did not appear under HG's name until 1788, by which time she was generally acknowledged its author. When Samuel Johnson denied in April 1778 a claim that John Hill had written the book, he did not intend to support HG's authorship. Instead he suggested jocularly that the work (with which he was evidently familiar) gave recipes too unscientific to have come from Hill or any other educated man, who would never speak of saltpeter and *sal prunella* as two different substances, and he expressed a desire to write a better cookery book of his own, practical like HG's but based on the exact and economical compoundings of pharmacology. Some items in *The Art of Cookery* are quaint: eels stewed in broth is recommended for "weakly and consumptive constitutions"; a recipe for "hysterical water" includes a quarter-pound of dried millipedes; a concoction called "plague water," reported efficacious against the London plague of 1665, is made from 47 different roots, flowers, and seeds. Others, such as the recipe for seed cake that calls for seeds, four pounds each of butter and flour, and 35 eggs, beaten together for two hours, are impractical today. Before modern refrigeration, HG's gauge for freshness of eggs (touch the tip of the tongue to the large end of an egg to see if it is still warm) must have been based on useful personal experience. Her directions, on the whole, are clear, sensible, and still timely: "All things that are green should have a little crispness, for if they are overboiled, they neither have any sweetness or beauty." She gave explicit advice for choosing good, fresh ingredients and for proper preparation of different foods in Continental as well as English cooking styles. Later editions of her book also considered menus appropriate for different seasons and the attractive presentation of food. American editions included special recipes for native foodstuffs and instructions for more self-sufficient households. In her own time and for many years after, HG's book must have done much to raise the standard of cooking in homes in the English-speaking world.   M.D. and B.B.S.

GLOVER, Jean (1758–1801), poet, was born at Kilmarnock, Ayrshire, the daughter of a weaver. She and her husband became strolling players; she was a good singer and she played the tambourine in the streets to attract customers to her husband's juggling act. She was described as "a roughly hardened tramp, a wilful, regardless woman." She composed "Ower the muir among the Heather," which was written down by Robert Burns; its first verse, anglicized, is as follows: "Over the moor and among the heather / Down among the blooming heather, / By sea and sky! she shall be mine, / The bonnie lass among the heather." JG probably died in Co. Donegal.   J.T.

GOMERSALL, Mrs. A. (fl. 1789–1824), novelist and poet, lived in Leeds, Yorks., and wrote three novels that were published between 1789 and 1796. Although little is known about her life, her work justifiably gained some critical praise in its time. AG's novels are superior to those of most other female writers of the period. The *Monthly Review* recommended *Eleonora* (1789), an epistolary novel, and *The Citizen* (1790) as entertaining and accurate portrayals of middle- and lower-class life, distinguished by touches of humor, effective characterization, and "a happy facility in sketching familiar conversations." Although *The Disappointed Heir* (1796) was not as highly praised, it proves interesting for its female characterization. Avoiding the stereotype of the victimized woman, AG depicts female characters who are both intelligent and resilient. A heroine disobeys her stepfather, proclaiming that "I can patiently sustain *injuries*, but I inherit a mind which scorns to bow to *insult*." And the "wronged woman" realizes that she and her children are better off than if she were married: "To you, Sir Philemon, I have been such in every thing, but the name; and, pardon me, if I add, your unmanly behaviour has made me long cease to regret I do not bear *that*." AG's final work was a poem entitled "Creation" (1824).   M.A.B.

GOOCH, Elizabeth Sarah (1756–post 1804), writer of autobiography, novels, poems, and essays, was born in Edwinstow, Notts. In 1759 the death of her father, William Villa-Real, of a wealthy Sephardic-Jewish family, left her an heiress, but contact with her paternal family was discouraged by her mother. EG's arranged marriage to William Gooch, second son of Sir Thomas Gooch, produced two sons but soon ended disastrously with mutual recriminations. Taken to France and abandoned there, she lived partly on an annuity steadily diminished by Gooch and partly from the support of various gentlemen. She shuttled between France and England as her relationships and finances dictated until 1787, when she was imprisoned for debt. EG began to write about her experiences to earn her release. By 1802 she was sufficiently reestablished in society to dedicate her "Monody to the Memory of his Grace the Duke of Bedford," an effusion full of Johnsonian echoes, to the Duke of Norfolk "and Other Members of the Whig Club." Her earlier life is echoed in her novels, in which naive, imprudent heroines are abandoned by unfeeling husbands after a minor misunderstanding, are supported by other men and lose their social position, but are shown to be superior in character and delicacy of sentiment to their more respectable counterparts.

An Appeal to the Public, On the Conduct of Mrs. Gooch . . . Written By Herself (1788), composed in Fleet Street Prison, is a self-justification and a plea for help. Her experiences before and after marriage are treated more fully, including additional lovers, in *The Life of Mrs. Gooch*, in 3 vols. (1792), in which vivid anecdotes about French and English society are combined with moments of pathos: "Without one assisting friend, how is it possible for me to stem the torrent of adversity that is pouring in upon me from every side?" In *Poems on Various Subjects* (1793), consisting chiefly of elegies (one on Sir Joshua Reynolds) and a few sonnets, pathos predominates: "Will then my suff'rings never cease / But lies in death my only road to peace?" In EG's novels sentiment is combined with sensationalism. In *The Contrast*, 3 vols. (1795), EG traces the love relationships of Lady Jane, whose mind is "by nature susceptible of tender sentiments and soft impressions," who is cast off by her husband and falls in with disreputable people, but who is eventually pitted against her scheming young step-mother-in-law to show the contrast between "unavoidable error and premeditated vice." *Truth and Fiction*, 4 vols. (1801), mingles invention with fact that is scarcely distinguishable from fantasy. This complicated epistolary novel is side-tracked into a long gothic tale about a hermit guilty of murder and another tale about "the luckless Theodora" whose Portuguese-Jewish ancestors are clearly modeled on EG's own. *Sherwood Forest*, 3 vols. (1804), using material from EG's native Nottinghamshire, first contrasts the families of a solid Scottish gentleman and of a nouveau-riche English peer, then focuses on a young recluse vaguely modeled on Robin Hood who is maltreated by the peer's son but rescued by a benevolent wandering Jew, and also introduces a flighty society lady corrupted by a wicked woman friend. In addition, EG wrote the novel *Fancied Events: or, The Sorrows of Ellen*, 2 vols. (1799), and completed Thomas Bellamy's novel, *The Beggar Boy* (1801). Her earlier essay collection, *The Wanderings of the Imagination*, 2 vols. (1796), already reveals her sympathy for beggars and other unfortunates and primitives, such as a blind Welsh harpist. EG is noteworthy not for her novels, which suffer from excessively episodic plotting, or for her poems and essays, which are unrelievedly sentimental, but for her autobiography, which vividly presents the dilemma of a spirited young woman unprotected by husband or family.   M.K.D.

GOODHUE, Sarah Whipple (1641–81), American writer from New England, composed her last testament, *The Copy of a Valedictory and Monitory Writing*, seven days before she gave birth to twins, because "I have had of late a strong persuasion upon my mind, that by sudden death I should be surprized." Three days after childbirth, she died. *Valedictory* was published in the same year and reprinted in 1770, 1805, and 1830. SG was obviously an educated woman. Her final 3000 words, although fairly crude, are not the product of an unpracticed hand. Her *Valedictory* includes couplets, often using a 17-syllable line, addressed to members of her family (she bore ten children): "My first, as thy name is *Joseph*, labour so in knowledge to increase, / As to be freed from the guilt of thy sins, and enjoy eternal Peace."   C.C.

GRAHAM, Isabella (1742–1814), devotional writer, was born in Lanarkshire, Scotland, daughter of John and Janet Hamilton Marshall. She was educated at boarding school and influenced by the strict Calvinism of her family and by Dr. John Witherspoon, later president of the College of New Jersey (Princeton). When she was 17 she made a total commitment to her faith, which sustained her throughout her life. She married a widower, John Graham, in 1765; two years later she traveled with him to Canada, where he was posted as surgeon to the Royal American Regiment and served at Quebec, Montreal, and Fort Niagara. He died on a mission to Antigua (1762–63), leaving IG virtually penniless and the only

provider for their three daughters and a son born after his father's death. IG returned to Scotland, but her family was unable to help her, and she lived in poverty in a cottage at Cartside until, with the help of her friends, she opened a boarding school at Edinburgh in 1780. In addition to her teaching of young ladies, IG relieved the poor and promoted her religion by organizing a society for the relief of the destitute sick and becoming a patron of the Society for the Promotion of Christian Knowledge and Piety. She traveled to New York in 1789 and there founded a school for young women. She also helped to establish an orphan asylum (1806), a Magdalen society dedicated to helping females in lunatic asylums (1811), and, in the last year of her life, a Sunday school for adults and for young people working in factories, and a society for promotion of industry among the poor. She died in New York City at the home of her daughter, Joanna Graham Bethune. IG's writings, along with her biography, were published after her death by Mrs. Bethune under the title *The Power of Faith, Exemplified in the Life and Writings of the Late Mrs. Isabella Graham* of New York (1817). This popular collection of biography, correspondence, devotional exercises, journal entries, and religious poems required four editions and was circulated widely in Britain. Mrs. Bethune also published *The Unpublished Letters and Correspondence of Mrs. Isabella Graham* in 1838. While the works are primarily private and inspirational in nature, they reflect a strong, determined woman forced into the role of single parent, who not only supported her own family but also devoted much effort to helping the needy. IG's meditations reveal the depth of her dedication to the Scriptures, a dedication echoed in her religious poetry, as in her hymnlike "Jordan." Her prose style resembles that of contemporary sermons. In "My Last Journey Through the Wilderness" she identifies herself with the displaced Israelites and members of the early Christian church in her own journey to salvation.   E.N.

GRANT, Anne [Macvicar] (1755–1838), poet and non-fiction writer, was born in Glasgow, Scotland, but spent her early years in New England, where her father, a British army officer, was stationed. There she was raised and educated mainly by the influential Schuyler family. In 1768 Anne and her parents returned to Scotland, and 11 years later she married Grant, an army clergyman; they lived at a manse in Laggan in the Highlands. In the following years she not only raised eight children but also actively participated in her community, where she was known for her acts of charity. She also spent time studying local customs, which became the subject of several of her works. In 1801 Grant died, leaving his wife almost penniless. She had further reason to be discouraged in her later life—seven of her children died and in 1820 she suffered an injury that kept her on crutches for her remaining years. Yet she was known for her wit and high spirits, which adversity apparently could not destroy. AG published her first volume, the verses she had written over the years, in 1802 to ease her financial problems after her husband's death. Four years later, again for financial reasons, she published the three-volume *Letters from the Mountains*, selected from her correspondence which had long been admired by her acquaintances for its liveliness. The work was very well received. Also popular was her next work, *Memoirs of an American Lady* (1808), a record of her childhood memories of Mrs. Schuyler and the new nation. ("Self-interest, eagerly grasping at pecuniary advantages, seems to be the ruling principle of this great continent.") The book is interesting for its minute depiction of colonial life, although it is flawed by a general romanticism, especially concerning slavery. In 1811 "Essays on the Superstitions of the Highlands" appeared, followed in 1814 by "Eighteen Hundred and Thirteen: A Poem." After her death a fragment of her autobiography was brought out by her son. AG was respected and praised by many of her literary contemporaries; Scott called her "an excellent person," and a literary friend spoke of "her great good nature and such strong good sense, mingled with a natural talent, plain knowledge, and good taste." She wrote the popular words for "Where and O where is your Highland laddie gone?" The first stanza answers the question thus: "He's gone to fight the foe for King George upon the throne, / And it's O in my heart that I wish him safe at home."   D.L.

GRANT, Elizabeth (1745?–1814?), song writer, was the daughter of Lieutenant Joseph Grant of a Highland regiment; she was probably born near Aberlour in Banffshire, and about 1763 she married her cousin, Captain James Grant of Carron, near Elchies, on the Spey. He died in 1790 and EG married Dr.

Murray, who lived in Bath, where she died. EG's songs were very popular in her time, mentioning places and people near EG's home and including traditional ballad elements. The most famous song is the one to which Robert Burns refers, "Roy's Wife of Aldivalloch"; in it a rejected lover complains of being deserted for another but, remembering his lover's many attractions, ends by being well-disposed toward her: "Her hair sae fair, her e'en sae clear, / Her wee bit mon'sae sweet and bonnie! / To me she ever will be dear, / Though she's for ever left her Johnnie."   J.J.

GREEN, Sarah (fl. 1790s), novelist, is reputed to be the author of twelve novels, in addition to a didactic tract, *Mental Improvement for a Young Lady* (1793). It is ironic that this work condemns all novels save those of FANNY BURNEY. Great emphasis is placed on diligence and chastity.   L.F.

GREVILLE, Frances (1730?–1789), occasional poet and author, was the third of the four daughters of James and Catharine Coote Macartney of Longford, Ireland. FG was formidable for both wit and beauty. Her goddaughter FANNY BURNEY noted her fine "feminine" feature, "masculine" understanding, croaking voice, manner of lounging at ease "in such curves as she found most commodious, with her head alone upright," her eyes fixed "with an expression rather alarming than flattering" on her object. To outsiders she appeared pedantic, sarcastic, supercilious; to her own circle, kind and good-humored. In 1747, still a minor, she made an unlucky conquest of the patron of Dr. Burney, Fulke Greville (1717–1808?) of Wilbury House, Wilts., a man constitutionally inconstant, who lived with the splendor of a Renaissance prince and followed the modes for sports, music, dancing, and above all gambling (which would ruin him). FG eloped with Greville, who had been catapulted into temporary passion, not permanent commitment; they married the same year. "Mr. Greville has taken a wife out of the window when he might just as well have taken her out of the door," said FG's father. FG's favorite child, Frances-Anne, later the beautiful Mrs. Crewe, must have been born soon after, and five sons followed. FG seems not to have established homes for long or to have become a Bluestocking hostess; instead she was a traveler and a guest. The couple was in Italy in 1749 and in 1757. Greville had so ruined his finances by 1763 that FG had to seek help of her old friend LADY HOL-LAND, who noted that FG would prefer a place for her husband to one for herself. Greville spent the years 1764–70 as Envoy Extraordinary to Bavaria. Meanwhile FG and her daughter traveled restlessly between Britain and the Continent, where she established friendships with Mme. du Deffand and Mme. de Mirepoix. In 1766 FG married her daughter to John Crewe of Crewe Hall—"a pumpkin fricaseed in snow," said FANNY BURNEY—and in 1770 FG's father died, leaving his Irish estate between his three living daughters. In her later years Mrs. Crewe was FG's closest companion; Lady Holland noted that FG cared little for her husband and sons, but she spent much of her later years in Ireland, often in company with her youngest son, Charles (b. 1762), making extended visits to LADY LOUISA CONOLLY at Castletown and to her own connections at Pakenham House. Although FG was rarely noted in company with her husband, Fanny Burney describes a 1776–77 meeting at the Burneys' house of the Gre-villes and Mrs. Crewe with Dr. Johnson that shows the husband and wife to have been on amicable terms. Despite Fanny Burney's claim that thinness quite early destroyed her beauty and despite her con-stant nerves and low spirits, FG was ha-bitually followed and surrounded by ad-mirers—perhaps because she could not travel alone. Mrs. Selwyn, in Burney's *Evelina*, is almost certainly her portrait in later years. *Gentleman's Magazine* (August 1789) vaguely reports her death as "lately."

FG enjoyed a great contemporary rep-utation for wit and authorship, to which she was indifferent; she left little evidence of her ability. R.B. Sheridan dedicated *The Critic* (1781) to her, the author of "most elegant productions of judgment and fancy." In 1756, in full expectation of being ac-claimed a second de Rochefoucault, Fulke Greville published his *Maxims, Characters, and Reflections*. Critics found it odd but enjoyable, and readers delighted in the char-acters of FG as Camilla, her husband as Torrismond, Mrs. Garrick as Flora, ELIZ-ABETH MONTAGU as Melissa, and Lord Chatham as Praxiteles. There were 1757 and 1768 editions. Horace Walpole, who had complimented FG as "Fanny" in *The Beauties*, noted that she was generally thought to have collaborated on *Maxims*, and libraries frequently catalogue it as a joint work, but neither husband nor wife ever acknowledged this. FG's fame rested on her "Ode to Indifference," one of the most celebrated popular poems of the time. The ode was composed fairly early in her married life (Mrs. THRALE said after the accidental death of her eldest son, but Bur-ney hints that her husband was sufficient cause) and circulated privately for some time before it found publication. Lady Hol-land sent in 1758 FG's "exceedingly pretty" verses to her sister, adding that she had not got the COUNTESS OF CARLISLE's poem. Since FG's good friend Lady Carlisle wrote "The Fairy's Answer" to the "Ode" (see *Elegant Extracts* for both), very likely the reference marks the appearance of FG's verse. The ode was also printed in Fawkes and Woty's *Poetical Calendar* (1763) and frequently thereafter. In 1767 General Fitz-william boasted he had written and dis-tributed 40 copies. A plea for surcease from the pains of sensibility, the ode now seems both affecting and affected: "take this treacherous sense of mine, / Which dooms me still to smart; / Which pleasure can to pain refine; / To pain new pangs impart." FG left behind an unfinished novel, which Mrs. Crewe asked Burney to finish. "It has much spirit, knowledge of human nature, and gaiety in most of its parts," said Burney, but did not complete it. *Notes and Queries* in 1873 recorded the possession by FG's descendants of some unpublished pieces, as well as verses by her in the guest book at Crewe Hall.   B.R.

GRIERSON, Constantia [Cawley? Phil-lips?] (1706–33), poet and scholar, was uni-versally acknowledged the most gifted of the circle of women wits around Swift, which included MARY DELANY, LAE-TITIA PILKINGTON, and MARY BAR-BER. CG was born at Graiguenamanagh, Co. Kilkenny, to a poor illiterate country family. Observing her pleasure in books, her father tried to furnish her with suitable volumes and she quickly mastered the clas-sical languages. CG herself recounted of her education that she "had received some little instruction from the minister of the parish, when she could spare time from her needle-work, to which she was closely kept by her mother." At 18, CG was apprenticed to Dr. Van Lewen, a well-known Dublin physician, to learn midwifery. He was the father of Laetitia Pilkington, who remembers of CG: "She wrote elegantly both in verse and prose; and some of the most delightful hours I ever passed were in the conversation of this female philosopher." Dr. Delany's comic poem referring to these women suggests that CG was small and blond, for he gives to "Letty, one filbert to regale, / And a peach for pale Constance to make a full meal." Soon after coming to Dublin she married George Grierson, a Scottish bookseller who was the King's Printer and an associate of George Faulkner, Swift's bookseller. This alliance not only gave her access to an excellent library, but made available to her the direct means for publishing her own work. She issued three editions of Latin classics: Virgil (1724), Terence (1727), and Tacitus (1730). Of the last, the classical bibliographer Dr. E. Harwood wrote: "I have read it twice through, and it is one of the best edited books ever delivered to the world. Mrs. Grierson was a lady possessed of singular erudition, and had an elegance of taste and solidity of judgment which justly rendered her one of the wonderful, as well as amiable of her sex." She was working on an edition of Sallust when she died at 27. CG had two sons. One died young; Mary Barber refers thus to her sorrowing verses: "This Mourning Mother can with Ease explore / The Arts of *Latium*, and the *Grecian* Store." Her other son grew up to be George Abraham Grierson, who, following in his father's footsteps, was King's Printer from 1753–55. Like his mother he died at 27, after a brief period of recognition as a man of "uncommon learning and great wit and vivacity." Dr. Johnson admired him and often observed "that he possessed more extensive knowledge than any man of his years he had ever known."

Of CG's poems, few have survived. Seven occasional poems praising her friends and patrons are collected in George Colman and Bonnell Thornton's *Poems By Eminent Ladies* (1755). "The Art of Printing" is quoted in C.H. Wilson's *Brookiana* (1804), and there is reason to believe it was printed as a broadside and distributed on Lord Mayor's Day in 1732 by Swift's friend John Barber. Laetitia Pilkington rated CG's literary talent above that of any other woman writer of the time. "I remember she wrote a very fine poem," says Pilkington, "on Bishop Berkeley's Bermudian Scheme." The poem praises St. Paul and Berkeley: "Tis he from words first rids philosophy, / And lays the dull material system by, / Affrights the daring libertine to find / Naught round him but the pure, all-holy mind; / The blushing sinner from his covert draws / Of matters various forms and motions laws, /

His only fortress from the atheist takes, / And his atomic world at once unmakes." The poem saw the Bishop as a true ambassador of Christ, prophesying his great success in the conversion of the Indians. R.P.

GRIFFITH, Elizabeth (1727–93), playwright and author, was born probably in Dublin, the daughter of Thomas Griffith (1680?–1744), celebrated comedian and manager of the Theatre-Royal in Aungier Street, and Jane Foxcroft Griffith (1694–1773), daughter of Richard Foxcroft, rector of Portarlington. Her father's parents were from Wales, her mother's from Yorkshire. EG was educated in polite literature and French, but not the classics; in the writing and recitation of poetry; and in the imitation of the bearing, propriety, and wit of a fine lady. At her father's death she was left with insufficient guidance and fortune. In 1746 she met a well-connected but poor Kilkenny farmer and libertine, Richard Griffith (1716?–1788). He and EG fell in love, but, since his father expected him to marry a fortune, he attempted to seduce her. She guided him toward marriage. "I have often wondered that a person, who has as much wit, spirit, and wildness in her imagination, as any one I know," he lamented, "should have, in reality, more delicacy in her sentiments, and more decency in her expressions, than I ever met with in any other woman." From 1749–51 EG played major roles with the Smock-Alley Theatre company. Her private and secret marriage to RG, witnessed by Lady Orrery, took place ca. 1751. A son was born ca. 1752; a daughter ca. 1756. In 1751 RG had established a linen manufacture at Maidenhall, Bennettsbridge, Co. Kilkenny, and was struggling with the enterprise. With her marriage still a secret, EG, as Mrs Griffith, essayed the stage at Covent Garden from March 1753 to May 1755, without progressing beyond minor roles. Soon after, the linen manufacture failed. In 1757 EG and RG published by subscription *A Series of Genuine Letters between Henry and Frances*, admitting the public to the secrets of the conduct of their courtship and marriage. The wit, variety, and politeness of the letters made them famous, and in 1760 the Duke of Bedford provided RG with employment. Finally possessed of her own home, EG was dissatisfied with her husband's "no scheme of life" and in 1764 moved to London, settling in 1766 into a house in Hyde Street, Bloomsbury, while RG was often in Ireland campaigning for his political friends Lord Charlemont and Henry Flood. Their separations ensured the continuance of both their politeness and their correspondence, which was issued in four additional volumes. In 1770 they equipped their son to venture to India; by 1780 he had returned very rich to Ireland, where he married well, purchased Millicent, an estate at Naas, Co. Kildare, and sat in the Irish Parliament. RG may briefly (as ANNA SEWARD averred) have eloped with an heiress in his sixties, but he died at Millicent in 1788. EG died there also in 1793.

The second two volumes of the *Letters* were published in 1767, the final two in 1770; these were the basis for EG's considerable reputation for politeness and decorum, sprightliness and wit. Her translations from the French include *Memoirs of Ninon de l'Enclos* (1761), *Memoirs, Anecdotes, and Characters of the Court of Louis XIV* of Mme. de Caylus (1770), *The Shipwreck and Adventures of Monsieur Pierre Viaud* (1771), *The Fatal Effects of Inconstancy* (1774), A *Letter from Mons. Desenfans to Mrs. MONTAGU* (1777), *The Princess of Cleves* (1777), *Zayde, A Spanish History* (1780), and some volumes of a 1779–81 edition of Voltaire. She edited *A Collection of Novels* (1777), and *Novellettes* (1780), which included 13 stories by EG originally published in the *Westminster Magazine*. She wrote three popular epistolary novels, *The Delicate Distress* (1769, a companion volume to RG's *The Gordian Knot*), *The History of Lady Barton* (1771), and *The Story of Lady Juliana Harley* (1776). Two late moral works were *The Morality of Shakespeare's Drama Illustrated* (1775) and *Essays Addressed to Young Married Women* (1782). But she worked hardest as a playwright. *Amana, A Dramatic Poem* (1764) was published as a poem but never produced. *The Platonic Wife* (Drury Lane, 1765) was not well received, and EG's friends labored to secure six performances. But *The Double Mistake* (Covent Garden, 1766) was a hit; EG printed the motto "Depressa resurgam" on the title page. She now used her old weapon, letters, to cajole Garrick into helping her adapt Beaumarchais's *Eugénie* into *The School for Rakes* (Drury Lane, 1769), another great success. The production of *A Wife in the Right* (Covent Garden, 1772) was ruined by the drunkenness of an actor, but was published by subscription. A translation of *The Barber of Seville* (1776) was never produced. *The*

Times (Drury Lane, 1779), adapted from Goldoni's *Bourru Bienfaisant*, was moderately successful. EG, whose best friends were Kitty (CATHERINE) CLIVE and Peg and Mary Woffington, was constrained in her works to play the moralist and guide to women. Vivacious, free, and full of sensibility when young, she adopted more and more the persona of the cultivated, polite, well-bred, decorous duenna, interpolating moral comments even in her translations. A few critics found her affected and over-nice. She was diffident about her writing and had to be coaxed to attempt original work. But she claimed in the prefaces to her novels to have had much acquaintance with the world and to have drawn her characters and situations from life: "I felt as I wrote, and *lived along the line.*" In fact, the packet boat to Ireland and the storm, the shipwreck, the secret marriage of her plots derive from her own life, although they are narrated in a romantic mode that modern readers find unrealistic. But the psychological distresses of her womanly and decorous heroines are still compelling; she wrote "conducting the heroine between the Scylla and Charybdis of female frailty and unfeeling perfection so that one trembles for her sensibility, admires her virtue, and sympathizes with her distress," as one reviewer put it. In 1747 she complained to RG that men vainly believe they are imbued with greater sense and nobler souls and "in order to preserve this unjust dominion to themselves . . . they concluded no Salique law so effectual, as to fetter and inslave our minds, by such a narrow, domestic, and partial education, as should bury the seeds of sense and philosophy." In 1782, in her last published work, she advised young married women: "A love of power and authority is natural to men and wherever this inclination is most indulged, will be the situation of their choice."   B.R.

GRIFFITHS, Isabella (1713?–1764), editor and probable reviewer for the *Monthly Review*, was the wife of Ralph Griffiths, a nonconformist Staffordshire watchmaker who arrived in London ca. 1740, worked for the bookseller Jacob Robinson, and then set up at the sign of the Dunciad in St. Paul's Churchyard, then Paternoster Row. In 1749 he published the first number of the *Monthly Review*, a journal which survived to 1845. Earlier literary reviews devoted to polite and Continental literature had slighted the English publications on which the *MR* concentrated; reviews at this time consisted largely of abstracts from the works reviewed. Most reviewing did not require a university education; when it did, Griffiths had assistance. Both *MR* and the *Critical Review* left reviews unsigned, in attempts to maintain a pretense that the reviewers were a set of disinterested and independent gentlemen. At the outset Griffiths was principal reviewer, assisted by William Rose and John Cleland. IG undoubtedly assisted her husband significantly with the *MR* from its inception; he could scarcely have run a thriving bookshop, published numerous books, pamphlets, newspapers, and magazines, and edited the *MR* without the assistance of a competent partner. Oliver Goldsmith is the originator of charges that IG both edited and wrote for the *MR*. He lived in her house from May to October 1757 and wrote for the *MR*, afterward complaining that both Griffiths had dared to emend his work, a charge supported by a 1790 letter from Thomas Campbell reporting that both the Griffiths altered and interpolated Goldsmith's writings, and that Griffiths "at a time when the Review was not very profitable . . . was not disposed to pay another for doing what filled up so much space with little labour to himself, or as we are told, to his wife." Campbell added, of this information, "My conscience bids me report it, but my fears whisper to me that all the Reviews will abuse me."

Goldsmith's complaints were further strengthened by Tobias Smollett in November 1757 in the rival *CR* in an attack addressed "To the Old Gentlewoman who directs the Monthly Review"; it carried on for three pages the jest of supposing IG (then 44, seven years her husband's senior) the editor. In 1759 Smollett rejoiced that the *CR* was not written by hirelings "under the restraint of a bookseller and his wife who presume to revise, alter, and amend," that the *CR* writers were "unconnected with booksellers, unawed by old women." He further described IG as an "Antiquated Female Critic." In 1762 Griffiths denied IG's having written a review to a friend: "Hark! how my good woman scolds at you for thus persisting in the joke about her (alleged) exploits in the literary way. . . . She says this is carrying the matter too far . . . I can with the most sacred truth declare that there never was a single word written for the R- - - by a female pen" (although he then excepted ELIZABETH CARTER). If Goldsmith can be believed, Griffiths's

statement cannot be true. (He was, after all, a man who lied for professional advantage whenever he thought it necessary.) The review of which Griffiths spoke was written by one "N," whom Nangle, in his catalogue of the *MR*'s reviewers, cannot identify, but who contributed from 1757–63 and again from 1766–94; it is therefore possible that IG was the first of two separate reviewers identified by her husband as "N." Goldsmith's contumely was owing to his indignation not that a woman should write, but that she should presume to edit and evaluate the writings of men. For this reason the politic assertion that his wife had never written for the *MR*, made by Griffiths, should not be considered conclusive.

Of IG little more is known. It was not she but Griffiths's second wife who was memorialized by Sir Richard Phillips as his "literary wife, in her neat and elevated wire-winged cap." IG had moved with her husband to Linden House, Turnham Green, before she died in 1764. B.R.

GRIFFITTS, Hannah (1727–1817), American poet, came from a Quaker family; she was the daughter of Mary Norris and Thomas Griffitts, a lawyer and mayor of Philadelphia. Her grandfather Isaac Norris was a wealthy merchant who amassed a large library, and HG may have made use of it, since she seems to have received a reasonable education. In the 1760s she alludes to financial difficulties. In the 1780s she remained in Philadelphia during the British occupation. HG corresponded with SUSANNA WRIGHT, ELIZABETH GRAEME FERGUSON, and DEBORAH LOGAN, her cousin, and exchanged verses with them. She was urged to publish but refused, although the revisions on her more than 200 manuscript poems suggest that she took her work seriously. HG's poetry is primarily religious and patriotic; the latter concerns the events and people of the revolutionary period. In "'Beware the Ides of March,' said the Roman Augur to Julius Cesar [sic]," she exhorted her countrymen to "sacrifice to Patriot fame, / And give up tea by way of healing. / This done, within ourselves retreat, / Th'industrious arts of life to follow, / Let the proud Nabobs storm and fret, / They cannot force our lips to swallow." Poems celebrate great men like Benjamin Franklin, whom she called "a Newton" who soared in science to "a summit before unattain'd"; and friends and fellow poets like Susannah Wright, whose genius and character are, on her death, warmly commended: "For genius, thus distinguish'd and admir'd, / Above ambition's low contrasted care, / She walk'd with wisdom, in the 'vale retir'd,' / And left the world its tinsel and its glare." Her religious poems preach acquiescence; one on the death of her parent prays: "In this, and all the future strokes from Thee, / Oh may I bow, in deep humility." Other poems consecrate her muse to God.   J.T.

GUNNING, Susannah [Minifie] (1740?–1800), novelist and family apologist, was the daughter of James Minifie, D.D., and at the publication of her first novel in 1763 lived in Fairwater, Somerset. Five years later, she married Captain (soon to be Lieutenant-General) John Gunning, the articulate and spoiled brother of the famous beauties, whose mother was the daughter of a viscount. Gunning's parents had so successfully advanced his sisters through marriage that SG may have attempted a parallel coup for her daughter, born in 1769. Her plans went awry, however (see ELIZABETH PLUNKETT), resulting in the hullabaloo of forgeries and adulteries which Horace Walpole called the "Gunninghiad." At this time SG wrote of her husband, "I have been so long in a scene of mysteries, of which he is the artificer, that I never expect to get out of them as long as I live" (*Letter from Mrs. Gunning*, 1791). Not long after, General Gunning, who had maintained a high moral tone during the family crisis, was himself fined £5,000 for "criminal conversation" with his tailor's wife (*Trial between J. Duberly, Esq., Plaintiff, and Major General G.*, 1792). Gunning and his mistress hastened to Naples, where he wrote an *Apology* (1792) in which he boasted of myriad, detailed, and exaggerated conquests, especially of aristocratic women. In 1797, in response to a letter from his daughter, he altered his will the day before he died, leaving £8,000 to her and to his wife, and his Irish estate to the latter. During this final period SG wrote steadily. At her death she left an unfinished novel, *The Heir Apparent*, which her daughter revised and published two years later.

In all, SG wrote 13 novels (six of them epistolary), one long poem, and a defense of her daughter's conduct. She and her sister MARGARET MINIFIE initiated their own careers in 1763, publishing by subscription their collaborative *Histories of Lady Frances S- - - and Lady Caroline S- - -*. Commercial publishers printed the next five novels, which followed in quick succession: *Family Pic-*tures (1764), *The Picture* (1766—with Margaret), *Barford Abbey* (1768), *The Cottage* (1769), and *The Hermit* (Dublin, 1770). *Family Pictures* claims to be "literally true" and is addressed to the "female part of this metropolis." In fact, however, the plots of these early novels are conventional (distressed virgins achieve aristocratic marriages), and the language formal. When after 15 years of marriage SG published her next novel, *Coombe Wood* (1783), the satiric element had increased, and marriage itself was the occasional object. Since Lady Lucy, for instance, considers marriage an "encumbrance," she plans to wed a £200,000 man in spite of "a detestable dapperness wriggled into his whole person." The heroine loves her cousin but does not intend to marry him, a posture which even at this early date appears to reflect the situation which engendered the "Gunninghiad." Nine years later, in an advertisement prefacing the *Anecdotes of the Delborough Family* (1792), SG denied the allegation that she had included family details. Regarding the *Anecdotes*, the denial may stand, but the theme of her poem *Virginius and Virginia* (1792) is that a father and child should never "be debar'd," and in *Memoirs of Mary* (1793), where the heroine suffers because of a forged letter and the writing is notably more idiomatic, SG certainly plundered her daughter's life, if not her own. She tried a new direction in *Delves* (1796), "A Welsh Tale," which is a young boy's picaresque "Quixotting expedition." In the same year she also published *The Foresters*, a four-volume alteration from the French. Her last two books were novels of manners. *Love at First Sight* (1797) and *Fashionable Involvements* (1800) center on their titles, relying heavily on plot and stylized characters, including a rapacious Jewish moneylender named Isaac. SG was most pungent when she was fictionalizing her personal experiences, but her rather innocent novels do not truly reflect the lurid complications attendant on marriage to John Gunning.

In her most dramatic scenes, SG tends toward hyperbole, a habit for which Lady Harcourt coined the word "minific." In *Memoirs of Mary* Lord Auberry says of his daughter (the heroine's mother), "I would a thousand times rather see her dead, than the wife of your favourite Montague." Yet SG's satirically treated characters often speak with compressed vigor. Sir Ashton Montague writes to Mrs. Oxburn: "Was you ever hippish? Do you know anything about the vapours? I have an odd sort of feeling, and can't make out what it is; no wonder, for I am confined to a bed, where none but a dwarf can lie straight, in a room not ten feet square, half my body swathed with poultices, half-covered with plasters, and fed on milk-sops like a baby." Although SG here ascribes a feminine complaint to a male character, the sexual attitudes she reflects are otherwise unrelievedly conventional. Her women, in particular, consistently jibe at their erring sisters and rivals.

SG's plots are always predictable, her characters familiar. But the writing, although often prolix, is eminently capable. From the start she was widely appreciated. In 1773 Maria Burney wrote to FANNY BURNEY about a thatched cottage which "would make a very great figure in Miss Minifie's hands" (*Early Diary,* I). The writer of SG's obituary claimed that her works "rank among the middling class of novels" (*Gentleman's Magazine,* ii, 1800). J.Th.

H

HALE, Mrs. (fl. 1800), poet, was "a lady of fashion and fortune" (*Monthly Review,* June 1800), whose only publication, *Poetical Attempts* (1800), was sold by subscription to benefit a clergyman's family. H's motley collection traces "Each passion which from youth to age / Mark the heart's progress stage by stage." Weddings, motherhood, friendship, and religion provide poetical subjects for which she good-humoredly claims attention; even if critics "Declare I'm to no muse related, / At all events I here present ye / Variety!—let that content ye." Reviews noticed "the effusions of a truly amiable heart, expressed with ease, and sometimes with sprightliness" *(MR).* G.B.

HALKETT, Anne, Lady (1622?–1699), devotional writer and autobiographer, was born in London, daughter of Thomas Murray, provost of Eton and former tutor to Charles I, and Jane Drummond, once governess to the Princess Elizabeth. Educated by tutors under her mother's supervision, AH also learned medical skills, which she put to good use during the Civil War, treating wounded soldiers of both armies. Her independent spirit was shown early, when she organized a group of friends to attend plays together without male escorts. A Royalist sympathizer, AH was actively involved in several political intrigues during the Civil War period and in 1648 contrived the escape of the Duke of York by dressing him in female disguise. From 1650 onward she lived among Royalist families in Scotland, while undertaking a lawsuit for the recovery of her mother's estate. After two unhappy love affairs, one with the Royalist agent (and would-be bigamist) Colonel Bampfield, AH married (1656) Sir James

Halkett (d. 1670), later losing three of four children in infancy. Having received, at the Restoration, only token compensation for her lost estate, AH supplemented her income, after 1683, by tutoring children of the Scottish aristocracy. In 1685, James II awarded her a pension.

AH wrote copiously over many years and at her death left more than 20 manuscript volumes of devotional writings, dating from 1649 onward, and an autobiography, written 1677–78. Selections from her religious writings *(Instructions for Youth, Meditations and Prayers upon the First Week,* and *Meditations on the Twentieth and Fifth Psalm),* were published shortly after her death (Edinburgh, 1701) together with an anonymous biography based in part on her memoirs. Her autobiography itself was first published in 1875. Her meditations, evidently written for private use, provide an insight into her political as well as her religious convictions, her concern with historical events of the period being closely connected with reflections on her personal and spiritual life. On the death of her second child in 1661, for example, she wrote: "What a sad journey hath this beene hether to mee into England where I expected greatest sattisfaction: 1st in seeing the King and Royall family restored, and then in seeing my relations and friends; and to mitigate these joys the Lord is pleased dayly to send mee new afflictions, and to take away allmost the cheefe comforte of my life, which is my deare children . . . and all to teach mee nott to love the world or anything that is in itt." Her autobiography, notable for its vividness and attention to detail, similarly combines the record of political events with a narrative of her own adventures and emotional experiences. Both the meditations and the autobiography are of interest as historical documents and as examples of the candid, almost self-analytical style in women's writing which, during this period, characterized not only many devotional works, but also the writings of such autobiographers as the DUCHESS OF NEWCASTLE.   R.F.

HALL, Sarah [Constantia, Florepha] (1761–1830), American essayist, was born in Philadelphia to Hannah (Sergeant) and Rev. John Ewing, pastor of the First Presbyterian Church, tutor in the College of Philadelphia and, from 1779 to 1802, provost of the University of Pennsylvania. She was self-taught from conversations with her learned father, from overhearing her brothers' Greek and Latin lessons, and from listening to discussions among intellectual visitors. In 1782 she married John Hall, a planter, secretary of the land office, and U.S. marshall; he died in 1826. Of their 11 children, nine reached maturity. SH wrote for such periodicals as *Port Folio,* founded by Joseph Dennie in 1801. The only other woman contributor was ELIZABETH GRAEME FERGUSON. SH's eldest son edited this journal for ten years after her son Harrison acquired it in 1816. Two other sons also wrote for it. In 1811, at the age of 50, she began to learn Hebrew in preparation for a book that was to have one British and three American editions. In 1818 her *Conversations on the Bible* was published anonymously. In its 365 pages, "Mother" explains the Bible to "Fanny" and "Catherine." The narrator defines words, describes places mentioned, discusses local customs, summarizes the events, paraphrases ideas, and associates them with the life of her own times. This biblical commentary had to be disguised as dialogue because SH had no status as a scholar.

Three years after her death, Harrison published her prayers, book reviews, poems, and excerpts from her letters in *Selections from the Writings of Mrs. Sarah Hall, Author of Conversations on the Bible, with a Memoir of Her Life* (1833). In one of these essays, "On Female Education," she advocated a traditional role for women. Her conventionality can be seen in her urging women "to act with propriety the part assigned to us by Providence"; "retirement is her element, domestic and social life is her proper sphere," while "the superior strength of the man declares that he is designated to wrestle with the world." Another essay, "On the Extent of Female Influence," limits a woman to being a wife and mother; a childless woman like HANNAH MORE, however, may become an educator, a worker for charity, or a distributor of tracts, because it is a duty to use the gifts bestowed by the creator. SH's writing was praised for its clarity and liveliness, and it was said that she "displayed remarkable ability in controversy."   R.R.

HAMILTON, Elizabeth (1758–1816), essayist, poet, satirist, and novelist, was born in Belfast. Since her life was in many ways uneventful, it is important to note her own assessment of her personality: "I have always found myself in more danger of being forsaken by my prudence than my spirits." Her mother, Katherine MacKay, was Irish, but her father, Charles Hamilton, came from a distinguished though poor Scottish family, and worked as a merchant. EH was their third and last child. Her father died within the year, her mother when she was nine. From the age of six she lived in Stirlingshire, Scotland, with her paternal aunt Mrs. Marshall, who had defied family pride by marrying a worthy and dignified farmer. EH became a tomboy, climbing over the countryside in summer and sliding over it in winter. Although she did not receive a classical education, she studied until the age of 13 under a master in a mixed school. She was happy with the Marshalls, but she realized that she was intellectually superior to her surroundings, and she idolized her brother and sister. As she was finishing her formal schooling, her brother left for a 14-year tour of military duty in India. Their voluminous correspondence constituted what her friend and biographer ELIZABETH BENGER called "a *second* education." In 1788 Charles Hamilton returned from India to translate the *Hedaya,* one of the two chief commentaries on Moslem law. When EH visited her brother in London, she realized she had at last met a group of people who were her intellectual equals. Her aunt had died in 1782, and, after her uncle's death in 1790, she moved to London to live with her brother. Although two years later he also died, he was undoubtedly the chief intellectual and emotional influence in her life, so much so that as late as 1803 she wrote, "With him, my every hope of happiness expired." EH was resilient, however, and she had made other friends, including Dr. George Gregory, who combined his religious and artistic interests by writing sermons, translations, a life of Chatterton, and a number of books on literature, taste, and education. Dr. Gregory and his wife advised and encouraged EH in all her literary ventures. After her brother's death, EH lived in England with her married sister Katherine Black, and she settled ultimately in Edinburgh in 1804, a move which inspired her vernacular poems, including "My Ain Fireside" and a feisty welcome to old age. She held weekly literary gatherings, won a government pension, and was generally recognized as a powerful intellectual force. Although inhibited by weak eyes and at times nearly incapacitated by gout, she helped to found a house of industry for women and continued publishing works on education. Her infirmities at last forced her to move to London, where she died.

From the start EH had always been ambitious; she wanted to be known beyond her own circle. While in Stirling she wrote a journal of a tour through the Highlands, which to her surprise her aunt caused to be published. She also began an historical novel about Arabella Stuart, which is most remarkable for a series of letters between two sisters who have been separated and yearn to meet. In 1785 she published essays and poetry in the *Lounger.* One of these essays warned women that they could expect "an inexhaustible source of delight" in learning, but that they would not thereby attract men. EH published three novels, differing widely in form. The first, *Letters of a Hindoo Rajah* (1796), uses the device of satiric Oriental letters, following Montesquieu and Goldsmith. This book, which she called "my black baby" (her books were her metaphorical children: she called *Letters on Education* "my bantling"), contains a long and learned preface, but its chief theme is that women need not faint at the sight of blood nor engage in other fashionable timidities—they can be strong and competent. The book attracted excellent reviews. Her second novel was *Memoirs of Modern Philosophers* (1800), a satiric spoof of the Godwin circle, which raced through a number of editions. The anti-heroine Bridgetina Botherim, who soon became "a proverbial point in conversation" (*Gentleman's Magazine,* 1816), represents MARY HAYS. Botherim is stupid, headstrong, deformed, and metaphysically inclined. She recklessly attempts to force men to love her. By following similar principles, her unfortunate counterpart, the sweet and lovely Julie Delmond, allows herself to be seduced and abandoned, and finally commits suicide. One of EH's most effective satiric

techniques is to put Godwin's literal words into the mouth of Julia's seducer, Vallaton. Interestingly, in spite of EH's usually loyal support of her own sex, the most evil character in this book is her *femme fatale* Emmeline, of whom she says, "the wickedness of even the worst of men seldom equals the wickedness of woman" (4th ed., 1804). When Emmeline tires of Vallaton, she conveniently betrays him to the guillotine. The objects of EH's satire seem chiefly to have been the extremists of the modern philosophers, among whom she did not include MARY WOLLSTONECRAFT. Her third novel was *The Cottagers of Glenburnie* (1808). Here, the commonsensical Mrs. Mason comes to stay with her well-meaning but lazy and disorderly cousin Mrs. MacClarty, and, although Mrs. MacClarty proves resistent, Mrs. Mason eventually organizes and reforms the whole neighborhood, introducing ideals of cleanliness, economy, and education. The characters speak in the vernacular and are eminently believable. The MacClarty family's refrain, *"I cou'd no be fashed"* (I couldn't be bothered), became a saying of the day, and F. Jeffrey in the *Edinburgh Review* suggested that the book be circulated among Scottish cottagers themselves, providing them with a more vivid and subtle encouragement to change their ways than HANNAH MORE's *Cheap Repository Tracts,* which were too condescending (12, 1808).

Interspersed among her novels, EH published a number of other influential works. Her *Letters on Education* (1801) went through eight editions by 1837. Here, her concern was chiefly that women, as mothers, should raise their children intelligently, treating boys and girls equally, nurturing their moral and intellectual life primarily by monitoring their early associations of ideas. Her biography of *Agrippina, the Wife of Germanicus* (1804) was an important attempt to deal seriously with the life of an admirable Roman woman, although EH's lack of a classical education hindered her researches. After living for six months as the invited tutor in an aristocratic household, she published *Letters Addressed to the Daughter of a Nobleman on the Formation of the Religious and the Moral Principle* (1806). It is worth noting that her religious beliefs were non-sectarian, which is not surprising considering her varied upbringing. Her last two books were *Exercises in Religious Knowledge* (1809), a "series of popular essays illustrative of principles connected with the improvement of the Understanding, the Imagination, and the Heart" (1813), and *Hints Addressed to the Patrons and Directors of Schools* (1815).

Although initially EH's chief intellectual mentors were male, she had many women friends, including JOANNA BAILLIE and MARIA EDGEWORTH. She directed all of her books primarily to her own sex, whose qualities of mind she admired and defended. Her books were popular, and Jane Austen was pleased that such a "respectable writer" had read *Sense and Sensibility.* After EH's death Maria Edgeworth praised her "as an original, agreeable, and successful writer of fiction," but argued that her works on education were of a "higher sort," chiefly because they opened a new field of investigation to women, metaphysical study, which was "not only practicable, but pleasant; and not only pleasant, but what is of far more consequence to women, safe" (*Gentleman's Magazine,* ii, 1816). J.Th.

HAMILTON, Lady Mary (1739–1816), novelist, was born in Edinburgh, youngest daughter (by his second wife, Elizabeth) of Alexander Leslie, fifth Earl of Leven and fourth Earl of Melville. She married Dr. James Walker of Innerdovat in 1762; after his death, she married Robert Hamilton of Jamaica, with whom she settled in France before the Revolution. They had two daughters; one married the dramatist Jouy, and the other General Thiébaut. After Hamilton's death, MH moved to Amiens, where she spent the rest of her life. While at Amiens, she sustained a close relationship with Sir Herbert Croft, who lived in a country house near her chateau, and addressed to her a poem, "On the death of Musico, a piping bullfinch belonging to the Right Honorable Lady Mary Hamilton." Through Croft, MH met Charles Nordier, who acted as her translator and rewrote one of her novels in French. MH wrote five novels, all of which show considerable erudition and campaign for women's right to learning: *Letters from the Duchess de Crui* (1776), *Memoirs of the Marchioness de Louvoi* (1777), *Munster Village* (1778), *The Life of Mrs. Justman* (1782), and the *Duc de Popoli* (1810), rewritten by Nordier in two parts entitled *La Famille du duc de Popoli, ou Mémoires de M. Cantelmo, son frère* (with a dedication to Croft, 1810), and *Auguste et Jules de Popoli* (1810). The works, which are either entirely or partially epistolary, have a strongly philosophical tone and are often close to conduct books: they adhere to clearly presented moral standards. *Letters from the Duchess de Crui* complains of the "mistaken idea" men form of a learned lady, while female characters in several novels compare operas and speak knowledgeably of Newtonian philosophy, chemistry, and classical and contemporary writers. Typically, the works are loosely structured around the lives of several correspondents with some central organizing principle, like setting, family relationships, or a primary narration, providing order. Richardson's influence is strong but MH's novels lack his complexity and skill. MH intends to provide a format flexible enough to accommodate abrupt shifts in tone and movement from one topic to another, reminiscent of periodical literature. The novels always sustain several conventional romantic plots marked by frequent instructive digressions on learned matters, such as a discourse on classical authors, or the exhaustive architectural description of the chapel of Roslin in *Louvoi,* whose preface recommends "the love and practice of virtue, and a taste for the study of the sciences." One issue often treated is the problem of marriage for aristocratic women. The heroine of *Munster Village,* MH's best novel, founds a type of utopian academic retreat and dedicates herself to philanthropy: "Her buildings, manufactures, academies of painting, sculpture, astronomy, architecture, with many other establishments, too great indeed for a subject, are particularly described" (*Gentleman's Magazine,* Sept. 1778). Her life earns authorial approbation: "Living entirely in the country, she sought in the beauty of nature, in science, and the love of order, that satisfaction which in the world (where people are the *slaves of apology and the dupes of caprice*) is eagerly pursued but *never found.*" The tone and the sentiment are characteristic of MH, whose work generally criticizes the world of fashion, and finds worth in the life of study, domesticity, and charity. K.S. & G.B.

HANDS, Elizabeth (fl. 1789), poet, possibly a Dissenter, was married in 1789 when she published her volume of verse, *The Death of Amnon. A Poem. With an Appendix: Containing Pastorals, and other Poetical Pieces.* Her poems, published in Coventry, reveal that she was a maidservant before marriage, probably in London. They mention her fond husband and the birth of a daughter. In a dedication to Bertie Greatheed of Coventry she characterizes herself as "born in obscurity, and never emerging beyond the lower stations in life," and grateful for the help of patrons. Her very substantial subscription lists the names of many of the eminent, including ANNA SEWARD, and of people surnamed Hands at Napton and Stoneleigh, both near Coventry, which was probably the home of her husband and the place where she was settled. Dr. and Mrs. Loveday, the patrons of MARY LATTER, subscribed, as did Samuel Blencowe and his wife, of the family which patronized MARY LEAPOR. EH's volume of poetry reveals versatility and originality of outlook, if not of form. *The Death of Amnon,* an epic in five cantos, is her most ambitious piece. The story of Amnon, son of David, begins "The Royal Youth I sing, whose sister's charms / Inspir'd his heart with love; a latent love / That prey'd upon his health; he droop'd, so droops / A beauteous flow'r, when in the stalk some vile / Opprobrious insect 'bides." Amnon becomes a sentimental lover, whose "tim'rous tenderness" is mocked by the villain. After her rape, his sister laments that she would have preferred murder, for "he that robs a woman of her honour, / Robs her of more than life," and she accepts completely that she is defiled. EH's more appealing poetry is in the appendix to the volume. In "On the Supposition of an Advertisement in a Morning Paper, of the Publication of a Volume of Poems by a Servant Maid" and "On the Supposition of the Book having been published and read," she reveals what she knows of the talk of her betters as they discuss the scribbling servant: "I know something of her, says Mrs. Devoir, / She liv'd with my friend, Jacky Faddle, Esq. / 'Tis sometime ago though; her mistress said then, / The girl was excessively fond of a pen; / I saw her but never convers'd with her—*though* / One can't make acquaintance with servants, you know." EH's pastorals tend to present contests between shepherdesses rather than shepherds; she wrote verses to female friendship and composed a piece "On An Unsociable Family": "O what a strange parcel of creatures are we, / Scarce ever to quarrel or ever agree; / We all are alone, though at home altogether, / Except to the fire constrain'd by the weather . . . / To comfort each other is never our plan, / For to please ourselves, truly, is more than we can." G.I.C.

HANSON, Elizabeth (?–1741?), American autobiographer, lived in Dover, N.H. Her maiden name was Meader, but there is no record of her birth or death in Dover. She married John Hanson, a Quaker, in 1703, and had eight children. John Hanson was not mentioned in his father's will, probably because of his Quaker affiliation. In 1724 or 1725 EH's house was attacked by Indians while her husband was away. (He had refused to move to the safety of a less-exposed area of the settlement.) Two children were killed and scalped immediately and EH, a baby of 14 days, a son, two daughters, and a servant were captured and taken to Canada. All except one daughter were ransomed and eventually released, and in 1727 John Hanson died on his way to rescue her. EH's only published work is a narrative account of her capture and deliverance, which she dictated in 1726 to Samuel Bownas, a preacher from England who was touring America at the time. Entitled *An Account of the Remarkable Captivity of Elizabeth Hanson,* it was published in Philadelphia (1728) and London (1760); according to Bownas, the narrative was "in her own words." Later editions were entitled *God's Mercy Surmounting Man's Cruelty.* The account also appears in S. G. Drake's collection of Indian captivities, *Tragedies of the Wilderness* (1824), and in Joseph Robson's *The British Mars* (1763), which includes methods of fortifying houses so that women and children in "British settlements in America and other places" could protect themselves. As Robson writes, "I was put upon this sort of fortification by reading an account of a man's wife and children being carried away by the Indians and some of them cruelly murdered." EH initially did not intend to publish the narrative but then changed her mind: "I hope the merciful kindness and goodness of God might thereby be manifested; and the reader stirred up with more care and fear to righteousness and humility; and then will my purpose be answered." This is typical of EH's attitude and the tone of the narrative. She appears to be a deeply Christian woman who has a strong sense of the justice of God and, while she recalls the horrors of her experience, she also mentions the kindness of the Indian women and men who played a part in her survival and that of her children. It is strange that throughout the narrative EH refers to her Indian captor as her "master" and seems to have served him with a truly Christian devotion to duty. EH's style has a certain immediacy, and she vividly retells the horrors of her captivity, the harshness of their living arrangements and the "guts and garbage" they were given to eat. EH's narrative is one of the many stories of Indian captivities, but it is remarkable for her calm acceptance of the tragedies in her life, her desire to use the account of her sufferings as a moral lesson, and her unwavering faith in the goodness of God. She accepts the cultural differences between Indians and settlers and does not judge Indian customs and traditions by the values of her own society.   J.B.

HANWAY, Mary Ann (fl. 1776–1814), novelist and journal writer, was apparently a resident of London; her first work, in which she speaks of the "juvenile mind" being excited by publication, was the result of a trip to Scotland. She was persuaded by an anonymous benefactress to publish a volume of her letters home, and these subsequently appeared as *A Journey to the Highlands of Scotland* (1776). Her first novel, purportedly written to "draw off her mind from dwelling too poignantly on a recent calamity," was *Ellinor; or the World as it is* (1798). It was followed by *Andrew Stuart* (1800), *Falconbridge Abbey: A Devonshire Story* (1809) and *Christabelle, the Maid of Rouen* (1814). Her Scottish journal is generally dull, with tedious historical reflections, trite moralizing, and conventional reticence ("a truce with politics, they ill become a woman's pen"). A dilettante observer of manners and scenery, she comments in a typically naive way that in Glasgow the mercantile spirit "produces those effects in the appearance of the people, which commerce never fails to bestow,—industry, content, and opulence; whilst in Edinburgh, there is a poverty, and a sort of Northern misery in the very features of the commonalty." *Ellinor,* which centers on the mystery of the heroine's birth, is written against the overpowering of judgment by the "susceptibility of the heart" or the "ebullitions of improper passions." The characters are functions of the prevailing genre, and MH cannot handle sensational incidents other than sensationally: "He had taken off his mask when he first declared himself. Ellinor saw his face enflamed, his eyes flashing fire, his hands that held her trembling, with passions that threatened her *ruin.*" The novel nevertheless received qualified approval from *Critical Review* (May 1798): "The story is interesting; and the sentiments are unexceptionable. We sometimes meet with an unpleasant pertness in the style; but it would be well if circulating libraries contained no worse books than Ellinor." *Andrew Stuart* again demonstrates the marriage of correct principles with crude emotionalism. Falconbridge Abbey tells of the enslavement of the pliant, good-natured Henry Falconbridge by the artful, machinating orphan Eliza, who is supposedly representative of a particularly degenerate kind of contemporary female. The novel is as sentimental and sensational, and uses language as "warm, flowing and dangerous" as any criticized by MH in her preface: "Sir Henry, in the embraces of his fair enslaver, forgot everything but herself; by the necromantic power of her potent charms, she still held his ductile mind in chains, subjugated his will, and moulded the plastic clay, bidding it take whatever form best suited her present or future purpose." *Christabelle* is an historical adventure set against the backdrop of the *ancien régime* and the revolutionary era in France. It is violently anti-revolutionary, as evidenced when Christabelle's guardian is arrested by a group of *sans-culottes:* "He did not flatter himself with making any impression on the putrescent hearts of regicide monsters, whose employment was the oppression of their species, whose eyes were daily, hourly, momentarily glutted with the blood of their fellow-creatures!" The novel proceeds by the familiar stratagem of persecuting the heroine, and couples this with the themes of obscure birth, the restored lover, etc. It has few virtues other than a tireless capacity for narrative obstruction and incident. Although MH nominally aligns herself against decadence in morals and literature, her own sensibility appears at one with the coarsest of the age.   R.J.

HARBISON, Mercy [Massy] (1770–?), American autobiographer, was born in New Jersey, the daughter of a revolutionary soldier, Edward White. In 1783 she moved to Pennsylvania, where in 1787 she married John Harbison and settled near the Allegheny River. In 1791, when the Indian Wars broke out, Harbison enlisted under General St. Clair, while MH stayed washing and working for the scouts. Later he was engaged as a spy and, while he was absent, she and her children were captured by Indians. A child of three was killed and scalped, while MH was taken to an island where one of the other two children, a boy of five, was also scalped. With the last child at her breast, MH was made to march with the Indians, until she managed to escape. She then traveled without food for four days until she arrived, starving and almost naked, near Fort Pitt; there she made a deposition for the magistrates, which was published in two versions in 1792. The first, entitled *Capture and Escape of Mercy Harbison,* is a crude first-person account reminiscent of the captivity narrative of MARY ROWLANDSON, while the second is a third-person summary of the events. Sensational sections from this second work formed part of an anthology of Indian atrocities called *Affecting History of the Dreadful Distresses of Frederic Manheim's Family.* MH recovered, was joined by her husband, and resumed her life of washing and cooking for the soldiers. In 1795 when the country was settled, the couple went to Bull Creek and then to Buffalo Creek where they remained until 1822, when John Harbison died. MH worked until she was 65, when she became too frail. In the next year, 1836, appeared another first-person account of her Indian sufferings, but this time in a sentimental literary style, closer to MARY KINNAN than to Rowlandson. Entitled *A Narrative of the Sufferings of Massy Harbison from Indian Barbarity . . . communicated by herself,* it was "edited" by John Winter, who described MH as a poor widow whose suffering ought to be remembered. To MH's account, Winter adds information on the history, laws, religion, and cruelties of the Indians. *A Narrative* gives an emotional color to MH's experiences, absent in the first version, and there is an insistence on horror: "The inhuman butchers dashed the brains of one of my dear children out on the door-sill, and afterwards scalped him before my eyes; . . . they took and tomahawked, scalped, and stabbed another of them before me, on the island;—and . . . with still more barbarous feelings, they afterwards made a hoop, and stretched his scalp on it." J.T.

HARRISON, Elizabeth (fl. 1756), poet, occasional writer, and author of didactic and religious works, seems to have worked as a teacher or governess. One work attributed to her, *The Friendly Instructor,* includes a preface by P. Doddridge in which he refers to the author as "a Lady, with whose valuable character I have been acquainted for many years, and who has been long employed in the education of children." In her earliest publication, *A Letter to Mr. John Gay, on His Tragedy Call'd "The Captives"* (1724), EH defends the play, replying to Gay's critics via her own detailed critique. Appended to the *Letter* is a short poem in which EH praises the Princess of Wales for favoring *The Captives. The Friendly Instructor; or A Companion for Young Ladies, and Young Gentlemen . . . in . . . Dialogues* was published in two volumes, apparently beginning in 1741, the date of Doddridge's preface. The author states that the aim of her dialogues is to prepare children for "usefulness in life, and happiness after death." Typical titles of these short prose pieces, which were meant to be read aloud by two children, are "On keeping the Sabbath," "On the Death of a Child," and "On Diligence and Obedience to Parents." Small woodcuts illustrate the stories, adding much to the appeal of the books. That they were popular is evident from the appearance of a 10th London edition by 1790. Many American editions were published, with the words "young masters and misses" sometimes being substituted for "young ladies and gentlemen" in the title, the latest recorded of these appearing in Boston as late as 1822. *Miscellanies on Moral and Religious Subjects, in Prose and Verse* (1756), which EH published to raise funds for the support of her mother, includes the names of CHARLOTTE SMITH and Samuel Johnson in its 28-page subscription list. Although the collection is described as "produced by the contribution of many hands," only a small number of the works is identified as written by others. Moreover, most of the works not thus identified are similar in tone and theme to EH's other writings, emphasizing biblical teachings concerning the punishment of sin and the reward of virtue. The prose pieces are short moral fables, homilies, or reflections on topics common to the period. "On the Creation" begins, for example, "In the visible things of the creation, we should see the glory of the invisible God." A few fictional letters are included, two of these being described as a sequel to ELIZABETH ROWE's fictional letters. The verse selections include hymns, dialogues, fables, paraphrases of the psalms, and imitations of Horace. An advertisement appears at the end of the volume for *Meditations Upon Various Subjects Religious and Moral . . . design'd for Persons in Younger Life,* described as just published by the same author; however, this work is not listed in standard reference works. One contemporary critic refused to evaluate the *Miscellanies,* stating: "As this publication is the work of benevolence, and a sacrifice, not to vanity, but to pious old age, and industrious poverty;

it has a natural claim upon us, to an entire exemption from any criticism that might tend, in the least, to obstruct the progress of so worthy an intention" (*Monthly Review* 14, 1756). Samuel Johnson commented: "The authors of the essays in prose seem generally to have imitated or tried to imitate the copiousness and luxuriance of Mrs. Rowe; this however is not all their praise, they have laboured to add to her brightness of imagery her purity of sentiments. The poets have had Dr. Watts before their eyes" (*Literary Magazine* vi, 1756). Although Johnson quotes four complete prose pieces and three poems from EH's book, he devotes the remainder of his review to a discussion of Rowe and Watts and general praise of didactic writing. J.F.

HARRISON, Susanna (1752–84), poet, was from a large family, probably resident in Ipswich. On her father's death, when she was still a child, the family was left in very poor circumstances. SH received no formal education but taught herself to read and write after entering domestic service at the age of 16. The Bible and Watts' hymns became her favorite books. Four years after she began domestic work, SH developed a severe illness from which she did not expect to recover and therefore gave a collection of her poems to the Rev. John Condor for posthumous publication. Although her health did improve, she was unable to return to her previous work and suffered from illness and poverty for the remainder of her life. In 1780 the Rev. Condor edited SH's poems and they were published under the title *Songs in the Night; By a Young Woman under deep Afflictions.* The work was well received, with two more editions being published before the author's death. A fourth edition in 1788 (Ipswich) included SH's last poems and a prose supplement and was used for the first American edition in 1802. The continued popularity of *Songs* until well into the 19th century is evident from the number of editions—six American by 1821 and fifteen British by 1823. SH was possibly also the author of *A Call to Britain,* a popular broadside.

The complete edition of *Songs* includes 133 hymns, 18 religious poems, and 16 meditations in blank verse. Although nowhere is there any statement concerning SH's religious affiliation, her works are markedly evangelical, and as the Rev. Condor was a Congregationalist it is assumed that SH was one likewise. Each work is based upon a specific biblical text, and throughout the book there is an emphasis on solifidianism. Hymn LXVI, based on the text "By Grace are ye saved," is typical; composed in six quatrains, it begins with the lines: "No more of works I vainly boast, / Nor so employ my tongue; / Jesus alone is all my trust, / Free grace my only song." Some of the later compositions express greater emotional intensity, as in Hymn CXXXII, which is based on Psalm CV, 4,5: "Yes, for my eyes would ever gaze / On beauty so divine; / My heart with love would burn and blaze, / And be for ever thine." The subjectivity of many of the pieces, especially the later ones, displays the same belief in personal salvation as expressed in the hymns and poems of ANNE STEELE. Little originality of form is found in the works. Although he criticized her "county phraseology," John Condor praised SH's "uniformity of sentiment, the propriety with which she useth words less common and the general smoothness of her versification" (*Songs,* vi). J.F.

HASTINGS, Susannah Johnson (1730–1810), American autobiographer, was born to the Willards of Lunenberg, Mass. In 1742, her parents moved to Charlestown, N.H., when it was still known as settlement no. 4; SH joined her parents in 1744. She was married to Mr. Johnson, since the age of ten an indentured servant of her great uncle, Joshuah Willard. SH lost several relations, including her father, to hostile Indians in the years preceding the French and Indian War. In 1754 SH herself was taken captive, along with other Charlestown settlers, including her husband and their three children. During the course of her four-year ordeal, SH gave birth to a fourth child, whom she named Captive, and became separated from her family, before being sold at St. Lawrence, Canada, to the French. A ransom for her return was paid by her husband, who had been released in 1758. *The Captive American,* which first appeared in 1779, is SH's sole literary effort, and an account of her experience. The dictated work, which came to be known as *The Narrative of Mrs. Johnson's Captivity,* was popular in both Britain and America. It was widely reissued in ever-expanding editions on an audience eager for just such narratives. SH married Mr. Hastings after Johnson's death, and she died in Charlestown. SH's aim was clearly stated: "The simple facts, unadorned, is what the reader must expect; pity for my sufferings and admiration for my safe return is all that my history can excite." The narrative rarely departs from its journalistic intention and, while this equanimity of tone lends authenticity to the work, it also drains it of any possible dramatic interest. No effort is made to exploit the emotional center of the story, and SH offers few insights, other than a guarded comment or two that the settlers were not treated "with cruelty in a wanton way." Later editions of SH's work become increasingly weighted down with superfluous, but probably authentic, biographical material. A collection of Indian narratives, published in 1854, purported to tell the "real" story of SH's adventure, but was only a well-edited version of the late editions.   D.T.

HAWKINS, Laetitia Matilda (1759–1835), miscellaneous writer, novelist, and memoirist, was born in London. Her father, John (later Sir John) Hawkins, who came from a family which LH herself characterizes as of "no eminence" in 1753 had married Sidney Storer, the daughter of his wealthy employer. In 1759, the year LMH was born, Mrs. Hawkins inherited additional money which enabled LMH's father to retire from his career as advocate, accept the position of magistrate for Middlesex, and pursue his literary and musical interests. LMH grew up, therefore, in affluence, with houses both in Twickenham and London. Her father, who edited Izaak Walton's *Compleat Angler,* compiled *A General History of the Science and Practice of Music* (1776), and wrote a *Life of Samuel Johnson* (1787), carefully supervised her education, prohibiting novels and other popular volumes until he had formed her taste as he wished. She and her brothers John Sidney (1757–1842) and Henry (c. 1761–1841), were frequently allowed into the family drawing room, where they observed many of the famous intellectuals of the day; they were, however, not permitted to speak unless they felt they could solve a problem or add an important fact to the conversation. LMH was so fiercely addicted to learning that she would often study instead of exercising, with the result that she suffered from occasional bouts of neurasthenia. She had little extra time, since her father made his children act as amanuenses, and LMH took over the task of copying Walton when her brother John went to Charterhouse. Although she copied for six hours a day for her father, and read aloud to her mother "nearly as long," before the age of 30 she clandestinely wrote a novel. This novel,

which concerns "manners and situations of which I knew little but by hearsay," and which she never names, was published by Thomas Hookham. LMH appears never to have revealed her venture into authorship to her father, or to anyone else except her younger brother. Although the original secrecy resembles FANNY BURNEY's early literary efforts, the continued secrecy does not. LMH claims that she "wrote many subsequent volumes," but since she mentions the titles of none of them, there is no way to trace them. She herself cannot really explain her continued diffidence, although she says she was "certainly afraid of some displeasure and ashamed of my employment." Her father died in 1789, and her mother four years later. Soon, she moved in with her brother Henry, called "Classic Harry" for his intellectual accomplishments, in Twickenham. She never married, remaining at Twickenham for the rest of her life.

The first work which has been securely attributed to LMH is the anonymous two-volume *Letters on the Female Mind* (1793), a book reflecting LMH's complex and at times inconsistent attitudes about women. In the initial ten letters, LMH speaks generally about female capacities; the last ten reply to HELEN MARIA WILLIAMS's *Letters from France.* At the start, LMH carefully distinguishes the male mind from the female. Women have "less strength but more acuteness" of intellect, and a "vivacity of imagination, and a concatenation of invention that disdains all limit." She argues that women are capable of mastering any field of study, and emphasizes snobbishly that they should do so in an "elegant home," rather than collecting "the gewgaws of an indiscriminating boarding school." Yet she continually stresses that women, by their nature and experience, are incompetent in certain endeavors. In LMH's view, they should not attempt to be sailors, architects, lawyers, or doctors. Least of all should they venture as Williams has done into politics. LMH counsels caution, conformity, and cheerful obedience: "I do not warn young ladies from the study of politics, only because it may hinder their becoming wives, but because it will make them less amiable *companions,* and less respectable members of society." Women must find their happiness within, chiefly by "the virtuous cultivation of the mind." Williams has been so flattered by the fact that she has been allowed to observe the National Assembly that she has failed to notice the rapacity and confusion in the country at large, and failed to sympathize with the royal family. "Let not susceptible Helen," LMH archly warns, "who in scenes of joy weeps tears of luxury, be ranked with the viragos of party." Starting at the age of 53, LMH, published three novels under her own name and one anonymously: *The Countess and Gertrude; or Modes of Discipline,* 4 vols. (1811), *Rosanne; or, a Father's Labour Lost,* 3 vols. (1814); *Heraline; or Opposite Proceedings,* 4 vols. (1821); and *Annaline; or, Motive-Hunting,* 3 vols. (1824). LMH felt that Richardson had allowed Clarissa too many imperfections. By contrast, in all her novels, the heroines are perfect—outspoken and fearless, yet judicious, godfearing, and polite. They are also lucky. Although they are impoverished, men are eager to marry them, and they turn down titled offers, even when they have no other secure prospects. In the end, each finds a rich and gentle husband, although, like Jane Austen, LMH avoids scenes where the lover actually makes his declaration. As the titles imply, each novel supports a theme: how to raise children, how a daughter through the love of God can save a father, or how being outspoken is more laudable than concealing. The first three novels take place in England and contain details from LMH's experience. Children are raised by her own family's principles, and in footnotes she expands on points in the text. In the middle of one novel, she suddenly refers to her brother's opinion: "We join in our merry friend Harry Classic's aversion to those rough manners which, as he says, seem let loose on the world." *Annaline,* however, is an exception, a romance set in Spain and on ship-board to South America, swift-moving and swashbuckling. Perhaps this was a revision of an earlier work, or a return to an earlier style. LMH is also thought to have written *Sermonets Addressed to Those Who Have Not Yet Acquired the Inclination to Apply the Powers of Attention to Compositions of a Higher Kind* (1814), and *Devotional Exercises Extracted from Bishop Patrick's Christian Sacrifice* (1823). In these endeavours to popularize religion, LMH may be compared to HANNAH MORE, whom she had mentioned in the *Letters* with admiration and approval. LMH's volumes of reminiscences, the *Anecdotes* (1822) and the *Memoirs* (1824), straddled her last novel. The *Anecdotes* chiefly describe the members of her father's circle. The *Mem-*

oirs, written as a distraction from illness, is a miscellaneous assemblage of observations and experiences. LMH never prided herself on careful organization, and in her last book she allowed herself to ramble. In both books she defends her father, whom others besides Johnson found "unclubbable," especially promoting his *Life of Johnson,* although she ultimately admits that Boswell's *Life* is better. She also prints pieces by her brother Henry. When De Quincey mildly ridiculed the *Anecdotes* in a review, LMH was hurt only by his implication that Henry's Latin was imperfect. Along with these attempts to further the memory of her male relatives, however, she recreates her contemporaries in deft and devastating portraits: Horace Walpole "always entered a room . . . knees bent, and foot on tiptoe, as if afraid of a wet floor"; Bennet Langton was always "sitting with one leg twisted around the other, as if fearing to occupy more space than was equitable" and George Stevens "was a frigid calculator, a sort of by-stander to his own actions; and in his neighbourhood, as his true character unfolded itself, his attentions to young women were considered not as in themselves seductive, but as a blasting mildew which would injure their estimation." Her memories of Johnson are those perhaps most often quoted and need not be repeated here. Henry Skrine's *Gossip About Dr. Johnson and Others* professes to abridge *Anecdotes* and *Memoirs* but is in fact largely rewritten.

Although LMH worshipped the men in her family and without question subjected her will to theirs, she valued her own education above all things, fearing that, if women too brashly flaunted their learning, men would rescind their right to such knowledge. She passionately admired women who had educated themselves and who triumphed in adversity, and went out of her way to explain that poverty had driven MARY ROBINSON and Emma, Lady Hamilton, to their illicit connections. She dedicated all her novels to women, and respected their minds even when uneducated. LMH herself achieved a firm reputation. Her books were reviewed occasionally with approbation: *British Critic* (January 1821), *[Heraline]; BC* (August 1824), *[Memoirs];* and occasionally with irritation: *New Monthly Magazine* (August 1821), or amusement, as by De Quincey. Her readers linked her with Mary Brunton, whose works enjoin similar moral virtues, especially self-control. Austen found *Rosanne* "Very good and clever, but tedious," adding, "and, as to love, her heroine has very comical feelings." LMH's primary gift was for sharp, realistic character portrayal. It is unfortunate that she expended most of her energies writing in genres which were incompatible with this gift.   J.Th.

HAYDEN, Anna Tompson (1648–?), American poet, was born in Braintree, Mass., the sister of the poet Benjamin Tompson. Her one or possibly two elegies appear in Joseph Tompson's journal before 1715, published in 1827. They are crude, pious pieces, tending to doggerel: the first, on ATH's niece who died in 1712, calls the dead girl a "lovely flow'r cropt in its prime" and warns others of their end, while the second, on Benjamin Tompson, said to be by a friend, begins "Ah, my dear brother, though your gone, / I do often think upon, / Of your great kindness shown to me / In my greatest extremity"; like the first poem, it insists on attention to death: "O happy they, that are prepar'd to die."   J.T.

HAYDEN, Esther (1713–58), American poet, married Samuel Hayden of Braintree, Mass., and had nine children. She left a deathbed message in verse of 167 lines to her family and friends, urging them to Christian devotion and expressing her own religious difficulties and doubts. Entitled *A Short Account of the Life, Death and Character of Esther Hayden* (1759), it exists now in a Brown University collection. In her verse, EH bewails her mental and physical afflictions, her "wasting sickness," her "fear to die" and her "horr'r and grievous sorr'w."   J.J.

HAYS, Mary (1760–1843), novelist and polemical writer, was born into a Dissenting family. In 1778 she fell in love with John Eccles, who lived close to her in Southwark, but marriage was opposed by MH's widowed mother and by Eccles' father. The pair exchanged many letters until objections to their marrying were overcome. Before the wedding could occur, however, Eccles died. MH comforted herself by reading novels and religious works, guided in the latter by Robert Robinson, a rational Dissenter who later became a Unitarian. Through Robinson MH met other notable Dissenters and liberal thinkers, including William Frend and George Dyer. Toward the end of the 1780s, MH attended lectures on religion and politics at the new Dis-

senting academy at Hackney. When Gilbert Wakefield, a teacher at the academy, attacked Dissenting public worship, she defended it in a pamphlet entitled *Cursory Remarks on an Enquiry into the Expediency and Propriety of Public or Social Worship* (1792), signed "Eusebia." Her argument stemmed from biblical texts and from her own beneficial experience of communal worship. The pamphlet was well received and went into a second edition. Thereafter MH was closely associated with radical Dissenters and became acquainted with the circle of Joseph Johnson, the publisher, which included William Godwin, William Blake and Thomas Paine. In 1792 MH read MARY WOLLSTONECRAFT's *Vindication of the Rights of Woman* and its feminist arguments influenced her greatly. In the following year she published *Letters and Essays, Moral and Miscellaneous,* a work sent to Wollstonecraft before publication for criticism; this was frankly given and MH followed Wollstonecraft's advice not to plead female weakness in the preface. MH developed close relationships with Godwin and Frend, who had arrived in London after his dismissal from Cambridge for Unitarian teaching. She wrote a large number of letters to Godwin anatomizing her emotions and ideas and fully describing her unreturned passion for Frend, to whom she also wrote. In 1796 when Wollstonecraft returned to London, MH renewed the friendship and, to revive her friend's low spirits after the suicide attempt, she invited her to meet Godwin again, a meeting which led to marriage. MH remained on intimate terms with both. In 1796 she published her first novel, *Memoirs of Emma Courtney,* a frank and self-pitying description of a woman's unrequited love, based on the relationship with Frend and using some of the correspondence with Godwin, who appears in the novel as Mr. Francis. During 1796 and 1797 MH wrote for the *Monthly Magazine,* entering the controversy about environment and education and stressing women's intellectual equality with men. When Wollstonecraft died in 1797, MH wrote a warm tribute to her for *MM,* praising her virtue and bravery, and noting her painful struggle against prejudice. Shortly after, MH quarreled with Godwin; they were later reconciled but never again intimate. As the times grew more conservative, hostility to liberals and radicals increased and MH was often attacked. Ridiculed in Charles Lloyd's *Edmund Oliver*

(1798) as Lady Gertrude Sinclair and as Bridgetina Botherim in ELIZABETH HAMILTON's *Memoirs of Modern Philosophers* (1800–1801), she was labeled "Wollstonecraftian" by Richard Polwhele and frequently mocked by the *Anti-Jacobin Review. Appeal to the Men of Great Britain in Behalf of Women* was published anonymously and ascribed to MH; similar to *The Rights of Woman* in its demand for female education to prove intellectual equality, it differs from the earlier work in its Christian emphasis. In 1799 appeared *The Victim of Prejudice,* MH's second novel, which attacks those moral conventions that victimize women. During this year MH corresponded with her former critic, Charles Lloyd, who spread the story about that MH loved him and had, like Emma Courtney, declared her passion. Coleridge, Lamb, Southey and Godwin were all involved in the dispute. In 1800 MH's second obituary of Wollstonecraft appeared in *Annual Necrology, 1797–1798;* it called women "the victims of vice and superstition," but was less eulogistic of its subject than the first. In 1802 MH published *Female Biography; or, Memoirs of Illustrious and Celebrated Women, of all Ages and Countries,* which showed a movement from her radical feminism of the 1790s but still a sympathy with women's concerns. She corresponded regularly with Henry Crabb Robinson and ELIZA FENWICK during these years. In 1804 she published a selection from Henry Brooke's novel *The Fool of Quality* (1766) to stress the hero's education; it was entitled *Harry Clinton; or a tale of youth.* MH moved several times over the next years, being for a short period a teacher in Oundle. In 1814 she was staying in Clifton, where she came to admire HANNAH MORE and MARIA EDGEWORTH; in the next years her work shows the influence of their moral concerns. In 1815 More published MH's *The Brothers; or Consequences. A Story of what happens every day* and in 1817 *Family Annals; or the Sisters,* both intended for the edification of the poor. In 1821 *Memoirs of Queens* was issued, much of the material taken from the earlier biographical work of 1802.

The letters to Eccles show MH's early concern with education and with women's failure to gain it. Her novel *Memoirs of Emma Courtney* shocked the public by its frank use of autobiography and by the passionate nature of the heroine, who does not follow convention by waiting for a male declaration of love. Unfortunately the exaggeratedly sentimental style in which MH wrote often dissipates the emotion she wishes to convey: "My imagination was raised—methought the lively colours of the complexion had faded, the benignant smile had vanished . . . I uttered a faint shriek, and fell lifeless into the arms of my friend." There is, in addition, much intrusive self-pity: "Torn by conflicting passions—wasted in anguish—life is melting fast away—A burthen to myself, a grief to those who love me, and worthless to every one." Despite its excesses, the novel remains a remarkable work in its unusual plea for female emotional emancipation and in its passionate desire to break through the "magic circle" of restriction and prejudice. *Letters and Essays* owes much to Wollstonecraft, as MH acknowledges; it argues against despotism in religion, in society, and in relations between men and women. Some reviewers praised it for its religious tendency, few applauded its feminism. The *English Review* termed MH "the baldest disciple of Mrs. Wollstonecraft" and one of her essays "an abortion." MH's later works show her feminism has mellowed but, as late as 1821, she reveals herself still believing in human perfectibility and hoping for increased opportunities for women. J.T.

HAYWOOD, Eliza [Fowler] (1693–1756), novelist, playwright, translator, and writer of periodicals, was born in London, the daughter of a small shopkeeper. Details of her early life are not known, but she claimed to have been better educated than most girls. She married Valentine Haywood, a clergyman with a Norfolk living, and their son was baptized in London in 1711. EH was in Dublin in 1715 and made her stage debut in Smock-Alley as Chloe in *Timon of Athens; or the Man Hater.* Her first novel, *Love in Excess* (1719), went through four editions before appearing in the collected *Works of Eliza Haywood* (1724). A translation from the French of Bursault's *Ten Letters from a Young Lady of Quality,* published by subscription in 1720, had 309 subscribers. In January 1721, an advertisement inserted by Valentine Haywood in the *Post-Boy* announced that EH had left him without his consent. Thereafter she supported herself by acting and writing. In the 1720s three of her plays were performed: *The Fair Captive,* a tragedy, at Lincoln's Inn Fields in 1721; *A Wife to be Lett,* a comedy in which she acted, at Drury Lane in 1723; and *Frederick, Duke of Brunswick-*

Lunenburgh, a tragedy, at Lincoln's Inn Fields in 1729. In the 1720s, EH's most prolific decade, her novels ranged in price from 1s to 3s and were dedicated to various people in the hope of gaining patronage. EH's friends included actor and playwright William Hatchett, who collaborated with her on *The Opera of Operas* (1733); Aaron Hill, who wrote an epilogue to her first play; Richard Savage, who praised her in verses prefixed to *Love in Excess* and *The Rash Resolve* (1724); and James Sterling, who wrote a complimentary poem *To Mrs. Eliza Haywood on her Writings.* She may have had a personal acquaintance with Steele, to whom she dedicated *The Surprise* (1724). EH was believed to have lived as mistress with various men, and was said to have two illegitimate children. In Book II of Pope's *Dunciad* (1728) she is depicted as the prize in a contest between the book-sellers Curll and Chetwood. Pope's work spread her reputation as a licentious woman. In the following decade she wrote little but appeared in several plays. In Hatchett's *Rival Father,* at the Haymarket in 1730, she played Achilles' cast-off mistress Briseis; and in *Arden of Feversham* (1736), an adaptation which she may have written herself, she played Mrs. Arden. She acted in *The Blazing Comet* in 1732 and *A Rehearsal of Kings* in 1737. She was involved in Henry Fielding's anti-Walpole campaign, acting in his *Historical Register* and its afterpiece *Eurydice Hiss'd* from March to May 1737. Her stage career ended when the Haymarket closed down after the Licensing Act. Later, EH attacked Fielding and his plays in *Betsy Thoughtless* (1751). She wrote her own attack on Walpole, *The Adventures of Eovaii* (1736), and dedicated it to his opponent the DUCHESS OF MARLBOROUGH, whom she had lampooned in the scandal-novel *Memoirs of a Certain Island* (1725). In the early 1740s EH set up as a publisher at the Sign of Fame, Covent Garden, but this venture was short-lived. In the 1740s and 1750s she wrote novels, periodicals, and conduct books. She continued writing until not long before her death.

EH's biographer, G. H. Whicher, lists 67 single works by her, although the authorship of a few of these is not certain, and she probably wrote additional works which have not been identified as hers. Her versatility is remarkable and her list includes four dramatic pieces, a volume of poetry, and seven translations, mostly from French. EH's periodicals were *The Female Spectator,* published monthly from April 1744 to May 1746; *The Parrot,* published weekly from August to October 1746; and probably *The Young Lady,* three numbers of which appeared in January 1756. Her conduct books are *A Present for a Servant-Maid* (1743), *The Wife* (1756) and *The Husband* (1756). *The Tea Table* (1725) is an essay commenting on modern manners through presenting the conversation of a lady and her visitors. *Epistles for the Ladies* (1749) is a collection of letters. *A Spy Upon the Conjuror* (1724) is a fictionalized account of the fortune-telling of the deaf and dumb prophet Duncan Campbell. Some novels, claiming to be true accounts of the actions of famous people, were designated "secret histories." *Memoirs of a Certain Island,* her most famous scandal novel, modeled on the *New Atalantis* of DELARIVIÈRE MANLEY, contains a key for the reader to identify the people referred to by fictitious names. *The Court of Carimania* (1727) is a similar work. Many of EH's "secret histories," however, were as fictitious as the works named as novels on their title-pages, and prose fictions formed the largest group among EH's large, varied output. *Love in Excess* was followed by *The British Recluse* (1722), *The Injur'd Husband* (1723), *Idalia* (1723), *Lasselia* (1723), and *The Rash Resolve,* which appeared separately and in the collection of 1724; *The Surprise, The Fatal Secret* (1724) and *The Force of Nature,* which appeared in *Secret Histories, Novels and Poems* (1725); *The Mercenary Lover* (1726), *The Fruitless Enquiry* (1727), *Philidore and Placentia* (1727) and many other novels. They are stories of love, similar in some ways to 17th-century French romances. Characters named Placentia, Lasselia, Idalia, or Cleomelia establish the unreal atmosphere of romance. The scenes are set in various countries, but without circumstantial detail. Seductions, attempted seductions, disguises, male infidelity, female friendship, and female rivalry make complicated plots but a simple message: the world is a dangerous place for a young woman. EH's extravagent style with its use of epithets, and her favorite theme of women's vulnerability in love, are exemplified in this quotation from *Lasselia:* "the generous Fair had too great a tenderness for her lovely Undoer, to press him to take off the Reproach she suffer'd by making her his Wife." The novels often contain letters between lovers, whose emotional rhetoric can be seen in this extract from Amena's letter to Delmont in *Love in Excess:* "know, thou Undoer of my Quiet, tho' I have lov'd and still do love you with a Tenderness, which I fear will be unvanquishable, yet I will rather suffer my Life, than my Virtue to become its Prey." In *The British Recluse* EH announces her intention to show "a sad Example of what Miseries may attend a Woman, who has no other Foundation for belief in what her Lover says to her, than the good Opinion her Passion has made her conceive of him," a description which would fit most of her early novels. In this novel the recluse, Cleomira, and Belinda, both betrayed by the same lover, reject the world and retire together to the country, where their friendship makes amends for their disappointments in love. Rejection of the uncertain and deceitful world is a common attitude in the early novels. EH's later novels, published in the 1740s and 1750s, are different in many respects from the early works. They show the influence of both Richardson and Fielding. The greater emphasis on moral teaching is probably learned from Richardson, though EH was not among his first admirers and is the likely author of *Anti-Pamela* (1741), an attack on his first novel. Some imitation of Fielding's tone is found in *Betsy Thoughtless,* which has facetious chapter headings in his manner. EH's later novels are concerned with realistic details of modern life and manners. *The Fortunate Foundlings* (1744) and *Life's Progress Through the Passions* (1748) are similar to her early work, but show signs of change. *The Fortunate Foundlings* contains depictions of ordinary contemporary life not found in the earlier novels, exemplified in minor characters such as the landlady, "a good motherly sort of woman," who tells Louisa "that she was pleased with her countenance, or she would not have taken her in without enquiring into her character." *Betsy Thoughtless* belongs more to the new realistic tradition. It tells the moral tale of the troubles the heroine brings on herself by vanity and coquettish behavior. Because of Betsy's imprudence her lover, Trueworth, marries another woman. Betsy is foolish, but unlike many of EH's earlier heroines she is not seduced. This would be inappropriate to the new tone of propriety EH is cultivating. Betsy marries Munden, who is mean, morose, and unfaithful, and eventually leaves him. Cured of her faults, Betsy is rewarded when, after her husband's and Trueworth's wife's deaths, she marries her

first love. For the romantic names found in the early novels, *Betsy Thoughtless* substitutes names which reveal personality: Betsy Thoughtless, Trueworth, Lady Trusty, Mr. Goodman, Miss Forward. Scenes in London society life replace the vague romantic settings of earlier novels. This story of the mistakes of a foolish but virtuous girl seemed to *Monthly Review* "a barren foundation" for a novel, but the formula became popular and was used in FANNY BURNEY's novels. In EH's last novel, *Jemmy and Jenny Jessamy* (1753), the hero and heroine become engaged, but Jenny, made aware of the seriousness of marriage by witnessing marital infidelity and disharmony, suggests delaying their wedding until they know more of the world. A false friend causes misunderstandings between them, but eventually they are happily married. EH's new sober, moralizing tone is demonstrated in her statement that "flames which burn with rapidity at first are soonest wasted . . . a gentle, and almost imperceptible glow of pure affection, when once raised up by any extraordinary incident, sends forth a stronger and more lasting heat." EH's later nonfiction displays her new moral stance. *The Female Spectator,* supposed to be written by a group of four women, and *Epistles for the Ladies* give moral advice to women. In *The Wife,* conventional advice is given to wives about striving to please their husbands; but, unconventionally, EH advises a wife to leave her husband if he proves impossible to please. This idea receives support in *Betsy Thoughtless* when Betsy leaves Munden, and EH's attitude is clearly a result of her own experience of marriage and separation. *The Wife's* moral advice is given for practical purposes. A wife trying to convince her jealous husband of her fidelity should "never fly into extravagancies, nor give any violent marks of her resentment; for clamour and loud words neither become the character of a wife, nor will avail to gain the point she aims at." EH still wrote some fiction in her earlier vein, and *The Invisible Spy* (1755), a miscellany of narratives and letters, is similar to her early scandal novels. Contemporary opinions of EH varied. In a note to the *Dunciad* Pope called her one of "those shameless scriblers . . . who in libellous Memoirs and Novels, reveal the faults and misfortunes of both sexes, to the ruin or disturbance, of publick fame, or private happiness." To Swift, she was a "stupid, infamous, scibbling woman."

Nevertheless, her early novels were very popular. The later change in her writing, which shows her adaptability and sensitivity to a changing literary market, was hailed as a moral conversion. CLARA REEVE, in *The Progress of Romance* (1785), wrote that EH "repented of her faults, and employed the latter part of her life in expiating the offenses of the former," and added "may her first writings be forgotten, and the last survive to do her honour!" However, EH's panegyrist James Sterling referred to her early novels when he wrote that "Born to delight as to reform the Age, / She paints Example thro' the shining Page." He considered that EH, APHRA BEHN, and De-larivière Manley formed "the fair Triumvirate of Wit." J.S.

HEARNE, Mary (fl. 1718–19), novelist, wrote *The Lover's Week* (1718), dedicated to DELARIVIÈRE MANLEY, and *The Female Deserters* (1719). The novels were reprinted in 1720 as *Honour, the victory; and love, the prize. Illustrated in ten novels by Mrs. Hearne* (with other novels, published by E. Curll). Both works celebrate the right of women to take lovers, and they see marriage as "a piece of Formality, introduced to bring Profit to the Church": "Let spiteful Maidens, talkatively chaste / Condemn those joys they slily wish to taste / Whilst the fair Nymph whom no false Fears restrain / Folds in her tender Arms th'Enamour'd Swain." L.F.

HELME, Elizabeth (fl. 1787–1814), novelist connected with the Minerva Press, was married to William Helme, a schoolmaster of Brentford. She wrote in a variety of genres. Her sentimental and gothic novels began with *Louisa; or The Cottage on the Moor* (1787), a popular work that ran to at least five editions and was reprinted as late as 1840. Like most of her novels, it is a romance with several interpolated episodes. *Critical Review* called it "a pleasing little artless tale, much superior, both in its plan and conduct, to the numerous productions of this class." *Clara and Emmeline* (1788) followed, with *Duncan and Peggy* (1794). All three were short works, fairly informal in tone, but *The Farmer of Inglewood Forest* (1796) was more ambitious, with lofty lyrical passages in the manner of ANN RADCLIFFE. Influenced by Restif de la Bretonne's narratives and William Godwin's philosophy, it yet has a firm, pious morality, for which it was praised by *CR* and the *British Critic. Albert; or The*

Wilds of Strathnavern (1799) showed EH's usual able plot construction; *CR* (Apr. 1800), remarked that it had "little originality or strength of character; but it is amusing in its story." *St. Margeret's Cave; or The Nun's story* (1801) is possibly EH's most successful romance. *St. Clair of the Isles* (1803), like many of her novels, revealed EH's knowledge of medieval customs and her fascination with Ossian. *Pilgrim of the Cross; or The Chronicles of Christabelle de Mowbray* (1805) and *Magdalen; or The Penitent of Godstow* (1812) are again on medieval subjects. *Modern Times; or The Age we live in* was published posthumously in 1814. EH also made translations of François Le Vaillant's *Travels from the Cape of Good Hope* (1790) and J.H. Campe's book on the conquest of Mexico (1799). She was the author of many books for children, *Instructive Rambles in London* (1798), *James Manners, little John, and their dog Bluff* (1799), *The History of England* (1805), *The History of Scotland* (1806), *The History of Rome* (1808), *Maternal Instruction* (1802) and *The Fruits of Reflection* (1809). EH was one of the better light-romance novelists of her time, and her works were reprinted until the late 19th century. Although derivative of other writers, such as Radcliffe and Marivaux, she tells her tales well and smoothly, and her conventional plots, of fair maids, noble sons, hidden identities and aristocratic property rights, hold the reader's interest without much recourse to suspense and horror. Occasionally EH writes in the exaggerated gothic style of the time: "His features assumed a ghastly paleness, a universal tremor shook his whole frame, the drops of cold perspiration hung upon his hollow careworn cheeks." Mostly, however, her tone is more restrained and elevated: "The lady Adelaide is not formed to create loose desires. Had you seen her, you would have felt the truth of what I assert; for dark indeed must that heart be, that could regard her with less reverence that that with which she inspired me." J.T.

HERBERT, Lady Lucy (1669–1744), devotional writer, was abbess of the Augustine nuns at Bruges. She came from a politically powerful and turbulent Catholic family: her father, William Herbert, had the Jacobite title Duke of Powis, and was outlawed from England; her sister Winifred, Countess of Nithsdale, engineered the escape of her husband from the Tower of London the night before his intended execution. LH authored a number of short works suggesting appropriate methods of devotion, including "Meditation for each Sunday of the month" and "Motives and practices of humility for every day of the month" (Bruges: John de Cock, 1722). Her longest and most popular work, *Several Excellent Methods of Hearing Mass . . .* , was originally published by John de Cock in 1722, republished by him in 1742 and by his widow in 1743, and again published in 1791. In *Several Excellent Methods* LH explains the importance of mass and gives sample ideas and personal prayers for worshipers to think about and use during the service. She makes much use of parallelism: her sentences are long, flowing accumulations rather than terse aphorisms. Ever striving to make the abstract concrete, she employs brief biblical similes: "The weary'd and thirsty stagg desires not so much the cooling streams, as my heart do's this victime [Christ], which is the source of grace." She quotes the Bible and Church fathers, especially St. Augustine, to reinforce her points. The struggles of the Catholics in England are reflected in her suggestions for prayers: at one point she says it would be appropriate to pray on Wednesdays for the conversion of England, and at another she prays to God, "Grant that England, and all misbelieving kingdomes may be converted to the true faith." The clarity and reasonableness of her explanations are convincing, but more impressive are her passionate prayers for forgiveness: "'Twas not so much Judas that betray'd you, as my treacherous heart; not so much the soldiers that struck, reviled, and spit upon you, as did my passions. 'Twas my sensuality that scourged you; my gluttony that gave you gall; in short, 'twas my sins that nail'd you to the cross, drew all the blood from your veines, and bereaved you of life."   A.W.E.

HERON, Mary (fl. 1786–92), poet, seems to have lived in the north of England. She published *Miscellaneous Poems* in 1786, and these were followed by *The Mandan Chief: A Tale in Verse* (1791) and *Odes, etc., on Various Occasions* (1792). Her first collection contains mostly occasional and nature poetry, together with less-than-successful attempts to write in more sophisticated forms such as the Pindaric ode. The lyric "Summer" is representative of her reliance on well-laundered poetic diction: "But first the fragrant spring, / With odoriferous wing, / Balmy perfumes has wafted through the grove; / The tuneful feather'd throng, / In soft melodious song, / Revive

their fond harmonious notes of love." *The Mandan Chief* is a tale of tribal warfare clearly inspired by contemporary literature on the American Indians; it sits rather awkwardly with the author's own Christian worldview. The most topical of the 1792 *Odes* is the "Ode to Reformation," by which MH misleadingly refers to the French Revolution. In her preface she expresses doubts as to whether, as a woman, she is competent to write on such a subject, but argues: "When rebellion spreads its ravages, and war renders the land one horrid scene of destruction, are not women often the first victims? Why then should they be excluded from giving their humble opinion and expressing their wishes for safety, before it is too late." The Ode itself evinces a qualified sympathy for the Revolution—the leaders have pressed their "zeal" to the point where "anarchy, confusion and disgrace / Involve the wretched realm they meant to save"— together with the common reactionary fear for the stability of England. The rest of the odes are on conventional themes and written in the same decorous, epithetical style as her earlier work.   R.J.

HERSCHEL, Caroline Lucretia (1750–1848), astronomer, sister of Sir William, aunt of Sir John, was born in Hanover. Her father, Isaac, secretly gave her violin lessons, since her mother, Anna Ilse Moritzen, restricted CH's education to useful accomplishments, such as knitting. After her father's death in 1767, CH escaped household drudgery by joining William, a favored brother and music teacher in Bath, England. He tutored her in English, arithmetic and singing. Together, they performed oratorios to public acclaim—she singing, he conducting—until 1782, when William's interest in astronomy took precedence over her career. CH trained as an "assistant-astronomer" to help William, who became astronomer to George III in 1783. CH's duties included making and recording all necessary astronomical calculations, as well as running William's Windsor household. In 1783, while "sweeping" (with telescope) on her own, CH discovered three nebulae, one the well-known companion to the Andromeda nebula. Between 1786 and 1797, she discovered eight comets, five with undisputed priority. The first money she considered her own was her £50 assistant's salary, awarded by the King. In 1788, the Royal Astronomical Society published her revision of the *Index to Flamsteed's Observations of the Fixed Stars,* including her "errata" and catalogue of 561 previously omitted stars. CH continued as William's assistant, nursed her ailing brother Dietrich, attended royal events at Frogmore (1816, 1817), and socialized with Princess Sophia (autumn 1818). Upon William's death in 1822, she returned to Hanover, where she continued her work for another quarter of a century and where she was buried, near her parents.

CH unselfishly supported William's astronomical research and the work of others. The published revision of *Flamsteed's Observations* was a reference to every observation of every star in the British Catalogue. Her unpublished "Reduction and Arrangement in the Form of a Catalogue in Zones of All the Star Clusters and Nebulae Observed by Sir William Herschel" provided indispensable background to her beloved nephew John's work. Her comet observations are contained in *Philosophical Transactions of the Royal Society,* 77 (1787), 79 (1789), (1792), (1794) and (1796). CH's descriptions of her "sweepings" are in Mrs. John Herschel, *Memoir and Correspondence of Caroline Herschel* (1876), which contains her day-book entries as well as a portrait. Her correspondence, chiefly with her nephew, continued into 1845, when she writes to tell of the Gold Medal for Science awarded her by the King of Prussia in recognition of her "valuable services rendered to Astronomy . . . as the fellow-worker of your immortal brother." Earlier awards had included election as an honorary member of the Royal Astronomical Society (1835) and the Royal Irish Academy (1838). CH never saw herself as more than "the mere tool" of William; in 1826 she wrote, "Saying too much of what I have done is saying too little of him for he did all." Practical, organized, and self-effacing even in death, CH arranged her funeral and wrote her own epitaph: "The eyes of Her who is glorified were here below turned to the starry Heavens. Her own Discoveries of Comets, and her participation in the immortal Labours of her Brother, William Herschel, bear witness of this to future ages." J.C.K.

HERTFORD, Frances Seymour, Countess of (1699–1754), poet and letter writer, was the daughter of Henry Thynne Viscount Weymouth of Longleat, and wife to Algernon Seymour, Earl of Hertford and Duke of Somerset. The C of H saved Savage from the gallows, and served with the COUNTESS OF POMFRET as Lady of the Bed-

chamber to Queen Caroline before retiring to the rural life she described, along with court gossip, in her series of letters. Some of her verses appeared in *The New Miscellany* (1725), others in Isaac Watts's *Reliquiae Juveniles* (1734), where their authorship is concealed beneath the name "Eusebia." More poems are included in *Select Letters between the Duchess of Somerset, Lady Luxborough, William Shenstone, and others,* 2 vols. (ed. Thomas Hull, 1778), and *Correspondence between Frances, Countess of Hertford (afterwards Duchess of Somerset) and Henrietta Louisa, Countess of Pomfret, between 1738 and 1741,* 3 vols. (ed. W. Bingley, 1805). The C of H also published in 1738 the poem *The Story of Inkle and Yarrico,* based on "a most moving Tale from the Spectator" by Richard Steele, and "An Epistle from Yarrico to Inkle After he had left her in Slavery." *The Story* tells of a poor boy who goes abroad to seek his fortune and is shipwrecked. When cannibals eat his friends, he is helped by a beautiful Indian virgin: "With tygers speckled skins she deck'd his bed, / O'er which the gayest plumes of birds were spread." They live an idyllic life but Inkle longs for the luxuries of Europe and, when a boat comes, he takes it and sells the Indian into slavery, although she is expecting his child. "An Epistle" reveals Yarrico tormented less by slavery than by man's ingratitude, still loving—"My faithful Soul for ever doats on thee"—but taking some comfort from Christianity.

C of H's letters to her son, the Viscount Beauchamp, are particularly pleasing. His death in 1744 at 19 reinforced the religious melancholy that she shared with her friend of 25 years, ELIZABETH ROWE, who celebrated her in prose and in verse. A patron of poets of sensibility, C of H was immortalized in Thomson's *The Seasons* as "the blooming, the benevolent Hertford." She counted Watts, Shenstone, LADY LUXBOROUGH, CATHERINE TALBOT, and ELIZABETH CARTER among her friends. Horace Walpole wrote in his *Catalogue of Royal and Noble Authors* (1759) that she had "as much taste for the writing of others, as modesty about her own." Her most attractive poems report simply on her life in the country: "Sometimes we trace Armida's bowers, / And view Rinaldo chain'd with flowers. / Often, from thoughts sublime as these / I sink at once—and make a cheese." J.H.

HERVEY, Elizabeth (1748?–1820?), novelist, was the daughter of Francis and Maria March. Her maternal grandfather was the Hon. George Hamilton who, with his brother, the Hon. Charles Hamilton, were members of the household of Frederick, Prince of Wales; their sister, Lady Archibald Hamilton, was the Prince's mistress. In 1756, after the death of EH's father, her mother married William Beckford, an immensely rich MP; EH grew up in his establishment and was half-sister to William Beckford, author of *Vathek.* In 1774 EH married Col. Thomas Hervey, natural son of the Hon. Thomas Hervey by Lady Hanmer. Her husband had gambled himself into insolvency by 1777, when the couple went abroad to avoid creditors. He died near Liège in 1778; EH eventually returned to England where she became a novelist, probably in an attempt to support herself.

EH's first novel, *Louisa,* in two volumes, was published in London (1790). Her second, *The History of Ned Evans* (sometimes erroneously attributed to JANE WEST), was published in London and in Dublin in 1796. It takes a boy from childhood to adulthood. The style is plain but circumstantial and there is much description of eating and drinking: "At dinner he could hardly eat anything, tho' he had taken a long ride, and though Mrs. Evans had provided something that she knew he liked. However, she did not urge him but when the cloth was removed, Mrs. Evans proposed drinking one of the bottles of wine, which had been left by Lady Cecilia, to her health, and to the hopes of speedily hearing some good account of her. Ned's eyes brightened a little at this proposal; and the wine being brought, he turned over a full bumper to the toast, seemingly with great satisfaction. 'Hah, Hah! young man,' said Mr. Evans, 'I see what source it is that whets your appetite—Had it been the custom to eat healths, as well as drink them, I fancy the hare we had today would not have gone away so whole.'" *Monthly Review* found the novel somewhat imitative and not the production of a first-rate writer, but pleasant, realistic, and interesting; "the good and bad . . . blended so as to present a natural image of the world, with that preponderance of the agreeable which leaves the mind under a pleasing impression. The sentiments are uniformly pure and laudable; and indeed, the work is distinguished by the religious air pervading it." *MR* noted that local descriptions of Wales, Ireland, and North America indicated the author's

having resided there; "the details of military scenes might infer a personal acquaintance with them, were that supposed compatible with the detestation of war, and the regard to the rights of mankind, which are warmly expressed in various parts of the book." *The Church of St. Siffrid* (1797) chronicles the sufferings of the daughter of a Welsh baronet of ancient pedigree and small understanding, who married her to an adventurer. In the end she is rewarded for her sufferings. *The Mourtray Family* (1800) is a morality piece: "The History of the Mourtray family evinces that on the proper regulation of our passions, our fate chiefly depends," wrote EH. In the novel various characters represent the qualities of vanity, avarice, dissipation, passion, and voluptuousness. At the end the virtuous are rewarded with happiness. *Amabel; or Memoirs of a Woman of Fashion* (London, 1814, 1818) was EH's last known work.   C.R.

HERVEY, Mary, Lady, (1700–68), letter writer, was born in Suffolk, the daughter of Brigadier-General Nicholas Lepel[l] and Mary Brooks. Her father had been page of honor to Prince George of Denmark. According to the DUCHESS OF MARLBOROUGH in 1737, MH's father made her a cornet "in his regiment as soon as she was born . . . and she was paid many years after she was a maid of honour." Pope states that by 1717 she was maid of honor to the Princess of Wales, despite lifelong Jacobite feelings. She was famous at court for her wit and beauty; both Pope and Gay praised her, as did Voltaire, who addressed to her the only surviving English verses he wrote. In 1720 she married John Hervey, afterward Lord Hervey, politician, supporter of Robert Walpole, influential at court, and famous for his quarrel with Pope. Although Hervey was noted for his infidelities and was often absent, MH lived amicably as his wife and had eight children. In 1721 Lord Hervey's great friend LADY MARY WORTLEY MONTAGU noted "the ardent affection" shown her by "Mrs. Hervey and her dear spouse." He died in 1743 and was ungenerous to his wife in his will. In later life MH suffered from gout but continued her social life, and she was admired for her looks and charm, even in her sixties. In 1750 Lord Chesterfield told his son in Paris to "trust, consult, and to apply" to MH, and he praised her good breeding, stating that she knew more than a woman needed "for she understands Latin perfectly well, though she wisely conceals it." To her

Horace Walpole dedicated his *Anecdotes of Painting in England* and he wrote the epitaph on her tombstone. From accounts and from the evidence of her letters, MH seems to have been a lively, intelligent person and, for many, the model of the cultured woman of fashion. Her letters written between 1742 and 1768 to the Rev. Edmund Morris, former tutor to her sons, were published in 1831 as *Letters of Mary Lepel, Lady Hervey,* and those to the Countess of Suffolk were published in 1821.

The letters to Morris concern literary matters and affairs of state, along with domestic events, bereavements, and illnesses. They display remarkable elegance, wit, and detachment. On the prospect of a French invasion, MH writes: "The conduct of the French seems to me as unaccountable as our own: we have had every thing to fear, without taking any precautions; they have had the greatest designs, and have pursued them with no vigour: we had been asleep, and they have not been well awake." She occasionally reveals the prejudices which, as a member of the court, she could hardly have avoided, as in her entry for 1 April 1745: "It is true, the whole seems in disorder; but the universe itself was once a chaos (as you tell us), and yet out of that disorder came forth order; at least, such order as we ever had. All I ask or wish is but to be kept from civil war and democracy; the two worst things I have any notion of." Her sense of humor emerges in remarks made after the earthquake in 1750: "The newspapers are filled with accounts of a hundred little subaltern earthquakes, which have been felt in many different places, but which I take to be only the ghosts of the more considerable one, which haunt the timorous. There is nothing truer than what you say, that fear is an epidemical distemper: there is hardly anything more contagious." J.T.

HIGHMORE, Susanna (1690–1750), poet, was born in Effingham, Surrey, the only surviving child of Elizabeth and Anthony Hiller, a yeoman farmer of some means. The family were probably Congregationalists. In 1716 SH and Joseph Highmore, by then a young portrait painter just out of articles as a solicitor's clerk, were married and lived in St. Swithin's parish, London. When their circumstances improved, they leased a house in Lincoln's Inn Fields, where they remained for the rest of SH's life. They had one son, Anthony, and a daughter SUSANNA HIGHMORE DUNCOMBE, both of whom were given good educations by their parents. SH inherited her father's property, which, along with her husband's success as a portrait painter, made them prosperous. Samuel Richardson, Hawkins Browne, Isaac Watts, and William Duncombe were among her literary friends. SH's surviving literary works are limited, but reflect a ready wit and a thoughtful curiosity. An extempore "On Seeing a Gate Carried by Two Men through Lincoln's Inn Fields, 1743," eventually published in Nichol's *Select Collection,* vol. 8, is a spoofing imitation of Alexander Pope's "On an Old Gate Erected in Chiswick Gardens," which was not yet in print when she wrote. Her couplet "On Reading the Essay on Satire, occasioned by Mr. Pope's Death" (June 1745), took the opportunity to praise Hawkins Browne: "That providence is kind, let none disown. / When heav'n recall'd her Pope, she lent us Browne." Her deistic disdain for religious intolerance and some knowledge of church history are evident in her sonnet "A Calvinistical Reflection" *(Gentleman's Magazine,* December 1749). When Isaac Watts died, SH wrote the obituary for the *London Evening Post,* November 1748. Before her own death, she hid notes about the house telling her husband how deeply she loved him, moving him the week after she died to write a letter to *The Rambler,* which he hoped would become an essay in that periodical, but Samuel Johnson did not use it (*GM,* January 1816). W.M.

HOLFORD, Margaret (fl. 1785–1814), playwright and poet, was the daughter of William Wrench of Chester. She married Allen Holford of Davenham, Cheshire, and became the mother of Margaret Holford, also a playwright and poet. MH wrote five-act comedies, *Neither the Man,* acted at Chester (pub. 1799), and *The Way to Win Her,* which was printed in 1814 but probably not performed. The latter play, collected in *The New British Theater,* is a sprightly comedy of manners boasting lively repartee and a thoroughly engaging heroine, Julia, modeled on Restoration heroines. Julia is not a sophisticated tease, but a genuine, forthright character whose bluntness and freedom of spirit compensate for the rather conventional mistaken-identity plot. MH is also credited with novels: *Fanny, A Novel In a Series of Letters,* 3 vols. (1785), *Calaf: A Persian Tale,* 2 vols. (1790), and another "tale," *Fanny and Selina,* published with *Gresford Vale and Other Poems* (1798). In addition, *First Impressions, or The Portrait* (1801) has also been attributed to MH.   E.N.

HOLLAND, Lady Caroline, [née Lady Georgiana Caroline Lennox] (1723–74), letter writer, was the beautiful eldest daughter of Charles, second Duke of Richmond, and Sarah, daughter of William, Earl Cadogan. Her parents objected to her attachment to the politically ambitious Henry Fox (1705–74), and following her elopement with him in 1744 refused to see her until after the birth of her son Stephen in 1745; but the marriage was a good one despite Fox's initiation of his three sons into his own favorite dissipations. During the course of the marriage, Fox held various key cabinet positions and became fabulously rich as paymaster-general during the Seven Years' War. CH, intelligent, with quiet domestic tastes, maintained her place in society and bore with, although she disliked, the frenetic and luxurious life at Holland House, Kensington. She enjoyed a country retreat at Kingsgate and occasional trips to the Continent. She suffered from nerves and low spirits, and was tried by perpetual demands made of her. Her adored eldest son suffered from the aftereffects of rheumatic fever; her sister the DUCHESS OF LEINSTER had successfully married off one of their orphaned sisters, LADY LOUISA CONOLLY, but Lady Louisa and her husband were chagrined by their own failures with LADY SARAH BUNBURY. Henry Fox was, as LADY LOUISA STUART said, remarkable for disclaiming contempt of women, and was so openly dependent on his wife's wisdom that when discussing public measures with Bute he would say, "Well, I will go home and talk it over with Lady Caroline before I make up my mind." The Foxes' middle son was Charles James (1749–1806), the famous politician. As a reward for her husband's political services, CH was made Lady Holland in 1762; in 1763 her husband became Lord Holland. He died in 1774, the year he paid off £140,000 of his sons' gambling debts; CH died of cancer in the same year.

CH's letters to her sister, the Duchess of Leinster, which were saved by the recipient, have been edited by Brian Fitzgerald and published by the Irish Manuscripts Commission. They reveal CH as a devoted wife and a careful mother, whose first concern was the health of her family. She watched over the family affairs of her two brothers, the Duke of Richmond and Lord George Lennox, and worried about her younger sisters and the Duchess of Leinster's expanding family. She was a great reader and commented on the fiction of the day, *The Vicar of Wakefield,* Swift's letters, Percy's *Reliques,* and *Fingal:* "I think there are some pretty things in *Fingal,* but upon the whole 'tis tedious and tiresome, and as Lord Tyrawley told Lady Bute . . . the most *fee faw fum* stuff he ever read." She kept a careful eye on fashion, while reminding herself of her matronly position. She commented on the social scene and was particularly attentive to the arrangement of marriages, being stirred by misalliances, although she was later to conclude that interference with young people about matches is dangerous: "You can't imagine how much I reproach myself having in any degree (which I certainly did) put a stop to Mr. Macartney's flirting with Lady Susan; it might and I believe would have come to something . . . Mrs Digby's uneasiness at her son's love for Lady Diana Clavering gave a different turn to his way of life. Who knows, had he married her when he liked her so much he might have been alive now? . . . 'Tis my firm persuasion that a too prudent foresight in us shortsighted mortals is the most imprudent way of acting for one's own happiness." Politically, she is informed and terse: in December 1761, "There seems to be an end of Mr Pitt, I think; my opinion is he will have a fit of the gout this day sevennight; the House of Commons shew'd he had no one to support him there." In one of her last letters she wrote, "Do, dearest sister, let us pass the evening of life together as much as our different situations will admit of, and call back the pleasing remembrance of younger days"; but within a few months illness had killed both CH and her husband.   B.R.

HOOTEN, Elizabeth, (1600?–1672), polemicist, was born in Nottinghamshire, where she was living in 1646 when she became one of George Fox's first converts to Quakerism. Soon afterward, although about 50 years old, she began her travels to preach the Quaker message in England and America. Because she attacked formal Christianity and disrupted public order with the injunction to obey the authority of Inner Light, she suffered frequent assaults and imprisonments. She was a persistent petitioner, both in person and by letter, for the civil rights of Quakers. Letters still exist in manuscript to Cromwell, Charles II, the Duke of York, the Bishops of London and

Canterbury, the Lieutenant of the Tower, as well as to eminent Quakers such as Fox and MARGARET FELL. In one letter, EH pleaded for prison reform. Her lively polemics confronted not only Anglicans but also defectors from Quakerism and other sectarians like the Muggletonians; in another letter, for example, EH addresses, "You bawling women from the Ranters." In the early 1660s, when her letters and visits to Charles II failed to win his permission to set up a Quaker house in Massachusetts, a place infamous for persecuting Quakers, EH was moved to go before Charles in sackcloth and ashes. Even though she finally obtained the King's permission, the magistrates at Cambridge imprisoned her when she arrived and kept her in jail for 48 hours without sustenance. A passage from her narrative describing the event illustrates how she was able to use accounts of her sufferings to further the cause of the Quaker movement against oppressive governments. At Cambridge, the magistrates "made a Warrant to whip me for a wandring vagabond Quaker—at three towns—10 stripes at whipping post in Cambridge and 10 at Waterdown and 10 stripes at Deddam at the Cartstail with a 3 corded whip 3 knotts at end, and a handful of willow rods at Waterdown on a cold frosty morning. So they put me on a horse and carried me into the wilderness many miles, where was many wild beasts both bears and wolves and many deep waters where I waded through very deep but the Lord delivered me." She walked out of the forest to safety and continued her travels. In 1670, EH went with Fox and other Quakers on a mission to Jamaica, where she died.   S.B.

HOPTON, Susanna [Harvey] (1627–1709), devotional writer and philanthropist, was born into the country gentry of Staffordshire. She married Richard Hopton, lawyer and Restoration judge (d. 1696), and lived for many years in Kington, Hereford. Childless and wealthy, SH devoted much of her means to the relief of the poor and of impoverished Anglican clergymen. Her own devout lifestyle and her interest in theological debate gained her the admiration and friendship of clergymen-writers George Hickes and Nathaniel Spinckes. SH was largely self-taught but, although she deplored the defects in her education, was acclaimed by Hickes as having attained a theological learning "not much inferior to that of the best divines." Converted in youth to Roman Catholicism, she returned to the

Church of England in 1661, persuaded both by her husband and by her own close study of many theological treatises. Her subsequent keen defense of Protestantism is epitomized in a long expository letter to her former mentor, Father Turbeville, published posthumously in Hickes's *Second Collection of Controversial Letters* (1710).

SH's other works consist mainly of prayers, meditations, and religious verses. They were published anonymously, but her authorship was disclosed by Hickes after her death. Her first book, *Daily Devotions* (1672, four editions to 1700), a collection of meditations and prayers, had earlier been thought the work of a deceased Anglican clergyman. Her second, *Devotions in the Ancient Way of Offices* (1700), was a "reform" of John Austin's work of the same name (Paris, 1668) to render it comfortable to Church of England usage. A collection of daily psalms, hymns, and prayers, reprinted five times in the 18th century, was edited by Hickes, with a preface acclaiming the author while concealing both her identity and her sex. SH's other two works, *Meditations and Devotions on the Life of Christ* and *An Hexameron,* a collection of meditations on the creation, were published posthumously by Nathaniel Spinckes, with a reprint of *Daily Devotions,* as *A Collection of Meditations and Devotions* (1717), and prefaced by a biographical account of the author. SH's somewhat austere religious practice is reflected in her writings. Her meditations ask, for example: "Our Affections, have they been set on things above, or altogether on things of the Earth? Our Senses, how have they been disciplin'd, or have they been loose or wanton, wandring, especially our Eyes?" Her literary style, despite the "improvements" undertaken by Hickes, shows an occasional lack of balance between enthusiasm and readability. Her "printed books" were mentioned in Hickes's epitaph for SH only as showing their author herself to have been "a great Example of Devotion"; they are important among 17th-century devotional manuals written by women, however, in that, unlike the similar works by such writers as ANNE, LADY HALKETT and ELIZABETH BURNET, they appear to have been composed not only for private use, but for publication.   R.F.

HOSKENS, Jane [Fenn] (1694–1760?), autobiographer, was born in London and raised in a pious Anglican household. During an illness she heard these words: "If I restore thee, *go to Pennsylvania.*" In 1712 she went to Philadelphia as a servant. While employed as a governess by a Quaker family in Plymouth, Penna., she first attended Friends' meetings. She was led to speak at meetings in Haverford, Radnor, and nearby towns. Encouraged by David and Grace Lloyd of Chester (whom employed her as a housekeeper) and other prominent Quakers, in 1722 she became a traveling preacher; she toured the American colonies, England, and Ireland with Elizabeth Levis, Abigail Bowles, and other "public Friends." She married in 1738. JH's *Life and Spiritual Sufferings* (1771) illustrates this principle: "we poor short-sighted mortals may propose many things to ourselves, but Providence can disappoint, and all for our good, if we patiently submit." Sometimes rebellious, often overcome with feelings of unworthiness, JH was helped by friends and guided by the Inner Light; thus she could avoid Satan's "snares" and ignore his "bitter whisperings." In the manner traditional with this genre, she focuses on her experience as a Christian, naming individuals who have contributed to her spiritual development and saying nothing about herself as woman and wife. Her generally matter-of-fact style is varied by biblical phrasings, exclamatory passages, and dialogue. (She quotes the inner voice, "the old accuser," and the Friends who recognized her as a preacher before she had accepted her call.) Included in the *Friends' Library* in 1837, the highly readable *Life* was reprinted in Manchester, England, some time before 1867. JH says more about inner peace and the joy of human fellowship than does the spiritual autobiographer BATHSHEBA BOWERS, who more vividly portrays the Quaker life as a war against the forces of darkness.   M.D.J.

HOWE, Jemima (1725?–1805), American autobiographer, left various, sometimes conflicting stories of her adventures. She was born Jemima Sawtelle and was married in the early 1740s to William Phipps, who was killed by Indians in Vermont in 1745. She was left with two infant daughters, Mary and Submit. About 1746 JH married Caleb Howe, an army sergeant discharged in 1749, and lived near Hinsdale, Vt. The Howes had five sons; William, Moses, Squire, Caleb, and an unnamed infant. In 1755 Indians killed Howe where he was working in a field, took William and Moses prisoners and then, surprising a small stockade, took its party of women and children, including JH and her remaining children. After her

capture, JH kept her baby, who later died, but her other children were distributed among various Indian families. JH was sold to M. Saccapee, a French officer in St. John. When JH had trouble fending off M. Saccapee's young officer son, Col. Peter Schuyler (who had already rescued her two daughters from marriages to Indian braves by spiriting them into a convent) came to her aid. Schuyler now gathered together JH's sons and for 2700 livres ransomed JH and her children and put them into the hands of Israel Putnam, who marched them safely back to New England. One of the daughters married a French officer; the other eventually returned home. Putnam told the story of JH and her adventures to David Humphrey, the author of *An Essay on the Life of the Honorable Major-General Putnam* (1788). JH apparently took exception to Putnam's version of her story and recounted her own to Bunker Gay, a Boston pastor, who published it in 1792 as *A Genuine and Correct Account of the Captivity, Sufferings and Deliverance of Mrs. Jemima Howe, of Hinsdale, in New-Hampshire.* JH's actual story accounts for four of 35 pages, since Gay used it to introduce a description of the barbaric lifestyle of the Indians as a preparation for a description of the even more barbaric practices of the Americans, who, "once our own people, but now intermixed with savages and negroes, have lately been at war with Great Britain, their mother country." In Gay's version (purportedly JH's own), JH was twice married. Her first husband was killed, and her second, Captain Howe, now a British officer, stationed at a garrison at Fort Dunmar, Canada, was killed in a night raid. From this point the story proceeds more or less as Putnam told it, with M. Saccapee's fervors reduced. Both Putnam's and Gay's accounts were frequently republished. In 1843 John Fellows published *The Veil Removed,* an attack on Putnam which attempts to discredit his whole career by showing that he lied about JH. Fellows notes that he revised the Saccapee story, toning it down in consecutive editions, but he also insists that Col. Schuyler, not Putnam, escorted JH home from Canada. JH and her husbands were almost certainly Americans. Fellows also adds the detail that JH was married a third time, to Amos Tate, or Tute.   J.R.

HUGHES, Anne (fl. 1784–90), poet, novelist, and dramatist, published *Poems* in 1784. Three novels followed: *Caroline; or,* *the Diversities of fortune* (1787), *Henry and Isabella* (1788), and *Zoraida* (c. 1787). The poems are mainly occasional and epistolary verses, ballads, and pastoral poems; for example, "On my arm thou shalt gently recline, / Sweet converse shall shorten the hour; / The magic of love shall refine, / And add sweets to each gale and each flower." They are entirely unremarkable. *Caroline* is a sentimental novel following the fortunes of the eponymous heroine; her unpresuming, dependent passivity, and the air of mystery surrounding the affairs and intentions of men, are premonitory of modern pulp romance: "The certainty of being tenderly beloved by the only man in the world to whom her heart could give a preference, could not but be attended with pleasure, yet the apprehension of never beholding him more, and the strange mystery in which a part of his sentiments towards her were involved, clouded the sunshine of her future hopes." Ultimately the social knot unties to her satisfaction and material advantage, and she marries the knight of her choice. AH's final work was *Moral Dramas. Intended for private representation* (1790), consisting of three tragedies, *Cordelia, Constantia* and *Aspacia.* The first is a dull work, typically high-principled and heroic; it concerns a battle between the tyrannous king, Segbert, and Prince Edgar, the people's hope. Cordelia, Segbert's daughter, is torn between filial affection and love for Edgar, who is accused of being swayed immoderately by passion: "Is it a time to sink in softening bliss, / When duty calls thee to the glorious dangers, / The steepy paths of patriotic virtue?" Cordelia is prevented by the guile of a loyal servant from destroying herself on a misunderstanding, and she and Edgar are united. R.J.

HUGILL, M. [Harley], (fl. 1786–98), novelist, produced six romances between 1786 and 1798 and lived for a time in London. She began her literary career with an anonymous novel, which was privately printed and sold through subscription, but eventually gained enough popular success to have her works published by reputable printers in London and Dublin. Some time between 1794 and 1797 she changed her name from Harley to Hugill, presumably as a result of marriage.

Although she achieved a certain commercial success, MH's first two works offered literary promise that her later works failed to fulfill. Her first gothic novel, *St.*

Bernard's Priory (1786), was published anonymously but was well received. Critics of the time remarked on the indebtedness of MH'S gothic to SOPHIA LEE's *The Recess,* but her novels reflect traits of the gothic dating back to Horace Walpole. The reprinting of *St. Bernard's Priory* (as *The Priory of St. Bernard*) in 1789 by William Lane of the Minerva Press attests to its popularity and MH's rising fortune. Like many of her contemporaries, MH increasingly emphasized historical and oriental aspects in her tales of females victimized by family and friends. She is at her best when dealing with typically gothic heroines, as in *The Castle of Mowbray* (1788): "Ah! cruel father, that by the most premeditated artifices could deceive thy child; and, cruel husband, who, forgetful of the sacrifice, and unmindful of the many hours, when misery had worn thee almost to desperation, I threw aside every thought of my own unhappiness, soothed thy woe-worn soul, and hushed it into calmness. Now whither shall I turn myself for shelter, when all join to persecute the helpless wanderer?" *Juliana Ormeston* (1793) and *The Prince of Leon* (1794) followed in quick succession, with *Isidora of Gallicia* (1797–98) translated into French as *Le Chateau de Gallioe. The Countess of Hennebon* (1789) is apparently now lost. MH has also been erroneously credited with writing *Augusta Fitzherbert* (1796), a novel claiming to be by the author of *St. Bernard's Priory,* but MH herself denied authorship. Most likely it was an attempt by the publisher to capitalize on her popular success. Her early works justifiably garnered some critical praise. The *Critical Review* (July 1789) commented that, while *St. Bernard's Priory* was obviously the work of a novice, "in the midst of the glitter we perceive marks of something richer, something more valuable than foil." But eight years later the same periodical (April 1798) condemned *Isidora of Gallicia* because "the incidents also are so confused, and the story so complicated, that it is difficult to trace the plot, or unravel the perplexity." M.A.B.

HULL, Elizabeth (fl. 1790), American autobiographer, printed her book in Newburyport, Mass., probably in 1790. Raised in a pious environment, she considered herself a Christian. But as conflict with Britain became imminent and it was rumored that the colonists would be deprived of their religious liberty, she examined her commitment to Christ—and realized that it was motivated by a fear of damnation.

Enlightened by sermons, the Scriptures, the catechism, hymn texts, and Christian friends, she at last made public profession of faith and entered into the covenant, becoming a member of the Second Church of Christ in Methuen, Mass. Written "for [God's] glory, and the good of others," *A Relation of the Religious Experience of Miss Elizabeth Hull* attests to "the importance of experimental religion" and the futility of "a legal spirit" resting on self-righteousness. Like many other spiritual autobiographers, EH traces her passage through the conversion process. In periods of darkness "intermixed with light and comfort," she learned to love and trust God. Preparing for death "in hopes of a glorious resurrection," the conscientious convert still examines and questions her relationship with God. At the end of the narrative is a hymn addressed to the members of her church, exhorting them to raise their children in the fear of the Lord. Thoroughly conventional, the *Relation* illustrates the effect of Calvinism on the "New England conscience." EH's hymn shows some ingenuity in the use of internal and approximate rhyme.   M.D.J.

HUME, Sophia (1702–74), American polemicist and Quaker minister, was born in Charleston, S.C., the daughter of Henry and Susanna (Bayley) Wigington. Her father was a well-to-do landowner, and her maternal grandmother was the renowned Quaker MARY FISHER. SH, however, was brought up as an Anglican, the religion of her father. In 1721 she married Robert Hume, a lawyer and noted citizen of Charleston. The couple had two children, Alexander and Susanna; her husband died in 1737 and seems to have left most of his estates to his relatives, rather than to his wife and children. Throughout her youth and marriage SH liked the finer things of life, including clothes, jewelry, books, music, balls, and plays. After two illnesses, one several years after her husband's death, she became concerned that her love of elegance was a threat to her soul. She turned toward the religion of her mother and grandmother and went to England, where she joined the Society of Friends. Six years later she returned to Charleston and urged its citizens to more righteous conduct. In 1748, her work, *An Exhortation to the Inhabitants of the Province of South Carolina,* was published. SH visited her fellow Quakers in Philadelphia and then returned to England, where she became a Quaker minister and published

other religious writings. In 1767 SH again appeared in Charleston, this time to attempt to revive a faltering Quakerism. Failing, she returned to London, where she died.

In the *Exhortation,* a poorly constructed work, SH pressed the people of Charleston to give up their elegance and live simple lives, wear modest clothes, and pursue worthwhile amusements; women were warned not to neglect the care of their children. The work quotes liberally from Scripture and remarks on the author's past life and conversion. While in England, SH wrote *A Caution to Such As Observe Days and Times to Which Is Added an Address to Magistrates, Parents, etc.* (1760), in the appendix of which she advises magistrates, parents, and others in authority to look to Christ, show good conduct, and regulate those in their charge; parents especially should be concerned with the souls of their offspring. Also in 1760 appeared *Extracts from Divers Ancient Testimonies of Friends and Others, Corresponding With the Doctrines of Christianity.* Excerpts from the work of William Penn and George Fox are presented, as well as passages from Rutty's *History of Ireland,* the "Epistle of A. Rigge," and Gerard Croese's "Account of Friends." In 1765 *A Short Appeal to Men and Women of Reason, Distinguished by Title . . . Or By Riches* was published. SH found problematic women's traditional role, which she presented in her works, and her own activities as a Quaker minister. During her life she was hard-pressed to resolve the conflict; she was also afraid that her being a woman might hinder the reception of her message.   A.N.

HUNTER, Anne (1742–1821), poet, was the eldest daughter of the surgeon Robert Home of Greenlaw, Berwickshire. Her parents' love match offended his relations, so AH's family relied on his profession for their livelihood, becoming more comfortable as time passed. After a long engagement, in 1771 AH married John Hunter, a distinguished anatomist and surgeon. In the next five years, she gave birth to four children, only two of whom survived childhood. Her married life is always characterized as happy, despite the partners' widely divergent interests. John Hunter avidly collected specimens of various sorts, making theirs a most unusual house to manage. In addition, it was home for large numbers of servants, relatives, and students. While Hunter was involved in pursuing his medical and scientific curiosity, AH's interests were literary. Her conversation parties were considered among the most enjoyable of the time, lacking affectation, formality, and pedantry. Her friendships were among women with similar literary interests: ELIZABETH CARTER and MARY DELANY were friends of long standing, as were ELIZABETH MONTAGU and FANNY BURNEY. AH did not affect deep learning and preferred to be known as a good housewife and amiable member of society. In this she was successful; contemporaries referred to her sagacity, good taste, amiability, and sense of humor. She was described as delicately fair, tall, and dignified, with a cultivated mind and special gifts for poetry and music. Circumstances altered greatly with her husband's death in 1793. The terms of Dr. Hunter's will and his accumulated debts required the sale of their house and left her without home or livelihood. She found herself reliant upon the Queen's bounty, through which she had a pension for two years. For seven of the difficult years she was companion to the two wealthy wards of her husband's friend, Dr. Maxwell Garthshore. The sale of her husband's effects in 1799 helped to repair her situation. The last year of her life were lived quietly near her nephew, Dr. Matthew Baillie, maintaining contacts with close friends until her death after a lingering illness.

AH began composing lyric poetry in her youth. "Adieu Ye Streams that Swiftly Glide" as a setting to the old air "The Flowers of the Forest" was published in *The Lark* (Edinburgh) in 1765. The first public effort was acclaimed, and she continued to write throughout her marriage. But she shared her efforts with friends rather than printing them. Haydn, a close friend, set some of her work to music, among others the ballad "Mother Bids Me Bind My Hair," originally written to an air by Pleydell, and "The Mermaid's Song," freely translated from the Italian. Nares claimed she became Haydn's muse and "all of his beautiful English canzonets were composed on words which she supplied." She wrote a libretto for his "Creation," which was discarded in favor of one originally written for Handel by Lidley and adopted by Haydn. In 1802, on the suggestion of friends, AH published some of her odes, ballads, and songs. Her preface shows that most of the pieces were already well known, and she admitted that she was induced to publish because of the popularity of lyric verse and her own earlier success. In addition to better known ballads,

Poems contains birthday verses, poems addressed to her children, and others of family interest relating to the death, education, or marriage of her children. These poems seem to belie the assertion by Roodhouse Gloyne, her husband's biographer, that the children played little part in her life. And although she later became estranged from her son, her daughter was one of her chief supports. Although not usually deep, AH's poetry does have a simplicity of expression, a fluency, and a sense of unaffected natural feeling. A later volume, *The Sports of the Genii* (1804), additionally provides evidence of her sense of humor and fancy. Written in 1797, *Genii* was issued in memory of Susan MacDonald, the young daughter of the Lord Chief Baron, whose etchings illustrate the book. AH's last identifiable lyric was "A New Ballad Entitled the Times" (ca. 1804), which contrasted the marital values of village folk and Londoners. AH's work generally drew praise from journals such as the *British Critic* and the *Gentleman's Magazine*. *Blackwell's Magazine* wrote, "All of her verses are written with elegance and feeling, and her Death-Song is a noble strain, almost worthy of Campbell himself." Others were harsher. *The Edinburgh Review* (Jan. 1803) wrote "Poetry really does not seem to be her vocation, and rather appears to have been studied as an accomplishment than pursued from any natural propensity."   D.L.L.

HUNTER, Maria (fl. 1774–99), actress and novelist, in the 1770s appeared often on stage in, for example, Dublin, Liverpool, and Norwich, but principally in London, where she had permanent engagements at Covent Garden Theatre and at the Theatre Royal in the Haymarket. She frequently played Mrs. Oakly in *The Jealous Wife,* Widow Brady in *The Irish Widow,* and the Queen in *Hamlet* and *Richard III.* MH's husband may have been a fellow actor. MH was mistress to General John Hayes St. Leger from 1777, and went with him to the West Indies 1781–82. Her engagements in the 1780s became sporadic; only a few performances are noted in the 1790s, the period from which MH's novels date. In the preface to one novel MH records that "in a life of disappointment and vicissitude, she has found her only stable comfort, and steady amusement, in an habit of study."

Two novels appeared under the name MH: *Fitzroy; or, Impulse of the Moment* (1792) and *Ella; or, He's Always in the Way* (1798), both published by Lane's Minerva Press. Both are sketches of manners and morals set in contemporary England. MH's purpose is "to give a true and useful picture of human life.—To divest her characters, not of the veil which every man in society wears, more or less, over his manner—but to tear away the covering from his intentions. To shew men as they appear,—and tell you what they are." Her protagonists are young people forced to be on their own in a heartless society shaped by love of property and wealth. *Fitzroy* contains abundant moral reflection on gambling, impulsive behavior, and English chauvinism. *Ella,* highlighting the perils of an unprotected virtuous girl, presents satirical vignettes about lawyers and aristocrats, along with admonitions about the importance of female self-sufficiency. Despite conventionalities of plot and characterization, MH's novels show a good ear for language, and some episodes have the liveliness of reportage, e.g., an account of a conniving theater manager. *Fitzroy* was well received: "This publication has all the appearance of being produced by a thinking mind" (*Gentleman's Magazine,* 1792), and "Mrs. Hunter seems to possess talents and acquisitions much beyond modern authoresses, or the ladies of the drama, with whom she ranks. Her language is easy and elegant. . . . the characters scarcely start from the canvas with sufficient spirit. But, on the whole, her work is very pleasing and entertaining, and the little disquisitions, with which the narrative is interspersed, shew much ingenuity and no inconsiderable share of learning. We trust this will not be the last time that we shall meet the lady on this ground" (*Critical Review,* 1792). For *Ella,* the *CR* (1798) had no praise: "The plan of this novel has little regularity. It seems to have been intended only as a vehicle for the introduction of characters from what the authoress calls *nature.* Some of these, as well as the incidents, are delineated with the pen of a caricaturist; and, with the exception of a few just though trite reflections on education and seduction, the moral tendency of the work is not very obvious." A.B.S.

HUNTINGDON, Selina Hastings, Countess of (1707–91), Methodist leader and letter writer, was the daughter of Earl Ferrers. In 1728 she married the Earl of Huntingdon, half-brother of Lady Elizabeth Hastings, who patronized MARY ASTELL; the couple lived at Donington Hall in Leicestershire. C of H had four sons and three daughters, but survived all except one of her children, as well as her husband, who died in 1746. She was converted to Methodism and was a member of the first Methodist society formed in Fetter Lane in 1739. In 1748 she appointed George Whitefield her chaplain, opening her London house for him to preach. He described the pious routine of her life in the 1740s: "We have the Sacrament every morning, heavenly consolation all day, and preaching at night. This is to live at Court indeed." In 1749, C of H tried to reconcile Whitefield and the Wesleys, with all of whom she was intimate; when she failed, she sided with Whitefield and his more-Calvinist doctrines. C of H used her position as a peeress to further the Methodist cause. She appointed Methodist chaplains, especially for the Connexion, which she founded; this consisted of missionary associations connected by spiritual affinity and common aims. In 1768 she opened Trevecca House in Wales to train her ministers. She saw her Connexion as mediating between Dissent and the Church of England, but in 1779 she was opposed, and her chapels (about 67 in number) were forced to become registered as Dissenting places of worship. She left the Church of England in 1781.

C of H was an indefatigable proselytizer and much admired by her followers; the hymn writer Augustus Toplady called her "the most precious saint of God" he ever knew. Her writing consists mainly of letters to her many chapel congregations and to Methodist leaders, inspiring them and describing her own spiritual progress: "Of late I have felt the most ardent desires for the exaltation of the Lord Jesus in every heart, and the most holy ardour of desire to promote his cause upon the earth. I seem to have done nothing, and would lie low in the dust before him, and lament my unfaithfulness, my unprofitableness, and unfruitfulness. May he increase my faith, animate my heart with a zeal for his glory, enlarge my sphere, and make me more faithful in the sphere in which I move." C of H also brought out a collection of hymns, *A Select Collection of Hymns to be Universally Sung in all the Countess of Huntingdon's Chapels, Collected by her Ladyship* (1780). The preface makes a large claim: "life, death, and immortality, they are all here." J.T.

HUTCHINSON, Lucy (1620–?), biographer, was born in the Tower of London, the daughter of Sir Allen Apsley, Lieutenant of the Tower, and Lucy St. John. She had a good education: she was taught French and English together and she recollected that, when she was about seven, she had eight tutors in language, music, dancing, writing, and needlework, but that her great interest was in books. She learned Greek and Hebrew and read widely in the classics, as well as in theology, thinking "it no sin to learne or heare wittie songs and amorous sonnetts or poems." In 1638 she married John Hutchinson; they lived for some months in London and then moved to Enfield, where she bore twin sons in 1639. The following year the family moved to Owthorpe Notts., Hutchinson's family home. LH translated the six books of Lucretius into English verse "out of youthful curiosity to understand things which she heard so much discourse of at secondhand": "I turned it into English in a room where my children practised the several qualities they were taught with their tutors, and I numbered the syllables of my translation by the threads of the canvas I wrought in, and set them down with a pen and ink that stood by me." In 1675 the translation was dedicated to the Earl of Anglesey. In politics, Hutchinson sided with Parliament against King Charles and became involved first in state affairs and then in war. He became governor of the castle in Nottingham and in 1646 a member of the Long Parliament. He was reluctantly made one of the King's judges but, after the execution, he played little part in public because of poor health and because of his opposition to Cromwell's aggrandisement; he held no office under the Protectorate. In 1659 he was summoned to Parliament and was there when Charles II was welcomed. After the Restoration a servile letter was written on his behalf, which LH claims that she composed, much to his displeasure. Although, with the help of royalist relatives, he did not initially share the fate of other regicides, he was uneasy in his freedom, and he refused to flee or apply for further protection. In 1663, on a trumped up charge, he was arrested and imprisoned in the Tower, but removed soon to a prison in Kent, where LH and two of their children followed him. He died shortly afterward, leaving to LH his last message: "Let her, as she is above other women, show herself in this occasion a good Christian, and above the pitch of ordinary women." Between 1664 and 1671 LH wrote *The Memoirs of the Life of Colonel Hutchinson* (published 1806) "to moderate my woe, and if it were possible to augment my love." It was prefaced by a fragment of autobiography, "The Life of Mrs. Lucy Hutchinson written by herself," and by a eulogy of Hutchinson, "Mrs. Hutchinson to her children, concerning their father 'To my children.'" After her husband's death, LH struggled against poverty, but managed to keep her interest in learning. It is not known when she died. Among her other works are two books on religious subjects for her daughter; one, *On the Principles of the Christian Religion,* was published in 1817.

LH's biography is eulogistic of her husband, inaccurate on many national political matters, but reliable on the events and personalities of Nottinghamshire. It provides a moving description of LH's marriage and courtship. It seems that, before he met her, Hutchinson was attracted to LH's learning and reserve and had noted in a song of hers an intelligence "beyond the customary reach of a she-witt." When friends tricked him into believing her married, he turned "pale as ashes, and felt a fainting to seize his spiritts." On finally meeting, he found his heart "prepossesst with his owne fancy," while she, usually indifferent to men, was "surpriz'd with some unusuall liking in her soule, when she saw this gentleman." On the day of their intended marriage she had small pox, which disfigured her temporarily, but he married her as soon as possible despite her appearance. The relationship that followed is presented lovingly: "if he esteem'd her att a higher rate then she in herselfe could have deserv'd, he was the author of that vertue he doted on, while she only reflected his own glories upon him: all that she was, was *him,* while he was here, and all that she is now at best but her pale shade." So constant was he in his love, she claims, "that when she ceast to be young and lovely, he began to shew most fondnesse." LH's own devotedness and bravery emerge from her narrative, especially after her husband's imprisonment when she and her children moved to Deal, "from whence they walk'd every day on foote to dinner and back againe at night, with horrible toyle and inconvenience"; to keep him amused in his solitude she brought him cockle shells to arrange and sort. Although always complimentary of Hutchinson, LH does allow a picture of him to come through her appreciation; an upright, punctilious, proud man, given to anger, but "never outrageous in passion."   J.T.

I-J

INCHBALD, Elizabeth (1753–1821), playwright, novelist, and critic, was born a farmer's daughter at Stanningfield, near Bury St. Edmunds, Suffolk. Her parents were Catholic, and EI was the youngest but one of seven daughters and two sons. She received no formal education, but after the death of her father (1761) picked up what learning she could from books at home. The theater was loved by the whole family, who visited the little Bury theater and occasionally the Norwich playhouse. EI had a pronounced stammer but taught herself elocution by reciting passages of declamation then in vogue on the stage, writing down the words that caused her difficulty, and mastering them one by one. Later she was able to cope on stage, but never overcame her impediment in ordinary speech. After her brother George joined a theater company, she applied unsuccessfully to Richard Griffith, manager of the Norfolk theater, for engagement as an actress. When 19 she visited her married sisters in London, where she met various people connected with the stage, including her future husband, Joseph Inchbald, an actor and portrait painter 17 years her senior, with two illegitimate sons. In April 1772 she ran away from home to seek her fortune. She had a great deal of beauty but little money, and took lodgings in London while she applied to actors in turn. After two refusals, James Dodd offered to assist her, but when she called on him to ratify their agreement, he attempted to molest her. Thoroughly frightened by this, and by the obvious dangers of London, she sought protection and agreed to marry Inchbald, whose proposals she had earlier rejected. He too was Catholic, and they were married in June 1772 at her sister's house. On the following day

they were married in church according to Protestant rites, as was required by law. EI made her debut in Bristol as Cordelia to her husband's Lear. She repeated the role at Glasgow and, during the next four years, played many roles in Scottish towns, often lodging meanly and traveling on foot. Inchbald early gave her cause for jealousy; she too attracted admirers, and they had petty quarrels. In addition to working hard at her career, EI tried to acquire more education, studiously making notes on all she read, and taking French lessons. In July 1776, after Inchbald had quarreled with the Edinburgh audience, the couple moved to Paris, where he tried to earn a living as a painter, and she to write comedies. They returned to Brighton in September, so poor that they often picked turnips directly from the fields instead of dining. They could obtain no work in London and in October proceeded to Liverpool, where they became friends with Mrs. Siddons and her brother John Philip Kemble. EI fell in love with Kemble, although their friendship never proceeded to an affair. After a visit to Canterbury, the Inchbalds were reunited with these friends at York in January 1778 and were engaged by Tate Wilkinson to play in several Yorkshire towns. In June 1779 Inchbald died suddenly of a heart attack. In the years to follow, EI turned down all offers of marriage, hoping that Kemble would propose, but he never did. She made her London debut at Covent Garden in October 1780 as Bellario in *Philaster*, but met with no great success. Never more than a competent performer, she retired from the stage in 1789 and devoted herself to her writing. EI had early written farces and after 1784, when a play of hers was performed, she gradually made her name as an author. A shrewd businesswoman, she invested her earnings, which eventually brought her an annual income of more than £260. She had a great fear of poverty and was extremely parsimonious. Yet she was equally generous, and as her family grew more dependent on her, she often stinted herself to provide for them. She was popular in literary and fashionable society and acquainted with ANNA LAETITIA BARBAULD and MARIA EDGEWORTH, who admired her novels. She was particularly friendly with Holcroft and Godwin, although never so radical in her principles. Both men proposed to her and were refused. Later, EI petulantly objected to Godwin's marriage to MARY WOLLSTONECRAFT, which occasioned a temporary coldness between them. EI led an independent, if at times lonely, existence in lodgings in London, except for a brief experiment in 1803 when she entered Annandale House, Turnham Green, a kind of convent without vows for single Catholic ladies. She retained her beauty until late in life and, despite her many admirers, her name was never associated with any scandal. She died a devout Catholic, although during the most hectic years of her career she had lapsed in her religious duties. Her last refuge was Kensington House, a genteel establishment for Catholic ladies, where she died. On the advice of her confessor, she burnt her much sought-after memoirs, on which she had worked for many years.

EI began writing farces in her early years as an actress, but when she sent the MSs to Harris and Colman, neither manager took any notice of them. In 1784, Colman paid her 100 guineas for *The Mogul Tale, or the Descent of the Balloon*, which he revised and produced at the Haymarket in July, keeping the authorship secret, lest it fail and damage her reputation as author and actress. EI herself played a small part in the comedy and almost broke down. Inspired by the craze for ballooning, it was a great success and ran for ten days. Thereafter EI obtained high prices for her sentimental comedies and farces, only three of which were never printed: "All on a Summer Day" (1787) bombed the first night, "Hue and Cry," a farce (1791), and "Young Men and Old Women" (1792). Two of her plays were never staged and were printed from MSs in 1833. These were *A Case of Conscience* and *The Massacre*, her only tragedies, written in prose. In the former, the action is well-conceived, and EI focuses

the attention through five acts on a single intrigue. In the latter, EI gestures towards realism and attempts to deal with the horrors of the French Revolution. She wrote at the height of the period when the English theater was coming under the influence of European drama, and seven of her plays are adaptations of French and German authors—the latter at third hand, since she knew no German. EI was ambitious, adaptations were popular, and she could produce them as rapidly as her original works. She succeeded rather better than rival authors working on the same plays because her adaptations were dramatic rather than literal translations. Her experience as an actress had given her a good understanding of what would please an English audience, and she modified her originals to suit the English stage. She even anglicized names of characters, as in her two plays from Kotzebue: *Lovers' Vows* (1798) and *The Wise Man of the East* (1799). It is odd that she even transferred the setting of one play, *The Widow's Vow* (1786), an adaptation of Patrat's *L'Heureuse Erreur*, from France to Spain; she may have desired greater license, since the plot contains improbabilities. Also Spanish comedy was in vogue, and its practice of naming characters by their christian names would enable an English audience to identify them more easily. In her adaptations, EI tended to simplify the intrigue, suppressing minor characters and incidents not necessary to the main action. She frequently condensed five acts to three, as in *The Married Man* (1789), from Destouches' *Le Philosophe Marié*. Yet her sense of structure was such that in *The Widow's Vow* she divided Patrat's one-act play of 32 rapid scenes into a two-act play of five scenes. EI worked hard for verisimilitude and psychological realism but, while she avoided servile translation, she was able to change or invent episodes and remake characters without damaging the essence of the original. Her other adaptations are *The Midnight Hour* (1787), from Damaniant; *The Child of Nature* (1788), from Mme. de Genlis; and *Next-Door Neighbours* (1791), from *L'Indignant* of Mercier and *Le Dissipateur* of Destouches. Of EI's original plays, some are light-weight, although ingenious, farces; e.g., *Animal Magnetism* (1789?) and *Appearance is Against Them* (1785). Her most accomplished comedies are *I'll Tell You What* (1786), which her friend Francis Truss called a "pretty, light, summer piece, likely to pay her very well for the time and anxiety" she had undergone but nothing more than that; *Such Things Are* (1788), about John Howard, the prison reformer, and the only one of her plays with a definite social thesis, although most contain reflections on social injustice; and *Everyone has his Fault* (1793). In drama, "the Rules" were no longer strictly imposed, but EI tried to keep to unity of time. In *To Marry or Not to Marry* (1805), this leads to absurdity, since the events could not possibly take place in the time allotted. Her principal themes are love and marriage, and their effect on women in society. Although she achieved independence herself, she thought the wisest course for most women was to seek the security of marriage. In *Wives as they were, and Maids as they are* (1797), her speaker refuses to desert her husband for her lover: "And what shall I have gained by the exchange, when *you* become churlish, when *you* become ungrateful? My children's shame! the world's contempt! and yours!" Nevertheless, EI did show the usefulness of divorce in her plays, which for a woman at this time was especially daring. EI was one of the better dramatists of her age; her characters are varied and her intrigues well managed, although her dialogue is not as spritely as that of her predecessor, SUSANNA CENTLIVRE. Individually, none of her plays compares with the masterpieces of Goldsmith or Sheridan, but the latter thought highly of her work. He commissioned and actually paid in advance for *The Wedding Day* (1794).

Today EI is regarded as a novelist. Her first novel, *A Simple Story*, was begun under the encouragement of Kemble and its first draft completed in 1779. It was revised and not published until 1791, when a second edition was ordered within three months. The book spans two generations and has been criticized for the 16-year break in the middle. The heroine of the first part, Miss Milner, displays many traits of EI's own character, while the hero, Dorriforth, resembles Kemble, so it is likely that their relationship was the initial inspiration for the book. The second part, dealing with Dorriforth's treatment of his banished daughter, is less vivid, but reinforces the moral that education determines character. The didactic element may have been intensified when the plot was altered in deference to Godwin's advice. The book was praised as original by *Gentleman's Magazine* (61.1, 1791) and as dramatic *Monthly Review* (IV, 1791) but EI's experience of the theater, while ensuring that individual scenes would have impact, offered no guidelines as to how these should be linked, and she connects them with stilted narrative. All the same, MARIA EDGEWORTH declared: "I never read any novel that affected me so strongly, or that so completely possessed me with the belief in the real existence of all the people it represents." EI's second novel, *Nature and Art* (1796), may have taken its origins from the moral of *A Simple Story*, and shows that education is responsible for the contrasting characters of two cousins, William and Henry. EI is indebted to Rousseau (she had undertaken a translation of his *Confessions* in 1790), and much of her thought can be found in Godwin's *Social Justice*. But Godwin was reputedly dissatisfied with the book, which points out social injustice but concludes by appealing to the poor to be content with their lot. In the novel, EI becomes more involved with the plight of Agnes Primrose, seduced and abandoned to prostitution. She may have been attracted to this theme because she had been unable to save her own sister, Deborah, from dying a wretched prostitute. Sympathy for humanity pervades *Nature and Art* rather than the radical philosophy of Holcroft and Godwin. *MR* (19, 1796) wrote of it, "The sentiments are just; and the satire is keen and pointed without descending to personality." EI has also been credited with *Emily Herbert; or Perfidy Punished* (1787), an epistolary novel, but her name does not appear on the title page. Once EI acquired literary fame, publishers and magazine editors were eager to give her work. She contributed to *The Artist*, wrote several articles for *The Edinburgh Review*, and Longman employed her to write critical prefaces to his edition of *The British Theatre*, 25 vols (1806–9). These prefaces are interesting for the insight they give into the criticism of the time. EI displays the prejudices of her age regarding Shakespeare (which is not surprising since she saw only the stage versions of Dryden, Garrick, Tate, and Cibber) in her concern for the moral, in her elegance of manners, and in her admiration for characters "new to the stage." But when she was able to draw on her own acting experience, in her remarks on the comedies, her perception is acute. She championed the female cause, noting in the preface to Rowe's *The Fair Penitent* that "whatever reasons may be urged against the more elevated instruction of the sex at present . . . , one good consequence at least accrues from it—they are better qualified than heretofore to choose their lovers and husbands." She took care to be objective but, even so, her remarks on the plays of the elder Colman involved her in a dispute with his son, who sneered at her scanty education. In an open letter on his play *The Heir-at-Law*, celebrated for its comic pedant, EI replied: "I willingly subscribe myself an unlettered woman, and as willingly yield to you all those scholastic honours which you have so excellently described in the following play." *A Collection of Farces*, 7 vols (1809), and *The Modern Theatre*, 10 vols (1811), were simply selected by her. EI was diffident, being conscious of her position as the first female drama critic. But Byron for one valued her opinion, declaring her praise of *The Giaour* pleased him "more than anything, except the *Edinburgh Review*." M.S.

IRWIN, Anne Ingram, Viscountess (before 1696–1764), poet and letter writer, is primarily known for a defense of women against Pope's satiric attack. She wrote some published verse, more still in manuscript, and interesting and extensive letters to her father. The second daughter of Charles, third Earl of Carlisle, and Lady Anne Capel, daughter of the Earl of Essex, AI spent most of her life at Castle Howard, the estate in Yorkshire designed for her father by Vanbrugh, and at court in London. In 1717 she married Richard, fifth Viscount Irwin (or Irvine), but their married life was short and blighted by financial reverses in the South Sea Bubble. Her husband was appointed Governor of the Barbados in 1720, but died in April 1721 before leaving to take up the post. The widowed AI was involved in London social and intellectual life, and numbered among her acquaintance Pope, LADY MARY WORTLEY MONTAGU and Horace Walpole. Her letters on her travels on the Continent with her sister Lady Elizabeth, who was married first to Nicholas Lechmere and then to Sir Thomas Robinson, remain mostly unprinted. AI was appointed Lady of the Bedchamber to the new Princess of Wales in April 1736 and escorted her to England. She married Colonel William Douglas against the wishes of her family in 1737; he died in 1748. AI died, childless, in 1764.

AI's printed poems are limited. They include a banal tribute to George III on his accession (*Gentleman's Magazine*, February 1761) and a poem on constancy, a reply to extempore verses by Montagu urging AI to encourage the "pretty fellows" (*Additions to the Works of Alexander Pope, Esq.* London, 1776). A longer poem, *Castle Howard*, was published anonymously in 1732. It is both a description of the gardens and landscape at her father's seat and an encomium on his virtue as shown in his retreat from the world and his devotion to his estate. Her best known poem, "On Mr. Pope's Characters of Women," can be found in *The New Foundling Hospital for Wit*, pt. 6 (1773), but it probably circulated earlier, since it earned AI a place in Duncombe's *Feminead* (2nd ed., 1757). The satire claims that women are trained to be foolish by the customs of society and their education: "If wealthy born, taught to lisp French, and dance, / Their morals left, Lucretius-like, to chance: / Strangers to reason and reflection made, / Left to their passions, and by them betray'd: / Untaught the noble end of glorious truth, / Bred to deceive, ev'n from their earliest youth!" The poem ends with an appeal to Pope, "who know[s] th' arcana of the soul [and] who can instruct as well as please," to rescue women from this "Gothic state" of ignorance. AI's letters to her father reveal a lively mind and give us useful information on the intellectual life of an aristocratic woman. She was a keen if not uncritical reader of Pope, and regarded him and Addison as "antidotes" against the ignorance and affectation at court. She was interested in theater, music, history, politics, and astronomy, and attended Desagulier's lectures on the last subject in 1737. Her approach to literature was classical and conservative. Montagu, not overly tolerant of her own sex, summed her up as being vain and full of false pretensions, and yet "on the whole I think her better than many other women" (*Letters* III, p. 162). P.J.G.

JACKSON, Sarah (fl. 1754), author on housekeeping, wrote *The Director, or The Young Woman's Best Companion* (London, 1754). It was republished in 1755 and may first have been printed in America, since the title page states: "The following receipts were inserted in the Carolina Gazette / May 9, 1750 / James Irving." There is also, in a medical section at the back of the book, reference to a "Negro *Caesar*'s Cure for Poison, and likewise his Cure for the Bite of a Rattle Snake," also signed "James Irving." *The Director* is a simple work "Containing above Three Hundred easy receipts in; cookery, pastry, preserving, candying, pickling, collaring, physick and surgery; to which are added plain and easy instructions for chusing Beef, Mutton, Veal, Fish, Fowl and other Eatables. Directions for Carving, and to make Vines; Likewise Bills of Fare for every Month in the Year." A typical recipe is "Chickens Surprise": "Take half a Pound of Rice, set it over a Fire in soft Water, when it is half boiled put in two or three small Chickens trussed, with two or three Blades of Mace, and a little Salt; take a Piece of Bacon about three Inches square, and boil it in Water till it is almost enough, take it out, pare off the Outsides, and put into the Chickens and Rice to boil a little together; (you must not let the Broth be over thick with Rice) then take up your Chickens, lay them on a Dish, pour over them the Rice, cut your Bacon in thin Slices to lay round your Chickens, and upon the Breast of each a Slice. This is proper for a Side-dish." The medical section employs chiefly spices and herbs. Plague water begins with sage, rue, celadine, rosemary, wormwood, the herb Waselis, mugwort, pimperhill, dragon's scabious, egremony, balm, scardium, carduus benedictus, betony flowers and leaves, and continues with nine more ingredients, the whole to be steeped in wine and distilled. "A most excellent Receipt for Deafness" is to "Take the Whites of three Eggs, beat them, and fry them in a clean Pan, with the Quantity of a Nutmeg of the purest *May* Butter over a slow Fire till they begin to be hard; then strain them. Drop three Drops of this excellent Oil into the Ear every Night and Morning, and stop it with black Wool." M.S.

JAMES, Elinor (fl. 1675–1715), writer of broadsides and pamphlets, was the wife of a prosperous London printer, Thomas James. She was also his working partner, which was not uncommon in the Stationer's guild. She published 15 to 20 of her own broadsides and five to eight brief pamphlets about current events, all signed boldly with her full name. In these ephemera, EJ took conservative positions and sided with the established Church, whether it was to defend the oaths of supremacy required of all Catholics and Dissenters, to give thanks to Queen Anne and to Parliament for the deliverance of the "high flyer" Dr. Sacheverell, or to advise against union with Presbyterian Scotland. Dryden refers to her in an amused tone in the preface of *The Hind and the Panther* as if her eccentric pro-Church po-

lemics were an institution. John Dunton (*Life and Errors,* 1705) refers to her husband as one of the best printers in London, but adds that he is "something the better known for being Husband to that She-State-Politician *Mrs. Elianor* [sic] *James."* In 1689 she was briefly committed to Newgate for dispersing polemical papers supporting James II and resisting the settlement of the Glorious Revolution. The British Library has a letter which she subsequently wrote to William III in 1691, a mixture of flattery and admonishment, which is probably an attempt to rectify this earlier stance. EJ's daughter Jane James married Thomas Ilive, and their son Jacob Ilive was also a printer and controversialist whose published discourses in 1755 denying the divinity of Christ and "all revealed religion" landed him in the house of correction at Clerkenwell for three years. The one other daughter, Elizabeth, married a Mr. Saunders.

EJ's broadsides and pamphlets are: "To the Right Honourable, the Lord mayor and Court of aldermen, and all the rest of the loyal citizens . . ." (about fasting) (London? 1683); "May it please Your Most Sacred Majesty, seriously to consider my great zeal and love that I have always had for his late Majesty and Kingdoms, and my fervent constancy to the Church of England" (about fasting) (London, 1685); "Most dear sovereign, I cannot but love and admire you, because I see those graces in you, that bespeaks you to be a gracious prince . . ." (comments on Charles II's copies of two papers written by the late King) (London, 1686); "My Lord, I thought it my bound duty to return your Lordship thanks for the great care you have taken in preserving the peace and prosperity of this city, and for your loyalty to my late soveraign lord the King and his brother . . ." (London, 1687); "Mrs. James's Defence of the Church of England in a short answer to the canting Address; with a word or two concerning a Quakers good advice to the Church of England . . ." (London, 1687); "Mrs. James's Vindication of the Church of England, in an answer to a Pamphlet, entituled: A New Test of the Church of England's Loyalty" (London, 1687); "An Address of Thanks, on behalf of the Church of England, to Mrs. James, for her worthy vindication of that Church" (London, 1687); "Mrs. James's Advice to the Citizens of London" (that they should continue loyal to James II) (London? 1688); "To the Right Honourable Convention" (exhorting the members of the

Convention Parliament to be loyal to King James II) (London, 1688); "An injur'd prince vindicated, or, A scurrilous and detracting pamphlet answer'd. By Mrs. E.J. in Hartfordshire" (1688); "My Lords, I can assure your Lordships" (letter to Lords advising them to "use all pious endeavours to do the King good . . . to reclaim him by . . . gentle means and not to suffer Priests and Jesuits to come about him") (London, 1688); "My Lords, You can't but be sensible of the great zeal I have had for King and Kingdom . . ." (against taking the crown from James II to bestow it on William Prince of Orange) (London, 1688); "This being Your Majesty's Birth-Day, I thought no time more proper than this to return you thanks . . . for declaring, that the Church of England is one of the greatest supports of the Protestant Religion . . ." (London, 1689?); "Sir, My Lord Mayor and the Aldermen . . ." (complaint about the practice of throwing firecrackers about the streets of London) (London, 1690?); "Mrs. Jame's [sic] Apology because of Unbelievers" (London, 1694?); "To the Right Honourable the House of lords" (defense of the East India Company) (London, 1701); "Octob. the 20th, 1702. May it please Your Lordships, Seriously to Consider what Great Things God has done for You and for the Kingdom . . ." (London, 1702); "Mrs. James's Consideration to the Lords and Commons; wherein she plainly shews, that the True Church has been, and always will be in danger . . ." (London, 1705); "Mrs. James Prayer for the Queen and Parliament, and Kingdom too . . ." (occasioned by the impeachment of Dr. Sacheverell) (London, 1710); "Mrs. James's letter of thanks to the Q- - -n and both houses of Parliament for the deliverance of Dr. Sacheverell" (24 March 1710); "Mrs. James's reasons humbly presented to the Lords spiritual and temporal. Shewing why she is not willing that at this time there should be any impeachment" (London, 5 November 1715); "Mrs. James's thanks to the Lords and Commons for their sincerity to King George" (London, 1715). The best known of these is a pamphlet defending King James' 1687 Declaration of Toleration called "A Vindication of the Church of England, in an answer to a Pamphlet entituled, A New Test of the Church of England's Loyalty" (1687): "I know their [King and court] Loyalty and have been a Labourer with them therefore I have the greater Reason to Plead for them: but I know you will say *I am a Woman,*

and why should I trouble my self? Why was I not always so, when I pleaded with the Parliament about the *Right of Succession,* and with *Shaftesbury,* and *Monmouth,* and at Guild-Hall, and elsewhere." EJ's printed broadsides and addresses were concerned with issues other than Anglican piety. One complained to the mayor and aldermen of London about the unrestrained use of fireworks in public streets; another was addressed to the House of Lords trying to discourage an intended tax on the Old East India Company. Probably the most interesting was an address to the printers' guild about the then current practice of taking in other men's apprentices as boarding servants, which put the master-apprentice relationship onto a wage basis too soon ("for giving him money makes him a journeyman before his time"), thus destroying the traditional paternal and pedagogic nature of the apprentice relationship and undercutting the journeymen's wage scale and professional status. EJ was not a careful or intellectual writer. But her belief in her right to be heard and her bombastic language give her writing a refreshing energy. She was aware of her anomolous position as a woman in public life; so, although she was considered a crank by her contemporaries, her self-conscious perception of herself as an active, participating citizen must have had the psychological effect of opening up to other women the possibilities of addressing the reading public.   R.P.

JEBB, Ann (1735–1812), political writer, was born in Ripton-Kings, Hunts., to James Torkington, rector of Ripton-Kings, and Lady Dorothy, daughter of the second Earl of Harborough. A petite and animated woman, AJ had little formal schooling but educated herself by reading extensively. In 1764 she married John Jebb (1736–86), a clergyman. The marriage was without issue. She was a devoted wife and found her metier as a writer in defending her husband's causes. Jebb embraced Unitarianism, which led to his leaving the clergy and becoming a physician. The Jebbs became political radicals as well and worked with the perennial reformer John Cartwright. After her husband's death AJ remained active in radical causes, kept up an extensive correspondence with the leading Dissenters of the day, and was involved in prison philanthropy.

AJ's writing is characterized by classic discipline rather than emotionalism, and her gift for irony appears in most of her works. In 1772–74 as "Priscilla" she published a series of letters in the *London Chronicle* supporting her husband's effort to end mandatory subscription to the Thirty-Nine Articles by Anglican clergymen and members of the universities. In 1774 she produced an anonymous pamphlet defending another of her husband's causes, the establishment of general examinations for university students: *A Letter to the Author of the Proposal for the Establishment of Public Examinations.* In 1793 as "W. Bull" she published a popular tract, *Two Penny-Worth of Truth for a Penny* (two editions), to answer the virulent anti-Jacobin and prowar propaganda of the day. "I suppose," Mr. Bull remarks, "you know they talk of a war; and, what is more surprising, of a war without fresh taxes; but you and I are too old to be so caught: we should as soon expect a war without men." Although virtually forgotten today, AJ was rather widely known in her time as an effective political writer. While her life was exemplary, Richard Polwhele considered her activities sufficiently forward to warrant mention in his anti-feminist *The Unsex'd Females.* George Wilson Meadley published an extensive obituary in the *Monthly Repository of Theology and General Literature* (1812), which was reissued with the addition of a bibliography of her works as *Memoirs of Mrs. Jebb* (1812).   G.T.P.

JEMISON, Mary (1743?–1833), American autobiographer, the fourth child of Thomas Jemison, was born on board ship to Philadelphia, from which her father went on to Adams County, northwest of Gettysburg, to farm. Here two more sons were born. In 1758 a raiding party of French and Indians captured the family (except for the two eldest boys who escaped) and some visitors, took a supply of food, and marched off westward. After a day's march, encumbered by too many prisoners, the Indians chose tiny golden-haired MJ and a neighbor boy and killed and scalped the other prisoners. Her mother's parting injunction was to remember her name and language. Having reached Fort Duquesne, MJ was sold to two Seneca women and taken to the Mingo Bottoms, an Indian village below Steubenville, Ohio, where she was adopted by her purchasers to replace a brother lost in battle. As a member of the Seneca tribe MJ was well treated, learned the tongue, and gradually lost the desire to leave her new family. In 1760 her sisters married her to a Delaware named Sheninjee, whom she

came to love. In 1762 she bore Thomas Jemison and then, with him on her back, trekked to Cuylerville, New York, to visit her foster mother and sisters, where she learned she was a widow. Several times she hid out to avoid being returned to white civilization. In about 1765, in Genishau, near the Genessee River, she married a 57-year old Seneca, Hiokatoo, with whom she lived for almost 50 years, bearing him four girls and two sons, John and Jesse. In 1779 American forces led by General John Sullivan raided and razed her village. MJ moved her family to a cabin in Gardeau and survived the winter; she and her children were rejoined after the war by Hiokatoo. Again in 1780 MJ refused to return to her old people. In 1797 she was deeded almost 18,000 acres of the Gardow flats, where she had been homesteading; most of this land she leased out. In 1811 her son John killed his older half-brother Thomas in a fight, and in 1812 he killed Jesse; finally he too was killed in a brawl. In 1823 MJ sold most of her land for cash and a $300 annuity, keeping two square miles on which she lived with her three daughters and their families. In 1831 she moved to a Seneca reservation on Buffalo Creek. Here, from a missionary's wife she relearned, weeping, the Lord's Prayer which in her infancy her mother had told her always to remember. Although she required nothing further of Christianity and always remained stoutly loyal to her Indian family, she joined the Christian party on the reservation and was given Christian burial at her death. In 1874 her body was removed to a grave in Letchworth State Park on the site of her old land grant, near her daughter's log cabin. Nearby is a bronze statue of her as she may have looked arriving in New York State with an infant on her back.

In 1823 MJ's story was recorded by James Seaver and published in 1824 as *A Narrative of the Life of Mrs. Mary Jemison, Who Was taken by the Indians . . . Carefully taken from her own words, Nov. 29, 1823.* The narrative was reprinted in England in 1826 and 1827, and has had numerous editions since.   C.W.

JEMMAT, Catherine (?–1766), poet and autobiographer, was born in Exeter, the daughter of Admiral John Yeo, of Plymouth. According to CJ's *Memoirs,* published in 1762, 1765, and 1771, her mother died when she was quite young, and her father married a 19-year-old woman. CJ attended a boarding school with her sister and was taught

French. Her *Memoirs* allude to a great number of suitors and a subsequent loss of reputation. She married Jemmat, a Plymouth silk mercer, who used her money to pay his creditors, drank, and abused her physically. He died before the first edition of the *Memoirs* appeared. She mentions giving birth to one daughter, about whom nothing else is known. CJ's efforts to portray herself as an "injur'd and oppressed female" are so strenuous that she strikes one as spoiled, self-pitying, and melodramatic. There are several poems appended to the *Memoirs,* one of which is LADY MARY WORTLEY MONTAGU's "Written extempore in Company on a Glass Window." In 1766 CJ published a subscription *Miscellanies in Prose and Verse.* Among the subscribers are the Queen and an unusual number of names from the nobility. CJ states in the preface that the *Miscellanies* had to be swelled by contributions by other hands. Some of the borrowed prose pieces are acknowledged, but it is not indicated which of the poems are not her own work. The poetry is made up chiefly of epigrams, songs, light occasional pieces, paraphrased psalms, and epitaphs. Some of the more interesting pieces are "Question, on the Art of Writing," originally published anonymously in Dodsley's *Collection of Poems by Several Hands* (1758) and two epigrams against the bill to facilitate the naturalization of the Jews, which was defeated in 1753. Perhaps most interesting is the "Essay in Vindication of the Female Sex." In it CJ confesses to a juvenile taste for debauchery and laments the irretrievability of reputation once lost. She states that: "notwithstanding I am now sufficiently convinced of my indecent behaviour, and have for some years past carried myself in the most irreproachable manner, yet am I still considered as a vile wanton, and am afraid I shall be esteemed so as long as I live. This rash and uncharitable disposition, in continuing a perpetual odium on our sex if we once transgress, is too partial and unjust, when we consider that men have the liberty of continuing in the most lewd and debauched actions, without being branded, for the remaining part of their life, as a scandal and reproach to human nature." An obituary in the *London Magazine* (November 1766) records CJ's death.   T.C.S.W.L.

JOHNSON, Elizabeth (1721–98), diarist from Bristol, became a Methodist; *An Account of Mrs. Elizabeth Johnson* (1799) is a biography containing extracts from her diary—a record of her religious feelings after conversion to the Wesleyan faith. Her writings reveal both a deep self-hatred and an intense sexual longing: "In the night He came down—He filled me—He filled me— I had no distinct perception—but it was God diffusing himself through all my soul— I said, Lord art thou about to take me to thyself? And hesitated, whether or not I should awake my maid who slept in the same room; but determined I would enjoy my God alone."   L.F.

JOHNSON, Esther (1682–1728), poet and letter writer, best known as Swift's "Stella," was born in Richmond, Surrey, the eldest of three children of Bridget and Edward Johnson. She was christened "Hester," a form she used in her girlhood. According to a biographical account written by Swift at the time of her death, EJ's father came from a good Nottinghamshire family, but her mother was "of low degree." EJ grew up in the household of Sir William Temple at Moor Park, where her mother, who had remarried after her husband's death, was a servant of Lady Giffard, Temple's sister, and her stepfather was Temple's steward. EJ's place there was nonetheless a special one, perhaps because she was bright, amiable, and docile. Her teacher was Swift, who was Temple's secretary from 1689 to 1694 and again from 1696 to 1699, when Temple died. Swift instructed EJ in "the principles of honour and virtue, from which she never swerved in any action or moment in her life" and encouraged her taste for history and philosophy. The legacy EJ received upon Temple's death—lands in County Wicklow, Ireland, worth £1000— ensured her status as a gentlewoman, but also led to a rumor that she was Temple's natural daughter. In 1701 the 21-year-old EJ left England, together with her life-long companion, Mrs. Rebecca Dingley, to make her home in Ireland, where she could maintain a lifestyle out of reach in England and be close to Swift. She then had hair "Blacker than a raven," and was "beautiful, graceful and agreeable . . . only a little too fat." Gossip that EJ and Swift enjoyed an irregular union, that they either planned to marry or were indeed already married has no basis in any known fact, but has persisted. Their friendship, although always conducted with discretion, was undoubtedly very close. EJ was Swift's confidante, hostess, amanuensis, correspondent—most notably of the *Journal to Stella*—inspiration for the wry and tender birthday poems, and instigator of much of his other occasional verse. Swift was the center of her world, but EJ was also much sought out for herself. As a young woman she had several suitors, but apparently refused them all. She kept a kind of salon in Dublin much frequented by local literati, luminaries of the Church of Ireland and other "persons of the graver sort" and was greatly admired for her unassuming manner, politeness, and wit. Her later portraits show a handsome woman, no longer by any means fat, with fine, intelligent eyes. After a long period of declining health culminating in a year-long illness, EJ died, leaving Swift and her other friends disconsolate.

Few of EJ's writings remain. Nothing is known of the 39 letters addressed to Swift at the time of the *Journal to Stella*. Of the works attributed to her, two short poems, "Jealousy" and an untitled poem, were printed in Mathew Concanen's *Miscellaneous Poems* (1724) as "By a Lady" and "By the Same." A longer poem, "To Dr. Swift on his Birth-day, November 30, 1721," thanks Swift for his tutelage: "You taught me how I might youth prolong, / By knowing what was right and wrong; / How from my heart to bring supplies / Of lustre to my fading eyes; / How soon a beauteous mind repairs / The loss of changed or falling hairs; / How wit and virtue from within / Sends out a smoothness o'er the skin." This appeared for the first time in Deane Swift's *Essay upon the Life, Writings, and Character of Dr. Jonathan Swift* (1755). M.D.

JONES, Mary (?–1778), poet, was the daughter of Oliver Jones of Oxford. She did not marry but lived with her brother, Rev. River Jones, Chanter of Christ Church Cathedral, Oxford. She had a wide range of friends, including Samuel Johnson and the Rev. Thomas Warton. In 1755 the editor of *Poems by Eminent Ladies* stated: "Her uncommon merit early recommended her to the notice of the polite world; and she has the honour of the friendship and acquaintance of Her Royal Highness the Princess of Orange; as well as an intimacy with many of our *English* Nobility." That she was keenly sensitive to the difference between her own social standing and that of her wealthy friends is seen in a letter written at Windsor Castle in October 1743: "Except religious Works . . . there are, you say, generally but two reasons for printing; Vanity and Poverty. Mr. Pope's expression, I think, is 'Hunger, and Request' of Friends—My Vanity I shall say but little of: You, who can raise it, can at any time sufficiently humble it; but as to my Poverty, I could write a Volume upon that Subject. For alas! I've only all the Necessaries of Life, and a few of the Conveniences; while my Betters . . . are rolling in Riches. Now 'tis plain, Gold is the only Good, because everybody seeks after it; and the first Question people ask you, when you come into a room, is 'Are you rich?'—'If you are, sit down.' The Virtues follow immediately. See! they paint themselves upon your Garment, thick as the deadly Sins upon an Inquisition Petticoat. Everybody bows, and acknowledges 'em."

MJ published only one volume, *Miscellanies in Prose and Verse* (Oxford, 1750). This, she says, was an effort to raise funds for a relation "grown old and helpless," and it probably succeeded because the list of subscribers takes up 46 pages. Approximately one third of the collection is verse and the remainder short prose pieces and letters. One ballad, "The Lass on the Hill," had been issued as a broadside about 1740; and "A Letter to Dr. Pitt," a parody of a medical paper, had been published separately about 1745. Sixteen poems from the *Miscellanies* were later included in Volume One of *Poems by Eminent Ladies* (1755). Many of MJ's poems and letters are addressed to either Charlot Clayton or the Hon. Miss Lovelace, both of whom were apparently close friends of the author. The poems demonstrate MJ's gift for composing witty pieces on common domestic situations, as, for example, in "The Fall," "The Spider," and "The Heel-Piece of her Shoe." In addition to occasional poems of this type, the collection includes epistles, epitaphs, elegies, and two translations from Italian; most are written in couplets or quatrains. MJ's more serious verse can be illustrated by the following lines from "Verses to the Memory of Miss Clayton": "If thy friendship lives beyond the dust, / Where all things else in peace and silence lie, / I'll seek Thee there, among the Good and Just, / 'Mong those who living wisely—learnt to die. / And if some friend, when I'm no more, should strive / To future times my mem'ry to extend, / Let this inscription on my tomb survive, / 'Here rest the ashes of a faithful friend.'" James Boswell in his *Life of Johnson* quotes Thomas Warton as stating of MJ: "She was a very ingenious poetess . . . and, on the whole, was a most sensible, agreeable, and amiable woman." J.F.

JORDAN, Dorothy (1761–1816), playwright, composer and actress, was the natural daughter of Francis Bland, the son of an Irish judge, and Grace Philipps, an actress and daughter of a minister. Like her mother, DJ became an actress, playing in *The Virgin Unmasked* in Dublin in 1779. When family troubles arose, she turned for help to her theater manager, Richard Daly, who seduced her. She fled to Yorkshire, where she bore a daughter and continued her acting career, eventually moving to London. In 1785 she fell in love with Richard Ford, the son of the court physician who had a large financial interest in the Drury Lane Theatre. She bore him three children (two daughters survived). Although she would have preferred to marry Ford, she became the mistress of the Duke of Clarence (later William IV) in 1790. They lived together for 20 years and "Dora" bore him ten children. The Duke and DJ were devoted to one another; between theatrical engagements she reigned as mistress at his estate Bushy Park. In 1811 the Duke left her to marry and provide an heir for the throne. Without his protection DJ's family problems worsened. Her oldest daughter Frances and son-in-law Frederick March bled her of all her money. When March was found guilty of fraud, she fled to France to negotiate with her creditors and died in poverty in St. Cloud. During her lifetime she was lauded and loved as a great comic actress. As Sarah Siddons was to tragedy, DJ was to comedy. Her letters to the Duke and to her children have been collected in a volume by A. Aspinall (*Mrs. Jordan and her Family,* 1951). The Duke was always kind to their children, and the present Earl of Munster is her descendant.

Although DJ was very concerned about her reputation as an actress and as a mother, she showed little concern for her own compositions. As a result, it is difficult to trace exactly what she wrote. We know that three of the songs she sang were composed by her: "My Father, A Ballad," "The River Queen," and "'Twas in the Solemn Midnight Hour" (all available at the New York Public Library). She is supposed to have written the music to the very popular "The Blue Bells of Scotland," although most song collections list the music as "popular Scottish air." In 1789 a collection of all the songs performed by DJ since her appearance in London—*Jordan's Elixer of Life, and Cure for the Spleen*—was published. Only two of the songs are attributed to any author; perhaps DJ wrote some of these as well. One of DJ's most popular roles was Little Pickle in the farce *"The Spoiled Child,"* which she may have written. Little Pickle is a prankster who bedevils the life of his maiden aunt, to the amusement of his grandfather. The piece is littered with word play; allusions to Shakespeare; comments on marriage, love, women poets, and actors; and sprightly songs. The best of the songs is a jolly ditty sung by Little Pickle while disguised in a sailor's suit: "Our Foes subdued, once more on shore, / We spend our cash with glee, Sir, / And when all's gone, we drown our care, / And out again to sea, Sir."   A.W.E.

K

KEIR, Susanna (1747–1802) novelist, was born Susanna Harvey; she married James Keir, a chemist and poet, friend of Erasmus Darwin and Joseph Priestley, and supporter of the French Revolution. While writing her novels she lived in Edinburgh, although her husband was involved in manufacturing in Birmingham and Dudley. Their only child, Amelia, wrote a sketch of James Keir's life, which was privately printed in 1859. Neither of AK's novels bears her name. *Interesting Memoirs* (1785) was written "by a lady" and went through four editions plus a reprinting in Boston in 1802. *The History of Miss Greville* (1787) was written "by the author of *Interesting Memoirs*" and was published separately in Dublin, Edinburgh, and London. Both novels, largely in epistolary form, are long on moralizing and short on action. *Interesting Memoirs,* SK claims in the preface, was written to counteract the "most fatal poison" which novels convey to the heart and to inspire virtuous aims and pious sentiments in the minds of youth. The story is "partly fictitious": Louisa, taken under the wing of Lady Granville after her mother's death, is courted and eventually won by Lady Granville's son. The majority of the letters in the novel are written by simple and modest Louisa, a pious and tedious friend, and a lively and beautiful friend Lady Charlotte Villiers, the most interesting character. A notable aspect of the novel is the reference to science. In one scene, Louisa and Lady Granville chat in one part of the room while the gentlemen perform chemical experiments in the other. On another occasion, Lord Granville expresses his pleasure that his son has chosen to pursue science rather than literature, for the "possessors of the former are ever modest and reserved; those of the latter are generally proud and loquacious." In *The History of Miss Greville* SK has wisely chosen to make her witty and charming character the heroine and to enliven her morality with scenes of abduction and robbery. Yet, as in the earlier novel, letters of strict moral advice bury the active scenes, and the final effect is moralistic. A.W.E.

KELLY, Isabella (fl. 1794–1815), novelist, poet, and educational writer, was married to Col. Kelly. His death and the death of an infant furnished matter for warm, simple verses about domestic afflictions composed for a subscription edition, *A Collection of Poems and Fables* (1794, 1807)—"the effusions of a heart under the pressure of a variety of domestic calamities" (preface). IK wrote romantic novels for the Minerva Press circulating libraries, then later turned to writing children's educational books. She married Hedgeland some time before 1819. Frequent allusions to and various uses of the name "Avon" in her work, and her use of a setting in Wales, suggest she knew the west of England well. Prefaces to her work make clear she wrote to support and instruct her own children, and in response to encouraging patronage. IK's ten romances, beginning with *Madeleine, or the Castle of Montgomery* (1794), are composed largely "In humble imitation of the well-known novels of Mrs. RADCLIFFE" *(Critical Review).* Gothic towers, crumbling cloisters, waning moons, and unspeakable apparitions support thin plots that leave readers suspended among the skeletons hidden in family closets and the elaborate machinery engaged to reveal them. *The Abbey of St. Asaph* (1795) is a gothic novel set in Wales. Ominous shrieks through the howling blast warning "murder—save—spare the infants" introduce *The Ruins of Avondale Priory* (1796). *Jocelina, or the Rewards of Benevolence* (1797) drags the pale, melancholy heroine through improbable distresses—including singing ballads at St. James's coffee house—before she finally marries an MP. *Eva* (1799) and *Ruthinglenne, or the Critical Moment* (1801) were followed by *The Baron's Daughter: A Gothic Romance* (1802), in which IK hopes "that the moral blending with my improbabilities, will be found to have no improper tendency." This romance is set vaguely in the western districts of Scotland in the 14th century. *A Modern Incident in Domestic Life* (1803) combines a Barbados plantation setting, male/female disguises, didactic moralizing, and the clumsy narrative devices of the gothic novel: "*Why* Mrs. Courtney uttered such a frantic shriek, or *what* caused such violent emotion, the reader is left to imagine"; only at the end, in the manner of Radcliffe, is all explained. *The Secret* (1805) and *Jane de Dunstanville, or Characters as they are* (1813) are IK's final novels. Although in language "her imagination sometimes hurries her beyond the bounds of propriety" *(Monthly Review),* it was generally agreed that IK's conventional gothic fiction was "entitled to a decent rank in the circulation libraries" *(CR),* and her romances were fairly well received. IK's educational writings are *The Child's French Grammar, Intended as an Introduction to the Practical French Grammar of Nicolas Wanostrocht* (1805); *Literary Information consisting of Anecdotes, Explanations, and Derivations* (1811); and *Instructive Anecdotes for Youth* (1819), composed of several hundred alphabetical entries. G.B.

KER, Anne (fl. 1799–1800), novelist, wrote *The Heiress di Montalde; or, the Castle of Bezarto* (1799); *Adeline St. Julian; or, The Midnight Hour* (1800); *Edric the Forester; Emmeline, or the Happy Discovery;* and *Modern Faults.* AK was a good craftsman. Her deadpan narrative sustains the melodramatic action of the gothic novel, in which her characters have such disordered intellects that they seek refuge unknowingly in the domain of their enemies and may be terrified by the simplest revelation. They are constantly on the brink of madness through their fear and ignorance, and they refuse to recognize truth or facts. In *Edric the Forester,* for example, everyone refuses to light a lamp to find his or her way into the dreaded North Gallery. AK's distressed

victims prefer to grow eloquent upon the insufficiencies of language in *Edric,* parodying their own passivity in their refusal to command a simple sentence: "But what language can explain the affliction that racked her breast when she heard her daughter's recital, prisoners as they were in the castle, in the power of a wretch, who knew not how to exercise it, unless to oppress the innocent, or gratify his passions; the thought drove her almost to madness. Often did they implore the mercy of heaven to release them from his tyranny, or to send their beloved Edric or Rosenberg to effect their deliverance." William Hazlitt admired AK's work sufficiently to anthologize *Edric* in the Romancist and Novelist's Library (London 1841). D.S.G.

KILLIGREW, Anne (1660–85), poet and painter, was born in London. Her father was Dr. Henry Killigrew, a Royalist, theologian, and occasional dramatist, who was related to the other "theatrical Killigrews"—AK's uncles, Thomas and Sir William, and her cousins, Thomas and Charles. As chaplain to the Duke of York, Dr. Killigrew was able to place AK as a maid of honor in the household of Mary of Modena, the Duchess of York, where Anne Finch, COUNTESS OF WINCHILSEA, became her companion. Soon after AK succumbed to smallpox at 25, Dr. Killigrew prepared a memorial edition of her papers, prefaced by Dryden's *Ode.*

AK's work takes its cue from her life at court, particularly reflecting the dour mood of Mary of Modena, who sorrowed much over her unpopularity. AK reveals a cultivated and eclectic taste in literature, choosing her subjects freely from both classical and scriptural sources, although most often selecting figures who experience great loss and sorrow, such as Penelope. AK's *Poems* were printed for Samuel Lowndes in London, 1686. Moral and scriptural topics seem to predominate over courtly affairs. In contrast with her contemporaries, she takes a firm, evangelical tone, attempting to inspire piety rather than resignation in the reader. Although she is typically didactic and derivative of other writers, she took an aggressive interest in poetic theory, praying in *Alexandreis* for the "frozen style" to be warmed with a "Poetique fire." Indeed, in her poem *On the Birth-Day of Queen Katherine,* she shows herself capable of a sophisticated sort of metaphysical paradox that breaks free of the frozen style. An angel soothes the troubled speaker of the poem:

"The Emblem thou hast seen, / Denotes the Birth-Day of a Saint and Queen . . . / . . . and such a Sable Morne / Was that, in which the *Son of God* was borne. / . . . God darkn'd Heaven, when He the World did save." Although AK remained an apprentice and never attained the discipline of mature craft, there are moments when she rises to Dryden's accolade: "Her Pencil drew, what e're her Soul design'd, / And oft the happy Draught surpass'd the Image in her Mind." D.S.G.

KILNER, Dorothy (1755–1836) and Mary Ann [Maze] KILNER (1753–1831), writers of fiction and informational works for children, were sisters-in-law, about whom very little is known, except that they lived quietly together in Maryland Point, Essex, now a suburb of London. DK was an acquaintance of SARAH TRIMMER, and it may be through this connection that she, and subsequently MAK, were encouraged to publish. Their works were issued by John Marshall, also publisher of the works of LADY FENN, a leading bookseller for children in London, who may have been looking for authors in the London area and sought them out. DK (pseudonym "M.P." or later "M. Pelham") was by far the more prolific of the two women, although the less imaginative; she issued 18 titles in all. Her works, including *The First Principles of Religion* (1781?), *The History of a Great Many Little Boys and Girls of Four and Five Years of Age* (1781), *The Good Child's Delight* (1782), *Letters from a Mother to her Children* (c. 1785), *The Rotchfords: or The Friendly Counsellor* (1785?), and *First Going to School: or the Story of Tom Brown* (1804), were sometimes simply informational and didactic. She may have written *The Village School* (1783) based on Sarah Trimmer's Brentford Sunday school, and she was known for her work on various Sunday school projects. *The Life and Perambulations of a Mouse* (1783–84) and *The Rational Brutes* (1799) were moralized animal stories of sprightly imagination, bearing strong resemblances to Trimmer's *Fabulous Histories;* other school stories exposed the vices of boarding schools. DK put an emphasis on play: in the *Mouse,* the children relate that "we danced, we sang, we played at blind-man's bluff, battledore and shuttlecock." MAK (pseudonym "S.S.") produced only six titles, but her works show an inventiveness and tendency to fantasize which was unusual for the time, although always subverted to the conventional moral end. *Memoirs of a Peg-Top* (1782) and *The Adventures of a Pincushion* (1782) are picaresque novels from the points of view of inanimate objects, showing real children both playing innocently and misbehaving. "So, when children accustom themselves to loll their elbows, stoop their heads, stand upon one foot, bite their nails, or any other ungraceful actions, it makes them disagreeable, and the objects of dislike to all their friends." R.M.

KINDERSLEY, Jemima [Wickstead] (1741–1809), travel writer, translator, and essayist called "Pulcherrima" ("most beautiful") married Col. Nathaniel Kindersley in 1762 in Great Yarmouth. Family records say she knew Samuel Johnson. *Letters from the Island of Teneriffe, Brazil, the Cape of Good Hope, and East India* (1777) begin as lively descriptions by an observant traveler, but later chapters form an informal treatise on India, with some observations on Anglo-Indian affairs. Publication prompted a pamphlet, *Letters to Mrs. Kindersley* (1778) by the Rev. H. Hodgson on a religious question in her *Letters.* JK translated *An Essay on the Character, the Manners, and the Understanding of Women* (1781) from the French of Antoine Léonard Thomas and appended two original essays written in hopes of teaching even "one woman to believe what great and good things she is capable of, and to raise herself above the follies with which she is surrounded." The first essay argues that secluded women have increased influence over their husbands; the second combats the masculine idea that women do not require training in reflection or knowledge. G.B.

KING, Sophia (1781?–?), novelist and poet, seems to have completed her writing career before the age of 25. While still in her teens she published *Trifles of Helicon* (1798), a volume of poems, jointly with her sister Charlotte King (1781?–?) and her own novels *Waldorf; or, the Dangers of Philosophy* (1798) and *Cordelia; or, a Romance of Real Life* (1799). In 1801 appeared two gothic novels, *The Fatal Secret, or, Unknown Warrior* and *The Victim of Friendship, A German Romance.* In the preface to the former she refers to herself as a "weak sapling of nineteen years growth"; she lashes out at the "sordid caprices and frigid parsimony of the low-minded affluent" and self-dramatizingly joins with the popular literature of the day: "Oh, welcome then ye little elves, ye ruined abbeys, and tranquil moon-beams; come all ye artillery of glorious Radcliffe." She seems to have married some time during this period, and published *Poems, Legendary, Pathetic, and Descriptive* (1804) as Mrs. Fortnum. She returned to the profitable genre which she had mastered with *The Adventures of Victor Allen* in 1805, after which she seems to have diverted her prodigious energies elsewhere.

The *Trifles of Helicon,* to which SK contributed less than CK, displays a jejune experimentation with poetic diction. *Monthly Review* noted the youth of the writers; not destitute of talent, they should, in the reviewer's opinion, have waited for greater maturity before going into print. *Critical Review* (March 1798) also emphasized the extreme youth of the authors and noted errors of language and poetics; they seemed captivated by words more than substance. Yet the reviewer did find felicities and praised CK's poems on sleep, one of which has the conventional invocation: "Oh, Sleep! kind god, approach thy gentle wand, / And strew thy poppies round my aching head, / Lay on my lids thy soft composing hand, / And pour thy brightest visions round my head."

SK found her niche with *Waldorf,* in which the hero is converted to atheism and indirectly causes the death of two women who come under his influence. One has two brothers who vow revenge on Waldorf, although one is killed himself. Another woman, Helena, lives with Waldorf and bears him a child, but subsequently deserts him. The second brother kills the child and is murdered in turn by Waldorf, who fails to prevent an innocent man being executed for the crime. Although he is acquitted on a charge of atheism owing to his father's influence, Waldorf later commits suicide on hearing of the death of a repentant Helena. *CR* (Sept. 1798), decided that among the work's various errors, "the radical defect is, that its philosophy, by which the writer means atheism, is not represented as false." The same journal found in *The Victim of Friendship* evidence of a "luxuriant imagination," although the *Anti-Jacobin Review* thought the language "inflated" and the tale of no interest. A luxuriant imagination is certainly at work in *The Fatal Secret,* a 12th century gothic romance which hinges on the repeated visits of the mysterious Unknown Knight to the Abbey of St. Modred. His appearance at the heroine's nuptials amply demonstrates SK's talent for melodrama: "in the midst of this revelry, the gates of the abbey echoed with violent knocking, and in a few seconds the mirth of all was suddenly, and to all appearances without reason arrested. The folding doors of the apartment were thrown open, and the mysterious warrior still in armour, and with plume of ebon die, solemnly and with gloomy aspect at once entered," The Unknown Knight enslaves the heroine, binding her to sacrifice everything at a point in the future to release him from a spell; meanwhile he prevails on her to murder her husband-to-be and her sister. He eventually reveals himself as the Devil and claims her soul. The full panoply of gothic horror ensues upon the surrender to sexual passion: the full resources of the genre are apparently directed to the intimidation of women and the suppression of their sexuality. In the 1804 *Poems,* as SK herself writes, the "fantastic imagination roves unshackled" amid the "horrible" and "extraordinary." The sensational *Adventures of Victor Allen* narrates the persecution suffered by an orphan, brought up to beggary and slavery, who finally settles his account with society. SK's work is third-rate, but it exhibits vitality and an irresistible juvenile readiness to contemplate moral extremity and perversion. R.J.

KINNAN, Mary ("Polly") (1763–1848), American writer of a captivity narrative, was born near Basking Ridge, N.J. Her father, Zephaniah Lewis, was a farmer of Welsh descent. Ann Doty, her mother, was descended from a non-Pilgrim passenger on the *Mayflower.* It is said that MK once supped with George Washington, a distant relation, when the Continental Army was at Morristown. At 15 MK married Joseph Kinnan, a local former and a soldier in the Revolutionary War. In 1787 they moved their family to Tygarts Valley in Randolph County, Va. (now W. Va.), choosing that part of the frontier as unlikely to be harassed by Indians. "Our house was situated in a beautifully romantic and agreeable place, called Tiger's [sic] Valley," MK wrote in her *Narrative.* "Here I would mark nature progressing, and the revolution of the seasons; and from them would turn to contemplate the buds of virtue and of genius, sprouting in the bosom of my children. Employed in such a pleasing occupation on that [May 1791] evening, I was startled by the bursting open of the door." Indians entered. Moments later her husband had been shot dead, her oldest daughter scalped, her brother and her sons had fled, and MK was running into the woods with her infant daughter in her arms. She hid the child in the bushes, but its cries brought Indians upon them; they dashed its head against a tree and hustled MK across half Ohio almost without stopping. Impressed by her bravery, her captors did not add her scalp to those of her family at their belts. For three years she lived with the Delawares, cooking, sewing, and attending an old squaw as her slave. By means of a trader MK was finally able to send a letter to Basking Ridge. The town's Presbyterian Church commissioned her brother, Jacob Lewis, to rescue her. Lewis discovered his sister in an Indian encampment near Detroit. They fled at night and MK, dressed as a man, passed unrecognized through a crowd of Indians to a boat. She spent the rest of her life in Basking Ridge, closely associated with the Presbyterian Church, supported by her nursing and, later, by a pension given widows of Revolutionary War soldiers. She never remarried and retained throughout her life two traits acquired during her time with the Indians: she never salted her vegetables, and she never spoke outdoors to anyone without putting her back to a tree or other protection. The year after her escape, while she still enjoyed telling her story—as later she did not—MK dictated a 15-page account, *A True Narrative of the Sufferings of Mary Kinnan* (1795), to a publisher, Sheppard Kollock. Probably Kollock polished its more extravagant sentiments, while to MK is due its briskness, its attention to chronology and geography, and its concentration on her long frustrated hopes for release. She tells little of her Indian life beyond noting its misery. *A True Narrative* displays the hallmarks of the Indian captivity genre, from the unearthliness of the hush the Indians interrupt, the smashing of children against trees, to the author's denial of rape. S.M.

KNIGHT, Ellis Cornelia (1758–1837), scholar, historian, novelist, translator, and poet, was born in Westminster and raised in London. Her father, Sir Joseph Knight, a rear-admiral of the white, was knighted in 1773. Her mother, Phillipina Knight, took special care with her daughter's education. ECK attended a seminary for girls, where she learned French, Latin, Greek, mathematics, geography, and history. In addition, a Swiss pastor tutored her at home. The Knights were drawn into the Johnson and Reynolds circle through the friendship between ECK's mother and Frances Reynolds, Sir Joshua's sister. As a young woman, ECK knew LAETITIA MATILDA HAWKINS, ELIZABETH CARTER, ELIZABETH MONTAGU, Edmund Burke, James Boswell, and Oliver Goldsmith. In 1775 her father died and she and her mother went to live abroad, principally in Rome and Naples. They were an odd pair, and HESTER THRALE remarked that she pitied ECK, who was doomed to live always with "that strange, old, drunken mother." ECK was conventional and respectable, politically anti-revolutionary and staunchly Bourbon in her later years, and quite argumentative. Dr. Johnson teased her for her lack of humor. In 1799, after her mother's death, ECK returned to England with Lady Hamilton and Nelson, who called her his poet laureate. In 1805 ECK was appointed companion to Queen Charlotte at Windsor, and in 1813 she exchanged that post for a position in the household of Princess Charlotte, from which she was dismissed in 1814. ECK's autobiography and journals, not published until 1861, are an important source of information for court history in this period. In 1816 she again went abroad and spent the rest of her life on the Continent except for occasional visits to England. ECK died in Paris. A portrait of her painted in 1793 in Rome by Angelica Kauffmann now hangs in the City of Manchester Art Gallery.

ECK's principal work, still highly regarded, is *A Description of Latium, or La Campagna di Roma* (1805), with 20 etchings by the author. Her first book was a sequel to Johnson's *Rasselas,* entitled *Dinarbus, a Tale* (1790). She also wrote *Marcus Flaminius, or a View of the Military, Political, and Social Life of the Romans* (1793), a didactic epistolary romance, and *Sir Guy de Lusignan. A Tale of Italy* (1833), a romance. A series of volumes was privately printed at Windsor during ECK's tenure with the royal household, including *Chronological Abridgement of the History of Spain* (1809); *Chronological Abridgement of the History of France* (1811); *Translations from the German, in Prose and Verse* (1812), a selection of prayers and hymns; and *Miscellaneous Poems* (1812). In addition, she wrote a number of poems and verse translations, many on military and historical topics, which were variously printed. She seems often to have retreated into poetry, as for example when, after a walk with Lady Hamilton and Nelson, she addresses "Ye gentle shades, ye soft Sicilian bowers

/ Where anxious care and deep solicitude / Awhile repose, and lull'd beneath the shade / Of verdant arches yield, a moment yield / Their place within a heart, too prone to beat, / To bless'd tranquillity." ECK's books never sold well although she earned praise for her erudition and her skill with languages.   J.L.E.

KNIGHT, Henrietta, Lady Luxborough (1700?–1756), letter writer, friend and correspondent of William Shenstone, was the only daughter of Henry, Viscount St. John, and his second wife, Angelica Magdalene Pellisary, a Frenchwoman whose father held a high position under Louis XIV. The family home was in Battersea, but HK often visited her half-brother, Lord Bolingbroke, in France. In 1727 she married Robert Knight, eldest son of the cashier of the South Sea Company, who was created Baron Luxborough in 1746. After her marriage she was frequently summoned to France to run the household of her father-in-law, who had left England at the time of the South Sea Bubble and whose wife was in poor health. Acting as hostess for the senior Knight at his frequent parties was a duty HK greatly disliked, and she looked forward to the visits of her husband, then the MP for Sudbury. The Knights had a successful marriage until about 1736 when, it appears, HK was unjustly accused of adultery and banished to a small Warwickshire estate owned by the Knight family. She was forbidden to travel within 20 miles of London and remained separated from her three children for 13 years. While living in isolation she wrote the letters included in *Letters Written by the Late . . . Lady Luxborough to William Shenstone, Esq.* (1775). Shenstone's estate, "The Leasowes," was about 14 miles from the Knights' house and the poet became HK's closest friend, with the exception of the COUNTESS OF HERTFORD, whom she was unable to visit because of travel restrictions and who had care of HK's three children. HK lived alone on the estate until her death.

The *Letters,* dating from 1739 to 1756, provide a glimpse of the life of an 18th-century woman as she writes about her friends and family, her favorite authors, and her plans for improving the house and estate. We learn that she and Shenstone exchanged gifts of poems and books; and on one occasion he even sent her a greyhound; but above all, they exchanged ideas and advice about home decorating and landscape gardening. Shenstone gave several of HK's poems to Dodsley for inclusion in his *Collection of Poems by Several Hands.* These are identified only as having been written by a "Lady of Quality," but the opening lines of "Written at Ferme Ornee near Birmingham; August 7th, 1749" clearly express HK's approach to the art of landscape gardening: "'Tis Nature here bids pleasing scenes arise, / And wisely gives them Cynthio, to revise: / To veil each blemish; brighten every grace; / Yet still preserve the lovely Parent's face." When writing to Shenstone, HK seldom complains about her situation; in a letter dated April 1748 she states: "If I was fond of London and its amusements, or had a taste for public places, I feel that it would give me pain to see St. James's, Vauxhall, Ranelagh, etc. etc. represented in so lively a manner as I see them through an optical glass which I have lately purchased, now that I am absent from them: but as I never was fond of a crowd, I enjoy those places as much as I desire them in this reflected way, without wishing myself at them; and I can look on the buildings and gardens of Stowe in the same manner, and with pleasure, because I never was there." The *Letters* received a very favorable notice in *Critical Review* (Dec. 1775): "Every successive Letter affords the reader fresh entertainment. What greatly adds to their value, is the evidence they contain of an amiable sincerity and goodness of heart that are seldom found united with so much knowledge of the world, so much politeness, and we may add, in a person who had felt so much unmerited obloquy, as this highly accomplished and truly respectable lady had experienced."   J.F.

KNIGHT, Sarah Kemble (1666–1727), American diarist, is remembered mainly for her remarkable account of a business journey made alone in 1704 from Boston to New York. Born in Boston, the daughter of Elizabeth Trerice and Thomas Kemble, and married to a shipwright, Richard Knight, of whom there is no further record after their seventh year of marriage, SKK maintained a large household and engaged in para-legal activities such as witnessing documents and settling estates. New England tradition holds that she was the writing teacher of young Samuel Mather and Benjamin Franklin. In 1713 she bought and operated farms in Norwich and New London, Conn., where she also speculated in Indian land and kept a shop and a tavern. Upon her death she left a significant estate to her daughter. Even before her journal was published almost 100 years after her death, she had been described in Hannah Mather Crocker's *Observations on the Real Rights of Women* as evidence that "the wise Author of nature has endowed the female with equal powers and faculties . . . as he gave to the male." Crocker mentioned neither journey nor journal, but that SKK had been famous as a teacher of writing, was a "smart, witty, sensible woman and had considerable influence."

In the fall and winter of 1704–05, to settle an estate for a relative, SKK traveled by horse from Boston to New York, stopping at inns and post houses, and hiring guides along the way. She kept a journal throughout her hazardous and uncomfortable journey, which was published in New York in 1825 with the title *The Journal of Madam Knight, and Rev. Mr. Buckingham* and was instantly popular. The *Journal* showed characteristics that were to become well-known traits of American travel, local color and humorous writing, where the classic situation is that of the easterner making a trip westward, which affords the occasion for humor. As later writers were to do, she uses stock characters such as the country bumpkin or the laconic New England farmer. She also shows a relish for touches of gothic horror and an occasional tendency to compare the rudeness of the colonial world with the grandeur of Europe, both of which were to become repeated notes in American fiction. An outstanding feature of the work is its mock-epic quality, with its heroine in the role of a questing "knight." In fact, in the 19th century, it was sometimes thought that "knight" was a generic term for the narrator. The work is counterpointed with verses in styles then fashionable in England and in the Colonies, which also contribute to the mock-epic tone. Of her guide from the town of Dedham, hired for a half a piece of eight and a dram—which he instantly downed—she writes, "His shade on his Hors resembled a Globe on a Gate post. . . . Hee entertained me with the Adventurs he had passed by late Rideing, and eminent Dangers he had escaped, so that, Remembering the Hero's in Parismus and the Knight of the Oracle, I didn't know but I had met with a Prince disguis'd," a passage showing her habit of juxtaposing the homely and the heroic, as well as her headlong and brisk writing style. The *Journal* is important as a secular work in a period dominated by Puritan literature.   L.Y.

L

LANSDELL, Sarah (fl. 1796–98), novelist, identified her home as Tenterden on the title page of her first novel. She was probably of a family whose head, John Lansdell, made a fortune in the Ordinance Office, bought the manor of Halsted in Kent, sold it in 1738, and died in 1739, dividing his fortune between his sons John and Chrysostom. Nothing else is known of her except that she was a young woman when she published her two novels in 1796 and 1798, that she apologized for her inexperience, and that she dedicated the second to a Mrs. Marriott. SL's first novel, *Manfredi, Baron St. Osmund*, appeared in 1796. Written in simple style, it is a medieval romance in the gothic tradition, with CLARA REEVE's *Old English Baron* its particular model. It contains the familiar elements of castles, night walks, mysterious knights in black armor, minstrels, buried crimes, unsolved mysteries, a tower chamber, and a romantic pair: "'Eldred,' cried she at length, 'and can you leave me?' 'Did you not bid me adieu in our last cruel meeting?' 'I here retract, and ask you to stay for my sake.'" The plot originates in the buried guilt of the father, who has committed a crime for an inheritance. The daughter, innocent but enterprising, must cope with the suspense and danger of a macabre and mysterious world whose secrets she does not know. The father attempts to force upon his daughter a villainous suitor, although she loves a good man who is her father's victim. In the end general justice prevails and supernatural incidents are naturally explained. The second novel, *The Tower, or The Romance of Ruthyne* (1798), has similar elements and characters but displays a greater imagination and psychological insight into the heroine's sensibilities. Several subplots are interpolated with some skill. The novel is further complicated by the doubling of the heroine; one daughter who loved gaiety soon goes mad (but later recovers), while the other who loved the contemplative life is rewarded with tranquility, true love, and an inheritance. Some time after the publication of *Manfredi* as a novel in two volumes, a short chapbook version of 30 pages was issued, very probably not by SL herself.   R.S.

LATTER, Mary (1722?–1777), miscellaneous writer, is probably the ML christened at Frilsham, Berks., in 1722, daughter of George and Mary Latter. By 1740 ML lived with her mother in Reading, where in that year, in a rhymed newspaper advertisement, she disowned some satiric verses on Reading ladies. Later she recollected a happy girlhood spent roaming the countryside and reading good English authors, but lamented the disadvantages of a female education. Very probably ML and her mother managed the linen draper's and millinery business in Butcher-Row of which ML was the proprietor after her mother's death in 1748; she also took in boarders. The letters and fiction of her first volume suggest that she led, when young, a varied and even gay social life, but that a well-established young man to whom she was engaged terminated the relationship. From this early period date her popular light verses "To Capt. - - - of Ld- - -'s, Dragoons; on his falling from his Horse, and breaking his Nose. Written extempore and sent with a Nose of Clay." Meanwhile she had acquired local reputation as an author and, through the interest of the schoolmaster, had attracted important friends and patrons, including the antiquarian John Loveday and his wife, Penelope. When her business faltered, ML published, by subscription, *The Miscellaneous Works, in Prose and Verse, of Mrs. Mary Latter*, proposals for which were advertised in January 1759. There were two editions in that year of the volume, which included a short epistolary novel, essays, letters, and verses, and ended with the dramatic blank-verse "Soliloquies on Temporal Indigence" and the consolatory "Retrospective View of Indigence: or, the Danger of Spiritual Poverty." *Critical Review* (Aug. 1759) allowed her "some strokes of genius"; *Monthly Review* (July 1759), noting her sex and circumstances, compared her unfavorably to MARY JONES and ELIZABETH CARTER. Meanwhile, her business failed and she spent some time in debtors' prison, a shock from which she barely recovered. Early in 1761 John Rich, manager of Covent Garden Theatre, who had read her unfinished tragedy, *The Siege of Jerusalem*, gave her money, invited her to stay with him in London to study the forms of theater, and organized a subscription to publish *A Miscellaneous Poetical Essay in three parts* (1761) dedicated to Lord Lyttelton; the first part describes her development as an author, and the second and third parts reconcile her, through a vision of Content, to her poverty. In the fall ML went again to live with Rich and his wife, working for him on the alteration of various theatrical pieces, but Rich died in November before he could produce her tragedy, and his heirs rejected it. In 1763 ML published the play preceded by "An Essay on the Mystery and Mischief of Stage-Craft," an account of her Covent Garden misadventures. In 1768 the tragedy was produced in an unsuccessful benefit for ML at Reading, and in 1774, following Garrick's refusal of the play at Drury Lane, she tendentiously defended its "title to perfection" and promised support for it from her "extensive connexion." "Fine & conceited" Garrick noted privately on her letter. Her other publications include "A Lyric Ode, on the Birth of his Royal Highness, the Prince of Wales, written in August 1762," and "published by particular desire" (1763), and a satiric poem, "Liberty and Interest" (1764), recommended respectively by *CR* and *MR* as the best imitations of the Hudibrastic style, and as having masculine beauties more in Swift's manner and spirit than anything seen in some time. Finally, in 1771 ML published "Pro and Con, or the Opinionists, an ancient fragment," a disjointed collection of critical, political, and hermetic pieces described by *MR* as "the ravings of a deranged imagination." She died in 1777 and was buried near her mother in the churchyard of St. Laurence, Reading.

ML enjoyed a share of the patronage of the great, and considerable local celebrity in Reading, but never achieved general acclaim or security; in her self-appraisal she alternated between abject apology for having, through her necessities, ventured into male terrain, and an over-estimation of her poetic abilities. She sometimes complained, disconcertingly, of persecution, and the charge of mental derangement made by *MR* about her last volume is not completely unreasonable. Nor did she settle on the best genre for her gifts. The self-pitying verses of her middle years, focused on weeping and trauma-struck muses, fail to make poetry of their bid for sympathy and support: "See! hungry Creditors, like rav'ning Wolves, / Impatient for their Prey draw mutt'ring on, / And meditate Destruction." More successful is the epistolary novel of her 1759 volume, which is humorous, good-humored, and realistic, with an engaging social satire that anticipates FANNY BURNEY and Jane Austen. B.R.

LEAD, Jane (1624–1703), mystic and prophet of the Philadelphian movement, was born Jane Ward and raised in Norfolk in a respectable Anglican gentry family. At 15 she was suddenly seized with a religious melancholy during Christmas festivities and began her lifelong search for inner spiritual peace. In 1642–43, she frequented the Independent conventicles of London and became sympathetic to the millennial hopes of radical Puritanism. Of her 27-year marriage to William Lead (d. 1670) she wrote, in her spiritual diary *A Fountain of Gardens* (1697), that he was a hindrance to "my marriage with the Lamb." In 1663 she met John Pordage (1607–81), one of the first English systematizers of the philosophy of Jacob Boehme. Some time in 1670, JL began to experience ecstatic visions of Sophia, the Goddess of Wisdom. Sophia, the central figure in one bypath of Christianity based partly on the Books of Wisdom, plays a prominent role in Boehme's theosophy. Although JL lived obscurely in London with only a small following, by the 1690s her tracts were being eagerly translated into Dutch and German for the thriving theosophical movements on the Continent. To propagate her prophecies, JL and her spiritual son, the nonjuror Francis Lee, initiated the Philadelphian society (fl. 1694–1703), which was named after the city Christ chooses as his New Jerusalem in Revelation 3.

In her first two books, *A Treatise of the Soul's Union with Christ* (1680) and *The Heavenly Cloud Now Breaking* (1681), JL began her assault on her contemporaries' faith in reason. She warns that reason, the natural self-centered perspective, prevents us from apprehending from a higher perspective, which she calls "Wisdom." In *Revelations of Revelations* (1683) and elsewhere, JL writes that the trinitarian God had a Virgin hidden within Him from all eternity. "The true Divine Masculine," she claims, is male and female. Because God created Adam "in His own image," Adam was an androgynous "virgin spirit" before he fell into division (Adam and Eve). In *Enochian Walks with God* (1694), she prophesies heretically that, since God's love (but not His wrath) is eternal, He will restore all of lapsed creation to its original divine state. JL and her followers expected a Third Coming, a return of the Virgin Wisdom, to initiate a renewal of God-like similitude in individuals. JL was influential in theosophical millennial circles because she experienced, at times nightly, visitations from Sophia which she describes in *Fountain of Gardens*. After JL died, the Philadelphian movement fell into disunity, although it continued to exist for some time in the more Quietistic climate of Germany and although another nonjuror follower, Richard Roach, continued to vindicate JL's teachings until his death in 1730. Influences of the Philadelphian movement can be traced in the work of such diverse writers as William Law (1686–1761), JOANNA SOUTHCOTT (1750–1814), and William Blake. JL's vision revitalizes a countertradition within Christianity, always present in mysticism, which emphasizes the female attributes of the God of Love. S.B.

LEAPOR, Mary (1722–46), poet, was born at Marston St. Lawrence, Northants., on the estate of Judge Blencowe, where her father, Philip, was gardener. Five years later the family moved to Brackley, nearby, where Philip Leapor kept a nursery and worked for local landowners. The family's resources were slight, and Molly—as ML was called even after her death—was educated only enough to read and write; when at ten or eleven she began scribbling verses, her parents attempted to break the habit. For a model she used chiefly Pope. Her library at her death consisted of only 16 or 17 volumes, including part of Pope's works, Dyrden's *Fables*, and some volumes of plays. She was once sent as cookmaid to the family of a "gentleman" who later described her as emaciated and swarthy, with a long crane neck, the body of a bass viol, and the propensity to scribble while the meat scorched. Her health was poor, and after the death of her mother, ca. 1742, ML kept house for her father and still contrived to produce a considerable body of writings. Through the local circulation of her verses and fame, about 14 months before her death she attracted the attention of Bridget Freemantle, daughter of a former rector of Hinton. This patron ("Artemesia" in ML's verses) tried to raise a subscription to enable ML to devote more time to writing, but before she could succeed, ML died of measles and was buried in Brackley. She asked that her poems be published for her father's benefit. Proposals, perhaps written by Garrick, were published in 1747, and *Poems upon Several Occasions* appeared in 1748. In 1751 a second volume with the same title was published, edited by Isaac Hawkins Browne with the aid of its printer, Samuel Richardson.

ML's history and writings attracted wide attention, and her pieces were much republished, particularly in *Poems by Eminent Ladies* (1755); she was honored by inclusion in Duncombe's *Feminead* (1754). William Cowper in 1791 remembered her, noting of another "natural" poet that he had not seen such talent in any disadvantaged poet since ML. She had a good ear, but the couplets in which she wrote moral epistles, fables, religious verse, and epitaphs, compared to those of Pope, are diffuse, less pointed, and better humored. In her own favorite work, the unproduced play "The Unhappy Father," a domestic melodrama imitative of Nicholas Rowe, ML may speak her own aspiration through her hero Polonius: "Ere Nature cuts the slender Twine of Life, / I'd fain do something worthy of my Birth; / Something that may inform a future Age, / Polonius liv'd; and Thus and Thus did he." Freemantle discerned a self-portrait in "Essay on Woman" although ML refuted the notion: "Pamphilia's Wit who does not strive to shun, / Like Death's Infection or a Dog-Day's Sun? / The Damsels view her with malignant Eyes: / The Men are vex'd to find a Nymph so wise; / And Wisdom only serves to make her know / The keen Sensation of superiour

Woe." Because she represented to the public the untutored poet denied the advantages of art, and figured partly as natural wonder, partly as laboratory in which might be revealed the different contributions to genius of nature and education, ML's works were well known after her death. Conscious of her quick response to any stimulus or encouragement, most readers were in agreement with Freemantle's summation: "her friends are now left to lament her loss, and that so great a part of a short and valuable life was spent in obscurity." B.R.

LEE, Harriet (1757–1851), novelist, was the daughter of an actress mother who died young and the actor and manager John Lee; she was born in London and brought up by her sister SOPHIA LEE. From 1781 to 1803 she helped her sister run a successful school in Bath. Her epistolary novel *The Errors of Innocence* (1786) attacks injustice to women. Her lively social comedy, *The New Peerage* (produced and published 1787), was moderately successful; but her melodramatic tragedy, *The Mysterious Marriage* (1798), was never acted. She published a second novel, *Clara Lennox*, in 1797. By far her best work is in *Canterbury Tales*, written in collaboration with Sophia and published with both their names. Harriet wrote most of Volumes I (1797) and III (1799) and all of Volumes IV (1801) and V (1805). HL was a kindly and unusually attractive woman, brilliant in conversation. William Godwin was one of several suitors; she rejected him for his egotism and lack of orthodoxy in religion. She was not altogether conservative, however, for she sympathized with the moderate supporters of the French Revolution.

HL's *Canterbury Tales* is distinguished by dry satiric comments, interesting characters, and enlightened views. "The Landlady's Tale" is a sympathetic account of an unwed mother, and "The Wife's Tale" places the blame for a young wife's errors squarely upon her selfish parents and husband. Sixteen-year-old Julia was too immature to resist her parents' pressure to marry a rich man of fifty. Since he was not choosing "a companion, a friend [or] a wife . . . but a mere expensive bauble to decorate his house with, and outshine his acquaintance," he required nothing from her except attentiveness to him; he forgot "that the virtues are rarely solitary; and that he who insists only on the one amongst them which conduces to his own convenience, may thank his fortune rather than his prudence if he

does not miss them altogether." Unable to love her husband and too inexperienced to reject his teachings, Julia becomes completely vain and worldly and fails to form any moral principles. Naturally she moves toward an adulterous affair, and he coldbloodedly prepares to punish her for it: he "contemplated without remorse the prospect of . . . marking with disgrace, a creature whose propensity to excellence he first had blighted, and whom he had purchased of herself, before she knew her own value." HL's comment on the plight of Julia's empty fashionable parents, after they had lost their accustomed station in life by squandering their money, throws light on an enduring difference in the situations of men and women: Julia's father can find nothing to do with himself, but her mother, "no way superior to him in abilities," found occupation because she "had the good luck to fall in with two or three notable housewives"; "she was of that fortunate sex which can sink to trifles without losing its dignity." HL's best story is unquestionably "The German's Tale: Kruitzner," a penetrating analysis and moral evaluation of a man destroyed by his own egotism. Kruitzner's pride nourishes itself by every circumstance and in spite of every failure; he attributes the distinction he enjoys as son of Count Siegendorf entirely to his own personal merits and fails to recognize what he owes to the extrinsic advantages of education, rank, and money. Dismissed from military command for insubordination and irresponsibility, he is indignant rather than ashamed, absconds from his country, and considers treason. His still-loving father's efforts to persuade him to return merely confirm his "idea of his own value in society," for he cannot recognize them as "simply the effect of paternal fondness." Instead of feeling dismay when his selfishness finally alienates his father, he rejoices in his new freedom from control and criticism. Nevertheless, Kruitzner is not a villain. He feels guilt for his failings, although never sufficiently so to reform. He can manifest self-control and fortitude under favorable circumstances, is capable of love and honorable feeling, and is incapable of calculated crime. Yet he is forced to recognize, when his beloved son commits a premeditated murder, that he is in a way responsible. Conrad resembles his father in following his own wishes over all other considerations and learns from him to excuse excesses of passion on the grounds that they are impossible to resist. The character of Kruitzner is convincing and fully engages our sympathy, whether we are exasperated by his throwing away opportunities and then rationalizing his failures; hope he will not be punished for crimes he did not commit, however consistent with his character they might seem; or sympathize with his agony over the vicious son for whom he is and is not responsible.

The outstanding value of HL's work is its good sense—evident in satirical comments on society, in penetration into human motives, and in judicious moral evaluation of situation and character. HL was remarkably free of the conventions which, in general, governed women's fiction in her day; "Kruitzner" is practically the only example which does not focus on romantic love. HL's work displays none of the sentimentality and silly fantasy so blatant in the work of her sister Sophia. Contemporary critics praised the *Canterbury Tales*, but without much discrimination, as they failed to note the differences between her work and Sophia's or the obvious superiority of "Kruitzner." The *Critical Review* (October 1801) admired its Germanic gloom and "impressive and striking" incidents, but wished for a simplistic poetic justice (which would have destroyed HL's moral point). The *Monthly Review* dismissed the tale as nothing but gloom and unwholesomeness. Byron was the first to recognize the merit of "Kruitzner," which he dramatized as *Werner, or The Inheritance* (1822): "this tale . . . made a deep impression upon me, and may, indeed, be said to contain the germ of much that I have since written."   K.R.

LEE, Sophia (1750–1824), fiction writer, was born in London, the eldest child of two actors. After her mother's death, Sophia took over the upbringing of her four sisters and one brother. She was educated by her father, an able but quarrelsome man who managed various provincial theaters as well as acting. Her comedy *The Chapter of Accidents* (produced and published 1780) proved a lasting success. With the profits she set up a girls' school in Bath, which ran successfully from 1781 to 1803 and was her main source of income. Her historical novel *The Recess* (1783–85) was well received. It was followed by *Warbeck* (1786), a romance similar to *The Recess* which she translated from the French; *A Hermit's Tale* (1787), a dull pseudo-medieval ballad; and *Almeyda, Queen of Granada* (1796), an

overblown tragedy which lasted for only four nights, despite the presence of SL's friend Sarah Siddons in the leading role. In 1797, she and her sister HARRIET LEE began collaboration on *Canterbury Tales*, a collection of short fiction. SL contributed the pleasantly humorous introduction to Volume I (1797), "The Young Lady's Tale: The Two Emilys" (Volume II, 1798), and "The Clergyman's Tale" (Volume III, 1799). Her epistolary novel *The Life of a Lover*, actually her earliest work, was published in 1804; and her comedy "The Assignation" failed on production in 1807 and was never printed. Good-looking and an excellent conversationalist, SL met most of the English and foreign celebrities who came to Bath. Her works were generally published with her name.

The Chapter of Accidents is a pleasant comedy combining the humor of amusingly crass servants with the sentiment of a self-sacrificing heroine, who is essentially virtuous although she has allowed herself to be seduced. SL's most characteristic work is sentimental fiction. Her flashes of sardonic social satire (as in the opening of "The Two Emilys") are soon drowned in displays of tender, pathetic, or noble emotions, expressed in stilted language. "The Two Emilys" depicts a world of overwrought feelings—delicate characters affected only by emotional distress, often contrived by themselves. The heroine, Emily Arden, is so exquisitely sensitive that if her fiancé utters a thoughtless word or her father forces her to face a painful fact, she shrinks into retreat for years. Female strength and competence appear only in the villainous woman. SL not only exalts Emily's inadequacies, but shows them triumphing in the real world. Although Emily is too sweet and submissive to dispute her husband's wishes, she manages to dominate him completely, as well as to confine him to the private world of the family. By the end, "Virtue and sweetness, personified in Emily, formed the center of a wide circle" of male relatives who looked to her as an example and were never tempted, through her long life, "to diverge from the sphere of so dear an attraction." In every way, the tale affirms feminine values narrowly defined: private life over public, sensitivity over plain sense, meek passivity over enterprise, fine feeling over useful action, intuition over reason. When Emily's maid cannot understand her, SL exclaims: "How to the gross of soul can delicate minds explain that acute sensibility

. . . discriminating as reason, yet impulsive as sensation . . . It knows not how to qualify—descends not to contention—disdains to be soothed—given to dignify existence, even though it entails sadness on those who have it." In implying that masculine values are coarse, in extolling those traditionally associated with women, in showing triumph through weakness and submission, SL blatantly appealed to feminine wish-fulfilling fantasy.

Although it expresses the same values, *The Recess* is a far more engaging work, as its historical setting distracts from the trite sentimental agonies and is in itself interesting. Despite a few glaring inaccuracies, *The Recess* attempts far more seriously than most gothic novels to recreate a historical period. Most of the prominent members of Queen Elizabeth's court are woven into the plot, in general consistently with their careers and characters (Sidney is chivalrous, Leicester selfish and ambitious). Love overwhelms the scene, motivating the most scheming politicians: Elizabeth executes Mary Queen of Scots because Leicester prefers Mary's daughter to herself. The novel centers on Matilda and Ellinor, twin daughters of Queen Mary by a secret marriage to the Duke of Norfolk, who are miracles of beauty, virtue, and sensibility. First one and then the other is relentlessly put through every misfortune known to woman. And they are exquisitely aware of their plight: "You will be astonished," Matilda says, "at my surviving such unceasing complicated misfortunes . . . I regard it myself with wonder, and impute [it] solely to the knowing no pause in my sufferings." Matilda and Ellinor are more appealing than Emily, partly because their harrowing adventures are more colorful and not self-generated, partly because SL was here realistic enough to show sweet dependency being trampled in the actual world. The perpetual abuse of these loving, inoffensive women by those with power expresses a truth about women's helpless position in 16th-century and even 18th-century England.

Although one can enjoy *The Recess* by abandoning one's mind to it, SL's work is of mainly historical interest. Her intensely "feminine" world is limited both by its caricature of female values and its lack of connection with real life. Emily's opposition to reason and lack of active virtue make her a reductive ideal; SL's exclusive concentration on refined feelings produces shallow and tedious fantasy rather than a significant representation of reality. Fiction such as hers could only reinforce preconceptions about intrinsic limitations to women's work. Contemporaries found SL's weaknesses more tolerable than we do. HESTER PIOZZI thought "The Two Emilys" "a very beautiful book," though unrealistic in exaggerating the devotion of Emily's husband. The reviewers generally agreed. The *Monthly Review* praised the tale for "a great variety of incidents, with many striking and affecting scenes," but condemned its "artificial concealments" and "indulgence of absurd and unaccountable prejudices" as grossly improbable (December 1798). Reviewers made similar points about *The Recess* and also objected to its unrelieved distress (*MR*, 1786). The *Critical Review* praised its innovative mingling of fiction with history, pointing out that the counselors and generals of Elizabeth are intrinsically more interesting than the stock heroes of fiction (1783). K.R.

LEINSTER, Emilia Mary Fitzgerald, Duchess of (1731–1814), letter writer, was the second surviving daughter of Charles Lennox, second Duke of Richmond, and his wife Sarah, daughter of William, Earl Cadogan. She was the most beautiful of four beautiful sisters, and Horace Walpole awarded her the supreme prize among beauties because she alone could still blush. "Let me go where I will . . . into all kinds of ill, I shall ne'er see such a beauty as she is," wrote her husband of 15 years in 1762. Habituated to the great world, at 15 she fixed on a love match with James, the Irish Earl of Kildare, and, against her parents' wishes, married him in 1747. Simultaneously her husband was made a peer of Great Britain. The marriage was unusually happy. The bride, who as a child had been clever and agreeable but pert and wild (according to her elder sister LADY HOLLAND), became a sweet, kind, considerate, tactful woman—a poor-spirited creature unable to keep a grudge, she called herself—entirely fitted for the many-faceted life she led. Her one fault was her extravagance; she was the most expensive woman in the world, said MARY DELANY. The couple made themselves popular by living in Ireland where the Earl was leader of the Popular Party and his wife, who also played a significant political role, became known as the unofficial queen of Ireland. They finished and decorated two magnificent houses, Leinster House in Dublin and Carton in Co. Kildare, and begot 19 children.

D of L also raised her three orphaned sisters, two of whom survived her (see LADY LOUISA CONOLLY and LADY SARAH BUNBURY). Kildare became Duke of Leinster in 1766. In November 1773 he died, leaving his wife with 12 surviving children. Soon afterward the widow departed for France with her younger children and their tutor, William Ogilvie, and in October 1774 married him there, making of him, said Mrs. Delany, an honest man. By her second husband she had several daughters. In 1780 the Ogilvies returned to Dublin, where Ogilvie was found a parliamentary seat; he made a severe stepfather, father, and husband. Because of his dislike for Ireland, and to establish their daughters, the family moved to England in 1790.

The D of L kept her correspondence, and 1770 of her letters were acquired in 1933 by the National Library of Ireland. Of these, less than half have been published in three volumes, edited by Brian Fitzgerald, who has also published a biography of D of L. Of her own letters, only those to her husband and preserved by him have been published in the *Correspondence*; but letters to Ogilvie, to her earliest friend Anne Hamilton, and to others, are included in the biography. The Duchess was beloved of both her husbands, the favorite of all her sisters, and a general favorite in society. Her letters to her husband ("my dear Angel") show her as generous, lively, and intelligent. "You are vastly good to me, my dearest Jemmy, in writing so constantly, so kindly, and so particularly, but I believe I need not tell you how happy it makes me, and you may have the satisfaction to know that those little marks of your love and attention for me are not thrown away upon me." She dearly loved each of her children: "I have a cheerful and pleasant prospect before my eyes within doors: the dear little brats are, thank God, so well, so merry, so riotous, so hardy, and so full of play from morning till night that it wou'd enliven the dullest of mortals to see them. The two nurses . . . are the best play-fellows for children I ever saw; they invent some new diversion every night. . . . Henry naked is the dearest little being on earth." She decorated and planted, relying on her sisters and others to relay the materials (sometimes smuggled) to Ireland. "I cou'd look at nothing, mind nothing, think of nothing, but the India taffeta. . . . What sweet furniture it is— there is nothing half so pretty for the country!" She gossiped about society, which always interested her: "By the way, 'tis a secret, but Sir James Lowther has desired Mr Fox to propose to him for Lady Betty Spencer. He is violently in love, poor man, and they don't behave quite well to him and are for putting it off for two years. . . . It is a vast match for her, but the Duchess is odd about it; the Duke wou'd be reasonable enough if it was not for her, and, in short, the whole thing is just a second part of the affair between you and I, which makes me interest myself prodigiously about it, and we talk of nothing else." Especially from Holland House, where she often stayed, she sent her husband advice: "There is a thing I am sorry for and which is a secret, and that is I am afraid Mr Fox and Mr Pitt have had some difference," or "I saw a letter from Harry to Ned Sandford with still a more particular account of your affairs than you give me in yours, and I think it all looks well. Stick to the Primate, and I think it must end so, if our own friends play us fair, which I shou'd be apt to have my doubts about, and wou'd watch them narrowly." The careful preservation of her correspondence suggests D of L's awareness of its real historical importance.   B.R.

LENNOX, Charlotte (1729?–1804), novelist, translator, magazine editor, poet, and playwright, was born in Gibraltor or New York province; she spent her childhood in New York, particularly in the Albany-Schenectady region, where her father, James Ramsay, was stationed as captain of an Independent Company of Foot. Although as an adult CL claimed that her father had been the governor or lieutenant governor of New York, there is no evidence for this. Judging from her work, at some point in her youth she received an unusually good education for a woman. James Ramsay apparently died around 1743 without providing for the family. CL's mother remained in New York until her death in 1765; CL went to England shortly after her father's death to live with an aunt. Later accounts indicate that she found her aunt senile or deranged, incapable of acknowledging her. Some time thereafter, CL came under the patronage of the Countess of Rockingham and Lady Isabella Finch, to whom she dedicated her first publication, a volume of poems (1747), printed by William Strahan, whose assistant, the Scotsman Alexander Lennox, she married in the same year. Lennox's chronic shiftlessness and, reportedly, his harsh treatment of his wife contributed to the unhappiness of their debt-plagued marriage; although the patronage of the Duchess of Newcastle secured Lennox later employment as a Deputy Kings Waiter (1773–82), he did little to relieve the family's indigence. During the years 1748–50, CL made a few unsuccessful appearances as an actress, a profession for which, according to Horace Walpole, she had no talent. She then turned to writing. For the rest of her life, which was one of unremitting struggle and poverty, CL wrote and translated to support herself, her husband, and her children. Despite her Grub Street existence and struggles with poverty, by 1755 CL was one of the most famous and highly praised writers in England, benefiting from the friendship and assistance of such notables as Samuel Johnson, Samuel Richardson, and John Boyle, Earl of Orrery. Johnson was her lifelong friend and mentor; he held an all-night party to celebrate the publication of her first novel, and was tireless in praising and recommending her work. Boswell quotes his famous tribute to CL: speaking of FANNY BURNEY, ELIZABETH CARTER, and HANNAH MORE, Johnson remarked, "Three such women are not to be found: I know not where I could find a fourth, except Mrs. Lennox, who is superior to them all." Johnson wrote proposals and dedications for CL and gave her ideas; their friendship lasted until his death, more than 30 years. But although CL was admired by many famous literary men of her day, she was generally disliked by women. She was close to the actress Mrs. Yates, but was not part of female literary circles. HESTER THRALE, reported Burney, pronounced that, although CL's books "are generally approved, nobody likes her." A reputed bad temper combined with poverty no doubt contributed to her estrangement from genteel Bluestocking groups, yet she received sympathy from men. Richardson as early as 1752–53 noted in a letter to Lady Bradshaigh that CL "has been unhappy," and Fielding later spoke of her as "shamefully distressed." Despite her literary successes and the assistance of others, CL's later years became increasingly difficult. Her daughter predeceased her; her son was forced because of misconduct (encouraged, CL said, by bad company and the irresponsibility of his father) to emigrate to America, perhaps to relatives of the Ramsays in Baltimore. By 1792, CL, probably separated from her husband and suffering from the illness which continued for the rest of her life, began to receive some small yearly assistance from the Royal Literary Fund, but her last years were spent in extreme poverty. She died, destitute, in Dean's Yard, Westminster.

Most of CL's fame rested upon her reputation as a novelist and translator. During her career she produced five, perhaps six, novels: *The Life of Harriot Stuart* (1750), *The Female Quixote* (1752), *Henrietta* (1758), *Sophia* (1762; serialized in *The Lady's Museum* as "The History of Harriot and Sophia," Mar. 1760–Feb. 1761), and *Euphemia* (1790). Also recently attributed to her is *The History of Eliza* (1766). She translated at least six works from the French: *The Age of Lewis XIV* (1752; from Voltaire), *The Memoirs of Maximilian de Bethune, Duke of Sully* (1755), *The Memoirs of the Countess of Berci* (1756; a romance), *Memoirs for the History of Madame de Maintenon* (1757), *The Greek Theatre of Father Brumoy* (1760; two chapters were translated by Johnson and one by Boyle), *Meditations and Penetential Prayers*, by the Duchess de la Vallière (1774). Her other works were *Poems on Several Occasions* (1747), the plays *Philander* (1757; never staged), *The Sister* (1769; based upon *Henrietta*, rejected by Garrick but staged at the Covent Garden Theatre with an epilogue by Goldsmith; it was withdrawn after one night, when the audience jeered it, an attack reputed to have been planned), and the adaptation of Jonson, Chapman, and Marston's *Eastward Hoe!*, entitled *Old City Manners* (1775; staged by Garrick at Drury Lane, it enjoyed a successful run of six nights).CL also published the controversial *Shakespeare Illustrated* (1753–54), a translation of his primarily Italian sources, and a critical commentary on his use of them. She edited a magazine, *The Lady's Museum* (1760–61), which follows a miscellany format, containing a variety of features, many written by her, which varied from a serialized novel to articles on science; it is one of the most intelligent and valuable early women's magazines.

Like many 18th-century novels written by women, CL's are directed particularly to a female audience, although her best work received high praise from men as well. They are novels of manners, designed to promulgate virtue, to edify as well as entertain. (Johnson's consistent high praise for even her mediocre works can perhaps be traced to his approbation of their moral purpose.) A typical CL heroine is pious, beautiful, and virtuous: Euphemia is characteristic, eliciting this description from an older male character: "Young as she is, she is strict in the performance of all her duties, yet she affects no peculiar gravity in her aspect and manners, but tempers her reserve with so much sweetness, that, without endeavoring to please any she pleases all the world." So much do CL's heroines please, in fact, that young men regularly fall in love with them: some are honorable, some not, and the plot of a CL novel often follows the machinations of lovers, conflict, virtue, and attempted seduction, and, of course, marriage. Marriage is not always treated kindly, however, and generally speaking it is the touches of realism like Euphemia's unhappy (but not tragic or melodramatic) marriage which separate CL's novels from many other 18th-century novels and romances. CL brings to her work obvious intelligence and education; at its best, it contains fine descriptive passages, a realistic attitude about human (especially male/female) interaction, witty character sketches, and effective, light satire. At its worst, it echoes the sentiments of "ladies' novels," pays tired tribute to virtue, and pursues a plot line heavily dependent upon coincidence and complication.

CL's first novel, *Harriot Stuart*, and her last, *Euphemia*, are noteworthy for their American settings. Drawing upon her background, CL places the novels around Albany and Schenectady, and both pay enough attention to American natural and social background to support recent claims for CL as "America's first novelist." Neither novel is her best, but both, through the explicit or suggested epistolary format, present their British readers with a view of the exotic American landscape (which includes, of course, Indians). The situation of her heroines' adventures in a foreign setting follows conventional romances (although, like APHRA BEHN in her *Oronooko*, CL is describing geography with which she is familiar). CL also echoes romance in the sudden plot complications and suitably extreme language. "When I went to France, I left you rich and happy; the reputed heiress of a large fortune, both your beloved parents alive, and every prospect brightening before you. What a reverse, in the space of a few months! An orphan! Your inheritance lost! married; and, in consequence of that marriage, becoming an exile from your country, doomed to waste your days in America!"

CL's major novel, which won her immediate acclaim and is the prime reason she deserves a place in modern considerations of 18th-century fiction, is *The Female Quixote*, which gives ample rein to her satiric talents. In writing this novel she received advice from both Richardson (who printed it) and Johnson (who may have written the penultimate chapter). One of the reasons for its success is its double function as both a romance (complete with love interest and a conventionally happy ending, though too quickly achieved to be convincing) and a satire on romances; thus Arabella is both a heroine and a mock-heroine. The novel, based very loosely upon Cervantes, presents a heroine raised in isolation on French romances and therefore inhabiting, Quixote-like, a fantasy world of exaggerated gestures and impossible plots; she sees ravishers or heroes in every male passer-by. This device produces much good comedy, especially through Arabella's speech, in which CL parodies the language of romance. In no other novel does CL sustain such a high level of satiric sophistication, but *Henrietta* and *Sophia* are both well constructed and both carry on CL's defense of virtue. Nearly all of CL's work was well received and elicited good reviews. Johnson wrote of *The Female Quixote* for *Gentleman's Magazine*, and Henry Fielding praised it highly, calling it "a most extraordinary and most excellent Performance. It is indeed a Work of true Humour, and cannot fail of giving a rational, as well as very pleasing, Amusement to a sensible reader, who will at once be instructed and very highly diverted." *Memoirs of Sully* became accepted as a standard history, and *Shakespeare Illustrated* excited interest and controversy.   K.S.

LETCHES, Mrs. (fl. 1792), poet, is the supposed author of *Poems on Several Occasions by a Lady* (Bristol, 1792). The work indicates that the author had at least four children, one of whom, a boy, reached eight years of age. Three others died in infancy. The author refers to herself as "Helena" in one poem. The 27-page volume comprises mostly occasional poems. In one, "Evening Reflections on Brandon Hill," the author denounces slavery. "The Skull's Harangue" is one of several morbidly religious poems: "Why look aghast—and turn at sight of me? / My hollow Scalp doth no harsh terrors bring; / It would persuade in soothing artless strain; / And teach you to disarm Death of his Sting." *Poems* is dedicated to the citizens of Bristol.   T.C.S.W.L.

LITTLE, Janet (1759–1813), poet and milkmaid, claimed to love the Muses, although "I cannot boast of any favours they have deigned to confer upon me as yet; my situation in life has been very much against me as to that." She received a fair education for one of her class, and while in charge of the dairy at Loudon Castle came under the patronage of Robert Burns's friend Mrs. Dunlop. Burns's example encouraged her to write in both English and Scots: she wrote him "an epistle, part poetic, and part prosaic . . . a very ingenious but modest composition." Although he offended Mrs. Dunlop by refusing to read her poetry, Burns made amends by filling up the subscription bill (which includes himself and James Boswell) when the *Poetical Works of Janet Little, the Scotch Milkmaid* was published in Ayre, 1792. She is said to have made £50 by the publication. She married a widowed laborer, John Richmond, who had five children and was 20 years her senior. JL's poems show spirit but little real accomplishment. She looks to LADY MARY WORTLEY MONTAGU and ELIZABETH ROWE as inspiring female predecessors and, imagining what critics will say about her as an unlearned author, pleads mercy for herself as a "crazy scribbling lass": "May she wha writes, of wit get mair, / An' a' that read an ample share / Of candour ev'ry fault to screen, / That in her dogg'ral scrawls are seen."   J.H.

LIVINGSTON, Anne Hume [Home] (1763–1841), American diarist known as Nancy, was the indulged child of William and Alice Lee Shippen. Her father was appointed Director General of all military hospitals of the Armies of the U.S., and as a result their home was the meeting place for the officers of the Continental Army. General Washington often dined and had tea at the Shippen home. As the belle of Virginia AHL fell hopelessly in love with Louis Guillaume Otto, attaché to the French Minister to the US. Possessing little money and just starting his career, Otto nonetheless proposed and AHL accepted. Owing largely to the Shippen's financial difficulties, AHL's father insisted she marry instead the very wealthy Colonel Harry Livingston. The match was disastrous owing to her husband's violent and jealous rages, and in 1783 AHL returned to her parents' home

in Virginia. Accompanying her was their daughter Margaret Beekman (Peggy). Soon after this, AHL began her journals. Edited by Ethel Armes in 1935 as *Nancy Shippen Her Journal Book*, they are composed mainly of the everyday life of a well-to-do colonial woman of Virginia and her views on various subjects. On marriage AHL writes "marriage to give delight, must join two minds not devote a slave to the will of an imperious lord." Daily entries involve mundane and ordinary topics, such as parties, menus, local gossip, current reading materials, teas, sicknesses, weather, toothaches, card-playing, and descriptions of her friends and daughter. In 1793, however, AHL writes about the heartbreak of letting her daughter return to her husband's mother. On May 16 she records, "Papa told me this morn^g at breakfast that I must send my darling Child to its Grandmama Livingston. I told him I cou'd not bear the Idea of it, that I had sooner part with my life, than my Child. She is my all & I must part with her! cruel cruel fate. Aug. 21—I have been in such a state of misery since I left my beloved Child . . . August 23—But now I can only think of her & cry for her, & be the most miserable creature existing for her." Her journal continues with entries about her renewed love for Otto: "Heard last night that Leander [Otto] who has been some time at Anapolis is return'd. I feel happy to think that I shall soon see so dear a friend one that is as much my friend in adversity, as in prosperity." In 1789 AHL formally started divorce proceedings and, in retaliation, her husband spread scandal and attempted to gain custody of Peggy. Peggy was spirited away by her mother to live in retreat under a fictitious name. AHL's parents failed to support her at a critical time in the divorce and she was faced with two choices: divorce her husband and marry Otto and as a result lose custody of Peggy, or drop the divorce case and retain some voice in Peggy's future. She chose the latter. After waiting eight years for AHL, Otto remarried in 1790. His name never again appeared in her journal. Her final entry in 1791 reflects her mood: "I consider'd my life so uninteresting hitherto as to prevent me from continuing my journal & so I shall fill up the remainder with transcriptions." When Peggy reached 16 she forsook the Livingston fortune and went to live permanently with her mother in seclusion. AHL lapsed into a religious depression from which she never emerged. In 1817, S. Man-ning privately published *Sacred Records* for AHL. This work consisted of some of the parables and miracles of Christ abridged in verse. Peggy also became extremely pious and died 23 years after her mother; they were buried in the same grave.   P.P.

LOCKE, Mary (fl. 1790), poet, describes herself in the preface to *Eugenius; or, Virtue in Retirement: A poem* (1791) as "young, uneducated and inexperienced." Although links between women's oppression and slavery remain unspoken, her poetry explores themes of captivity through white tyranny in Africa and imprisonment in England: "Untaught by Art, bold, generous and free / They knew, they felt the sweets of liberty. / Man, tyrant man, usurps what nature gave / Tramples on rights, and makes a king a slave."   L.F.

LOGAN, Deborah Norris (1761–1839), American diarist and chronicler of Pennsylvania history, was born in a Philadelphia mansion whose grounds were adjacent to the State House. Members of her family, especially William Penn's secretary James Logan, and Speaker Isaac Norris, were distinguished Quakers who influenced Pennsylvania's early history. Throughout her life, DNL fraternized with the country's most eminent citizens. She knew Washington, Jefferson, and all the signers of the Declaration of Independence; John Dickinson, C.W. Peale, Charles Thomson, and Fanny Kemble were among her close friends; and she met Harriet Martineau, Catherine Maria Sedgewick, and the infant Louisa May Alcott. In addition to enjoying a high social position, DNL received the benefit of a good education as a student at Anthony Benezet's Friends' Girls' School. Although she did not distinguish herself there, shortly after leaving she developed an extensive self-imposed reading course that formed the foundation of her scholarly pursuits. She did not abandon her interests after 1781, when she married George Logan and moved to Stenton, his ancestral home. A reluctance to neglect her family obligations motivated DNL to rise before dawn to accomplish her time-consuming editorial tasks. She managed to be a devoted wife and mother, an efficient manager of her large household, a charming hostess, and a zealous preserver of state history. DNL became the first female member of the Historical Society of Pennsylvania.

DNL's great service to history was the preservation of the letters she found in the attic at Stenton, the correspondence between James Logan and William Penn. The 11-quarto manuscript that was the result of her meticulous editing of the worn, delicate papers was published as *Correspondence of William Penn and James Logan* (2 vols., 1870–72). Other works include *The Norris House* (1867) and *Memoir of Dr. George Logan of Stenton* (1899). DNL also contributed numerous historical articles and poetry to *The National Gazette, The Philadelphia Gazette* in which in 1798 she published a defense of her husband's controversial peace mission to Paris, and *Poulson's American Daily Advertiser*. Some of this material can be found in her diary, a 4,000-page, 17-volume work she started in 1815 and concluded shortly before her death. She described the diary as a record of "whatever I shall hear of fact or anecdote that shall appear worthy of preservation. And many things for my own satisfaction likewise that may be irrelevant to others." Although the text's "worthy" portions include lively anecdotes about men who influenced the nation's early history, it is the "irrelevant" personal material that dominates the diary. Together with all of DNL's published and unpublished work, the diary is located in the Historical Society of Pennsylvania.   M.B.

LOGAN, Maria (fl. 1793), poet, wrote *Poems on Several Occasions* (1793). This insubstantial production consists largely of humdrum and stylized occasional and epistolary verses. The preface refers to "Seven Tedious Years of Uninterrupted Sickness," and the poem "To Opium" indicates one way in which ML alleviated her sufferings: "Be mine the balm, whose sov'reign pow'r / Can still the throb of Pain; / The produce of the scentless flow'r / That strews Hindostan's plain." She speaks of opium as a stimulus to Fancy and Memory, but there is little sign of inspiration in this volume.   R.J.

LONG, Anne (fl. 1718), poet, is described in *Letters, Poems, and Tales Amorous, Satyrical and Gallant* (1718) as a "celebrated Toast." The collection contains only one poem certainly attributable to her, addressed to Lady Mary Chambers; it is notable for its stress on women's political exclusion: "That Laws for Publick Justice meant / Should pass by General Consent: / And pray, what Woman did appear / To vote for this? I ne'er cou'd hear."   L.F.

LUCAN, Margaret Bingham [Smith], Lady (?–1814), poet, is better known as an amateur artist. *Verses on the Present State of Ireland* (London, 1778) is her only known work. In 1760, she married Sir Charles Bingham, Bart. (1735–99), who was created Baron Lucan of Castlebar, Co. Mayo, in 1776. According to the notes that follow the *Verses*, she lived in Ireland for several years. ML is frequently mentioned in the letters of Horace Walpole, Samuel Johnson, and MARY DELANY. For 16 years she worked at illustrating a five-volume edition of Shakespeare's plays with "a truth, delicacy, and finish of execution which have been very rarely imitated." She bore five children: Lavinia, who married the second Earl Spencer in 1781, Eleanor Margaret, Louisa, Anne, and Richard. ML's intention in writing *Verses on the Present State of Ireland* was to call the attention of the English people and in particular Queen Charlotte, whom she addresses directly, to the sufferings of the Irish. She is aware of "its being objected that the subject was not suitable to a female pen: and her performance perhaps proves it; but she is willing to suffer every critical censure, provided any benefit accrues to the cause for which she endeavours to plead" (*Verses,* p. ii). Her argument is simply expressed in 219 lines of heroic couplets. "The food of thousands is to roots confin'd! / Eternal fasts that know no taste of bread; / Nor where who sows the corn, by corn is fed." She argues that English restrictions on the wool industry and the interdiction of the wool trade have crippled the Irish economy, and she deplores the persecution of Irish Catholics. Her political fervor and acuity and her ease of expression make one regret that she wrote so little.   T.C.S.W.L.

M

MACARTHUR, Elizabeth (1768–1850), Australian letter writer and journalist, was born Elizabeth Veale in North Devon. In 1788 she married a Scottish ensign, John Macarthur, who in 1789 was made a lieutenant in the New South Wales Corps, founded to keep order in the convict settlement of Sydney Cove. EM travelled with her husband, her six-month-old baby and a thousand convicts. She left with mixed feelings: "we have every expectation of reaping the most material advantages," she wrote to her mother, perhaps to allay her fears, while also admitting elsewhere that the prospects seemed "terrific and gloomy." On the voyage she kept a diary for part of the time, describing the "filth and vermin" in the passages and the sickness and death. In mid-1790 she arrived at Sydney Cove at a time when many settlers were close to starvation. At first she lived in primitive housing, where she bore a premature baby who died. Gradually she grew accustomed to the place, although lamenting the lack of female friends "to unbend my mind to," and moved into a better house. Homesickness was lessened by the arrival of other congenial women, including MARY ANN PARKER, and by increasing prosperity. Her husband was made paymaster of his regiment and began to breed sheep, which he rightly saw as the future of New South Wales, and soon the Macarthurs became the biggest private landowners in the colony. By the end of the century EM knew Australia to be her home, although her sons were sent to England for schooling. In 1806, a new governor arrived and quarreled with the irascible Macarthur, who was jailed. Freed by soldiers, who arrested the governor, Macarthur had to return to England for his part in the affair, and he left EM to run the farm alone with her daughters for nine years. In 1817 he returned with his sons, by which time Sydney had become a more substantial colony. By 1830 EM was so firmly rooted in Australia that she could not think of a visit to England: "The time is too far past." Her main tie there was one son whom she did not see for 30 years; his death in 1831 depressed her husband, who never recovered from the blow and died in 1834.

EM's letters and diary reveal a matter-of-fact unemotional woman, suited to coping with the difficulties of early colonial life and with a choleric and depressive husband. They show quick adaptation; at one time they record the near starvation of the settlers and note the Aborigines' unhelpful ignorance of Australia—"All their knowledge and pursuits are confined to that of procuring for themselves a bare subsistence"—while at another they seriously depict the snobbery of colonial life, as EM claims that freed convicts were not acceptable company at dinner.   J.T.

MACAULAY, Catherine [Sawbridge] (1731–91), historian and pamphleteer, was descended on both sides from wealthy Whig mercantile families. She was born at her father's estate in Kent and educated privately at home. In 1760 she married the physician Dr. George Macaulay, a member of the Scottish circle in London, where CM came to live; he was a friend of Tobias Smollett and William and John Hunter. He was also intimate with the radical or "Old Whig" circle, whose most prominent member was the republican barrister Thomas Hollis. Macaulay died in 1766, leaving his wife and daughter in comfortable circumstances. CM had meanwhile begun to publish her *History of England from the Accession of James I to that of the Brunswick Line.* Her first volume appeared in 1763, and the second in 1767. Subsequent volumes appeared in 1768, 1771, 1781, and 1783. The *History* defended the Whig interpretation of the Stuarts and the Civil War; it reflected the republican, or commonwealth, sympathies of Hollis and others who saw in the political situation of the early reign of George III the betrayal of the English constitution. CM was not interested merely in the 17th century; in 1767 she published a pamphlet, *Loose Remarks on Certain Positions to be found in Mr. Hobbes' Philosophical Rudiments of Government and Society. With a Short Sketch of A Democratical Form of Government in a Letter to Signior Paoli.* She disagreed with everything Hobbes said; the suggestions for a constitution for Paoli's new Corsican state were a positive statement of her ideas. She saw a republic with universal male suffrage, constant rotation of office holders, and equal inheritance of land as the ideal form of government. By the following year she was actively engaged in British politics, closely associated with John Wilkes and his friends. The Wilkites opposed what they saw as the domination of Parliament by the King's men, who would destroy the individual liberties of Englishmen. The Parliamentary contests of the sixties were fought primarily over election petitions. CM's brother, John Sawbridge, was elected to Parliament as a Wilkite, but her position in the radical cause was the result of her own activity. She was its primary link to the more theoretically minded commonwealth men and became herself the most important spokesperson for the radical view. In 1770 she replied to Edmund Burke's pamphlet on the *Present Discontents* with *Observations on a pamphlet, entitled Thoughts on the Cause of the Present Discontents,* in which she attacked his solutions and proposed such measures as frequent elections, extension of the suffrage, and elimination of placemen. Her final effort for the Wilkite cause was the pamphlet of 1775, *Address to the People of England . . . on the Present Important Crisis of Affairs.* The crisis was the one in America; CM and her friends were sympathetic to the American cause and had many correspondents in the Colonies. Among those with whom she exchanged letters and views were John and ABIGAIL ADAMS, MERCY OTIS WARREN, Ben-

jamin Rush, and Ezra Stiles. CM was the only woman pamphleteer active in the political controversies of the sixties and seventies.

In the early 1770s, CM closed her radical salon in London and in 1774 settled in Bath. The same year she published her least effective work, *A Modest Plea for the Property of Copyright.* At the spa she lived in the house of the Rev. Dr. Thomas Wilson, the absentee rector of St. Stephen Walbrook in London and also a Wilkite. There was much gossip about the relationship of CM and Wilson. In 1777 he staged an elaborate birthday celebration for "the female Thucydides," as she was often called. Another participant in the party was Dr. John Graham, who was one of Bath's leading quacks. Wilson climaxed his honoring of CM by erecting a marble statue of her as Clio in the chancel of his London church. (This statue, removed from the church in 1779, is now in the Warrington, Lancs., Town Hall.) In 1778 she dedicated to Wilson the first volume of a new work, *History of England from the Revolution to the Present Time.* This work was critical of William III, Robert Walpole, and others in the Whig hierarchy; it was poorly received, and she wrote no more of it. At the end of 1778 CM left Bath to become the bride of William Graham, brother of John and 26 years her junior, a step even more unforgiveable in the public's eye than her liaison with Wilson. From this point on, it is difficult to find any favorable mention of her by a Briton.

The Grahams lived in Leicestershire where CM completed her *History . . . from the Accession of James I* and in 1783 published *A Treatise on the Immutability of Moral Truth.* In 1784 the couple went to the U.S. for about a year. Americans were much more hospitable and admiring than the Grahams' countrymen. An especially close relationship developed between CM and Mercy Otis Warren. The Grahams visited in Boston and New York and spent ten days with Washington at Mount Vernon. After their departure from the U.S. they probably spent some time in France before settling in London in 1787. They moved to Binfield, Berks., in 1788. Warren suggested CM might write a history of the American Revolution, but the Englishwoman replied that "my present thoughts are employed on education." In 1790 her *Letters on Education* appeared. The beginning of the French Revolution took CM back to politics; her last work was a reply to Burke, *Observations on the Reflections of . . . Burke on the Revolution in France* (1791), of which she mailed copies to her American friends shortly before her death.

In her own time CM was most widely known for her *History . . . from the Accession of James I* and her political pamphlets. The *History* was generally regarded as the best counter to David Hume's *History of Great Britain,* the main Tory version. Later writers have usually made Smollett's *History* the answer to Hume, but their contemporaries chose CM. Hers was the first history of the 17th century written by a woman and by a republican. There was of course considerable amazement that a woman would write such straightforward constitutional history rather than court gossip. She used and cited contemporary documents and pamphlets, many of which came from Thomas Hollis or from collections in the British Museum. Within the framework of her republican ideas, she did not shy away from judgments or conclusions; her friends were dismayed both by her sympathetic account of the death of Charles I (although she condemned all his policies) and by her view of Cromwell, "the most corrupt and selfish being that ever disgraced human form," who killed the Commonwealth, "the brightest age that ever adorned the page of history." The sources for her ideas about government were her wide reading in Greek and Roman history and in the 17th-century political theorists, especially James Harrington. Her real hero was the people, intelligent and rational, who should determine what government exists. "To plan a form of government perfect in its nature, and consequently answering all its just ends, is neither morally impossible in itself, nor beyond the abilities of man," she wrote in *Observations on the Present Discontents.* This pamphlet, like *Loose Remarks, Address to the People,* and *Observations on the Reflections,* is written from the same philosophical base as the *History,* applied in the shorter works to contemporary events.

In the 19th century CM was hardly known. The triumph of Tory ideas, the failure of the Wilkite and other 18th-century political reformers, and the new conditions of industrialization all pushed the views of CM and her friends into obscurity. If she was remembered at all, it was through the unkind Tory remarks of Dr. Johnson, James Boswell, HANNAH MORE, and others.

Most accounts of 18th-century historiography simply ignored her, or at best condemned her for being unscientific. Since no 18th-century historian was "scientific" in the modern sense, there was no reason, except her sex, to single her out. Her best press came from those writing about the American Revolution; her correspondence with American leaders and her defense of the Colonies usually earned her at least a brief mention. Recent interest in CM has centered on her *Letters on Education,* partly concerned with theology (the subtitle is *with Observations on Religious and Metaphysical Subjects,* a revision of the earlier *Treatise on Moral Truth*). Here for the first time CM appeared in print as a feminist. She said that the only difference in the sexes is physical, "there is but one rule of right for the conduct of all rational beings; consequently that true virtue in one sex must be equally so in the other." If boys and girls were to be educated in the same way, women would not be inferior or subject to men in any way, for the "vices and imperfections" generally attributed to women are not sexual in origin, but "entirely the effects of situation and education." The reforms she proposed were not simply to educate girls like boys; all education should be changed. Boys should be taught needlework, girls sports; both should read the same books and learn the same languages. In this way, "both sexes will find, that friendship may be enjoyed between them without passion." When the time comes to marry, "Your sons will look for something more solid in women than a mere outside"; daughters will not seek male admiration simply by coquetry and ornamental graces. The new plan of education would reform both men and women and thus society. It is not surprising that MARY WOLLSTONECRAFT admired the *Letters;* she discussed it in *Vindication* and at length in the *Analytical Review.*   B.B.S.

MacCARTHY, Charlotte (fl. 1745–68), novelist and religious writer, left few memorials of her life save scattered references in her five known works. Her early life was spent in Ireland. Her father, a gentleman "who had served the government justly, near fifty years," died when she was young, leaving her destitute. She recounts a miraculous religious experience undergone while sitting up all night with her mother's body. A lone Protestant child, frightened at the threats of Catholic children, she was later convinced that a Jesuit, by deliberately poisoning her, had ruined her health and earning capacity. At one time she gave lessons to young ladies. CM's earliest known publication, *The Fair Moralist* (1745), was her best known. A pastoral romance with romantic passions, seduction, betrayal, reversals, and discoveries, the novel is moralistic but includes illicit affairs, the rehabilitation of a fallen woman, and a lively, indecorous, Boccaccio-like episode. The volume also contains some competent occasional poetry. A second edition of the work (1746) includes a preface by CM expressing her surprise at the novel's popularity, and the addition of a few more poems, as well as "The Author's Observations: or, A Looking-Glass for the Fair Sex," incorporating advice against such feminine pitfalls as gossip, censure, fashion, fortune-telling, whining, cruelty, and revenge. In the summer of 1749 CM's lodgings next door to the theaters in Twickenham and Richmond were noted in newspaper advertisements as the place of ticket sales for the company playing in both villages alternately. Conceivably CM was the author of the company's "Celia, or the Perjured Lover," but the play apparently reached neither London nor a publisher's. CM's next known published work, *News from Parnassus,* was a slight ballad addressed to the Duke of Bedford while Lord Lieutenant of Ireland (Dublin, 1757). A note at the end announces CM's *Justice and Reason, Faithful Guides to Truth* as ready for the press. That book, dedicated to George III, did not appear until 1767. In 1765, CM published in London *The Author and Bookseller,* a short dramatic piece explaining why the booksellers would not undertake *Justice and Reason,* as prelude to proposals for issuing it by subscription. The subscription list includes more than 800 names, most of them those of merchants. Unable to publish her work in Ireland, CM had collected subscriptions there to pay her way to England, and had proceeded by collecting in Liverpool, Chester, Manchester, then London, visiting shopkeepers as most easy of access. *Justice and Reason,* "the effusions of a chimerical imagination . . . thrown together in a promiscuous manner" *(Critical Review),* consists of short sermonical chapters that argue against various vices and Roman Catholicism. "Letters Moral and Entertaining" concludes the volume. *CR* and *Monthly Review* both attribute to CM as well *A Letter from a Lady to the Bishop of London* (1768), signed "Prudentia Christiania," in which the author attributes the badly fallen moral state of England to the effects of the methodistical endorsement of faith without works. *MR* found this pamphlet "most singular." Despite her eccentricities, extravagance of opinion, and often unrestrained imagination, CM's argumentative style is plain and clear. She displays in her first two works a refreshing coarseness unusual in women writers of the time, and had, despite her piety, an irrepressibly strong streak of humor, as when she anticipates *The Screwtape Letters* in "From a Daemon, to his Friend in the Infernal Regions," in "Letters Moral and Entertaining." She usually signed her works and did not apologize for being a woman author: "I am neither weak, nor superstitious: no, not even so much as most Men are." Her fate after 1768 is unknown.   B.R.

MACKENZIE, Anna Maria (fl. 1783–1811), novelist, was the daughter of an Essex coal merchant, Wight. She married a gentleman called Cox, who died after having been duped out of most of his assets, leaving his widow and four children dependent on relatives. AMM became an assistant at a ladies' boarding school, a position she left to take up writing. While she spoke of her "confined education," her teaching position and her knowledge of history suggest that she was as well-educated as most middle-class women of her time. Friends reportedly considered her "pleasing in conversation" and remarked on the "justness of her repartee." AMM herself speaks of her love of writing. Although she is reported to have written essays for a variety of magazines, it was as a novelist that she achieved success. Her first novel, *Burton Wood,* was published in 1783. Some of her works were published anonymously, but title pages, signed prefaces and dedications, and comments of reviewers make it possible to follow to some extent her literary and marital career. By 1789 she was writing as Mrs. Johnson and by 1795 as Mrs. Mackenzie. She published *The Neapolitan* (1796) under the pseudonym Ellen of Exeter. While at least 16 novels can be attributed to her, she mentions in her preface to *Feudal Events, or, Days of Yore* (1800) that she had by that time published 28 volumes.

AMM wrote primarily for William Lane and his circulating libraries, and she had a good appreciation of what her readers wanted. She wrote sentimental and romantic fiction, at times verging on the gothic, and moved into the newly popular area of historical fiction. Her most popular novels mingle romance and adventure with history including elements of mystery and surprise, sometimes improbable events and coincidences, and the usual instances of mistaken identity and episodes of cruelty and horror. Most of her novels are long, with many subplots and stereotyped characters. *Monmouth: A Tale, Founded on Historical Facts* (1790) is better than most library novels in its sympathetic portrayal of Monmouth as brilliant and imprudent. *Slavery: or, The Times* (1793), also somewhat better than the usual library novel, contains romance and suspense and, in its story of the education in England of a young African prince, gives a Rousseauistic depiction of the noble savage in corrupt society; it comes out strongly against slavery. *The Danish Massacre; an Historical Fact* (1791), set in the time of Ethelred, is told from the viewpoints of both Britons and Danes, the scene shifting back and forth by means of lengthy journals and letters; it is a bleak tale of bloodshed, cruelty and death. A later novel, *The Irish Guardian; or Errors of Eccentricity* (1809), merits attention because of the character of the "Irish Guardian," a bluff, good-hearted, courageous Irishman who complicates the plot and aggravates the problems by his imprudence and quick temper. The Irishman speaks in dialect and provides an element of humor, a characteristic lacking in most of AMM's works.

Many of AMM's novels received lengthy reviews. The *Critical Review* (Oct. 1789) gives the early *Calista* (1789) high praise: "We have not in our late career, met with many better works, and few which possess so much merit, or which we can with less exception recommend." The *Monthly Review* praises *Mysteries Elucidated* (1795), set in the reign of Edward II, as "diversified by pleasing description, and told in correct language," and commends the author for having "successfully combined a series of perplexing and mysterious events, which are in the same issue happily disentangled and elucidated." *MR* also praises the "natural and animated language" of *Slavery; or, The Times,* but finds (Oct. 1797) that *The Neapolitan* "drags heavily, with tedious minuteness." It is AMM's gothic tendencies which *CR* most dislikes, commenting that *The Neapolitan* consists of detached scenes of horror, cruelty, and revenge; it notes the author's "Radcliffian manner" and (in Oct. 1798) criticizes *Dusseldorf; or, the Fratricide* (1798) as an imitation of ANN RADCLIFFE: "but she is far from being equal to that lady in this branch of composition." *CR* had earlier objected to *Orlando and Lavinia* (1792) because the heroine "though the victim of seduction is raised to the highest rank." Writing in the age of proliferating, poorly written sentimental fiction, AMM at times stands out from the crowd in her adroit blending of fiction and historical fact, and in her developing skill in structuring her novels, shifting scenes, and weaving together complicated plots. As she so frequently states in her prefaces, her writing always defends virtue and preaches morality. She rightly says that, while some of her contemporaries left her "quite in the shade," her novels "were at least harmless."   L.M.

MADAN, Judith (1702–81), poet, was the only daughter of Judge Spencer Cowper, MP, and Pennington Goodere. Judge Cowper, younger brother of the first Earl Cowper, Lord Chancellor, also served as Attorney General to George II. John, the third of Judith's four brothers and father of the poet William Cowper, served as chaplain to George II. While living on the family estate, Hertingfordbury Park, near Hertford, JM began corresponding with Alexander Pope through a common friend, Henrietta Howard, later the Countess of Suffolk. This correspondence continued for more than a year, between 1722 and 1723, but there is no evidence that the two poets ever met. The letters to JM were published in 1769 as *Letters to a Young Lady*. In 1723 JM married Captain Martin Madan, a career officer whose duties, which later included a period as Equerry to Frederick, Prince of Wales, kept him from home for long periods. After marriage she continued to live with her parents. The first of her nine children (two daughters and seven sons) was born at their town house in Bond Street, London. On the death of JM's mother in 1727, the Madans moved to London and in 1745 bought a house in Bond Street, only one year before Martin retired with the rank of Colonel. Throughout his life Martin Madan was a poor money manager and he never provided JM with the personal allowance of 100 guineas per year specified in her marriage settlement. Despite financial problems and long periods of separation, the marriage appears to have been a very happy one. JM converted to Methodism prior to her husband's death in 1756, and after that date she spent an increasing amount of time with her Methodist friends, who included the COUNTESS OF HUNTING-

DON and John Wesley. JM was buried at Grosvenor Chapel, Mount Street, Grosvenor Square.

Although only five of JM's poems have been published, 45 exist in manuscript, 22 of which were written before her marriage. "Verses Written in Her Brother's Coke Upon Littleton," a witty 14-line poem, appeared anonymously in a 1721 issue of the *Free-Thinker.* "Abelard to Eloisa," a 178-line response to Pope's "Eloisa to Abelard," written by JM in 1720, was included in the posthumous works of William Pattison, published in 1728. A year later James Ralph published the 87-line "To the Memory of John Hughes" in his *Miscellaneous Poems by Several Hands.* This poem was also included in *The Flower-Piece: A Collection of Miscellany Poems* (1731), John Hughes' *Poems* (1735) and F. Fawkes' *Poetical Calendar* (1764). JM's most ambitious work, "The Progress of Poetry," was first published in 1731 in *The Flower-Piece.* This poem, 264 lines of heroic couplets, is a revised and expanded form of a 1721 composition; Dodsley's 1783 edition of the poem is the earlier unrevised version. JM's poems first appeared under her name in *Poems by Eminent Ladies* (1755; 1757) and Dodsley's *Collection of Poems by Several Hands* (1766). "A Funeral Hymn" was published in her son Martin's *Hymns* (2nd edition, 1763, and later editions). Attributed to her is a poem in Dodsley's 1758 *Collection,* "A Fit of the Spleen, In Imitation of Shakespear," but this work is not on the list of manuscript poems. "Abelard to Eloisa" focuses upon Abelard's conflicting emotions: "My tortur'd heart conflicting passions move, / I hope, despair, repent—yet still I love." The poem rivaled Pope's in popularity and appeared in *Letters of Abelard and Heloise . . . To which are now added The Poems of Eloisa to Abelard, by Mr. Pope, And Abelard to Eloisa, by Mrs. Madan . . .* 11th edition (London, 1773). JM apparently was also a prolific letter writer, and about 500 letters to her husband and her elder daughter, Maria, exist in manuscript.

Apart from the long poems, most of JM's works are either occasional verse or love poems addressed to her husband; her most common form is the heroic couplet, clearly modeled after Pope. John Duncombe mentions her in *The Feminead; or Female Genius* (1751), and says of "The Progress of Poetry": "Praise well-bestow'd adorns her glowing lines, / And manly strength to female softness joins." Commenting on "Abelard to Eloisa," the editor of *Poems by Eminent Ladies* states: "A very affecting tenderness runs through the whole epistle from Abelard, and whether we consider the numbers, diction, or sentiments, it is certainly much superior to all those pieces that have appeared on the same subject; and indeed this Lady's Abelard is no mean companion to Pope's *Eloisa.*" Dodsley's 1783 edition of the unrevised "Progress of Poetry" received mixed reviews, one critic stating: "He must be a very indulgent critic, who can discover either fancy or invention in it; or who can think the characters not faintly and imperfectly drawn. It is in short little better than a muster-roll of some of the principal poets in chronological order, from Homer down to Granville and Rowe" (*Monthly Review* 68, 1785). Another reviewer comments: "In the present performance . . . we look in vain for brilliancy of fancy or originality of thought; but if pure description, perspicuity, and an easy flow of verse, entitle a writer to approbation, she deserves it." This reviewer particularly praises the lines on Addison even though he believes that Addison, in addition to Garth and Denham, "has no right to be enrolled in the list of our first-rate poets" (*Critical Review* 55, 1783). Much of JM's later work was deeply religious in tone. Her daughter, MARIA COWPER, recited her mother's funeral hymn, "In this world of sin and sorrow," on her deathbed.   J.F.

MAKIN[S], Bathsua [Pell] (1612?–1674?), polemical writer and educational reformer, was born into an educated, upper-class family, the only daughter of John Pell, a rector in Southwick, Sussex, and Elizabeth(?) Holland. Both parents died before BM was ten years old. Thomas, her brother, was appointed gentleman of the bedchamber of Charles I. In 1635 he left for America. John, the younger brother, became an esteemed mathematician and fellow of the Royal Society. A 1668 letter bearing BM's signature mentions her husband, Makin, and their unnamed son. BM's substantial correspondence with her brother John documents some of her proposals and activities concerning the education of young girls of the English gentry. Other facts of her life substantiate her reputation as a female disputant and learned lady. About 1641, BM was appointed tutor to Princess Elizabeth, the six-year-old daughter of Charles I. Most of BM's adult life was spent in the arena of educational and social reform. A vague reference in John Evelyn's *Diary* for April 1649 suggests that she may have been the superintendent of the exclusive Putney School for young English gentlewomen. In her seminal work, *An Essay to Revive the Antient Education of Gentlewomen* (1673), she states that she is the governess of a newly opened experimental school for young women of the upper classes, located four miles outside of London at Tottenham High Cross. Combining features of the "masculine" and "feminine" curricula of the day, the new school offered a larger, more advanced curriculum than that at Putney. The curriculum BM designed offered the standard "female" classes in domestic arts, singing, dancing, music, writing, reading, and basic arithmetic, and subjects before offered only to boys, languages (Latin, Greek, Hebrew, Italian, French, and Spanish, all of which BM knew), astronomy, geography, botany, and experimental philosophy. BM's impressive circle of associates included such well-educated women as Lady Elizabeth Langham, daughter of the Earl of Huntingdon and wife of Sir James Langham. BM celebrates Lady Langham's wit and beauty in an elegy on her death in 1664, "she/In Latin, French, Italian happily Advanc'd with pleasure." BM may have been associated with John Dunton and his circle of "Athenians," which included ELIZABETH ROWE, the "Pindarick Lady." A reference in the *Athenian Mercury,* quite likely to BM'S *Essay,* begins, "A little tract that I have lately read, very much encouraged women to be studious" (I, 1690). A principal influence on BM was the celebrated "Virgin of Utrecht," ANNA MARIA VAN SCHURMAN (1607–78), considered the most universally accomplished woman scholar of the 17th century. It is likely that BM met Van Schurman through John Pell when he was professor of mathematics at Amsterdam and Van Schurman was studying in Utrecht. Undated letters in Greek between Van Schurman and BM document their friendship. Van Schurman's treatise on woman's intellectual capacity, *Dissertatio De Ingenii Muliebris ad Doctrinam et Meliores Litteras Aptitudine* (1641), was subsequently translated into English by C[lement] B[arksdale] as *The Learned Maid* (1659), possibly under BM's auspices.

Works attributed to BM include *The Malady and Remedy of Vexation and Unjust Arrests and Actions* (1646), "Upon the much lamented death of the Right Honourable, the Lady Elizabeth Langham" (1664), and *An Essay to Revive the Antient Education of Gentlewomen, In Religion, Manners, Arts & Tongues. With An Answer to the Objections against this Way of Education* (1673). Genres represented in her work include elegy, formal essay, and *dissertatio.* Unarguably, BM's *Essay* stands as the first published feminist statement in English belles lettres. A pamphlet of 43 pages, it attempts to correct and controvert repressive assumptions of the day concerning woman's intellect and place in society. Two major influences in BM's *Essay* are John Amos Komensky (Comenius), a Czech philosopher and educationist, who visited London in 1641–42, and Van Schurman, his disciple, who transmitted his proposals into English feminist ideology through BM. Countering the contemporary masculine ideal of passive English womanhood with an egalitarian feminine model, BM's *Essay* begins strenuously, "The Barbarous custom to breed Women low, is grown general amongst us, and hath prevailed so far, that it is verily believed (especially amongst a sort of debauched Sots) that Women are not endued with such Reason, as Men; nor capable of improvement by Education, as they are." Anticipating MARY ASTELL's *Serious Proposal* (1694), BM's *Essay* is programmatic in its approach to educational reform. In the "Proposal," BM presents a new model of female education, her own school at Tottenham High Cross. Drawing upon the scholastic organization of Van Schurman's *Dissertatio,* BM anticipates the reproaches of her opposition by creating an adversary who raises such objections as "It is against Custom to educate Gentlewomen thus; those that do attempt it will make themselves ridiculous." She neatly lists her interlocutor's several objections and answers them. The argumentative strategy BM employs is the authority of precedent. She lists historical and contemporary women of achievement, several educated along the classical lines she proposes. Organized around seven major headings, BM's *Essay* writes women back into history by celebrating outstanding women in the arts, languages, oratory, philosophy, logic, mathematics, and poetry. Two radical points BM raises are woman's ability to govern and her need to secure economic independence through education: "As for unmarried persons who are able to subsist without a dependance, they have a fairer opportunity than men, if they continue long in that estate." BM's interest in reform also extended to social conditions. In an earlier essay, *Arrests and Actions* (1646), possibly occasioned by the imprisonment of her impecunious brother, John Pell, she appeals to Parliament to repeal laws calling for the imprisonment of debtors. While her pleas went unanswered, her essay illustrates an understanding of larger social issues: "Speedily . . . provide some good and wholesome laws for the preventions and utter abolishing of all vexations and unjust actions and arrests for pretended debts, by which many thousands families are undone, and many able and well-minded men at this day cast and lie in the devouring prisons under a miserable servitude and oppression." BM is a crucial figure in the evolution of early English feminist ideology, especially as it concerns educational opportunities for women. Her early *Essay* pointed the way for subsequent feminist discourse by MARY ASTELL, HANNAH WOOLLEY, John Locke, Nahum Tate, and Daniel Defoe, all of whom challenged contemporary notions of woman's inferiority to men by demonstrating that *femina rationis capax.* M.M.

MANLEY, [Mary] Delarivière (1663–1724), author of "scandal novels," political tracts, plays, and poetry, was born in Jersey, the daughter of Sir Roger Manley, who fought for Charles I and was made Lieutenant-Governor of the island under Charles II. He was also the author of a history of the wars in Denmark, 1657–60, and a Latin work, *De Rebellione* (1686). The only source for many of the details of DM's early life is her fictionalized autobiography, *The Adventures of Rivella; or, the History of the Author of the Atalantis* (1714). She writes that she was educated at home, where she was strictly chaperoned. She did, however, spend a short time with one of her two brothers at the house of a Huguenot minister, learning French. DM had the misfortune to be born plain between two sisters who were handsome. As a child she was marked by smallpox and tended to put on weight easily. Later in life she became extremely corpulent. When her father died in 1688, he left her an orphan with £200 and a share in the estate. About this time she was seduced into a bigamous marriage by her cousin John Manley, and bore him a child. When he left her, she went to live for a time in the household of the Duchess of Cleveland, where she doubtless picked up much gossip which she later used in her books. The Duchess soon quarreled with her on the pretense that she had in-

trigued with her son, and in 1694 DM retired for two years to Exeter and other places, during which time she wrote two plays. Both were put on in the same year, 1696, after some contention between managers. Her comedy, *The Lost Lover, or the Jealous Husband,* appeared first; written in seven days, and acted at Drury Lane, it was not a success. Her tragedy, *The Royal Mischief,* was brought out by Betterton at Lincoln's Inn Fields, and fared better. Following this DM had affairs with Sir Thomas Skipwith of Drury Lane Theatre and John Tilly, Warden of the Fleet. In 1705, DM, together with Mary Thompson, a woman of bad character, was involved in an attempt to obtain money from the estate of a man named Pheasant. She also pursued her literary career and became renowned for her wit and conversation. Society often misrepresented her, and DM had no compunction in slandering many people of note in her works, especially those who were also Whigs. On 29 October 1709, following the appearance of her most famous book, *Secret Memoirs and Manners of Several Persons of Quality, of both Sexes. From the New Atalantis,* she was arrested, together with the two publishers and the printer. Her own account is that she acknowledged herself to be the author in order to free the others. They were released on 1 November, and DM was granted bail on 5 November. When examined, she refused to disclose the source of her information, declaring that if indeed her book referred to particular characters, it must have been by inspiration. The case was dismissed on 13 February 1710. DM was involved in other disputes. She fell out with Richard Steele when he repaid her friendship with ingratitude, and when he refused assistance when she was in financial trouble. She attacked him in *New Atalantis* and was in turn attacked by Swift in *Tatler* no. 63. Steele denied writing the paper and confessed his earlier debt to DM. When DM published *Memoirs of Europe towards the Close of the Eighth Century* in 1710, she dedicated the work to Isaac Bickerstaff, i.e., Steele, printed his denial, with alterations, and added fresh accusations. The return of the Tories to power in 1711 brought better times to DM. In June 1711 she succeeded Swift as editor of *The Examiner* and, in July, Swift seconded her application to Lord Peterborough for some reward for her service to the Tory cause by writing *New Atalantis* and suffering imprisonment. In January 1712, DM was ill with dropsy and a sore leg. Swift wrote: "I am heartily sorry for her, she has very generous principles for one of her sort, and a great deal of good sense and invention." In May 1713, when Steele quarreled with Swift, he attacked DM in *Guardian* no. 53. She retaliated in her next two political works, *The Honour and Prerogative of the Queen's Majesty Vindicated,* 14 August, and *A Modest Enquiry,* 4 February 1714. She was eventually reconciled with Steele and dedicated her last play to him, with apologies for her previous attacks. This was *Lucius, or the First Christian King of Great Britain,* brought out at Drury Lane on 11 May 1717. Steele in turn wrote a prologue for the play. DM had been living for some years as the mistress of "Alderman" Barber, who treated her badly, although he benefited from her assistance in various ways. She died at Barber's printing house on Lambeth Hill and was buried at St. Benet's, Paul's Wharf. Her will (1723) describes her as being of Berkeley, Oxfordshire, where she had a house, and as "daily decaying in strength," so she had been ill for some time. In her will she refers to Swift as "her much honoured friend."

DM began as an author with her two plays: *The Lost Lover,* in prose, and *The Royal Mischief,* in blank verse. While these were being rehearsed, in 1696, her first work of fiction, *Letters written by Mrs. Manley,* was printed without her knowledge. DM suppressed the book, and authorized it to be published only after her death, when it appeared under the title *A Stage-Coach Journey to Exeter* (1725). DM was influenced by French fiction, the *chronique scandaleuse* and the *roman à clef,* then in vogue. Her first work of this nature was *The Secret History of Queen Zarah and the Zarazians* (1705), a straightforward satire on the DUCHESS OF MARLBOROUGH. The preface testifies to the change in market for prose narrative, to a distaste for long-winded heroic romance, and a preference for "little Histories" of the sort offered. DM recommends plainness of style and verisimilitude, indicating the limited capacities of an expanding readership rather than a movement toward modern realism. Her "History" still depends for its effects on stylized scenes familiar in romances, as do her later scandal novels. The work was so successful that "Zarah" and "Zarazians" became popular epithets for the Duchess and her political associates. DM's *New Atalantis,* published in 1709, was also extremely popular. A second volume followed in the same year, and the work went through seven editions as well as a French version printed at the Hague, 1713–16. It is poorly constructed and obviously written at top speed in the same ranting style of her earlier book. Yet the public was diverted, as the number of references to *New Atalantis* in the literature of the period testifies. Pope refers to it in *The Rape of the Lock,* and LADY MARY WORTLEY MONTAGU was concerned when the "unfortunate authoress" was taken into custody. *New Atalantis* also had a specific political aim: to attack prominent Whigs and praise the Tories. Yet the popularity of the work outlasted its notoriety because DM's themes were drawn from widely held assumptions concerning contemporary society. She dramatized the conflict between the aristocracy and the middle classes; she also exploited the popular mythology of innocent maiden seduced by aristocratic libertine. Her familiar themes smoothed the reader's entry into her fantasy world, while the erotic details with which she embroidered the narrative satisfied the basic demand that fiction supply a love-interest. In 1752 DM was still praised for the "peculiar vivacity" with which she treated "the passion of love." Her reputation, however, was more securely based on her portrayal of opposing moral values, distorted by Toryism and the clichés of romance, but rooted in basic economic realities. In *New Atalantis,* she concludes her satire on the first Earl of Portland (who has seduced and deserted a friend's daughter entrusted to his care) with a moral comment: "The remainder of her Life was one continu'd Scene of Horror, Sorrow, and Repentance. She dy'd a true Landmark, to warn all believing Virgins from Ship-wracking their Honour upon (that dangerous Coast of Rocks) the Vows and pretended Passion of Mankind." DM wrote her own sequel to this work in 1710: *Memoirs of Europe, Towards the Close of the Eighth Century. Written by Eginardus, Secretary and Favourite to Charlemagne; And done into English by the Translator of the New Atalantis.* This sequel was printed in 1720 and 1736 as volumes III and IV of a four-volumed work called simply the *New Atalantis.* In 1711 she brought out *Court Intrigues in a Collection of Original Letters from the Island of New Atalantis* in which again her political design gives unity to her racy scandals. In the same year Defoe published a brief political tract called *Atalantis*

Major in which he refers (perhaps ironically) to the great success and usefulness of the *New Atalantis.* DM's career as a political hack was furthered when she took over the editorship of *The Examiner.* Already, in April 1711, she had written *A True Narrative of what passed at the Examination of the Marquis de Guiscard . . .* , which concerned Guiscard's attempt to murder Harley. She worked from notes given her by Swift, who revised the whole, but who did not wish his name to appear on the title page. Later in 1711 DM published other political pamphlets: *A Learned Comment on Dr. Hare's . . . Sermon, A True Relation of the Several Facts and Circumstances of the Intended Riot and Tumult on Queen Elizabeth's birthday* (widely but erroneously attributed to Swift, who may have supervised it), and *The Duke of M- - -h's Vindication.* The last shows her growing proficiency in this kind of writing, and Swift says it was entirely her own work. In 1713 she wrote *The Honour and Prerogative of the Queen's Majesty Vindicated,* sometimes attributed to Defoe, and in 1714 *A Modest Enquiry,* a pamphlet in dialogue form which accuses certain Whigs of preparing to take advantage of the precarious political situation during the Queen's last illness. In 1714 DM also published *The Adventures of Rivella; or, the History of the Author of the Atalantis.* This was reissued for E. Curll in 1717 under the title *Memoirs of Mrs Manley. Containing not only the history of her adventures but likewise an account of the most considerable amours in the Court of King Charles IId.* A key was included at the end. In 1725, after DM's death, a fourth edition of *The Adventures of Rivella* was printed under the title *Mrs Manley's History of her own Life and Times.* In an address to the reader, Curll explains how the work came to be written. In 1714 Mr. Gildon, out of pique, wrote an account of DM's life, but two sheets only had been printed when she heard it was in the press. Suspecting that it was an invective on her conduct (as it was), she arranged a meeting with Gildon through Curll which led to a suppression of the work. In return DM promised to write her own history, which she completed in secret and in great haste. The work, published under a pseudonym, is in the form of a conversation and purports to be a translation from the French. This disguise was adopted because DM thought "though the World may like what I write of others, they despise whatever an Author is thought

to say of themselves," and she insisted that the secret of authorship be kept during her lifetime. The work appears to be an honest one. DM does not make light of her faults, nor does she make extravagent claims for her obvious generosity and loyalty to friends. The speaker notes that there is much to praise and blame in DM's conduct, yet she was often heard to say, "if she had been a Man, she had been without fault." She recognized with a sense of injustice that "what is not a crime in Men is scandalous and unpardonable in woman." DM showed concern at the position of women in society in two tragedies in blank verse, *Almyna: or the Arabian Vow* (1707), and *Lucius, the first Christian King of Britain* (1717). Both plays have a strong love interest and demonstrate male prejudice and men's willingness to exploit women. DM's religious and patriotic statements in these plays are orthodox and conservative; in her scandal novels she often paused to denounce the immorality of the age, using the conservative rhetoric natural to a Tory propagandist: "Did Mankind confine themselves only to what was necessary, reasonable, or proper, there would indeed be no occasion for most part of the great Expence they are at" *(New Atalantis).* In 1720 DM published *The Power of Love in Seven Novels,* affirming in the dedication that some of these short chronicles are founded on truth but that "divers new Incidents" have been added. Once again these tales show her facility for mixing romance, intrigue, and scandal. In the same year verses by her appeared in Antony Hammond's *A New Miscellany of Original Poems.* Many of these are complimentary verses, short, composed in simple lyric metres, but fluent and lively. At her death DM left a MS tragedy called *The Duke of Somerset* and a comedy, *The Double Mistress.* She is also credited with contributions to *The Female Tatler* (1709), with *Bath Intrigues: in four letters to a friend in London* (1725), and with *The Court Legacy,* a ballad opera (1733). Her main achievement was to naturalize the French "chronique scandaleuse" to the political controversies of the day, and during the first two decades of the century she had no living rival in the production of amatory fiction. As for her style, Swift wrote to Addison (August 1710) that it seemed "as if she had about two thousand epithets and fine words packed up in a bag, and that she pulled them out by handfuls, and strewed them on her paper, where about once in five hundred times they happen to be right." M.S.

MANNERS, Catherine Rebecca [Grey], Lady (1766?–1852), poet, came from Cork, Ireland. She married William Manners, afterwards Talmash, Lord Huntingtower of Leicester, in 1790, and was buried at Leamington, Warwick. CM published two volumes of poetry. *Poems* (1793) shows a romantic sensibility; it consists of moralistic tales of lovers in Norman times, nostalgic Irish landscapes, and contemplative odes to Solitude, Virtue, and delusive Hope. Language and versification are simple and melodious. The *Gentleman's Magazine* called CM a "most accomplished lady." On her second volume, *Poetry, Ancient and Modern* (1799) it noted that CM characterizes succinctly the thematic and moral concerns of poets from "matchless Homer" to "enlightened Johnson." The extensive catalogue of ancient poets, including Pindar, Theocritus, Lucretius, and Tasso, and English poets since Chaucer, reveals discerning intelligence and wide reading. Poetry is enlisted to lead the way to moral truth; "Addison's enlighten'd page / Charm'd while it reformed the age"; and "Piety's seraphic flame / Mark(s) enlighten'd Johnson's name" (*GM*, Aug. 1799). G.B.

MARISHALL, Jean (fl. 1766–89), novelist, first published an epistolary novel, *The History of Miss Clarinda Cathcart, and Miss Fanny Renton* (1766). She was later to record how, on journeying south to London for the first time in the sixties, she had failed to attract a higher offer than five guineas for the novel; and her even greater mortification when, on presenting the Queen with a copy, she received ten guineas instead of the expected patronage: "Ambition lay crushed under the weight of Disappointment, and Hope durst not venture to show her face." Undeterred for long, however, she published another novel, *The History of Alicia Montague,* the following year. She made an unsuccessful venture into drama with *Sir Harry Gaylove; or, Comedy in Embryo* (1772), which was never performed. *A Series of Letters* (1789) appears to have been her last work. *Clarinda Cathcart* deals with the social comings and goings of a spirited girl confined to the country for four months to stay with a maiden aunt, much to her displeasure: "I am already arrived at the age of eighteen, and have never had one serious lover, nor ever been once se-

riously in love." It is a piece of respectable matrimonial foreplay which is never allowed to get out of hand. *Alicia Montague* is in a similar vein, although the heroine, an orphan, is more passive and self-abasing. She admonishes herself for entertaining thoughts of Lord L.: "Could I ever look up with consciousness of doing what I ought, were I to encourage his addresses? I, who am a poor unhappy orphan, who have no relation to countenance me, and am a humble dependant on his aunt's bounty." *Critical Review* (Mar. 1767) found her "a young lady of a most amiable character" and thought the other characters, "though not drawn in such full proportions," to be "supported with sufficient propriety, and represented in colours abundantly expressive." *Sir Harry Gaylove* is a play in the sentimentalised Restoration ethos current in the 18th century. Of the *Letters,* a substantial number are written to "a young gentleman who had been eight years under her care," and are as banal as any such letters: fault-finding, gentle reprimands, etc. Others, written for publication, range in subject-matter from parental responsibilities to the organization of the state. On marriage she comments that "were we to live in common, we should soon degenerate into creatures the most wretched that can be conceived. All right to succession must necessarily cease, and sloth and indolence be the undoubted consequence." She displays in these letters, which are probably her best work, an adventurous if limited intelligence. R.J.

MARLBOROUGH, Sarah Churchill, Duchess of (1660–1744), essayist, letter writer, and politician, was born in a suburb of St. Albans, Herts., the last of nine children. Her father, Mr. Jennings, was the owner of the Sandridge estate and, by some accounts, a locally influential politician. Mrs. Jennings, the daughter of Sir Gifford Thornhurst, was responsible for the prudent introduction of two of her daughters into court society as maids of honor to Anne Hyde, the Duchess of York. After the Duchess's death, D of M continued to serve her successor, the Princess of Modena, during which time she became the intimate of Lady Anne, the daughter of Anne Hyde. Independent and headstrong, D of M demonstrated a precocious ability to manipulate other people when, in 1676, she compelled the Duchess to expel Mrs. Jennings from court. D of M determined to marry John Churchill, the son of Sir Winston Churchill.

Neither had any money, but they were both opportunists and were very much in love. She dissuaded John from a more economically sound match and, aided by the Duchess, they married secretly in 1678. During the years 1679–90 D of M bore eight children, five of whom survived infancy—four daughters and one son. Despite her busy household, D of M continued to be the confidante of Princess Anne, who devised the pseudonyms "Mrs. Morley" and "Mrs. Freeman" for herself and D of M, respectively, that they might better converse as equals. The politicization of the Churchills began with their marriage, and by 1685 D of M had become the highly influential First Lady of the Bedchamber, while John had become a Gentleman of the Bedchamber to King James, who named him Baron Churchill of Sandridge. In 1688, upon the coronation of William of Orange, the Churchills' religious opportunism and foresight—they hid themselves and Princess Anne during the exile of Roman Catholic James—earned John the positions of Earl and Privy Councillor. During the early 1690s their fortunes reversed when John attempted to reingratiate himself with the exiled James; he was stripped of his posts and sent to the Tower. After Queen Mary's death in 1694, William was reconciled with Anne, who had left court to defend D of M's continued presence during John's disgrace. Subsequently, William was reconciled with John himself. The year 1702 marked the acme of their political influence during which D of M prevailed as a warring Whig alone among a majority of antiwar Tories. Her influence over Queen Anne prevented the cessation of the War of Spanish Succession which John was conducting. The Churchills' subsequent financial and titular rewards were excessive: D of M, for example, added £1,500 per year to the £6,000 she received already, plus an annuity of £5,000 for life to sustain the expenses of John's dukedom. In 1703 their fortunes soured again, this time because D of M tired of being Anne's confidante and carelessly absented herself from court too often. Anne began to favor D of M's cousin, Abigail Hill, as D of M's replacement. Abigail, in turn, conspired with Robert Harley to undermine D of M's influence and to purge the Whigs from court. To her credit, Anne appealed to D of M and the Duke of Marlborough to renew their loyalty, but when D of M responded, it was only to be tactless. The Marlboroughs fell out

of favor, and D of M was much maligned and lampooned by Tory pamphleteers. In 1710 she at last tried to appeal to Anne, but they parted bitterly without a reconciliation. Meanwhile, the ministry was yielded to the Tories and so the Marlboroughs lost all political advantage. Although both appealed humbly and often, Anne refused to listen and she demanded the return of the golden key of the Mistress of the Robes, ending forever D of M's influence. In 1711 John was dismissed from all his posts and the wearied Marlboroughs decided to live abroad, possibly in John's Bavarian principality. In 1714 they returned to England on the day of Queen Anne's death and, thanks to John's ingratiating efforts toward the Electorate, were again welcomed. The Duke died in 1722 and D of M survived him by another 22 years, descending to a series of bitter quarrels with family, friends, public personages, and pamphleteers. Despite two attractive marriage offers, she preferred to remain a widow. Her outspokenness and toughness created a trail of celebrated detractors, including Robert Walpole and Dr. Johnson, and defenders, especially Henry Fielding, who published *A Full Vindication of the Duchess-Dowager of Marlborough* in 1742. She died a wealthy but bitter, lonely woman, one of whose last acts was to arrange for the suppression of Pope's *Ethic Epistles (Moral Essays)* because she learned that, despite her generous financial assistance to him, he had ungraciously patterned his character "Atossa" on her own life: "Oblige her, and she'll hate you while you live." Sadly, D of M, too, had ceased to care: "one great happiness there is in death, that one shall never hear any more of any thing they do in this world."

In collaboration with Nathaniel Hooke, D of M produced *An Account of the Conduct of the Dowager Duchess of Marlborough* (1742); after her death were published *The Opinions of Sarah Duchess Dowager of Marlborough* (1788, eds. Sir David Dalrymple, Lord Hailes, MS notes by W. Seward); *Private Correspondence of Sarah, Duchess of Marlborough, illustrative of the Court and Times of Queen Anne* (1838); and *Letters of Sarah Duchess of Marlborough* (1875). D of M availed herself of the letter, the essay, and the belle-lettrist genres, generally defending herself against the accusations of other politicians and writers. The following passage from *Opinions* illustrates both her simplicity of style and

Johnson's caveats about the audacity of the author of the *Conduct:* "it would be making myself no great compliment, if I should say, her chusing to spend more of her time with me, than with any of her other servants did no discredit to her [Anne's] taste. . . . she at length distinguished me by so high a place in her favour, as perhaps no person ever arrived at a higher with queen or princess. And, if from hence I may draw any glory, it is, that I both obtained and held this place without the assistance of flattery; a charm . . . my temper and turn of mind would never have suffered me to employ." Her brief note on "Women" concludes intuitively upon the subject of her lifelong rancor; D of M refused to be subordinated or confined within the natural limits of her position: "Women signify nothing unless they are the mistress[es] of a Prince or a first Minister, which I would not be if I were young; and I think there are very few, if any women, that have understanding or impartiality enough to serve well those they really wish to serve." D.S.G.

MASHAM, Damaris, Lady (1658–1708), theological writer, was born in Cambridge where her father, Ralph Cudworth, famous Platonist and philosopher, taught for 43 years. DM was raised in a spirit of intellectual independence and early in life was distinguished for her knowledge and keen mind. In 1685 DM married Sir Francis Masham, third baronet of Oates, Essex, and acquired nine step-children. Her only son, Francis Cudworth Masham (b. 1686) grew up to become accountant-general to the Court of Chancery. DM's most influential friend and mentor was the philosopher John Locke, whom she met in 1682 when 23 years old. Locke instructed DM in philosophy and divinity, and in 1691, when his health was failing, he became a part of the Masham household, living at Oates until his death in 1704. His presence there greatly influenced DM, both in her writing and in her role as mother. She raised her son Francis according to Locke's *Thoughts Concerning Education,* teaching him Latin without knowing it herself when she began, and bravely following Locke's instructions regarding thin-soled shoes and exposure to sun and fresh air in an age when children were kept protected from the elements. Locke, a man who weighed his words, said of DM, "The lady is so well versed in theological and philosophical studies and of such an original mind, that you will not find many men to whom she is not superior in wealth and knowledge and ability to profit by it." DM was buried in the center aisle of Bath Abbey.

DM defended the life of reason against those who believed that this life ought to be spent in preparation for the next, and those who thought women had no business being reasonable. In 1696 *A Discourse concerning the Love of God* was published anonymously, but it was widely known to be by DM. The volume, translated into French by Pierre Coste in 1705, was in part written as an answer to certain religious theories put forth by Rev. John Norris, the Platonist who, under the assumption that DM had gone blind, had dedicated his *Reflections Upon the Conduct of Human Life* to her. In *A Discourse,* DM shows herself to be a true disciple of Locke: she argues that the cultivation of the mind is not only consistent with the doctrine of Christianity, but an integral part of it. If, DM wrote, as Mr. Norris maintains, "we are to have no desires but after God, the several societies of mankind could not long hold together, nor the very species be continued." Nor was she troubled, as was MARY ASTELL, correspondent of Rev. Norris, over whether the "love of the creature should exclude the love of God; any more than that the love of cherries should exclude the love of our friend that gives them us." Her second volume, written in 1700, defended the rational life against social prejudice. In *Occasional Thoughts in reference to a Vertuous or Christian Life* DM exhorts women to acquire as much knowledge as possible despite parental apprehension that learned daughters "might be in danger of not finding husbands," for she felt that an enlightened household could not exist without the participation of educated women. "Girls, betwixt silly fathers and ignorant mothers, are generally so brought up that traditionary opinions are to them, all their lives long, instead of reason." But what fate awaited the educated woman of DM's day? Not an easy one, according to DM: "Her understanding of the Christian religion would go near to render her suspected of heresy even by those who thought the best of her: Whilst her little zeal for any sect or party would make the Clergy of all sorts give her out for a Socinian, or a Deist: And should but a very little Philosophy be added to her other knowledge, even for an Atheist. The Parson of the parish, for fear of being ask'd hard questions, would be shy of coming near her, be his reception ever so inviting." DM also wrote an account of Locke in the *Great Historical Dictionary.* And it is Locke who, perhaps more than anyone in DM's life, recognized her intellectual acuity when he wrote, "I know few who can bring such clearness of thought to bear upon the most abstruse subjects, or such capacity for searching through and solving the difficulties of questions beyond the range, I do not say of most women, but even of most learned men." R.R.

MASON, Sarah or Charlotte (fl. 1772), writer on cooking, was apparently for many years a housekeeper to families of position. She wrote *Mrs. Mason's Cookery, or The Lady's Assistant,* published first by J. Walter in London in 1772 and reprinted at least eight times in the next 24 years. SM was named author of the first, second, and sixth editions; Charlotte Mason was named author of the fourth, fifth, seventh, and eighth editions. Two distinct editions of the third were printed by J. Walter in 1777, one signed Charlotte and the other Sarah. *The Lady's Assistant* contains all the information necessary for a beginning cook to serve an acceptable meal. SM provides menus for family dinners of two, five, and seven dishes. A typical dinner of seven dishes includes haddock stuffed and broiled, fish sauce, soup santé, roast leg of mutton, cauliflower, french beans, and a light pudding. SM gives explicit instructions: "As neatness is a most material requisite in a kitchen, be particularly careful to keep all the utensils perfectly clean, the pots and saucepans well tinned, or lined with silver; let all meat boil gently and always use soft water, if to be had: put the meat into the vessel while the water is cold, unless it is not salt enough (if beef or pork) then put it into hot, or boiling water." With the recipes are monthly charts of foods in season, and in later editions SM adds an appendix on kitchen poisons in which she quotes various doctors consulted, and another appendix on the properties of different kinds of water, hard and soft, and which kind is best for assorted purposes. SM's book was noted enough to have been reviewed in the *Monthly Review* (July 1773): "What can we add in favour of the *Lady's Assistant,* but a hearty recommendation of the book to all young wives, and inexperienced housekeepers; many of whom may profit by as attentive observance of the good instruction with which it is fraught, so as, perhaps, in time, to merit the honour of entertaining even a reviewer, at their tables." M.S.

MASTERS, Mary (1706?–1759?), poet and letter writer, seems to have passed her life unmarried in Norwich. In the preface to her 1733 *Poems on Several Occasions* she states: "The Author of the following Poems never read a Treatise on Rhetorick, or an Art of Poetry, nor was ever taught her English Grammar. Her Education rose no higher than the Spelling-Book, or the Writing-Master: her Genius to Poetry was always brow-beat and discountenanc'd by her Parents, and till Merit got the better of her Fortune, she was shut from all Commerce with the more knowing and polite Part of the World. If therefore no Grammatical Mistakes be found in these Compusures, she is free to acknowledge it owing to the Assistance of a Friend who revis'd the Work." This friend is probably Rev. Thomas Scott, a Dissenting minister and hymn writer who contributed six poems to the work. James Boswell's statement that Johnson revised MM's volumes and "illuminated them here and there with a trace of his own genius" cannot apply to this volume, for Johnson was still in Lichfield. Boswell also quotes Francis Barber, Johnson's servant, as mentioning that MM visited Johnson at Gough Square in 1752, while he was mourning the death of his wife, and described her as living with Edward Cave, her publisher. In 1755 MM brought out *Familiar Letters and Poems on Several Occasions.* She remarks in the preface that, after publishing by subscription in 1733, she "for a while lived content and quiet, but the Death of some Friends, and Treachery of others, rendered my Situation very inconvenient and uncomfortable: in Hopes of redressing it, I was prevailed upon to make a second attempt." Among the subscribers to this volume were ELIZABETH CARTER, CHARLOTTE LENNOX, MARY JONES, John Duncombe and John Hawkesworth. The familiar letters are chiefly addressed to other women and contain much feminist sentiment. MM deplores the lack of educational opportunities for women, insisting that "*a Woman is equal to a Man,* as being of the same Species, and endow'd with every Faculty which distinguishes him from the Brutes." In one letter she recommends to a friend the works of MARY ASTELL, CATHARINE TROTTER, and ELIZABETH ROWE; another letter shows that MM was well acquainted with Elizabeth Carter. Included in MM's poems are Gray's "Ode on the Death of a Favourite Cat" and Dryden's "Catullus and Lesbia." Those by MM herself include several paraphrased psalms and three "Short Ejaculations," one of which, "'Tis religion that can give / Sweetest pleasures while we live," can be found in most hymnals.   T.C.S.W.L.

MATHEWS, Eliza [Kirkham] (?–1802), poet, novelist, and miscellaneous prose writer, was a teacher by profession. She published *Constance: a novel* in 1785 as the "first literary attempt of a young lady," and followed it with *Argus; the house-dog at Eadlip* (1789), *Arnold Zulig: a Swiss story* (1790), *The Count de Hoensdern; a German tale* (1793) and *Simple Facts; or, the history of an orphan* (1793). In 1797 she married the popular actor, dancer, mimic, and comedian Charles Mathews, and did not resume her writing career until 1801 with *Mornings' Amusement; or, Tales of animals, etc.* A volume of *Poems* appeared in 1802, along with *Anecdotes of the Clairville Family; to which is added the History of Emily Wilmont.* She died in May 1802 of consumption; her husband speaks of a "withering sickness" marking her in the womb and bringing on her death as she reached her prime. After her death were published *Griffith Abbey, or Memoirs of Eugenia* (1807), *Ellinor: or The young governess. A moral tale* (1809); and *Afternoon Amusements; or, tales of birds* (3rd ed. 1809).

Constance, a sentimental novel, portrays a passive heroine launched into an unfamiliar world of male desires and stratagems. She has been brought up "with a total insensibility to the misfortune of being deprived of those pleasures which are so eagerly pursued by almost all of her age, rank and expectations," and on narrowly escaping rape she is in "a state of trepidation that almost dislocated her joints." She eventually marries the man she loves after participating under duress in a null marriage to a brutal lord who subsequently reforms. *Arnold Zulig* is a bloody romance with touches of gothic horror, which traces the results of the hero's disenchantment with his life of repose in Switzerland to involvement in the religious wars in France. The moral is that "he who is driven by excessive zeal from the straight paths of moderation and charity, will sooner or later feel that he is sinning under the appearance of virtue." *Critical Review* attacked the novel's improbabilities with customary savagery: "The escapes, indeed, of the hero and his friend are astonishing; and such have been the

surprising recoveries, which we have witnessed, of persons not only dead, but even buried, that our grief, at the conclusion of the piece, is considerably alleviated by the pleasing hope, that the Baron and his Lady, who were drowned in our sight, are by this time restored to life." EM's *Poems* comprise sonnets, odes, and elegies on a variety of well-worn themes. *Ellinor* is an episodic story of a young woman, urged by her mother to cultivate self-reliance and industry, who becomes a governess. Her response to one of her charges' killing of an insect is typical of her "judicious manner" of instruction: she reproves the girl—"let this incident teach you never more to seek amusement from the *captivity* or *death* of any created being"—but continues opportunistically: "Since the poor little animal is free from pain . . . dry your eyes, Amelia, and let us examine its structure." The work attempts to predicate the most pompous assertions of Christian morality on such trivial or bathetic instances of juvenile misdemeanor. It is, unfortunately, representative of EM's work as a whole.   R.J.

MEADES, Anna (1734?–?), novelist, probably came from Cambridgeshire; she mentions enjoying the diversions of Bath and London between 1749 and 1757. When 19 she wrote *The History of Cleanthes, an Englishman of the Highest Quality and Celemene, the Illustrious Amazonian Princess* (1757), a confection of romance, shipwrecks, and slavery, written, according to the preface, to pass the time and imitate old romances. Letters (printed in T. C. Duncan Eaves and Ben D. Kimpel's *Samuel Richardson: A Biography* (1971) indicate that AM in January 1757 wrote to Samuel Richardson under the pseudonym of Cleomira, wishing him to read *Cleanthes* and help her with another novel, written in imitation of his works since she had heard he planned to write no more. Begging for correction of "any very gross error, or striking faults," she asked Richardson to print the revised book and receive half the profits; she herself was not in great financial need, she declared, but would nonetheless like to earn from her writings. To Richardson she described the new book as quite distinct from *Cleanthes,* for it was "a description of modern life." She worried that the letters of her male characters contained "many passages not altogether free from what might be stiled improper to flow from the Pen of a Woman." Later in 1757 AM sent Richardson a copy of the published *Cleanthes,* asking him to detail its faults so that she could in future avoid them. In reply Richardson praised AM's imagination, but admitted that "a due Attention is not always given to Nature & Probability." In July, AM called on Richardson and was impressed; she noted his "eyes with a charming Benignity" and praised his condescension: "I could converse with you without Fear, so obligingly did you in the course of our conversation submit to talk with me upon a level." The novel with which he helped was probably *The History of Sir William Harrington* (1771) "written some years since, and revised and corrected by the late Mr. Richardson," also attributed to T. Hull. The Richardsonian connection was denied, but the editor in the second edition reasserted it, declaring that Richardson's notes had been left for many months with a bookseller for general inspection.

Sir William Harrington is an epistolary novel set in 1766 and imitating *Clarissa* and *Sir Charles Grandison.* It tells of the rather tame progress, reformation, and marriage of a group of rakes, endowed with sentimental feelings; one comments on a good man's death: "what a pattern does he set us, of true piety and resignation! And such behaviour at the close, is the effect of a life well spent." The women mainly stand for virtue, like Constantia, or spirit, like Julia, and there is much debate over female behavior in love: "In us, a modest reserve is what you men admire: can you really love me, and yet seek to destroy, what if I possess, will render me more worthy of your love?" The plot is slow-moving and unexciting, but the book is enlivened by occasional details such as Julia's ruse to discover an intrigue at table: she drops a toothpick so that she can bend down to see if the guilty pair are pressing each other's feet. If Richardson were involved in the revision of the work, it may have been partly owing to the frequent flattering allusions to his novels in the text: when Constantia accuses her brother of leading their sister into bad company, she asks, "would *Sir Charles Grandison,* think you, have carried *his sister* into such company, and to such a place, as *you* did *yours?*" *Monthly Review* (March 1771), reviewing the novel, commented on the large number of Richardsonian imitators and implied that AM was copying the wrong aspects of her model, not the well-drawn characters and knowledge of human nature, but the "prattling, gossiping style" and minute description. *Critical Review* (February 1771) was more complimentary, while noting the borrowing of characters from Richardson, and praised both the realism and the morality of the novel.   J.T.

MEARS, Martha (fl. 1797), medical writer and trained London midwife, was a cultivated woman of good family and influential medico-literary connections. Unlike her sister-disputants in the 18th-century English midwifery debate—ELIZABETH CELLIER, ELIZABETH NIHELL, and JANE SHARP—MM established an exemplary and beneficial camaraderie with such eminent medical men of her day as James Douglas, Thomas Denman (her midwifery teacher), John Armstrong ("the poet-physician"), and Francis Willis. In her principal work, *The Pupil of Nature* (1797), MM says she is pleased "to strain her feeble voice to swell the note of public praise which they [the medical men] have so justly deserved" for assisting medical women in their midwifery practice. Denman, for example, had prepared obstetrical charts for woman-midwives, and instructed them in the use of various birthing instruments. MM's particular interest in the pregnant woman's health and hygiene was influenced by the practical advice of Armstrong, expressed in his long, didactic poem, "The Art of Preserving Health" (1744), which she cites in her discussion of the mother's diet, exercise, and eating and bathing habits. MM's women friends probably included LADY MARY WORTLEY MONTAGU, FANNY BURNEY, and HANNAH MORE, all of whom advocated Armstrong's regimens. MM's commitment to smallpox inoculation may have been prompted by Montagu's own efforts to introduce this practice into England, after she herself was stricken in 1715. Through MM's writing and associations, she upgraded the image of medical women and, more important, made it possible for them to study with medical men at the new lying-in hospitals of the day.

MM's principal work is a book-length study of 161 pages, *The Pupil Of Nature; Or Candid Advice To The Fair Sex, On The Subjects Of Pregnancy; Childbirth; The Diseases Incident To Both; The Fatal Effects Of Ignorance And Quackery; And The Most Approved Means Of Promoting The Health, Strength, And Beauty Of Their Offspring. By Martha Mears, Practitioner In Midwifery* (1797; German trans. by E. Henschel, 1804). The work's epigraph from Pope sounds the theme "Take Nature's Path, and mad Opinions leave." In 11 individual "Essays" MM sets out to combat prejudice and error by discussing proper pre- and postnatal care of mother and child, and by dispelling long-held fallacies concerning pregnant women: "A state of pregnancy has too generally been considered as a state of indisposition or disease: This is a fatal error and the source of almost all evils to which women in childbearing are liable." Because obstetrical instruments were readily purchasable after 1773, MM emphasizes the judicious use of forceps and calipers, especially by relatively untrained lay-midwives. Like Elizabeth Nihell (*The Art of Midwifery,* 1760) and Margaret Stephen (*The Domestic Midwife,* 1795), MM speaks out against artificially induced labor ("dispatching the mother"), and urges woman-midwives to maintain high standards in their professional and personal lives. Eager to quash the image of the midwife as a "doting, dram-drinking matron," MM discourages medical women from drinking cordials and giving them to patients as a medicament. MM's work, the last major contribution by a woman-midwife to the English midwifery dispute of the 18th century, is significant because it points the way for holistic health care of pregnant women. While her observations are eclectic, her *Pupil of Nature* is useful because it conveniently summarizes the obstetrical theory of the day advanced both by male and female midwives. M.M.

MEEKE, Mary (?–1816?), novelist and translator, was a prolific writer of gothic fiction. Very little, however, is known about her life. She may have been the wife of the Rev. Francis Meeke, whose widow died in October 1816 at Johnson Hall, Staffs. If so, two of her novels were issued posthumously. "Grabrielli," a pseudonym she used often, may have been her maiden name, which would suggest Italian descent. We can ascertain from her work that she wrote quickly and entertainingly and, as she was published by the Minerva Press, she was probably able to earn a good living as a writer. She was intelligent, widely read, and highly industrious, and it is apparent from her work that she took an interest in religion and in European languages. MM was primarily concerned with the demands of her reading public when she composed her novels, and in the preface to one of them (*Midnight Weddings,* 1802) she advises aspiring fellow novelists to consult their publishers as to how best to satisfy the public taste of the moment. MM became a favorite

author of both Lord Macaulay (Lady Trevelyan wrote that "he all but knew [Mrs. Meeke's romances] by heart") and of Mary Russell Mitford.

Most of MM's novels present a similar plot: a mystery surrounding a seemingly poverty-stricken, humble youth who inevitably proves to be the son of a wealthy aristocrat. MM's heroes receive typical gentleman's educations at public schools and Oxbridge, visit exotic places, and fight with patriotic zeal for the mother country. MM plays on the prevailing sentimental style of the day, as in her description in *Count St. Blancard* (1795), her first novel, of a lovers' tête-à-tête: "Dubois's breath, which had almost forsook him, returned, and he ventured to press the hand he held, to his lips, and bathed it with his manly tears." Her recognition scenes tend toward spectacular melodrama, as for example in *Ellesmere,* when Clement answers an advertisement for a missing noble son who "bears the mark of two vowels": "He had been unbuttoning his breeches knee while he was speaking, and now, forcing down his stockings, he discovered the very two letters the Marchioness was so choice of, who caught him once more to her bosom, calling him her dear Albert Ormond—her long regretted long lamented son." Other novels published under her own name include *Palmira and Ermance* (1797), *Which Is the Man?* (1801), and eleven others published between 1803 and 1823. As "Gabrielli" she published *The Mysterious Wife* (1797), *Harcourt* (1799), *The Mysterious Husband* (1801), *Independence* (1802), *Something Odd* (1804), and *Something Strange* (1806). *Count St. Blancard* was called "an entertaining and well-connected story" by the *Critical Review.* MM's second novel, *The Abbey of Clugny* (1795), was praised as "told with ease and vivacity" by the *Monthly Review.* MM also translated a number of works from French and German, including *The Unpublished Correspondence of Madame du Deffand* (1810), Sophie de Cottin's *Elizabeth, or the Exiles of Siberia* (1814), and Klopstock's *Messiah* (1811). Though a minor novelist concerned primarily with surface and plot, MM won popularity because she cultivated middle-class Cinderella stories in modish sentimental gothic narratives. J.L.E.

MILLER, Anna Riggs, Lady (1741–81), poet and travel writer, was born in London and became the sole heiress of her wealthy grandfather, Edward Riggs, who was a commissioner of revenue, privy councillor, and member of the Irish House of Commons. AM's father was made a commissioner of customs in London in 1741, and her mother, Margaret Pigott, came from an old Shropshire family. AM married John Miller, a poor Irishman, in Bath in 1765, and Miller adopted his wife's maiden name before his own. They had two children. The couple built an extravagant villa outside Bath, at Batheaston on the Avon, where they were visited by Horace Walpole and FANNY BURNEY. When they were forced to economize by living abroad, they went to France and Italy in 1770–71. In 1778, Miller was created an Irish baronet, and AM instituted a literary salon at Batheaston. Her guests were each invited to place a *bout-rimé* (a 6-line poem) in an antique Roman urn the Millers had brought back from Frascati. The salon was visited by Walpole, Anstey, Garrick, ANNA SEWARD, Dr. Johnson, Fanny Burney, MARY DELANY, and HESTER THRALE. The Batheaston gatherings are described by Philip Thicknesse in his *New Prose Bath Guide* (1778). AM died suddenly at Bristol Hot Wells and is buried in the Abbey Church, Bath. On her monument is a verse epitaph by Anna Seward.

AM edited four volumes of the verses written at Batheaston, and published them under the title *Poetical Amusements at a Villa Near Bath* between 1775 and 1781. These volumes contain several verses by AM herself. In 1776 she published her three-volume *Letters from Italy, Describing the Manners, Customs, Antiquities, Paintings, & c. of that Country,* which went into a second edition in 1777 and is at once a memoir, a travel guide, and a series of art-historical reflections and architectural sketches; AM calls the Piazza San Marco in Venice, for example, "the only spot one can call *terra firma* in this city," and describes its cathedral as "in the old absurd Gothic style." The verse AM wrote and cultivated in others is light and relies on puns; in a *bout-rimé* of her own titled "Enigma," she began "Crush'd by oppression's weight" to suggest a shoe. Charles Dickens used her as the original of Mrs. Leo Hunter in *Pickwick Papers,* the woman who writes the "Ode to an Expiring Frog." Her contemporaries made fun of AM: Mme du Deffend found her boring; Horace Walpole wrote to Lady Aylesbury, "Alas! Mrs. Miller is returned a beauty, a genius, a Sappho, a tenth Muse, as romantic as Mlle. Scuderi, and as sophisticated as Mrs. Ve-

sey"; Fanny Burney described AM as "a round, plump, coarse-looking dame of about forty, and while all her aim is to appear an elegant woman of fashion, all her success is to seem an ordinary woman in very common life, with fine clothes on." AM's desire for social prominence earned her ridicule, but her salon and Thursday Parnassus fairs were popular for about six years, and she introduced to England the idea of poetical contests.   J.L.E.

MINIFIE, Margaret (fl. 1763–80), novelist, daughter of James Minifie, D.D., was the less famous sister of SUSANNAH GUNNING. With Susannah, MM gathered nearly 800 subscribers for their first book, many of whom committed themselves to two or three sets. They called their epistolary novel *The Histories of Lady Frances S- - -and Lady Caroline S- - -* (1763), informing their dedicatee, Lady Tynte of Haswell, Somerset, that "Here your Ladyship will see a helpless Orphan, conducted by the hand of Providence to the guardian and director of her tender years, perfected and completated with all the ornaments and embellishments human nature is capable of receiving." The sisters collaborated again on *The Picture* (1766). In 1780, however, MM alone published the epistolary *Le Count de Poland,* which was distributed by Dodsley. This book fulfills its French title only through a few scenes abroad. Otherwise, the plot is familiar in that the orphaned Olivia eventually marries a lord. MM carefully distinguishes some of the influences of sex and class. Her women are particularly ungenerous, one of them referring to Olivia as "a dirt-sprung girl." The Osmonds foolishly allow their daughter Emily to be raised by "a family of quality," and the effect of this education is "only to subvert her understanding, and vitiate her principles," meaning that she is concerned with money and position instead of love and honor. MM's style and content resemble her sister's, and even contemporaries failed to distinguish clearly between the two Minifies. Reuss's *Register of Authors* (1791) lists only one Minifie (with an ellipsis for a given name), and Maria Burney in 1773 referred to "Miss Minifie" in the singular only.   J.Th.

MIXER, Elizabeth (fl. 1730s), American religious autobiographer, was the daughter of a deacon in Ashford, Mass. In 1736 she wrote *An Account of Some Spiritual Experiences and Raptures* as part of her soul searching before entering the Ashford Church. In this work she describes her pious upbringing and her enthusiasm for religion, as well as three visions: of Christ in the Heavenly City, of Christ coming to her at night, and of the Last Judgment. Her ecstatic undoctrinal account and her visionary experiences connect EM with the Great Awakening.   J.J.

MOLLINEUX, Mary [Southworth] (1651–95), poet, became famous seven years after her death as the author of *Fruits of Retirement or Miscellaneous Poems Moral and Divine,* which went through six editions in England and at least four in Philadelphia before 1783. The date of her birth is computed from the date of her marriage in 1685, when she was said to have been 34 years old. The preface to *Fruits of Retirement,* which first appeared in 1702, by her cousin Frances Owen, describes her as an only child, "who, in her Childhood was much afflicted by weak eyes, which made her unfit for the usual Imployment of Girls; . . . her Father brought her up to more Learning, than is commonly bestowed on our Sex; in which she became so good a Proficient, that she well understood the *Latin Tongue,* fluently discoursed in it; and made a considerable progress in *Greek* also; wrote several *Hands* well; was a good *Arithmetician,* yea, in the best Arithmetick; *for she so numbred her days as to apply Her Heart unto Wisdom;* as also to the study of several useful Arts; had a good understanding of Physick and Chyrurgery, the Nature of Plants Herbs and Minerals." From the age of 12 she wrote pious exhortations in verse to members of her family. In 1684 MM was imprisoned at Lancaster Castle for taking part in a Quaker assembly, and in 1685 married one of her fellow prisoners, Henry Mollineux, at Penketh, near Warrington. From this time her poetic output nearly ceased, except for the Latin poems she sent her husband when he was in prison. In 1690 Henry Mollineux was arrested again for nonpayment of tithes. MM approached the Bishop Stratford in June 1691, and pleaded her husband's case so well that "the Bishop, his Chaplain, and the Chaplain's brother, a Lawyer were all put to silence." Her husband was released on that occasion and almost immediately rearrested. Despite their frequent long separations and MM's delicate health, there were children of the marriage. The manner of her death in 1695 is recounted in affecting detail by her husband, including the odd circumstance that she spoke to him in Latin whenever there were other people present. "Learning of Christ the Truth, to be *lowly in Heart* she chose rather to appear little to Men" and would not publish her work in her lifetime. Henry Mollineux claimed that he published only in order than others might be edified by her example. Tryall Ryder offers additional evidence: when he had seen her verses, before she was married, he had suggested that "they might be of service, if made Publick in Print." Her posthumous reputation is due entirely to the wishes of the Quakers to keep her example before the Society of Friends.

MM has been dismissed as a "facile writer of pious verse": the truth is rather that her verse is crude and often clumsy, while her utter lack of exhibitionism leads her into diction which is positively gaunt. Her friendship with one of her cousins, F. R., (perhaps the initials of Frances Owen before her marriage), inspires some of her most characteristic writing: "Methinks a Spring should be / From Winters chilling force, more free / Than to be Frozen! Inbred Heat / Is then, with purest Springs, more great; / And with its Current soon doth glide / Through Ice besetting either side. / Let Love spring up, that we may see / The same effects, dear Friend, in thee."   T.C.S.W.L.

MONCK, Mary (1677?–1715), translator and poet, was the second daughter of Robert, first Viscount Molesworth, and first wife of George Monck of St. Stephen's Green, Dublin. She taught herself Latin, Italian, and Spanish and read much English literature. After her death at Bath from a lingering disease, several poems and translations were discovered in her desk and published by her father under the title *Marinda. Poems and Translations upon Several Occasions* (1716). The book contains 63 poems, 11 of which are addressed to Marinda (MM's coterie name), while some are translations by MM of earlier poets, including Tasso, Della Casa, Guarini, Quevedo, Marino, and Petrarch (printed with the originals). Her preferred themes include sleep, death, women and, of course, love. Several of her translations and poems are reprinted in Colman and Thornton's *Poems by Eminent Ladies* (1755), which also includes an unpublished poem written to her husband while MM was on her deathbed. This poem ends: "And should'st thou grieve that rest is come at last? / Rather rejoice to see me shake off life, / And die as I have lived, thy faithful wife." Her major talent lay in her ability to translate other poets gracefully, economically, and precisely. Many of her poems are set in the typical neo-classical framework preferred by the coterie, with her own acquaintances disguised as nymphs and swains in pastoral settings. Her selection of Quevedo's story of Orpheus and Euridice to translate and the subject matter of some squibs indicate her occasional misogyny.   T.C.S.W.L.

MONTAGU, Elizabeth [Robinson] (1720–1800), essayist, hostess, patron, and letter writer, was the eldest daughter of wealthy and well-connected parents. Her younger sister was SARAH SCOTT. The sisters grew up on family estates in Cambridgeshire and Kent, and they were educated at home, partly under the direction of the scholar Dr. Conyers Middleton, their grandmother's second husband. They read widely in English, French, and classical literature. In 1742 EM married an MD, Edward Montagu, a grandson of the first Earl of Sandwich. He was 28 years her senior and extremely wealthy. Despite the disparity of age and character, the marriage was a success. Their only child, a son, was born in 1743 and died the following year. Although the center of a wide and lively circle of friends, EM accompanied her husband regularly to his estates and coal mines in the north of England as well as to the more pleasant Sandleford estate in Berkshire. She cared for him in his last long illness and at his death in 1775 inherited a fortune worth about £7,000 a year. She continued to supervise the various estates and mines, which on her death passed to her nephew, Matthew Robinson Montagu, later fourth Lord Rokeby. EM lived in London, first in her husband's house in Hill Street and then at Montagu House in Portman Square, which she built in 1781. Always a patron of the latest artistic and literary fashions, EM commissioned her town house in the classical style; it was designed by "Athenian" Stuart and decorated by Angelica Kauffman and others. It was destroyed in World War II. At Sandleford, her favorite country seat, she built, also in 1781, a major gothic addition by James Wyatt and hired "Capability" Brown to improve the grounds. These houses were the settings for EM's salons, which gained her the title "Queen of the Bluestockings." With several other women, similarly well educated, well connected, and wealthy, she promoted evening gatherings where the main feature would be informed and lively conversation participated in by both sexes. There was no gambling, no dancing, and no drinking. Respectable persons of wit and learning were welcomed. The model for these salons was French. The English women did not succeed in being as influential as their French sisters, or in reforming society as a whole, but they did provide gatherings where people interested in the arts, literature, and even politics could come together and exchange views. Through these gatherings EM extended her wide circle of friends, introduced young writers to the great world, and brought her friends together. One of her first female friends was Lady Margaret Harley, later Duchess of Portland; other Bluestockings and friends included Elizabeth Vesey, FRANCES BOSCAWEN, MARY DELANY, ELIZABETH CARTER, HESTER MULSO CHAPONE, HESTER THRALE, Samuel Johnson, David Garrick, Edmund Burke, Horace Walpole, Lord Lyttleton, Sir Joshua Reynolds, and the Earl of Bath. EM boasted of her distant family connections with both Henry Fielding and Lawrence Sterne. Among writers patronized by her were James Beattie, ANNA LAETITIA BARBAULD, HANNAH MORE, and FANNY BURNEY. EM often traveled: she visited Scotland and made frequent stays in Bath and Tunbridge Wells; she went to France several times, as well as visiting the Low Countries and the Rhineland.

During her lifetime EM published two works: three of the eighteen *Dialogues of the Dead* (1760) and *An Essay on the Writings and Genius of Shakespear* [sic] (1769). The *Dialogues* are criticisms of modern society; Lord Lyttleton wrote the other fifteen. In EM's first, Hercules and Cadmus discuss the virtues and uses of wisdom. In the second, Mrs. Modish, a "modern fine Lady," tells Mercury she cannot come as she is "engaged, absolutely engaged," not with husband and children but with countless diversions, "the business of my Life." Her conduct dooms her to be forever excluded from the Elysian Fields. In the final dialogue, a modern Bookseller tells Plutarch how much money he has lost on an edition of the Latin author's *Lives*. What modern readers of both sexes want are books "void of Facts and Doctrines," and the writers comply; only a few try to teach as they entertain, among these Richardson and Fielding. The *Essay on Shakespear* was a defense of the English dramatist against attacks made by Voltaire. It is full of nationalist pride. Shakespeare is compared to French and Greek playwrights, none of whom has all his virtues, for "Such is his merit, that the more just and refined the taste of the nation has become, the more he has encreased in reputation." The *Essay* was highly regarded in its own time, even by Johnson, and was translated into both French and Italian. It is analytical and comparative rather than critical, so that modern writers have paid little attention to it, even when studying 18th century criticism.

The best of EM's writings are her letters, which are not yet completely published. Her nephew published four volumes in 1809 and 1813, which cover only the years to 1761. They were widely read, but they were not admired in the first half of the 19th century for they aimed not to teach but to entertain and communicate. Her epistolary style was formed in the first half of the 18th century; it is frank and lively—much closer to LADY MARY WORTLEY MONTAGU's, for example, than to Hannah More's. The charm, wit, intelligence, and friendly affection that captivated so many in her lifetime are reflected in the letters. In 1782 she wrote to Elizabeth Carter about a friend: "I really believe she was just like Eve before she eat the apple, at least she answers to Milton's description of her. She would have preferred her husband's discourse to the angels. I am afraid you and I my dear friend should have entered into some metaphysical disquisition with the angel, we are not so perfectly the rib of man as woman ought to be." They tell the modern reader about the writer, her ideas and her life, and her friends and the society in which they lived.   B.B.S.

MONTAGU, Lady Mary Wortley (1689–1762), newspaper author, essayist, poet, and letter writer, was born in London to Evelyn Pierrepoint and Lady Mary Fielding. Her father became Earl of Kingston, then Marquess of Dorchester, and finally fifth Earl and first Duke of Kingston. She had two sisters and a brother. Her mother died when MWM was four. MWM was brought up by her father's mother, near Salisbury, in London, and at Thoresby, Notts. Mainly educated by a governess, she taught herself Latin and later was tutored in Italian and carving. In 1709 she began a correspondence with Edward Wortley, brother of her friend Anne, and when Wortley did not accept her father's marriage terms, eloped with

him in 1712. Her son Edward was born the next year. MWM and her husband, an MP, were Whigs and frequented the court. Her literary interests developed early, and some of her poetry was printed by Edmund Curll without her permission. She knew Congreve, Arbuthnot, and Addison, and had a close friendship with Pope and Gay. In 1715, MWM contracted smallpox and was left with no eyelashes and deeply pitted skin. In 1716 she journeyed to Constantinople with her son and husband, the Ambassador to Turkey, where she wrote her *Embassy Letters.* In 1718 she gave birth to Mary and vaccinated Edward for smallpox. They returned to England, where she enlarged her circle of friends to include the DUCHESS OF MARLBOROUGH, MARY ASTELL, Lord Hervey, Lady Stefford, and Mary Skerritt (Sir Robert Walpole's mistress) and acted as a patron for Edward Young and her cousin Henry Fielding. In 1728, Pope wrote his first attack on her, caused most likely by her rejection of him, and for eight years continued these attacks, which she ignored. Her son Edward became troublesome in his teens and never thereafter was a person she could accept. Her daughter married the well-born but not wealthy John Stuart, Earl of Bute, and of their children, LADY LOUISA STUART became MWM's favorite and eventually wrote a recollection of MWM. In 1736, at 47 years, MWM became enamored of Francesco Algarotti, a 24-year-old, bisexual Italian with literary talents; Lord Hervey was also in love with him. After Algarotti left England, MWM wrote nine issues of a paper *The Nonsense of Commonsense* to refute the Opposition's *Common Sense,* although she was not identified as the author. In 1739, when Algarotti returned to England, MWM made plans to live with him in Italy and left England for that purpose. When Algarotti finally reached Florence, it was 1741 and the frustrating two years had cooled MWM's ardor. For the next 20 years MWM lived abroad, mainly in Italy. She occupied herself with reading, writing, visiting, and gardening, and was so content with her life, and her husband with his, that in his three trips to the Continent they made no effort to see one another. In January 1761 Wortley died, leaving a remarkably large estate; in September MWM began her return trip to England. In June 1762 she developed breast cancer and died two months later, sedated with hemlock.

MWM did not want her works printed during her lifetime, because, as she told her daughter, "I write only for myself." Her dislike of acclaim and attention, her preference for privacy, and her sense of her position in society suggested this posture. In 1791 on her way home from Italy, she left a copy of her *Embassy Letters* (as yet unpublished) with Rev. Benjamin Sowden "to be disposed of as he thinks proper," because she knew her daughter would try to stop their publication, as indeed she did. MWM wrote in various genres: a critique for Addison of his *Cato,* poems as letters for friends, a translation of the *Enchiridion* from a Latin text, a letter to the *Spectator* from "Mrs. President," letters to Margaret of Navarre in French, a fairy tale in French, poems to Algarotti, court poems, the letters in *The Nonsense of Common Sense,* and her own personal letters. One of her first writings, the criticism of *Cato* and the Epilogue, indicates her variety of tone: the criticism is polite and gentle, whereas the Epilogue, as was customary, is cynical: "Poets write morals—priests for martyrs preach— / Neither such fools do practise what they teach." Caught between what she considered her position in society and her perceptive view of human foibles and passions, MWM's life and her literary stance reveal the Stoicism of the *Enchiridion,* which she translated when she was 21. In "An Answer to a Lady," MWM wrote: " Long since the value of this world I know; / Pitied the folly, and despis'd the show; / Well as I can, my tedious part I bear, / And wait dismissal without pain or fear." That she knew the sophisticated life of England and could write about it as wittily as her male contemporaries is evident in her "Eclogues" printed by Curll: "Damon is practis'd in the modish life, / Can hate, and yet be civil to his wife: / He games, he drinks, he swears, he fights, he roves; / Yet Chloe can believe he fondly loves. / Mistress and wife by turns supply his need; / A miss for pleasure, and a wife for breed." This was truly MWM's vision of marriage. Pope wrote of lovers killed by lightning, "Victims so pure Heav'n saw well pleas'd, / And snatch'd them in celestial fire"; whereas, MWM wrote a cynical epitaph to the lovers and later one on the death of a newly married woman, "Three months of rapture, crown'd with endless rest. / . . . To you the sweets of love were only shown, / The sure succeeding bitter dregs unknown." She chided women for not taking a rational interest in politics because of their "little Vanities with which they amuse themselves." But this characteristic of women MWM laid squarely on their lack of education: "Most people [arc] confounding the ideas of sense and cunning, though there are really no two things in nature more opposite: it is, in part, from this false reasoning, the unjust custom prevails of debarring our sex from the advantages of learning, the men fancying the improvement of our understandings would only furnish us with more art to deceive them, which is directly contrary to the truth." Education for women also had a private, more important value: "it is in the power of study not only to make solitude tolerable, but agreeable." Of the education of her granddaughter, MWM writes: "If she has the same inclination (I should say passion) for learning that I was born with, history, geography, and philosophy will furnish her with materials to pass away cheerfully a longer life than is allotted to mortals." MWM looked at other cultures without prejudice. She describes a chamber of a palace in Constantinople "wainscoted with mother of pearl fastened with emeralds like nails" and concludes of the Turks: "they have a right notion of life; while they consume it in music, gardens, wine, and delicate eating, while we are tormenting our brains with some scheme of politics, or studying some science to which we can never attain, or, if we do, cannot persuade people to set that value upon it we do ourselves." MWM was known during her lifetime as a woman of wit and after the publication of her *Embassy Letters,* the year after her death, as a woman of charm and perspicacity. S.M.S.

MOORE, Jane Elizabeth (1738–?), poet and autobiographer, published *Genuine Memoirs of Jane Elizabeth Moore, Written by Herself* (1785) and *Miscellaneous Poems* (1796). Her *Memoirs* contains a fascinating account of her work as a clerk in her father's business and her commentary on "the trade, manufacturers, laws and police of this country"; it also reveals her disillusionment with her husband: "I . . . informed Mr. Moore that I was fully determined, (in the true sense of the word), not to be obligated to any man breathing." L.F.

MOORE, Milcah Martha (1740–1829), American poet and pedagogical writer, was the daughter of a Quaker, Richard Hill. In

1767 she married Dr. Charles Moore of Philadelphia but, because he was her cousin, the Quakers would not sanction the marriage, although the couple remained Quakers all their lives. In 1769 the *Pennsylvania Chronicle* published a poem "The Female Patriots. Address'd to the Daughters of Liberty in America, 1768," probably by MM since a version of the poem exists in her commonplace book. The work blames men for insufficient patriotism and for a degenerate interest in trade rather than liberty. It urges "the Daughters of Liberty" to arise and the people of America to become self-sufficient and scorn British goods. When the War of American Independence began, MM and her husband left for their country house at Montgomery Square, where they stayed for most of the time until Charles Moore died in 1801. MM reveals her life at Montgomery Square in her commonplace book; while her husband practiced medicine, she opened a school for poor girls. She became notable as a teacher, partly because of the moderate popularity of her compilation, *Miscellanies, Moral and Instructive* (1787), of which Benjamin Franklin much approved. It was reprinted in America and Britain. In 1801 MM moved to Burlington, N.J., to live with her sister, and remained there until her death.   J.J.

MOORHEAD, Sarah Parsons (fl. 1741–42), American religious polemicist, married the Rev. John Moorhead of Boston. She wrote poetry during the 1740s that formed part of the controversy of "the Great Awakening." "Lines . . . Humbly Dedicated to the Rev. Gilbert Tennant" appeared in the *New England Weekly Journal* of March 1741, signed Mrs. S.M. and presumably by SPM; they express fear at the excesses of the "Awakening": "dear sacred Tennent, pray beware, / Least too much terror, prove to some a snare." In 1742 James Davenant had left his congregation in Long Island to become a wandering preacher and critic of established ministers, whom he accused of hypocrisy and worldliness. SPM's "To the Reverend Mr. James Davenport on His Departure from Boston, By Way of a Dream" (1742) criticizes Davenport for his public quarreling, although it praises him as well: "I love the zeal that fires good Davenport's breast." SPM is uneasy at the extreme emotionalism Davenport exhibits and which marks the "Great Awakening" in general: "Conversion is become the drunkard's song; / God's glorious work, which sweetly did arise, / By This unguarded sad imprudence

dies." In the dream, Davenport is warned not to think grace confined to himself and exhorted to "let charity unclose thy drowsy eyes"; impressed by the warning, he is made to repent and pray for the unity of the churches he has "rashly rent." While emphasizing God's love, the poem insists on belief in "free grace" without which there is only damnation.   J.T.

MORE, Hannah (1745–1833), poet, playwright, and religious writer, was born at Stapleton, Bristol, the fourth of Jacob More's five daughters. More was headmaster of the free school at Fishponds, Stapleton, and a Tory and high churchman, although tolerant toward sects. His daughters were all influenced by their domineering father and his principles. Since he could afford no dowries, he trained them to be teachers from an early age. HM was a delicate and precocious child, and when More began to teach her Latin and mathematics, he was "frightened at his success." He believed women's brains were more delicate than men's, and, although HM begged to continue the lessons, he would only compromise and resume the Latin. Mary, the eldest daughter, took French lessons in Bristol and instructed the others on her return. Later, HM perfected her colloquial French by talking to French officers living on parole in the neighborhood. In 1757 Mary set up a girls' boarding school in Trinity Street, Bristol, in which she was joined by her sisters. There HM continued her Latin and learned Italian and Spanish. She also attended public lectures in Bristol. The school was a success, and in 1762 the sisters built larger premises at 43 Park Street, where they enjoyed a lively and intellectual social life. HM was jilted by a Mr. Turner, 20 years her senior, who had a fine estate outside Bristol. They had become engaged when HM was about 22, but Turner kept postponing the marriage until, after six years, the Mores asked a clergyman friend to intervene. The engagement was broken off in 1773 and, after this humiliation, HM vowed never to marry; she was able to demonstrate her resolve when she later received an offer from Lord Monboddo. Turner, as was the custom, offered to make reparation by settling on her an annuity of £200. This was accepted without her knowledge, and later she was induced to make use of it. Throughout her life, when crises occurred, HM took refuge in bouts of ill health. This time she recovered at Uphill, where she became friends with the poet John Langhorne. In 1773 or 1774, HM made the first of a series of annual visits to London, taking two sisters, Sarah and Martha ("Patty"). She had some connection with Sir Joshua Reynolds and his sister Frances, who introduced them to London society. HM became an intimate friend of David Garrick and his wife, and after 1777 always stayed with them during her London visits. She met ELIZABETH MONTAGU and was admitted to the society of the Bluestockings. She also became friendly with Samuel Johnson, a friendship which grew stronger in mutual flattery, and she made the acquaintance of Edmund Burke. Turner used to say that Providence had reserved HM for a happier fate than marrying him, and might have added that his annuity enabled her to grasp this fate. She became a professional writer and met with early success. After Garrick's death in January 1779, she gradually lost interest in the gaieties of the town. When, after consoling Mrs. Garrick, she took up social life again, it consisted mostly of the company of the Bluestockings and their guests, Gibbon, Beattie, and Horace Walpole, whom she met in 1781. This intimate association with elderly persons meant that intellectually HM belonged to a generation already passed and, when she later met Southey, Coleridge, and De Quincey in Bristol, she was prejudiced against them. In 1784, she discovered that a Bristol milkwoman, ANNE YEARSLEY, wrote poetry, and HM edited a collection of her work to raise money for her: the two women later quarreled. HM became increasingly concerned with humanitarian projects; as her London circle died, she deepened her friendships with evangelicals of the Clapham Sect—John Newton, Zachary Macaulay, and William Wilberforce. The last urged her to set up a school at Cheddar, during a visit he made in 1789 to her cottage at Cowslip Green, near Wrington, Somerset. The scheme grew, and with her sisters (who had retired in 1789) HM promoted women's friendly societies. In 1800 she was involved in the "Blagdon controversy." The curate of Blagdon, where she had set up a school, complained it had a Methodist tendency. The dispute lasted two years, and grew out of all proportion. HM was attacked personally in pamphlets and had to dissolve the school. On the request of Beilby Porteus, bishop of London, HM wrote *Village Politics* (1792), the first of her tracts for the poor, intended to counteract the radical influence of the revolution in France. She began another series in 1817, during the critical period following the peace. HM had moved with her sisters in 1802 to a larger house, Barley Wood, in Wrington. After her last sister died in 1819, she retreated into ill health and kept to her room. Her servants cheated her unmercifully, and in 1828 friends persuaded her to move to Clifton. There she received admiring visitors and was cosseted until her mind failed in 1832. At her death she left £30,000, chiefly to charities and religious societies.

The successive interests of HM's life can be traced through her writings. *The Search After Happiness* (1773), "a Pastoral Drama for Young Ladies," is a conversation rather than a drama, written in heroic couplets and interspersed with songs. Its aim was to promote "a regard to religion and virtue in the minds of young persons, and afford them an innocent, and perhaps not altogether unuseful amusement in the exercise of recitation." The sentiments are platitudinous, but *Dodsley's Annual,* which printed the lyrics separately, recommended the play as suitable for elegant females, and it attracted patrons to the More sisters' school. *The Inflexible Captive* (1774) started as a language exercise and was based on her own translation of *Attilio Regolo,* one of Metastasio's less well known lyrical dramas. It was produced at the Theatre Royal, Bath, on 19 April 1775. Langhorne composed the prologue, and Garrick, who was present on the first night, the epilogue. Her sister Sally wrote: "Never was a piece represented there known to have received so much applause." HM's early poetry was written to please individuals. The "Ballad of Bleeding Rock," relating the death of a nymph deserted by her lover, was written during her engagement to Turner (when she also wrote the inscriptions to be placed on statues in his grounds); it was published with the more popular ballad "Sir Eldred of the Bower" in 1776. This poem confirms HM's interest in the current ballad revival and tells of jealous love, madness, and death. Dr. Johnson was so delighted with it that he wrote his own stanza, which was duly included. "The Ode to Dragon," Garrick's dog, laments Garrick's retirement from the stage; it received so much praise when circulated in 1776 that HM published it the following year. Her two tragedies, *Percy* (1777) and *The Fatal Falsehood* (1779), were also inspired by her devotion to Garrick. *Percy* takes its theme from "Chevy Chase" and concerns the feud between the Douglas and

Percy families. The action is melodramatic and the motivation now seems far-fetched. The heroine, Elwina, is forced by her father to break her engagement with Lord Percy and marry Percy's enemy, Earl Douglas: "He dragg'd me trembling, dying, to the altar, / I sigh'd, I struggled, fainted, and— complied." Elwina, punctiliously virtuous, afterwards prates of wifely duty and her unsullied reputation. The exasperated husband kills the lover, the wife takes poison, the husband stabs himself, the father repents, and the curtain falls. Garrick, who wrote the prologue and epilogue, revised the whole and helped with the play's production. The cast was good and it was a huge success. The first edition, 4000 copies, sold out in a fortnight. *The Fatal Falsehood* was unfinished at Garrick's death, and he criticized only the first two acts. A melodrama of love, it purports "to shew the effect of passions uncontroll'd." It was well-produced; the first night was a success, the critics were kind, but the play ran only four nights. Later Mrs. Siddons added it to her repertoire, but it was never as popular as *Percy*. HM came to think playgoing wrong; in her *Collected Works* she prefaced her plays with a denunciation of drama, which she thought could not even be read without the heart being "dissolved by amatory scenes," the mind "warped by corrupt reasoning," or the heart "inflamed with seducing principles." During the period of grief after Garrick's death, HM wrote "Sensibility," a poem in heroic couplets: "Ne'er shall my heart his loved remembrance lose, / Critic, guide, guardian, glory of my muse!" This was published in 1782, together with *Sacred Dramas,* which she began years before and was prophetic of her later absorption in religion. These are Bible stories in dialogue form, intended to be read, not staged. The critics were only lukewarm in their praise, but the book ran into 19 editions and was much translated. In 1784 HM wrote "The Bas Bleu" in octosyllabic couplets, a witty description of the Bluestocking Club. Johnson said, "there was no name in poetry that might not be glad to own it." This was published in 1786, together with "Florio: a Tale for Fine Gentlemen and Fine Ladies," written in the same metre and dedicated to Horace Walpole. It relates how an irresponsible youth-about-town marries and becomes a conscientious squire. The moral, "Florio escap'd from fashion's school, / His heart and conduct learns to rule," does not overshadow the story, which is charming and light-hearted. In 1789 HM wrote *Bishop Bonner's Ghost,* an amusing trifle, footnoted in pseudo-scholarly style, an indirect compliment to Bishop Porteus. Her later work is more serious. "The Slave Trade" (1790), first published as "Slavery, a Poem" in 1788, a long poem in heroic couplets, was praised as a contribution to the abolitionist cause. *Village Politics, by Will Chip, a Country Carpenter,* a dialogue in colloquial language, was written to placate the uneducated who clamored for reform. Her other political works dealing primarily with government are: *Remarks on the Speech of M. Dupont* (1793), an indignant reply to Dupont's atheistic speech in the National Convention at Paris, 14 December 1792, in favor of establishing anti-religious public schools; *The History of Mr. Fantom, the New Fashioned Philosopher and his Man William* (1795?), a dull tract warning of the harm done by Thomas Paine's doctrines; and "The Riot: or Half a Loaf is Better than no Bread," one of her best story-poems, written in 1795, "a Year of Scarcity and Alarm." This is a dialogue in which Jack explains to Tom that the famine conditions are from the weather, not misgovernment; that the less one has, the harder one should work: "the gentlefolks too will afford us supplies, / They'll subscribe—and they'll give up their pudding and pies." The ballad was reported to have stopped a riot near Bath. HM accepted authority; any questioning of church, government, social distinctions, or distribution of wealth shocked her. She believed that it was against God's benevolent plan for the poor to be ambitious— they should be taught that joy in heaven was their reward for deprivation on earth. Her *Cheap Repository Tracts,* a series of readable moral tales, edifying ballads, and special Sunday readings of sermons, prayers, and Bible stories, are founded on this belief. Their aims and sentiments are now unacceptable but, as many passages are drawn from life, they have historical value. Her best-known tract, *The Shepherd of Salisbury Plain* (1795), gives an accurate description of the interior of a peasant cottage of the period. HM wrote 49 of the first 114 pamphlets, signing them "Z". They sold by thousands, and these *Cheap Repository Tracts* and the tracts of 1817 were reprinted in 1819 as *Stories for the Middle Ranks of Society, and Tales for the Common People.* The books HM considered her most important contribution to ethics and literature are today her least interesting work. *Thoughts on the Importance of the Manners of the Great to General Society* (1788) urges the upper classes to set an example to the poor. It ran through seven editions in a few months, the third edition selling out in a few hours. *An Estimate of the Religion of the Fashionable World* (1790), attacking the neglect of Christianity, was equally popular. Both works lack structure (HM wrote with dreadful ease and seldom revised), yet they contain shrewd insights. In the *Estimate* HM questions whether the age can justly be termed "the Age of Benevolence": "a general alteration of habits and manners has at the same time multiplied public bounties and private distress; and it is scarcely a paradox, to say that there was probably less misery when there was less munificence." HM's books on education were enthusiastically received. Her first prose work, *Essay on Various Subjects, principally designed for Young Ladies* (1777), enjoyed a rapid sale but was used in other works and not reprinted in her collected edition. *Strictures on the Modern System of Education* (1799) went through 13 editions and sold 19,000 copies. HM's views were in advance of most of her time. She scorned "accomplishments": "The chief end to be proposed in cultivating the understandings of women, is to qualify them for the practical purposes of life." But she had no sympathy with MARY WOLLSTONE-CRAFT: "Rights of women! We will be hearing of the Rights of Children next!" Women, she believed, had their own sphere, should subdue passion, and be trained in self-denial. Bishop Porteus's fulsome praise of this book antagonized John Wolcot (Peter Pindar), who published six satires on the subject. *Hints for Forming the Character of a Princess* (1805) was designed for the education of Princess Charlotte, who is said to have approved the book. *Coelebs in Search of a Wife* (1809), HM's only novel, sets out the qualities she thought necessary in a model wife. HM finished her writing career with *An Essay on the Character of St. Paul* (1815) and three books on Christian Duties: *Practical Piety, or the Influence of the Religion of the Heart on the Conduct of Life* (1811); *Christian Morals* (1812); and *Moral Sketches of Prevailing Opinions and Manners, Foreign and Domestic, with Reflections on Prayer* (1819). All sold with a rapidity which seems extraordinary today. *Bible Rhymes* (1821) has no literary merit, and *The Spirit of Prayer* (1825) is made up of extracts from previous work. HM is also remembered as a hymn writer, although she wrote only three, the most famous being "O How wondrous is the story / Of our blest Redeemer's birth!" HM's opinions are no longer fashionable, yet her work encouraged philanthropy and raised the general culture of the nation, although its political effect on the poor may not have been all she desired. Those who learned to read tracts could equally read Paine, and frequently did. Bishop Porteus was not exaggerating greatly when he praised her writing as appealing "equally to the Cottage and the Palace."   M.S.

MORTON, Sarah Wentworth (1759–1846), American poet, was born in Boston into a distinguished family. When she was nine, her parents James and Sarah Apthorp moved to Braintree, where they became socially active with their neighbors the Adams, Quincys, and Hancocks; in this cultural and political climate SWM received an unusually good education for a girl. In 1781, she married the lawyer Perez Morton and later gave birth to five children. They moved to Dorchester in 1797, where SWM became the center of a literary and political circle. But her wealth and social position could not protect her from painful experiences, including the deaths of two children and an affair between her husband and her sister, which resulted in the latter's suicide. The scandal became the plot of the first American novel, *The Power of Sympathy;* the book greatly upset SWM, but for years it was falsely attributed to her. (The actual author was William Hill Brown, a neighbor). Her suffering is a major theme in her poetry. Yet despite such a trial, she continued to devote herself to her husband; family pride often surfaces in her works. In 1837, after Morton's death, she returned to Braintree and was active until her death in Christ Church (Episcopal).

In 1789 SWM published her first poems, "Invocation to Hope" and "Philander: A Pastoral Elegy," in *Massachusetts Magazine* under the pseudonym "Constantia." (She later used "Philenia.") The next year "Ouâbi: or The Virtues of Nature" appeared, a long poem sentimentally portraying American Indians as "noble savages"; SWM herself claimed the poem was realistic. Both her romanticism and her goal of writing about subjects "wholly American" surfaced in her next works, the epic poem "Beacon Hill" (1797) and "The Virtues of Society" (1799). Dubbed "the American Sappho," SWM published in various periodicals between 1800 and 1823, including *Mass. Mag.* and *Columbia Centinel.* She wrote some of the earliest American sonnets ("Sonnet to Gen. Lincoln" and "The Retrospect"), and was the only woman included in the first anthology of American verse. She was also a chief literary spokeswoman for abolition; for example, the last stanza of "The African Chief" reads: "Let sorrow bathe each blushing cheek, / Bend piteous o'er the tortured slave, / Whose wrongs compassion cannot speak, / Whose only refuge was the grave." In later years she mainly wrote occasional verse and hymns, in which she exhibits religious tolerance. Her last work, the only one published under her real name, was *My Mind and Its Thoughts,* (1823), a collection of poems, essays, and fragments. Although by modern standards many of her works seem overwritten, SWM was widely read and highly praised in her time; "Ouâbi" was very favorably received in England and *Mass. Mag.* called her early work "truly sublime." Her later writings were not as flamboyantly praised.   D.L.

MOXON, Elizabeth (fl. 1749), wrote a spectacularly popular early cookery book, *English Housewifery. Exemplified in above four Hundred Receipts, Never before printed, etc.,* first published in 1749, which went through 14 editions by the turn of the century. In later editions it contained a supplement of recipes "Collected by a Person of Judgement." The work includes instructions on how "To Dress Cod's Zoons" and "To fry Parsnips to look like Trout," and recipes for such curiosities as "Quaking Pudding" and "Cupid Hedge-Hogs."   R.J.

MURRAY, Judith Sargent (1751–1820), American essayist, playwright, and poet, was born in Gloucester, Mass., the daughter of a prominent merchant and shipowner, Captain Winthrop Sargent, and Judith Saunders. During her youth she had the opportunity of studying with her younger brother, Winthrop, as he prepared for Harvard. In October 1769 JSM married Captain John Stevens, a sea-trader, and remained in Gloucester where she began writing essays and occasional verse. Meanwhile Rev. John Murray began his Universalist ministry in Gloucester in 1774, and eventually numbered JSM and the Sargent family among his converts. Their conversion was viewed as heretical by Gloucester's First Parish Church, and thus the Stevens and

Sargent families were suspended from the Church. In 1780, with a congregation of former members of the First Parish Church, Murray built the first Universalist church in America, on land which JSM's father contributed. As the Revolutionary War progressed, the economy of Gloucester declined, and Captain Stevens found himself so severely in debt that in 1786 he was compelled to leave his wife and sail for the island of St. Eustatius in the Dutch West Indies to avoid imprisonment. He died shortly after his arrival. JSM then married John Murray in 1788. No children were born during her first marriage, but her second marriage produced two: George, who died in infancy, and Julia Maria. Throughout her marriage, JSM accompanied her husband on his preaching tours while continuing to write, and from 1789 through 1794 she published a number of her poems and essays in the *Massachusetts Magazine.* In 1793 the Murrays moved to Boston, where JSM would eventually write two plays. Growing financial difficulties, brought on in part by the decline of her husband's health, led JSM to collect a number of her essays (previously published in *Mass. Mag.*) and the two plays and publish them as *The Gleaner* (3 vols., 1798). John Murray's health worsened and in 1809 he suffered a paralytic stroke. With their daughter's marriage in 1812 to wealthy Mississippi planter Adam Louis Bingamon, the Murrays were at last afforded some relief from their financial worries. JSM edited her husband's letters and sermons for publication (1812–13), and in 1816, the year after his death, she completed and published the autobiography he had begun. JSM moved to Natchez, Miss., that year, and lived with her daughter until her death.

JSM began writing during her twenties and tried her hand first at poetry, but, coming from a religiously liberal family and reaching adulthood in New England during the dawn of the Revolution, she turned to the essay form to convey her growing awareness of the rights of man. Her interest in women's rights and her advocacy of educational opportunities for women, evident in an unpublished essay she wrote in 1779, reveal JSM to have been a kindred spirit with her contemporaries ABIGAIL ADAMS and MERCY WARREN. Her first published essay, "Desultory Thoughts upon the Utility of Encouraging a Degree of Self-Complacency, Especially in Female Bosoms" (1784), appeared in the Boston periodical *Gentle-*

man and Lady's Town and Country Magazine and was signed "Constantia." In it she contended that young women would not see marriage as a haven from spinsterhood and a means of gaining respectability if they had sufficient respect for themselves as individuals. After her marriage to John Murray, JSM contributed a number of poems to *Mass. Mag.,* beginning with the January 1790 issue. Between February 1792 and August 1794 the magazine published JSM's principal literary achievement, a popular series of essays entitled "The Gleaner." These essays are remarkable for their concern with ideas traditionally considered "masculine," such as nationalism and federalism. Using a fictitious character named "Mr. Vigilius" as her persona, JSM encouraged her readers to be Americans, and not Francophiles or Anglophiles as was then considered fashionable. She was a thoroughgoing nationalist, both in literature and in politics, and emphasized the value of the American plays of Royall Tyler and Mercy Warren for American audiences. She asserted that her countrymen should place more importance on the study of their own language than on the classics, noting that "National attachment should . . . dictate the studious cultivation of a national language; and it may be worthy the exertions of an enlightened legislature, to erect a standard, to raise, to dignify, to perfect and to polish a common tongue." Still, she saw a value in studying classical literature and found many heroes in Plutarch (although she was displeased to find their accomplishments often martial ones). So she maintained that "It is by the careful investigation of proper, great and virtuous actions, as performed by others, that the glow of emulation is enkindled in our bosoms." In other of her "Gleaner" essays, JSM found that the concept of liberty was closely aligned with restraint, and explained "that *licentiousness* too often assumes the sacred name of liberty." Instead, since liberty for JSM required subordination, she explained in a poem that "*Necessity* her various grades designs, / And with subordination *peace* combines." Thus she held that "the best part is always the least, and of that best part the wiser is always the lesser." Underlying these ideas was JSM's defense of a federalist government which permits the good and well born to govern in order to ensure liberty. Another significant theme of these essays is that women and men should be considered as intellectual equals. JSM

shared many of the feminist views of MARY WOLLSTONECRAFT and, like her English contemporary, she hoped that women might be allowed to receive an education that would not only make them well informed, but also enable them to support themselves financially. She hoped that girls among her readership would become part of "a new era in female history." When the Murrays moved to Boston in 1793, midway through the publication of the essays, JSM began work on her first play. While this comedy entitled *The Medium, or A Happy Tea-Party* (published as *The Medium, or Virtue Triumphant*) may well have the distinction of being the first American play produced at the Federal Street Theater, it was not a success and closed after its one performance in March 1795. Her only other theatrical effort, *The Traveller Returned,* was also unsuccessful, although it played two performances in March 1796. Robert Treat Paine, Jr., criticized *The Traveller Returned* for being pedantic and tedious, and thought that John Murray was in fact the author. Still, the dialect in both plays makes them noteworthy extensions of the literary nationalism JSM advocated. In 1798 *The Gleaner* was published by subscription in Boston, and chief among the 750 subscribers was George Washington; JSM dedicated the work to President John Adams. After this, she published eight more poems, seven in the *Boston Weekly Magazine* (30 October 1802—19 March 1803) and one in the *Boston Magazine* (14 December 1805), and devoted her literary energies thereafter to editing her husband's *Letters, and Sketches of Sermons* (3 vols., 1812–13) and his autobiography, *Records of the Life of the Rev. John Murray, Written by Himself, with a Continuation by Mrs. Judith Sargent Murray* (1816). Her essays rank among those of her contemporaries Joseph Dennie, Philip Freneau and Noah Webster.　F.J.B.

MURRAY, Hon. Sarah [Macsc] (1744–1811), topographical writer, was married first to the Hon. William Murray, then to George Aust; she died at Noel House, Kensington. *A Companion and Useful Guide to the Beauties of Scotland, to the Lakes of Westmoreland, Cumberland, and Lancashire, and to the Curiosities in the District of Craven . . .* (1799) went through three editions. It is a first-person narrative, occasionally reflecting on customs and manners, but primarily informative about distances, inns, road conditions, and sights of interest. The Advertisement boasts, "the present work differs from any other publication of the kind: for no writer of Tours has hitherto taken the trouble of ascertaining what *may* be seen, worthy of notice, in the Course of a Traveller's journey." G.B.

MURRY, Ann (fl. 1778–99), poet and children's author, is known only through what can be inferred from her writings. *Mentoria: or, The Young Ladies Instructor* (London, 1776), her first and most popular work, was originally written for her pupils; it was enormously successful, going through 11 editions, and inspiring *Sequel to Mentoria* (1799) and *Mentorian Lectures* (8 vols., 1809). AM's other work for young people is *A Concise History of the Kingdoms of Israel and Judah* (2 vols., 1783). In *Mentoria* a governess named Mentoria presents subjects of instruction and answers the questions of her students, two girls and their brother. Mentoria makes her lessons interesting by developing them with anecdotes, similes, sample situations, and examples. Drawing mainly on classical and biblical stories for her examples, she also invents such modern character types as Sir Charles Dupe. Many of her lessons end with a poem summarizing the moral content of the lesson: the majority of the poems are AM's, although she also uses Milton, Thomson, and Pope. Her lessons include reflections on virtue (industry, the duties of life) and manners (how to entertain guests and make conversation), factual information (grammar, geography) and religious instruction. The only time Mentoria fails to answer any request of her students occurs when one girl expresses interest in geometry. Mentoria bluntly replies, "It is not a part of female education." AM's religious and political biases occasionally manifest themselves in *Mentoria.* Mentoria believes in subordination and the chain of being. She condemns the Roman Catholic Church for being founded on a system of "pretended miracles and supernatural events." Mohammed is called "Mahomet the Imposter"; and, although Jews are to be pitied rather than execrated, they "must and will remain fugitives on earth" for rejecting Christ. AM condemns slavery as a "heinous crime" and sympathizes with the rebelling American colonies, blaming the disunion on the "unhappy plan of taxing, and changing the government over them." *Sequel to Mentoria* is at once more factual, more religious, and less concerned with manners than *Mentoria.* Its subjects are astronomy, physics, and geology; unlike *Mentoria* it has no poetry. Its stated intention is to "enlarge the Ideas, and inspire just Conceptions of the Deity from the Contemplation of the general System of the Universe." The question of the limits of man's knowledge inevitably arises. Mentoria acknowledges the omnipotence of God and man's dependence on His will but also urges her pupils to use their senses as instruments of instruction, "as there is scarcely any branch of knowledge that is wholly unintelligible, or that may not in some degree prove a valuable attainment." Most of AM's factual information is based on the then current findings of Dr. Herschel and on Adams's lectures. In addition to her work for juveniles, AM published a volume of poetry, *Poems on Various Subjects* (1779), which lists 425 subscribers, including David Garrick, the Duchess of Bedford, and the Countesses of Darnley, Harcourt, and Marchmont. Some of the poems are meditations; others are satires on the foibles of society, much like those written by JANE BRERETON or LADY MARY WORTLEY MONTAGU. In "A Familiar Epistle, To the Author's Sister," AM pictures a modish lady sitting in her easy chair "Intent to fabricate and deck her hair; / A Compound vile, of powder, paint, perfumes, / Adorned with diamonds, and with lofty plumes." Another important satire of AM's is *The Card Party: A Town Ecologue,* in which she mimics the prattle of frivolous ombre players. Behind AM's satire is clear moral intent: she says her poems are meant to impress on others the instability of human happiness and the necessity of directing the mind to the hope of obtaining heaven. Her first poem is addressed not to a muse but to the Supreme Being. In "Damon and Thyrsis" she sounds much like Samuel Johnson on happiness: "Alas, my Thyrsis, short and vain's the date, / Of human happiness, prescrib'd by Fate; / Our views are boundless, circumscrib'd our gains; / By Hope we are elated, scourg'd by pains." AM celebrates the glories of heaven in many of her poems. She is very much the 18th-century writer in her themes, her morality, and her heavily endstopped couplets. A.W.E.

N

NEWCASTLE, Margaret Cavendish, Duchess of (1623–73), author of a dozen books in almost as many genres, was born into a wealthy country family as the youngest child of Elizabeth and Thomas Lucas of Colchester, Essex. Her childhood was secluded, and she was allowed to indulge herself in daydreams and flamboyant dress of her own design, a habit she continued into adulthood. Her education at home by tutors was undisciplined and left its mark on all her writing; she never absorbed some elementary principles of grammar, and she was innocent of the idea of revision. After the Civil War broke out, she volunteered, in spite of her chronic bashfulness, to serve as maid of honor to the distressed Queen Henrietta Maria in Oxford, and from there followed the Queen into exile in France. In Paris she met and fell in love with the handsome, gallant, urbane William Cavendish, then Marquis, later Duke, of Newcastle, 30 years her senior. After their marriage in 1645 D of N shared her husband's exile for the next 15 years, during most of which time they lived on credit in Antwerp. In 1651 D of N journeyed to England with her brother-in-law in an attempt to raise money and retrieve what she could from the Cavendish estates; she was alone during most of her unsuccessful 18-month stay in London and began writing poetry to console herself. At the Restoration the Newcastles returned to England and, when the Duke was excluded from Charles II's government, retired with great contentment to the family estates. Their marriage was happy and also particularly fortunate for D of N as a 17th-century woman writer. The Duke, whom she idolized, was himself an amateur poet and playwright, and a generous patron of writers, philosophers, and artists. He encouraged and assisted his young, beautiful, and childless wife in her writing, which she described as her "chiefest delight and greatest pastime." She praised the Duke for his unusual tolerance: "You are pleased to peruse my works, and approve of them so well, as to give me leave to publish them, which is a favour few husbands would grant their wives; but your lordship is an extraordinary husband." Although D of N had produced a good deal of juvenilia, she began writing with a view to publication only after her marriage. She was motivated by ambition and saw literature as the only avenue to renown for a woman: "I confess my ambition is restless and not ordinary, because it would have an extraordinary fame; and since all heroic actions, public employments, powerful governments, and eloquent pleadings are denied our sex in this age, or at least would be condemned for want of custom, is the cause I write so much." She was widely regarded as eccentric when she published her works and then proceeded to bestow copies on friends and upon the university libraries; her extravagant dress confirmed the general opinion of her oddity. When, because of her passionate interest in natural philosophy, she arranged to be invited to visit the Royal Society in 1667, both her purpose in the visit and the opulence of her equipage laid her open to ridicule. Although people laughed at her behind her back, they flattered her because of her rank. At her death she was buried in the Newcastle tomb in Westminster Abbey; her epitaph, written by her husband, describes her as "a wise, witty, and learned lady, which her many books do well testify; she was a most virtuous and a loving and careful wife, and was with her lord all the time of his banishment and miseries, and when he came home never parted from him in his solitary retirements." As a further tribute, the Duke had compiled and printed in 1676 a collection of the letters and poems written in praise of the Duchess.

D of N was the first Englishwoman to publish extensively; several of her books appeared in multiple editions, with the later editions sometimes expanded and altered. Her first book, *Poems and Fancies* (1653), contains verse not only about the fairy kingdom but also about an atomic theory of matter. *Philosophical Fancies* (1653), a small volume of verse speculations about natural philosophy, appeared in a revised and expanded form in 1655 as *Philosophical and Physical Opinions*. Although her theories are often nonsense, she was the first Englishwoman to write about science; her lifelong passion for natural philosophy was characteristic of the age. The letter dedicating the *Opinions* "To the Two Most Famous Universities of England" is a passionate defense of women and the century's most moving appeal for women's education. She laments that women are "become like worms, that only live in the dull earth of ignorance, winding ourselves sometimes out by the help of some refreshing rain of good education, which seldom is given us, for we are kept like birds in cages to hop up and down in our houses, not suffered to fly abroad to see the several changes of fortune and the various humors ordained and created by nature, and wanting the experience of nature, we must needs want the understanding and knowledge, and so consequently prudence and invention of men." D of N went on to write essays on a wide variety of subjects, published in a disorganized collection, *The World's Olio* (1655), a mixture or stew, as the title indicates. She attempted another genre in her collection of tales, *Nature's Pictures Drawn by Fancy's Pencil to the Life* (1656). At the end of the volume is a little masterpiece, "A True Relation of My Birth, Breeding, and Life," the first autobiography published by a woman in England. "A True Relation" gives a charming picture of a large, closely knit, aristocratic family and of its strong and capable head, the widowed Elizabeth Lucas, "very skillful in leases and setting of lands, and court keeping, ordering of stewards, and the like affairs." D of N was one of the many who wrote closet drama while the English theaters were closed. In 1662 she published a collection entitled

Plays, followed in 1668 by *Plays Never Before Printed*. The first volume includes 14 plays, several in two parts; the second includes five plays and various dramatic fragments. The plays depict heroines who win fame as soldiers and scholars, but the strikingly original content is undercut by the chaotic form. Often the individual scenes have no beginning, middle, or end; one scene simply stops abruptly and an unrelated scene follows. Choosing a more congenial form, D of N wrote *Orations* (1662), but these are less interesting in content. Her *Sociable Letters* (1664) is a charming volume because the informality and brevity of the form suit her fanciful and undisciplined talents. D of N displays here more than elsewhere her humor, good sense, and occasionally shrewd social observation. She continued to write about her scientific interests in *Philosophical Letters* (1664), which disputes the theories of Hobbes, Descartes, Henry More and Van Helmont; *Observations upon Experimental Philosophy* (1666), which reacts to Robert Hooke's work with the microscope; and *The Description of a New Blazing World*, which is a bizarre science fiction tale appended to the *Observations*. Her finest work is *The Life of the Thrice Noble, High and Puissant Prince William Cavendish, Duke, Marquess, and Earl of Newcastle* (1667), the first biography of a husband to be published by an Englishwoman, which caused Samuel Pepys to describe her as "a mad, conceited, and ridiculous woman." Far from ridiculous, the biography made a contribution to the then underdeveloped art of biography. Focusing on the Duke during the Civil War and the Interregnum, the *Life* gives a portrait of the loyal nobleman in war and exile, the ideal aristocrat serving his king. Although she did not write a separate critical piece, a good deal of literary criticism is scattered throughout D of N's works. She is always enthusiastic and sometimes perceptive in her assessments of earlier English writers, Shakespeare being her particular favorite. Her own writing is characteristically weak in form and style. All her works are flawed by errors in grammar, spelling, and punctuation; her verse is often defective in meter and rhythm; her long works are idiosyncratic and often chaotic in structure and organization. She was aware of these defects and so diffident about them, and about her temerity as a woman writer, that she armed her books with numerous prefaces, prefatory letters, and introductory verses, explaining and apologizing for herself and her writing. At the same time, the folio volumes are ascribed resoundingly to "The Thrice Noble, Illustrious, and Excellent Princess, the Duchess of Newcastle" and often prefaced with an engraving of the author's picture. In spite of their defects, her works compel attention and sometimes admiration for their catholic concerns, unusual for a woman of D of N's generation, and for their social and historical interest. Her works display a genuine affection for country life, and her love of animals manifests itself in an unusually early humanitarian feeling for their sufferings. She was the most outspoken feminist of the century, and her feminist aspirations are responsible for the originality in her fictions. Her tales and plays typically center on a heroine rather than a hero: usually an orphan, she travels to distant lands and amazes a foreign prince with her wit and wisdom, usually assuming rule or a share of the rule; or she wins acclaim and immortality with the pen or the sword. These fictions are the thinnest of disguises for D of N's own life and daydreams and as such show us, as no other documents, the interior life of the 17th-century lady. In *The Common Reader* Virginia Woolf wrote of D of N, "Though her philosophies are futile, and her plays intolerable, and her verses mainly dull, the vast bulk of the Duchess is leavened by a vein of authentic fire."   N.C.

NIHELL, Elizabeth (1723–?), medical writer and midwife, was an educated and prosperous woman of good family and influential connections. She was encouraged in her medical work by her husband, James Nihell, M.D., a surgeon-apothecary and medical writer. Although a Protestant by birth, EN obtained dispensation by royal decree of the Duke of Orleans to study midwifery under Roman Catholic teachers at the famous Hôtel Dieu, Paris, where midwifery was taught without the supervision or intervention of medical men. During her two-year apprenticeship, EN claimed to have assisted at 900 births where she put into practice the natural birthing methods of her teacher, Mme. Pour, the head *accoucheuse.* The French woman-midwives at this time emphasized manipulation over the use of "modern" instruments, such as the fashionable but potentially fatal forceps, the iron crochet, and the fastening hooks. After her training in Paris, EN returned to London and with her husband opened a medical office in the Haymarket. She is most noted

for her *Treatise On The Art Of Midwifery* (1760), a lively contribution to the 18th-century midwifery dispute, in which she attacks Dr. William Smellie, a leading Scottish man-midwife, teacher, and medical writer. Tobias Smollett, the Scottish novelist and a former London surgeon (during 1714), defended Smellie and ridiculed EN in his *Critical Review* (1760).

EN's works and attributions are: *Traité des eaux Minerales de la Ville de Rouen* [Treatise on the Mineral Waters of the City of Rouen] (1759), on hydrotherapy; *A Treatise On The Art of Midwifery* (1760, French trans. 1770); "An Answer to the Author of *The Critical Review,* For March 1760, Upon the Article of Mrs. Nihell's *Treatise*" (1760) (EN's response to Smollett's attack); and *Observations on the Impropriety of Men being Employed in the Business of Midwifery* (post. publ. 1827), possibly adapted from EN's *Treatise.* EN's *Art of Midwifery* answered Smellie's *Treatise on the Theory and Practice of Midwifery* (1751) and his case-history volume of 1754. Smellie's midwifery practices represented to EN the height of masculine arrogance, exploitation of female ignorance, and abuse of human life. During the latter half of the 18th century, medical men like Smellie, aided by the Royal College of Physicians and the Corporation of Surgeons, attempted to "professionalize" midwifery by establishing licensing regulations, which eventually resulted in the subversion of medical women's traditional claims to midwifery. Because 18th-century women were denied university-level training, they lacked formal medical instruction (esp. in anatomy) and, thus, were debarred from licensed practice. With the invasion of mercenary medical men, woman-midwives found themselves robbed of employment and "professional" roles. Smellie discredited woman-midwives for haphazard training and asserted the superiority of man-midwives who, through training and licensing, were able to purchase such "necessary" birthing instruments as the speculum, scapel, lasso, and tenacula which, he argued, aided the delivery of the child and travail of the mother. In Part I of her *Treatise,* EN registers her contempt for Smellie and his tribe of "Instrumentarians" who choose to "cut their Way in, with iron and steel." Man-midwives, she argued, are naturally inferior to woman-midwives, whose smaller hands can more easily turn the child and whose temperaments are more compassionate and patient:

"The common and gentlest methods are the hands of women, who ought therefore to be preferred to men, and to be restored to their antient and rightful possession." EN employs a standard feminist strategy, drawing up a catalogue of women-worthies. She cites Agnodice, Cleopatra, and Aspasia as distinguished midwives of antiquity. EN also draws support from contemporary medical men who lectured or published against the medical "Moderns." In Part II, EN anticipates "Victorian" attitudes toward the naked female body when she discourages the practice of medical men "touching" women during examinations and childbirth (hence, under-the-sheet deliveries) (cf. Philip Thicknesse, *Man-Midwifery Analysed*, 1764, a parallel essay). Historically, EN's work follows that of Peter Chamberlen the Elder, Nicholas Culpeper, ELIZABETH CELLIER, and JANE SHARP, all of whom urged independent woman-midwives to incorporate and upgrade their practice. EN's medical writing precedes that of MARTHA MEARS, whose *Pupil of Nature* (1797) stands as the woman-midwives' final pronunciamento.   M.M.

NORMAN, Elizabeth (fl. 1789), novelist, wrote one work which appeared in 1789 and was quickly forgotten. Nothing is known about her life. *The Child of Woe* is an epistolary novel with little plot or characterization, a turgid style, and overblown sentiments; it is also marred by EN's predilection for trivia, which results in minute descriptions of women's apparel and the recording of mindless chatter. Eliza, the "child of woe," is not introduced until p. 88, when she begins to tell her own melodramatic story: "Sad Eliza lives to say— her fond, her faithful Edward lives no more— o'erwhelmed by briny waves, for ever from my sight. I must lay down my pen, and for a while indulge the silent drops of sorrow that chace [sic] each other down my pallid cheek. When the melancholy suffusion is subsided, I will again resume it." *The Analytical Review* article (probably by MARY WOLLSTONECRAFT), which terms *The Child of Woe* "a truly feminine novel," makes use of the opportunity to criticize women writers and the largely female public to which they cater: "Unnatural characters, improbable incidents, sad tales of woe rehearsed in an affected, half-prose, half-poetical style, exquisite double-refined sensibility, dazzling beauty, and *elegant* drapery, to adorn the celestial body (these descriptions cannot be too minute) should never

be forgotten in a book intended to amuse the fair" (April, 1789). The *Critical Review* criticizes EN for "prose almost run mad" and, "on the whole, an insignificant and insipid work."   M.A.B.

NORTHUMBERLAND, Elizabeth Percy, Duchess of (1716–76), diarist, was the daughter of Algernon Seymour, seventh Duke of Somerset. Lady Betty, as she was called, married Sir Hugh Smithson in 1740; the couple lived at Stanwyck until the death of her brother, Lord Beauchamp, in 1744 turned her into her parents' only heir. Thereafter she and her husband lived at Alnwick Castle in Northumberland, Syon House in Middlesex, and Northumberland House in London, the scene of frequent and lavish entertainments. Sir Hugh was made Earl of Northumberland and, on his father-in-law's death in 1750, Duke of Northumberland. D of N had conflicts with her grandfather, the old Duke of Somerset, until his death in 1748. He criticized her interest in education, calling her "a prig and a bluestocking." He so disapproved of her marriage that he attempted, but failed, to have her disinherited. D of N was a Lady of the Bedchamber to, and a personal friend of, Queen Charlotte. She was exceptionally proud and loved the pomp and splendor of her status. It is said that she was once reprimanded by the Queen for traveling with a greater retinue than the Queen herself. On 5 July 1764 she entertained 1500 guests at Northumberland House in celebration of George III's birthday. D of N and her husband were politically active, taking a prominent part in the Westminster elections of 1767 and gaining unpopularity for opposing John Wilkes. D of N had considerable literary taste and entertained the noted writers of her era. James Boswell considered himself privileged to correspond with her as "a woman of the first consequence." Her pride derived from the Percy name, inherited from her mother; Horace Walpole considered such pride absurd, as her claim was the result of the lack of surviving male heirs. D of N had two sons, Hugh (b. 1742), later second Duke of Northumberland, and Algernon (b. 1750), created Earl of Beverley in 1790, and a daughter, Elizabeth, who remained unmarried. In later years failing health forced D of N to resign her position as Lady of the Bedchamber. It had been predicted that she would die before she reached the age of 60; she died on her 60th birthday in Alnwick.

D of N's diaries, written between 1752 and 1776, were published in 1926 as *Diaries of a Duchess*. The original journals are at Alnwick. They record her London life and her travels throughout England and abroad. D of N could remark informally on the passing scene. In July 1761 she wrote: "Ld. Huntingdon, Groom of the Stole, & Ld. Ashburnham, Lord in Waiting to the King, had great altercation on the subject of giving the King his shirt. A quarrel also happened this Evening at Ranelagh between Poll Davis & Kitty Fisher, two very pretty Women of the Town, (the first kept by Lord Coventry, the second by Mr. Chetwynd), in which the former not only boxed the others Ears, but also hit Ld. Coventry a slap on the Face, for which she was turned out of Ranelagh & forbid to come there any more." She could also consciously write history, as on the occasion of the royal marriage: "At half-an-hour after Seven, everybody assembled at St. James's. The Peers, Peeresses & Peers Daughters waited in the King's Levee Room, till the procession begun & proceeded down the great Stairs, which was lined with a double Row of Horse Guards (as was the Cloisters) in their Shoes, to the Chappel in the following Order: First Drums & Trumpets, then the Serjeant Trumpeters. . . . The Bride was dressed in a Silver Tissue, stiffen body'd Gown, embroidered & trimmed with Silver, on her Head a little Cap of purple Velvet quite covered with Diamonds." During a trip to Holland D of N noted that Antwerp women were "as ugly as the devil." Walpole accused her of being mischievous while pretending to be frank. Energetic and curious, she loved travel, witnessing on one of her visits to France the marrige of the Dauphin to Marie Antoinette. She visited Voltaire in Switzerland and received presents of a pineapple and a melon.   M.My.

NORTON, Frances, Lady (1640–1731), de-votional writer and poet, was born in Wiltshire, third daughter of Ralph Freke. By her first marriage (c. 1672) to Sir George Norton, FN had three children, of whom Grace (later LADY GETHIN) survived infancy. FN, who had ceased to live with Norton, composed her two devotional treatises, *The Applause of Virtue* and *Memento Mori: Or, Meditations on Death*, after the death of this daughter in 1697. She was apparently also instrumental in the publication, in 1699, of her daughter's collected manuscript papers as *Misery's Virtues Whet-Stone* (reprinted 1700 as *Reliquiae Gethinianae*), praised successively by Congreve, Ballard, and Edmund Gosse. FN twice remarried in her later years: in 1718 to Colonel Ambrose Norton (d. 1723) and, in 1724, to William Jones. She was acclaimed for her piety and for her extensive benefactions to the church. FN's two devotional works, although initially intended for her own "melancholy divertisement," were published in 1705, bound in one volume. Consisting in large part of quotations from ancient and modern writers, they are of more value in illustrating the extent of FN's learning and reading, which apparently included Greek and Latin authors in the original, than as demonstrating any great facility in the composition of "divine and moral essays." She also composed a number of pious verses, which she then embroidered on the backs and seats of chairs and stools. These poems were published as *A Miscellany of Poems* (Bristol, 1714). While the composition of religious "essays" and poems was, like the transcription of devotional materials, a not uncommon practice among devout women of the period, the signed publication of such works during the author's lifetime was comparatively unusual, and distinguishes FN from most of her contemporaries among the devotional writers.   R.F.

O

O'BRIEN, Mary (fl. 1790), poet and playwright, has been identified only as the wife of Patrick O'Brien. The title page of *The Political Monitor, or the Regent's Friend* (1790) cites MO as the author of *Charles Henley*, a novel in two volumes. MO has also been identified as the author of a comic opera, *The Temple of Virtue*, undated. *The Political Monitor* is a collection of poems inspired by the agitation in the regency crisis during George III's "indisposition" (1788). Several poems are satiric attacks on William Pitt, including "Paddy's Salutation to the Right Honorable William Pitt," bouncy verse in ballad stanzas, "Freedom of John Bull" ("Jacky Bull" is dragged by the nose by "Billy Pitt") in rhymed couplets, and "Paddy's Opinion: An Irish Ballad." Occasional verse is represented in an "Ode for the Prince of Wales's Birthday" and "On the Birthday of Her Royal Highness, the Princess Royal," in octave stanzas. The verses are competent but mediocre, the diction conventional: "Pomona hails thy birth" and "Happy the day / That gave Charlotta birth." MO celebrates a wedding in "A Pastoral Ode to the Duchess of Rutland," using traditional arrival-of-spring imagery. She is more inspired in another satire, "Lines on a Bishop" ("bishops may be mended"), and in an "Ode to Milton," as she suggests that his blindness should not be featured in a London monument, but rather "his lamps of light" that "in higher regions burn" should be emphasized. MO has also been suggested as the author of *The Fallen Patriot: a Comedy in Five Acts* (1790), and *The Pious Incendiaries, etc.* (poetry, 1783). E.N.

OGLE, Margaret (fl. 1742), poet, wrote *Mordecai Triumphant: or, The Fall of Haman . . . An Heroic Poem* (1742) as satire and warning to the prime minister Robert Walpole, who, she hopes, may "swing on Tyburn, with the Approbation / Of all true Britons" since he "has sold the nation." With wooden couplets and an excessive number of run-on lines, the poem tells the story of Vashti and Esther: "*Vashti* I thought in Beauty far excell'd / But lovely *Esther* is unparallel'd." J.J.

O'NEIL, Henrietta (1758–93), poet, was the daughter of Viscount Dungarvon. She married John O'Neil of Slanes Castle in Co. Antrim. She was a friend of CHARLOTTE SMITH, who preserved her poems, publishing one in her book *Desmond* and another in her own second volume of poetry. The first entitled "Ode to the poppy" is a melancholy lyric lamenting the passing of "Love and Joy" and praising the poppy for its "potent charm" that can "agonizing Pain disarm; / Expel imperious Memory from her seat, / And bid the Throbbing heart forget to beat." The second poem, "Verses written on seeing her two sons at play," is marked by a similar melancholy, urging the boys to "revel long in childhood's thoughtless joys" when they can find happiness "centered in the bounding ball." A mother, however, knows that "the dark train of human ills" will soon come, "a sad certainty of future sighs." The poem ends gloomily: "For ah! how few have found existence sweet, / Where grief is sure, but happiness deceit!" J.T.

OPIE, Amelia [Alderson] (1769–1853), novelist, was born at Norwich where her father, a medical doctor, was a leading member of local intellectual society. Brought up as a daughter of "rational dissent," she made the acquaintance of William Godwin in 1794 when he visited her father's house and saw him frequently, on his regular visits to London, over the next few years. Wishing to become an actress and playwright, she knew Holcroft, ELIZABETH INCHBALD, Mrs. Siddons, and others connected with the theater, although she never fully shared their libertarian views. She had an immense admiration for MARY WOLLSTONECRAFT, whom she knew and with whom she corresponded. The often-repeated story that Godwin asked her to marry him is based on a misunderstanding of the entry in his journal for 10 July 1796 "Propose to Alderson," which refers to Godwin's successful efforts to raise money from Dr. Alderson for the poet Robert Merry, who was then under arrest for debt. In 1798 Amelia married the Cornish painter John Opie, then a fashionable portraitist despite his rough country manners, and shortly afterward began to publish books of poems, tales, and novels. After Opie's death in 1807 AO returned permanently to Norwich, where she was converted to Quakerism and devoted much of the remainder of her life to charity and religion.

AO's chief published works are *The Dangers of Coquetry* (1790), brought out anonymously; *Father and Daughter* (1801); *Adeline Mowbray* (1804); *Simple Tales* (1806); *Valentine's Eve* (1816); and *Madeline* (1822), all novels or "tales," as she preferred to call them; a volume of *Poems* (1802); a memoir of John Opie attached to his *Lectures on Painting* (1809); a number of moral works, including *Illustrations of Lying* (1825) and *Detraction Displayed* (1828); and finally a further volume of poems, *Lays for the Dead* (1834). The most interesting work is *Adeline Mowbray, or the Mother and Daughter, A Tale*, first published at a time when reaction against the theories of Godwin and Wollstonecraft was at its most bitter, which relates the succession of disasters which befall Adeline in her attempts to live out in practice the advanced views of "Glenmurray." Some modern readers have taken it as secretly glamorizing the liberated life—and certainly the descriptions of conventional marriage do not inspire respect—but there is no doubt that AO genuinely intended her tale as a warning, drawing on the actual experience of Wollstonecraft and other friends to point her lesson. Her other novels are most concerned with love and seduction in high life and, although the writing is sometimes lively,

the moral purpose is never adequately concealed, and few of the characters have credible individuality. "In his dealings with men, Sir Patrick was a man of honour," AO wrote of a boorish husband, "in his dealings with women, completely the reverse: he considered them as a race of subordinate beings, formed for the service and amusement of men; and that if, like horses, they were well lodged, fed, and kept clean, they had no right to complain." W.S.C.

OSBORN, Sarah (1714–96), American autobiographer and letter writer, was the daughter of Benjamin and Susanna Haggar. The family emigrated to America and settled first in Boston and then in Newport, R.I., where SO met and, in 1731, married Samuel Wheaton. Two years later, he was lost at sea, leaving her with one child. She remarried and in 1737 was admitted to the Congregational Church in Newport, where she encountered SUSANNA ANTHONY, with whom she became friendly. In 1755 she wrote her spiritual autobiography *The Nature, Certainty, and Evidence of True Christianity*, which outlined her life from 1743 to 1753. This was expanded with the help of the minister Samuel Hopkins to become *Memoirs of the Life of Mrs. Sarah Osborn* (1799). SO suffered during the Revolutionary War and found herself at times sick and desolate. In addition she had to come to terms with the deaths of her husband, father, brother and only child. In 1807 her letters, together with those of Susanna Anthony, were published as *Familiar Letters Written by Mrs. Sarah Osborn and Miss Susanna Anthony*. SO's religious writing is typical of 18th-century American women; less intellectually robust than that of earlier periods, it is more given to excessive sentiment and ecstatic piety. Her letters from the period 1740 to 1779 to her "very dear and lovely friend" urge both of them to greater spiritual effort: "Oh, my friend, trust, love, and live upon, this good, and faithful God." Although usually in the effusive religious mode, SO's letters yet seem more given to doubts or "murmurings" than her friend's, and there is fear that SO will be left alone "in this howling wilderness." But she claims to derive much benefit from Anthony's comfort and rebukes during her times of sickness, misery, and doubt. J.T.

OSBORN, Sarah (1693–1775), letter writer,

was the daughter of Admiral Sir George Byng, a distinguished naval hero created Viscount Torrington, and Margaret Master Byng. SO was born at Southill, Beds., one of a family of eleven sons and four daughters. In 1710 she married John Osborn of Chicksands Priory, eldest son of Sir John Osborn and great-nephew of Dorothy Temple. SO had five children, but only Danvers (b. 1716) survived; in 1719 John Osborn died, a blow which SO felt all her long life. Having to become executrix of his ill-managed estate and guardian to her only surviving son forced SO to learn business and money management. With advice from her father and her brother Robert, she improved the estate until her son, now Sir Danvers, came of age. In 1740 Sir Danvers married Lady Mary Montagu, daughter of the Earl of Halifax. They had two sons, George (1742) and John (1743); during the latter birth Lady Mary died, and Sir Danvers traveled continuously thereafter, eventually dying in America in 1753 when governor of New York. At 60 SO once again assumed the duties of managing the inheritance of minors and for ten years devoted herself to her grandsons' welfare, relying on advice from their uncle, Lord Halifax, whose household she managed. SO's fourth brother, Admiral John Byng, was court-martialed and then executed at Portsmouth in 1757, on charges of neglect of duty in a battle with the French in 1756. Voltaire, who referred to this unjust and politically motivated execution in *Candide*, worked strenuously for a lesser sentence, as did SO, in many letters and memorials. Her grandson George Osborn entered the army; John entered the diplomatic service.

SO's familiar letters have been twice published, first by Emily F.D. Osborn in 1890, and then with an introduction by John McClelland in 1930. Their style is easy and comfortable. Subjects range from politics, requests to have bills paid, to excursions to the opera. To her brother Jack she wrote, "Don't laugh when I tell you there has been one of our men of war sent from a port in the East Indies in search of an island which they had the fortune to find, and landed some of the crew to discover the sort of people upon it. They found them a strong, robust people eight feet and a half high. A girl of thirteen was seven foot, and others in proportion." In a typical letter, "Mother Osborn," as her friend Horace Walpole affectionately called her, could discuss Parliament and the engagement of FRANCES GREVILLE's beautiful daughter, who would not marry LADY HOLLAND's eldest son, Stephen Fox: "Your brother has run away, and left me to add that the House sits every day, till half after ten, but last night till 2 this morning. I think there must be a fresh set soon, for these will all be demolished. . . . Mr. Fox was certainly refused (whatever was thought abroad) when he made his last proposal here to Miss Greville. She could not bring herself to consent, and therefore he told his friend Crew she was the woman to make him happy. He followed his advice and proposed immediately, was accepted, and the conclusion to be directly, to the amazement of the town that one so much in love as Fox was, should not only resign but give her to another. She, however, is a lucky girl, and the envy of all the young women in town" (1766).   J.A.G.

P

PAKINGTON, Dorothy, Lady (?–1679), moralist, was the youngest daughter of Thomas Coventry, Lord Coventry (1620–80) and one of the most learned ladies of her time. She was the wife of Sir John Pakington and the contemporary of other accomplished women, such as the DUCHESS OF NEWCASTLE, KATHERINE PHILIPS, and LUCY HUTCHINSON. Before, during, and after the Restoration, DP made remarkable contributions to religious and intellectual activities by establishing her husband's home at Westwood, Worcs., as the center for discussions by the most learned Church of England divines. She herself had been tutored by the noted scholar Sir Norton Knatchbull and was apparently of superior intelligence, wit, and literacy. She moved in the most exclusive social circles and was loyal to the Stuart cause; contemporary historians feel that she must have stimulated the publication of many treatises even if she may not have had an active part in the actual writing itself.

For many years she was the supposed author of a series of books including the extremely popular *Whole Duty of Man,* the *Gentleman's Calling,* and the *Ladies' Calling.* When the first edition of the *Whole Duty of Man* was published anonymously in 1658, it was prefaced with a statement by Dr. Henry Hammond, who lived at DP's home from 1649 until his death in 1660, and the general supposition was that she had written it. Various incidents and statements supported this belief for several decades, but studies of internal evidence during the 19th century made it seem that it was probably written by Richard Allestree, although all admit that DP was fully equal to the task; certainly she may be the author, excluded on the grounds that so popular a

book is unlikely to have come from a female pen. DP was an acknowledged expert in the history of pagan and Christian systems of thought, and she spent years in the company of Royalist divines, including Dr. Hammond, Bishop Fell, Bishop Morley, Bishop Pearson, Bishop Henchman, Bishop Gunning, Canon Richard Allestree, and the amanuensis William Fulman. The *Ladies' Calling* is the book with which her name is most persistently linked. Written in protest against the improprieties of the Restoration court (as indeed was the whole series), it extols the virtues of modesty, meekness, sobriety, piety, and restraint in manners and speech. It would indeed be ironic if, in espousing these qualities, LP prevented recognition of her own authorship. M.P.

PALMER, Charlotte (fl. 1780–1800), novelist and children's author, was also a teacher, "having Myself taught Writing to young Ladies above nine years," she wrote from Hendon in 1797. She relied on this experience in producing instructive books for children, in addition to two novels and an allegory. Her first published work was *Female Stability; or the History of Miss Belville* in five volumes issued by Francis Newbery in 1780. Following the vogue for epistolary writing, it was undertaken in CP's youth for personal amusement and was claimed to be unrevised. The heroine who refused to marry after the death of her lover epitomizes female tenderness and generosity, and her character represents an idealized femininity removed from the vagaries of the daily world. Although the title page of the work refers to her as the "late Miss Palmer," other books are attributed to her, including in 1792 *It is or it is not,* a two-volume novel, and *Integrity and Content, an allegory,* neither published with Newbery. In 1797, CP returned to the family publishing firm when Elizabeth Newbery issued her *A Newly Invented Copybook* and *Letters on Several Subjects from a Preceptress to her Pupils who have left School addressed chiefly to real characters;* intending it for schoolmasters and private tutors and their more skillful pupils, CP claimed it was "an easy and speedy Mode of attaining and retaining the Principal Parts of Speech." Laid out with examples at the top and rules at the bottom of each page, it was quite literally a "copybook." Having intended it for the use of male tutors, she apologized for presuming to tell a man how to teach: "I hope I shall not be considered as having encroached on an Employment belonging to the opposite sex, nor as endeavouring to diminish their superiority." *Letters* included conventional instructive pieces addressed to young ladies aged 15 to 20 to encourage them to continue their education after leaving school. It accepted the traditional modes of behavior for middle-class girls and this guaranteed the critical acclaim of the *Gentleman's Magazine* (Aug. 1798), which concluded "with most heartily recommending these very sensible Letters of Miss Charlotte Palmer to the notice of the publick, and particularly to the Ladies." CP's *Three Instructive Tales for Little Folk; Simple and Careful, Industry and Sloth, and the Cousins,* listed in Newbery's 1800 *Catalogue,* has the same conventional moral values and the same easy tone of *Letters,* although directed toward a younger audience. The children are characterized according to adult gender roles.   D.L.L.

PALMER, Mary (1716–94), dialect author, was the eldest daughter of Samuel Reynolds, master of the grammar school at Plympton Earl, Devon, and Theophila Potter. MP was the sister of Sir Joshua Reynolds (b. 1723), who was influenced by her love of drawing; she assisted him financially in his career. MP married John Palmer of Torrington, Devon, in 1740. He was educated for a solicitor but never practiced. In 1752 he built the house later known as Palmer House at Great Torrington, and there Samuel Johnson stayed when visiting Devon with Sir Joshua. MP had two sons, who both became clergymen, and three daughters. The eldest, Mary, inherited Sir Joshua's fortune, and her sister Theophila often sat for him, notably for "Strawberry Girl."

FANNY BURNEY often met the two sisters at Sir Joshua's house. MP long survived her husband, who died in 1770. Sir Joshua painted her twice, once in about 1741, and again when she was apparently about 60. MP wrote *A Devonshire Dialogue,* "the best piece of literature in the vernacular of Devon." During her lifetime the MS was shown to a few friends, who made extracts from it, some of which were later inserted in various periodicals without acknowledgment. In 1837 an incomplete version was published with a glossary by J.F. Palmer. In 1839 the complete work was edited by Mrs. Gwatkin (Theophila), and there is an edition dated 1869. The advertisement for the 1837 edition states: "the Author's conduct through life is perhaps the best guarantee for the excellent moral which pervades the whole." In the *Dialogue,* Betty, a servant maid, discusses her master, Farmer Hogg, with Robin, her lover. Hogg is a drunken lout who mistreats his long-suffering wife and half starves his apprentice. Yet the work is humorous, was many times reprinted, and was still sold by local booksellers at the turn of the century.   M.S.

PARKER, Mary Ann (1760?–?), travel writer, set sail for the coast of New Zealand aboard "The Gorgon," an English man-of-war, in 1791. Her husband, Captain John Parker, had received a commission to bring badly needed supplies to the colonists who had settled there. The ship, for private commercial reasons, was also to make stopovers in various ports lining the coast of Spain and Africa. This voyage and the adventures encountered along the way provided the rich material for MP's chronicle, *A Voyage Around The World.* In her book, she describes the exotic people and places she visited with such a lack of bias and such grace, good humor, and insight that the reader is captivated by her personality. She is as adaptable to the foothills of Santa Cruz and an overattentive guide as she is to the rainforests of New South Wales and a picnic with its armed and potentially fierce natives. She writes of her experience in Santa Cruz, "It may afford a smile to my readers to add, that, after it was found out that I could speak Spanish, I entered into conversation with my muleteer, which made him so proud of his charge, that, previous to our entering any town or village, he, with great form, requested me to sit upright, and then spread my hair very curiously over my shoulders. Poor fellow! Could I be displeased with his request;

since it arose, without doubt, from a desire of making me appear to the greatest advantage?" Of her experience with the startling and warriorlike people of New South Wales, she writes that she "never felt the least fear when in their company," since she comported herself in a fashion that her hosts would view as polite and amiable. An example of MP's ability to admire what would normally be outside the range of an Englishwoman's 18th-century world is found in this description of an African woman: "The beauty of one of the females particularly struck my attention; the elegance of her deportment, the symmetry of her features, and the pleasing curl of her fine dark hair, could not pass unnoticed by any, excepting those who were unwilling to pay that tribute to the simplicity of nature, which all the assistance of art could not place them in possession of." MP's voyage was not entirely a pleasurable one. She witnessed a great many tragedies, such as the loss of men at sea and the brutal conditions aboard prisoner ships where the mercenary captains were paid for a prisoner delivered dead or alive. She suffered through storms at sea when great fireballs came hurling through the sky and journeyed for weeks through islands of ice. Her greatest hardship, however, occurred on her return to England. During the voyage home, John Parker contracted yellow fever and died when he arrived in England. This left MP griefstricken and nearly destitute. At the suggestion of a friend, she decided to publish her account of the voyage as a means to support her small family. Her writing was also a labor of love, since she devised it as an affectionate memorial to her husband.   D.B.

PARRY, Catherine (?–1788), novelist, signed her one epistolary novel from "Montgomeryshire, North Wales," claiming "some affecting circumstances happened in America" which induced her to write *Eden Valley* (1784). Criticism of the American Revolution, "this scene of desolation and distress," does indeed comprise a subplot in which brother kills brother, but the main sentimental and clichéed plot tells of the loves of two sisters—giddy, humorous Louisa and quiet, sentimental Emma. A brother kills his sister's clergyman lover in defending her honor; the seductress of the clergyman penitently dies of fever at the news, but not before leaving her fortune to the wronged Emma, who devotes her life to charitable activities.   G.B.

PARSONS, Eliza [Phelp] (1748?–1811), novelist, daughter of a Plymouth wine merchant, married Mr. Parsons, a turpentine distiller, of Stonehouse. She had eight children. The family lived comfortably until Parsons suffered business losses during the American Revolution. They then (1778–79) moved to London, where Parsons began to rebuild his business. In 1782 fire destroyed his entire property; he died within about five years. EP, left without property or resources, began writing to support her family. EP's numerous novels are: *The History of Miss Meredith* (2 vols., 1790), *The Errors of Education* (2 vols., 1792), *Woman as She Should Be, or The Memoirs of Mrs. Menville* (4 vols., 1793), *The Castle of Wolfenbach, A German Story* (2 vols., 1793), *Ellen and Julia* (2 vols., 1793), *Lucy* (3 vols., 1794), *The Voluntary Exile* (5 vols., 1795), *The Mysterious Warning* (4 vols., 1796), *Women as They Are* (4 vols., 1796), *An Old Friend with a New Face* (3 vols., 1797), *The Girl of the Mountains* (4 vols., 1797), *Anecdotes of Two Well-Known Families* (3 vols., 1798), *The Valley of St. Gothard* (3 vols., 1799), *The Miser and His Family* (2 vols., 1800), *The Peasant of Ardenne Forest* (4 vols., 1801), *The Mysterious Visit* (4 vols., 1802), *Murray House* (3 vols., 1804, also attributed to MARY MEEKE), and *The Convict; or Navy Lieutenant* (4 vols., 1807). A farce, *The Intrigues of a Morning,* was produced at Covent Garden and published in 1792. In 1804, *Love and Gratitude: or Traits of the Human Heart* was published as a translation of six tales of La Fontaine. Other novels attributed to EP are *The Wise Ones Bubbled: or Lovers Triumphant* and *Rosetta,* both undated. EP's novels are sentimental and didactic. Some are full-fledged gothic novels: *The Castle of Wolfenbach* and *The Mysterious Warning* are among the seven "horrid novels" recommended to Catherine Morland in Jane Austen's *Northanger Abbey;* others use gothic settings and characters. Some are epistolary. Her novels are, above all, moral. They warn against the dangers of violent passion and the corruptions of fashionable society, and preach the value of prudence, simplicity, proper education, and filial and wifely obedience. In the words of one of her heroes, "out of a thousand instances of wretchedness in a marriage state, there is scarcely one that does not originate from the imprudence of youth, in forming connexions contrary to the advice and inclination of their parents and friends.

Parents may *sometimes* be selfish, arbitrary, and unfeeling; but youth is *too generally* impetuous, obstinate, and inconsiderate. They permit their passions to lord it over their reason, and are only convinced, by sad experience and painful consequences, of their own too hasty determinations in such points, as must decide their future happiness or misery." The value of both moral and social conformity is evident in the words of a self-condemned young widow: "Warned by my example, let not any young woman suppose if she is conscious of no crime, she may indulge the gaiety of her heart, take pride in the admiration she excites, and sacrifice the public opinion to the gratification of her own vanity, with impunity: 'tis not sufficient to be *really* virtuous, 'tis a duty we owe society to *appear* such, and the neglect of it is sure to be attended by the contempt of the world, and unavailing repentance to ourselves." EP also values sentiment; evidence of a good heart and true feelings often guarantees a character's virtue. EP was especially concerned with the status and problems of women. Her women are stereotypical. The virtuous take their vocations as wives and mothers seriously. The heroine of *Woman as She Should Be* successfully repels a rake by reminding him that "I am a wife . . . I am a mother. These sacred characters, the duties they imprint on my mind, shall ever regulate my conduct through life." On the other hand, power in the hands of women is dangerous: women, prone to pride and passion, must be controlled. EP's tormented heroines frequently blame themselves, rather than their persecutors, for their misfortunes, as does a character in *The Mysterious Warning:* "I shall relapse into sorrow or madness if haunted with recollections that pain me to my very soul; a fugitive daughter, whose conduct perhaps hastened a parent's death, who died without blessing or forgiving me; he might be arbitrary, prejudiced and cruel, but he was my father, to whose goodness I owed every comfort in life, and to whose parental care of me in my infancy, I was indebted for my very existence. What sacrifices had not such a parent a right to demand?" Women's weakness increases the necessity of education, which will prepare them to accept their rank and fortune, restrain their desires, and submit to be ruled. Yet EP's treatment of women betrays a concerned awareness of the female dilemma. The novels repeatedly stress the

dangers of female dependence and women's need for security, particularly as economic and moral dependence render women sexually vulnerable. In fact, while EP asserts that daughters must obey their fathers in all things, her plots and characters demonstrate that obedience is often dangerous. In style and structure, EP's novels show the pressures of haste and necessity. Although she uses the flashback effectively, and can convincingly portray mental agony, her work is characterized not by depth of development, but by incident and repetition. She frequently uses interpolated tales, and this habit reinforces the tendency to repeat plots and character types, even within a single novel. She also sometimes relies heavily on such works as Richardson's *Clarissa* or the gothic romances of ANN RADCLIFFE. Her efforts at terror and suspense often fail, as she explains the supernatural too quickly. Finally, her moralizing overwhelms every other impulse and effect. EP's books were reasonably well received. The *British Critic* described *The Mysterious Warning* as "agreeable but most melancholy"; *Ellen and Julia,* in the *Monthly Review* (Aug. 1794), was considered "a success chiefly on its moral merit." The *Analytical Review* (Sept. 1794) praised "the variety of wonderful incidents" in *Lucy,* but found its "moral sentiment trite." And an unidentified critic, who found *Errors of Education* "natural, pathetic, and interesting," recommended it to parents who might be tempted to mis-educate their daughters.   R.R.F.

PEACOCK, Lucy (1785–1816), children's author, was probably born in London, where she later operated a bookshop on Oxford Street. She is associated with a group of strongly didactic authors whose commissioned works for children began to appear in 1780. Many of LP's stories appeared originally in magazines, particularly the *Juvenile Magazine,* and were occasionally published anonymously. Her first book, an allegory for children, appeared in 1785 and was entitled *The Adventures of the Six Princesses of Babylon in the Travels to the Temple of Virtue. Friendly Labours* (1786) was followed by *The Knight of the Rose* (1793), and *Visit for a Week* (1794). LP also published *Patty Primrose* (1813) and *Emily, or the Test of Sincerity* (1816). She translated from the French two books of Veyssière de la Croze, *Historical Grammar* (1802) and the *Abridged Chronology of World History* (1807). *Visit,* with its seven reprintings, was by far LP's most popular work, and its story is typical. Paying a first visit to their aunt, Mrs. Miller, two children discover that learning can be exciting, and that old Mrs. Miller is not half as dreadful as they had imagined. Mrs. Miller beguiles the children with stories on a variety of subjects, including the history of Richard II and the social organization of bees, finding time to stop for moral discourses on the necessity of fighting for one's country, and the debt we owe to carpenters. To her credit, LP's morality lessons do not begin with the self-evident, and *Visit* is not without charm.   D.T.

PEARSON, Susanna (fl. 1790–94), poet and novelist, wrote one novel, *The Medallion* (3 vols., London, 1794); she is better known for her poetry. Her *Poems* (Sheffield, 1790) is dedicated to the Countess Fitzwilliam. The majority are sonnets on such diverse subjects as nature, love, the pain of memory, reviewers, poet friends, and Sarah Siddons. One sonnet on a controversial political topic praises the Prince of Wales for complying with proposed restrictions in the Regency Bill. Few of SP's poems have religious themes, with the exception of one of her best sonnets, "To the Setting Sun," which sees God's handiwork in the glory of the sun: "But when from western skies thy beauty flows, / His mercy in thy soften'd splendour glows, / And fills my pensive soul with love divine!" Her longer poems exhibit a wider range of poetic skill. In the gothic "Lines Found on the Stairs of the Tour de la Chapelle of the Bastile," a prisoner awaiting death is visited by specters of famous tortured prisoners; "Clessamora" is an imitation of Ossian; "Zara and Sebastian" and "Viola and Alonzo" are imitations of old Spanish ballads; and, in perhaps her most interesting poem, *An African Tale,* the Edenic love of Zarad and Zilea is tragically destroyed by slave hunters. SP points out the irony of the slavetraders' claims in a speech of Zilea's: "Oh! ye false strangers! that from many a coast / Hasten to bind a guiltless world in chains, / And even while ye lock their fetters, boast / How Liberty still revels on your plains." To enforce her message, SP adds a sardonic footnote, commenting that from the eagerness with which the "sanguinary commerce" of slavery is pursued, "it must appear to the artless natives that the Europeans are necessitated to obey the injunction of some remorseless deity; and not merely impelled by a prospect of gain." The poem

closes with a prophecy of the future rise of Africa. Neither the images nor the language of SP's poetry are striking, but she can be admired for the variety of meters and forms used.   A.W.E.

PEDDLE, M. (fl. 1785–89), miscellaneous writer, was married, had several children, and may have lived near Sherborne, Dorset, where her first book was published by subscription. *The Life of Jacob. In Ten Books* (1785) was an early example of an historical novel, although MP would have objected to the word "novel." The *Monthly Review* (August 1785) called it a fictitious narrative based on historical fact, and "one of the most successful attempts we remember to have seen." He found the conception natural, the diction "sufficiently elevated, without perpetually swelling into bombast." MP's purpose in writing the fictional life of Jacob is made clear in her statement about the dangers of novel reading in her next work. "I have never known a young person who was fond of novels, capable of relishing any thing superior to them. For my own part, I had rather see a girl wholly ignorant of the alphabet, than attached to that species of writing; for I am convinced that *infinitely more* have erred in the conduct of life for that cause, than from any other." This second work, signed "Cornelia," was *The Rudiments of Taste; in a Series of Letters from a Mother to her Daughters. By the Author of the Life of Jacob* (1789). *MR* (October 1790) called the author "no friend to singularity and affectation, no enemy to innocent cheerfulness and enjoyments; but it is her earnest wish to guard her fair readers against the errors into which fashion and false taste may lead them." Her advice includes "Rest assured that in the exercise of social and religious duties, the mind will find her solid happiness. . . . Never lose sight of this truth, that there is no happiness adequate to the capacities of the human soul, but what is found in the exercise of piety and virtue; nor any praise worthy her regard, but what results immediately therefrom. . . . When reason and religion have given the clue to your pleasures, resolve always to have them of your own chusing, and not of other people's." MP wished to raise the standards of politeness but to preserve sexual distinctions which she felt divinely ordained. "The Mahometan sentiment which prevailed some years ago of the inferiority of the female mind, seems exploded in this age of universal refinement; and a woman of cultivated understanding is no longer a phenomenon.—The paths of knowledge are rendered accessible; men of learning have stooped from the elevations of science to accelerate the improvements of the other sex; they abridge, compile, explain. . . . Make all the use you possibly can of such advantages, and be convinced that the cultivation of the mind will exalt you in the estimation of rational beings; will open to you exhaustless sources of amusement and delight, of which the ignorant can have no conception: yet be careful, my dear girls, never to overlook one feminine grace or accomplishment—There is a line of character drawn between the sexes which neither can pass without becoming contemptible." *The Rudiments of Taste* was a popular work. It was republished in 1790 with the COUNTESS OF CARLISLE's *Thoughts in the Form of Maxims.* In 1790 there were Dublin and Philadelphia editions; a third American edition was published in Philadelphia in 1797, and another in Litchfield, Conn., in 1799.   E.T.

PENINGTON, Mary [Proud] (1625?–1682), autobiographer, was orphaned at three and grew up with Anglican guardians of noble rank in Kent. Early in adolescence, MP rebelled against formalized religion and began to seek personal spirituality. In 1642 she married a vehement Puritan, William Springett, who died shortly afterward during the Civil War. In 1654 MP married Isaac Penington (d. 1679), and together they were converted to Quakerism after hearing George Fox preach in 1657. Although "Quaker aristocrats," they were persecuted with their fellow Friends, and also lost a good part of their estate. Isaac was a reclusive writer of mystical tracts. MP was the practical one and spent her last years restoring their estate for themselves and their descendants. Although MP wrote *A Brief Account of some of my Exercises from my Childhood* for the private edification of her descendants, it has since been recognized as a literary legacy in the genre of the spiritual autobiography. Of its three parts, the first, written some time before 1668 for her daughter Gulielma Maria Springett, recounts her early spiritual struggles and conversion to Quakerism. In the second section, MP describes her efforts from 1669 to 1673 to renovate their Woodside property, as well as her mental turmoil in trying to reconcile her obvious pleasure in restoring their outward estate with her calling to the inner life. The third section is a letter to her grandson, Springet Penn,

containing an exemplary life of her first husband, his grandfather. This paragraph describing her first marriage illustrates her skill at vividly depicting the religious passions which inflamed the 17th-century: "We lived together about two years and a month. We were zealously affected, and daily exercised in what we believed to be the service and worship of God. We scrupled many things then in use amongst those accounted honest people, viz.: singing David's psalms in metre. We tore out of our Bibles the common prayer, the form of prayer, and also the singing psalms, as being the inventions of vain poets. . . We looked into the Independent way, but saw death there, and there was not the thing our souls sought after." That she was able to achieve a fresh approach to the conventional form of conversion-narrative is demonstrated in her account of the democratic vision which foreshadowed her introduction to Quakerism: "I dreamed that I was sitting alone, retired and sad . . . I stood still at a great distance, at the lower end of the hall, and Christ was at the upper end, whose appearance was that of a fresh, lovely youth, clad in gray cloth, very plain and neat . . . I saw Him embrace several poor, old simple people, whose appearance was very contemptible and mean, without wisdom or beauty . . . for He must behold some hidden worth in these people, who to me seem so mean, so unlovely and simple."   S.B.

PENN, Hannah (1671–1726), letter writer, was born in Bristol, the sixth of the nine children of the Quaker button manufacturer and linen draper Thomas Callowhill and his wife, Anna. At 14 she was the only surviving child and was carefully educated in accounting, business, and merchandising. At 24 she was courted by the Proprietor of Pennsylvania William Penn (1644–1718), then recently widowed. His children, Springett, Letitia, and William Jr., all urged HP to marry their father, which she did in 1696 in Bristol. The relationship was based on equality and mutual respect. HP bore eight children during the marriage, of whom three died. Those that survived were John (b. 1700), Thomas (b. 1702), Margaret (b. 1704), Richard (b. 1706), and Dennis (b. 1707). In 1699 William Penn, HP, Letitia Penn, and James Logan, Penn's private secretary, journeyed to Pennsylvania and took up residence for two years at Pennsbury, a large estate 24 miles from Philadelphia. Here HP learned about the Province at first hand. In 1701 problems with dishonest agents forced the Penns' return to England, where Penn was eventually imprisoned for debt, and the family settled near Reading. HP did not leave England again. In 1712 HP's parents died and Penn suffered the first of a series of strokes. He had already decided that William Jr. was incapable of managing the Province, and in his will he named HP his executrix and left her and her children most of his own lands there. HP was now forced to settle her parents' estate and to manage her husband's affairs. By correspondence with the councilmen in Philadelphia and guided by Logan's advice, she participated in the government of the Province, eventually decided not to surrender it to the Crown, a question that had been pending since Penn had wished to be rid of it in 1703. After Penn's death in 1718, his son William Jr. instituted a long and expensive law suit against HP, which she eventually won, thereby preserving their Pennsylvania inheritance for her children. In 1721, weakened by illness, HP left much of the business of the Province to an agent and to her son John, but continued to interest herself in her charge, concluding in 1724 an agreement with Lord Baltimore about the Pennsylvania-Maryland border, and finally determining that family responsibility demanded that the territory should not be returned to the Crown. Her descendants held the Province until the Revolution.

HP's letters have not been collected and published, nor has an authoritative biography been written. The following extract demonstrates the extent to which she was active in management and the tact with which she took advice: "since those, in whom I have most reason to confide for justice and friendship, have advised a change of governor we have all concurred and joined our helping hands to make you easy therein and looking over all other difficulties have, at your requests, got William Keith commissioned . . . though he was pretty much a stranger to me yet his prudent conduct and obliging behaviour, joined with your observations thereon, give me and those concerned good hope to believe that he will prove the man you recommend him for." Most of the letters and papers written by her and her contemporaries about Pennsylvania affairs are in the Historical Society of Pennsylvania at Philadelphia. Some of her letters have been published in the *Pennsylvania Magazine of History and Biography,* in *Correspondence between*

William Penn and James Logan (1872), and in Sophie Drinker's *Hannah Penn and the Proprietorship of Pennsylvania* (1958). M.Ma.

PENNINGTON, E[lizabeth] (1734–59), poet, daughter of the Rev. John Pennington of Huntingdon and friend of FRANCES SHERIDAN and Samuel Richardson, is respectfully mentioned, along with her friend MARTHA FERRAR, in John Duncombe's *Feminead.* She died at 25. Her "Ode to a Thrush" appeared in Dodsley's *Collection,* and her "Ode to Morning" in Alexander Dyce's *Specimens of British Poetesses* (1827). The latter is a competent but conventional invocation to morning: "The dew-drops, daughter of the Morn, / With spangles every bush adorn, / And all the broider'd vales"; it ends with a warning about the transience of life. EP's best known and most skillful poem is "The Copper Farthing" written in the style of John Philips's "The Splendid Shilling": "Happy the boy, who dwells remote from school, / Whose pocket or whose rattling box contains / The Copper Farthing!" It was printed in Fawkes and Woty's *Poetical Calendar* (1763) and in Dilly's *Repository* (1777). Two other poems appear in Nichols's collection of poetry. J.H.

PENNINGTON, Sarah, Lady (?–1783), author of conduct books, letters, and epistolary fiction, began writing as a direct result of her unfortunate and notorious personal life. Her mother having died before SP was 19 and with a distant and otherworldly father, SP by her own account grew up without benefit of social instruction. She married Sir Joseph Pennington of Water Hall, Yorks., probably in 1746, and separated from him and their several children nearly 12 years later, settling in Bath. The reasons were never explicit, but they concerned marital discord fostered by her social conduct (she speaks of behaving like a coquette) and his intolerant, even brutal, response. His accusations and attempts to deprive her of a small inheritance brought the situation into public scrutiny; although SP confessed to social sins, she insisted on her moral innocence. She wrote all of her works after the separation in a spirit of remorse and self-vindication, seeking (successfully) to restore her reputation. Most of her books contain explicit autobiographical references; at least one was written out of financial necessity, to pay a debt arising from litigation. Perhaps because of her public appeals and the high moral tone of her conduct writing, the world exonerated her and even made her a martyr. Her obituary in *Gentleman's Magazine* illustrates her reputation at the time of her death by referring to her "extraordinary abilities," her "piety, charity, and benevolence," and the "resignation" with which she sustained "a series of very severe and uncommon afflictions." She is buried in Fulmer, Bucks.

SP wrote four works, the most important of which is her first, written in direct response to the separation, *An Unfortunate Mother's Advice to Her Absent Daughters; in a Letter to Miss Pennington* (1761); often appended to later editions is her "Letter to Miss Louisa on the Management and Education of Infant Children." Later works are *Letters on Different Subjects, in Four Volumes; Amongst which are interspers'd the Adventures of Alphonso, After the Destruction of Lisbon* (1766) and *The Child's Conductor* (1777), a religious text written ostensibly for her grandchildren. *The Unfortunate Mother's Advice* was popular immediately (it went into three editions in the first year and at least seven more before 1800) and throughout the 19th century, when it was frequently printed in editions with HESTER CHAPONE's *Letters* and Dr. Gregory's *Advice*. Far from damaging her credibility, SP's notoriety endowed her with additional authority to give advice, for she could speak with the voice of experience about the importance of public opinion to a woman's life. Her writings echo conventional conduct-book morality, emphasizing virtue and propriety. As an exile of sorts, she was particularly able to provide the traditional warnings about the world's cruelty: "You are just entering, my dear Girl, into a World full of Deceit and Falsehood, where few Persons or Things appear as they really are: Vice hides her Deformity with the borrowed Garb of Virtue . . . and it requires a long Experience, and a penetrating Judgment to discover the Truth." Although she attempted epistolary fiction in *Adventures of Alphonso,* SP's primary strength is the conduct book: practical, motherly advice in the voice of experience. K.S.

PENNY, Anne (1731–84), poet, was the daughter of Owen Hughes of Bangor, Caern. In 1746 she married Thomas Christian (1716–51), captain and owner of a privateer who had acquired an Oxfordshire estate with the proceeds from the capture of Spanish galleons. Her second husband, Peter Penné (or Penny) is described both as a Frenchman working in a customs house and as a naval man who had lost a leg. In 1771, AP published by subscription *Poems with a Dramatic Entertainment;* the dedication to the traveler and philanthropist Jonas Hanway is dated "Bloomsbury Square, May 13, 1771." The poems are principally occasional pieces, notably elegies upon the deaths of the great, and versifications of selections from diverse prose sources, such as Evan Evans's *Specimens of Welsh Poetry* (1764), Macpherson's *Ossian* (1765), and "Anningait and Ajutt," a tale of two lovers who "Both flourish'd sweet on Greenland's rigid coast, / Pure as its snow and constant as its frost" which appeared in *The Rambler,* nos. 186 and 187 (December 1751). The earliest dated poem is "On the Royal Nuptials" of 1761. A letter from Michael Lort to Horace Walpole dated May 1779 mentions proposals for a new subscription, AP's husband "being lately dead" and she "left in great distress." In 1780 the collection reappeared with a few deletions and additions, including a series of odes commissioned by the Marine Society founded by Jonas Hanway, to be sung by boys' choirs marching among the tables at their annual commemorative dinners. T.C.S.W.L.

PENNYMAN, Mary (1631–1701), religious polemicist, was the daughter of Nicholas Bond of London. She married Henry Boreman, a Quaker, who died in prison in 1662. MP went to live with other widows at Tottenham, dissociated herself from the Quakers, and moved toward the Philadelphians like JANE LEAD. She was associated with the notorious John Pennyman, who embraced Quakerism and then in the early 1660s grew dissatisfied with it and held meetings of his own outside the organization. His mysticism and eccentricity worried George Fox and other Quakers, who disowned him. Pennyman married Dinah, MP's sister as his second wife. After her death, MP moved in with Pennyman in 1671, in response to divine prompting. Pennyman hired a hall, provided victuals for 250 people, and announced their marriage. The event was much mocked, for example in "Ye Quaker's Wedding" mentioned by REBECCA TRAVERS. In 1672–73, again under divine influence, they walked through Essex and Hertfordshire. In 1691 they went to live with Pennyman's son-in-law in Bishopsgate but later moved into the country. MP died after a long illness. Pennyman published *Some of the Letters and Papers* which were written by Mrs. Mary Penny-man, relating to an Holy and Heavenly Conversation, in which she lived to her Dying-Day (1701–02). MP collaborated with Pennyman on tracts such as *The Ark is begun to be opened (the waters being some-what abated) . . .* (1671), *John Pennyman's Instruction to his Children* (1674), and *The Quakers Rejected* (1676?).   J.T.

PHILIPS, Katherine (1631–64), poet and playwright, was dubbed by her admirers "The Matchless Orinda." She was born in London, where her father John Fowler, who died when she was 11, was a successful merchant. She was educated at Miss Salmon's school, Hackney. When in 1646 her mother, born Katherine Oxenbridge, married Sir Richard Phillips, the family moved to Pembroke, Wales. At the age of 16 KD's own marriage was arranged with 54-year-old James Philips. He was a kinsman of Sir Richard's and had been previously married to Sir Richard's own daughter. KP bore two children, a son who died in infancy and a daughter, also named Katherine. In the quiet countryside of Wales KP began producing poems as early as 1651. These were mostly dedicated to friends addressed under classical pseudonyms. Much of this poetry celebrated her intense platonic love for Mary Aubrey, "Rosania," and Anne Owens, her "dearest Lucasia." A Society of Friendship is mentioned, which has suggested to historians that she actually conducted a salon, but her rural isolation makes this unlikely. In the ensuing years James Philips's rise to prominence in Cromwell's Parliament afforded KP several opportunities to visit and socialize in London. After the Restoration, despite her Puritan affiliations and her husband's political difficulties, KP was able to participate in the literary renaissance emanating from the court of Charles II. Her admirers included Dryden and Cowley; she corresponded with the Earl of Rochester and the DUCHESS OF NEWCASTLE; the Earl of Orrery was her patron, and Sir Charles Cotterell, the Master of Ceremonies at Charles's court, was her confidante. She maintained a voluminous correspondence with Cotterell whom she addressed as "Poliarchus." On a trip to Dublin in 1662, at Orrey's suggestion, KP translated Corneille's *La Mort de Pompée*. This work established her reputation. It was produced at the Theatre Royal in Smock Alley, Dublin, in the 1662–63 season. Its fame, it is said, was due to the unprecedented presentation of a play by a woman, but it was

still on the London stage as late as 1678. KP next undertook Corneille's *Horace* but, having completed nearly four acts, she contracted smallpox and died in London at the age of 32 at the height of her productivity and success. Sir John Denham completed *Horace,* which was performed before the King in the London season 1668–69.

Despite her fame, "The Matchless Orinda" managed to escape the social censure that stigmatized her contemporary APHRA BEHN ("The Incomparable Astrea"). "Orinda" and "Astrea" were often compared in literary commentary—usually to the detriment of the latter, whose lifestyle was considered less than exemplary. In an age when the writing of poetry, not to mention its publication, was considered not in a woman's sphere, KP protected herself with protestations of modesty ("Sometimes I think that employment [poetry] so far above my reach, and unfit for my sex . . ."), and a personal life that was above reproach. In his *Diary* John Evelyn summed up the general consensus on her character when he referred to her as the "virtuous" KP. She never sought publication or publicity; on the contrary, she had an almost morbid fear of losing reputation through being published: she, "who never writ any line in my life with an intention to have it printed," claimed to have suffered a "sharp fit of sickness" on learning that purloined rough copies of her poems had been published without authorization. It was only then, in self-defense, that she allowed Cotterell to supervise a correct edition. *Pompey,* KP's version of *La Mort de Pompée,* was published in Dublin in 1663. Later that year it came out in London, at about the same time as a version by Edmund Waller, Charles Sedley, Lord Buckhurst and other "wits" was in circulation. KP's adaptation from alexandrines into heroic rhymed couplets was considered the more faithful to the original. *Pompey* and the incomplete version of *Horace* are included in the collection of KP's poems, *Poems. By The Most Deservedly Admired Mrs. Katherine Philips, The Matchless Orinda* (1667). This collection also contains KP's original poems and some translations from French poetry. Her original work reflects KP's royalist sympathies; it laments the execution of Charles I and celebrates the return of Charles II to England. The best of KP's poetry, however, is more personal in nature, marking signal events in her life and investigating and analyzing her deepest feelings about her personal relationships. Friends and friendship were idealized. KP's style shows the influence of the Précieuse school (the literary movement originating in France and brought into fashion in England by Charles I's French Queen Henrietta Maria; the movement espoused refinement of language and elevation of literary themes). Platonic love was a prominent theme, and classical pseudonyms were employed. In KP's case the love object was another woman. Her exquisite and mystical concept of love / friendship had metaphysical, religious overtones; it is exemplified in the lines from "To Mrs. Mary Awbrey": "Soul of my soul, my Joy, my Crown, my friend, / A name which all the rest doth comprehend; / How happy are we now, whose souls are grown, / By an incomparable mixture, one." Her enthusiasm may have overwhelmed the recipients for, in "To My Lucasia, in Defense of Declared Friendship," she assuages the other's reticence regarding outspoken affection: "O My Lucasia, let us speak our Love, / And think not that impertinent can be / Which to us both doth such Assurance prove." This same Lucasia is the "Calanthe" referred to in *Letters From Orinda To Poliarchus* (1705), many of which concern the unsuccessful suit of the young widow by KP's friend Cotterell. Her cult of friendship would have reached its epitome if KP could have brought about the marriage of two of her closest friends.

KP's entire output consists of few works, but she was highly esteemed in her lifetime. In an encomium included in the posthumous edition of her works, Cowley states: "But if Apollo could design / A woman Laureate to make, / Without dispute He would Orinda take." She was hailed as a pioneer, a model, and an inspiration by the women writers at the end of the century. DELARIVIÈRE MANLEY, LADY PIERS, the COUNTESS OF WINCHILSEA, and CATHARINE TROTTER all praised her in their own poetry. Trotter in particular cultivated comparison, carefully guarding her reputation from notoriety. In a commendatory poem before her play *The Unhappy Penitant* (1701), Lady Piers reminded her of her illustrious predecessor: "Thus like the morning star Orinda rose / A champion to her sex, and wisely chose / Conscious of female weakness, humble ways / T'insinuate for applause, not storm the Bays."   C.C.

PHILLIPS, Catharine (1726?–1794), polemicist, poet, and autobiographer, was born at Dudley, Worcs., the youngest child of Henry Payton, a Quaker minister; she was his companion in his later invalid years. Educated at home and at boarding school, CP read poetry, history, and philosophy and wrote poems, but abandoned these after she received her call to the ministry in 1748. At the age of 23 she began her travels in the ministry, which took her to Ireland, Scotland, Holland, and America, and which continued until nine years before her death, when she was confined by illness. As an example of her relentless pace, in one fifteen-week period she attended 117 meetings and traveled 1230 miles. In England one of her companions was RACHEL WILSON. In 1772 she married William Phillips (d. 1785) and settled in Cornwall. She had always been wary of writing, because "I was early afraid of my mind and services being tarnished with vanity," but here she began to produce her tracts. With the exception of *An Epistle to Friends in Ireland (on vital religion),* written in 1758 and published in 1776, CP's works were published only a few years before her death or posthumously. *An Address to the Principal Inhabitants of the County of Cornwall who are about to assemble at Truro . . on the mining concerns of that county* and *Considerations on the Causes of the High Price of Grain and Other Articles of Provision* appeared in 1792. *Reasons why the people called Quakers cannot so fully unite with the Methodists, in their mission to the negroes in the West India Islands and Africa, as freely to contribute thereto* (1792) disagrees with Methodists over payment of tithes, baptism, prohibitions against female ministers, and qualified support of the Church of England. *To the lower class of people in the western part of the county of Cornwall* followed in 1793. *The Happy King: a sacred poem. With occasional remarks . . . addressed to George the Third* (1794) is a compendium of views on the obligations of a just king, opinions and advice on foreign affairs, and encouragement for missionary activity in the growing British Empire. It is noteworthy chiefly for a tirade against the slave trade: "Let it depart, / From Britain's commerce; too long stain'd, / With such a wicked trade; / Sources for wealth enough remain, / When this just law is made." It is so sincere in its ineptness that it is almost palatable, certainly more so than the cluttered and fanatical verse of like-minded ANNE DUTTON. The preface refers to the author as "an old woman, bending under a weight of bodily infirmities." More interesting than the tracts are her own *Memoirs* (1797), largely a journal of her travels in the ministry, which reveals the workings of a Quaker mind. Her account of her relationship with Phillips, for example, is riddled with doubts as to his piety and religious circumspection: "our minds were clothed with awful caution of stepping forward without Divine direction." And she notes of her marriage itself: "we did not marry until the 15th of Seventh month, 1772; when, in a large and solemn meeting held at Bewdley, we took each other in the real fear of the Lord, and therein had a strong evidence of his favour." Some of CP's more popular discourses were bound with those of her friend Samuel Fothergill in 1803. R.J. and A.W.E.

PHILLIPS, Teresia Constantia [Con] (1709–65), memoirist and courtesan, was born in West Chester, the eldest daughter of Thomas Phillips, Captain of the Grenadiers in Lord Longford's regiment. After her father left the army, his financial situation steadily declined. He moved his family to London in 1717, where he depended on relations and friends for support. The Duchess of Bolton was TCP's godmother, and she provided for her education at Mrs. Filer's boarding school in Prince's Court, Westminster. TCP's mother died in 1721, and shortly afterward her father married the family servant. TCP found her stepmother intolerable, and she moved to the lodgings of Mrs. Douglas, where she met "Thomas Grimes" whom she held responsible for her life as a courtesan. In a published letter to the Earl of Chesterfield of April 1750 she writes: "Who denies Mr. 'Thomas Grimes' to be a Man of Honour and Integrity; yet this very Man, first betray'd and ruin'd the unhappy Miss Phillips, basely, nay villainously, ruin'd her, and after that abandoned her to Sorrow, Misery, and Infamy; which was the Source of all the Ruin and Unhappiness that has since befallen her." The Dictionary of National Biography deduces that "Thomas Grimes" is Lord Chesterfield, yet this connection is not explicit in TCP's memoirs. After "Grimes" abandoned her, she married Francis Delafield in 1722 to avoid imprisonment for debt. This marriage was annulled, and she married Henry Muilman in 1723. In 1724, Muilman, threatened by his father with financial ruin unless he left TCP, started annulment proceedings. Commentary on these proceedings form a large part of TCP's memoirs. From 1724 until 1748, she was kept by various aristocratic paramours. The publication of her only literary work in 1748, *An Apology for the Conduct of Mrs. Teresia Constantia Phillips, more particularly that part of it which relates to her Marriage, with an eminent Dutch Merchant,* brought a brief period of financial independence. The *Apology* excited considerable controversy and went through four printings by 1761. Still she continued to live beyond her means, and was imprisoned for debt on several occasions. In 1754 she moved to Jamaica, where she was married three times and where she died.

The *Apology* is an effective account of the abuses suffered by a kept woman in the 18th century. TCP's writing is dramatic, often witty, yet incisive prose. She condemns the hypocritical attitudes of a society in which a man who keeps a woman is viewed as the victim and the woman as the perpetrator. She argues that it is the woman, rather than the man, who suffers unjustly. "But the error of women ruining men is a mistake the World runs away with so frequently, that we cannot avoid taking into our consideration the absurdity of such an opinion. If an Idle young fellow takes it in his head to keep a woman, and blindly runs into all Extravangies and Follies that can be possibly thought of must his ruin be imputed to her? A mistress is oftentimes but the least part. If she is ornamented it is to make his Follies and Expences the more conspicuous: He may drink, game and riot Etc. but these are never laid to his account: When undone, the woman has ruin'd him! and all his other Vices and Extravagancies are absorb'd in her only!" TCP's *Apology* influenced Jeremy Bentham, who wrote, "It was the first, and not the least effective, in the train of causes in which the works by which my name is most known had their origin." On the merit of the *Apology*'s thesis, an anonymous critic referring to himself as the Oxford Scholar observed: "these admirable Adventures, will afford indisputable Proofs that Pleasure was the reigning Taste; that Profusion passed for Magnificence; that Show and Equipage gained Admittance every where; that Money was the one thing necessary, and that all Ways of coming at it were esteemed lawful amongst those who lived in a continual State of Dissipation." H.A.

PICKERING, Amelia (fl. 1788), poet, wrote *The Sorrows of Werther,* a melancholy, contemplative poem of 178 Sicilian quatrains. It was one of a spate of works founded on Goethe's novel about Werther's despairing, distracted love for Charlotte. Abstractions of Youth and Disappointment float through verdant vales as Werther, who, longing for sleep and death and dwelling on man's transience and the idle pomp of the world, struggles against madness: "Each social joy from me for ever gone; / The tyrant Love now holds my heart in chains, / And Reason abdicates her falling throne." Versification is serene and competent, never brilliant. *Monthly Review* cited some "elegant and pleasing stanzas" but added, "we cannot flatter our fair authoress (though she deserves much praise) with being equally favored by the Muses throughout her whole performance." G.B.

PIERS, Sarah, Lady (?–1720), poet, was the daughter of Matthew Royden, Esq. She married Sir George Piers of Kent, who was an officer under the Duke of Marlborough. There were two sons, the eldest of whom died in childhood. SP was a member of a circle of women writers that included MARY PIX, DELARIVIÈRE MANLEY, CATHARINE TROTTER, and SARAH EGERTON. She was the intimate friend of Trotter, who dedicated her tragi-comedy *Love at a Loss* (1701) to her, praising SP's "taste in poetry and delight in the muses," and alluding to her unusually happy marriage with her liberal-minded husband, "Who so well recommends his own worth by his respect and value for you . . . and has found his felicity in making yours."

SP represents Urania, the muse of Astronomy in *The Nine Muses,* a collection of poems, eulogizing Dryden after his death in 1700. Several women poets contributed, including those mentioned above. A set of verses by SP is included in the printed edition of Trotter's *The Unhappy Penitent* (1701), in which she likens Trotter to "Orinda," as KATHERINE PHILIPS was known, and praises her above "gay Astrea," referring to APHRA BEHN. Prefixed to Trotter's tragedy *The Fatal Friendship* (1698) is a poem "To My Much Esteemed Friend" in which SP praises Trotter in self-deprecating terms: "Were I judge enough, I'd do thee right / Though yet much more I want poetic flight; / And twere his folly to repeat anew, / Who lights a taper the bright sun to shew, / Should I attempt your praise; but as a friend, / T'express my thoughts is all that I intend." She tags her poems with a wordplay on the title of the play: "O heav'n this my fondest wish decree! /

Our mutual friendship may ne'er fatal be." The above poems were unsigned; the only published poem to bear SP's name is "George For Britain," celebrating the accession of George I in 1714. SP seems to have been more of a patron than a creative force in the literary set of which she was a part at the end of the 17th century. Now she is known more for the people she gathered around her than for her own accomplishments. C.C.

PILKINGTON, Laetitia (1712–50), autobiographer, was born in Dublin to Van Lewen, a man-midwife of Dutch descent, and a gentlewoman (née Meade) related to several well-connected Anglo-Irish and English families. The salient events of her life were her friendship with Jonathan Swift, to whom she was distantly related—her grandmother's sister married Swift's uncle—and her marriage to Matthew Pilkington, his abandonment of her with their two children in Ireland, her pursuit of him to London, separation, and divorce, after which she supported herself on "Nothing but Poetry," her attempted suicide, confinement in debtors' prison, failure as the proprietor of a little book and print shop, employment as a ghostwriter for a portrait painter who, years earlier with Matthew's permission, had tried to seduce her, and a pamphlet war with Matthew. Her life is chronicled in her *Memoirs,* 3 vols. (vol I, 1748), the work upon which her contemporary reputation and notoriety were established. Most of the information about her life stems from her own writing, whose accuracy is problematical. Virginia Woolf said of her and her work in *The Common Reader* (1925), "It is her duty to entertain; it is her instinct to conceal."

The *Memoirs* is a way of asserting control over her life and of salving what she terms her "scribbling Itch." Writing is important throughout the narrative, informing events and phrases, for example, "poor I, have been for many Years a Noun Substantive, obliged to stand alone." Volume I established the work's contemporary impact: in its attempt to be "instructive to the Female Part of my Readers" and to restore the lost "Jewel" of "Reputation," it presents the memoirist as a learned woman writer victimized by her sex and aspiration. The major event of LP's childhood becomes her father's discovery of her at the age of five, reading aloud from Dryden, and his encouragement of her despite her mother's opposition to her "strong Disposition to

Letters." She is attracted to Matthew Pilkington in part because he courts her with poetry. After marriage, she continues to read and write voraciously, but his increasing jealousy climaxes when she answers easily a stylistic question of Swift which Matthew does not understand. Soon he claims that "the Dean had made me mad . . . and that a Needle became a Woman's Hand better than a Pen and Ink." LP illustrates the dilemma of her conflicting roles through examples of needle and pen, a metaphor she exploits, often ironically, throughout the *Memoirs* ("But to resume my Thread," "But once more to gather up my Clue," and "I must bring you a Simile from what I do not much deal in, that is, Needle-work"). Reading and writing directly precipitate her divorce. Having been discovered by her husband alone with another man "at an unseasonable Hour in my Bed-Chamber," she "solemnly" declares that "it was the attractive Charms of a new Book, which the Gentleman would not lend me, but contented to stay till I read it through, that was the sole Motive of my detaining him." Often ridiculed by commentators, this excuse makes sense in the context of a recreated life of a writing woman. LP introduces herself to Swift by sending him two birthday poems. The first, presented as a school exercise written for her brother, begins "O spotless paper" and images a sheet of blank paper as a virgin despoiled by the poet's writing "to please a Boy." In the second, the traditional pen/paper, male/female symbolism is reversed: the poet becomes a quill pen "Ambitious to transcribe your deathless lays." The introduction of her own poetry in the section on Swift is characteristic of LP's practice throughout the *Memoirs*—a demonstration that truly she "was most incorrigibly devoted to Versifying, and all my Spouse's wholesome Admonitions had no manner of Effect on me." The interpolated poems not only demonstrate her abilities but comment on her remembered life. For example, her poem "The Statues," a fable about male inconstancy, was not published until 1739, a year after her ecclesiastical divorce, but is inserted in her *Memoirs* during the early 1730s when she was friendly with Swift (upon whose unfamiliarity with physical love and playful instruction of women it comments) and when her relationship with Pilkington was beginning to disintegrate. Volumes 2 and 3 are primarily a vindication of past conduct and a display of acquain-

tances and abilities, to be used as a weapon against future attacks; so LP offers fewer details about her life and makes less effort to justify her interspersed poems and anecdotes about Swift and other luminaries such as Cibber and Richardson. By the end of Vol. 3, she is anticipating death: to her son John Carteret Pilkington, who edited this posthumous volume, she left her life's commitment to language, in the form of her *Memoirs,* "as the only Legacy I have." Her death in July in Dublin has been consistently misdated a month later by all secondary sources (*Gentleman's Magazine,* August 1750, and *Dublin Journal,* July 1750). Both her bequest and this mistake can be read as symbols of a life and career represented and misrepresented by language.

Before and after her death, LP's work provoked extreme reaction. In 1738 Swift, who had authorized her entry into literature, signaled the end of their friendship by labeling her "the most profligate whore in either Kingdom." About 1749 John Cleland wrote to Ralph Griffiths, publisher of Cleland and LP: "this woman would have, in all probability, been an irreproachable wife, had she not been married to such a villain, as her whole history shows her husband to have been: and indeed to do that sex Justice, most of their errors are originally owing to our treatment of them: they would be what they ought to be, if we [would be] to them what we ought to be." In 1748 *The Parallel,* a 66-page comparison of LP's memoirs with those of TERESIA CONSTANTIA PHILLIPS, found in LP's "the plain Appearance of an active Spirit that paints after Nature. . . . Her Ideas fall upon the Paper just as they rise in her Mind, and the Reader sees things as she saw them, and therefore sees them as they were. . . . The Detail she gives us of her own Misfortunes is very natural and affecting, tho' perhaps it may not be altogether ingenuous." *The Parallel* suggests that the *Memoirs* vacillates between the "ingenuous" and the "ingenious," and that the work reveals that for a woman "the only way to be safe is to be innocent." Eighteenth- and nineteenth-century response to the *Memoirs* often focused on the relationship between women and wit. The *Gentleman's Magazine* (1748 and 1754) excerpted and summarized all three volumes and characterized LP as "betray'd, like many others, by wit to Folly, and by pride to meanness." ELIZABETH MONTAGU thought LP's "turn of wit" "a dangerous quality" for "I am sorry to say the generality of women who have excelled in wit have failed in chastity." W.H.E.

PILKINGTON, Mary [Hopkins] (1766–1839), novelist, translator, and short story writer, primarily of works for children, was born in Cambridge. At the age of 15 on the death of her surgeon father, she was left dependent on her grandfather for support. In 1786, she married the successor to her father's practice, who later abandoned her to become a naval surgeon. She then supported herself for eight years as a governess to a family identified only as "W", gaining much of her experience with children that enabled her to write for them. She became a professional author, much in demand, as is evident from the publication of one of her more popular stories, *Marvellous Adventures; or, The Vicissitudes of a Cat,* by two competing booksellers. She was also something of an educational theorist, having translated works of Marmontel and Madame de Genlis and then using their intensely moral tales as her models. She was prolific, translating or writing and publishing about 40 works; among her best known are *Edward Barnard* (1797), *A Mirror for the Female Sex* (1798), *Tales of the Hermitage* (1798), *Biography for Boys* (1799), and *Biography for Girls* (1799), and *The Sorrows of Caesar, or Adventures of a Foundling Dog* (1813). The realistic, domestic stories resemble the fiction of Thomas Day and HANNAH MORE, being intensely moral and with little humor. MP employs the themes of hard work, obedience to parents, attention to studies, kindness to animals, Christian virtue (especially acceptance of life's vicissitudes), and proper social behavior, especially for girls. Her bad children are easily distinguished from her good ones, and the adult characters are right about all issues. She followed the successful models of a number of other writers for children, primarily SARAH TRIMMER in her tales of animals. Her works are highly imitative of her Rousseauistic models, as is clear from *Mentorial Tales* (1802), with their didactic emphasis on the value of fiction: "As the power of *habit* is allowed to be capable of counteracting the principles of *nature,* and the most amiable dispositions are often influenced by its effects, one of the first objects in the system of education ought to be that of giving a proper direction to the youthful mind." Although her exhibitions of vice were sometimes so vivid as to draw the adverse criticism of her contemporaries, her works are otherwise distinguished only for their quantity. R.M.

PINCHARD, [Elizabeth?] (fl. 1791–1816), writer of children's literature, was the wife of a Taunton attorney. A staunch Tory, she produced fiction designed to instruct young middle-class girls in the conservative virtues suitable to their sex and station: religion, reason, duty, kindness to servants and animals, and "true sensibility." Her opinions of herself and her vocation, as well as a suggestion of her style, are found in the preface to *The Blind Child, or Anecdotes of the Wyndham Family* (1791): "It has always been my opinion that a person of genius, who dedicates superior talents to the instruction of young people, deserves the highest applause, and the most enthusiastic admiration. To write with a constant attention to the limited understanding or information of children; to restrain a lively imagination, and employ a mind capable of the most brilliant pursuits on subjects of a puerile kind, seems to be a sort of heroic sacrifice of gratification to virtue, which I cannot doubt is acceptable to the Supreme Being." The popularity of P's early books shows that she was in some degree successful with her public. Along with *The Blind Child, Dramatic Dialogue, for the Use of Young Persons* (1792) and *The Two Cousins, a Moral Story* (1794) enjoyed numerous printings in England and the U.S. Some years later P. published several rather longer works: *Mystery and Confidence: A Tale* (1814), *The Ward of Delamere* (1815), *Family Affection* (1816), and *The Young Countess* (new ed., 1823). P.'s works are similar to the didactic juvenile literature produced by other writers of her time. She relied on fictional exposition to support her lessons, avoiding the incorporation of history or natural science that occasionally enlivened the works of MARY PILKINGTON and PRISCILLA WAKEFIELD. G.T.P.

PINCKNEY, Eliza Lucas (1722–93), American letter writer, was the daughter of George Lucas; she was educated in London. While her father was in Antigua with his regiment in 1739, she remained on the family's South Carolina plantation to be with her mother, whose health was delicate. By the age of 16, ELP was managing her father's estates, keeping house for her mother, and instructing her younger sister, Polly. ELP early took great interest in scientific farming. She wrote often to her father about crops, investigating which would be most profitable for export and experimenting with indigo for dye. ELP also had a full social life, joining in the elegant, English-type society of Charles Town; she was especially intimate with neighboring landowners, Colonel and Mrs. Pinckney. The society she describes was based on the slave system, which she did not question although she took pains to educate some blacks. In 1743 her father was made Lieutenant-Governor of Antigua and his family planned to move there. Before the move, Mrs. Pinckney died and ELP quickly became engaged to the 45-year-old widower. They were married in 1744. While Charles Pinckney pursued his duties as lawyer and politician in South Carolina, ELP continued to handle her father's property and experiment with silkworms and indigo; by 1747 chiefly through her efforts, Carolina was exporting large quantities of the dye. In 1745 a son was born; two more children followed. Her letters of this period describe a social life of pleasant hospitality, but also touch on the Indian wars, encouraged in the 1740s by the Spanish and French. In 1747, ELP's father died, a prisoner of the French, news which shocked her so deeply she miscarried. In 1752 Charles Pinckney became a commissioner for South Carolina in England, and the couple moved to London. There ELP contrived to meet George II and the Princess of Wales, whose informality she approved. She enjoyed the season in Bath and the London theater, and she claimed to have seen all Garrick's performances. She disapproved the English prisons and the passion for gaming. In 1756 war broke out in Europe and the Pinckneys, worried over its economic effect on Carolina, resolved to return. Leaving the two boys in England, they arrived back in 1758. Shortly afterward Charles Pinckney caught malaria and died, willing considerable property to ELP and the children. She set about reorganizing the estates, which had become neglected in her absence, and reclaiming her garden which had "gone back to woods again." Frequent letters kept her in contact with her sons, while her daughter grew up and married. In 1769 one son returned to America, while the other, after a short stay, went back to military school in Europe. Both sons figured notably in the Revolution. As relations between England and America worsened, ELP's letters commented more and more on political affairs; yet she still referred to England as "home" and she seemed optimistic about peace until war

actually broke out. ELP and her daughter wholeheartedly espoused the American cause, and in 1780 when Charles Town was taken by the British, the estates of ELP and her children were overrun. Soon she was reduced to poverty: "After the many losses I have met with, for the last three or four desolating years from Fire and Plunder. . . . I still had something to subsist upon, but alas the hand of power has deprived me of the greatest part of that and accident the rest." After the British withdrew, ELP remained impoverished for some time. When her daughter was widowed, she went to live with her on her property. By 1791 her fortunes had mended to some extent, and she was visited by George Washington.

ELP's letters, preserved because she kept duplicates of them, provide a good description of life in colonial America and during the Revolutionary War. Despite her London education, she was early aware of being an American: "I like this part of the world" she wrote to a friend in England, and "Charles Town . . . is a polite agreeable place, the people live very Gentile and very much in the English taste. The country is in general fertile and abounds with Venison and wild fowl." In England when she described the impropriety of sitting in the presence of the Princess of Wales, she wrote: "This you'll imagine must seem pretty extraordinary to an American." As well as depicting the crowded sociability of colonial life, the letters note the upheavals of the time, the wars and epidemics: for instance in 1760 she wrote, "A great cloud seems at present to hang over this province, we are continually insulted by the Indians and a violent kind of smallpox that rages in Charles Town almost puts a stop to all business." ELP's letters reveal her intellectually enquiring mind in matters of religion, science, agriculture, and literature. She consulted Locke "over and over," and was eager to educate according to "Mr. Locke's method," in which the child was "to play himself into learning."   J.T.

PIOZZI, Hester [Lynch, Salusbury] Thrale (1741–1821), diarist, memoirist, and travel writer, was born near Pwllheli, Caern., Wales, of landed gentry, and grew up mainly in London. She was educated at home by her mother and aunt, and subsequently studied Latin, logic, and rhetoric under Arthur Collier. She was much praised for her abilities, having by age 20 learned four languages and displayed precocious interest in scholarship and literature. Not later than 1762 she began publishing poems and other short pieces in newspapers, but this incipient literary career was interrupted by her father's death and her mother's decision to marry her (1763), against her will, to Henry Thrale, a wealthy brewer. The experience of being bartered (she felt) for the sake of his fortune to a man who did not love her embittered her deeply. So did its consequences: 13 pregnancies between 1764 and 1778 produced 12 children, eight of whom died in infancy. From 1763 to 1781 she divided her time between Thrale's town house in Southwark and his estate at Streatham, Surrey. In 1765 she was introduced to Samuel Johnson, with whom she and Thrale soon became intimate. With Johnson she translated poems by Boethius, and for one of his projects she wrote her best-known poem, "The Three Warnings" (1766). Johnson's presence at Streatham attracted other eminent people, most notably Giuseppi Baretti, Edmund Burke, Charles and FANNY BURNEY, David Garrick, Oliver Goldsmith, and Sir Joshua Reynolds. HTP became, and remains, celebrated as their hostess; in old age she was venerated by those who met her as "the woman who had entertained Johnson, Burke and Reynolds." In the later 70s she also became acquainted with ELIZABETH MONTAGU and her circle. All this celebrity turned to scandal, however, when after the death of Thrale (1781) HTP elected to marry (1784) Gabriel Piozzi (1740–1809), a highly respected musician but also an Italian and Roman Catholic, and therefore considered an inferior (even sinister) match for a well-bred Englishwoman. She made the decision in the face of violent opposition by her eldest daughter and Johnson, with neither of whom was she afterward reconciled; she did so convinced that, having "married the first Time to please my Mother," she must the second time make her own choice and "rise to the Rank of a human Being conscious of its power to discern Good from Ill." The marriage proved eminently satisfying. With Piozzi she traveled in France, Italy, and Germany (1784–87), writing poems for the *Florence Miscellany* (1785), edited by Robert Merry, William Parsons, and Bertie Greatheed, the so-called "Della Cruscans"; writing also her first, best-known, and best book, *Anecdotes of the Late Samuel Johnson* (1786); and collecting materials for her third book, *Observations and Reflections made in . . . a Journey through France, Italy,*

and Germany (1789). The creative outburst that started in Italy lasted more than 15 years and generated ambitious performances.

Her edition of Johnson's letters to her family (338 of them, 1788); "a two Volume Book of *Synonyms* in English . . . for the use of Foreigners, and other Children of six feet high" (*British Synonymy,* 1794); a political pamphlet, *Three Warnings to John Bull before He Dies* (1798); and *Retrospection,* a world history in popularized form (1801) were all published. Unpublished works are "The Adventurer. A comedy in two acts" (n.d., c. 1790: John Rylands Library); a short exposition of Anglican Church doctrine (1786); "Una & Duessa or a Set of Dialogues upon the most popular Subjects" (1791); "The Two Fountains," a masque "in the Manner of Milton's Comus" based on Johnson's tale "The Fountains" (1789: Houghton Library); a translation of the *Tableau Spéculatif de l'Europe* (1798) by Charles-François Dumouriez (1803: Rylands); and "Lyford Redivivus," a dictionary of Christian names (c. 1814: Hyde Collection). In 1795 HTP and Piozzi settled on an estate of their own building, Brynbella, near Denbigh in Wales, where they entertained numerous friends (among them the actress Sarah Siddons) and performed the duties of principal local landowners, visiting London and Bath for the winters. During the '90s HTP's domestic life was troubled by her husband's increasing ill health and by feuds with her daughters stemming from Thrale's will. In 1798, apparently despairing of her own children, she and Piozzi adopted his nephew, John Salusbury Piozzi; in later years HTP doted on this boy, whose failure to reciprocate her affection was a deep disappointment to her. Another was the failure, so complete that it virtually ended her writing career, of *Retrospection.* Her last years after Piozzi's death were lived in comparative—sometimes actual—poverty mainly in Bath; and although in public she maintained her legendary vivacity, in private she sank into neurosis and self-pity. In 1818 she met the actor William Augustus Conway—the last of a series of younger men who had for years found her fascinating—and developed an extravagant sentimental affection for him. She rarely sought to publish after 1801, but continued to write, sending letters, copying poems, and obsessively filling notebooks until almost the day of her death. She died at Clifton, of complications from an injury sustained in a fall.

HTP wrote numerous journals. Her most famous diary is *Thraliana* (1776–1809), valuable as a document of her social milieu. There are also three travel journals of Wales (1774), France (1775), and Scotland (1789: Rylands Library); a family diary, the "Children's Book" (1766–78); and two commonplace books, "Minced Meat for Pyes" (c. 1796–1820) and the "New Common Place Book" (1809–21: Hyde Collection). Some of these contain copies of her poems (in *Thraliana* alone there are 177 poems); other manuscripts, notably a five-volume collection known as the "Harvard Piozziana" (1810–14: Houghton Library) bring the total to at least 450.

In her choice of genres HTP made few concessions to the prevailing restrictions on women writers in her time. She steadfastly avoided the genre most practiced by women, the novel, partly because her abilities did not lie that way and partly from principle: like Johnson, she distrusted the moral influence of fiction. Endeavoring, in her own words, "to make Truth palatable," she directed her literary attention, as did Johnson, to the world of actual people and events, and to genres which deal with that world: anecdote, memoir, travel book, history, political oratory. In this she also resembled the Bluestocking writers Elizabeth Montagu and ELIZABETH CARTER; but she was bolder than they, and put herself directly into competition with such eminent male contemporaries as Edward Gibbon. In *Retrospection* she attempted nothing less than an answer to Gibbon's Whig, and "Infidel," *History;* the book failed in part because it was perceived to have overstepped the generic limits allowed to women writers—"history in dimity," one reviewer scornfully called it. Throughout her work HTP is concerned to uphold values she associates with Johnson and Augustanism: a judicious skepticism regarding human nature; belief in the moral force of literature; distrust of publicly eccentric behavior, or "individualism"; and deep distrust of innovation, especially in politics and learning. All her writing of the 1790s, regardless of its topic, was intended to defend the British status quo against the "levelling French Democrates." At the same time, she was by temperament many of the things she wrote against—impulsive, romantic, eccentric, imprudent, melodramatic. In her work this tension sometimes produces incoher-

ence, as when she casts a political pamphlet that is meant to be a Burkean call to moral action *(Three Warnings to John Bull)* in the form of her witty, folkish poem "The Three Warnings." At other times, however, its results are valuable, as when, in the *Anecdotes,* in utter defiance of the then-canons of biographical decorum, she tells such frank, unsentimental stories as this: "The trick which most parents play with their children, that of shewing off their newly-acquired accomplishments, disgusted Mr. Johnson beyond expression; he had been treated so himself, he said, till he absolutely loathed his father's caresses, because he knew they were sure to precede some unpleasant display of his early abilities." This candor she seems to have learned partly from Rousseau, whose work she admired as a penetrating commentary on human conduct and whose political radicalism she apparently managed to ignore. At the height of her career HTP enjoyed considerable literary celebrity: her *Anecdotes* were ranked with Boswell's *Journal of a Tour to the Hebrides* (1785) as one of the two most remarkable books about Johnson, and her edition of his letters was widely read (among its admirers was Jane Austen); *Observations and Reflections* was esteemed as an account of Italian society and customs; her published poems had a mixed reception, but "The Three Warnings" became popular as a recitation piece (and continued to be anthologized far into the 19th century). Her later works were less well received, and she lived to see most of her achievements belittled. In poetry, her association with the *Florence Miscellany* involved her work in the fate of the Della Cruscans: attacked savagely by William Gifford in *The Baviad* (1794), their reputations quickly expired, and hers with them. Even as a travel writer she did not escape Gifford's satire: "See Thrale's grey widow with a satchel roam, / And bring in pomp laborious nothings home." Her important work on Johnson was impugned by Boswell in his *Life of Johnson* (1791); only in the 20th century has its value been reaffirmed. The *Anecdotes* is now recognized as one of the three most authoritative early memoirs of Johnson and, although esthetically it is much inferior to Boswell's books, it is considerably more pungent and probing than they. Her editing of his letters, once held in great suspicion, has been at least partially vindicated by R. W. Chapman (1952). In her poetry, which is often occasional and kept pace with current taste, sounding at first like Pope and later like Southey, she is now remembered almost exclusively for her English "imitations" of two Latin poems by Johnson, "In Theatro" ("When sixty years have chang'd thee quite, / Still can theatric scenes delight? / Ill suits this place with learned wight, / May Bates or Coulson cry") and a set of verses to Dr. Lawrence ("Condemn'd to shun bright Sol's reviving ray, / While my tir'd sight shrinks at th' approach of day, / Each pleasing task become my present dread, / Chain'd down by darkness to a lazy bed"). As a letter writer she has always retained some fame, and since the publication of *Thraliana* she has acquired it as a diarist.   W.M.

PIX, Mary (1666–1709), playwright and novelist, was born at Nettlebed, Oxon., the daughter of Rev. Roger Griffith and the former Lucy Berriman. At 18 she married George Pix, a London merchant tailor, with whom she had one child, who died in 1690. She began to publish in 1696, writing her first plays for the patent company at Drury Lane. As a result, perhaps, of feminist commendatory verses she wrote for her colleagues CATHARINE TROTTER and DE-LARIVIÈRE MANLEY, MP was ridiculed in *The Female Wits* (1696), a dramatic burlesque performed by her own company. The play portrayed MP in the figure of corpulent, hard-drinking, good-natured Mrs. Wellfed. After this, MP's plays were produced by the rival company at Lincoln's Inn Fields, where she was befriended by Thomas Betterton and William Congreve, who supported her in a 1697 plagiarism dispute with George Powell, an actor with the patent company. After she sparred with Powell in print in 1698, MP's life, both private and professional, seems to have been inconspicuous. At her death, a benefit performance for her estate was given of the popular play *The Busy Body,* written by her friend SUSANNA CENTLIVRE.

MP wrote twelve plays: six tragedies and six comedies; these have not been collected or reprinted. She also wrote two novels, *The Inhuman Cardinal* (1696) and *Violenta* (1704). Although several of her tragedies were popular, they are poor stuff. Her first was a historical work, *Ibrahim* (1696), dealing with the amours of a Turkish emperor; the play is theatrical and achieved some success, being revived in 1704 and 1715. Her next tragedy, *Queen Catharine* (1698), took English history as its subject, reducing the Wars of the Roses to a love quarrel among Edward IV, Owen Tudor, and Catharine of France. MP's worst play was *The False Friend* (1699), a muddle of moralizing and melodrama intended as part of the stage reform movement. Also weak was *The Double Distress* (1701). *The Czar of Muscovy* (1701) is livelier, as is her last tragedy, *The Conquest of Spain* (1705). The tragedies show no originality, continuing the by-then-debased Beaumont and Fletcher tradition; three are imitations of Fletcher plays with very little new added. They were successful, however, probably because MP hit the popular taste with her knack for alternating scenes of heroic rant and melting love in which a mighty hero languishes at his lady's feet. Her tragedies look to the later stage in the prominence given to the heroine and to the fatal accidents to love. Their greatest weakness is their style, since MP was apparently unable to write decent blank verse. Her best works are her comedies, lively intrigue plays full of stage business, bustle, and surprises. The dialogue is usually flat, but the action never flags; the plays contain some pleasant songs, which were published separately or in contemporary anthologies. *The Spanish Wives* (1696) is an amusing farce with tellingly human marital repartee. The skillful double plot contrasts the situations of two wives, one with a trusting and generous husband, the other married to a jealous and avaricious man. According to Charles Gildon, "this farce had the good fortune to please"; performances are recorded as late as 1726. Also popular was *The Innocent Mistress* (1697), in which an unhappily married man finds happiness in a platonic relationship. In *The Deceiver Deceived* (1697) the cuckolding intrigue is undercut by a sentimental twist to the plot. *The Beau Defeated* (1700), based on Dancourt's *Le Chevalier à la Mode,* is one of MP's best intrigue comedies, depicting the adventures of two wealthy widows. A Mr. Rich concludes the play with an encomium of the English merchant, a speech that suggests Lillo and the bourgeois drama of the next generation. *The Different Widows* (1703) comically contrasts two sisters, the idle and intriguing Lady Gaylove and the virtuous Lady Bellmont. *The Adventures in Madrid* (1706), a sentimentalized intrigue comedy that flirts with, but avoids, the depiction of adultery, is lively and theatrical. Forced or unhappy marriages appear frequently as a plot device in such comedies as *The Spanish Wives, The Deceiver Deceived, The Innocent Mistress,* and *The*

Adventures in Madrid, but, unlike APHRA BEHN, MP does not crusade against forced marriage. Her treatment of the unhappily married person is sentimentalized: either the *mal mariée* is rescued and married more satisfactorily, as in *The Spanish Wives* and *The Adventures in Madrid* (this also happens in a tragedy, *The Czar of Muscovy*); or, as in *The Deceiver Deceived* and *The Innocent Mistress,* the seemingly errant spouse is really virtuous. MP's use of sentimental characters in intrigue actions causes oddities of plotting, a characteristic of playwrights at the turn of the century who were under pressure for stage reform. Generally her comedies reflect the changing temper of the times, emphasizing virtuous love rather than cuckolding. Though not an important figure, MP achieved modest recognition; she worked quietly for ten years as a minor playwright of thorough professionalism. N.C.

PLANTIN, Arabella (1700?–?), novelist, left little record of her life, except that she was, apparently, a member of the Wharton family. Two works, *Love Led Astray: Or, The Mutual Inconstancy* (1727) and *The Ingrateful: Or, The Just Revenge* (1727), appeared in *Letters to the Lady Wharton, and Several Other Persons of Distinction* (printed for Curll). They were reprinted in *Whartoniana, or Miscellanies in Verse and Prose by the Wharton Family* (1727) and in *The Poetical Works of Phillip Duke of Wharton,* II (1731). The novels are built on conventional romantic themes, unrestrained passions, jealousy, betrayal of love, and the revenge of the jilted lover. The plots turn on the convoluted complications of the theater, such as dual sets of masked lovers, while village rustics act as choruses. Sidneian pastorals, pitifully underdeveloped, the novels are yet distinctive among those of APHRA BEHN's followers: AP rejected both the prurient interest of DELARIVIÈRE MANLEY and ELIZA HAYWOOD and also the ponderous moralism of ELIZABETH ROWE in favor of only a slight didactic tinge. Although unable to achieve realism in her own work, AP sensed the lack of both psychological and social verisimilitude in the romantic novels of her time. "Perhaps, I may be told," she writes of lovers who go to a temple to learn their marital fates, "that neither one nor t'other of them were much in love, since they did not appeal to their own Hearts upon the Matter," and she assures her audience that in such circumstances lovers hear an "Answer propitious to their Inclinations." Social verisimilitude, she believed, would be created by discarding the modish literary fashions of the period with their court settings and lofty titles in favor of a more middle-class realism: "It is not among the most exalted Characters, nor in the highest Rank of Life, that the strange Effects of Love most frequently appear. . . . I know that the Name of a Prince embellishes a Story . . . tho' that pompous Title is not always attended with all the Gallantry which is often found in a private Person." F.K.B.

PLUMPTRE, Anna (1760–1818) and Annabella, miscellaneous writers, were the daughters of Dr. Robert Plumptre, the president of Queens' College, Cambridge. Anna, whose output was by far the most significant, received a good education and became skilled in languages, particularly German. She performed an important service in making German literature accessible to an English audience, most notably the plays of the once-popular dramatist August von Kotzebue, including *The Count of Burgundy* (1798), *The Force of Calumny* (1799), and *The Horse and the Widow* (1799). Among other works she translated were J. C. A. Musaeus's *Physiognomical Travels* (1800) and F. C. Pouqueville's *Travels in the Morea* (1813). Her first original work was *The Rector's Son: A Novel* (1798), and this was followed by *Something New; or, Adventures at Campbell House* (1801). During the period 1802–5 she lived in France, and the fruits of her stay are contained in the *Narrative of a Three Years' Residence in France* (1810). She toured Ireland in 1814–15, and again published her impressions in *Narrative of a Residence in Ireland* (1817). In between she published another novel, *The History of Myself and a Friend* (1817). Her last work, published jointly with Annabella in the year of her death, was *Tales of Wonder, of Honour and of Sentiment, Original and Translated.* Annabella was the third daughter of the family. Her work is difficult to come by but included a novel, *Montgomery, or Scenes in Wales,* and a volume of *Stories for Children* (1804).

The Rector's Son is a sentimental novel with a prominent element of intrigue, a little-known forerunner of the modern thriller. It centers on the fortunes of Charles Meadows, long presumed dead in suspicious circumstances in India but ultimately resurrected to be reunited with his wife. *Critical Review* (May 1798) was dismissive: "Those readers who do not regard the probability of a story may derive pleasure from this work. Though we do not consider it as having any great merit, it is not altogether contemptible." The "something new" of her second, epistolary novel is an "ugly heroine," who "shew'd no symmetry of form, or face, / Though richly stored with ev'ry mental grace." This heroine is eventually married neither to the beauty-worshipper, who learns "to distinguish solid happiness from the tinsel joys of what is commonly called pleasure," nor to the fortune-hunter, who rediscovers an old lover; in the absence of normal credentials, she becomes "something superior to mortality." The French *Narrative* is noteworthy chiefly for its Revolutionary sympathies (Anna was a well-known democrat and a friend of HELEN MARIA WILLIAMS). It contains a spirited defense of Napoleon: "In all the governments where Bonaparte has any influence, he has uniformly been the means of procuring relief to the people from some of the most grievous of their oppressions." Her second *Narrative* is a detailed travelogue and commentary on Ireland, extending to its "civil and political state"; it minimizes the discontent. It was savaged by the *Quarterly Review* as "trash" and blamed for ignorance and inaccuracy, and for being "pedantic and dull." The joint *Tales of Wonder* roams widely over Europe for settings. Annabella's singly authored *Stories for Children* evinces a very tight and repressive juvenile morality. R.J.

PLUNKETT, Elizabeth (1769–1823), novelist and translator, was born in London, daughter of SUSANNAH [MINIFIE] GUNNING. Her mother and aunt MARGARET MINIFIE were veteran novelists. Both of her parents also attempted to act out their fantasies, a habit which EP may have inherited. The story goes that, to encourage the suit of her cousin the Marquis of Lorne, she forged a letter presumably from the Marquis of Blandford releasing himself from matrimonial intentions. Her mother refused to admit her daughter's authorship and published a 147–page *Letter* (1791) to Lorne's father the Duke of Argyll, who was Mrs. Gunning's brother-in-law, attributing the forgery to distant cousins named Bowen, in the service of her husband. General Gunning ejected both wife and daughter, and they moved to a house provided by the Duchess of Bedford, Blandford's grandmother, who had introduced EP's beautiful aunts to society and uncritically adored their niece. Society on the

whole sided with the General. Walpole dubbed these unseemly complications the "Gunninghiad." To define EP's mother's tendency toward "absurd hyperbole" Lady Harcourt coined the word "Minific"; Gillray produced a Gunning-cartoon; and this "Maiden all for-*Lorn*" engendered a new version of the nursery rhyme. After a brief stay abroad to escape legal repercussions, EP and her mother returned to London. In 1803, three years after her mother's death, EP married an Irish major "of slender circumstances" named John Plunkett.

EP began writing novels after the "Genninghiad," while she was living with her mother. It seems likely that her mother and aunt spurred her on to produce her first three novels, *The Packet* (1794), *Lord Fitzhenry* (1794), and *Memoirs of Mme. de Barneveldt* (1795—a translation), during which period Susannah Gunning published nothing. Although EP was heavily indebted to French techniques, her mother apparently influenced her throughout her early career. In the 1790s, for instance, both wrote books set in Wales. EP eventually surpassed her mother in sheer quantity and published, as well as nine novels, two collections of didactic stories for children, five translations or "alterations" of French novels, and one version of a French play. She also translated Fontenelle's *Plurality of Worlds* (1803), one of her father's favorite works. Inheriting her father's fortune did not seem to slow her down, nor did her marriage. Although EP frequently tried the epistolary form, she found it inhibiting, especially since she leaned toward the gothic rather than the satiric. *The Packet,* for instance, contains a gothic sequence in which the heroine is abducted and hidden in an unnamed country full of tigers and wolves. While occasionally claiming to be "founded in fact" (*The Gypsy Countess,* 1799), EP's novels usually end with a suitable marriage or two, a plot line that reflects traditional themes and not EP's own unfortunate experience. But her later works reveal her fascination with politics. In *Exile of Erin* (1808) her third-person dedication speciously claims that "As a woman she has avoided any thing like political discussion, well aware of how ill one of her sex must be qualified to enter on such a topic." In this epistolary novel, one of the characters apologizes, "I find my postscript is more like a state paper than a letter expressive of my approaching happiness." EP's themes were more wide-ranging than her mother's, but less fully embodied, and her language is less individual. Although many of her novels reached second editions, she was never able to equal her mother's reputation. Her brief obituary designated her as "a lady endowed with many virtues, and considerable accomplishments" (*Gentleman's Magazine,* 1823). J.Th.

POLWHELE, Elizabeth (?–1691?), playwright, may have been the daughter of a nonconformist minister, Theophilus Polwhele, was the wife of another, Stephen Lobb, and the mother of at least five children. She was one of the first women known to write for the professional theater. In about 1670 she composed a rhymed tragedy called "The Faithful Virgins" [Bodleian MS], probably performed by the Duke's Company. It is a play in the Jacobean style, with apparitions, an allegorical masque, and an ending of multiple deaths. With its improbable plot and wooden rhymes, it has little to redeem it. With the next play, *The Frolicks, or The Lawyer Cheated* (1671), EP changed with the times and turned to low-life realistic comedy. The work was clearly written for performance, but there is no record of its being staged. *The Frolicks* is a light play, relying much on song, dance, and boisterous action. It has a loose plot of stock figures: country bumpkins, a young country wife enamored of London and gallantry, a middle-aged husband easily fooled but always fearing cuckoldry, a good-hearted rake, and a scheming lawyer. The most interesting character is the witty heroine Clarabell, who notes that "Love is but a swinish thing at best" and who is called by her father "a pert, headstrong baggage." The dedication to Prince Rupert reveals EP's awareness of being an uneducated woman writer; the conventional stance of unworthiness mingles with her discomfort at trespassing in a male literary world: she has, she claims, thrown her "foolish modesty aside . . . I am young, no scholar, and what I write I write by nature, not by art." EP calls herself "an unfortunate young woman" who is "haunted with poetic devils," and she mentions the troubles in her life. She also refers in her dedication to another work of hers named *Elysium,* possibly a religious masque. J.T.

POMFRET, Henrietta Louisa Fermor, Countess of (1698–1761), letter writer, was the daughter of Lord Jefferys and Lady Charlotte Herbert. In 1720 she married Thomas Fermor, who became the Earl of Pomfret. He was made Master of Horse to Queen Caroline in 1727, while C of P became Lady of the Bedchamber, with the COUNTESS OF HERTFORD; both women were much attached to the Queen. C of P retired in 1737 and moved with her husband and two of their daughters to the Continent, possibly owing to financial difficulties. At first they lived near Paris, then moved to Italy. In 1740 in Florence she was visited for two months by LADY MARY WORTLEY MONTAGU, with whom she corresponded for some time in chatty letters; the two women admired each other's conversation and enjoyed their friendship. In Rome in 1741, C of P is said to have written a life of Vandyck. She returned to England late in 1741, and in 1753 the Earl of Pomfret died. In 1758 she gave Oxford University part of the collection of the "Arundel Marbles," purchased by her father-in-law. C of P was survived by four sons and six daughters.

When on the Continent, C of P exchanged weekly letters with the Countess of Hertford. These were published as *Correspondence between Frances, Countess of Hertford (afterwards Duchess of Somerset) and Henrietta Louisa, Countess of Pomfret between the years 1738 and 1741.* C of P's letters are pleasant in tone, often humorous about the pretensions of the great, and observant about people and places. They comment on towns such as Siena, which she found dull and expensive, and give graphic pictures of C of P's life. Of a lonely winter in France, she writes: "My neighbours are all gone to Paris; and that beautiful landscape, which my window presented to me, is become a dreary waste. The ground is russet, the trees resemble skeletons, and the castles remind me of ghosts. Nay, even the river, that gave life to the whole, now only serves to exhale thick fogs, which give additional horror to the scene." The letters also reveal C of P's enjoyment of society and of friendship, "the noblest sentiment of the soul." J.T.

PORTER, Sarah [Martyn] (?–1831), American poet, married John Porter, a physician, in 1767 in Boxford, Mass. In 1780 the Porters settled in Plymouth, N.H. Like her husband, who was admitted to the bar in 1784, SP was celebrated for her intellectual attainments. Mother of five, she published one volume of poetry. She was widowed in 1813 and died in Williamstown, Vt. Based on 2 Sam. 12:1–23, *The Royal Pen-*

itent in three parts. To which is added David's Lamentation over Saul and Jonathan (1791) depicts King David's remorse for having Bathsheba's husband killed so that he might possess her. The once-great leader, characterized by description and dialogue, is haunted by the thought of Uriah, "the hero and the patriot join'd." His torment unrelieved by "court's licentious joys," David longs for the contentment known only to those who eschew luxury. Written in elegant heroic couplets, the poem begins with the invocation of the "Celestial Muse" and, having portrayed the King's sincere repentance, ends with a vision of the millenium: "Upon the verdant grass, the fearless lamb, / Shall, with the wolf, lie down as with its dam." Without referring explicitly to her own nation, SP uses the biblical story and the traditional contrast of court and country life to explore issues of concern to the new republic: justice, the uses of power, and the corruption of virtue. "David's Lamentation over Saul and Jonathan" (1793) is an elaborate paraphrase of 2 Sam. 1:17–27. With the Old Testament chronicler, SP exclaims, "How are the mighty fall'n!"—perhaps alluding to fallen patriots. Like MERCY OTIS WARREN and other sophisticated women writers of her day, she used classical and biblical parallels for contemporary social and political issues. The publication of her works indicated New England's growing acceptance of women's ability to speak on subjects other than religion.   M.D.J.

POYNTON, Priscilla [Pickering] (1750–1801), poet, native of Lichfield, lost her eyesight when she was 12 "occasioned by a violent Headache." She claimed to have been kept as a child under "the strictest subjection by an aged parent" and without an amanuensis. Yet her first publication, under the well-worn title *Poems on Several Occasions,* was issued in 1770 with 50 pages of subscribers' names, including Lucy Porter, Samuel Johnson's step-daughter. In 1789, canvassing for patrons to her second volume, she admitted that she had "sustained many Losses in the year 1770, through unavoidable contingencies." The *Poems* (1794) contained a large proportion of verses by the editor, J. Weston, and J. Morfitt. Little else is known about PP except her marriage to Mr. I. Pickering, a saddler of New Street, Birmingham, in 1788. *The Birmingham Gazette,* 15 June 1801, noted her passing only briefly: "Died—Mrs. Pickering, of this town, who some time ago pub-lished a volume of poems by subscription. She had been blind about 50 years." Much of her poetry is autobiographical, such as her first one describing her loss of sight. Milton and Homer could find inspiration in noble authors; she must find her instructor in Nature. Consoling herself that being blind she is immune to earthly temptations, she pathetically anticipates a heavenly change: "There, instantaneous, be restor'd to sight, / And fill'd with perfect permanent delight." She also wrote celebratory odes, such as that to George III on his recovery, in 1789, which he answered in kind, calling her "Sweet Philomena." She responded in verse on the least provocation, sending several poems to the *Gazette.* Weston criticized this generosity, which made it difficult to collect adequate material "to aid the poor unfortunate woman." PP's verses lack any light natural touch and are frequently self-conscious and verbose, with jog-trot rhythms and obvious rhymes. One odd little poem complains of social gatherings where a woman is without respite for six hours and more: "Tea, wine, and punch, Sir, to be free, / Excellent diuretics be."   J.H. and D.L.L.

PYE, Joel-Henrietta [Jael] [Mrs. Hampden Pye] (1737?–1782), occasional poet and author, was born Jael Mendez, daughter of a rich Jewish merchant of Red Lion Square, Holborn. By 1760, when she published her first known work, she was familiar with Twickenham, birthplace of her first husband, John Neil Campbell, of Milton Ernest, Beds., admitted to Lincoln's Inn in 1755. The first marriage in 1762 was brief, for in 1766 at Farringdon, Berks., JP married Robert Hampden Pye, a second son and an ensign in the fashionable 1st Foot Guards; she was about 30, her "little volatile lord and master" about 10 years younger. His father, MP for Farringdon, had died in March, leaving debts of £50,000. JP admits having spent her own fortune with profligate abandon, and by 1774, when she began writing a series of letters to Garrick from France, she was living alone with her young daughter almost in poverty, often unable to afford a theater ticket. In a word portrait in French (1777) she describes herself at 40 as above middle height with a small head, penetrating black eyes, pretty jet-black hair, a well-formed chest, good legs, and a noble walk; she was a lover of adornment, seemed haughty, but was sweet and compassionate, and longed to excite admiration. When JP's husband was ordered to America, the couple were hard-pressed to raise the money for his necessities, and Garrick had to lend her 60 guineas to pay the school fees in Dijon of her son. She complained that her husband's mother and brother (Henry-James Pye, Poet Laureate in 1790) would not help, and then resented their taking her son off her hands. Garrick, who always did what he could for her, introduced her to Mme. Riccoboni, who befriended her, reported she knew not ten people in France, defended her when she was slandered in the papers in 1777 (apparently as a reprisal by people who believed that she had done similarly to them), and found her sweet, honest, and exact in conduct. After her many misfortunes, JP told Garrick that she was looking forward to a quiet old age to be spent reunited with her husband, but she died before this occurred.

JP's first known publication was a 19-page pamphlet, *A Short Account of the Principal Seats and Gardens in and about Richmond and Kew* (Brentford, 1760). She describes briefly the most imposing houses in the neighborhood, sometimes including their interiors. Pope's former villa is depicted in "Some Account of a little Kingdom on the Banks of the Thames." The descriptions of Horace Walpole's and Garrick's villas are flattering; also included are the houses of Mrs. Pritchard, Mrs. Clive, the Dukes of Argyll and Newcastle, and the Earls of Radnor and Portmore. The pamphlet was twice reprinted, once with her *Poems* (1767) and again as *A Peep into the Principal Seats and Gardens in and about Twickenham* (1775). The volume includes competent complimentary verses from JP to Walpole in 1760 about his Strawberry Hill. Envy visits the villa: "Through well rang'd chambers next she bends her way, / Gloomy, not dark, and chearful, though not gay: / Where to the whole each part proportion bears, / And all around a pleasing aspect wears" and concludes, addressing Walpole in her own name: "Th' applause

which thou so gladly would'st receive, / The candid and the wise alone can give, / Taste, though much talk'd of, is confin'd to few; / They best can prize it who are most like you." Walpole called the lines "Violent compliments in verse," and addressed an equally violent return to her: "No, 'twas Parnassus did her fancy fill, / Which the kind maid mistook for Strawberry-Hill; / Whilst Modesty persuaded her to place / Another on that mount, she ought to grace." He later characterized JP's book as silly, inaccurate, superficial, and blundering, and dismissed her as "a Jewess, who has married twice and turned Christian, poetess and authoress." In 1767 JP printed privately a 36-page pamphlet, *Poems.* In 1771 Garrick produced her farce, "The Capricious Lady," at Drury Lane; it had one performance only and was not published (in the Larpent Collection). Also in 1771 JP brought out *Poems. By a Lady,* (2nd ed. 1772); it was approved by *Critical Review,* which liked her modernized version of Childe Waters, with its refinement of language and suppressed indelicacies, and found her other poems remarkable for purity and refined taste. Other poems are personal epistles, referring to visits, shared experiences, and events of note ("On the Report of Dr. Sterne's Death, in the Year 1760"). In one poem addressed to Garrick she laments being forced to decline for propriety's sake an invitation to appear on stage in a masquerade ball scene: "In haste I flew to gain admission; . . . / A phantom met me on my way, / And sternly urged a moment's stay: / A formal, antiquated dame, / And WORLDLY PRUDENCE was her name." In 1777 JP reported to Garrick that she was about to assist Le Tourneur with his translations of Shakespeare (which began to appear in 1781). In 1786 was published, probably by her husband, *Theodosius and Arabella. A Novel. In a Series of Letters. By the late Mrs. Hampden Pye,* a two-volume work which *CR* found overpriced and bathetic.   B.R.

R

RADCLIFFE, Ann [Ward] (1764–1823), novelist, was born in London, the only child of business people who had connections with the landed gentry. In her uncle's home she met HESTER PIOZZI and ELIZABETH MONTAGU. When her family moved to Bath, she probably attended a school kept by SOPHIA and HARRIET LEE. At 23 she married William Radcliffe, a journalist who became owner and editor of the *English Chronicle,* and settled near London. They had no children. Encouraged by her husband, she wrote during the long evenings when he was away on business. Her first work, *The Castles of Athlin and Dunbayne* (1789), is a clumsy medieval tale with much melodramatic action and virtually no development of character or atmosphere. In *A Sicilian Romance* (1790) she made better use of gothic architecture, exotic atmosphere, and suspenseful flights through dark vaults, while in *The Romance of the Forest* (1791) she first developed a solid responsive central character. Although popular, these works were overshadowed by the extraordinary success of *The Mysteries of Udolpho* (1794), for which AR received the then-enormous sum of £500. *Udolpho* brought to a culmination the gothic terror, romantic charm, and picturesque scenery in which she excelled. AR's romantic descriptions of French, Swiss, and Italian scenery were not derived from observation, however, but from landscapes and travel books. She left England only once, recording her experiences in *A Journey Made in the Summer of 1794, through Holland and the Western Frontier of Germany . . . To which Are Added Observations During a Tour to the Lakes* (1795). With the same sensibility that created her novels, this book describes the "awful pleasure" inspired by the Alps, a ruined fortress made "interesting" by its romantic history and still more so "by the shadowy hour and the vesper bell of a chapel on a cliff below," and the vaults of Brougham Castle under which are probably laid the bones of the victims of a tyrant's will. For *The Italian* (1797), the most grim and powerful of her romances, AR was paid £600. In 1802 she wrote *Gaston de Blondeville, or The Court of Henry III,* in which she made more effort at historical verisimilitude than in her earlier romances. It was published after her death (1826), along with *St. Alban's Abbey. A Metrical Tale.* Like her heroines, AR was studious, sensitive, proper, and passionately responsive to music and natural scenery. Her marriage seems to have been happy; her *Journey* shows a congenial couple enjoying their trip and sharing all their responses. She was conservative in religion and politics, but expressed indignation at injustice, oppression of the poor, and the slave trade. She was shy in company and took no part in literary society, although she did put her name on the title page of all her books after the second edition of *The Romance of the Forest.*

The most interesting character in *The Romance of the Forest* is La Motte, a man of feeling gone wrong. Because he has never learned to control his passions, La Motte has slipped from weakness into vice; he is unkind not from natural cruelty, but from self-indulgence compounded by guilt. His rational principles are further weakened by an overactive imagination, which "often dazzled his judgment." Although AR capitalized on the love of wonder, and depended on feeling and imagination, she constantly insisted that such impulses must be controlled. She made her villains conspicuously hard and prosaic, but she firmly opposed superstition and feeling divorced from principle. Emily in *Udolpho* must exert herself to control her excess sensibility, and Schedoni, villain of *The Italian*, plays upon that of the hero, Vivaldi. Accordingly, AR's heroines are tremblingly sensitive to music, natural beauty, and tender or harrowing emotions; simultaneously they are rational and firm, resisting aggression with resolution and dignity. They are clearly although not deeply characterized and provide a definite consciousness at the center of the novel. This is essential to AR's effects, which depend not on objective horrors but on the consciousness that experiences them. Her villains are violent, overbearing men, impervious to natural beauty, tender emotions, and the promptings of imagination. Forceful and superior to ordinary vanity or frivolity, they easily dominate others and are strangers equally "to pity and to fear." Mazzini in *A Sicilian Romance* is typical, convinced of female weakness and sure that imagination and sensitivity are marks of weakness. The monk Schedoni, the most impressive of the stern villains, appears "almost superhuman" "as he stalked along, wrapt in the black garments of his order"; and his piercing eyes "seemed to penetrate, at a single glance, into the hearts of men." His self-command enables him easily to manipulate more emotional characters. He is ashamed as well as amazed when, for the first time, he lacks resolution to kill. But although almost immune to tender emotions, he is himself the slave of ambition and revenge.

More artistically than any of her contemporaries, AR appealed to her readers' taste for sentiment, scenery, and terrifying thrills. Sensitive, admirable young ladies, with whom one easily identifies, almost forget their misfortunes as nature's sublimity is spread before them. The site of San Stefano, the convent where Ellena in *The Italian* is about to be imprisoned, "overlooked the whole extent of plains . . . with the vast chain of mountains, which seemed to form an insurmountable rampart to the rich landscape at their feet. Their towering and fantastic summits, crowding together into dusky air, like flames tapering to a point, exhibited images of peculiar grandeur, while each minuter line and feature withdrawing, at this evening hour, from observation, seemed to resolve itself into the more gigantic masses, to which the dubious tint, the solemn obscurity, that

began to prevail over them, gave force and loftier character." The silence and deep repose of the landscape is then made even more impressive by the vesper service of the monks, softened by the sweet voices of the nuns. AR works up terror by withholding essential information, ingeniously delaying the outcome, and combining actual perils with supernatural fears that are plausible in context. Soon after arriving at Udolpho, Emily looks behind a black veil to see a dreadful object (not identified until the end of the book). Alone at midnight in her isolated room with a door that cannot be locked, she imagines that her room communicates with the room of the black veil. She hears a repeated sound—that seems to come from the door. "While Emily kept her eyes fixed on the spot, she saw the door move, and then slowly open, and perceived something enter the room, but the extreme duskiness prevented her distinguishing what it was." Slowly the form, which she could now see "appeared to be a human figure," approaches her bed. We are actually relieved to discover, at length, that it is merely a human ruffian, come to abduct Emily and forcibly marry her. Often AR draws her terrors from the familiar effects of nightmare, such as the scene where Ellena cannot run away from the seaside house where she expects to be murdered, but seems compelled to go back and forth on the beach, shadowed by the villain. For AR and her contemporaries, the combination of refined sensibility, sublime scenery, and terror was a natural one. On Emily's going to investigate the veiled object, AR comments: "a faint degree of terror . . . occupies and expands the mind, and elevates it to high expectation." In an essay published posthumously in the *New Monthly Magazine* (VII, 1826) AR writes: "Terror . . . expands the soul, and awakens the faculties to a high degree of life," while horror "contracts, freezes, and nearly annihilates them." Horror can never be "a source of the sublime, though . . . terror is a very high one." Since terror is enhanced by uncertainty and obscurity, AR sought her effects by generating clouds of sinister suggestion; she eschewed the supernatural events and grisly tortures of contemporary gothic novelists such as Matthew "Monk" Lewis (though he claimed inspiration from *Udolpho*). Her terrors are firmly controlled: as her eerie events are rationally explained, her heroines' feelings are restrained by decorous good sense, and her harrowing perils are brought to a poetically just ending.

As the preeminent writer of fiction that unites exotic thrills with irreproachable morals, AR enjoyed a fame unprecedented among novelists. *The Romance of the Forest* was generally praised, and *The Mysteries of Udolpho* received prominent favorable reviews in all the magazines. The *Monthly Review* praised its "correctness of sentiment and elegance of style . . . rich vein of invention, which supplies an endless variety of incidents to fill the imagination of the reader [its evocation of suspense and] the strongest sympathetic emotions, whether of pity or terror" (November 1794). The *European Magazine* found her descriptions prolix, but partly redeemed by the vigor of her imagination (June 1794). Some reviewers considered *The Italian,* now recognized as her most powerful work, less successful than *Udolpho;* although *MR* particularly praised the scenes at the lone house by the seaside (March 1797). Although Walter Scott poked gentle fun at AR's hairraising devices in Chap. 1 of *Waverley,* in his *Lives of the Novelists* he said she had never been equalled in fiction which appeals "to those powerful and general sources of interest, a latent sense of supernatural awe, and curiosity concerning whatever is hidden and mysterious." AR exerted her spell on most of the Romantics, most conspicuously on Byron (who acknowledged it in *Childe Harold's Pilgrimage,* IV, xviii). His impressive doomed heroes, such as Manfred and Lara, were inspired by hers, although she would never have condoned his sympathy with Satanic defiance.   K.R.

RADCLIFFE, Mary Ann (1745?–1810?), polemical writer and autobiographer, inherited considerable property on the death of her father, who had made his money in trade. Her place of birth and early places of residence are not known. When aged 15 she married Mr. Radcliffe, a Catholic, 20 years her senior, with no property of his own, in a secret ceremony in London, to the disapproval of her mother and guardians. Although raised a Catholic, MAR became a Protestant, and religious differences affected her relations with family and friends. MAR's life was filled with financial problems, and she saw herself as being "the shuttlecock of fortune." Her patrimony was slowly eaten away by the expenditures, of her husband, whom she describes as benevolent but of "a natural inactive turn," and eventually they separated for financial

reasons. To provide for her eight children, MAR gradually sold off her remaining property and sought employment, often having to live apart from her family. Her jobs included serving as a lady's companion, governess, and household manager; she sold patent medicines from her own shop, was proprietor of "The Ladies' cheap Shoe Ware-House" in Oxford St., London, and ran a pastry shop for three years in later life at a seaside resort. Housebound with illness from 1805 to 1810, and having unsuccessfully sought asylum in a hospital, she finally found refuge in Edinburgh with a female friend.

MAR meant to issue *The Female Advocate; or, An Attempt to Recover the Rights of Women from Male Usurpation* (1799) anonymously, but the publisher wanted to capitalize on the similarity to ANNE RADCLIFFE's name. The pamphlet addresses itself to MAR's own plight, that of the middle-class woman without male protection who cannot find work. Like PRISCILLA WAKEFIELD and others in the 1790s, MAR argues that employment opportunities for women should be enlarged, particularly in shops which feature female merchandise. MAR's overarching concern is with the circumstances that can lead women of good family and education into prostitution, and her language is suitably dramatic: "they pass their time in sorrow, till they meet the fatal alternative, either to be passive under the horrors of a prison, or compound for their preservation, by entering under the infernal roof of vice for protection." MAR, identified in a contemporary biographical dictionary as "one of the Wollstonecraft school," writes at times with the fervor of MARY WOLLSTONECRAFT, but her roots are principally in her own bitter experience rather than in late 18th-century thought. The epistolary *Memoirs of Mrs. Mary Ann Radcliffe* (1810), which includes a second edition of *The Female Advocate,* began as a private autobiographical account to a female friend, with repeated warnings about the dangers of precipitous marriage. The *Lady's Monthly Museum* praised MAR's "special pleadings" for her sex in *The Female Advocate:* "Her animadversions on men-milliners, and all that effeminate tribe who monopolize occupations that were better appropriated to the weaker sex, have . . . our entire approbation, and we hope may have a good effect on such as have sufficient influence in society." The reviewer suggests, however, that "unjust usurpations" may not be specific only to women: "Do not the other sex injure and oppress one another as well as her's? Perhaps she quarrels more with the lot of humanity in general, than the many ills one class of rational creatures inflict on another" (1799). Of the *Memoirs,* the *British Critic* (1812) commented: "The reader will find a narrative by no means ill written, of an unfortunate individual, whose life exhibits a useful moral, and lessons of important concern to the thoughtlessness of her own sex." A.B.S.

RADCLIFFE, Mary Anne (fl. 1790?–1809), novelist, was often confused, perhaps deliberately, with ANN RADCLIFFE. Attributed to MAR are *The Fate of Velina de Guidova* and *Radzivil,* both published by William Lane (1790). MAR wrote *Manfroné, or the One-Handed Monk* (1809) and issued *Radcliffe's New Novelist's Pocket Magazine* (1802), a chapbook compilation and condensation of gothic fiction. Her place of residence is identified in the latter as Wimbledon, Surrey. No other biographical information is available. *Manfroné* is derived substantially from the novels of Ann Radcliffe, with doses of the lurid anticlerical gothic of "Monk" Lewis. MAR's heroine of fortitude and good sense is subjected to kidnappings, attempted rapes, paternal tyranny, and isolation from her noble lover. The complex plot drips with clichés of the genre, such as dungeons, mysterious monks, and a severed hand. Sexual frustration and sexual fears are more explicit than in other gothic novels; the vengeful villain Manfroné tells the heroine that if she will not marry him, "I will gratify by force the longings of my bosom, and then, Rosalina, you may die." MAR combines gothic sensationalism with a moral tale. Her purpose is "by shewing the true image of vice, and the baneful effects of indulging vicious passions and inclinations, in their proper colours, disrobed of their deceitful garbs, [to] present a picture to youth, from whose deformity they may start with increasing horror!" MAR deftly imitates the Radcliffian novel in *Manfroné,* but does not approach the richness of Ann Radcliffe's characterizations and nature descriptions. About *The Fate of Velina de Guidova* a reviewer declared: "The incidents in this novel are common, the circumstances improbable, and the dénouement improperly hurried." (*Town & Country Mag.,* 1790), *Manfroné* was equally dismissed: "We meet with nothing new or striking. The style is unequal, and seems to have depended a good deal upon the last books which the authoress had been reading immediately previous to taking up her pen" (*Le Beau Monde,* 1809). A.B.S.

RAMSAY, Martha Laurens (1759–1811), American diarist and spiritual autobiographer, was the daughter of Henry and Eleanor Ball Laurens. Her father, who was a political leader in South Carolina, was from a French Huguenot family and her mother from English stock. Her mother died when MLR was eleven, and she and her sister were looked after by an aunt while her father took her brothers to Europe until 1774. During this time, she corresponded with her father and wrote of the approaching war. She had an active childhood and was very interested in mathematics. Religious from an early age, at 14 she composed a "Covenant with God." She made the "resolve to surrender and devote my youth, my strength, my soul, with all I have, and all I am to the service of that great and good God." In 1775 she went to England, destroying much of her devotional writings before she left. In England she feared the "gay," "worldly" and "profane," and was contemptuous of the "vain visits" of the ladies and the "talk of laces, dresses, ornaments, and finery." Life often appeared a "dreary wilderness" and she feared for her faith, although later she was happy to meet many pious people including the COUNTESS OF HUNTINGDON. As the American War of Independence grew fiercer she found it difficult in England, and her uncle took her and her sister to France until peace was restored. In 1780 her father was imprisoned in England. On his release she saw him in Paris after a separation of seven years; there she became the head of his diplomatic household. She remained pious and was much concerned with the religious education of the poor. After peace was established MLR, her aunt and sister returned to Charleston, where in 1787 she married the revolutionary patriot David Ramsay and had eleven children, eight of whom survived her. In her married life she read pious and educational works and was much impressed with the theories of John Locke; she tried to bring up her children according to modern and pious principles. She also studied the classics and read books on science and medicine. Through a large portion of her life MLR kept a diary, recording her religious fears and her sorrow at the death of her three children. She worried over her sinfulness and her failing belief, and she laid great stress on grace and salvation through Christ. To strengthen herself, she wrote of faith and read much in hymns and religious poetry. To her children she sent instructive letters, and those to her son at college show both maternal tenderness and an understanding of politics. To her son in Princeton, she wrote, "I will do all in my power for my dear children, and must then leave the event to God and their own exertions." One of the last books she read was a life of ELIZABETH CARTER, whom she expected to meet in heaven. After MLR's death following a long illness, some of her writings were published by David Ramsay as *Memoirs of the Life of Martha Laurens Ramsay* (1811).   J.T.

REEVE, Clara (1729–1807), novelist and critic, was born in Ipswich. Her father, William Reeve, was rector of Freston and of Kerton, Suffolk, and perpetual curate of St. Nicholas, Ipswich; her mother, Hannah, was a daughter of William Smithies, goldsmith and jeweler to George I. CR was the eldest daughter of a large family. One brother, Samuel, became a vice-admiral, and another, Thomas, became master of Bungay grammar school. CR's father, described by her as an "Old Whig," educated her and made her read at an early age parliamentary debates, Rapin's *History of England,* Greek and Roman histories, and Plutarch's *Lives.* These studies, she later reported, formed her principles. She learned Latin and later translated Barclay's *Argenis,* published as *The Phoenix* (1772). After her father's death in 1755 CR, her mother, and two sisters moved to Colchester. Little is known about CR's adult life. Her first publication, *Original Poems on Several Occasions* (1796) reveals her early literary ambitions. She explains that she had been afraid of the prejudice against female writers, until the success of a number of women had encouraged her. In one poem, written in 1756, CR argues that women are generally inferior to men as writers, but she nevertheless praises KATHERINE PHILIPS, ELIZABETH CARTER, and CHARLOTTE LENNOX. She also complains that her own literary talents have brought her unhappiness through the scorn or envy of others. It is not clear how far CR depended on writing for income. Her most famous work, the gothic novel *The Old English Baron,* did not bring her much money. When first published as *The Champion of Virtue* (1777), it was printed for the author, and later she

sold the copyright for £10. She abandoned a translation of the *Letters of Aza,* commissioned by the *Lady's Magazine,* on learning that she would not be paid for the work. CR's political views are evident in *The Old English Baron*'s praise of an older, more hierarchical society, and even more so in her other gothic novel, *Memoirs of Sir Roger de Clarendon* (1793), where the belief in subordination, characteristic of the 14th century, is favorably contrasted to the modern ideas that produced the French Revolution. Her interest in politics extended to the writing of a pamphlet in 1792, arguing against the "anti-saccharites" who were refusing to buy West Indian sugar because its purchase supported the slave trade.

The majority of CR's fictions are set in her own time. *The Exiles* (1788) is a tale of bigamy and tragedy strongly influenced by the French writers Prévost and D'Arnaud. *The Two Mentors* (1783), *The School for Widows* (1791), *Plans of Education* (1792), and *Destination* (1799), have domestic settings and show CR's interest in education. CR wrote one work of criticism, *The Progress of Romance,* which is in the form of a discussion among three characters. CR's *Castle Connor, an Irish Story* was lost on the Ipswich-London coach in 1787 and never recovered. *Edwy and Edilda* (1783), a gothic tale in verse, was attributed to her, but is in fact by Thomas S. Whalley. *Fatherless Fanny* (1819) was also misattributed to CR, although it is possible that an unknown manuscript of hers was plagiarized for parts of the composition. Although *The Old English Baron,* which went through ten editions before 1800 and was translated into French and German, made CR a famous writer, she had few literary acquaintances. ANNA SEWARD, who considered that CR's *The Progress of Romance* (1785) praised Samuel Richardson's *Pamela* too highly at the expense of his later works, corresponded with CR about this in the *Gentleman's Magazine.* Martha Bridgen, one of Richardson's daughters, revised and corrected *The Old English Baron* for the second edition. CR died at Ipswich and was buried there, at her own request, near her old friend the Rev. Mr. Derby, in St. Stephen's churchyard.

CR is principally remembered for *The Old English Baron,* one of the first gothic novels, which draws on Horace Walpole's *Castle of Otranto* (1765). In the preface to the second edition she writes that, like Walpole, she intends to unite the ancient romance and modern novel. She claims that *Otranto*'s excessive use of supernatural horrors arouses laughter rather than terror, and expresses the belief that a gothic tale should keep within the bounds of possibility. Her tale concerns Edmund, who is brought up as a peasant. His father was murdered by a usurping tyrant, and his mother fled from the murderer and died soon after Edmund's birth. The truth is revealed through various incidents, few of them deserving the title supernatural. Edmund stays in a reputedly haunted chamber, where his parents appear to him in a dream and predict that he will gain his rightful inheritance. Mysterious groans, falling armor, and the ghost of Edmund's father provide supernatural elements, but do not create an atmosphere of terror, because it is soon evident that any mysterious forces at work are on the hero's side. As Edmund discovers his true identity less than half-way through the book, the element of suspense is greatly reduced. Walpole complained that the novel was "so probable that any trial for murder at the Old Bailey would make a more interesting story." CR's interest in realistic matters such as the exact details of the transfer of property to the hero renders the past accessible, not remote or mysterious. Her emphasis is on the moral, rather than mystery or excitement. The story describes the triumph of law, virtue, reason and Christianity over usurpation, unkindness, and superstition. Edmund's behavior in the haunted room demonstrates that in CR's world the supernatural cannot terrify the true Christian: "he kneeled down and prayed earnestly, resigning himself wholly to the will of Heaven; while he was yet speaking, his courage returned, and he resumed his usual confidence; again he approached the door from whence the noise proceeded." With this tale CR establishes a particular type of gothic novel, which, despite its historical setting and hints of the supernatural, deals with 18th-century concerns and upholds 18th-century morality. *Memoirs of Sir Roger de Clarendon* follows in this tradition. CR's praise of medieval society for lacking cards, dice, swearing, and drunkenness is not based on historical evidence, but on her desire to criticize the present. Her 18th-century, middle-class standard of judgment is evident when she writes that Edward, the Black Prince, "possessed all the social and domestic virtues." These same virtues are recommended in the novels with a contemporary setting. In *The Two Mentors,* a virtuous tutor and an unprincipled guardian both try to influence a young man. Women's moral influence, one of CR's favorite themes, is seen when he preserves his virtue by resisting the temptations set by a wicked lady and falling in love with a modest young virgin. CR's standards of female decorum are strict, and she recommends a quiet life, away from the influence of fashionable London, as the best way to preserve female virtue. Her statement in *The Two Mentors* that "an early attachment to a virtuous and amiable woman cultivates and ripens every noble quality; an attachment to a bad woman leads to a life of folly, vice and misery" illustrates her belief in female influence and her simplistic moral division of women. Statements in this balanced, rather heavy style are replaced in parts of *The Exiles* by more emotional, exclamatory utterances, such as "Oh, how one false step leads to another!—the story of Cronstadt would be a warning to all that believe—Polygamy is capable of increasing a man's pleasures or happiness!" Despite the differences in style these two novels share the didactic purpose of recommending marriage with a good woman as a man's best chance for a virtuous life. Mrs. Strictland and Mrs. Darnford, good wives to bad husbands, establish female virtue as the central theme of *The School for Widows.* In her widowhood Mrs. Darnford founds a school for girls and rescues a third widow from mental breakdown. The novel explicitly endorses female subordination, but its most powerful images are of women united for mutual protection against men and immorality. Widowhood brings the freedom to enjoy female friendship, which is celebrated in this scene described by Mrs. Strictland to Mrs. Darnford: "Suppose me sitting at a table, with Mrs. Bailey on one side, and Mrs. Martin on the other—Mary Martin opposite—listening to the praises of Mrs. Darnford from all of them, and gaining little circumstances of her life and character that delight my very soul." This group of friends joined together to praise a virtuous woman is Richardsonian, and the scene could almost be taken from *Sir Charles Grandison.* CR admired Richardson, as her *Progress of Romance* shows. This critical work is a defense of fiction undertaken by Euphrasia in opposition to Hortensius, who believes that fiction has an immoral influence. Euphrasia claims that the best fiction upholds morality. She distinguishes romances from novels. She criticizes 17th-century romances for falsifying history, but adds in their favor that they foster chivalry toward women. Euphrasia assesses novels on moral grounds. She disapproves of APHRA BEHN, DELA-RIVIÈRE MANLEY, and the early novels of ELIZA HAYWOOD. Marie-Jeanne Riccoboni, SARAH FIELDING, Charlotte Lennox, FRANCES SHERIDAN, FRANCES BROOKE, SARAH SCOTT, and ELIZABETH GRIFFITH are all praised. Henry Fielding is considered a highly talented but not always moral writer. Smollett's work is found to have a generally moral tendency despite improper scenes, and Rousseau appeals to the heart despite being a dangerous and improper writer. Circulating libraries are condemned for encouraging indiscriminate reading, and a list of fiction suitable for young people is provided. In *Plans of Education* CR expounds her educational ideas within a framework of letters written by the characters of *The School for Widows;* the theme of *Destination* is the correct mode of education. As in all CR's novels, the didactic intention is paramount.

In her own time CR was praised chiefly for *The Old English Baron. Critical Review* (1778) called it "no common novel" and compared it to *Otranto. Monthly Review* called it an imitation of ancient romance and found it agreeable and capable of rousing the reader's feelings, although it expressed some reservations about the introduction of ghosts. CR's later novels, although praised for their morality, were considered to show a decline in her talents. The *British Critic* compared the *Memoirs of Sir Roger de Clarendon* unfavorably to *The Old English Baron.* Introducing CR in *Ballantyne's Novelists Library* (1823), Walter Scott wrote that she lacked a rich imagination, that parts of *The Old English Baron* are "tame and tedious, not to say mean and tiresome," but that all her novels show "excellent good sense, pure morality, and a competent command of those qualities which constitute a good romance." J.S.

RIDDELL, Maria [Banks] (1772–1808), poet, editor, and travel writer, was the daughter of William Woodley, Commander and Governor of St. Kitts and the Leeward Islands. While in the West Indies in 1791 she met and married Walter Riddell of Glenriddell, the younger brother of Robert Burns's patron, Captain Robert Riddell. The same year Walter Riddell purchased the estate Goldielea near Dumfries and renamed it Woodley Park for MR, who soon bore him two children, Alexander and Anna Maria. Owing to what Rev. Charles Rogers, one of Burns's biographers, called MR's "strong literary aptitude," Woodley Park was the scene of many gatherings at which the Riddells encouraged the fashionable talent of the day, among whom was Burns, who became an ardent admirer of both MR's beauty and her literary talent. He and MR were close friends and critics of each other's work from about 1792 until early 1794. In that year, at a celebration for Walter Riddell's homecoming from the West Indies, Burns became intoxicated and made a rude overture to MR. He begged her forgiveness the next morning, but she deeply resented his behavior and the Riddells and Burns quarreled so intensely that Burns never again saw Robert Riddell, his patron, who died in 1794. Burns was reconciled with MR and her husband in 1795. He wrote several love songs for MR, for example "The Last Time I Came O'er the Muir" (1793), which was censured for its blatantly amorous language. During his quarrel with the Riddells, he composed several epigrams on both of them. When Burns died in 1796, MR published an article about him in the *Dumfries Journal,* which flattered both Burns's character and her own writing. Walter Riddell died at the end of the century after losing Woodley Park and another property; MR moved to England with her two children. Alexander died at their apartments at Hampton Court in 1804. MR married Phillips Lloyd Fletcher, a Welsh landowner, in 1807 and died the following year. She is buried in the Fletcher family vault at Chester.

MR started her career at 19 when Burns gave her an introductory letter to his printer, William Smellie, for the publication of the account of her travels, *Voyage to the Madeira and Leeward and Carribean Isles, with Sketches of the Natural History of these Islands* (Edinburgh, 1792). Smellie compared her book favorably to the "flippant romances" of the day and pronounced it a work of "science, minute observation, accurate description, and excellent composition." Contemporary reviewers found MR's book lacking in novelty of subject matter, but unique in its descriptive approach. Even though she was not considered proficient in natural history, her observations were deemed scientific. Indeed, MR seems to have studied wildlife of the islands with an exacting eye: "The wood-flare is one of the most venomous reptiles found in these islands. A gummy fluid exudes from all his pores which blithers and ulcerates the skin of those who touch it. And under each claw is a small bag filled with a thick blue-coloured matter, which is said to be the chief ingredient used in the composition of the famous Malay poison, well known in the East Indies." MR was contrasted to other women who traveled abroad as one who enlightened herself with knowledge of practical things. She edited *The Metrical Miscellany, consisting chiefly of poems hitherto unpublished* (1802; 2nd ed. 1803) in which she published 18 of her own poems and the poems of some of her fashionable literary and political contemporaries. Among the contributors were the dramatist and statesman R. B. Sheridan, the poet and wit William Spencer, and GEORGIANA, DUCHESS OF DEVONSHIRE. Burns called MR "a votary of the Muses" and described her verse as elegant and "always correct."   N.E.S.

ROBERTS, Eliza (fl. 1780–88), poet and translator, wrote two poems which appeared in the *Lady's Poetical Magazine* (1781–82): "Effusions of Melancholy" (vol. I) and "On a Supposed Slight From a Friend" (vol. II). In 1788 she published translations of short excerpts from Rousseau's works, *The Beauties of Rousseau. Selected by a Lady* (2 vols.): presented without editorial comment, the selections cover a wide range of subjects from "Arts and Sciences" to "Wealth and the Wealthy." In the preface the author reveals her name but gives no other personal information. *The Beauties of Rousseau* received a good review: "The Lady to whom we are obliged for this agreeable and moral selection, had no occasion, in this instance, to plead her sex, in order to obtain the indulgence of the public. Her merit entitles her to their approbation and encouragement. She has shewn much judgment in the selection, and faithfulness in the translation of the various passages which compose these volumes" (*Monthly Review* 80, 1789).   J.F.

ROBERTS, R. (1730?–1788), translator, poet, and sermon writer, was a daughter of William Roberts of Bristol, whose family earlier possessed the manor of Abergavenny, Mon. A kinsman, William Hayward Roberts, put up a marble tablet in Abergavenny church describing the family genealogy for 300 years; RR's brother William appended some Latin hexameters. RR had at least one sister and two brothers: William, who published *Thoughts upon Creation* (1782) and *Poetical Attempts* (1784), and Richard, headmaster of St. Paul's from 1769 to 1814. At the time of her earliest known publication (1763), RR was said to be living in Gloucester. Little is known of her own life. She was of the same religious and poetic turn of mind as her brothers, and occupied her leisure in writing. She may well have known HANNAH MORE, with whom the two daughters of her brother William, Mary and Margaret, had a close friendship.

RR's earliest noted publication was an anonymous translation of four tales from Marmontel, *Select Moral Tales* (1763). In 1770 she published *Sermons Written by a Lady,* undertaken when a clergyman "between jest and earnest" promised he would preach any sermon she wrote. The *Monthly Review* judged that, while a lady might not harangue an audience from the pulpit, she might "without the least imputation or indelicacy exhibit exhortations and rules of morality," so why not in sermons? *Critical Review* commended the benevolence of her defense of fallen women. The book was republished in Philadelphia in 1777 as *Seven Rational Sermons.* In 1771 RR published an abridged translation of Millot's *Elements of the History of France,* intended for use by school-girls. *MR* did not find the translation worthy of its purpose, but *CR* thought it most proper. In 1774 appeared RR's translation of Madame de Graffigny's *Peruvian Letters,* with an additional volume extending the story; RR wished the Indian princess heroine to be converted to Christianity and the virtuous hero to be rewarded. *MR* judged the additions commendable and thought there would probably never be a superior translation of the work. In 1779 RR published, in competent blank verse, an unproduced tragedy, *Malcolm.* RR's last known work was *Albert, Edward, and Laura, and the Hermit of Priestland, Three Legendary Tales* (1783), for which Hannah More's "Sir Eldred of the Bower" was almost certainly the model. These were ballad-style medieval tales, composed, *MR* complained, of the usual ingredients—love and murder. *CR* found in them "the cold unpoetical virtue" of mediocrity. Two of these tales were inspired by romantic settings encountered on visits, one to The Friary in East Barnet, the other to Hampshire.   B.R.

ROBERTSON, Hannah (1724–1800?), autobiographical and instructional writer, was the daughter of a Mr. Swan, whom she alleged in her autobiography to have been born in Windsor Castle, the son of Charles II. Her father, she stated, was named Swan by a nurse and raised by a Scottish family. HR was one of the six children of his second marriage. Soon after HR's birth her father died and her mother established a linen manufactory at Ormeton, but remarried and moved to Glasgow when HR was six. In 1736 the family moved to Perth. HR's first fiancé, a Captain B- - -, died fighting at Ghent. Her second fiancé, a Captain Johnstone, was reportedly lost in a shipwreck. In compliance with her family's wishes, she was about to marry the affluent Mr. Robertson when Johnstone reappeared. HR determined to sacrifice herself to Mr. Robertson, but the marriage was not a happy one. Her eldest son died; her husband, neglecting his business to attend to her in her resulting distracted state of mind, went bankrupt in 1756 and was jailed for debt. HR, however, opened a successful tavern in Aberdeen and paid off her husband's debts. In 1771 her husband froze to death in a storm. HR lived in Edinburgh, instructing in "the various arts I understood," taught filigree in boarding schools in York, moved to London in 1782, gave lessons in Northampton, and then settled in Birmingham. Her elder daughter, Anna, had lived with a moneyed wastrel, eloped with a lover rather than emigrate to America, remarried an attorney, and died of cancer. Minia, her younger daughter, had married a midshipman, opened a successful dress shop to support him, and died. Her younger son, a successful artist, had died; and her elder son had left her and gone off to France. At the time of the publication of her autobiography (1791), HR was sick and poor, and living in Birmingham with two dependent grandchildren. It is not known what happened to her thereafter.

HR's first printed work was *The young ladies school of arts; containing a great variety of practical receipts, in cookery, pastry, puddings, marketing, &c. &c.* (Edinburgh, 1766), apparently published during her teaching days there. A second enlarged edition appeared the next year. The recipes were plain and clear: "To make Pork sauseages Take two or three pounds of the thick of a leg of pork, the same quantity of fat as lean; mince it well together, and season it with pepper, nutmeg, and salt; you may put sweet herbs in, if you like it,

and a few crumbs of bread; take the smallest hogs guts, and clean them well; to fill them, smooth them with your hand; make them what length you think fit, to fry them. N.B. Make beef or mutton the same way." HR's second work, *The young ladies school of arts. Containing a great variety of practical receipts, in gum-flowers, filigree, japanning, shell-work, gilding . . . &c.* gave directions for the various kinds of fancy work she taught. A second edition was issued with her first book in Edinburgh in 1767. A fourth edition was published at York in 1777, apparently while she taught filigree in schools there. Her last work was her autobiography, the title page of which read *The Life of Mrs. Robertson, (A Tale of Truth as well as of Sorrow) Who, Though A Grand-Daughter of Charles II has been reduced By a Variety of very Uncommon Events, From splendid Affluence to the greatest Poverty. And, after having buried nine children is obliged, At the age of Sixty-Seven To earn a scanty Maintenance for herself and two Orphan Grand-Children By teaching Embroidery, Filigree, and the Art of making Artificial Flowers.* The volume, signed and dated "Hannah Robertson. Birmingham, Oct. 15th, 1791," was published in Derby by J. Drewry and reprinted the following year in Edinburgh. The volume begins, "I am grand daughter of Charles II. My father was born in Windsor castle, towards the close of the reign of that prince, his mother being a daughter of the D- - - family, a name too much distinguished to appear in the same narrative with mine," and ends with HR's declaration that she will next present her case (presumably with a copy of her book) "to the court, to the Dukes of Richmond, and of Grafton; who are each, like me, descended from a King; but not like me, the miserable inheritor of his misfortunes!"   J.P.G.

ROBINSON, Mary [Darby] ("Perdita") (1758–1800), poet, novelist, and actress, was born in Bristol to a mother of genteel background and a father who was a prosperous merchant with a spirit for adventure. Her early education was in a school run by HANNAH MORE and her sisters. Family circumstances changed with marital and financial turmoil; for a short while MR's mother ran a school herself, in which MR was an instructor. MR's beauty and talents led to the suggestion that she choose the theater as a profession; Garrick was ready to take her on as a pupil. In 1774, aged 16, she married Thomas Robinson and entered his world of high living and debt. In debtors' prison with him, she looked after her baby daughter Maria and wrote verses. MR went on the boards at Drury Lane Theatre with her husband's encouragement in 1776, and during the next four seasons played 26 parts, including nine Shakespearian roles. Her second daughter, Sophia, was born during her time of great popularity as an actress; the baby died when six weeks old. In 1778 the Prince of Wales, then 17, saw her as Perdita, and a liaison gradually developed that was widely recorded and satirized and that many felt was arranged for her financial advantage. MR was the Prince's mistress for one year, living luxuriously in a house he bought her. When he abruptly ended the affair, she insisted on payment from the bond of £20,000 he promised her when he came of age; she was accused of blackmailing the Prince with his letters if he failed to pay. In 1781 she was granted a lifetime annuity of £500. Debt plagued her from then on. By 1783 she had entered into a relationship, which lasted ten years, with Col. Banastre Tarleton, a cavalry hero of the American campaigns. She went with him to France and was honored as "la belle Anglaise." A chill during the return journey led to a fever and paralysis of her legs (perhaps rheumatic), from which she never recovered. The last 17 years of her life she sought health cures in England and on the Continent. Cut off from the beau monde, supporting her daughter and widowed mother, MR turned to writing as consolation and as essential supplement to her annuity and to funds from Tarleton. In the 1790s her work was admired and she was called the "English Sappho." For her liberal opinions Richard Polwhele listed her among his "unsex'd females." She enjoyed the friendship of William Godwin and Coleridge in her later years, and the latter wrote several poems in her honor. MR died in a cottage in Windsor Park and was buried in Old Windsor Graveyard. When the *Lady's Monthly Museum* (1801) ran an adulatory biographical sketch of MR, one reader protested, "we surely want not public panegyrics upon characters which have been lost to decency and shame," and another reader saw MR's life as being "a caution to young women against being dazzled with false splendours."

MR's literary work has seldom been separated from her life. Her notoriety affected the sale and reception of her poetry, novels, and plays, and her writing has many autobiographical touches. MR's earliest publications were *Poems* (1775) and *Captivity, A Poem; and Celadon and Lydia, A Tale* (1777). In 1790 under the pseudonym "Laura Maria" she published "Ainsi va le Monde," a poem inscribed to Robert Merry. From 1790 on she contributed verse to newspapers under the names "Laura," "Laura Maria," "Oberon," and "Tabitha Bramble." She is said to be the author of the pamphlet *Impartial Reflections on the Present Situation of the Queen of France; by a Friend to Humanity* (1791). Verse collections from this time are *The Beauties of Mrs. Robinson. Selected and Arranged from her Poetical Works* (1791), the two-volume *Poems* (1791–93), and *Sight, The Cavern of Woe, and Solitude* (1793). MR wrote odes, sonnets, elegies, ballads, and light satiric verse. Her most substantial poetry reflects on such subjects as health, vanity, melancholy, and ingratitude. MR's first novel, *Vancenza; or, the Dangers of Credulity* (1792), sold out on its day of publication and was immediately reprinted. This moral tale in the guise of a historical romance shows "the dangers and deceptions of a world, where virtue struggles midst a maze of snares, wove by the cunning hand of dark duplicity." MR portrays dissolute women of the world and a virtuous but doomed heroine who wishes her education had included the useful rather than the elegant, to "enable her to enjoy the tranquil hour of Blessed Independence!" Other novels followed rapidly: *The Widow, or a Picture of Modern Times* (1794), and *Angelina, Hubert de Sevrac* and *The Wanderings of the Imagination* (1796). MR wrote one farce, "Nobody," acted in 1794, and one five-act tragedy, *The Sicilian Lover,* published 1796 but not performed. A prominent theme in MR's writing is the struggle between reason and passion. *Sappho and Phaon* (1796) is a series of 43 sonnets on phases of love; it ends by welcoming "returning reason's placid beam." In *Walsingham, or the Pupil of Nature* (1797) the world-weary protagonist sees himself as the victim of a convoluted family history and also of his own erratic emotions. This novel uses sentimental language to express Enlightenment ideas about injustice, oppression, and the importance of education; for example, "The fibres of my heart quivered with that emotion which never failed to wring them when I beheld a weaker object in the power of a stronger. To aid the wretch who was sinking beneath the stroke of inhumanity was natural." MR also presents deft social comment on gaming aristocrats, physicians, and literary critics. Later novels were *The False Friend* and *The Natural Daughter* (both 1799). Other poetry was *Lyrical Tales* (1800) and, under the pseudonym "Laura Maria," *The Mistletoe, A Christmas Tale in Verse* (1800). *Effusions of Love* (n.d.) purports to be her correspondence with the Prince of Wales. Attributed to MR are a pamphlet *Thoughts on the Conditions of Women* (n.d.) and *Letter to the Women of England on the Injustice of Mental Subordination* (1799). Her daughter Maria E. Robinson completed *Memoirs of the Late Mrs. Robinson Written by Herself* (1801) and gathered her mother's poetry together in three volumes as *The Poetical Works of the Late Mrs. Mary Robinson* (1806). Reviewing *Vancenza, Gentleman's Magazine* (June 1793) wrote "amongst the abundance of trash which, under the appelation of Novel, is poured upon the publick, we eagerly seize any opportunity which may offer of discriminating from the heterogeneous mass good writing or moral sentiment. Mrs. Robinson's work is more remarkable for the latter than the former. The sentiment is unexceptionably good; of her style we cannot speak as we could wish." Of MR's *Poems* (1791) the *Analytical Review* wrote: "If a great variety of refined sentiments, sometimes of the tender but more commonly of the plaintive kind, adorned with rich and beautiful imagery, and expressed in sweetly harmonious verse, can entitle the Poetical Productions of a Female Pen to public praise, Mrs. Robinson's Poems will obtain no inconsiderable share of applause." The *English Review* (1792) commented about the same collection: "The poems now before us are the elegant effusions of a mind which seems to feel too much for its own peace."   A.B.S.

ROCHE, Regina Maria [Dalton] (1764?–1845), novelist, was born in Co. Waterford. She married Mr. Roche in 1794. Few circumstances of her life are known. She received public celebrity and royal notice for her writing in the late 1790s. Then came changes in fortune and poor health, and she eventually found consolation in religion. She lived in retirement in Waterford for many years.

Many of RMR's books were published by Minerva Press and reflected prevailing tastes in popular novels, combining the plots, characters, and moral tone of Richardson and Mackenzie with settings and episodes in the gothic mode, especially as interpreted by ANN RADCLIFFE. As Regina Maria Dalton RMR wrote *The Vicar of Lansdowne* (1789) and *The Maid of the Hamlet* (1793). Her best-known work was *The Children of the Abbey* (1796; 11th ed. 1832), which approached the popularity of *The Mysteries of Udolpho. Clermont* (1798), listed among Jane Austen's Northanger "horrid" novels, features gothic machinery of terror. *The Nocturnal Visit* (1800) subordinates gothic elements to a romance of sensibility. RMR's heroines are young and virtuous, raised in retirement, and educated to have "resources against despair." They find themselves without male protection and suffer physical, mental, and moral vicissitudes through libertines and perfidious aristocratic women who seek to rob them of "a pure and spotless fame." Love, benevolence, and fortitude triumph over selfishness, vanity, and an untutored imagination. Settings are variously picturesque, melancholy, and sepulchral. The style is often histrionic: "The horrors of her situation all at once assailed her mind, . . . she leaned her throbbing head upon her hand, and a deep groan burst from her agonizing heart" *(The Children of the Abbey)*. Later works are *The Discarded Son* (1806), *Alvondown Vicarage* (1807), *The House of Osma and Almerida* (1810), *The Monastery of St. Colombe* (1812), and *Trecothic Bower* (1813). RMR's one collection of short stories is *London Tales* (1814); *Anna, or Edinburgh* was published that same year. Subsequent novels are *The Munster Cottage Boy* (1819), *Bridal of Dunnamora, and Lost and Won* (1823), *The Castle Chapel* (1825), *Contrast* (1828), *The Nun's Picture* (1834), and *The Tradition of the Castle* (1824). Of *The Maid of the Hamlet Critical Review* (Apr. 1794) said, "there is nothing in the story . . . which will contaminate the mind," and the *British Critic* (Jan. 1798) was able to "safely recommend" *The Children of the Abbey* to its female readers: the "character of Adela is very well drawn, but somewhat romantic; yet by many readers, this will perhaps be thought the very essence of its merit, and the best part of our commendation." On later novels *CR* was harsh; regarding *Anna, or Edinburgh:* "Mrs. Roche is a veteran in the novel service, but does not exactly, by her writings, confirm the proverb—'that practice makes perfect.' Romantic plot—marvellous incident—platonic love—soaring language—lofty imagery—with all its *sublime* accompaniments! The tale is not, however, uninteresting; particularly, to those who delight to sigh over passionate love scenes, and sentimental distress" (1815). A.B.S.

ROGERS, Susanna (1711?-?), American poet, lived in Boxford, Mass. She was engaged to Jonathan Frye, chaplain to Captain Lovewell's military unit, but his family seems to have opposed marriage because of her "want of property and education." In 1725 when SR was about 14, Frye was killed in an encounter with Indians, and SR wrote her "childish lines": "The Mournful Elegy of Mrs. Jona[than] Frye." It was mentioned by Samuel Knapp in 1829 in his lectures on American Literature, and printed in 1861. The poem is a crudely rhyming account of the pious Jonathan and his end: "He served the Lord whilst he was young, / And ripe for Heaven was Jonathan." With some gusto, it describes how he was wounded and then left "in the wood / Some scores of miles from any food; / Wounded and famishing all alone, / None to relive or hear his moan." The poem ends by advising the bereaved father to "kiss the rod" and "Remember this the hand of God." J.T.

ROLT, Elizabeth (fl. 1768), poet, of Chesham, Bucks., was the author of a single volume, *Miscellaneous Poems* (1768), with the imprint "Printed for the Author, and sold by H. Turpin, Bookseller and Stationer, at the Golden Key, in St. John's St., West Smithfield, and J. Catling, Bookseller, at Chesham, Bucks." *Monthly Review* (July 1778) commented: "We are very sorry, that, notwithstanding our warm prepossession in favour of every production of a lady's pen, we cannot possibly say any thing in praise of the poetical performances of Mrs. Elizabeth Rolt." The volume has sometimes been confused by cataloguers with the three-volume *Miscellaneous Poems* anonymously published (also in 1768) by PHILLIPINA BURTON, because the two works have the same title and publishing date. Burton's was reviewed by *MR* in February 1768, ER's in July. B.R.

ROWE, Elizabeth (1674–1737), poet and religious writer, was born in Ilchester, Somerset, the eldest of the three daughters of Walter and Elizabeth Portnell Singer. From her father, a Dissenting Presbyterian

preacher and later a prosperous clothier of Frome, she received intellectual encouragement and pious example that formed her character. Little is known of her childhood and youth, but she appears to have rejected boarding school after brief attendance and gained a more academic education from members of the noble family of Henry Thynne at Longleat, Somerset, who were her intimate friends and patrons throughout her life, and from the Anglican Bishop Thomas Ken, who had retired at Longleat. Her attainments included drawing, French, Italian, Latin, and appreciation of music. She was well-read in poetry and works of devotion and philosophy; despite her belief that plays and imaginative fiction weakened the character, she read widely in drama and romance, preferring didactic and sentimental works. She was especially influenced by Shaftesbury's moral and ethical views and his attitudes on solitude and retirement. Among her friends were the COUNTESS OF WINCHILSEA, the fifth Earl of Orrery, Matthew Prior, and Isaac Watts, the last two of whom showed both literary and romantic interest in her. Especially valuable to her was a close friendship with Frances Thynne, later COUNTESS OF HERTFORD, with whom she shared enthusiasm for religion and good works, interest in poetry, and a love for nature and pastoral solitude. Though not a "regular beauty," ER possessed, as well as her independent spirit, a charm and benevolence that won her many admirers. In 1710 she married Thomas Rowe, a vigorous, pious, intense scholar of history, 13 years her junior, and moved with him to London. She was deeply affected by his death of consumption in 1715, after which she returned to Frome. There she lived the last third of her life in reflection and seclusion, corresponding with her friends and performing acts of charity.

Between 1691 and 1697 ER's poems appeared regularly in a succession of journals published by the Athenian Society as the works of "Philomela" or "the Pindarick Lady." She did not identify herself to the editor, John Dunton, until 1695, and was not publicly identified until 1705. These early poems were largely pastoral lyrics in an exuberant, personal voice that project Platonic conceptions of friendship and romantic love but also deal with death and the fate of the soul in the hereafter, the themes most commonly associated with her later work. Two issues of *The Athenian Mercury* were dedicated exclusively to her verse (one in 1694 and one in 1695), and her contributions were collected in *Poems on Several Occasions, by Philomela* in 1696. Dunton reprinted her poems in several anthologies, but by 1718, having come to feel that these early verses, with their erotic overtones, misrepresented her outlook, ER asked him to cease even referring to her in his works. Part Five of Tonson's *Poetical Miscellanies* (1704) contains work of hers from her early period, and Matthew Prior's *Poems on Several Occasions* (1709) includes both a poem by her and one by Prior about her. Meanwhile, ER began writing poetical paraphrases of the Scriptures, of which *The History of Joseph* was published in 1736. Also, probably under the influence of Bishop Ken, she developed mystical proclivities that led her to translate "Thoughts on Death" from the moral essays of the Port-Royal authors and to write the work for which she became best known, *Friendship in Death, or Letters from the Dead to the Living* (1728). This series of imaginary prose epistles and its companion work, *Letters Moral and Entertaining* (Pt. I, 1728; Pt. II, 1731; Pt. III, 1732), were highly regarded by Samuel Richardson and Dr. Johnson, was very popular during the 18th century, and passed through many editions during the next century in both England and America. Written in the personae of various persons who had died and addressed to imaginary friends still living, the letters proffer hope of the soul's salvation, recommend friendship, love, and devotion to God as the highest moral virtues, and extol the value of rural solitude in promoting the moral life. ER uses themes and techniques of early 18th-century prose fiction in *Friendship;* in *Devout Exercises of the Heart* (1738), the influence of 17th-century mystical literature predominates. These meditations in prose and verse were sent at her death to her friend Isaac Watts, the hymn writer, with her request that he edit and publish them, making of them, in effect, another set of letters from the dead to the living. The personal, fervid, rapturous style of these meditations embarrassed Watts, who apologized in his preface for their romantic, zealous, mystical character, and also Lady Hertford, who declined to be mentioned by name in Watts's dedication of the book to her. These meditations, like ER's other works, imply a relation between divine and human love and show a distaste for the earthly world and a longing for death: "Come, Lord Jesus, come quickly; oh come, lest my Expectations faint, lest I grow weary, and murmur at thy long Delay. I am tired with these Vanities, and the World grows every Day more un-entertaining and insipid." *Devout Exercises* had a large following, however, and was praised by Dr. Johnson in the *Literary Magazine* (1756). Theophilus Rowe published a two-volume collection of her works, *Miscellaneous Works in Prose and Verse,* which contained a laudatory biography begun by her friend Henry Grove and completed by Rowe. This collection had reappeared at least four times by 1772 and was expanded later to four volumes (1796; reprinted 1820). ER's writings and her life were well known and respected in England and abroad during the century after her death, and received favorable mention from Samuel Richardson, Colley Cibber, James Thomson, and ANNA LAETITIA BARBAULD, among others. Her works were examples of piety and propriety that, in an increasingly urban, secular, scientific age, offered Christian believers hope of the soul's immortality.   D.W.M.

ROWE, Hannah (fl. 1785), poet, wrote *A Pindaric Poem. Consisting of Versified Selections from the Revelation of St. John* (1789) and, apparently, a similar versification of some of the Psalms. The ode reflects the contemporary vogue for imitation. It is extremely bad, travestying all the intricate symbolism of Revelation. The following is a version of Chapter 17: "Me then he took (swam my rapt giddy head) / And swift into the wilderness, on whistling wings I sped; / Where, falling roses round her strew'd, / I a scarlet harlot view'd. / There flaunting on a rampant beast / She sat in pomp and splendour of the east; / In a spangled luring vest / Shone the earth's audacious pest." Elsewhere the ode appears as a very gauche transliteration of biblical idiom into 18th-century poetic diction.   R.J.

ROWLANDSON, Mary (1635?–1678?), American autobiographer, was a new England settler whose life is known to us only through her famous *Narrative;* she was probably born in England. The wife of Rev. Joseph Rowlandson, she lived in the village of Lancaster at the time of the confrontation with the Indians known as King Philip's War. She and her three children were captured, as her narrative describes, and forced to wander nearly 12 weeks through the forests of Massachusetts and New Hampshire. She describes how her six-year-old son died in her arms, how she bartered her skills for food—knitting stockings for peas and a shirt for a piece of bear meat—and how she met the Indian, King Philip. After considerable diplomatic bargaining, she and her remaining children were released for ransom. It is likely that she died two years later, before the first publication of her *Narrative*. Published at Cambridge as *The Soveraignty and Goodness of God, Together with the Faithfulness of His Promises Displayed; Being a Narrative of the Captivity and Restauration of Mrs. Mary Rowlandson* (1682), the narrative is organized around a series of 20 "removes" or journeys from one place to another. Historians have praised the work for its detailed picture of Indian life and for its "pure, idiomatic and sinewy English." But the book was far more than a mere history to the author and to the readers of the thirty-odd reprints that appeared on both sides of the Atlantic; it was a Puritan spiritual autobiography, as a typical passage shows. "Then we came to a great swamp through which we travelled up to our knees in mud and water, which was heavy going to one tired before. Being almost spent I thought I should have sunk down at last and never got out; but I may say, as in Psalm xciv.18, *When my foot slipped, thy mercy, O Lord, held me up.* Going along, having indeed my life but little spirit, [King] Philip . . . took me by the hand and said 'Two weeks more and you shall be Mistress again.'" The *Narrative* reveals an admirable Puritan "plain style" and a fine sense of dramatic timing.   L.Y.

ROWSON, Susanna (1762–1824), British/American novelist, actress, and educator, was born in Portsmouth to Lieutenant William Haswell, R.N., and his first wife, who died in childbirth. As a child she was brought to Massachusetts, where her father was serving as a customs officer. The voyage to America, ending in shipwreck off Boston Harbor, was later recounted in her novel *Rebecca, or Fille de Chambre* (1792). In 1775 the family was interned as loyalists and their property confiscated. Permitted to leave in 1778, they returned to London, where SR briefly became governess in the family of the DUCHESS OF DEVONSHIRE. She published many stories and poems and, in 1786, her first novel, *Victoria*. She married William Rowson in 1787, and continued writing: *The Inquisitor* (1788); *Mentoria* (1791); *Charlotte: A Tale of Truth* (1791; reprinted as *Charlotte Temple* in

America); and *Rebecca*. Having begun acting, the Rowsons were booked for an American tour and, after performing in Annapolis, Philadelphia, and Baltimore, settled in Boston in 1796. In addition to singing, dancing, and acting, SR wrote songs, musical shows, and dramas, including the operetta *Slaves in Algiers, or a Struggle for Freedom* (1794) which declared "Women were born for universal sway, / Men to adore, be silent, and obey"; *The Volunteers* (1795), a musical farce; and *Americans in England* (1797), a three-act comedy. In 1797 she retired from the stage and opened a Young Ladies Academy. She taught for the next 25 years, continuing at the same time to write poems, essays, novels, dramas, and textbooks on geography, history, and biography for her students; in these she praised the fiction of MARIA EDGEWORTH, FANNY BURNEY and HANNAH MORE. She died in Boston in 1824, leaving behind the manuscript of *Lucy Temple, or the Three Orphans* (1828), also known as *Charlotte's Daughter.*

Despite her varied career, SR's main claim to fame is as a novelist. Her fiction is sentimental, combining the most successful features of her popular 18th-century contemporaries—Richardson, Fielding, Goldsmith, and Sterne. Although she criticized the frivolity of novel reading and writing, SR insisted upon the moral purpose of her own fiction, written "for the perusal of the young and thoughtless of the fair sex." *Victoria* announces that it is "calculated to improve the morals of the fair sex by impressing them with a just sense of the merits of filial piety." Interspersed with poetry and sermons, this epistolary novel tells of the consequences of eloping with a libertine. *The Inquisitor* advocates sensibility; *Mentoria* preaches filial obedience and dutifulness. Although most of SR's novels teach her readers the consequences of disobeying parents, yielding to seducers, or defying social constraints and barriers, some present young women who are no more than victims—of their own naiveté or of others' thoughtlessness or malevolence. Both *Trials of the Human Heart* (1795) and *Sarah* (1813) put their heroines through numerous adverse experiences. Lucy Temple's sufferings are a result of her parents' sin. Although the heroine of *Charlotte Temple* is naive and disobedient, she is victim of both a seducer and two false friends: "Spoilt by a mistaken education . . . thrown on an unfeeling world without the least power to defend themselves from the snares not only of the other sex, but from the more dangerous arts of the profligates of their own." Of all SR's work, *Charlotte Temple* was the most successful. Although it tells in highly sentimental prose the archetypal seduction story, it also allows some detachment through a third-person narrator who, while dealing in tears and distress, imagines a reader objecting, "I shall never have patience to get through these volumes, there are so many ahs! and ohs! so much fainting, tears, and distress." When it was first published in America, the book sold over 25,000 copies. By 1812 Matthew Carey noted that "the sales of *Charlotte Temple* exceed those of any of the most celebrated novels that ever appeared in England." E.G.

RUSSELL, Lady Rachel (1636–1723), letter writer, was the daughter of the Earl of Southampton and widow of Lord Vaughan; she married William Russell in 1669. In recognition of their difference in rank and wealth, she remained Lady Vaughan until Russell became a lord following his brother's death in 1678. Along with intense loyalty and love, RR brought property and influence to this union "of perfect trust and happiness." Unhesitantly, she used her position to advance Whig values. RR's support for her husband was tested when Lord Russell's activities in opposition to government policy resulted in the charge of high treason. Taking notes at the trial to be later used for her husband's defense, RR was yet unable to persuade Charles II to intercede on Russell's behalf, despite her reminder of her father's devoted service to the Crown. Lord Russell was executed in 1683. A disconsolate widow, RR expended her energy in restoring her husband's lost reputation (a reversal of the attainder was secured in 1689), arranging socially and financially successful marriages for their three children, and in securing patronage positions for friends and family. She was highly regarded by men of influence in the political sphere, and consulted as a "person held in high opinion by the new sovereigns William and Mary." The record of RR's life, also found in MARY BERRY's *Some Account of the Life of Rachel Wriothesley, Lady Russell,* is most poignantly expressed in RR's own letters. In 1773, George Ballard first published RR's letters from her widowhood. They were widely read and went through several editions; their popularity led to the publication in 1817 of RR's earlier

letters to her husband. The depth of the affection between husband and wife is obvious to the reader. One may note RR's insistence that her husband take care in political matters, which unfortunately Russell did not follow. RR's affecting but not literary letters are best described in the opening advertisement in the 1819 edition: "Their merit must arise entirely from a previous knowledge of the character-habits of this writer, and from the interest which the subsequent circumstances, in which she was placed, inspires."   M.Ma.

RYVES, Elizabeth (1750–97), poet, playwright, and novelist, was born in Ireland, then moved to London to pursue a literary life after she was cheated out of her property. Known for her good nature and generosity despite her poverty, she died destitute in her apartments in Store Street, London. Isaac D'Israeli mentions her sympathetically in *Calamities of Authors* (1812), when he describes her sinking "by the slow wastings of grief, into a grave which probably does not record the name of its Martyr of Literature."

ER published seven small volumes of poetry and drama, a novel, and several translations. Odes and elegies are her favored forms. In her most significant collection, *Poems on Several Occasions* (1777), tribute verses addressed to the king and to patrons invoke "rural shades" and complain of the unequal favors handed out by love, fortune, and fame. On the whole ER's elegies and songs are conventional in diction and sentiment, but occasionally they achieve some persuasiveness, for example the sensitive poem, "Elegy Written in a Convent": "And wandering thoughts, and a rebellious heart, / Renounce that peace repentence would impart." Graveyard poetry themes run through much of the verse; odes address Sensibility, Hope, and Friendship, with a sense of life's transience and the momentary tranquility provided by the muse. Other published poems are "Ode to the Rev. H. Mason" (1780), "Epistle in Verse to Lord John Cavendish" (1784), "Dialogues in the Elysian Fields, Between Caesar and Cato" (1785), "The Hastinad, an heroick poem" (1785), and "Ode to Lord Melton" (1787). *Gentleman's Magazine* observed of ER, "Her poetical compositions are distinguished by vigour, taste, and even an air of originality." ER also wrote plays and fiction. *The Prude* (1777), a comic opera set in Elizabethan times, was never performed, nor was *The Debt of Honour,* although Drury Lane paid ER £100 when they accepted it. *The Hermit of Snowden* (1789), a novel, purports to be copied from an old manuscript; ER employs gothic conventions in these "memoirs" of a dissolute youth turned hermit. The unfortunate Lavinia, who "had been deprived of her birthright by a chicanery of law" is a partly autobiographical figure who attempts to write for the stage. ER also translated Rousseau and Raynal, and started a translation of Froissart.   G.B.

S

SANDERS [SAUNDERS], Charlotte Elizabeth (fl. 1787–1803), novelist, poet, and children's writer, spent at least part of her life in Bath. The few biographical facts available indicate that she was a young, unmarried woman when her first novel appeared in 1787. She continued to use her maiden name on all of her subsequent works. The preface to *The Little Family* (1799) suggests that she was childless, as she speaks of the joy of relating stories to her friends' children. All of her books first appeared in London. CS began her literary career with the publication of the novel *Embarrassed Attachment* (1787), followed one year later by a book of poetry, *Poems on Various Subjects*. Both received negative reviews. *Critical Review*, appraising her first attempt, stated: "To recover a lover, supposed to have been drowned, and a father cast on the coast of Guinea, are too much for one work. We would recommend better employment; for as an author, Miss Sanders will never succeed." The review of her poetry was even more severe: "We cannot, with any degree of justice, compliment Miss Sanders as a poetess. She may be a lover of the Muses, but she is not qualified for their services, in any other capacity than that of the meanest of handmaids." Not until 1799 did CS reappear in print, when she became a regular contributor to *Children's Magazine*. In addition to numerous poems, she submitted two stories that became part of a third book, *The Little Family* (1799). As a children's writer CS achieved some success. *Edmund; A Tale for Children* followed in 1802, and in 1803, *Holidays at Home*. This last work went through at least three printings, the second in 1806 and the third in 1812; and an edition appeared in Boston in 1804. CS's attitude toward her earlier failures is perhaps reflected in this couplet from *Edmund*: "Let wiser heads for science claim degrees, / Be mine an humbler task, the young to please." K.C.

SCHAW, Janet (1737?–1801?), journal writer, was one of six children of Gideon Schaw and Anne Rutherfurd. Schaw was a customs official, and the family undoubtedly lived near some of his posts. JS almost certainly stayed for a few years at her father's 14-acre farm near Edinburgh and was also living in Edinburgh in 1778. She was a distant cousin of Sir Walter Scott. Her elder brother Robert emigrated to the Cape Fear section of North Carolina, where he became a successful planter. In 1774, her brother Alexander also emigrated, to take a position as searcher of the customs in St. Christopher, and at the age of 35 or 40 JS elected to travel with him. All other facts about JS are derived from her *Journal of a Lady of Quality*, the record of this trip, covering the 16 months from October 1774 to February 1776. Although not published until 1921, the manuscript seems to have been circulated privately. The *Journal* divides into four parts, all directed to an unnamed Scottish friend, probably a woman. The first describes the tempestuous crossing itself with its gothic and comic elements; another concerns the months in North Carolina. The other two sections, dealing with JS's stopovers in the West Indies and Portugal, are less unified although equally vivid. In North Carolina JS saw a number of prominent Scottish emigrés, and she recounts through the eyes of a staunch Presbyterian and loyalist the early stages of the rebellion in the South. Of what she takes to be the American peasantry, she says,

"Their feet are flat, their joints loose, and their walk uneven. . . . For tho' there is a most disgusting equality, yet I hope to find an American Gentleman a very different creature from an American clown." Colonel (later General) Robert Howe, although "very like a gentleman," was also a "woman-eater." When JS inveigled him into reading aloud Shakespeare's description of Falstaff's ragged crew (with the implication that his fellows were a similar lot), Howe warned her that she risked being tarred and feathered. As the tension grew, JS learned to put her feminine "delicacy . . . on and off like any piece of dress," and she headed the military patrol one night to be sure that some neighboring Negroes had returned safely home. Eventually, by pretending that she was going on a fishing excursion, she managed secretly to embark for Portugal. Although JS's prejudices are blatant, her sense of detail is dramatic, and her personality intense. She was extremely well educated, and had read nearly every available book on the countries she visited. On the basis of her preconceptions and her learning, she energetically proclaimed her public feelings, while remaining reticent about her private life. Her portraits of women reflect her sensitivity to similar conflicts in their lives and to their need to play contradictory roles.   J.Th.

SCOTT, Elizabeth (1708?–1776), hymn writer, was born in Norwich, the daughter of an Independent minister; in 1751 she married Elisha Williams, rector of Yale College from 1726 to 1739, and traveled to Connecticut, where, after her husband's death, she married William Smith of New York, by whom she was again widowed. She died at Wethersfield, Conn. Before her first marriage, ES wrote many hymns, which circulated in manuscript; some of these were later printed in English hymn books. Nineteen of the hymns in the Baptist *Collection of Hymns* of Ash and Evans are signed "S", while twenty signed "Scott" appear in John Dobell's *New Selection of Seven Hundred Evangelical Hymns* of 1806. Almost all are in a Yale College manuscript entitled "Hymns & Poems by Eliz. Scott," dedicated in 1740 to her father. The manuscript includes ninety hymns, while two probably by ES occur anonymously in the Unitarian *New Collection . . . for the Use of Protestant Dissenters in Liverpool* (1763). ES's hymns are more poems than congregational songs; they are written with literary language and often contain very poor rhymes. Suggesting quiet sadness and restrained happiness, they avoid emotional extremes and preach peace and loving kindness. The most successful ones are poems of praise: "Great God, thy penetrating eye / Pervades my inmost pow'rs; / With awe profound my wond'ring soul / Falls prostrate, and adores."   J.T.

SCOTT, Mary (fl. 1774–1788), poet, wrote *The Female Advocate; a poem occasioned by reading Mr. Duncombe's Feminiad* (1774), an important poem about women of the past. The facts of MS's life are somewhat sketchy. Around 1786 her relationship with a Dissenting minister John Taylor, her future husband who converted her to "the truth of Arian principles," caused such dissension in her home that she broke with her parents. Nonetheless, according to ANNA SEWARD's correspondence, MS's mother died in her arms, possibly in 1787 (see *Gentleman's Magazine*, Nov. 1787). After MS's marriage to Taylor some time between 1787 and early 1789, she went to live in the house formerly owned by an earlier Dissenting poet, ELIZABETH ROWE. MS's long friendship with Anna Seward is evident from their correspondence. In the 1780s they approvingly discuss a poem against the slave trade by a common friend, HELEN MARIA WILLIAMS. MS was also a friend of ANNA STEELE, daughter of a Baptist lay preacher, to whom she refers in the preface to *The Female Advocate*. The ill-health MS also mentions in the preface continued after two births, by which time Taylor had renounced his earlier religious views; in 1793, he became a Quaker and subsequently took up schoolteaching in Bristol and Manchester. Their son, John Edward Taylor (b. 1791), who grew up to become an educator and political reformer, founded the *Manchester Guardian*. MS's politics are partly discernible from her exclusion from *The Female Advocate* of Roman Catholics and unbelieving women, as well as women of so-called unsound moral character, and from her paeon to the American slave writer PHILLIS WHEATLEY and the Whig-Republican CATHERINE MACAULAY: "thou MACAULAY, say, canst thou excuse / The fond presumption of a youthful Muse? / A Muse, that, raptur'd with thy growing fame, / Wishes (at least) to celebrate thy name; / A name, to ev'ry son of freedom dear, / Which patriots yet unborn shall long revere."

The Female Advocate was possibly the only late 18th-century poem by a feminist to follow earlier mid-century male writers, such as George Ballard and John Duncombe, in praising learned and creative women. MS's list of exemplary women is much longer than Duncombe's, for she seeks to redress the imbalance of historical knowledge about women caused, in her opinion, by male prejudice and female educational deprivation. She calls on women to exercise their talents and on men to welcome women into learning. The thesis of the poem is that, if men can be brought to recognize that women can write as well as men, they must in time admit women to the sciences and to equal education. MS asks in the preface, "How much has been said, even by writers of distinguished reputation, of the distinction of sexes in souls, of the studies, and even of the virtues proper for women? . . . Do they not regard the woman who suffers her faculties to rust in a state of listless indolence, with a more favorable eye, than her who engages in a dispassionate search after truth?" She then characterizes and compliments several women in history, as well as the DUCHESS OF NEWCASTLE, ANNE KILLIGREW, CATHARINE PHILLIPS, LADY RACHEL RUSSELL, LADY CHUDLEIGH, MRS. GRIERSON, MRS. BARBER, MRS. CHANDLER, MARY JONES, MARY MASTERS, SARAH FIELDING, ELIZABETH TOLLETT, CHARLOTTE LENNOX, ELIZABETH GRIFFITH, "THEODOSIA," MRS. GREVILLE, Phillis Wheatley, Mrs. Macaulay, ANNA WILLIAMS, LADY PENNINGTON, MRS. MONTAGU, MRS. CELESIA, CATHERINE TALBOT, MISS ROBERTS, MRS. PYE, and MRS. BARBAULD. She ends the poem with a vision of realized women: "One turns the moral, one th'historic page; / Another glows with all a Shakespeare's rage! / With matchless Newton now one soars on high, / Lost in the boundless wonders of the sky; / . . . From sense abstracted, some, with arduous flight, / Explore the realms of intellectual light; / With unremitting study, seek to find, / How mind on matter, matter acts on mind: / Alike in nature, arts, and manners read, / In ev'ry path of knowledge, see they tread!" *Monthly Review* (Nov. 1774) suggested that MS's temper had suffered a degree of injury from the ill health of which she spoke; *Critical Review* (Sept. 1774) found her address elegant and poetical and admired her ability to vary so many compliments. *Gentleman's Magazine* found her zeal fervent and rational, the writer amiable,

the poem just and elegant. *The Messiah* (1788), published for the benefit of the General Hospital at Bath, was inspired by William Hayley's "Poetical Epistles on Epic Poetry" (1782) in which he encouraged a national epic poem. MS decided to contrast the heroes of the world to the Messiah. *MR* found the poem of merit, the versification easy and harmonious, but the muse heretical.   M.F. and B.R.

SCOTT, Sarah [Robinson] (1723–95), novelist and historian, was the younger sister of ELIZABETH MONTAGU. Daughters of a wealthy and well-connected family, both were educated at home. After Montagu's marriage in 1742, SS traveled widely in England with her sister and alone. In 1752 she married George Lewis Scott, Sub-Preceptor to the Prince of Wales. The marriage was unsuccessful, and in 1753 the couple legally separated. SS lived with her close friend Lady Barbara Montagu in and near Bath until the latter's death in 1765. Thereafter SS traveled and moved her residence several times. The details of her life are few, since she ordered her papers destroyed after her death. Her works were all published anonymously or pseudonymously. The novels are *History of Cornelia* (1750), *Agreeable Ugliness* (1754), *A Journal Through Every Stage of Life* (1754), *A Description of Millenium Hall* (1762), *The History of Sir George Ellison* (1766), and *A Test of Filial Duty* (1772). The histories are *The History of Gustavus Ericson, King of Sweden* (1761), *The History of Mecklenburgh* (1762), and *The Life of Theodore Agrippa D'Aubigné* (1772). The novels, conventionally plotted and written, have mostly passed into deserved oblivion. The exception is *Millenium Hall* and, to a lesser degree, its sequel, *Sir George Ellison*. SS and Lady Barbara devoted themselves to charitable work; *Millenium Hall* is in part a fictional account of their life together. It tells of a group of wealthy women who, disillusioned with the world and with men, decide to establish a retreat for other victims of society: the elderly, poor girls of respectable family, widows, and the maimed and handicapped. The women create a female utopia; Ellison, whose chance visit offers the occasion for the novel, leaves to start his own version for boys. The descriptions of life, the inhabitants, and the setting of the estate are much more realistic and certainly more interesting to the modern reader than those of the other novels; Horace Walpole and others assumed that SS and Lady Barbara collaborated as authors on this book. The histories, or biographies, were well received at the time of their publication. *The History of Mecklenburgh* was occasioned by the marriage of George III to Charlotte of Mecklenburgh; it is now quite scarce. *Gustavus Ericson* and *D'Aubigné* are examples of mid-18th-century biography, history told in "the dispositions of individuals, . . . teaching the knowledge of men in a superior manner, while they acquaint us with facts." The stories are political, military, and diplomatic; there is almost nothing of the personal life of the men, who are presented as examples of individual conduct and public actions. B.B.S.

SEWARD, Anna (1747–1809), poet and letter writer, known as "the Swan of Lichfield," was born in Derbyshire, but moved to Lichfield, the city with which she is always associated, in 1754. Her father, a Canon of Lichfield Cathedral, was given a residence in the Bishop's Palace; AS lived there until her death. Educated at home, AS read French, Italian, and Latin. Her family knew Samuel Johnson before he left Lichfield; her sister Sarah was engaged to marry Johnson's stepson, but she died before the marriage took place. Lichfield was one of the major provincial literary centers in the later 18th century, and the Seward family was much involved in literature. Others in their circle included Thomas Day, Richard Lovell Edgeworth, and Erasmus Darwin. After Sarah's death, the Sewards adopted Honora Sneyd, to whom AS became devoted. She encouraged Honora's romance with Major John André, who was shot by the Americans as a spy in the Benedict Arnold affair. Honora was picked by Day, an enthusiastic disciple of Rousseau's ideas of education, to be trained as his wife, but when she grew up she refused to marry him. Instead she married Edgeworth, thus becoming the first of MARIA EDGEWORTH's stepmothers. AS seldom ventured far from Lichfield, but visited London a few times in her early adult life. She went occasionally to Bath, visited nearby country houses, and traveled to Wales in her later years. On these trips she became acquainted with a wider circle of literary figures, including HESTER THRALE PIOZZI and HELEN MARIA WILLIAMS, who were added to her large number of correspondents. She read continuously and widely, and was quick to encourage new authors. Her praise of Sir Walter Scott led to an acquaintance, and she bequeathed her literary works to him.

AS began writing poetry at an early age. Her first published poems appeared in LADY MILLER's *Batheaston Miscellany*. An enthusiastic versifier, she commemorated great and small events with poems, sent to periodicals or circulated among friends. In 1782 she published *Louisa*, a poetical novel. Her only prose work was *Memoir of Dr. Darwin* (1804). In 1810 Scott edited her *Poetical Works* in three volumes. In her own day, AS's most widely known poems were probably her elegies for André and Captain Cook. She called the first a "Monody," a form she claimed to have invented. Although herself a liberal Whig, and later sympathetic to William Godwin and MARY WOLLSTONECRAFT, AS's personal involvement with André led her to condemn the Americans. She blamed French influence for making American leaders refuse to negotiate, even though their generals wanted to stop the war. She especially blamed Washington in such lines as: "Oh Washington! I thought thee great and good, / Nor knew thy Nero-thirst of guiltless blood! / . . . Remorseless Washington! the day shall come / Of deep repentance for this barb'rous doom! / When injur'd Andre's memory shall inspire / A kindling army with resistless fire; / Each falchion sharpen that the Britons wield, / And lead their fiercest lion to the field!" Washington was so upset by her view of him that after the Revolution he sent letters and a personal envoy to explain that "no circumstance of his life had been so mortifying as to be censured in the Monody on André, as the pitiless author of his ignominious fate: that he had labored to save him." He sent her papers including a copy of the proceedings of André's court martial, a copy of his letter offering André in exchange for Arnold and of his letter to André advising him to expose Arnold's perfidy. AS was "filled with contrition." Perhaps the best of her poems are those about Lichfield, containing such descriptions as: "Ah, lovely Lichfield! that so long has shone / In blended charms peculiarly thine own; / Stately, yet rural; through thy choral day / Though shady, cheerful, and though quiet, gay." Her verses are on the whole perfectly conventional for their time.

AS's letters reveal her as an omniverous reader and a keen critic. They are much more interesting and far less conventional than her poems although they share the ecstatic, gushing tone of much correspondence of the period. She constantly introduced new books to her friends and especially sought out those by women. Unmarried herself, she strongly disapproved of the conduct books, such as Gisborne's *Duties of the Female Sex*, whose rigid formulae produced girls who knew so little that they would regard any marriage as better than none. Her liberal although not radical politics—she supported the French Revolution only in its moderate phase—and tolerant religious views, both at first somewhat surprising in a provincial cleric's daughter, are more understandable when read along with her views on women and their education. She left her letters to the Edinburgh publisher Archibald Constable with a request that Scott edit the whole for publication. He declined; in 1811 Constable issued six volumes of letters written between 1784 and 1807. B.B.S.

SHARP, Jane (fl. 1671), medical writer, was the first noted midwife to publish a popular work on the subject that would benefit other female practitioners. Entitled *The Midwives Book, or the whole Art of Midwifery discovered* (1671), the book went through several editions, its illustrated fourth edition in 1725 bearing a new title *The Compleat Midwives Companion*. It ends with the sentence "To God alone be all Praise and Glory. Amen. Jane Sharp." There is little information about how JS earned her skill, but customarily obstetrical knowledge was gained at first and second hand, by witnessing births and studying the literature. JS used Trotula's 16th-century Latin work on female physical problems for reference purposes, especially on uterine diseases and menstrual difficulties, in writing her own, and she was probably acquainted with the work on midwifery of the French Louise Bourgeois, midwife to the Queen of France, which was translated into English in 1655. To obtain translations of relevant French, Dutch, and Italian works, JS paid a considerable amount, an index to the difficulty of acquiring the kind of anatomical knowledge essential to good practice. She ordered her own work conventionally, following Nicholas Culpeper's book (1651), entitled *A Directory for Midwives: Or, A Guide for Women, In Their Conception. Bearing; And Suckling Their Children . . .*, which began "To the Midwives of England, Nicholas Culpeper wisheth success in their Office in this world, and a Crown of Glory in that to come." Culpeper advises women that, if they follow his rules, they "need not call for the help of a Man-Midwife, which is a Disparagement, not only to ourselves, but also to your Profession." Although JS uses several examples, such as the one on multiple births, from Culpeper's book, she also offers a number of independent observations, such as that there is a relationship between mental contentment and conception and that pregnant women want sex to prevent male infidelity, not because of the "curse," as Culpeper claims.

Resembling her contemporary ELIZABETH CELLIER, JS was dismayed by male usurpation of midwifery, traditionally a profession uniquely concerned with and practiced by women. The preface to the fourth edition of her book offers biblical evidence for women's prior claim to the profession, asserting that the practice of midwifery should be a right accorded by sex: "it being the natural propriety of women to be much seeing into that art; and though nature be not alone sufficient to the perfection of it, yet further knowledge may be gain'd by a long and diligent practice, and be communicated to others of our own sex." While she ridicules the pretenses of men who use Latin and Greek terms, JS acknowledges that both knowledge and experience are desirable for effective midwifery, for "she that wants the knowledge of Speculation, is like one that is blind or wants her sight; she that wants Practice, is like one that is lame and wants her legs." Book One examines female anatomy in detail, ending with two chapters entitled "Of the Womb it self, or Matrix" and "Of the Fashion, and Greatness of the Womb, and of the Parts it is made of." The next five books cover a wide range of topics, including signs of pregnancy, sterility, the management of labor, miscarriage, diseases of pregnancy, postpartum problems, and instructions to nurses in Book Six, which ends with "Discoveries of the Several Diseases Incident to Children, with the Cure." The pleas of JS and Cellier that midwives be offered a better education for greater proficiency were ignored. Still, JS's obviously admired book filled a need, created a demand, and publicized a growing concern for rapid, safe deliveries by women for women of all classes. M.F.

SHERIDAN, Frances (1724–66), novelist and playwright, was born in Dublin, the only daughter of Philip Chamberlaine, Archdeacon of Glendalough, and Anastasia Whyte, who died soon after her daughter's birth. Though her father opposed her learning to read and write, her brothers educated her in secret. Between the ages of 15 and 21, she composed two sermons and a prose romance while caring for her father, who had lapsed into madness, and went occasionally in secret with her brothers to the theater. Early in 1746 she published a verse fable, "The Owls," and a prose pamphlet supporting the Dublin actor and theater manager Thomas Sheridan, who was engaged in public controversy concerning audience behavior in his playhouse. Soon thereafter they met and in 1747 were married. When in 1754 Sheridan had more problems with his theater, they moved to London, where they lived for the next ten years in debt and uncertain circumstances. Between 1747 and 1759 FS bore four children, two of whom, Richard Brinsley and Alicia Lefanu, also became known as writers. In London FS knew such prominent figures as Boswell, Johnson, Young, Richardson, and Garrick, and was friends with SARAH FIELDING, Mrs. Cholmondeley, CATHERINE MACAULEY, and SARAH SCOTT. Her daughter's biography presents her not as a Bluestocking, however, but a wise, modest, patient, devoted helpmate to a well-meaning but much maligned husband, plagued by debt and bad fortune. In September 1764, for reasons of health and economy, the family moved to the South of France. FS died in Blois following a short illness. She was not a beauty in the conventional sense and was slightly lame from a childhood accident, but she was noted for certain beauties of person, evenness of temper, social grace, sensible conversation, and a spirited mind.

FS was best known in her time for her novel *The Memoirs of Miss Sidney Bidulph* (3 vols.), written furtively between household chores. It was published in March 1761 and, although its authorship was no secret, issued anonymously. Its sequel, *Conclusion of the Memoirs of Miss Sidney Bidulph* (2 vols.), was written at Blois and published posthumously (1767). The 1761 work is a fictional journal after the style of Richardson who, having seen the manuscript of the prose romance that she wrote in her teens (*Eugenia and Adelaide*, published posthumously in 1791), encouraged her to write. Portraying the ill-starred and unconsummated love between the title character and her devoted but misunderstood suitor, FS draws the moral that man must "use the good things of this life with that indifference, which things that are neither permanent in their own nature, nor of any estimation in the sight of God deserve . . . look forward for an equal distribution of justice, to that place only, where . . . our lot is to be unchangeable." Although to 20th-century tastes her novel is long and excessively sentimental, most of its characters are psychologically convincing, and the plot is alive with a wit, humor, and diversity that balance the pathos. It was approved by critics on its publication and enjoyed wide popularity on the Continent in translations by J.B.R. Robinet and the Abbé Prévost. Incidents from it are used in a French play by J. B. Mercier and also in *The School for Scandal* by FS's son. Early in 1763 she sent to Garrick the manuscript of a sentimentaal comedy, *The Discovery*, which he staged immediately, including in the cast both himself and Thomas Sheridan. The play is distinguished by witty manners in a subplot concerning the marital problems of a young couple and in the portrayal of Lord Medway, a philandering, out-of-pocket gentleman. It is marred for 20th-century taste, however, by the over-refined female characters and by the incredible conclusion of the main plot. Highly successful on the stage, largely because of Garrick's portrayal of the solemn, courtly, elocutionary Sir Anthony Branville, *The Discovery* was nevertheless criticized, even in the mid-18th century, for its sentimentality and contrived ending. Were FS less noted for sweetness of temper, one might suspect that in it she was satirizing her husband in the characters of both Lord Medway and Sir Anthony, and that in championing the piece, Garrick intended to embarrass Sheridan, with whom he was seldom on good terms. (An adaptation by Aldous Huxley in 1924 alters the action considerably.) *The Dupe*, which followed in December 1763, was retired from the stage at Drury Lane after three performances because a squeamish audience was offended by some of its language. It sold well in print, however, with slight alterations. Her third comedy, *A Journey to Bath*, was written at Blois and sent in unfinished draft to Garrick, who rejected it. Her Mrs. Tryfort of this piece is the prototype for Mrs. Malaprop in her son's play *The Rivals.* It was published in its unfinished form in 1902 by William Fraser Rae in an edition of plays by Richard Brinsley Sheridan. Her last completed work, *The History of Nourjahad*, is an Eastern tale on the vanity-of-human-wishes theme. Published posthumously in 1767, it was meant as the first in a series of didactic tales to be dedicated to the Prince of Wales. Very popular both in England and on the Continent and translated into French, Russian, and Polish, it was also adapted as a "melodramatic spectacle" in 1802 and staged as a musical play, *Illusion*, in 1813. Before her death FS attempted a dramatic version of the last two volumes of *Sidney Bidulph*, but the manuscript was lost and the work was never published.   D.W.M.

SHERWOOD, Mary Martha [Butt] (1775–1851), writer for children, was the daughter of a well-educated Church of England cleric who held several livings in Worcestershire. She was educated with her brother and sister at home by her parents. The family made frequent visits to Lichfield, where MMS met ANNA SEWARD and other literary figures. Her father encouraged her story-telling talents; she and her sister Lucy amused themselves by telling each other long romances and writing plays. In 1791 MMS was sent to Reading as a parlor boarder in the school run by M. and Mme. St. Quintin. (This well-known French emigré school later moved to London; among its pupils there were Mary Russell Mitford and Lady Caroline Lamb.) MMS returned home to Kidderminster in 1793 and began writing seriously, although she said she had "a horror of being a literary lady" as a result of knowing Seward and reading *The Tatler*. After the death of her father in 1795, she lived with her mother and sister in Bridgnorth, Salop. There she learned Greek at her brother's urging, organized a parish Sunday school, and continued to write. In 1799 she visited HANNAH MORE and her sisters in Bath. MMS married her cousin Henry Sherwood, an army officer, in 1803. When his regiment was sent to India in 1805, she accompanied her husband, leaving their baby daughter in England. The Sherwoods remained in India until 1816. MMS was not happy there, and, after the deaths of the first two children born there, she wished to return home. The bereaved mother was somewhat consoled by three daughters and another son who did survive Indian conditions. More important in her acceptance of her lot was her conversion to evangelical Anglicanism. Her religious convictions spurred her on to more extensive good works, especially in education. She began Sunday schools and regular schools for missionary converts and the children

of Britons in India, and she wrote many stories for use in these schools. She adopted several abandoned European children. When the Sherwoods sailed home their party included their own four children and nine adopted ones. The family settled near Worcester, where more children were sent to them by friends in India and relatives at home. MMS's own eighth child was born in 1819. In addition to supervising the education of her numerous family, she took female pupils for several years. Until her death in 1851 she continued to write stories and tracts and to be active in good works, especially of an educational nature.

All of MMS's published work was of a didactic nature and written primarily for children. *Susan Grey* (1802) was written for her Sunday school girls. She described it as "the first of its kind—that is the first narrative allowing of anything like correct writing or refined sentiments, expressed without vulgarities, ever prepared for the poor, and having religion as its object." But after her conversion, she felt it to be full of incorrect doctrine and revised it extensively. Many of her stories were brief and appeared as tracts and in magazines. A selection was published as late as 1891 in *The Juvenile Library*. The best known of her short stories was probably *Little Henry and his Bearer*, written in India. It introduced several generations of children to British India and was translated into French, German, Hindustani, Chinese, and Singalese. Many of her stories used her own and her family's experiences, which gave them a strong sense of realism. Of her longer works, *The Fairchild Family* (1818) was the one read most often, and it retained a place on nursery shelves well into the 20th century. It is the story of a lively, though highly moral, family of three children whose everyday life is full of playing, eating, and exciting, though often morbid, events. The sermons and morals drawn by the parents and other adults were increasingly edited out of the story in versions published after MMS's death. MMS herself edited SARAH FIELDING's *The Governess* in 1820, keeping the moral but removing the fairy stories, of which she strongly disapproved.   B.B.S.

SIMCOE, Elizabeth Postuma (1766–1850), diarist, came from the Welsh Herefordshire family of Gwillim. Her father, a soldier with General Wolfe in Quebec, died before she was born, and her mother died in childbirth. The orphaned ES inherited a considerable fortune. She was raised by her aunt at Hembury Hill near Honiton and educated in languages and drawing. In 1782 she married John Simcoe and went to live in Exeter. In 1784 they bought a 5,000-acre estate near Kentisbeare, where they built a new mansion and raised five daughters and a son. Simcoe was much concerned with Canadian affairs and was chosen as the first Lieutenant-Governor of the new Province of Upper Canada. In 1791, leaving her four small daughters, ES went to Canada with her husband, her youngest two children, and a bevy of servants and nurses. At first they stayed in Quebec and Montreal, where they found an elegant colonial society, and then proceeded to Kingston on Lake Ontario and Niagara,where conditions were more primitive. In her "canvas home" ES produced a seventh child, who died the following year. After two and a half years, Simcoe, fearing hostilities with the Americans, moved his wife and children back to Quebec, which ES left the following year to rejoin him in Kingston once peace was settled. In 1796, owing to a debilitating malaria, Simcoe requested leave, and the couple sailed for England. On the way back they encountered French warships and gales. "I had no idea what it was to be so frightened," ES wrote. They returned to Exeter and ES never again left England. By 1804 she had four more children. In 1806 Simcoe applied for a post in India to which ES was to accompany him; ordered instead to Lisbon, he fell ill and died in Exeter. ES's seemingly favorite son was killed six years later. For her daughters, hardly mentioned in her journal, she seems to have avoided marriage; none married before ES died, and only one did so afterward.

From her departure from England to her return five years later, ES kept a journal. She describes the rough crossing and the first dreary sight of Quebec: "I was not disposed to leave the ship to enter so dismal looking a town as Quebec appeared through the mist, sleet and rain." She records her later impressions of the Anglo-French society of the town and her enjoyment of the round of parties and theatrical entertainments. She also records in a matter-of-fact way the difficulties of life in more primitive places and the extremes of temperature to which she was unaccustomed. She notes the fears of the colony, the disturbances made by the war with France, by the immigrant loyalists from the US, and by the American threat. More interested in scenery than in people, she yet noted her surprise at finding the Indians so far from the noble savages they had been depicted: "They are an unwarlike, idle, drunken, dirty tribe," she asserted, and she found their ceremonial singing distasteful, "like a repetition in different dismal tones of he', he', he', and at intervals a savage whoop." ES presents an extraordinary picture of the colonial English lady creating, despite many hardships, an English atmosphere of tea and whist on the edge of the wilderness.   J.T.

SKINN, Ann Emelinda (1746?–1789), novelist, was born Ann Emelinda Masterman, the granddaughter of Henry Masterman of York. The only account of her life is found in her obituary, which was published in *Gentleman's Magazine* (April 1789). It states that she had every advantage of education, was pretty, and blessed with a shining personality. She was the only heir to her grandfather's fortune; however, before she reached the age of 16 she so enraged her grandfather that he disinherited her of £3,000 a year. Her first husband was Mr. Skinn, a lawyer. Her second husband, Nicholas Foster, was an officer in the army and the son of an Irish baronet. Mr. Foster deserted her and left her in extreme poverty. To support herself she kept a day school and did needlework, in addition to writing novels. She died at Margate, at 42. In the address to the reader in her epistolary novel *The Old Maid* (1771, probably postdated), AES states that the book is not autobiographical, although she does admit that some of the characters are drawn from family and friends, and some of the circumstances from real life. Much appears to be wish-fulfillment, contrasting with her hard circumstances. The work examines the social conventions of her time in a lively manner, alternating between comedy and bitter sarcasm. The overall tone is moralistic and AES constantly admonishes the reader on the inevitable consequences of bad living: "How terrible a thing is vice? It is amazing to me, the ill consequences which ever follow, do not deter people from running into it. . . . all perverse people, generally, are the greatest sufferers by their own folly." Although AES sometimes uses her authorial hand heavily to bring her characters to the recognition of these facts, the plot is interesting and, on the whole, skillfully worked out. The book, however, was not received well. *Critical Review* (Dec. 1770) found the characters "insipid . . . the circumstances unbelievable." *Monthly Review* (Dec. 1770) was somewhat more lenient: it claimed that, although the work would "disgust a critical reader," it might be acceptable to one who is "fond of novels and not too nice in the choice of them." AES's obituary states that she authored other works but does not mention them. P.H.

SLEATH, Eleanor (fl. 1810), novelist, wrote a gothic romance, *The Nocturnal Minstrel; or The Spirit of the Wood* (1810). The title page refers to other works: *The Orphan of the Rhine, Who's the Murderer?* and *Bristol Heiress. The Nocturnal Minstrel* is set in the time of Edward IV and Richard III, and focuses on a baroness who is still mourning the loss of her husband a year after his death, and who faces the threat of an enforced marriage since her estate is forfeited to the Crown. She is fascinated by the repeated visitations of an invisible minstrel since, "Nursed and bred on the very bosom of superstition, within the walls of a convent, from whence she had only recently been removed at her marriage with the Baron, her mind had acquired somewhat of a romantic cast, which the pageantry and priestcraft of the religion of the age had in no small degree tended to encrease." The minstrel turns out to be her long-lost husband, who had been deceived, like herself, into thinking his wife dead. The novel is lurid and sensational, and consists of a series of bizarre "supernatural" events that have equally improbable rational explanations. R.J.

SLOCUM, Frances (1773–1847), American autobiographer, was one of the ten children of the Quakers Jonathan and Ruth Slocum, who had come from Rhode Island to settle on the banks of the Susquehanna in 1777. When Indians raided in November 1778, Mrs. Slocum escaped with most of the children to the woods, but FS and her lame brother Ebenezer were captured. Ruth Slocum, emerging from hiding, managed to beg Ebenezer back, but saw FS carried away. On 16 December in a return raid Indians killed FS's father and grandfather. Meanwhile FS was adopted at Niagara by Delawares who wintered in Detroit. Her Indian family then moved to the Miami town of Kekionga, at modern Fort Wayne, Ind., where she married a Delaware, but then returned to her foster parents. Next she married a Miami named Shepancanah. Her two sons died; her two daughters survived her. In 1831 or 1832 her husband died, but she continued to live near Fort Wayne. In 1835 she consented to tell the story of her life to George Ewing, a fur trader who stopped the night in her cabin. Ewing wrote a letter about her to Pennsylvania on the chance that her relatives might still be living. Published two years later, the letter eventually reached connections of Joseph Slocum, FS's brother, who had never ceased searching for her. From 1784 to 1807 FS's mother had looked unrelentingly for her lost child, and on her deathbed in 1807 she had enjoined her children never to give up. Three surviving siblings, Isaac, Joseph, and Mary, now converged on FS's cabin. When they urged her to return to Pennsylvania, she refused. "I cannot. I am an old tree. I cannot move about. I was a sapling when they took me away. It is all gone past. . . . I shall die here and lie in the graveyard, and they will raise the pole at my grave with the white flag on it, and the Great Spirit will know where to find me." She was visited in 1839 by Joseph Slocum and his two daughters, one of whom described her as small, gray-headed, with clear and sprightly chestnut eyes, her face wrinkled and weather-beaten. Two portraits of her, by George Winter, commissioned by her brother, remain in Wilkes-Barre and Lafayette, Ind. In 1845, when the Miamis were forced to give up their lands in northern Indiana, FS successfully petitioned Congress for the land on which she lived. She was thereafter known to white settlers as "the white Rose of the Miamis." Her burial spot near her former home is now a state historical shrine.

FS's history has been given in many versions. The first was published by the Rev. John Todd in 1842, during her lifetime, as *The Lost Sister of Wyoming.* Todd's version was reprinted in several histories of the Wyoming Valley and in the Slocum genealogy (1882). James Slocum published *Frances Slocum, the Indian Captive* in 1876; Caleb Wright told the story in verse in 1889; and the *Biography of Frances Slocum*, by John F. Meginness, was published in 1891. A grandniece, Martha Phelps, published *Frances Slocum, the Lost Sister of Wyoming* in 1905, and Charles Slocum published the *History of Frances Slocum* in 1908. C.W.

SMITH, Anna Young (1756–1780?), American poet, was born in Philadelphia, Penna., to James and Jane Graeme Young. After the death of her mother, she was raised and educated by her aunt ELIZABETH

GRAEME FERGUSON at Graeme Park near Philadelphia. Ferguson, herself a poet and frequent hostess to many of Philadelphia's leading citizens, became a shaping influence for her niece: she encouraged AYS's writing by example and introduced her to other Philadelphia intellectuals and writers, many of them women. Ferguson's protégé responded in letters and verse, the earliest surviving example of which is an "Ode to Gratitude" written when she was 13. AYS married Dr. William Smith of Philadelphia in 1775, a match to which her father apparently did not consent. Some confusion exists as to the date and circumstance of her death. Ferguson's commonplace book, the source for most of AYS's extant poems, records that "this dear child died April the 3, 1780, in the child bed of her third child very sudden." Although at least two other sources give other dates, Ferguson's is probably the most reliable.

Fifteen (sixteen counting one uncertain attribution) of AYS's poems were copied into Ferguson's commonplace book, written for ANNIS STOCKTON, probably in 1787. Her first publication—"An Elegy to the Memory of the American Volunteers"—appeared in the *Pennsylvania Magazine* (1775). Eight poems (one a reprint of the "Elegy") were printed posthumously in the *Universal Asylum and Columbian Magazine* (1790–92). Adopting the pseudonym "Sylvia," AYS composed occasional verses on such themes as friendship, sensibility, grief, religion, love and courtship, nature and mortality. Although these subjects are common enough, her treatment of them is sometimes strikingly individual. Her "Occasional Verses on the Anniversary of the Death of [her] Grandfather, Dr. Thomas Graeme," for example, opens conventionally, but modulates into a love poem for her fiancé. AYS also addressed political issues. Ferguson recalled her niece as "a warm Whig" on matters relating to the American Revolution, a label supported by "An Elegy to the Memory of the American Volunteers": "Where e'er the barb'rous story shall be told, / The British cheek shall glow with conscious shame." The firmness of that statement is characteristic of AYS's later poems. Her response "On Reading Swift's Works" (1774), for example, reveals an anger later readers would call feminist: "Say when thou dipp'st thy keenest pen in gall, / Why must it still on helpless woman fall? / . . . Why are we drawn as a whole race of fools, / Unsway'd alike by sense or virtue's rules? / . . . thy harsh satire, rude, severe, unjust, / Awakes too oft our anger or disgust." P.C.

SMITH, Charlotte (1749–1806), poet and novelist, was born in London, the eldest child of Nicholas Turner, a landed gentleman, and Anna Towers. Her mother died when CS was three, and she and her sister, Catherine Anne, were brought up by an aunt. CS went to schools in Chichester and London. She showed enthusiasm for drawing, which she was taught by the artist George Smith, and for reading. Later she wished she had had a more rigorous education. She wrote from an early age, sending compositions to the *Lady's Magazine* when she was 14. Her father's second marriage probably hastened her own marriage to Benjamin Smith, the son of a West India merchant, in 1764 or 1765. Later, she wrote that she had been sold into marriage before she was old enough to realize its implications. Her first child died, and her second was born when she was 17. The Smiths lived in Southgate and Tottenham, and in 1774 they moved to Hampshire. Their family increased to ten children, but the eldest son died in 1777. In 1776 CS's father-in-law died, intending to leave his fortune to her children, but a dispute over his will prevented them from gaining any benefit from this. The unfavorable portraits of lawyers in CS's novels are a result of this experience. In 1783 Benjamin Smith was imprisoned for debt. CS began to write for money, and *Elegiac Sonnets*, published in 1784 at her expense, made a profit and was reprinted several times. CS joined her husband in Normandy, where he had gone to escape his creditors and where their last child, a son, was born in 1785. She translated *Manon L'Escaut* in 1785 but withdrew it from publication. Her translation of *Les Causes Célèbres* was published as *The Romance of Real Life* in 1787, the year CS left her husband. Later she wrote that the marriage had always been unhappy because of his infidelities and his temper. CS now had no money and nine children, eight of them dependent on her. She began to write novels, and *Emmeline* (1788) was immediately successful. The first edition of 1500 copies sold out, another edition was published that year, and the publisher, Cadell, increased his payment. CS published ten novels in ten years. The lawsuit over her father-in-law's property remained unresolved, and CS's letters reveal her resentment at having to write for a living. She depended on obtaining advances from her publishers, and was usually paid £50 a volume. She occasionally sent money to help her husband, but avoided meeting him and mentioned him with bitterness. She moved several times, spending time at Bignor Park, at Brighton, at Bath, and in Portman Square, London. In 1792 she stayed at William Hayley's house at Eartham, where she wrote part of *The Old Manor House* (1793) and read it aloud in the evenings to Hayley, Cowper, and the artist Romney. Joseph Cooper Walker and Sarah Rose became her close friends. She met Wordsworth, who admired and was influenced by her poetry, and Coleridge. CS's novels contain many autobiographical elements. She portrays herself as the virtuous wife of a vicious husband in Mrs. Stafford of *Emmeline*. Mrs. Denzil of *The Banished Man* (1794), a reluctant authoress of romantic tales, is another self-portrait. CS's favorite child, Anna Augusta, is idealized as Angelina of *The Banished Man*. Financial pressures did not lessen when CS's children grew up. In 1801 her daughter Lucy was left a penniless widow, with two children and expecting a third. CS continued writing, turning now to children's tales. Her son Charles lost a leg in the siege of Dunkirk and died of yellow fever in Barbados in 1801. CS's greatest grief was Anna Augusta's death in 1795. During her last ten years CS endured painful illnesses; she died, a few months after her husband, at Tilford, Surrey.

CS's reputation today depends on her novels, but she considered herself primarily a poet. *Elegiac Sonnets* went through several editions in the '80s and '90s, and a second volume was published in 1797. Her poems express her personal sorrows, her feeling for natural scenery, and compassion for the poor and oppressed. She presents herself as a melancholy figure, out of harmony with nature's happier moods, who finds her feelings expressed by storms and gales. "Another May new buds and flowers shall bring; / Ah! why has happiness—no second Spring?" she asks in Sonnet 2. In Sonnet 32, "To Melancholy," she writes "When latest Autumn spreads her evening veil, / And the grey mists from these dim waves arise / I love to listen to the hollow sighs, / Thro' the half leafless wood that breathes the gale." Some sonnets are adaptations of Petrarch; others are supposed to be written by Goethe's hero, Werther. Some poems appear in the novels, and indicate her per-

secuted heroes' and heroines' melancholy and appreciation of nature. The novels also contain scenic descriptions, often indicative of the characters' moods. Emmeline's pensive mood is reflected in her surroundings, where "a rich and beautiful vale, now variegated with the mellowed tints of the declining year, spread its enclosures, 'till it was lost again among the blue and barren hills." CS's novels belong to and add to the development of the sentimental tradition. *Emmeline, Ethelinde* (1789), *Celestina* (1791), *Montalbert* (1795), and *Marchmont* (1796) center on the experience of a heroine of sensibility. CS contributes to the development of the traditon of the sentimental heroine by stressing the intelligence, artistic powers, grace and sensitivity of heroines who became famous in the 1790s. Self-educated Emmeline's sweet, expressive countenance more than compensates for the lack of perfect regularity in her features, and she is refined, elegant, and pensive. *Desmond* (1792), *The Older Manor House, The Wanderings of Warwick* (1794), *The Banished Man*, and *The Young Philosopher* (1798) are more concerned with the hero's experience, although the sentimental heroine often plays an important part. Love is an important theme in all the novels; and poverty, family opposition, previous marriages, or mystery about the hero or heroine's true identity play their parts as temporary obstacles to love's fulfillment. Orlando's reverie in *The Old Manor House* demonstrates the emotive style sometimes used by lovers in the novels, and the typical sentimental concern with the conflict between love and duty: "Ah! why was it thus impossible to reconcile his duty and his love; and why should his attachment to Monimia be inconsistent with the attention his family would have a right to if—if his father should die?" CS's satirically portrayed minor characters—grasping lawyers, conceited fops, and pompous lords—are often livelier creations than her sentimental heroines. Her best satirical portrait is Mrs. Rayland of *The Old Manor House*, who is absurdly proud of her illustrious ancestors. Social criticism plays a large part in CS's novels. Many of her heroes and heroines are persecuted because of poverty or low birth, and suffer because of the pride, greed, and cruelty of rich, powerful people. CS often makes social criticisms through her portraits of minor characters. In *Desmond*, Lord Newminster's hatred of the French Revolution is the attitude of a powerful statesman who dotes on his pet dog and ignores the people who need his help. CS exposes disparaging attitudes to women in *Marchmont*, where Mohun, the heroine's unwelcome suitor, is described as "surveying Althea with the sort of look that a sagacious jockey puts on when he is about to purchase a horse." CS's feminist interests are evident in her attempt, particularly in the later novels, to portray strong heroines whose fortitude and intelligence show them to be the equals of men. In the preface to *Desmond* she defends a woman's right to be interested in politics, and in the preface to *The Young Philosopher* she expresses admiration for MARY WOLLSTONE-CRAFT. Many of CS's novels refer to political questions of her day. In *Desmond*, written during the early period of the French Revolution, she is a wholehearted supporter of its ideals. She makes her liberal sympathies clear by setting *The Old Manor House* in the time of the American War of Independence and making her hero criticize the British government's part in it. In *The Banished Man* her sympathies, like those of many early supporters of the French Revolution, have changed since the Reign of Terror. Her hero is an exiled French aristocrat, and the suffering the Revolution has brought to landowners and peasants is emphasized. A long blank verse poem *The Emigrants* (1794) also expresses sympathy for the Revolution's victims. In *The Young Philosopher* her support for radical ideas has returned. A benevolent character, Armitage, praises revolutionary ideals although he laments the excesses of the Revolution, and the hero rejects British high society, preferring a simple life of farming in America. CS was criticized for changing her political opinions, but her compassion for victims of oppression, which formed the basis of her political ideas, remained constant. Compassion motivated her description of a shipwreck, *A Narrative of the Loss of the Catharine* (1796), published by subscription in aid of one of the survivors. CS's other publications include children's stories—*Rural Walks* (1795), *Rambles Farther* (1796), and *Minor Morals* (1798)—which show her interest in natural history. A five-volume collection of narratives, *Letters of a Solitary Wanderer*, was published between 1799 and 1802. Three more works for children appeared: *Conversations introducing Poetry* (1804), *History of England* (1806), and *A Natural History of Birds* (1807). *Beachy Head, and other Poems* came

out in 1807. CS is sometimes considered a gothic novelist. Castles, old manors and abbeys, and rocky coastlines infuse a certain gothic atmosphere into the novels. Ethelinde believes she sees her father's ghost, Monimia in *The Old Manor House* fears ghosts, and in *Marchmont*, the hero in hiding is thought to be a ghost. Gothic elements, however, are not central to her work, and she is a realist, a satirist, and a sentimentalist more than a gothic writer. Her novels share some characteristics with those of ANN RAD-CLIFFE, who borrowed from her in creating her heroines. CS's landscape descriptions, based on places she knew, are usually more detailed and accurate than Radcliffe's. CS's work suffers because of hasty composition, but the fine first section of *The Old Manor House* (which book's quiet humor is similar in tone to Jane Austen) shows that with more leisure at her disposal she would have produced extremely good writing. Austen mocked CS's sentimentalism in *Northanger Abbey*, but may also have drawn on CS's work in developing her own style. In her own time CS was very popular. *Emmeline* was hailed as superior to most novels and hardly inferior to FANNY BURNEY's work. *Monthly Review* praised it as "simple, femininely beautiful and chaste." Reviewing *Celestina*, the *European Magazine* (Oct. and Dec. 1791), praised CS for touching "those springs that are most likely to excite emotions in the heart," while *Critical Review* pointed out that in this novel, "the delicacy of the drawing, the skill in distinguishing the minuter features of the mind, are generally displayed in the subordinate characters." *CR* objected to scenes in *The Old Manor House* where the hero and heroine meet at night in the heroine's bedroom. *CR* also disagreed with the political views in *Desmond*, but *MR*, *Analytical Review*, and *European Mag.* (July 1792) praised this novel, the last considering that CS had "vindicated the cause of French liberty with much acuteness." *CR*, reviewing *Marchmont* (in Mar. 1797), decided that CS's work was not as exciting as Radcliffe's, nor as amusing as Burney's, but was "more true to nature than either." J.S.

SMITH, Elizabeth (1776–1806), scholar and translator, was the second child and eldest daughter of an affluent banker in the West of England. She was born in Burn Hall, Durham, but moved often through her childhood, living in Suffolk and Bath and, from 1785, at Piercefield Park near Chepstow. She was talented in music and drawing, but was especially attracted to languages and mathematics, in which she became extremely proficient, despite little instruction. By the age of 13 she was a sort of governess to her younger siblings and was called by her mother "a living library." When still a child she wrote sentimental poetry in the manner of the day, and in letters commented excitedly on Ossian and Welsh bards. When her father's bank failed after the declaration of war in 1793 (he joined the army in 1794), ES and her sisters had to go to Bath, where she stayed with friends for some months, including the family of HENRIETTA MARIA BOWDLER. For many years ES had neither a settled home nor access to libraries, yet she managed to teach herself about history, poetry, the Bible, astronomy, and botany and to learn Arabic and Persian. In 1796 ES went with her mother to Ireland for some months to join her father; in 1798 she was in Conway in Wales, but returned with her mother to Ireland in 1799, leaving it again for the Lake District in 1800. By this time her enthusiasm for Ossian was overtaken by a stronger one for the classical writers, whose superiority she ascribed to the scarcity of paper: "Of course, they would think deeply, and consider their subject on every side, before they would spoil their parchment by writing what on reflection might appear not worth preserving." By 1803 ES's linguistic ability was known and she was appreciated by many including ELIZABETH HAMILTON. She was proficient in French, Italian, Spanish, German, Latin, Greek, Hebrew, Arabic, and Persian; she translated the Book of Job and was asked to translate the works of Klopstock. In 1805 she caught a cold, which lingered, and she became paralyzed; she died the following year.

After ES's death, Henrietta Maria Bowdler described her life and published the description with ES's writings as *Fragments in Prose and Verse by a Young Lady, lately deceased. With some account of her life and character by the Author of 'Sermons on the Doctrines and Duties of Christianity.'* The work went through many editions. It includes ES's informal chatty letters, full of learning, philosophical speculations, and enthusiasm for wild scenery. They are often lively: "To be good and disagreeable is high treason against virtue." Despite her own scholarly accomplishments, ES accepts female intellectual inferiority ("there never was among women a Milton, a Newton"), although she notes the necessity of favorable

circumstances for genius to flourish. ES's were hardly favorable, Bowdler insists in the memoir, and her great learning in the face of such odds makes her "an example, which may be useful to all her sex." In 1810 *The Book of Job, translated from the Hebrew by Elizabeth Smith* was published, and in 1814 appeared *A Vocabulary, Hebrew, Arabic, and Persian, by the late Miss E. Smith. To which is prefixed, A praxis, on the Arabic alphabet by the Rev. J.F. Usko. Memoirs of Frederick and Margaret Klopstock*, translated from the German, was issued in 1808, sometimes on its own and sometimes with an edition of *Fragments*. J.T.

SMITH, Elizabeth (fl. 1780–89), devotional poet, probably lived the first part of her life near Exeter, where in 1780 she published "Life Review'd: A Poem" about the churchyard in Truro. It is a typical graveyard poem describing dead townspeople and commenting sententiously on their common fate: "All, all, together join'd, their Force must fail, / Nor can the purest Virtues thus prevail. / Then what is Life? its pompous vain Parade? / The empty Shadow of a fleeting Shade." The poem ends with a vision of the last judgment, a welter of melting mountains, bloody waves, and open graves. "Life Review'd" is bound with an elegy on the curate of Truro, an "Heroic Christian," and lists 27 pages of subscribers. By 1787 ES was probably in Birmingham, where she published a biblical paraphrase called *The Brethren; A Poem*, which she "earnestly recommended to the attention of the rising generation," since it impressed on "the opening mind" the imitation of the "amiable character of early piety and virtue." In the preface, ES makes her "unfortunate situation" account for the defects in accuracy and eloquence. The subscription list includes ANNA SEWARD. In wooden couplets the poem tells the story of Jacob and his sons: "Far different passions now their bosoms move, / From pure affection and fraternal love; / High raging pride and malice unrestrain'd, / O'er Simeon's soul in dark conjunction reign'd." In 1789 ES published *Israel; a poem in four books.* Possibly she is also the author of *The Contrast: or, The Mayoralty of Truborough A Comedy*, published in 1790 by an E. Smith of Plymouth. J.T.

SMITH, Eunice (fl. 1791–92), American polemicist, lived in Ashfield, Mass. and wrote simple evangelical pamphlets, full of the loving kindness of Christ. Her first published work, *Some Arguments Against Worldly-Mindedness* (Boston, 1791) is a dialogue between two Christians, Mary and Martha. Their discourse is a consideration of the temporal vs. the spiritual world and the obstacles encountered on the road to salvation. Martha voices the practical concerns of the Christian; she is, however, encumbered by worldly cares and, as a result, her soul is undernourished. Mary plays the role of spiritual adviser and is always prepared to explain the seemingly inexplicable workings of divinity. For example, when Martha is distressed by the hardships in everyday life, Mary replies, "As a skillful physician would apply many medicines to a man afflicted with many sore diseases, some of the medicines might be sweet and some bitter, telling him all shall work for the good: so our dear Redeemer deals with us in wisdom and love." In *Practical Language Interpreted in a Dialogue between a Believer and an Unbeliever* (Ashfield, Mass., 1792) the author again creates dramatic foil characters. The Believer has found peace and satisfaction in this world by keeping a constant gaze toward the next, while the Unbeliever, at first complacent, comes to realize his profound wretchedness. In this vision a sinner can shrug off damnation simply by renouncing sinful pleasure and embracing the invitation of the gospel. ES's last and most accomplished work, *Some Motives to Engage Those Who Have Professed the Name of the Lord Jesus*, illustrates her deep commitment and talent for argument. She presents five inducements for righteousness: man was in a "state of death" before the redemption; we were redeemed through great sacrifice and pain; the promise of salvation and the glory of heaven offer the only true happiness; we are in constant danger of falling back into a state of disgrace; and our ingratitude for the gift of salvation would wound the "lovely Saviour" and, "the hearts of those who love Him." She ends with an acrostic:

"S weet is my lovely Saviour's voice,
M y soul in Jesus does rejoice,
I love to feel his grace;
T he happy day will surely come,
H is saints will all be gathered home,
  To see his lovely face."   D.B.

SNELL, Hannah (1723?–1792), memoirist, said she was born in Worcester, on St. George's Day, one of nine children of Sam-

uel Snell, a hosier and dyer and trustee of the Baptist Meeting House. Her parents having died, in 1740 HS settled in Wapping with her sister Susannah and brother-in-law James Gray, a carpenter. All the other Snell children, inspired by family tradition, entered the service or married servicemen. In 1744 HS claims to have married a Dutchman, James Summs, who abused and deserted her. Having buried her daughter of seven months at St. George's Middlesex (but this burial is not apparent in the register), HS in 1745 left Wapping in James Gray's clothing and in his name enlisted at Coventry in a regiment of foot. The regiment marched to Carlisle where HS incurred her sergeant's wrath and suffered 500 lashes without revealing her sex. She subsequently deserted and enlisted at Portsmouth in a regiment of marines bound for India. She fought at Morusus, Elacapong, and Pondicherry, where she was wounded by eleven balls in the legs and one in the groin; she claims to have removed the last of these herself, to continue her disguise. In June 1750 HS was discharged and revealed her secret to her incredulous comrades. An overnight curiosity and celebrity, she published her story, *The Female Soldier*, "done in a Hurry from HS's own Mouth," an account already finished and sworn by her to be authentic in late June. The Duke of Cumberland awarded her a pension. That summer and autumn she took to the stage at the New Wells in Goodman Fields and in Clerkenwell to sing and drill in her regimentals. During the winter she appeared at Simpson's Theatre, Bath. Within that year her memoirs, expanded by much romantic adventure, were republished. She opened a pub at Wapping at the sign of The Widow in Masquerade, or The Female Warrior, and announced her intention never to resume women's clothing. In 1759, as "spinster," she married an itinerant carpenter, Richard Eyles, in Newbury, Berks. She christened a son, George Spence Eyles, in 1765 at St. Luke's, Chelsea, and later opened a public house, the King's Head, in Jews-Row, Chelsea, near the hospital. Richard Eyles died in 1768; in 1772, HS "of Speen" married in Wickham, Berks., Richard Habgood of Welford. In 1789, judged insane, she was admitted to Bethlehem Hospital, where she died three years later; she was buried, at her own request, at Chelsea Hospital.

HS had been taught to read but not to write. She signed the 1750 affidavit and the

1759 marriage register with an X; in 1772 she could in halting fashion sign her name. She collaborated in, but was not the sole author of, her memoir; most of the facts of her career seem true, but their interpretation is much embellished, both romantically and salaciously, and some explanations are omitted. Mother Ross, an earlier Amazon, was excused her unwomanly ambitions because, in an excess of womanly dedication and failure of rationality, she had been pursuing her own husband. The same excuse has probably been borrowed for HS, who may never have married before 1759. Her memoir has been embroidered with an irrational devotion to a brutish husband, a modest travail to hide her sex at all costs, and the constant danger of exposure and offenses to feminine delicacy of shipboard life. But it also includes—the paradox not noted—her amours with various women, a popular motif much expanded in the second edition. It can be surmised that her enlistment was inspired by family tradition, economic necessity, and resentment at the limitations imposed on women. B.R.

"SOPHIA " (fl. 1739–40), defender of women's equality, has been surmised to be Lady Sophia Fermor (*Notes and Queries*, 1897). Lady Sophia was the daughter of the first Earl of Pontefract; she died in 1745, aged 24, shortly after her marriage to John Carteret, second Earl Granville. There is as yet little evidence for this or any other conjecture about "S's" identity. "S" first published a pamphlet entitled *Woman not Inferior to Man* (1739): "it must appear to everyone, who has but a degree of understanding above the idiot, a matter of great surprize, to observe the universal prevalence of prejudice and custom in the minds of the Men. . . . It is necessary to separate . . . *interest* and *prejudice* from justice and sound judgement. To this end therefore we must examine, in order, what are the general notions which the Men entertain of our sex. . . . Men seem to conclude, that all other creatures were made for them, because they themselves were not created till all were in readiness for them. How far this reasoning will hold good, I will not take upon me to say, but if it has any weight at all, I am sure it must rather prove that Men were made for our use than we for their's." She insists that, although there is gender in bodies, there is none in souls: "All the diversity then must come from education, exercise, and the impressions of those external objects which surround us in different circumstances." She does not intend to be incendiary: "What I have hitherto said has not been with an intention to stir up any of my own sex to revolt against the *Men*, or to invert the present order of things with regard to government and authority. No, let them stand as they are. I only mean to show my sex that they are not so despicable as the *Men* would have them believe themselves, and that we are capable of as much greatness of soul as the best of that haughty sex." A second corrected edition appeared in 1740; but an immediate response had come in 1739, *Man Superior to Woman; or, A Vindication of Man's Natural Right of Sovereign Authority over the Woman*. The author, an "accomplished gentleman," noted, "If, instead of making use of the little complaisances we have for their weakness to redouble their obedience and fidelity to us, they aspire to become our equals; ought we not, in justice to ourselves and for instruction to them, shew them that it has been owing to our generosity more than to any Right they can claim, that we have not hitherto treated them only as our less useful slaves? . . . Everyone will be able to guess that I am speaking of Sophia, that enlightened Lady, who . . . has surprizingly found out that Man is not Superior to Woman in any thing but what she pleases to call brutal strength." "S" responded in 1740 with *Woman's Superior Excellence over Men: or, A Reply to the Author of a Late Treatise, entitled, Men Superior to Woman*, in which "the excessive weakness of that gentleman's answer to *Woman not Inferior to Man* is exposed; with a plain demonstration of woman's natural right to superiority over the men in head and heart; proving their minds as much more beautiful than the men's as their bodies are, and that, had they the same advantages of education, they would excel them as much in sense as they do in virtue." "S" thus progressed from a claim of equality to a counterclaim of woman's superiority. Nothing further was heard from her. J. Robinson collected the three pamphlets and published them together as *Beauty's Triumph* in the 1740s and again in 1751. C.R.

SOUTHCOTT, Joanna (1750–1814), religious visionary, was born in Gittisham, East Devon, the fourth daughter of a poor farmer, William. Until she was 40, she lived as a working-class woman, first serving as a domestic and later becoming an upholsterer. Her detailed knowledge of even the most obscure books of the Bible was attributed to her continual study. On Christmas 1791, she joined the Wesleyans. On Easter Monday 1792, she predicted that the locusts of Abaddon would be loosed upon the world. Agitated and feverish for ten days, she retired to her sister's home in Plymtree, Devon, where she began to prophesy in "a mixture of doggerel verse and rambling prose." These prophecies were sealed and left with her sister when she returned to Exeter. There, in 1793, she wrote to all the local clergymen, from curates to bishops, to examine her forecasts. Only one minister supported her claims. Other prophecies followed, all couched in biblical language. Those of 1796, for example, ended "These are the promises; these are the threatenings. I am clear of the blood of all men. There is nothing covered, but shall be made manifest; there is nothing hid, but will be made known: for what hath been done in the secret chamber will be revealed on the house top. The night is far spent, the day is at hand, it is time to awake and be doing." In 1801, she invested £100, her life savings, in printing The Strange Effects of Faith. (The printer, T. Brice, included 2s.6d. in his bill "for correcting the spelling and grammar of the prophecies.") Colonel Basil Bruce introduced several clergymen to her text; Stanhope Bruce, Thomas Philip Foley, Thomas Webster, and William Sharp subsequently became her followers. At their urging, JS moved to London where, at High House, Paddington, she began to "seal" the faithful, eventually gaining 144,000 adherents. These were certified for the millenium, on half-sheets, backed by a red seal. Before her death, she had published 65 books, and had circulated enough manuscripts to fill many more. Her "Box of Sealed Writings," weighing 156 pounds, was held by her disciples, the Southcottians. She submitted to three trials: in the Guildhall, Exeter, January 1802; in January 1803 by 58 persons; and in December 1804, at Neckinger House. No dynamic evangelist but "a kindly, motherly creature, simple, aimiable and unaffected," she discredited attempts to make her "more than human." A chapel was opened for her in Southwark in the spring of 1805. As early as 1794, she had identified with the woman in Revelation, XII. Then, in October 1802, she had foretold that she would give birth to Shiloh, "the second Christ." In October 1813 she went into seclusion, seeing only two followers. Since her handwriting was nearly illegible, she dictated her rhymed prophecies to them. A letter appeared in the Times in the same month attacking those who mocked her as an imposter. In March 1814 she became ill: six our of nine doctors consulted said that she had symptoms of pregnancy. Her joyous followers advertised in the Morning Chronicle for "a large furnished house" for the lying-in; a crib, costing £200, was ordered. In November JS announced that she was dying and ordered all the presents to be returned. In December 1814 she died and was buried at St. John's Wood. Her tombstone promised: "Thou'lt return in greater power." When the Regent's Park explosion shattered it in 1874, this was taken as an augury of her return. Her defenders claim that she did have clairvoyant powers, and that many of her predictions have been fulfilled. Others attack her publications "all equally incoherent in thought and grammar." Although her verse has been ridiculed as "nothing more than doggerel," she was famous among poets. Blake, Southey, Byron, Keats, and Henry Crabb Robinson all knew of her. R.R.

SPAULDING, Mary (1769?–?), American autobiographer, was born in Chelmsford, Mass. Her father was Benjamin Spaulding, and her family was described as being "regular and respectable." In adolescence she experienced a succession of severe and painful illnesses that continued for eight years. During that time she underwent a spiritual crisis that ended with an affirmation of faith and a sudden physical cure. Her Remarkable Narrative (Boston, 1795), recounts her experiences. The 24-page Narrative is a testimonial presented in a plain style that occasionally achieves simple eloquence: "My distress and agony of soul were too great for language to express. Those who have experienced the same can feel better than I can describe them. When I looked up for mercy, it seemed that God and Christ were turned against me. The gate of heaven appeared to be closed, while the doors of hell stood wide open to receive me. My life appeared to be very short, and my mind was heaviness, and my heart was sorrow." G.T.P.

SPENCER, Sarah Emma (fl. 1788), novelist, identified herself on the title page of her one known novel as "Late Miss Jackson, of Manchester," and "Authoress of Poetical Trifles, Etc." Her Poetical Trifles has remained undiscovered, unless she is claiming a part in the volume generally attributed to Sir John Henry Moore, 1756–80, first published in 1777 as *A New Paradise of Dainty Devices; consisting of original poems, By different hands*, and then reissued in Bath and London in 1778 and 1783 as *Poetical Trifles*. Her mournful introduction to the novel, *Memoirs of the Miss Holmsbys* (1788), confesses that, although born to happier prospects, she had been plunged into the severest distress by the misfortunes of some of her family and the imprudence of others. Her humble education (which may nevertheless have included French) and her situation at the time of publication had excluded her from two very essential needs of a writer, company and books. She had no friend to correct her work, and she wrote at the bedside of a sick husband who had no support but her writings. The modest subscription list of just over one hundred includes many Manchester and London names (George Romney perhaps the most prominent), but no members of the Jackson or Spencer families.

The Memoirs of the Miss Holmsbys consists entirely of the letters of the three Holmsby sisters to and from their three respective women friends. It was almost certainly influenced by FANNY BURNEY's *Evelina* (1778). The sisters are the attractive daughters of a well-to-do London tradesman. Two are vain and ambitious, and the third is sensible and serious. Mrs. Holmsby and her two foolish daughters acquire new gowns, fashionable beaux, a coach, and a country box before Mr. Holmsby is ruined and the girls orphaned. In the many turns of fortune that follow, one wins a lottery prize, sets up as an heiress in London, marries and is bilked by a fortune hunter, becomes the mistress to a lord, and finally kills herself. Another discards a faithful, honest suitor for an unworthy baronet, is herself discarded as toadeater to her sister, and is seduced and ruined before she sickens and dies. The last, too sensible even to enjoy her days or prosperity, has been resigned throughout and eventually wins the hand of a duke. It is interesting that both her contemptuous sisters prefer death to the dishonor of her assistance. The story parallels *Evelina* in its use of tradespeople as characters and its preoccupation with rearranging the status of the characters according to their moral worth; but the events of SES's novel are far more improbable, the girls far more

ladylike, and the setting so vague that the sisters attend "a ball" but none of the other diversions of London. Nevertheless, the writing is lively and plain and has some merit. Andrew Becket, reviewing the book for *Monthly Review* (February 1789), recounted its author's misfortunes and added, "The writer stands not in need of the indulgence she solicits. Her Novel is generally interesting. There is a happy contrast of character in it; and the more prominent features of virtue and vice are depicted with considerable skill and judgment."   G.I.C.

STANHOPE, Eugenia [Pieters] (fl. 1760–86), editor and manual writer, secretly married Philip Stanhope, whom she met in Rome when he was on the Grand Tour. Stanhope was the natural son of the Earl of Chesterfield; he died in 1769 and left her with two sons. Despite the Earl's presumed disappointment with the match, which he discovered after his son's death, he was on good terms with ES, although the *Dictionary of National Biography* calls her "an unattractive woman of undistinguished position." He befriended her and educated and wrote to his grandchildren. After the Earl's death and despite opposition from his representatives, ES sold for £1500 the letters he had written to his son. They were published as *Letters written by the late Right Hon. Philip Dormer Stanhope, Earl of Chesterfield, to his Son* (1774) and dedicated to Lord North. The work speedily became popular. *Supplement to the Letters of the Earl of Chesterfield* was published in 1787, together with a statement that ES had intended bringing them out before she died. The work consisted mainly of early letters. Later in life ES appears to have written an advice book for wives entitled *The Deportment of a Married Life: laid down in a series of letters written by the Honorable E- - - S- - -* (1790), dedicated to the Countess of Derby and published posthumously. It went through several editions, including one of 1821 when it was called *A Guide to Matrimonial Happiness*.

The advertisement to the Chesterfield letters explains that they were written to the Earl's natural son to educate him from a "Boy" to a "Man." ES takes great pains to give the work a moral character; it shows, she announces, "a scrupulous adherence to the strictest Morality" and aims to lay in the earliest period of life "a firm foundation in good Principles and sound Religion." The authenticity of the letters is asserted, as is the worth of the writer of the Advertisement: "though a Woman, I have had the most real of all satisfactions,—that of being of some use to my Country." For later editions, ES added a postscript defending the Earl against charges of misanthropy and calculation; she even supported his recommendation of gallantry with married women by affirming that it was meant for foreign countries, was useful for learning the language, and helped keep young men from loose women. *The Deportment of Marriage* preaches conventional domesticity and subordination of wives: "There is only one Path by which a married Woman can arrive at Happiness, and this is by conforming herself to the Sentiments of her Husband"; it warns against the "sad Effects of the Independence of Wives." The advice is worldly and pessimistic, teaching wives how to manipulate and manage husbands and gossiping neighbors, and suggesting constant care in behavior and speech. Virtue in women is stressed because the reverse is socially uncomfortable, and the double standard is accepted because "Men constitute the World, and make its customs." *An Apology for Mrs. Eugenia Stanhope, editor of the earl of Chesterfield's letters to Philip Stanhope, Esq. addressed to that lady by an amateur du bon ton* appeared in about 1775; it is a satirical work damning the Chesterfield letters as an "inestimable treasure of fine breeding, fine sense, and easy morals," aimed to contract sensibility and promote French frivolity. It attacks ES by ironically seeing her as "rising superior" to the wishes of her dead father-in-law, who did not want his letters published.   J.T.

STARK, Marian[n]a (1762?–1838), playwright and travel writer, was the daughter of Richard Starke, for a time governor in Madras. The family later moved to Epsom, Surrey. MS's early life in India provided the background for her plays. *The Widow of Malabar* (1791) was produced at the private theater of MRS. CRESPIGNY, to whom the play is dedicated, and at Covent Garden; it is an inept melodrama, an imitation of a French play of M. Le Mièrre, but it proved fairly popular and went through several editions. *The Sword of Peace; or, the Voyage of Love* (1789), first performed at the Theatre Royal in the Haymarket in 1788, tells the sentimental stories of two virtuous girls who find love in India. There is much spirited criticism of the indolent and vulgar Englishwomen who come to

India in search of money and husbands. The preface consists of humorous speculation about the author: "I am credibly informed she is a grocer's daughter . . . a mere adventuress," says one speaker, while another asserts, "her father was a parson, and she had run away with a strolling player." Anonymity for a female playwright is justified: "A woman, however possessed of genius, wit, vivacity, or knowledge of the world, unless she continues to veil them under the modest, delicate reserve, which should ever characterise her sex, destroys their effects, and renders herself a being pitied by men of sense, envied, yet ridiculed by every woman of her acquaintance." *The Tournament* (1800) is a five-act tragedy in verse imitated from a German play by J.A. von Toerring und Kronsfed. MS also wrote the poem *The Poor Soldier; an American Tale: founded on a recent fact* (1789), again dedicated to Mrs. Crespigny. It recounts the misfortunes of a loyalist, persecuted in America and treated as a beggar in England; the horror of bureaucracy is graphically depicted as the luckless soldier tries to enter the Chelsea Pensioners' Hospital. Some sonnets of MS were published in her 1811 work *The Beauties of Carlo Maria Maggi Paraphrased.*

In later life MS primarily published travel guides, which proved extremely popular. For many years she lived on the Continent, during nine of which she tended an invalid relative. She witnessed the upheavals of the Napoleonic years, especially the entry of the French into Italy and the capture of Nice in 1792, when she left for Italy with her sick relative carried by porters. They arrived in Genoa in late 1792; by 1793 she was in Pisa and in 1796 in Florence, where she noted with distaste the spread of republican ideas. In 1797 and 1798 she saw the French in Rome. Some of these events were described in her *Letters from Italy, between the years 1792 and 1798, containing a view of the Revolutions in that country* . . . (1800). The book was revised and enlarged in 1815; apart from describing MS's experience, it gives practical travel advice, beginning with a warning of the dangers of travel at a time when disbanded soldiers were roaming as banditti. MS returned to England and lived in Exmouth, revisiting Italy, France, and Switzerland between 1817 and 1819 for the purpose of writing a new guidebook. *Travels on the Continent* appeared in 1820; begun as a supplement to the fourth edition of *Letters from Italy*, it developed into a new work. (Most of her subsequent works are revisions and enlarged versions of previous ones.) It relates MS's journeys and describes travel expenses and accommodation, detailing the improvements in lodging and transport since the end of the war and noting that furnished lodgings were easy to find because newly impoverished nobles were eager to let their palaces. In 1824 MS published *Information and Directions for Travellers on the Continent*, enlarged and republished many times before 1832; it grew into *Travels in Europe between the years 1824 and 1828 . . . Comprising a historical account of Sicily . . .* (1828), and into *Travels in Europe for the use of Travellers on the Continent, and likewise in the Island of Sicily. To which is added, an account of the remains of ancient Italy*, enlarged and illustrated with a map in 1833. These guidebooks included art objects and places of interest as well as advice on transport and money matters. MS died in Milan while traveling from Naples to Sicily.   J.T.

STEELE, Anna ["Theodosia"] (1717–1778?), American poet, was the eldest daughter of Rev. Mr. Steele, a Dissenting minister of Broughton, N.H. Because she was frail, AS seldom left home, particularly after her father's death, yet she authored many popular hymns, in addition to a version of the Psalms. Her editor, Caleb Evans, indicated that "the duties of friendship and religion occupied her time, and the pleasures of both constituted her delight." She is said to have welcomed her death with tranquility and joy as a reward for her piety. AS devoted all the profits from the 1760 edition of her work to charity, and her relatives consigned the eventual profits from Evans's edition to the Bristol Education Society, probably a project of Evans himself.

Under the name "Theodosia," AS published two volumes of *Poems on Subjects Chiefly Devotional* (1760), and a third was added to these in Caleb Evans's 1780 edition. Subsequent editions were published under her name in 1808, 1863, and 1882, and another work, *A Summer Journey in the West* (1841), is credited to AS. All her works are religious in implication or subject; for example, the disappointment that "On earth no solid joy is found" ("Desiring a taste of Real Joy") is countered in another poem by the conviction that "Faith leads to joys beyond the sky" ("Faith in the Joys of Heaven," after 2 Cor: 7). AS's "Imitation of Mr. Pope's *Ode on Solitude*" recasts his poem, which addresses a quite temporal "passion for rural life," to claim that there is no paradise on earth, no tranquil solitude. Quite often AS uses her own sickness as an emblem of spiritual challenge, and her meditations represent an aggressive attempt to heal herself, her illness being one of the "many trials" she must overcome with the help of God. AS's version of the Psalms is notable for its regularization of the poems into hymn meter, with each stanza resolving a spiritual crisis, as in Psalm 84, st. 6: "Through Baca's thirsty vale they go; / But God commands, and springs arise, / And showers descend with copious flow, / To yield the pilgrim full supplies." The frequent editions of AS's work attest to the popularity of her writings. Mr. Evans described her poems as "excellent" and inspirational, citing her epitaph: "But now in heaven she joins the angelic song, / In more harmonious, more exalted lays."   D.S.G.

STEELE, Elizabeth [Hughes] (1740?–1787), biographer, grew up in Westminster, London, where her father was the king's slater. At school she knew the royal sergeant-trumpeter's daughter who became, in Boswell's words, "that beautiful, insinuating creature, Mrs. Baddeley of Drury Lane." ES married and had children, but in 1769 she forsook domestic life in Oxfordshire to establish a ménage with Sophia Baddeley after the actress's marriage broke down. ES took a house in St. James's Place and lent Baddeley money and respectability. The two women lived at the full gallop that Baddeley calls "going like herself": according to ES, their "life was such a continued scene of bustle and dissipation, that I wonder how she looked so well. . . . Often, in summer time, have we returned from a place of amusement, at three in the morning; and, without going to rest, have changed our dress, and gone off in our phaeton [which ES often drove], ten or twelve miles to breakfast; and, have kept this up for five or six days altogether, without any sleep." Together they attended a naval review and Lord North's installation as Chancellor, and paid a cottager to christen her baby "Sophia Elizabeth." They went to one masquerade as Juliet and her nurse. To another ES happened, as part of her otherwise unknown costume, to carry a truncheon with which she brained a footpad on the way home. On a brief plunge into France, Baddeley, according to ES, attracted offers from Louis XV, while ES herself, alighting at an inn in man's dress, instantly struck the inn-keeper's daughter as the only man she could ever love. A long evening's farce followed: ES protested her womanhood to no avail until the girl, dragged from ES's bed, was given her two-and-a-half guinea whip as consolation. At length Baddeley's lovers grew stingy and abusive. These ES could generally restrain (although she claims to have lost a tooth to one of them) by threatening some with horsewhipping and by brandishing a pistol at others, but Baddeley's extravagance—three guineas a day for flowers, £8000 at the linen-draper's in two years—was uncontrollable. "I could only keep her within bounds, by soft-reasoning persuasion, and giving way to her folly in many things," noted ES. Folly won out as debts outran Baddeley's gifts. ES proposed to "work day and night" that Baddeley "should live like a gentlewoman," but Baddeley—whose heart ES knew to be "disengaged from the trammels of love"—drifted off, the common-law wife first of a sheriff and then of his servant. She died at 40 in Edinburgh. "I never could have survived her," ES had said on another occasion; nor did she for long. At the urging probably of Alexander Bicknell, a hack writer to whom the work is sometimes attributed, she dictated and published the *Memoirs of Mrs. Sophia Baddeley* (1787) within a year of Baddeley's death. A few months later, impoverished, alone, in hiding from a capital charge of forgery, ES died, as *Gentleman's Magazine* gloated, "in the most extreme agonies and distress."

The *Memoirs* was notorious. "Truly infamous," *GM* branded it. *Critical Review* expressed "contempt." Many guessed that it was meant to blackmail Baddeley's lovers. Indeed, more than 80 people are named, some 50 of whom—including the Lords Melbourne and Palmerston of the day—allegedly had received Baddeley's favors, as well as others, including Charles James Fox, whose "professions [were] neither desirable nor acceptable." ES points out, moreover, that she mentions "only those who are generally known"; to list everybody "would fill a dozen volumes." The six volumes unfortunately earned the *English Review*'s remark that "dullness is the characteristic of this performance." ES's note of lament grows shrill, deeply felt though it is. "I may, perhaps, be censured for living with her, after I found there was no reclaiming her, but I had still the hopes of doing it. I loved Mrs. Baddeley as my sister." Also attributed to ES is a rare translation, "Spring" (1787?), from St. Lambert's poem "Les Saisons." S.M.

STEWART, Helen D'Arcy (1765–1838), poet, was the daughter of the Hon. George Cranstoun. In 1790 she became the second wife of Professor Dugald Stewart, philosopher, teacher, and writer. The couple spent much time in Edinburgh, where their house attracted many scholars. In 1810, on Dugald Stewart's retirement, they left for Kinneil House on the Firth of Forth, the possession of the Duke of Hamilton. Dugald Stewart died in 1828 in Edinburgh, where HS also died. Two of her poems, "Returning Spring" and "The tears I shed" were published in Johnson's *Musical Museum* (1792). The latter, adapted to an air, was included in Alexander Whitelaw's *Book of Scottish Song* (1866); a skillful poem on slighted love, it begins: "The tears I shed must ever fall / I mourn not for an absent swain / For thoughts may past delights recall / And parted lovers meet again." J.T.

STOCKDALE, Mary R. (1769?–?), poet and translator, was the eldest child of John Stockdale of Cumberland and Mary Ridgeway of Cheshire. On moving to London, her father first worked as a porter for the publisher John Alman, but later developed a prosperous publishing and book-selling business of his own. His acquittal on a charge of libeling the House of Commons led to passage of the Libel Act if 1792. MS's eldest brother, John Joseph, also became a publisher who, like his father, was involved in a series of libel suits relating to his business activities.

MS's earliest collection of poems, *The Effusions of the Heart* (London, 1798), is dedicated to Queen Charlotte. In addition to pastorals, sonnets, and occasional poems, it includes a long gothic tale, "Henry and Mary," which is illustrated in a frontispiece engraving by Thomas Stothard. After calling herself "the Child of Solitude," the author accurately describes the content and tone of her verse: "Reader, if here thou expectest to find the delusive tongue of Flattery, or the flow of pompous words which avail nothing, lay down the book; it is not written for thee: but if the precious precepts of mild Religion, soft Humanity, meek-eyed Charity, and Fellow-feeling, ever warmed thy breast, fear not—take it up; for in it thou shalt find thy own sentiments recorded." One of the most interesting if ineptly written works is "The Remonstrance An Ode on His Majesty's Birthday, June 4, 1797," in which MS criticizes the King's behavior: "Great George was seen / To tread unhallow'd ground / With England's queen. . . . The stage of vice was by his presence grac'd, / And, at each side, a royal offspring plac'd." A two-volume edition of poems, *The Mirror of the Mind* (1810 and 1817), includes an autobiography. MS also published several long elegies. These include *The Unexpected and Affecting Death of . . . Princess Charlotte* (n.d.), *A Plume for Sir Romilly* (1818), *A Shroud for Sir Romilly* (1818), *A Wreath for the Urn* (1818), *The Christian Poet's Lament Over the Christian Statesman. An Elegy on the Right Hon. Spencer Percival* (1812), *A Wreath for the Urn: An Elegy on the Princess Charlotte, With Other Poems* (1818), a reprinting with additions, all published in London. *The Mother and Child* (1818) and *The Widow and Her Orphan Family. An Elegy* (1812) were also separately published. In 1826 she prepared *Miscellaneous Poems*, including those previously published, bound with a manuscript list of titles. In *The Widow* MS describes the poverty of a working-class family and solicits help for them from "the Nobility, Gentry, and others." In an "Advertisement" in the 1s. edition, the publisher states: "This little Poem made its first appearance in 'The Morning Post' of the 7th of December, 1811: and the interest it excited was so unusually great, that the large number printed of that paper, appearing in no respect adequate to gratify the public curiosity, and fears being entertained that the disappointment thereby created might injure the Charity, are reasons that induce Miss Stockdale to re-publish it in the present form." A 6p. edition was also published in 1812.

MS also published a translation from the works of Arnaud Berquin as *The Family Book, or Children's Journal . . . from the French of Berquin. Interspersed with Poetical Pieces Written by the Translator, Miss Stockdale* (1798; 2nd ed. 1799). She possibly contributed to two earlier Berquin translations published by John Stockdale: *The Children's Friend* (4 vols., 1787) and a one-volume selection from this entitled *Select Stories for the Instruction and Entertainment of Children* (1787). Two novels, *The Panorama of Youth* (1807) and *The Life of a Boy* (1821), supposedly written by Mary Sterndale, are often attributed to MS; however, there is no evidence that MS ever

used a pseudonym, and all the available facts indicate she did not write the novels. The melancholy tone of most of MS's poetry is indicated in her poem to Queen Charlotte in *The Effusions of the Heart*, where she asks: "how can Grief on Joy's light pinions soar, / Or Sorrow swell the strain of mirthful lore?" *Critical Review* (23, 1798) commented: "We are pleased with Miss Stockdale's affectionate and religious feelings, though we cannot much commend the poetry in which they are expressed." J.F.

STOCKTON, Annis Boudinot (1736–1801), American poet, was born into the Boudinot family, which had arrived in America as Huguenot émigrés in the late 17th century. They built connections with good colonial families by marriage and prospered in trade and the professions. Elias Boudinot, AB's father, served as silversmith, innkeeper, and postmaster in Princeton, N.J., where AS was born, grew up, and married another native, Richard Stockton (1730–81), of a prominent family; he was educated at the College of New Jersey (Princeton), where he later served on the board of trustees. He was a barrister and held extensive landed estates. Richard and AS lived at Morven, an elegant mansion that she helped design. The marriage was happy and close; their family included two sons and four daughters, one of whom married Benjamin Rush. On a journey to Britain for his health, Stockton was received by George III, and he also traveled to Scotland to offer the presidency of Princeton to John Witherspoon. In America he served as a judge during the colonial period and then as a member of the Continental Congress, and was one of the signers of the Declaration of Independence. The Revolutionary War brought tragedy to the family. Stockton, betrayed by the loyalists and imprisoned, had lost much of his wealth by the time of his release, and his health was broken. He remained an invalid, nursed by his wife, until his death from a cancerous growth in the neck. An executor of his will, AS managed the estate after his death, and with moderate success rebuilt it to prosperity.

AS composed poetry from her girlhood, sharing the verses with her friends and family. Some published specimens date from the closing years of the Revolution. A poem celebrating the British surrender at Yorktown was published anonymously in the *New Jersey Gazette* of November 1781. Two of her poems were included in the publication of Samuel Stanhope Smith's sermon preached at her husband's funeral. The first was, in the words of Smith, "a sudden production, the effusion of her heart while watching by his bed," although its language seems stilted. The poem laments Stockton's suffering, recounts his wife's helpless anguish, and closes with hope in the Redeemer. The second, an elegy, is somewhat more successful, although still conventional; after surveying her husband's virtues and public career, AS recalls that his private life was: "marked with every grace / That e'er illumin'd or adorn'd the place / Of *husband, father, brother, master, friend.*" She calls on nature to mourn with her: "Why does the sun in usual splendor rise / To pain, with hated light, my aching eyes? / Let sable clouds inshroud his shining face. / And murmuring winds re-echo my distress."   G.T.P.

STUART, Lady Louisa (1757–1851), memoirist and letter writer, was born in London, the 11th child of John, third Earl of Bute, briefly Prime Minister to George III, and granddaughter of LADY MARY WORTLEY MONTAGU. She spent much of a lonely childhood in her father's grand but isolated country house at Luton, and, as an adult, made regular visits to Scotland LS endured the taunts of her duller siblings at the slightest sign of intellectual aspiration; she learned to hide her writings and to carry on the life of the mind virtually in secret. Fascinated by politics, foreign affairs, and literature, LS read omnivorously but scrupulously observed the rules of conduct for an 18th-century aristocratic lady, which discouraged writing for publication or engaging in fierce political or literary polemics. She compensated for the deprivation with wide-ranging correspondence and vicarious participation in national affairs through a large circle of friends and relatives, spanning several generations. True to family and class, her political views were consistently Tory, although a ready wit and instinctive human sympathy tempered her conservatism. After the death of her mother in 1794, LS set up her own home in London, where she lived between visits to a round of country houses. Economically independent although far from rich by the standards of her class, LS maintained her own establishment, entertained whom she chose, and cultivated an extraordinary genius for friendship. She never married and died at 94, in full possession of her remarkable faculties.

LS is best known as the friend, correspondent, and critic of Sir Walter Scott. Her letters to and from Scott chronicle an abiding friendship and reveal her as a perceptive and candid literary critic whose opinions he valued highly. The two volumes of letters to Louisa Clinton (1901–3) (written 1817–1834), a young protegée, are written in the best Enlightenment tradition; they warn against the indulgence of reverie and self-consciousness and enjoin the necessity to examine all sides of a controversy in order to avoid the "mania" of public opinion, one of the recurring warnings of LS's correspondence. They also discuss politics, foreign affairs, and an enormous range of books. Decidedly not a feminist, LS laments that "woman has a natural dependence on man, which, do what she will, she can never quite shake off "; nevertheless, she harbors the feminist's contempt for inferior men and the intelligent woman's exasperation at the male predilection for silly women. The earlier letters to her favorite sister (1778–1813), published in *Gleanings From an Old Portfolio* (1895), disclose a developing mind and the young woman's successful efforts to come to terms with the limitations imposed on her intellectual life by class and gender. As a familiar biographer LS is unexcelled. Her *Memoir of John, Duke of Argyll* (1837, published 1899) includes a devastatingly funny portrait of her father's cousin LADY MARY COKE and her "propensity to give things a high *historical* coloring. Her actual situation, with all the terrific power that a husband may exert by strictness of English law about to thunder on her devoted head, was sufficiently grievous; and no very common case either. Yet still it wanted a certain grandeur of peril, which her imagination sought to supply by . . . directing her apprehensions to assassination and poison." The "Introductory Anecdotes" to *The Correspondence of Lady Mary Wortley Montagu* (1837) and the unpublished "Memoire of Frances Lady Douglas" also reflect their author's ability as an affectionate but worldly and honest memoirist. This same approach appears in her "Notes" to Jesse's *George Selwyn* (1843, published 1928), drawn from a characteristic combination of personal memory and remembered anecdote. LS's letters—including the large collection of unpublished correspondence at the Bodleian—memoirs, and moral fables provide some of the most spirited political analysis, incisive literary criticism, and witty social satire of this period.   J.R.

T

TALBOT, Catherine (1721–70), poet, essayist, and letter writer, came from a family of Church of England clerics. Her father, son of a bishop of Durham, died before her birth. Living with the Talbots was Catherine Benson, sister of another bishop, who in 1725 married Thomas Secker, a cleric. Mrs. Talbot and CT, who were not well off, lived with the couple. Secker was successively Rector of St. James Piccadilly, Bishop of Bristol, Bishop of Oxford, Dean of St. Paul's and, in 1758, Archbishop of Canterbury. He was a noted scholar and took charge of CT's education. She studied English Scripture, knew French, Italian, some Latin, and later taught herself German. The Secker household was much involved in the social and literary circles in London. CT knew, among others, ELIZABETH MONTAGU, Samuel Richardson, and Samuel Johnson. In 1741 she met ELIZABETH CARTER, who became her most intimate friend. The two constantly exchanged letters and visited together, mostly in London and Bristol. CT and her mother continued to live with the Archbishop after his wife's death. When he died in 1768 they received a large legacy. CT died in London; she was said always to be in delicate health.

CT wrote essays and some poetry and had a reputation for learning and talent. Despite the urging of friends and family, she published nothing during her lifetime except one paper in *The Rambler* (30, June 1750). After her death her mother gave her manuscripts to Elizabeth Carter, who published *Reflections on the Seven Days of the Week* (1770). Another book of essays and poems was published in 1772. The *Reflections,* vaguely theological essays, were quite popular and were reprinted a number of times. CT's collected *Works,* with a bio-graphical note, were edited by Montagu Pennington, Carter's nephew and heir, in 1809. CT's essays and poems are conventional in style and content; their equal, or superior, can be found in any literary periodical of the day. A single example, from an essay on "Literary Composition," illustrates the lack of originality. "Without at all pretending to criticism, it is almost impossible to read a variety of books, and not form some reflections on the variety of stile in which they are writ. One of the first and most obvious, to me, is that the plainest and least ornamented stile is ever the most agreeable to that general taste, which is certainly the best rule, by which an author can form himself. . . . The flowery ephitheted way of writing wearies the imagination, by presenting it with a multitude of wrong objects, in a way of simile and illustration, before it has half informed the understanding, of what was its main purpose. . . . Gold and Jewels do not become the muse herself, half so well, as an elegant simplicity. But elegant it must be, and noble, or else the stile of writing degenerates into mere chit-chat conversation." Without question, the source of CT's reputation is her friends, who always reported her as the "learned Miss Talbot." To be praised and admired by Carter, Richardson, or Montagu seemed to guarantee her worth. In the 19th century she and her friends were neglected; as an author she does not deserve any particular attention today.

CT's letters are far more interesting than her literary works. In 1809 Pennington published, in four volumes, *A Series of Letters between Mrs. Elizabeth Carter and Miss Catherine Talbot,* which reveal a CT much more lively, more conscious of society and the world and of their ironies and injustices than do her essays. Her formal work is sexless, but the letters show a woman who, like Carter, does not entirely agree with the assumed place of her sex. CT is important for the friendship and encouragement of Carter, who was given an entrée into the great world, a place to visit in London, and an intelligent correspondent.   B.B.S.

TAYLOR, Miss (fl. 1799), novelist, wrote *Josephine* (1799), her only known novel, for Minerva Press; it was signed "By an incognita." Its plot and characters have unexpected qualities of imagination, complexity, and humor. The plot tells how for generations the first-born of a certain wealthy country family has been a son named Joseph. Josephine enters, a woman who throughout the remainder of the novel exhibits a commendable spark of rebellion and aggressiveness. She is aware that, as a woman, she is supposed to be virtuous, meek, obedient, and silent; yet her intelligence and self-confidence are permitted free expression in a parade of iconoclastic observations—"As we females usually gain every point our wicked little hearts are fixed upon." When finally she agrees to marry the errant bridegroom, she considers that probably all will be well if he pays as much attention to her as to her mother's lapdog. The author thus makes it clear that the perfect woman is not only an uncorrupted child of nature, well-educated and sensible, but also a playful, cheerful companion and a witty conversationalist. Her opinion of the male is somewhat less sanguine: "Sir Joseph, rising, shewed himself to be a complete Englishman, by obscuring the light of the fire from all present."   M.P.

TAYLOR, Mrs. (fl. 1685?), poet, had several of her poems published by APHRA BEHN in her *Miscellany* of 1685. The poems in ballad stanza are songs of love, smoothly and skillfully written. One warns against giving up honor and virtue and begins, "Ye virgin powers, defend my heart / From amorous looks and smiles"; another candidly declares, "Strephon has fashion, wit, and youth, / With all things else that please: / He nothing wants but love and truth, / To ruin me with ease." Possibly Mrs. Taylor is a pseudonym for Behn. J.T.

TEMPLE, Anne Grenville, Countess (1709–77), poet, was the daughter and co-heiress of Thomas Chambers, and was married in 1737 to Richard Grenville, who in 1752

became the second Earl Temple. Only one small book of poems is known to have been produced by AGT (1764); it is a charming chronicle of a gay and sprightly woman who obviously was well-read and a loyal, generous friend. Her poetry was apparently only a pastime, socially acceptable and becoming to a lady, but she had a fair sense of rhythm and produced a few commendable poems in imitation of Pope's heroic couplets. Most noteworthy, she had a quick and infectious sense of humor that gives us a pleasant glimpse of the better characteristics of the 18th-century nobility. Horace Walpole prefaces her book with a 22-line poem in iambic pentameter couplets that lavishly praises the poet for touching Sappho's lyre and bringing forth the seeds of genuine poetry to wake them into life. He apparently was a good friend, for he mentions her in his letters.

Some of AGT's verse is inept, romantic musing that refers shyly to Venus, Mars, and the problems encountered in romance. Most tends to be imitative, such as "Marble-Hill," which uses the talking-animal theme popular in 18th-century poetry. Here she places the action at the residence of Henrietta, Countess Dowager of Suffolk at Twickenham and, using iambic tetrameter couplets, describes a fluttering company of birds who have gathered in a lovely grotto to celebrate the first of May. They are so intoxicated with its beauty and their bliss that when the president of the group, a raven, tries to lure them away, he is unsuccessful. "No orator was he, like Pitt." They have indeed become "Birds of Paradise." AGT also takes several popular fables and adapts them to couplets. In "The City-Mouse and the Country-Mouse," Lady Mouse journeys from Berkeley Square to her cousin's cottage and feeds on the last scraps of oatmeal, bacon, peas, and bread. They return together to town, where they admire themselves in endless mirrors, are surrounded by servants, and dine on elegant soups, ragout, and sweetmeats. When the dogs bound in to snatch at the scraps, however, the country mouse flees gratefully home to peace and security. In "The Lion in Love," the noble animal pleads ardently for the love of the evasive maiden, who deftly refers him to her father. The father in turn agrees to a match—providing the lion removes his claws and teeth and bestows upon the daughter half the forests of Libya—"Love bids the blinded Lion yield; / The articles are sign'd and seal'd: / The lawyers all she asks appoint her, / Half Libya's forests are her jointure." AGT also wrote a few clever poems in iambic tetrameter couplets commemorating her friends' birthdays. Most are lavishly laudatory both of the person and of Nature, with reference to the Druids, Pan, sacred woods, Prudence, Charity, and Love. In one poem to an ailing friend, she refers to "modern quacks [who] take their fee and write their bill, / In barb'rous prose resolv'd to kill." To one young bride of a year who apparently yearned for a new gown but had little money, she sent a length of "painted taffety" and an affectionate poem: "Since times are so bad and are still growing worse, / You may make this your own without sinking your purse." M.P.

TENNEY, Tabitha (1762–1837), American novelist and anthologist, was born in Exeter, N.H., the eldest of seven children of Samuel and Lydia Gilman. In 1788 she married Samuel Tenney, who had been a doctor during the American War of Independence and was interested in both science and politics. He died in 1816 and TT devoted her widowhood to elaborate needlework. TT published an anthology of classical literature for girls, *The Pleasing Instructor,* to "inform the mind, correct the manners, or to regulate the conduct." In 1801 appeared her popular *Female Quixotism: Exhibited in the Romantic Opinions and Extravagant Adventures of Dorcasina Sheldon,* dedicated "to all Columbian Young Ladies, who Read Novels and Romances." Written in the tradition of CHARLOTTE LENNOX's *Female Quixote* of 1752, it is part of the reaction of the late 1790s and early 1800s to sentimental literature and its seemingly idealized characters. In its presentation of an intelligent but foolish heroine, the novel makes a covert plea for a rational and serious education for women. J.T.

TERRY, Lucy [Prince] (1730–1821), American poet, wrote the earliest known poem by a black American; she was born in Africa and brought to New England as a slave. At the age of five she was sold to Ebenezer Wells in Deerfield, Mass., where she experienced an Indian raid in 1746. She described the raid in 14 couplets. In 1756 she married a free Negro, Abijah (or Obijah) Prince, who purchased her freedom. They became landowners and charter members of the town of Sunderland, Vt. When the oldest of her six children was of college age, she tried, unsuccessfully for three hours, to persuade the trustees of Williams College to change their segregation policy and admit him. When a neighbor tried to claim some of the Prince's land, she argued the case to the U.S. Supreme Court, where she won. Her home was a rendezvous for young people who enjoyed the many stories which earned her a wide reputation as a raconteur. Although it was known earlier, LT's one published poem, "Bars Fight," was not in fact published until 1855. It has been called doggerel because of awkward syntax, strained rhyme, bouncing meter, and fragmentary content, and has also been praised as vivid and dramatic, a good account of the bloody massacre it records, sometimes with macabre details ("Simeon Amsden they found dead, / Not many rods off from his head"). J.C.G.

THICKNESSE, Ann (1737–1824), miscellaneous writer, was born in London, the daughter of Thomas Ford, clerk of the arraigns. At an early age she became a noted musician, as both singer and instrumentalist, and her amateur Sunday concerts were fashionably attended. In 1758 FRANCES GREVILLE wrote to Dr. Burney about a performance in which AT sang a dirge "divinely well. . . . she is . . . the most pleasing singer I ever heard." AT's father disapproved of her public career and confined her in his house through a magistrate's warrant, but she escaped and in 1760 began a series of lucrative subscription concerts; her father tried to stop them by obstructing the roads near the hall, but he was opposed by Lord Tankerville. In 1761 AT was again singing, accompanying herself on musical glasses controlled by water. In the same year she went with Philip Thicknesse and his wife to a military post in Suffolk; on his wife's death in 1762, Thicknesse married AT, who followed him in his peripatetic life, living in various English towns, in Spain in 1776, and in Paris in 1791. The couple had a son and a daughter whom AT described as "unfortunate." In 1792 Philip Thicknesse died in France and AT was arrested and kept in a convent until 1794. Returning to England, she lived with a woman friend, Sarah Cooper, in London. It is possible that AT is the MISS F who wrote *A Letter from Miss F* (1761) complaining of her treatment by an elderly nobleman.

In 1761 AT published a manual, *Instructions for Playing on the Musical Glasses, so that Any Person Who has the Least*

Knowledge of Music, or a Good Ear, May be Able to Perform in a Few Days if not in a Few Hours. She also contributed to journals in the 1780s, writing, for example, anecdotes of Henry IV for the *London Magazine,* and published a novel, *The School for Fashion* (1800). Her main work is *Sketches of the Lives and Writings of the Ladies of France* appearing in 1778 (probably in three volumes) and in 1780–81. It had a noble subscription list and was dedicated to MRS. CRESPIGNY. The introduction begins boldly: "If women are thought to possess minds less capable of solid reflection than men, they owe this conjecture entirely to their own vanity, and erroneous mode of education." She proves that nurture, not nature, is at fault by giving the example of French women; England, she admits, has produced ELIZABETH CARTER, ANNA LAETITIA BARBAULD, HESTER CHAPONE, and ELIZABETH MONTAGU, but in France no less than 400 women have been renowned for literature. *Sketches* is a biographical dictionary, beginning with Heloise and Marguerite de Valois. The entries are evaluative, and sometimes denigrating; Anne Bins, for example, is called "a violent bigot." Footnotes generalize on female writers and education. Sentimental friendship is much praised and favored over turbulent passion; the height of friendship is seen not between women, who become rivals, but between men and women. French writers, whom she credits with both charm and intelligence, she values over English ladies, with their learning and wit.   J.T.

THOMAS, Elizabeth (1675–1731), poet and miscellaneous writer and "Curll's Corinna" in the *Dunciad,* was born in London to Emanuel Thomas, attorney of the Inner Temple, and Elizabeth, of the old Kent family of Osborne. Although ET lived in straitened circumstances after her father's early death, she was raised a gentlewoman in polite society. Mostly self-educated, she showed early aptitude in learning and poetry. On reading ET's poems, Dryden christened her "Corinna." In 1700 began her 16-year courtship by Richard Gwinnett, barrister and heir to a Gloucestershire estate; letters memorializing this love were published as *Pylades and Corinna* (1731–32). Among ET's friends were MARY, LADY CHUDLEIGH, MARY ASTELL and Pope's friend Henry Cromwell. (The received opinion that she was Cromwell's mistress appears to be incorrect.) Pope frequently mentions ET in letters to Cromwell, he visited her at least once, and Cromwell gave her Pope's letters, which later she published through Edmund Curll. Between 1714 and 1718 ET's uncle, mother, and Gwinnett died. Her last dozen years were filled with horrors: litigation, sickness, solitude, imprisonment for debt, hack writing, bitter controversy with Pope, and death in poverty.

ET's sensibility and interests—rational theology, platonic love, and science—were distinctively of the 17th century. She had nothing of the new sentimentalism and pietism of her contemporary ELIZABETH ROWE. She wrote for herself and for friends, only in the last years with a view to publication. Much of the writing is negligible, particularly the attack (with Curll) on Pope, *Codrus* (1728) and a dull satire, *The Metamorphosis of the Town* (1730). Her occasional poems were collected in the *Miscellany Poems* (1722), reprinted as *Poems on Several Occasions* (1726). These Drydenian panegyrics and satires lack Dryden's invention and sublimity. The literal-minded ET succeeds only when personal emotion, typically sorrow, seizes her and sometimes in satire. As a historian—or storyteller, since she loved to tell sensational anecdotes about the great—ET is inaccurate about the distant past but generally reliable about her own career. Her literary best may be seen in the *Pylades and Corinna* letters where sensibility balances good sense. The discussions with correspondents about moral and religious issues are clear, logical, and equable. The wit recognized by Gwinnett, Cromwell, and Pope is often evident. She draws a corrosive satiric portrait of the "gentle knight" Cromwell as a grotesque squab. Tactful whimsy distinguishes a letter to Gwinnett in the persona of his cat, who depicts the love anguish of his "landlady" in Gwinnett's absence. Her emotional outbursts to Gwinnett have the fire of Dryden's tragic heroines: "Truth, O Caesar, is the most beautiful Ornament of the Mind. . . . I have paid you a most exact and immaculate Fidelity . . . and little expected it would have been returned by such a Fallacy as you deceived me with Yesterday." Good sense, humor, and grace mark ET's best writing, even when she is pressed by adversity. That she appears in literary history a sluttish dunce is the unkindest cut she could have imagined.   T.R.S.

TIMBURY, Jane (fl. 1770–90), novelist and poet, may possibly have been a bookseller by trade. She published an epistolary novel, *The Male-Coquette; or, The Hisory of the Hon. Edward Astell*, in 1770, and subsequently ventured into verse with *The Story of Le Fevre, From the Works of Mr. Sterne* (1787) and *The History of Tobit; A Poem: With Other Poems, on various subjects* (1787). Her last known work, which seems to have been sufficiently popular to warrant a sequel, was *The Philanthropic Rambler* (1790). *The Male-Coquette* treats the reformed rake, who, after a number of amorous adventures, eventually marries the heroine, who had initially resisted his sexual advances ("I had flattered myself, I had faith! Harry, coxcomb as I was, that I had charms for all hearts; having never known one of the sex escape me before"). *The Story of Le Fevre* attempts to reproduce the affective qualities of Sterne's tale, but, as the *Critical Review* not unjustly put it, "The wrong side of tapestry . . . gives as good and as favourable an idea of the figures on the right, as the present travestie . . . does of Sterne's most happy production." *CR* thought better of *The History of Tobit*, a tale of the blind Tobit and the adventures of his son under the guardianship of the archangel Raphael in human guise; crediting her with a "pious and well-informed mind" and an "easy and perspicuous" diction, although the poem appears now clumsily to place the gridiron of the couplet over a flat narrative. The socially unaware *Philanthropic Rambler* consists of a series of episodes in which the wealthy Benevolus intervenes to good effect in the lives of various characters on the London streets. He befriends, for example, an extremely principled and articulate prostitute ("the value which our sex is taught to set upon chastity, leaves us inexcusable for the breach of it"), and reconciles her with her father, who has disowned her.　R.J.

TOLLET, Elizabeth (1694–1754), poet, was the daughter of George Tollet, commissioner of the navy during the reigns of William III and Queen Anne. She spent the early part of her life at her father's house in the Tower of London, moving later to Stratford and then to West Ham, where she died. She was well educated by her father in history and mathematics as well as the usual music, drawing, poetry, and languages, and she is said to have spoken fluent French, Italian, and Latin. Sir Isaac Newton, a friend of both ET and her father, was one of the first to read ET's work. She was described as "a little, crooked woman, but

a sharp wit." ET's poetry was published posthumously as *Poems on Several Occasions, with Anne Boleyn to King Henry VIII, an Epistle* (1755; 2nd ed. c.1760). This includes poems in a variety of forms in both English and Latin; many are biblical paraphrases or translations from the classics, and a musical drama, "Susanna, or Innocence Preserv'd." The original works often have physico-theological themes, as in "The Microcosm," a long poem which traces the influence of man's reasoning power upon the development of civilization. Other poems praise contemporaries such as Newton, Congreve, and Pope, and often show the influence of the last, as in the lines "Then let half-criticks veil their idle spite, / For he knows best to rail, who worst can write" ("To Mr. Congreve, on his Plays and Poems"). Perhaps Wordsworth knew ET's sonnet "On the Prospect from Westminster Bridge" (1750), which includes the lines: "See! to the skies what sacred domes ascend, / What ample arches o'er the river bend; / What seats above in rural prospect lie; / Beneath, a street that intercepts the eye; / Where happy commerce glads the wealthy streams, / And floating castles ride." ET impressively conveys her delight in other writers, including the COUNTESS OF WINCHILSEA, and in the pursuit of knowledge. To the question "Shall jealous Man to Woman then deny, / In these Debates her Faculties to try" she returned a determined negative. Robert Southey judged ET mediocre as a poet, and the *Monthly Review* (13, 1755) declined to rank her work, "in the first class," but stated: "Her numbers are generally harmonious, and her versification easy: her muse seems to have been delighted chiefly with serious or solemn objects, to which the turn of her expression is naturally suited." A later commentator, John Nichols, who reprinted her poems in his collection, was much more enthusiastic, finding the works full of "sentiment and simplicity. . . . Some of the poems indeed have such a philosophical cast, and so great a depth of thought, that they will scarcely be understood by the *beau monde*. The worthy author's head and heart concurred in promoting the cause of Good-manners, Virtue, and Religion" (*Poems,* 1780, vol. 6).　J.H. and J.F.

TOMLINS, Elizabeth Sophia (1763?–1828), poet, novelist, translator, and miscellaneous periodical contributor, was born in London, the daughter of Sir Thomas Edlyne Tomlins, an eminent and erudite solicitor, and the brother of Thomas Edlyne Tomlins, also an attorney and solicitor. A long life of scholarship and literary effort concluded with her death at her residence at Chalden, Surrey. EST's works include *Tributes of Affection: With Other Poems,* By a Lady and her brother (1797); a ballad entitled "Connell and Mary" for Langhorne's selection; the novels *Conquests of the Heart, The Victim of Fancy* (1787, translated into French by A. G. Griffet de Labeaume and F. Notaris as *La victime de l'imagination, ou l'enthousiaste de Werther), Memoirs of a Baroness* (1792), and *Rosalind de Tracey* (1799); a translation of the first history of Napoleon Bonaparte, which appeared in England as part of the *Universal History of Anquetil, &c;* and numerous pieces in periodicals (1780–1827). EST's early talent for poetry gave way to a preference for novel writing, and she concerned herself primarily with the sentimental novel of love and manners, chronicling the perils of the ingenue at court. EST writes to convince her reader that virtue will be rewarded and that *omnia vincit amor,* even though vanity is the "ruling passion not only of women but mankind." Although morally didactic, EST can sympathize with the misguided performance of her heroes and heroines, allowing them a nearly gothic anguish when they fail in virtue. Honorable to a fault, the Baroness d'Alantun suffers protracted melancholy rather than confess the error she has committed in marrying the Baron. Concerned, as is her contemporary Jane Austen, with the obstacles that impede a young heroine's progress, EST yet upholds the morality of the contemporary social code, although she refuses to sacrifice her ingenue upon the scaffold of ridicule, as FANNY BURNEY does. She promotes female friendship; near the close of *Memoirs of a Baroness* the narrator addresses the reader on the subject of candor between women: "There is no virtue which so surely commands our love, our esteem, and our respect; it is indeed the seal of nature on great minds.—It flings a splendour over our very errors, and adds an irresistible grace to every virtue. Cultivate it then my fair countrywomen, and whatever reserve may be exacted from you to the other sex, be it your pride never to forfeit your sincerity to your own." D.S.G.

TONKIN, Mary (fl. 1781–83), autobiographer, seems to have come from Portsmouth. She claims to have made 48 trips to France and to have been a trusted naval spy for the British. In 1781, during the American War of Independence, she was shipwrecked on the French coast. After returning to England in 1782, she wrote to the Admiralty about the movements of the French fleet. When she was finally summoned to the Admiralty she told them of spies working in England and asked Admiral Pye to hire her to investigate them, but he "grinned like a monkey" and prevaricated. Other letters brought no results, until she was asked by Charles James Fox to spy against the French. MT was taken as a spy in the Channel Islands but managed to escape by pretending marriage to an American. She brought back details of the French fleet, but found that, on her return, Fox was no longer in office. Refused payment, although she claimed she had spent £142 on her expedition and had nearly broken her leg, MT was described by a friend as a "cripple, ruined by the affair; between three and four hundred miles from home." Fox finally sent her a little money but, when back in office, refused to pay her properly. To draw attention to her plight and to gain some revenge on those who ignored her, MT published *The Female Spy; or Mrs. Tonkin's Account of her Journey through France, In the War, at the Hazard of her Life, at the Express Order of the Rt. Hon. Charles James Fox, Secretary of State; For which she has been refused any Indemnity or Compensation* (1783). Dedicated to the Queen, the pamphlet tells of MT's troubles with the authorities and of her spying career. It is written in a plain style: "I am no writer," MT explains in a footnote, "I describe people as I found them, in plain language; and write, as most people *speak,* of the characters in this pamphlet." The result is often vituperative. Government officials are slippery and squeaking; one is a *"lying, deceitful puppy,"* another a *"pitiful meanspirited Scotch pebble."* Although the events are presented in too rushed a fashion, and invective is substituted for description, the pamphlet conveys well the anger MT feels, as well as the desperation of her situation. J.T.

TRAVERS[E], Rebecca [Rebeckah] (1609–88), polemicist and letter writer, came from a devout Baptist household. She married William Travers, a tobacconist in Watling Street, London. In 1655 or -56, she heard a dispute between the Quaker James Nayler and the Baptists and felt the Baptists had been defeated in argument. She became a Quaker through intellectual conviction, although warned by Nayler: "Feed not on knowledge [since he] who feeds on knowledge dies to the innocent life." When in 1656 Nayler was whipped for blasphemy, she washed his wounds, reporting, "There was not the space of a man's nail free from stripes and blood from his shoulders near to his waist." After his release from prison in 1659, he stayed with her for some time. RT was a powerful preacher, who publicly questioned and confounded ministers on doctrine when she thought them mistaken. Possibly she was imprisoned three times in 1664 for her outspoken convictions. Prominent in women's meetings of Quakers, she was active in the care of the infirm and elderly; she was also a prison visitor in Ipswich and other towns. In 1671 she was named as one of the members of the "six weeks" meeting, a Quaker court of appeal. She was survived by a son and possibly a daughter. Her funeral sermon was preached by William Penn, who described her as "an aged Servant of God."

RT wrote at least ten tracts or pamphlets, as well as prefaces to Nayler's books. *A Testimony of the Light and Life of Jesus* (n.d.), an 18-page pamphlet, was written because she felt the need to exhort and preach. In 1658 in *A Message from the Spirit of Truth unto the Holy Seed, Who Are chosen out of the world, and Are lovers and followers of the Light,* she urged readers to humility and avoidance of spiritual and intellectual pride. Noting the growth of Quakerism, she underlined the Quaker emphasis on good works and proselytizing: "Wherefore dearly beloved of God, for his name sake I beseech you, be zealous for his appearance, and with meeknesse and fear instruct the ignorant, who oppose themselves." *A Testimony Concerning the Light and Life of Jesus . . . ,* a four-page pamphlet exhorting people to hold to the old spirit of Quakerism and to remember the sufferings of the past, appeared in 1663. *A Testimony for God's Everlasting Truth, As it hath been learned of and in Jesus* (1669) stressed the Inner Light of the Quakers and justified it through the description of Christ as the light. In this pamphlet, RT described herself as old and expecting death, "waiting quietly on my weak bed for the revelation of his will whom I serve in my spirit day and night." But by 1677 she was still describing the deaths of others, this time of a young Quaker girl in *The Work of God in a Dying Maid: being A short Account of the Dealings of the Lord with one Su-*

sannah Whitrow. About the Age of Fifteen Years, and Daughter of Robert Whitrow of Covent-Garden in Middlesex. Published as a warning for those still healthy, the work described the child's sorrow for her past vanity and her hope that her mother too might die and leave the wicked world. The pamphlet quotes Whitrow's own words of longing for the afterlife and concludes with testimonies to her saintly end.   J.T.

TRIMMER, Sarah [Kirby] (1741–1810), educational writer, was born in Ipswich and educated at a girls' school in the usual female accomplishments; she read extensively in French and English literature and was especially known for her skill in reading aloud. In 1756 the Kirby family moved to London when her father, an architectural draftsman, was appointed instructor in perspective drawing to the Prince of Wales, later George III. Kirby afterward instructed Queen Charlotte in the same subject. In London the family moved in artistic circles, and were friendly with Hogarth, Gainsborough, and Reynolds. Through Reynolds, ST met Dr. Johnson. He was said to be impressed that she had a copy of *Paradise Lost* in her pocket at a party. In 1759 Kirby was appointed Clerk of the Works at Kew. There ST met James Trimmer (d. 1792) of Brentford, whom she married in 1762.

ST lived in Brentford until her death. She did not move in London literary circles, although she corresponded with various writers, including ELIZABETH CARTER and HANNAH MORE. Nine of her children survived her. The best known was probably Selina, who became governess to the nursery of Georgiana, DUCHESS OF DEVONSHIRE. ST educated both her sons and daughters herself, except for sending the boys to a neighboring cleric for instruction in Greek and Latin. The publication of ANNA LAETITIA BARBAULD's *Early Lessons for Children* (1778) persuaded ST to publish her own *An Easy Introduction to the Knowledge of Nature and reading the Holy Scriptures, adapted to the capacities of children* (1780), a formal presentation of some of the material she used for her own children. This work went through many later editions. A devout evangelical Anglican, ST published several religious works for children, including *Sacred History* (1782), *Abridgements of the Old and New Testaments* (1793), and commentaries on the Catechism and Prayer Book.

ST was an early activist in the Sunday school movement. Her own school at Brentford was very successful; she was consulted by Queen Charlotte on setting up a similar institution at Windsor. In 1787 ST published *The Oeconomy of Charity,* a handbook for the establishment of such schools and their curricula. Her interest in the education of the "lower orders" continued. In 1788–89 she wrote and published *The Family Magazine* for "cottagers and servants," which included abridgements of sermons and instructive tales to encourage both patriotism and contentment. A volume of stories from this publication appeared in 1810 as *Instructive Tales.* ST apparently introduced the idea of teaching small children through illustrations as well as texts, and also compiled spelling books (one for girls and one for boys) for charity schools. From 1802 to 1806 she published *The Guardian of Education,* which in addition to moral essays included critical reviews of books for children and works on education.

ST's best known work is her *Fabulous Histories, designed for the Instruction of Children, respecting their treatment of animals* (1786), adaptations of which are still to be found in children's libraries. The book is didactic, clearly written, easily understood, and lively. ST did not approve of fairy tales, but she understood a child's interest in giving animals human traits, and was one of the first writers to attempt to educate children in the proper treatment of animals. *Fabulous Histories* concerns children who encounter, first, a family of robins in their own garden, and then other birds and animals as they explore neighboring farms and the countryside. It was the robin family that caught the fancy of most readers; by 1818 *History of the Robins* was the subtitle, and by 1819 it was the only title for the book; in later 19th- and 20-century editions only the robins section remains. ST's autobiographical work, *Some Account of the Life and Writings of Mrs. Trimmer* (1814), which was largely religious in content, conveys only a little of what must have been her pedagogical ability. B.B.S.

TROTTER, Catharine [Cockburn] (1679–1749), dramatist, poet, and moral and philosophical essayist, was born in London and attracted public notice as an adolescent because she wrote the first tragedy to be produced on the stage by a woman since APHRA BEHN. CT was the younger of the two daughters of Captain David Trotter and Sarah Ballenden, connected to the noble Scottish Ballenden family, as well as to the Maitlands and Drummonds. After her Jacobite father died unexpectedly from the plague on an expedition to Scanderoon following a distinguished career, the family was forced into a life of genteel poverty, dependent on connections and the promise of an Admiralty pension, which the death of Charles II temporarily delayed. Not until the accession of Queen Anne did the family finally receive the modest pension of £20 a year. These penurious years undoubtedly provoked the frequent reference to money in CT's writings and quite likely affected her choice of career. As part of her education she taught herself French and studied Latin and logic which helped her with her philosophical explorations. Despite her Protestant upbringing, she joined the Roman Catholic faith as a young woman, but reconverted to Anglicanism in 1707. In 1693 her first literary works appeared: a poem to celebrate a recovery from smallpox, and an epistolary tale, "Olinda's Adventures," which appeared anonymously in a miscellany of the bookseller Samuel Briscoe and was translated into French by 1695. Although the name "Mrs. Trotter" appears in the 1718 and 1724 editions, her authorship remains disputed. In 1695, CT's first tragic play, *Agnes de Castro,* was performed at the Theatre Royal, Drury Lane, to an enthusiastic audience. The following year it was printed anonymously and dedicated to Charles, Earl of Dorset. Owing to the influence of William Congreve, whom she met after her dramatic success, her next tragedy, *Fatal Friendship,* was produced in 1698 at the Lincoln's Inn Theatre. Dedicated to Princess Anne, its moral framework suggested that CT sympathized with the denunciation of stage immorality made in a 1698 essay by the non-juring clergyman Jeremy Collier; he admired the play. CT's contribution to the collective elegy *Nine Muses; or Poems Written by as many Ladies Upon the Death of the Late Famous John Dryden* suggests her public recognition as a writer. So does the supportive friendship of LADY PIERS, another contributor to the elegy and possibly a patron. Lady Piers wrote a prologue in 1701 to CT's next play, *The Unhappy Penitent,* which was produced at Drury Lane. Dedicated to Lady Piers, Trotter's only comedy, *Love at a Loss, or most votes carry it,* received a much cooler reception the following year, but she was to revive it with another title many years later. Not long after this disappointment, she went to live in Salisbury with her married sister and became close friends with Bishop Burnet's family. Through the Bishop's brother George, CT met John Locke, Nicolas Malebranche, and the French writer, Anne Lefevre Dacier. She also met John Norris, friend and correspondent of MARY ASTELL. In 1701 CT completed *A Defence of Mr. Locke's Essay on Human Understanding* (1702), which she sent to Leibnitz. After its publication, Locke sent her a gift of books in appreciation. In 1703 she wrote a letter (since lost) on the truth of the Christian religion. Through this activity, CT succeeded in establishing herself as a notable participant in European philosophical controversies. Her noble connections, as well as her intellectual curiosity, explain the correspondences she initiated with contemporary luminaries. She was so well acclaimed by this time that in 1704 Queen Sophia Charlotta of Prussia described her as the new "Scots Sappho" in a letter to George Burnet. In the same year CT wrote a poem to the Duke of Marlborough after his victory at Blenheim. Despite medical problems, CT was composing another play one year later. Dedicated to Marlborough's daughter Harriet Godolphin, *The Revolution in Sweden* flopped when it was produced at the Queen's Theatre in the Haymarket. In early 1708 she married a young Scottish clergyman, Patrick Cockburn, who resorted to teaching in an academy in Chancery Lane after he had refused to take the oath of abjuration in 1714 and was denied curacies for more than a decade. In the course of bearing and raising four children in straitened circumstances, CT's literary pursuits fell off considerably. She did, however, begin to revise her plays and she maintained a lively interest in literature: the writings of Pope and Dr. Samuel Clarke, whom she considered the greatest English metaphysician, particularly appealed to her. After Locke was again attacked, she came to his defense in an essay entitled *Vindication of Mr. Locke's Christian Principles* (1727). In 1732 she wrote a poem, "The Busts set up in the Queen's Hermitage," the Hermitage being Merlin's grotto which Queen Caroline had constructed at Richmond Lodge. In this poem she championed women's rights, including their right to earn their own living and proclaim their ideas. The Queen died before CT could find a person willing to present her with the poem, which was later printed in an altered version in the *Gentleman's Magazine* (May 1737): "Learning

deny'd us, we at random tread / Unbeaten paths, that late to knowledge led; / By secret steps break thro' th' obstructed way, / Nor dare acquirements gain'd by stealth display. / If some advent'rous genius rare arise, / Who on exalted themes her talent tries, / She fears to give the work, tho' prais'd, a name, / And flies not more from infamy than fame." In 1737 she wrote an essay upon moral obligation which appeared in the *History of the Works of the Learned* (1743). Her *Remarks upon Some Writers in the Controversy Concerning the Foundation of Moral Obligation* was begun in 1739 and finished in 1740. Two years before her death, despite incapacitating asthmatic attacks and deteriorating eyesight, she penned *Remarks upon the Principles . . . of Dr. Rutherforth's Essay . . . in Vindication of the Contrary Principles . . . of the late Dr. Samuel Clarke* (1747). Before she could publish her works by subscription, she died and was buried beside her husband and youngest daughter at Long Horsley near Morpeth, where Patrick Cockburn had served as curate during his final years. In 1751, Dr. Thomas Birth published her collected works, including miscellaneous pieces, letters, and poems.

Heroic tragedy was CT's major genre. *Agnes de Castro,* an orthodox fusion of court intrigue and heroic ideals, borrowed its theme from a French novel. In *Fatal Friendship,* a long pathetic tragedy also in blank verse, she introduced a domestic setting. *The Unhappy Penitent* focused conventionally on misunderstandings of love and honor, and enjoyed a success beyond *The Revolution in Sweden,* in which CT proclaimed her desire to reform the stage. In *The Female Wits: or the Triumvirate of Poets at Rehearsal,* a lampoon of CT, MARY PIX, and DELARIVIÈRE MANLEY, CT's flaunted intellectual pretensions were ridiculed, while her inclusion suggested her contemporary reputation as a scholar and playwright. One of the reasons for the lampoon was the support women dramatists extended to each other in their prefaces, which, by aiding unity, helped in their economic survival. CT's serious and vigorous correspondence with advanced philosophers of the age, such as Locke and Leibnitz, marked her as an intellectual woman, perhaps as much if not more than her other creative and ethical writings. She had a deep respect for philosophy, and in her late *Advice to a Son,* for example, she suggests its efficacy in training the mind;

she encourages her son to read Hugo de Groot and Samuel Clarke, with wisdom through self-improvement as a goal. ST was mindful of the triviality of most women's lives; in her *Vindication of Mr. Locke's Christian Principles,* for instance, she asserts: "Quadrille should then resign the tyrant sway, / Which rules despotic, blending night with day, / Usurps on all the offices of life, / The duties of the mother, friend, and wife. / Learning with milder reign would more enlarge, / To nobler aims improve the vacant hours / Be Newton, Clarke, and Locke thcir mattadores." CT peppered all her writings both in her early more prolific period and in her sparser later period with a defense of female intellectuality, capacities, and talents. M.F.

TUITE, Eliza Dorothea, Lady (1764–?), poet, was the niece of the Countess of Moira, Baroness Hastings, to whom she dedicated the 1796 edition of her poems. The Countess was probably the mother of Francis Rawdon Hastings, Adjutant-General to the British forces in America, who later became Commander in Chief in India. ET seems to have been living in Bath in 1796, perhaps in ill health and needing money, for in a prefatory letter to her aunt she indicates that her circumstances are far from ideal: "The relationship between us, is an honor I share with many; but the friendship that has so long united us, is one I partake of but with few—Circumstanced as we are, it can never be in my power to repay your kindness but by gratitude and affection . . . With the motive that induces me thus to appear before the public you are not unacquainted." *Poems by Lady Tuite* was published in London in 1796 (2nd ed. 1799). A third edition, with additions, was published at Bath in 1841 under the title *Miscellaneous Poetry.* ET also published a tale for young people, *Edwin and Mary* (1838). In addition to the usual occasional verse, *Poems* includes 16 songs in a wide variety of stanzaic forms. Both poems and songs tend to be patriotic in theme, with some of the longer poems providing vivid descriptions of social corruption and advocating reform. "Written at the Close of the Year 1794" gives an amusing picture of current fashions in dress. The young men "Do not take too much pains to dress, / (For that they have not time to spare, / A *Beau* disdains to comb his hair) / With breeches, half-way down their legs, / Coats loose, as tho' they hung on pegs, / Huge stocks their beardless chins to hide, / Huge

cudgels, dangling by their side, / Gigantic hats, on pigmy shoulders, / Enough to frighten all beholders." The author condemns this vanity, stating a few lines later: "Our gallant soldiers bleed in vain, / While luxury's destructive band, / Thus, locust-like, pollute the land." Another predominant theme is friendship. Following an apparently traumatic experience, alluded to only obliquely in a few poems, ET seems to have turned to a close friendship with an unnamed woman. In "To a Friend, Written, 1782," she writes, "The hand of friendship shall my sorrows heal. . . . Let Friendship then be hence my only theme, / For Hope is vain, and Love's an idle dream." The woman to whom these lines were addressed died before 1796, apparently while still quite young, and one of the longest poems in the collection is a moving elegy written to her memory; there is also a short poem titled "To the Memory of My Best Friend." J.F.

TURELL, Jane (1708–35), American poet, diarist, and letter writer, was born in Boston, the daughter of Benjamin Colman, the first liberalizing Puritan minister in Massachusetts. Educated by her father, JT was both intellectually precocious and early occupied with religious matters. In 1726 she married Ebenezer Turell, minister of Medford, Mass., where she lived until her death. Of her four children, only one survived her. Like Colman, Turell encouraged her intellectual development, but he, too, was primarily concerned with her spiritual state. Although she wrote regularly early in her marriage, JT apparently composed less poetry in later years, as she concentrated on spiritual self-examination. "I find my Inclinations to *Poetry* still continue, tho' I hope I do not follow them to the omitting more necessary Things," she wrote in 1731.

Only 15 poems of JT survive, published after her death, along with the only samples of her prose, in *Reliquiae Turellae, et Lachrymae Paternae. The Father's Tears over his Daughter's Remains. Two Sermons . . . To which are added, Some large Memoirs of her Life and Death by her Consort, the Reverend Mr. Ebenezer Turell, M.A. Pastor of the Church of Medford* (Boston, 1735). Additional biographical background is available in Ebenezer Turell's *The Life and Character of the Reverend Benjamin Colman, D.D.* (Boston, 1749). Her husband omitted from the *Memoirs* poems he thought too light or witty. The dominant religious concerns in the fairly simple, derivative poetry, are evident in her first lines (1718): "I fear the Great *Eternal One* above, / The God of Grace the God of Love," and in her last, an elegy on her mother (1731): "O *Quickening Spirit!* now perform thy Part, / Set up thy Glorious Kingdom in my Heart." The theme of poetry is also striking. "To my Muse" (1725), probably referring to her contemporaries, KATHERINE PHILIPS and ELIZABETH (SINGER) ROWE, reveals JT's aspiration to belong to a feminine poetic tradition: "O let me burn with *Sappho's* noble Fire, / But not like her for faithless Man expire. / And let me rival great *Orinda's* Fame, / Or like sweet *Philomela's* be my Name." In "On reading the Warning by Mrs. Singer," she praises Elizabeth Rowe ("Philomela"), a poet her father admired, and perhaps suggested to her as a model: "Inspir'd by Virtue you could safely stand / The fair *Reprover* of a guilty Land. / You vie with the fam'd *Prophetess* of old, / Burn with her Fire, in

the same Cause grow bold. / . . . A *Woman's* Pen strikes the Curs'd *Serpents* Head, / And lays the Monster gasping, if not dead."

JT's diary and letters reveal religious desire mixed with self-doubt, as in a 1732 entry: "I bless God that I have experienc'd more outgoings of Soul towards my Savior . . . to Day, and more of the divine Afflations comforting me and refreshing me than ever in my Life before. *I return'd home fill'd with Joy and Praise.* I think I could see my Interest in Christ, and the Father's reconciled Face shining on me. *My Beloved is mine and I am his! All things are mine!* O my God and Savior, let not this my Hope and Joy be that of the *Hypocrite* which shall perish; but that of the *Righteous* which abideth for ever." JT's more-flamboyant sister Abigail Colman Dennie (1715–45) rebelled against their father but ended her life with him after an imprudent marriage; she also wrote poetry, but only one short verse letter to JT seems to have survived.   R.R.F.

U-V

UPTON, Catherine (fl. 1780s), poet, grew up in Nottingham. She moved to Gibraltar probably as the wife of a soldier. Possibly widowed, she was left with several children, whom she endeavored to support by writing and teaching; in her book she calls herself "governess of the Ladies Academy" at Bartholomew Close. In 1784 she had printed *Miscellaneous Pieces in Prose and Verse; by Mrs. Upton, authoress of the Siege of Gibraltar*, dedicated to General Boyd, the governor of Gibraltar; she claims that she is writing not for fame but "to *support my children.*" The preface takes issue with the critics of "The Siege of Gibraltar" who have blamed it for poor language and versification; CU's defense is that, when Dryden and Pope take liberties with meter, they are praised, where she is criticized because she is "a *woman,* who pretends to no learning at all." Reviewing the work, *Critical Review* (October 1785) conceded a slightly different point: "Ladies seldom receive candid treatment from critics. The jealousy of the tyrant, who fears to be invaded on his despotic throne, is not less fatal than the complaisance of those tender judges who respect the sex, and all its errors." "The Siege of Gibraltar," first published in 1781, describes in pedestrian verse the Spanish attack on the British, "that terrific sight, / When Bourbon's force, array'd in warlike plight, / Rush'd on the waves, and cover'd all the bay." Other poems mention current events and leaders, although CU claims she is barred by her sex from writing much on politics. There are verse letters as well, including a rather engaging one called "A Letter from the Authoress in London to her Father in Nottingham" which describes CU's London life: "My love for scribbling still torments me here. / Though rattling coaches stun my ears with noise, / Whilst louder chimney-sweep discordant cries." CU's volume includes children's verse and prose passages; one concerning love and marriage shows irritation at the double standard which requires virtue only in women, while another on education, much approved by *CR*, pleads for more kindness in instruction and a separating of "teacher" and "tyrant." J.T.

VAN SCHURMAN, Anna Maria (1607–78), poet and polemical writer, was born in Cologne, the only daughter of Frédéric á Schurman (d. 1623) and Eve de Harf, both of noble families and professed members of the Reformed Church. AMVS's father, recognizing her vast talent, allowed her to develop without any particular formal training. She could read at three, and went on to distinguish herself as the most accomplished woman of 17th-century Europe. As a child and adolescent, AMVS enjoyed the advantages of two formally educated brothers, one of whom studied under Amesius. She excelled in the fine arts: her precise paper-cutting work is preserved in the Schurman Museum, Franeker, and she was accomplished on the violin and lute. AMVS's virtuosity as a linguist was predictable from her early skill in writing foreign alphabets. By the age of 30, she had begun serious study in languages, philosophy, and theology, and went on to master Latin, Greek, English, French, Italian, German, Ethiopian, Oriental languages, and Hebrew. She was equally gifted in the sciences. Among other scholars and musicians, her associates included Descartes, a close friend; Gisbert Voët, rector of the University of Utrecht, who taught her Hebrew; Dr. Rivet, a professor of theology, Leyden, and dedicatee of her *Dissertatio* (1641); John Amos Komensky (Comenius), Czech philosopher, educationist, and early influence; and Jan van Beverwijck, who oversaw the publication of much of AMVS's work and who dedicated his own feminist treatise, *De Excellentia Sexus Foeminei* (1639), to her. A modest woman, AMVS's friendship with eminent scholars took the form of a substantial correspondence from her small cottage in Utrecht. One woman friend and correspondent was BATHSUA MAKIN. From 1650, AMVS abandoned her studies and turned exclusively to theology, particularly mystical religion. She was attached to Jean de Labadie (1610–74), a controversial French theological writer and former Jesuit, and became a prominent member of his separatist religious community at Altona, which practiced principles of Quietism and Pietism. AMVS died at Weiwert.

AMVS's principal works include *Dissertatio, De ingenii muliebris ad doctrinam et meliores litteras aptitudine* (1641), translated into English by C[lement] B[arksdale] as *The Learned Maid* (1659); *Opuscula* (1642): self-portrait, *De vitae termino, Dissertatio, Epistolae, Poemata, Lettres; Question Célèbre* (1646); and ΣΤΚΛΗΡΊΑ (*Eukleria*) (1673; on Labadism). Genres represented in AMVS's work include the *dissertatio,* informal essay, and poetry (panegyric, epigram). Her principal feminist work, the *Dissertatio* of 1641, is a scholarly and syllogistically organized treatise asserting woman's capacity for scholarship and public roles, and refuting objections raised by adversaries, such as "Women are of weak Wits." The treatise reflects assumptions and arguments of 17th-century feminist thought, and concludes with a proposal for a classical educational model for females, featuring the liberal arts and sciences, previously offered only to males: "Our *Maid* should [not] be excluded from the Scholastick Knowledge and Thinking of those [Studies]; especially not from . . . *Politicks* or *Civil Government.*" Estimates of AMVS by English and European contemporaries note her intellect, virtuosity, and comeliness. *Gentleman's Magazine* (1761) praised her early artistic achievements. B[arksdale] describes her *Dissertatio* as a "*discourse* . . . very rational, and much tending to the *perfection* of [the female] Sexe." John Dunton in *Petticoat-Government* (1702) refers to AMVS as an outstanding "Philosopher, Poet, and Painter." Beverwijck described her as the most wonderful woman of her epoch. Caspar van Baerle eulogized her as "a second Sempronia, a better Sappho, a new Pallas." Jacob Cats wrote poems to AMVS as the age's "*Wunderkind.*" AMVS showed 17th-century Europe that a woman could, indeed, be scholar. She contributed inestimably to the status of learned women, and the evolution of early English feminist thought in particular. Her advanced views concerning larger educational opportunities for females demonstrably influenced the work of Bathsua Makin, whose own polemical tract, *An Essay to Revive the Antient Education of Gentlewomen* (1673), follows AMVS's *Dissertatio* in form and content. B[arksdale] states that his *Learned Maid* is the second English translation of the *Dissertatio,* revealing that, within 18 years of its publication in 1641, AMVS's treatise was forceful enough to go through two English editions. AMVS's objections to arguments of woman's superiority to men, advanced in works by such 17th-century *femmes savantes* as Mmes. Marinella, Gournay, and Guillaume, are recorded in her more egalitarian views on relations between the sexes.   M.M.

VANE, Frances Anne, Viscountess (1713–88), autobiographer, was the daughter of Francis Hawes, South Sea director of Purley Hall near Reading. Endowed with little fortune but much beauty, FV married first a poor nobleman and then the second Viscount Vane. Such were her extravagances and amorous adventures that she became an object of scandal. She spent the last 20 years of her life in bed, incapacitated by disease. FV paid Smollett to include her *Memoirs of a Lady of Quality,* written with the help of Dr. Shebbeare, in his *Peregrine Pickle* (1751). "This most impudent and repulsive narrative" as the *Dictionary of National Biography* calls it, fails to reveal any "rudiments of good feeling," but a certain Roxana-like resilience makes it not entirely unengaging. Indeed, art often seems to have invaded life: "Never was passion more eager, delicate, or unreserved, than that which glowed within our breasts. Far from being cloyed with possession of each other, our raptures seemed to increase with the term of our union."   J.H.

W

WAKEFIELD, Priscilla [Bell] (1751–1832), educational writer and philanthropist, was born in Tottenham, Middlesex, of a notable Quaker family. PW raised one daughter, two sons, and various grandchildren (her extant journals report on daily family matters). When she was 40, her husband Edward, a London merchant, fell on hard times, and her sons were in financial need, so PW began writing books. She wrote 17 during a 20-year period (a Quaker sense of service marked her other activity, social reform, as it did that of her niece, Elizabeth Fry, for female prison reform). PW established a lying-in charity for women in Tottenham and in the 1790s a Female Benefit Club and a Penny Bank for children, which together developed into the first savings bank (known as a "frugality bank") in England. PW strongly supported Joseph Lancaster's monitorial method for educating children. Her special interest was in enlarging educational and occupational opportunities for women; she made her views in this area known through her book on female education, through letters to the editors of various journals, and through reports on her philanthropic projects, which were published in volumes of *Reports of the Society for Bettering the Conditions and Increasing the Comforts of the Poor*. In later life, she moved to Ipswich, where she valued highly the company of ELIZABETH COBBOLD and the elderly CLARA REEVE. PW's last 15 years brought increasing illness and incapacity.

PW's writings include instructional dialogues, moral tales, and travelogues. In these books, principally for an audience of young people and their mothers/parents/governesses/teachers, she combines moral instruction with amusement. In *Mental Improvement: Or, The Beauties and Wonders of Nature and Art* (1794; 9th ed. 1814), father and children hold evening conversations on natural objects and their uses. *Leisure Hours: Or, Entertaining Dialogues, Between Persons Eminent for Virtue and Magnanimity* (1794–96; 7th ed. 1821) contains lessons about moderation and toleration through examples from history. *Juvenile Anecdotes, Founded on Facts* (1795–98; 8th ed. 1825) presents moral tales based in everyday life, such as "The power of a school-boy to relieve the unhappy." A later book, *Sketches of Human Manners, Delineated in Stories, Intended to Illustrate the Characters, Religion, and Singular Customs of the Inhabitants of Different Parts of the World* (1807; 7th ed. 1826), tells of people who, encountering troubles on life's path, finally arrive at wisdom and piety. PW also wrote texts on natural history for young people, and her books were among the first by a female author for this emerging, specialized market. Her texts on natural history are *An Introduction to Botany* (1796; 11th ed. 1841), *Domestic Recreation: Or, Dialogues Illustrative of Natural and Scientific Subjects* (1805), *Instinct Displayed, in a Collection of Well-Authenticated Facts, Exemplifying the Extraordinary Sagacity of Various Species of the Animal Creation* (1811), and *An Introduction to the Natural History and Classification of Insects* (1816). PW's best-known work was the first of her six travelogues, *The Juvenile Travellers: Containing the Remarks of A Family During A Tour Through the Principal States and Kingdoms of Europe* (1801; 19th ed. 1850). In the preface PW explains that writing travel books for young people means sidestepping the "immoral tendency" found in adult travelogues; the parental interlocutors in her narrative take their 12- and 14-year-old children on a European tour "with the hope of increasing their knowledge, and promoting their general improvement." The success of this format led PW to write other travel volumes, all based, like her first, on armchair study: *A Family Tour Through the British Empire: Containing Some Accounts of Its Manufacture, Natural and Artificial Curiosities, History and Antiquities* (1804; 15th ed. 1840), *Excursions in North America* (1806), and *Perambulations in London, and Its Environs* (1809). Two later travelogues follow the adventures of the son of a fictional family, already known to her readers from earlier books, as he journeys around Africa (*The Traveller in Africa*, 1814) and to India and China (*The Traveller in Asia*, 1817). Her travel books contain frequent criticism of superstition, bigotry, slavery, and anti-female practices throughout the world. PW's educational interest in young people expressed itself in two other genres: biography in *A Brief Memoir of the Life of William Penn* (1816), and the miscellany in *Variety: Or, Selections and Essays, Consisting of Anecdotes, Curious Facts, and Interesting Narratives, with Occasional Reflections* (1809). She declares in the latter that "the female sex will be the object of my peculiar attention," and indeed her commitment to improving women's lot is clear throughout her books for juvenile readers and in her one book for an adult audience: *Reflections on the Present Condition of The Female Sex, With Suggestions for Its Improvement* (1798; 2nd ed., with additions 1817). This belongs to the ameliorative mode of 18th-century thought on women. She argues forcefully for enlarging female intellectual and occupational opportunities, to enable women to work toward economic independence, but she believes that gender differences are "in the Order of Nature"; she believes, further, that women should be trained according to their class: "There are many branches of science, as well as useful occupations, in which women may employ their time and their talents, beneficially to themselves and to the community, without destroying the peculiar characteristic of their sex, or exceeding the most exact limits of modesty and decorum." Her vocational suggestions include teaching girls (and training them to teach, in special female seminaries), painting portraits and hand-coloring prints, serving in retail shops which sell female merchandise, and, interestingly, farming.

PW's books were reviewed widely, favorably, and regularly in periodicals, especially in the *British Critic* and *Monthly Review* (e.g., "The publications of this accomplished female, would of themselves form a respectable Juvenile Library"). PW herself was commended in her day for the power of her personal example (see *The Ladies' Monthly Museum*, 1818), and *GM* declared in her obituary: "In her efforts to improve the rising generation, by the publication of useful books for their perusal, she was eminently successful."   A.B.S.

WALLACE, Eglinton [Eglantine], Lady (?–1803), playwright, poet, and pamphleteer, was the youngest daughter of Sir William Maxwell, a Scots baronet. Beautiful, witty, and unconventional, she unsettled the many men she enchanted by her assumption of personal freedom and equality. "The woman content in the approbation of her own mind indulges an open sincerity often mistaken for the boldness of a woman of multiplied vices," she wrote to her son in 1792. She married Thomas Dunlop-Wallace, self-styled baronet of Craigie, in 1770 but divorced him in 1778 on the grounds of various adulteries. Educating men to honor and women to virtue and inner resourcefulness through an equal classical training became her most insistent theme. By 1787 EW figured in the social and literary life (as well as in the newspapers) of London, as she had in Edinburgh, but when her comedy, *The Ton*, was canceled before a fourth performance, she migrated to the Continent. Although she had committed women to "social retirement" in *A Letter to a Friend*, 1787, she was arrested in Paris as an English agent in October 1789; contracted a friendship at Brussels with Gen. Charles François Dumouriez in 1792; and on a return to England wrote political pamphlets exalting him and the Hanoverian monarchy, which (drawing parallels with the French Revolution) she saw threatened by the libertinism of the aristocracy. After her third social comedy, *The Whim*, was denied the royal license, she returned to the Continent and died at Munich. The elder of her two sons was Gen. [Sir] John Alexander Dunlop Agnew Wallace.

Although tediously didactic, EW's plays are imitative of Restoration comedy in plotting, themes, and characters. *Diamond Cut Diamond* (1787) alone is sprightly, but it is an adaptation of a new French comedy. *The Ton, or, Follies of Fashion* (1788), which opened with a strong cast to a large house at Covent Garden in 1788, was reduced to pantomime by rioting at the second performance. EW, acknowledging a lack of action, charged that a cabal which feared exposure of its vices had plotted to damn the play as indecent. (Later critics taxed it with dullness.) *The Whim* (1795) reversed the roles of master and servants, directed witty barbs against legal justice and the "great," reaffirmed the obligations of class, and ended with two pages of patriotic speeches. It was suppressed, nevertheless, on political grounds, which EW protested in an address to the public. She may have exposed a royal intrigue or drawn characters too close to the life. Her other known works are *A Letter to a Friend, with a Poem called the "Ghost of Werter"* (75 rhymed couplets [1787]), which condemns the heroine for coquetry; *Letter from Lady W-ll-ce to Captain - - -* (1792), moral advice to her son thick with commentary on international affairs; *The Conduct of the King of Prussia and General Dumourier Investigated* (1793), which contains some autobiographical notes; and *A Sermon Addressed to the People, pointing out the only sure method to obtain a speedy Peace and Reform* (1798). A rationalist committed to Pitt and the Establishment although tolerant of other religions, except Roman Catholicism, EW saw herself as a true Briton, missionary to the nobility. Love was a trap and dallying contemptible; even honest passion was to be subdued because it endangered property and social organization. Consciousness of personal rectitude compensated for the many "disappointments of life." I.S.L.

WARDLAW, Elizabeth, Lady (1677–1727), poet, daughter of Sir Charles Halket, Bart., married Sir Henry Wardlaw, Bart., in 1696. She circulated what purported to be a fragment of an ancient ballad of *Hardyknute,* which she possibly wrote herself. In 1719 it was privately published in Edinburgh and subsequently appeared in six more editions. As an authentic example of an ancient Scottish epic *Hardyknute* was inordinately praised (see John Moncreif's notes to the first London edition, 1740). EW probably prepared the versions of two other Scottish ballads which appeared in Percy's *Reliques of Ancient Poetry* (1763), "Sir Patrick Spens" and "Gilderoy." Whatever the truth about the provenance of the ballads, it seems that EW is one of the first movers of the ballad revival. *Hardyknute* may be a composite of genuine fragments

substantially reworked; such reworking is in the spirit of 18th-century antiquarianism.   T.C.S.W.L.

WARREN, Mercy Otis (1728–1814), American poet, dramatist, and historian, was born in Barnstable, Mass., the third of thirteen children and first daughter of James and Mary (Allyne) Otis. James Otis followed a variety of professions; as a farmer, merchant, lawyer, judge of the county court, and colonel of the militia, he and his wife were able to raise their large family in comfort. The Otis sons received their education from their uncle, the Reverend Jonathan Russell; the Otis daughters had no formal education beyond the elementary level, but they were allowed to attend their brothers' lessons and had liberal access to their uncle's library. It was at her uncle's suggestion that MW first read Raleigh's *History of the World,* an undertaking which demonstrates an early intellectual bent and diligent character. This book is said to have influenced her own historical work, *History of the Rise, Progress and Termination of the American Revolution.* In 1754, MW married James Warren of Plymouth, Mass. Like MW, James had been raised by ardent democrats with a history of political involvement. Upon his father's death, he inherited the post of High Sheriff, a position he held until the outbreak of the Revolution. Before and during the Revolution, the Warren household served as a meeting place for many of the leading political figures of the day. MW was not only hostess to such men as George Washington, John Adams, and Alexander Hamilton, but also confidante and consultant. Her opinions on political matters were esteemed as much for their wisdom as for the eloquence with which they were delivered. A suggestion of hers that was met with particularly marked respect was for Massachusetts to send a legislative body to the Congress of 1765. In her own words, "By the Plymouth fireside were many political plans originated, discussed, and digested." MW also gained fame as the Revolutions' first lady of letters. In 1772 her first play, *The Adulateur,* appeared in installments in the Boston newspaper *The Massachusetts Spy.* She satirizes Thomas Hutchinson, the governor of Massachusetts and a lackey of the British, as Rapatio, the tyrant of a mythical land named Servia, whose inhabitants desire nothing but their liberty. The play was followed by two others similiar in style, *The Defeat* and *The Group. The Blockheads* and *The Motley*

Assembly are also attributed to MW, although their authorship is not definite. In 1790 she published *Poems, Dramatic and Miscellaneous*, which includes verse and two tragedies, *The Sack of Rome* and *The Ladies of Castille*, both of which were highly praised by Alexander Hamilton and John Adams. If there is one theme that percolates throughout MW's work, it is her passion for liberty and self-rule, as illustrated in this excerpt from *The Ladies of Castille:* "Not like the lover, but the hero talk— / The sword must rescue, or the nation sink, / And self degraded, wear the badge of slaves. / We boast a cause of glory and renown; / We arm to purchase the sublimest gift / The mind of man is capable to taste." In 1805, at 27, MW published her major opus, *History of the American Revolution*, in three volumes. This work is valuable not only as a chronicle of the Revolution, but also for its lively and candid depictions of the famous men and women who were her friends and associates. Although he had been among the first to encourage MW to write her account, John Adams was not pleased with her unflattering portrayal of his political ambitions. "History," he remarked to Elbridge Gerry, "is not the Province of the Ladies." MW lived to the age of 86 and, although she was afflicted with blindness, her intellectual powers remained intact. When 80, she was described by a visitor as erect in person and still possessing the intelligence and eloquence in conversation for which she was well known in her youth. She was buried at Burial Hill in Plymouth, Mass.   D.B.

WARTON, Jane (1723–1809), poet and prose writer, daughter of the poet Thomas Warton the Elder and sister of Joseph and Thomas Warton, was born in Basingstoke, Hants. By 18, JW contracted what was probably rheumatic fever and consequently remained a cripple for the rest of her life, which was spent as a governess or companion in various families. JW never married; she was close to those she served and especially to her own family, to whom she wrote often, offering encouragement and literary advice to her brothers. JW's domestic experiences and interest in the education of young women inspired her two major works.

JW wrote an ode on the death of her father, published in his posthumous *Poems on Several Occasions* (1748), and may have been the author of *Adventurer* 87 (1753), a paper on good breeding. Other evidence suggests she may have contributed essays and short poetry to periodicals, and we know she published in 1796 a tribute to her brother Thomas in the *European Magazine* and further commentary on him in the *Gentleman's Magazine* (April–May 1803). More important, manuscript discoveries have shown that she was the anonymous author of *Letters Addressed to Two Young Married Ladies, on the Most Interesting Subjects* (2 vols., 1782) and a novel, *Peggy and Patty; or, the Sisters of Ashdale* (4 vols., 1783; 2nd ed. 1784). *Letters* offers advice to women on such domestic and personal considerations as religion, fortitude, charity, economy, amusements, affection due to a husband, and education of children, especially young females. Clearly written, *Letters* frequently follows contemporary thought regarding a woman's role in the family and society, but also gives feminist hints: "In all things, I would have you shew a *firm steadiness* of action: . . . it gives a degree of spirit to a mild, timid nature, which has too often the appearance of insipidity; it will dignify you in the eyes of every one: whereas a giddy, wavering, dissipated manner, has always the contrary effect. . . . Our sex is, and ever will be, exposed to suffer, because we are always in a state of dependance. Men are naturally tyrannical; they will themselves have pleasure and liberty, and yet always expect we should renounce both." *Peggy and Patty* depicts the adventures and misfortunes of two sisters who "by the aid of the most hellish potions and brutal force" become "the miserable victims of the worst passions of the vilest libertines." The sisters lose sight of their basic goodness and morality and become casual prostitutes, who are left destitute to beg for sustenance. A return to virtue cannot save them, and thus they die in each other's arms. Although it is filled with signs of a beginning novelist (e.g., awkward diction and strained or maudlin scenes), the novel reveals a woman attempting to educate her readers to the villainies of mankind and to their effect on young women. The tinge of rebelliousness and bitterness in the *Letters* and *Peggy and Patty* make JW a far more interesting figure than any of her contemporaries, who knew her only as a governess or a dabbler in literature, could have imagined.   J.A.V.

WARWICK, Mary Rich, Countess of (1624?–78), devotional writer and Puritan autobiographer, was born in Youghal, Ireland, seventh daughter of Richard Boyle of an old Herefordshire family, who rose to considerable wealth and eminence in Ireland, finally becoming the first Earl of Cork. After the death of her mother, Catherine Fenton, when C of W was two, she was sent to Lady Clayton, a "prudent and virtuous lady" with whom she was "soberly educated" in Munster until the age of 11. At that time she moved with her family to their estate in Dorset, where at 13 or 14 she was approached for marriage by a suitor whom her father welcomed but whom she disliked: "my aversion for him was extraordinary, though I could give my father no satisfactory account why it was so." In response to her refusal, he cut off her allowance. Later she met Charles Rich, a younger son of the Earl of Warwick; they became intimate despite her knowledge that her father would disapprove, and he "did insensibly steal away my heart." In 1641, when she was 15, they were married, and shortly afterward her father was reconciled to the match and provided his daughter with a dowry, although a smaller one than he had intended. With her husband, C of W moved to the Warwick estate, Leigh's Priory, near London, and enjoyed a full social life close to the court. She had a daughter, who died in infancy, and a son. Her husband was involved in the parliamentary cause during the Civil War, although she disapproved of military action. During his absence she helped preserve the house from looting by soldiers. In about 1647 she was deeply upset by her son's illness; at this time she grew more pious and more inclined to Quietism, influenced by the household chaplain Anthony Walker, her "soul father." In 1658 Charles Rich became the Earl of Warwick. Shortly afterward he began to suffer from gout and his temper grew soured with pain. In 1664 their son caught smallpox and C of W reports: "I sat up myself with him, doing all I could both for his soul and body." When he died both parents were grief-stricken: "I confess I loved him at a rate that, if my heart do not deceive me, I could, with all the willingness in the world, have died either for him or with him, if God had only seen fit, yet I was dumb and held my peace, because God did it," C of W wrote. The remainder of her life was spent in charity and piety, entertaining Puritan clergy and helping unfortunate neighbors. Social life and family commitments (she brought up her husband's three nieces) constantly pressed against her desire for soli-

tude and communion with God. Her love of her husband was sorely tried by his choleric temper during his long illness, and she came to see her suffering as punishment for her disobedient marriage and for "my having ever loved that indeared relation from which I now met with so much unkindness." Yet he seems to have retained respect for her, and after his death in 1673 she was his sole executrix, while on her side she mourned his loss despite her ill treatment.

After C of W's death, Walker preached a sermon at Felsted, Essex, entitled *The Virtuous Woman found. Her loss bewailed, and character exemplified . . .* , published in 1678 "With so Large Addition as may be stiled The Life of that Noble Lady," together with some of her "Pious and Useful Meditations." The work, which praises C of W for her "exemplary Piety," quotes also from the diary she kept for 12 years and which Walker calls "the hasty fruit of one or two interrupted hours after Supper." Her autobiography from a manuscript of the 1670s entitled "Some Specialties in the Life of M. Warwick," said to have been written in two days, was published, along with selections from her diary, as *Memoirs of Lady Warwick: also her diary, from 1666 to 1672* by the Religious Tract Society in 1848. The autobiography is primarily an account of her spiritual life, but it describes as well a sociable existence led in high places, with mention of courtiers and statesmen to whom C of W was related. Existence becomes a tension between the demands of the political, social, and domestic worlds and her desire for spiritual communion: "I delighted in nothing so much as being alone in the wilderness, that I might there meditate of things of everlasting concernment." The diary is a much rawer document, full of repetitive piety and conventional Puritan rhetoric. Its devotional imagery is often extreme and C of W constantly searches for ecstasy, reviling herself when she cannot achieve it: "I begged earnestly of God that he would this morning enable me to offer up my heart as a burnt offering in flames of love to Christ" or I "did endeavour to storm heaven in my importunate prayers." Weeping over sins becomes a ritualized comfort. Although most of the diary concerns the fluctuations of pious emotions, there is also mention of mundane matters, and C of W well conveys the difficulties of a religious lady in the free-speaking Restoration period. In 1666 she notes a "Fast-day for the plague . . . my heart was carried out in earnest desire for pardon for my own and the nation's sins." The fire also comes as divine judgment, and she begs to be allowed to help quench it with her tears. Her own daily round is often interrupted by "a very great glut of company" and by the need for her attendance on dying relatives and friends. One constant theme of the diary is her ailing and choleric husband and the strife between her strong-minded piety and his profanity. Diary entries for 1667, for example, read "After supper, my lord being choleric, I was so foolish as to dispute with him . . . but yet, by Gods mercy, was kept from saying anything to him that was unfit"; and again, "He fell violently passionate against me, which made me, wicked wretch that I was! speak passionate words softly to myself, unadvisedly with my lips." She takes him to task and "with much respect, but with great plainness, tell[s] him of his wicked swearing"; by late in the year she was so worn down that she was declaring she would rather be dead than subjected to his torments, a view which she lengthily repents. For her friend George Berkeley, C of W wrote "Rules for Holy Living," praising few diversions, cheerfulness, "gaiety of goodness," and the ability to be alone: "the way not to be alone is to be alone." Her "Occasional Meditations" is an early example of pious effusions inspired by ethical rules, trivial domestic events, and rural sights; for example: "Upon observing a snail, that where so ever it crept, it left some skin."   J.T.

WELLS, Helena (1760?–?), American novelist, was born in Charlestown, S.C., of Scottish parents, Robert and Mary Wells. To escape the tumult preceding the American Revolution, the loyalist Wells family moved to England in 1774. Louisa Wells, HW's sister, voiced their feeling at their arrival: "I could have kissed the ground on the Salt Beach! It was my land . . . The Isle of Liberty and Peace." England did not prove as congenial as the Wells sisters had hoped, and they experienced economic hardships and problems adjusting to English life. In 1789, HW and Louisa opened a boarding school "for those gentlewomen of fortune who are without female relations to introduce them into life." Forced to give up teaching by ill health, HW turned to writing and between 1789 and 1800 published two novels and an advice book. Little is known of her life after 1800, except that she married a man named Whitford, bore

him four children, and spent some years in Yorkshire.

HW is a didactic writer whose chief concern is female education. Rejecting the notion that a gentlewoman should be raised to a life of leisure, she advocates a practical education that prepares a woman to handle financial matters, to speak clearly and correctly, and to be sensibly virtuous. Her orphan heroines, Caroline Williams in *The Step-Mother* and Constantia Neville in *Constantia Neville*, embody these values. The test of Caroline's upbringing comes when she must provide for her step-daughters after her husband's death. In the first volume of *The Step-Mother*, her trials are those of day-to-day living—maintaining her financial independence and arranging her daughters' education. In the second volume, the focus shifts from Caroline to the romantic intrigues of her daughters, and the novel becomes more melodramatic and less unified. In the second novel, probably based on some of HW's English experiences, Constantia's trials take place in the amoral world of fashionable society. Equipped with "habits of reflection," a knowledge of bankruptcy laws, and a balance of sense and sensibility, she resists various assaults on her affections and virtue until she finds an intelligent, loving husband. In both novels, action is subordinate to thematic concerns, and the plots are slow-moving and diffuse. In an apologia for her method, HW writes: "I trust the majority of readers . . . will pardon the exuberance of zeal which prompts a writer to express sentiments irrelevant to her subject . . . her aim is to impress on the minds of all, the blessing attending a religious practical education." The requirements for a "religious practical education" are also the central issue of HW's last two books, *Letters for Young Females* and *Thoughts on Institutions for Unportioned Respectable Females*. The former consists of letters of instruction and advice addressed to HW's pupils on such subjects as "correct pronunciation and judicious choice of words" and "courteous demeanor." In *Thoughts*, she proposes the establishment of Episcopalian girls' schools. She discusses such practical matters as their physical plan, the subjects of instruction, the teachers, and even the students' diet and exercise. HW's pragmatic approach to the problems of a young woman's education is the most interesting aspect of her works, especially her emphasis on financial independence.   D.M.C.

WESLEY, Susanna (1669?–1742), letter writer, was the youngest daughter and 25th child of Samuel Annesley. She married the Rev. Samuel Wesley c. 1690 and bore him 19 children, including John and Charles Wesley, founders of the Methodist movement, and MEHETABEL [WRIGHT]. Eleven of the children died young. A remarkable educator, SW taught her daughters as she taught her sons; girls should learn reading before needlework "for the putting children to learn sewing before they can read perfectly, is the very reason why so few women can read fit to be heard, and never to be well understood." Despite Samuel Wesley's tendency to fecklessness, he always insisted upon his male pre-eminence; husband and wife seldom thought alike. SW directed her children's spiritual life and extended her pastroal care to the parish when Wesley was away, considering that "though I am not a man, nor a minister, yet if my heart were sincerely devoted to God, and I was inspired with a true zeal for his glory, I might do somewhat more than I do." She began to talk to friends and neighbors "more freely and affectionately" than before; her talent was such that by these means she soon had a congregation of "above two hundred. And yet many went away, for want of room to stand." On his return, her husband was somewhat dismayed at her success and objected that her preaching looked "particular" because of her sex. To this objection SW replied, "I cannot conceive, why any should reflect upon you, because your wife endeavours to draw people to church and to restrain them from profaning the Lord's day, by reading to them, and other persuasions. For my part, I value no censure upon this account. I have long since shook hands with the world. . . . As to its looking particular, I grant it does. And so does almost any thing that is serious, or that may any way advance the glory of God, or the salvation of souls."

In copious correspondence with her famous sons (letters available in *The Works of John Wesley,* 1975–), SW encouraged the Georgia experiment and matched theological arguments with her own from George Herbert, Jeremy Taylor, Bishop Kendal, Pascal, and Thomas à Kempis. In 1742 John Wesley records his visit to his dying mother, whose looks were, in his words, "calm and serene, and her eyes fixed upward." He called her "in her measure and degree, a preacher of righteousness"; he quoted with pride her letters on her vocation and on her educating of her children. In a 1711–12 letter she describes herself as "mistress of a large family" with each soul "a talent committed to me under a trust, by the great Lord of all the families." Another quoted letter (August 1732) describes her method of encouraging self-restraint in children: "When turned a year old, (and some before,) they were taught to fear the rod and to cry softly," by which means "that most odious noise of the crying of children was rarely heard in the house." As soon as they could the children joined the family dinner, but "were never suffered to choose their meal, but always made to eat such things as were provided for the family." SW notes that "In the esteem of the world they pass for kind and indulgent, whom I call cruel, parents, who permit their children to get habits which they know must be afterward broken." To form their minds, "the first thing to be done," in her view, "is to conquer their will, and bring them to an obedient temper. . . . As self-will is the root of all sin and misery, so whatever cherishes this in children, insures their after wretchedness and irreligion: whatever cherishes and mortifies it, promotes their future happiness and piety."   J.T. and J.H.

WEST, Jane (1758–1852), novelist, poet, and playwright, was born in London. When she was 11 her family moved to Northamptonshire, where she spent most of her life. She married Thomas West, a yeoman farmer of Little Bowden, Northants., and had three sons. Self-educated, she began writing poetry at 13, and later wrote to help support her family. Although she insisted that her duties as housewife took precedence over writing, she produced a large body of literary work. She supported the Church and Tory politics. Her friends included Bishop Percy, Robert Nares, and SARAH TRIMMER. Sensitive about her low social status, JW took pride in her husband's relationship to Gilbert West and Admiral West. Her youngest son, Edward, died in 1821, and her husband in 1823.

JW wrote in various genres. She published *Miscellaneous Poems* (1780), *Miscellaneous Poetry* (1786), a long poem, *The Humours of Brighthelmstone* (1788), *Miscellaneous Poems and a Tragedy* (1791), an elegy on Burke (1797), and a set of poems and plays between 1799 and 1805. In one 1791 poem she expresses fear that a woman of her class ought not to waste time writing poetry, but defends her writing because of its moral aims. Her Muse's advice is "Give to morality thy noblest lays / And fix thy hopes, where time destroys no more." JW follows this advice in all her writing. Three novels, published in the 1790s, convey the message that women should stifle their feelings in the interests of duty. In *The Advantages of Education* (1793), Maria learns to reject an attractive, immoral suitor, and to choose duty and a virtuous husband instead. JW's mockery of the typical sentimental novel with its emphasis on love and its perfect heroine enlivens this work. JW's usual technique is simply to state her moral, and she expresses one of her favorite ideas with typical solemnity here: "it cannot be too often inculcated, that the neglect of those little humble duties, which many contemptuously refuse to admit into the family of the virtues, leads to serious habits of error." The contrast in *A Gossip's Story* (1796) between Marianne, ruined by excessive sensibility, and her sensible sister Louisa anticipates the theme of Austen's *Sense and Sensibility*. Prudentia Homespun, the gossiping narrator, adds humor to the novel. JW's anti-Jacobinism is explicit in *A Tale of the Times* (1799) whose villain, a seducer, supports the French Revolution. JW's career continued into the 19th century with two conduct books, *Letters to a Young Man* (1801) and *To a Young Lady* (1806), five more novels, another long poem, a children's story, a translation, and a volume of scriptural essays. Her last work is *Ringrove* (1827). JW's determination to instruct rather than entertain robbed her work of much potential merit. The *British Critic*'s commendation of her second novel is typical of the praise given her by contemporaries: "Genius is here employed in its proper station, namely, in the defence of virtue." J.S.

WEYLAR, Maria (fl. 1770), poet, published *Reveries du Coeur, or, Feelings of the Heart. Attempted in Verse* (1770), intending, she writes, to "*serve*, and, perhaps, save a distressed Relation." MW's poetry is conventional in subject and treatment, with a sentimental preference for the pastoral life. Her praise of Wilkes as a defender of liberty carries over into her "Song" on the condition of women: "We're curb'd like any head-strong beast, / And all our wishes bridled— / Born, all our youth, to be opprest, / Or be by some-one wheedled." "This lady," wrote a reviewer crushingly in *The Literary Magazine* (29), "may be a most valuable woman for ought we know to the contrary, but we do not think her reveries

is much calculated to give her a literary reputation." J.H.

WHARTON, Anne (?–1685), poet, born in Ditchley, Oxon., was daughter and co-heiress to Sir Henry Lee. Her marriage in 1673 to Thomas Wharton (later Marquis of Wharton), to whom she brought a large dowry, proved childless. Apart from a year in Paris (1680–81) because of ill health, AW lived quietly at Winchendon, sharing neither Wharton's lifestyle nor his Whig politics. In 1682, she was dissuaded from leaving him by her regular correspondent, Bishop Gilbert Burnet. Burnet also reprimanded AW for exchanging complimentary verses with the "abominably vile" APHRA BEHN in 1681–82. AW also exchanged poems with Burnet himself, Edmund Waller, and Robert Wolseley. Praised by contemporaries particularly for her verse paraphrases of Scripture, AW is now remembered chiefly for her few lyric poems. Although these were not printed in her lifetime, they had a considerable private circulation: Burnet, for example, sent them to all his female friends. Subsequently, they were published sporadically in miscellanies; her elegy for Rochester and a reply to Waller's commendation of her paraphrase of Isaiah: 53 appeared in Nahum Tate's *Poems by Several Hands* (1685) within a month of her death. Her song "Spite of Thy Godhead Powerful Love," first published anonymously in *Vinculum Societatis* (1687) with music by Purcell, was often reprinted, although sometimes, as in Nichols's *Select Collection* (1780–82), misidentified as the work of Lucy, Marchioness of Wharton, Wharton's second wife. Poems by and to AW were appended to Edward Young's *Idea of Christian Love* (1688), while her commendatory poem to Wolseley appeared in the miscellany appended to Behn's *Lycidus* (1688). Other poems were included in Gildon's *Miscellany Poems* (1692), in *A Collection of Poems* (or *The Temple of Death*) (1693, 1695, 1701), in *Poems on Affairs of State* (1697), and in Dryden's *Miscellany Poems* (3rd ed. 1702). Her "Paraphrase on the Lamentations of Jeremiah" was first printed in full in *Whartoniana* (1727). AW also translated the "Epistle of Penelope to Ulysses," published in Tonson's *Ovid's Epistles* (1716), and wrote a five-act blank verse tragedy, "Love's Martyr, or Wit above Crowns" (MS in the British Museum) on the theme of Ovid's love for Julia, which, although entered in the Stationers Register, February 1686, was never printed or staged. AW was accused by Burnet of expressing an "atheistical" despair in her writing and, while often religious or moral in theme, her poems do have a melancholy tone. "Verses on the Snuff of a Candle, Made in Sickness" begins: "See there the taper's dim and doleful light, / In gloomy waves silently rolls about, / And represents to my dim weary sight, / My light of life almost as near burnt out." To Burnet's further criticism of her failure to correct and revise her work, AW replied that she lacked the necessary peace of mind for the task. Like Wolseley, Behn noted AW's literary, as well as familial, kinship with Rochester; Waller, however, acclaimed AW's poems as the pious antidote to Behn herself.   R.F.

WHEATLEY, Phillis (1753?–1784), American poet, was born in Senegal, West Africa, apparently of Fulani origin, and was brought to Boston, Mass., on a slave ship in 1761. PW was purchased by John Wheatley, a prosperous Boston tailor, as a special companion for his wife, Susannah. PW was educated in the Wheatley home with the assistance of the children, Mary and Nathaniel; when 16, she joined the Old South Church of Boston, then led by the Rev. Dr. Sewall, later a subject of one of her poems. In a letter of November 1772 to the English publisher of PW's poems, John Wheatley wrote that "by only what she was taught in the Family, she, in sixteen Months Time from her Arrival, attained the English Language, to such a Degree, as to read any, the most difficult Parts of the Sacred Writings, to the greatest Astonishment of all who heard her." Included in her studies were Greek mythology, Greek and Roman history, English poetry, and Latin. By the age of 13 PW was writing verses, and in 1770 her first poem was published. Always in precarious health, PW was taken to England in 1773 by Nathaniel Wheatley in the hope that the sea voyage and English physicians might effect an improvement in her condition. (Some sources claim that PW was manumitted at this time, but others say at a later date.) In England, PW was cordially received, especially by Selina Hastings, COUNTESS OF HUNTINGDON, with whom she had previously corresponded. Here she was urged to publish her collected poems and, within the year, *Poems on Various Subjects, Religious and Moral* (1773) appeared in print. PW's visit to England was shortened by the news that her mistress Susannah Wheatley was seriously ill. PW returned to Boston just before

Susannah died. When John Wheatley died in March 1778 she was left to her own resources. By this time the Wheatley daughter had married, and the son was living abroad. In April 1778 PW married John Peters, a free Negro of Boston, who, although possessed of some intellectual attainments, was unable to provide for her and three children born to them in the next six years (all died in infancy). For the first time in her life PW was compelled to accept menial employment. Under the strain of heavy manual labor and child bearing, PW's health continued to decline, and she died alone, in poverty.

PW's earliest poems were "To the University at Cambridge in New England" (1767), a 30-line poem in blank verse; "To the King's Most Excellent Majesty" (1768), 14 lines of heroic couplets praising the King for the repeal of the Stamp Act; and the 50-line "On the Death of the Rev. Dr. Sewall" (1769). Her first published poem was an elegiac tribute to the famous revivalist of the Great Awakening, entitled "On the Death of the Rev. Mr. George Whitefield." This poem of 46 lines of heroic couplets includes an internal dedication to the Countess of Huntingdon, whom Whitefield had served as chaplain: "Great Countess, we *Americans* revere / Thy name, and mingle in thy grief sincere; / *New England* deeply feels, the *Orphans* mourn, / Their more than father will no more return." PW's departure for England in May 1773 prompted perhaps her most lyrical effusion, "A Farewell to America: To Mrs. S.W.": "Adieu, *New England's* smiling meads, / Adieu, the flow'ry plain: / I leave thine op'ning charms, O spring / And tempt the roaring main." The publication of *Poems on Various Subjects* created something of a sensation in European literary circles. Voltaire wrote: "There is actually a Negress who writes very good verse in English," and the Lord Mayor of London presented her with a rare edition of Milton. *Poems* contains 39 pieces, one-third of which are on the subject of death. Five are addressed to clergymen, and four others have religious themes. Only two of the poems in the collection reflect PW's origins, one a tribute to the slave-artist Scipio Moorhead, "To S.M., a Young African Painter, On Seeing His Works," and the other, "On Being Brought from Africa to America," the most personal reference to her own condition among her verses. In 1775 PW published "To His Excellency General Washington" in Thomas Paine's *Pennsylvania Magazine* on the occasion of Washington's appointment as Commander-in-Chief by the Continental Congress. After having read the poem, Washington invited the poet to meet him in Cambridge in 1776. In 1777 *Poems on Various Subjects* was published in America and elicited an accolade from Jupiter Hammon, a slave-poet, who wrote: "An Address to Miss Phillis Wheatley, The Ethiopian Poetess of Boston, Who Came From Africa at Eight Years of Age and Soon Became Acquainted With the Gospel of Jesus Christ." One of her last poems, and one of only two published under her married name (Peters), was "Liberty and Peace, a Poem" printed in pamphlet form in 1784. After her death, her verse continued to be reprinted, especially by the abolitionist press in the early years of the 19th century. PW's poetry is on the whole imitative and conventional in sentiment and diction.   B.B.W.

WHITE, Dorothy (fl. 1659–63), polemicist, wrote the Quaker tracts *This to be delivered to the counsellors that are sitting in Counsel* (1659), *Upon the 22 day of the 8th Month, 1659, A Diligent Search among Rulers, Priests, Professors, and People, and a warning to all sorts high and low, that are out of the doctrine of Christ, and fear not God* (1659), *Unto all Gods host in England* (1660), *Lamentation unto this Nation; and also a warning to all people* (1660), *An alarm sounded to Englands inhabitants, but more especially to Englands rulers* (1661), *An epistle of love and consolation unto Israel* (1661), *A trumpet of the Lord of Hosts blown unto the city of London* (1662), *A Call from God out of Egypt, by his Son Christ the Light of Life* (1662), *To all those that Worship in Temples made with Hands, but more especially to them of Pauls, as a Warning to them to Repent* (1663), and others. Her tracts present the new nonconformism in its most uncompromising aspect. *A Diligent Search* uses terroristic tactics in its effort to save souls: "a woful day is coming upon you, a day of terrible vengeance upon all that are found striking against the Lord, and resisting his spirit, a day of desolation, and of swift destruction, a cup of endlesse wrath will the Lord pour out upon you, unless you speedily repent." The *Lamentation* is a piece of vatic eschatology delivered as if by authority of God: "A GREAT and TERRIBLE DAY approacheth, and in the Eternal Authority of the *Lord God*, it doth lie upon me to sound it forth, fore-seeing in the Eternal

Power of the Lord of Heaven and Earth, that the Approach of the *Great* and *Terrible Day* cometh, and that very swiftly." The tract *To all those that Worship in Temples*, which is signed from the "Counter Prison in Wood-Street," is a polemic against idolatrous worship and an exhortation to people to search their hearts "by the Candle of God" and discover whether they are led "by the Spirit of Truth." DW's work is written in the tones and cadences of the Bible; it is unremarkable, but has its place in the history of belief.   R.J.

WHITE, Elizabeth (1637?–1699), American autobiographer, was probably born near Boston. She published only one book, which supplies most of the known facts of her life: *The Experiences of God's gracious dealing with Elizabeth White* (1696). Self-doubt, uncertainty, soul-searching, despair, and religious questioning are the focal points of the work. Revealing herself as an unusually sensitive, conscientious Puritan, she examines with merciless honesty her moments of spiritual crisis—at her marriage, the birth of her first child, the overwhelming love she felt for the babe when she weaned it—and after much distress she finds comfort and salvation in the reality of Christ. Like other spiritual autobiographies of the 17th century, such as that of BATHSHEBA BOWERS, this account frankly admits the recurrence of periods of doubt and visions of hell, but EW repeatedly repents and finds her peace by placing trust in Christ. Her life as a wife and mother in Puritan New England was obviously an extremely difficult one. The goals of perfection and unquestioning submission to every burden and disaster were at times not only unattainable but unacceptable. Perhaps writing about her doubts helped to purge them, for she ultimately resolves her dilemma and feels a spiritual reassurance.   M.P.

WILKINSON, Eliza Yonge (fl. 1775–83), American letter writer, was the well-educated daughter of Francis Yonge, a Welsh immigrant, who had settled on Yonge's Island near Charlestown, S.C., as a slave-plantation owner. Six months after her marriage to Wilkinson, EYW was widowed. In letters to her confidante, Miss M- - - P- - -, EYW gives a lively emotional account of her experiences at the hands of the British and American soldiers during the Revolutionary War; for example, a violent encounter with the British and a subsequent misunderstanding with some American soldiers whom she mistook for British. EYW's *Letters* (1839) concern the spiritual and mundane circumstances of a gentlewoman's life in a war situation. "Hope springs eternal" and other clichés characterize the optimistic spirit of her reflections. Her naiveté about the horrors of war is betrayed by her literary retreats to Homeric narrative, "poor old Priam, King of Troy", and the disparity between the violence she alludes to—"The whole world appeared to me as a theatre, where nothing was acted but cruelty, bloodshed, and oppression, where neither age nor sex escaped the horrors of injustice and violence; where the lives and property of the innocent and inoffensive were in continual danger, and lawless power ranged at large"—and the scale of her personal experience: "upon first entering the house, one of them gave my arm such a violent grasp, that he left the print of his thumb and three fingers, in black and white, which was to be seen, very plainly, for several days after." Despite her frequent hyperbole, EYW conveys the anxiety that comes from awareness of an inevitable attack. She makes clear her patriotism and armchair interest in politics, as well as her feeling of helplessness and anger. She worries about the propriety of a woman writing, especially when the events she chronicles seem so uncontrollable: "What will the men say if they should see this? I am really out of *my sphere* now, and must fly to Homer for direction and instruction on household matters."   D.S.G.

WILLIAMS, Anna (1706–83), poet and translator, was born in South Wales, the daughter of an eminent physician, Zachary Williams, whose serious but inaccurate study of longitude reduced them to near poverty when they resided in London in 1730. AW lost her eyesight in 1740 owing to cataracts; this handicap seems to have spurred the publication of her translation, *Life of the Emperor Julian*, with Notes (1746). Dr. Johnson and his wife took an interest in AW and arranged for an operation on her eyes, which unfortunately failed. After her father's death in 1751, AW became a permanent member of Dr. Johnson's household because of her friendship with Mrs. Johnson's daughter, Lucy Porter. For many years after Mrs. Johnson's death, AW maintained Dr. Johnson's household, and her devotion to him was unshakable. He, in turn, credited her with being "a very great woman" and, in recommending her plans for a dictionary

to Samuel Richardson, he claims that AW "is certainly qualified for her work . . . as she understands chimistry and many other arts with which Ladies are seldom acquainted," and concludes his appeal emotionally: "a being more pure from any thing vicious I have never known." Other contemporaries were more critical, finding her excessively rigid in morals and unsympathetic to the faulty. Her income of £40 per year was derived from the kindness of other women, including Lady Philipps (of Picton Castle) and ELIZABETH MONTAGU. Johnson also came to her aid by requesting that Garrick give her a benefit-night at his theater in 1756. After unwillingly defrauding her subscribers several times, and tiring of the procrastination of Johnson and Goldsmith, AW eventually engaged a substantial subscription list that enabled her to publish *Miscellanies in Prose and Verse* (1766). Johnson was deeply saddened to learn that AW died during his absence from the house at Bolt-Court, Fleet St.

AW's poetry is mostly sentimental and devotional, in the form of epitaphs, odes, and lengthy meditations. It displays a literate, well-read, derivative sensibility. Most of it is didactic; it recommends "The joys which from religion flow" (*To Clara*) and denounces the "loose wits of a degenerate age" ("Verses Addressed to Mr. Richardson"). Her longer meditations aspire to visions of "eternal rest" and salvation, and in "The Nunnery" she longs for the security of the cloister to be made available to English women. Her longing for isolation and her didactic insistence upon the divine purpose of human labor are exemplified in her epitaph "On the Death of Stephen Grey, F. R. S. The Author of the Present Doctrine of Electricity." Although she assisted him and was the first to observe "the emission of the electrical spark from a human body," she recoils from the secular implications of that knowledge. AW's speaker imagines Grey to have ascended to a heaven populated by scientists (Bacon, Newton, and Boyle) who scoff at the slow pace of human discovery; yet she concludes piously: "Unblest the man whom philosophic rage / Shall tempt to lose the Christian in the Sage." Conventional in both rhyme and purpose, AW's verse harmonized with her conversations as reported by the Johnson Circle.   D.S.G.

WILLIAMS, Helen Maria (1761?–1827), chronicler and novelist, was born in London, elder of two daughters of a Welsh army officer and a Scottish mother, Helen Hay.

Her father died when she was still a child, and the family moved to Berwick-on-Tweed, where HMW was educated by her mother and soon began writing poetry. By 1781 she had finished her long work *Edwin and Eltruda*, with which she arrived in London; Andrew Kippis, a noted Dissenting minister, helped her publish it in 1782. After its success, her mother and sister, Cecilia, joined her in the capital. A persistent socializer throughout her life, HMW was soon surrounded by a group of acquaintances and patrons from FANNY BURNEY, who thought her affected, to ELIZABETH MONTAGU and Samuel Johnson, who were charmed by her. She became a frequent correspondent of ANNA SEWARD, and she later wrote to Robert Burns. She continued publishing fashionable sentimental poetry, often condemning slavery and idealizing political victims; in 1784 appeared *Peru*, concerning the conquest of the Indians, and in 1786 a collection of *Poems*, which included hymns and the "Sonnet to Twilight," which Wordsworth admired and anthologized. HMW's poetry was so popular that several people addressed verse compliments to her, including George Harding, Anna Seward, and the young William Wordsworth. In 1790 she published her novel *Julia*, in which was embedded a poetic interlude "The Bastille," which enthusiastically approved the French Revolution. Soon she was to see it at first hand. In 1786 she and her sister had met the wife of a French aristocrat, Madame du Fossé, who had been forced to leave France because of the displeasure of her father-in-law, who had imprisoned his son. On the death of the father and the outbreak of the Revolution, the du Fossés invited the Williams sisters to France. Their story became for her an example of past French tyranny and revolutionary hope; it is told in her first volume of accounts. HMW arrived in France eager to be impressed, just before the Festival of the Federation, enthusiastically described in *Letters written from France in the summer of 1790*: "The impressions of that memorable day have determined my political opinions." The work was widely read in England, which was eager for first-hand details of the Revolution. Over the next 25 years HMW would cover in her impressionistic way all the major political events of France; her *Letters* were published often in single volumes and then reprinted together, with much overlap in material and titles. She returned to England in late 1790, but was back in France the following year, acquainted now with most of the Jacobin and Girondist leaders, her closest tie being with Madame Roland. Late in 1792 the Williams family made a third trip to France, and there is no evidence that HMW ever returned to England. By this time the breach between Girondists and Jacobins had widened, and HMW was clearly associated with the former, whose opinions influenced her accounts. She also knew many expatriate sympathizers with the Revolution, including Thomas Paine, Gilbert Imlay, and MARY WOLLSTONECRAFT; during the winter of 1793 HMW's salon in Paris was a frequent meeting place. She collaborated with John Hurford Stone and Thomas Christie in one of the volumes of her *Letters* dealing with the French campaign of 1792. The worsening events of this time formed the basis of her four volumes of *Letters from France 1792–6*, which alarmed her friends in England, who could not understand her constant support for the revolutionary principles, despite her horror at Jacobin violence. Her attitude alienated many of her earlier admirers, such as HESTER PIOZZI and Anna Seward, and her reputation in England quickly declined. In the summer of 1793 the Girondists were defeated, and Madame Roland and other close friends were guillotined. HMW and her family were arrested in the round-up of British subjects in Paris, and her months in prison, along with the accounts of her fellow prisoners, form part of her next series of *Letters*. The family was freed through Athanase Coquerel, nephew of her friend Madame du Fossé and later husband of Cecilia. In 1794 she witnessed the passing of Danton to execution. After a law barred strangers from Paris, the Williamses moved near Versailles. Later in the year, fearing persecution for her anti-Jacobin stand, HMW went to Switzerland, just before the French intervention; she was accompanied by Stone, with whom she had a long relationship, possibly a marriage, which also caused much adverse criticism in England. A problem for later ages is her activity at this time and later in Paris, where she still managed to keep a salon despite the comparative failure of her later books. Possibly she was a spy for England; certainly she was watched by the Jacobin and later Napoleonic police. HMW spent about six months in Switzerland, giving her impressions in *A Tour of Switzerland, or a View of the present State of the Governments and Manners of those Can-*

tons, with comparative *Sketches of the present State of Paris* (1798). After the fall of Robespierre, HMW returned to Paris and in 1795 attended the trial of Fouquier-Tinville, the public prosecutor. Working on her second series of *Letters*, she also translated *Paul et Virginie* by her friend Bernardin de Saint-Pierre; later translations included the seven volumes of Humboldt's travels. In 1798 her sister died and left two small sons in her care. Raised according to HMW's Dissenting views, both became distinguished French Protestant leaders. In *Sketches of the State of Manners and Opinions in the French Republic towards the Close of the Eighteenth Century* (1801), HMW described her life under the Directory and Consulate, expressing the usual irritation at the former's inefficiency. At first impressed with Napoleon, she later condemned his ambitions; in 1802 she offended him with an ode on the Peace of Amiens, in which she referred favorably to British sea power. She and her family were detained for a day by the police. In 1801 she published *Perourou, the Bellows-Mender*, a lively tale satirizing rank by presenting a comic misalliance; it was adapted for the stage by Edward Bulwar Lytton as *The Lady of Lyons*. During 1803 she edited the forged correspondence of Louis XVI, which she thought genuine, making observations on each letter to replace the French editor's favorable attitude to the King with her own republican bias; she was violently abused by British periodicals for her efforts. HMW grew more politically despondent as French designs became clearly imperialistic. In 1815 she published *Narrative of Events which have taken place in France from the Landing of Napoleon Bonaparte . . . till the Restoration of Louis XVIII*. She welcomed the end of the Empire, and after Waterloo she reopened her salon. By this time Stone had failed in his publishing venture, and she seems to have been the main provider of income. In 1819 her last work, *Letters on Events which have passed in France since the Restoration in 1815*, completed her account of turbulent French history. In 1818 Stone died, and HMW and a relative, Persis Williams, went to live in Amsterdam with her nephew. Later she returned to Paris to live on a small pension from her nephew.

HMW's poetry, later overshadowed by her chronicles, is conventional and fluent, much given to sentimental tableaux of dying relatives and of father and daughter re-unions. Two devotional poems beginning "Whilst thee I see, protecting Power! / Be my vain wishes stilled; / And may this consecrated hour / With better hopes be filled" and "My God! all nature owns thy sway, / Thou giv'st the night, and thou the day" became congregational hymns. As a novelist, HMW had some skill when she was not unremittingly sentimental. Wollstonecraft noted the power of *Julia*, while condemning its simple characterization of the noble heroine; the lighter *Perourou* shows where HMW's strength lay, although she wrote little in this vein. Her main productions are her chronicles of France. These do not purport to be histories, but are eyewitness accounts and impressions of events, in which personal feelings are interwoven with public incidents. There are few nuances of emotion: HMW almost invariably either enthusiastically approves or harshly condemns people and events. The early years of the Revolution seem to her "the age of chivalry" reconstituted, not "in its erroneous notions of loyalty, honour, and gallantry" but "in its noble contempt of sordid cares, its spirit of unsullied generosity, and its heroic zeal for the happiness of others." Later she describes with horror and no effort at comprehension the Jacobin atrocities, but finds something to admire in the deportment of the victims, especially the women: "Among the victims of the tyrants, the women have been peculiarly distinguished for their admirable firmness in death. Perhaps this arose from the superior sensibility which belongs to the female mind, and which made it feel that it was less terrible to die, than to survive the objects of its tenderness." Madame Roland is much praised as the ideal of noble womanhood, while Robespierre becomes "this sanguinary usurper," later to be reincarnated in Napoleon. Although her accounts record a slow growth of disillusion and, although by 1815 she could look back wryly on her extreme libertarian enthusiasm, HMW nonetheless held to her liberal principles throughout her life: "Liberty is innocent of the outrages committed under its borrowed sanction." While her early poetry and early political accounts were all reviewed and much appreciated, her later work was reviled by British periodicals, as was her own character. The *Anti-Jacobin Review* presented her as a personification of Lechery, and *Gentleman's Magazine* claimed she had "debased her sex, her heart, her feelings." Horace Walpole wrote her off as a "scribbling trollop," and Richard Polwhele scorned her as "an intemperate advocate of Gallic licentiousness." HMW is unlikely to have written *A Residence in France, during the years 1792, 1793, 1794, and 1795; described in a series of letters from an English lady* ... (1797), attributed to her, since its anti-revolutionary tone is less in keeping with her sentiments than with those of John Gifford, the ostensible editor.   J.T.

WILLIS, Lydia [Fish] (1709–67), American letter writer, was born in Duxborough, Mass. She seems to have been self-educated, and she found that her learning allowed her to enter "the best society that her rural situation and times afforded." She is said to have had "a taste for reading" that was "almost singular, and she excelled most of her sex in a relish for works of genius, books written in taste." She married the Rev. Eliakim Willis and lived first in Dartmouth, N.H., and then in Malden, Mass. Her three children were stillborn or died in infancy, and she became close to a niece with whom she corresponded. LW's letters were selected and published after her death as *Rachel's Sepulchre; Or, a Memorial of Mrs. Lydia Willis, taken, Chiefly, from her Letters to Friends,* probably in 1767. The work was republished in 1788 as *Madam Willis's Letters and her Character. With some Strictures of Madam Ann Stockbridge's and the Character of Sarah Page.* The letters are pious and melancholic, mainly concentrating on family miseries, such as deaths and illnesses. They are self-pitying and self-condemning, and a poem inserted in one of them laments SW's "wicked, stupid heart" and her benighted faith.   J.J.

WILSON, Rachel (1720–75), journal writer, was the daughter of John and Deborah Wilson; she was born and brought up at Kendal in Westmorland, where her father was a tanner. She married Isaac Wilson, a shearman dyer, shortly before her 21st birthday, and her daughter (the first of seven) was born three years later. In 1744 she began a nine-month journey through England and Wales on horseback with a female companion. She was acknowledged as a Quaker minister at 18 and traveled widely in Britain as a preacher before finally crossing the Atlantic in 1768: "I've almost hourly a distant shore before my view, as if my lot must be to visit the churches in America." She was away for 17 months, returning in December 1769. In 1774 her eldest daughter

died and her own health began to fail; confined to her house for four months, she made a temporary recovery, but she died during a visit to London.

Her American journal gives a detailed account of the people and places she encountered through her travels in the ministry. It also contains more topical passages, such as an exhortation against the slave trade in Philadelphia: "it never was intended for us to traffick with any part of the human species, and, if there were no buyers, there would be no sellers." Her letters home, like the journal, generally speak of good health, energetic yet comfortable traveling, and kind and accommodating companions. But there is also the occasional intrusion of self-doubt characteristic of Quakers: "I am too well acquainted with my own weakness & frailty to be set up with empty noise; it was never pleasant to be so popular, but hath often deeply humbled my mind and caused me to drop some tears." Selections from her journal and private letters were printed in John Somervell's *Isaac and Rachel Wilson, Quakers, of Kendal, 1714–85* (1924). While on her tour of America RW delivered "A Discourse on the Duties and Importance of Religion" at a Friends meetinghouse in Beekman's Precinct, Duchess County, N.Y. Her words were taken down in shorthand and published without her knowledge or permission by Solomon Southwick of Newport, R.I., in 1769. Her sermon is based on Isaiah 40:6–8: "All flesh is grass. . . ." Like many religious speakers, she relies on exhortation, repetition, and frequent recital of Scriptures. She uses simple words and no imagery. She is preoccupied with the connection between man's reason, morality, and God's revelation: the word of God is plain to every man who has the "light" of reason, and "since morality is founded upon that reason which is a common gift to mankind, every man must answer for the use of his reason." The tract was apparently quite popular in the U.S.: it was reprinted as late as 1792 in Dover, N.H.   R.J. and A.W.E.

WINCHILSEA, Anne Finch, Countess of (1661–1720), poet, dramatist, and fable writer, was born in Sidmonton, near Southampton, of an ancient and distinguished Hampshire family, in royal service since the 12th century. She was the third child of Sir William and Anne Haselwood Kingsmill. When C of W was five months old, her father died; the following year her mother married Sir Thomas Ogle of Suffolk, with whom she had a daughter, Dorothy. Her mother died in 1664 and Sir Thomas in 1671. Left without close adult relatives at the age of ten, C of W and her half-sister, Dorothy Ogle, became intimate companions, and this bond lasted until Dorothy died in 1712. (Dorothy became "Teresa" in the poems and C of W, "Ardelia.") As daughters of a prominent family, C of W and Dorothy became maids of honor: Dorothy to Princess Anne, and C of W to Mary of Modena, wife of James, Duke of York, who became King James II in 1685. In this service she met another maid of honor, the poet ANNE KILLIGREW, friend and inspiration of John Dryden. In 1683 C of W met Col. Heneage Finch, captain of the halbardiers and gentleman of the bedchamber to the Duke of York. Although he was a commoner, Finch was the oldest living son of the Earl of Winchilsea and uncle of the heir, and was thus held in high esteem at court. Finch's initial attentions to C of W were at first resisted, but the couple was eventually married in 1684. In 1685, C of W wrote in a poem that Finch's unfailing passion had found the way "To win a stubborn, and ungratefull heart," and he became her life's "Crown, and blessing." A model couple, though childless, they displayed mutual love and fidelity, and C of W often praised her husband for showing both the passion of a lover and the duty of a spouse, a combination not often found in Restoration court circles. They resided in London, and C of W resigned her position; Col. Finch increased his considerable prestige through the reign of James II, even serving a year in Parliament. When James yielded the throne in 1688, the Finches, loyal to the departing Stuarts, could not swear allegiance to William and Mary and spent the next two years in various temporary family residences. They finally settled in 1690 at Eastwell Park, Kent, at the ancestral home of Charles, the new Earl of Winchilsea and Col. Finch's nephew, who had invited his relatives to the splendid estate, giving the future Lord and Lady Winchilsea (following Charles's death in 1710) a haven from politics and the folly of court life. Here they lived 30 years, except for brief trips and winters in London. At Eastwell, C of W found the pastoral seclusion for reflective poetry, for formulating reasoned responses to nature, and for cultivating a detached satirical perspective resulting in a rational, constructive rather than cynically negative appraisal. Here she

nurtured lasting female friendships, sharing views in love, politics, and aesthetics. Among notable friends were the much-admired poet ELIZABETH ROWE, and members of illustrious Kent families—Thanet, Thynne, Twysden—several providing C of W with poetic personages. Sustained by an enthusiastic coterie, C of W developed a new court, although in self-exile the Finches had to temper their Stuart leanings. The main poetic subjects for C of W were not politics, but nature and the consciousness of women. As a Restoration woman daring to assert her writing among men, she worked quietly, circulating poems in manuscript, contributing to miscellanies, and not publishing her own volume until 1713. But she insisted that women could be acceptable writers in public, and more than mere sex objects in private. Eastwell provided the matrix for C of W, blessed by a happy marriage, to emerge as a poet befriended by such contemporaries as Pope and Swift and dedicated to giving women of her time an intelligent and sensitive voice.

All of C of W's works were written after 1685: nature and love poems, translations from Italian and French, reworkings of verse from Scripture, two verse dramas, and several each of Pindaric odes, satires, and fables. The only published volume, *Miscellany Poems on Several Occasions, Written by a Lady* (1713)—her name was added on the 1714 title page—contained 81 poems. The modern definitive edition (1903) lists 165 separate pieces, adding manuscript items and those from miscellanies. C of W's main theme is nature. William Wordsworth made an anthology of her verse and praised her nature imagery in his "Essay Supplementary to the Preface" (1815), describing "A Nocturnal Reverie" as the only poem between John Milton's *Paradise Lost* and James Thomsons' *The Seasons* to contain "a single new image of external nature." Although C of W was mostly concerned with reason and order in nature, she does foreshadow those honest and simple descriptive qualities which Wordsworth deemed essential in understanding the external world. Direct yet evocative images abound: "When in some River, overhung with Green, / The waving Moon and trembling Leaves are seen" ("A Nocturnal Reverie"); "Poets, wild as thee, were born, / Pleasing best when unconfin'd, / When to Please is least design'd" ("To the Nightingale"); "Where is that secret Sylvan seat, / That melancholy, sweet retreat, / From whence, thou doest these notes repell" ("To the Eccho"); "Gay as the spring, gay as the flowers, / When lightly strew'd with pearly showers" ("The Bird"); "The *Shepherd* here, from Scorching freed, / Tunes to thy dancing Leaves his Reed" ("The Tree"). The sylvan and rustic images, concentrated in the shorter poems, infuse and liven virtually all her works. Nature meant retirement, peace, and balance, as she describes in "The Petition for an Absolute Retreat": "A sweet, but absolute Retreat, / 'Mongst Paths so lost, and Trees so high, / That the World may ne'er invade, / Through such Windings and such Shade, / My unshaken Liberty."

C of W's second theme, the role of woman, can be viewed as part of the general rationality of the Augustan perspective. She was devoted to reason as the basis of her poetry of love and nature, and in her life in general. In reply to Restoration and Augustan male attitudes toward woman as sex object and mistress, C of W expressed the balanced view of the rare happy marriage, seeing Heneage Finch as "The much lov'd husband, of a happy wife" in "A Letter to Daphnis." Her poems were explicit statements of female love for the male, and attacked both the motif of sex over love as well as the constraint on women poets to avoid personal expressions of passion: "They err, who say that husbands can't be lovers. / With such return of passion, as is due, / Daphnis I love . . . / . . . my hopes, my joys, are bounded all in you." She also criticized the failings of her own sex. In "Ardelia's Answer to Ephelia," Ardelia is accosted and detained by a foolish boor, much in the manner of Rochester's "Timon." But the object of the satire is not a courtly male figure, but a typical frivolous and subservient Restoration woman. Courtly intrigues and pretensions are generally satirized, as is the sentimentality of later Restoration drama, C of W arguing that not frivolity but "sence and Nature shou'd be found in Plays." "The Spleen" (an ode, and the most famous of her poems in her lifetime) condemns the presumed restriction of women to the domestic arts, while arguing against melancholy; and in "The Introduction" to a manuscript edition of her poems, C of W denies that women should be occupied by "Good breeding, fashion, dancing, dressing, play," and that "To write, or read, or think, or to enquire / Wou'd cloud our beauty, and exaust our time." She chose to champion women's literary and social rights but did not become a public voice, accepting the reality that women were not allowed to speak out, having no elected or appointed forum. Her works were influential, nonetheless, as she was respected by notable literary and political people. C of W also emulated her contemporaries and earlier writers, reading widely and doing verse translations and paraphrasings from Scripture. She made direct adaptations of fables from Aesop and La Fontaine. A noteworthy fable, "The Atheist and the Acorn," uses a comic incident from nature and chance—a falling acorn—to justify the ways of God. She also wrote parodies and imitations. In "Fanscombe Barn," for example, she imitates, perhaps even in burlesque, Milton's blank verse. She borrowed classical themes from contemporaries, with "The Petition for an Absolute Retreat" owing much to John Pomfret's "The Choice" and Andrew Marvell's "The Garden." This eclectic tone in her works extends, finally, to the two blank verse dramas, which C of W acknowledged were imitative of those of KATHERINE PHILIPS, too imitative since they almost become parodies. *Love and Innocence* is filled with Shakespearean overtones: two sets of beseiged lovers in two concurrent plots, precisely drawn characters of good and evil, and seemingly disastrous circumstances from which everyone is saved by a *deus ex machina* resolution at the very end. Also in the classical dramatic tradition is *Aristomenes*, a heroic tragedy following the model of Nathaniel Lee and Thomas Otway, in which the typical historical character is brought steadily to a tragic end. The verse dramas are important as serious attempts in an area formerly closed to women writers and serve to round out the broad compass of C of W's efforts to gain recognition.

C of W had a modest circle of admirers in the early 18th century. Matthew Prior wrote a poem in her honor, Nicholas Rowe praised her on several occasions, and Swift in his visits to Charles Finch came to know her personally, speaking well of her often and writing of her in "Apollo Outwitted." Her relationship with Pope, 20 years her junior, is curious. He had praised "The Spleen," for which C of W was grateful, but afterward he became more generally critical. The exact details in the relationship are vague, but Pope was explicit at least once, when complaining that he became ill during an after-dinner reading by C of W of one of her plays. Less definite is an apparent unkind portrayal of C of W in the farce *Three Hours after Marriage*, originally attributed only to Pope but later accepted as a collaboration with John Arbuthnot and John Gay. C of W may be represented in the character of the much-mocked "learned lady" Phoebe Clinket, an inkstained writer constantly promoting her own works and character as author. The view of the woman writer as a pedant was what C of W struggled to dispel throughout her brief career, hoping to prove women viable, important voices.   L.M.J.M.

WINSLOW, Anna Green (1759–80), American diarist, was born in Nova Scotia, the daughter of Anna Green and Joshua Winslow, Commissary-General of the British forces. She was sent to school in Boston, where she kept a diary for her parents. Published in 1895 as the *Diary of Anna Green Winslow: A Boston School Girl of 1771*, it records a young girl's life of parties, clothes and domesticity, together with notes on sermons heard. There is advice to herself to think of death and a short poem of "humble thankfulness" to her parents for allowing her educational opportunities unavailable to "the vulgar."   J.T.

WISEMAN, Jane (fl. 1701), dramatist, rose from humble origins to see her first and, quite probably, only play, *Antiochus*, performed on the London stage. During her youth, JW was employed as a servant in the household of William Wright, Esq., Recorder of Oxford, whose library provided her with an opportunity to develop her literary interests. While a member of Wright's domestic staff, JW began writing the play that established her dramatic reputation. Her immediate background remains obscure, but it is known that JW left Wright to settle in London, where she continued her writing and married Holt, a vintner. With the profits from *Antiochus*, she and Holt set up a tavern in Westminster. The date of the premiere of *Antiochus* is unknown, but it was performed at Lincoln's Inn Fields in 1701, with subsequent productions in 1711, 1712, and 1721. It was published as *Antiochus the Great. A Tragedy. As it is now Acted at the New-Theatre in Lincolns-Inn-Fields. By His Majesty's Servants. Written by Mrs. Jane Wiseman* (1702). In the play's Epistle Dedicatory to Lord Jeffreys, JW reveals that *Antiochus* was more successful with theater-goers than with drama critics, who found it too slowly paced and wanting in character development. Like many women writers, JW was charged with false authorship: "The Language they [the critics] are unwilling to believe my own: and have chose one of our best Poets for my Assistant, one I had not the Happiness to know, 'till after the Play was finished." This charge may have been prompted by the fact that the play's prologue and epilogue were "Writ by a Friend." Might JW's "Assistant" and "Friend" have been Charles Gildon? In the play's text, JW identifies Gildon as the author of the Dialogue sung in Act III. The success of *Antiochus* is understandable. JW shrewdly exploited the most theatrically appealing features of 17th-century "heroic" drama, the affective excesses and "sentimentality" of contemporary pathetic drama, and the controversial themes of woman-centered or profeminine drama as written by MARY PIX and SUSANNA CENTLIVRE. The action of *Antiochus*, loosely adapted from historical facts, is the revenge of Leodice on King Antiochus Theos II who, having seduced her earlier, has not repudiated her. The theme of female distress is carried by the discarded Leodice, torn between revenge and lingering love for Antiochus, and Berenice, whose secret affair with an Egyptian prince brings her more guilt than joy. The play's feminism derives from such themes as the sorry results of the arranged marriage between Antiochus and Berenice; the woman-centered nature of the play, which turns on the "manly" strength of Leodice; and the play's secondary moral, announced in the epilogue, "A Husband's Wrongs are always paid in kind; / Mens Stratagems but small Advantage get, / And injur'd Women seldom die in Debt." *Antiochus* is didactic and cautionary: all evil-doers, including Leodice, are eventually exposed and punished. Berenice, although an adulteress, is spared because she vindicates herself at the end of the play with a display of remorse and magnanimity.   M.M.

WISTER, Sarah [Sally] (1761–1804), American diarist, was born to a distinguished Philadelphia family in the house on High Street built by her grandfather, Johann Wüster, in 1744, after he became a prosperous wine merchant. SW's father, Daniel, simplified his name to Wister. SW's mother, Lowry Jones, was descended from Dr. Edward Jones, who came from Wales in 1682; her great-grandmother had been the daughter of Dr. Thomas Wynne, speaker of the first Pennsylvania Assembly. SW was educated with the daughters of the first families of Philadelphia, including DEBORAH NORRIS LOGAN. Their schoolmaster was the well-known Quaker Anthony Benezet. SW studied French, Latin, and English literature. She often quotes poetry, and occasionally published some of her own verses in the *Port Folio*. *Sally Wister's Journal, a true narrative; being a Quaker maiden's account of her experiences with officers of the Continental army, 1777–1778* (1902) was begun as a sort of letter to her friend, Deborah Norris [Logan]. The Wister family had moved to a farm 15 miles outside Philadelphia when the Revolutionary War began. In September 1777, when the British entered Germantown, she began her journal account of the daily events. In lively auditory images, she contrasts the sounds of the country, where she is waiting out the war, with the city sounds she misses—"the rattling of carriages of the streets—harsh music, tho' preferable to croaking frogs and screeching owls." The 16-year-old author presents a naive and frank account of what it felt like to be "surrounded by an army, the house full of soldiers, the yard alive with soldiers." She tries to come to terms with her ambivalent feelings toward them, noting that they "eat and talk like other folks." The insistence with which she assures herself betrays the strength of the opposite feelings: "So I will not be afraid of them, that I won't."   R.R.

WOLLSTONECRAFT, Mary (1759–97), polemical writer and novelist, was born in London, the second of seven children. Her grandfather was a prosperous weaver, whose wealth allowed his son to become a gentleman farmer. At this occupation he was unsuccessful, and the family moved frequently within England and Wales during MW's childhood. Between the ages of 9 and 15 she lived in Beverley, Yorks., where she gained some education and formed a close friendship with Jane Arden. During these years of declining fortune, her father's temper soured and MW became angered over the importance allowed to the eldest son, who, she felt, was given educational opportunities denied the rest of the family. At 16 when living in Hoxton near London, MW met Fanny Blood, an accomplished young woman from a poor family. MW was much impressed by her, and the two girls formed a plan of living and working together. This deep friendship was alluded to lovingly in late works and in the naming of MW's first child; it is anatomized more

sternly in MW's first novel, *Mary, A Fiction* (1788), where Fanny Blood's weakness of character is criticized. At 19 MW, in a bid for independence, became a companion to a wealthy widow in Bath; in this situation she bitterly noted fashionable life and struggled to maintain both the proper subservience and her own self-respect. In 1781 she was called home, now at Enfield, to care for her sick mother; after her mother died, MW felt responsible for the younger children and, through most of her life, she caringly, if sometimes heavy-handedly, promoted their welfare. At this time she moved in with Fanny Blood and her family, and helped with needlework in the daily struggle against poverty. Her stay was interrupted again by her own family, when, in a postnatal depression, her sister Eliza summoned her. Interpreting the situation as male tyranny, MW dramatically abducted Eliza from her husband and baby, knowing full well the social consequences for herself, if not the emotional ones for her sister: "I knew I should be . . . the *shameful incendiary* in this shocking affair of a woman's leaving her bed-fellow." She established her sister in secret lodgings and then planned, with Fanny Blood and later another sister, to open a school. In 1784 they chose Newington Green for their school; it contained a community of intellectual Dissenters, including the famous polemicist, Richard Price. The school prospered in a small way, until MW left for Portugal in 1785 to attend Fanny Blood who, long consumptive, had married and become pregnant. After Fanny Blood died she returned to England in 1786 to find her school foundering. To gain money she wrote a book on educating girls, *Thoughts on the Education of Daughters*, published by Joseph Johnson in 1787. The work earned her 10 guineas, which she gave to the Bloods. In the same year she became a governess to the daughters of Lord and Lady Kingsborough in Ireland, a life about which she had few illusions: "A governess to young ladies is . . . disagreeable. It is ten to one if they meet with a reasonable mother. . . . The children treat them with disrespect, and often with insolence. In the mean time life glides away, and the spirits with it." During her uncomfortable time with the Kingsboroughs, she wrote *Mary, A Fiction,* a self-pitying account of her childhood and friendship with Fanny Blood. Dismissed by Lady Kingsborough in 1787, she resolved to be a writer, "the first of a new genus," she excitedly thought, and she moved to

London to work for Joseph Johnson as translator and reader and later as reviewer and editorial assistant on the *Analytical Review*, a new liberal journal. He introduced MW to his political friends in London, Thomas Paine, Henry Fuseli, William Blake, and William Godwin. Between 1787 and 1790 she wrote two books for children, *Original Stories from Real Life; with Conversations, Calculated to Regulate the Affections, and Form the Mind to Truth and Goodness* and *The Female Reader*, a book of reading passages for girls; she translated Jacques Necker's *Of the Importance of Religious Opinions* and Christian Gotthilf Salzmann's *Elements of Morality for the Use of Children*; she reviewed novels, travel books, and educational treatises. A study of all these works suggests a radicalizing of her views during the early London years and, by the time Edmund Burke attacked both these views and her friend Richard Price in *Reflections on the Revolution in France*, she was ready to articulate them clearly. Her reply to Burke, the first of many, appeared in 1790, entitled *A Vindication of the Rights of Men*; in it she argued against satisfaction with British society and noted the trivialization of women within it. The latter was her theme again in her next book, *A Vindication of the Rights of Woman* (1792), a work growing from her own experience and from her appreciation of CATHERINE MACAULAY's *Letters on Education*, reviewed in 1790. *The Rights of Woman*, arguing for female education, was dedicated to Talleyrand, whose plan for French education MW wished to influence. While writing this work, she had become obsessed with the married Swiss painter and philosopher Fuseli and, after a period of frustration, she proposed living with his family. Rejected, she set off alone for revolutionary France in 1792, her sister commenting somewhat spitefully, "So the author of the Rights of Women is going to France . . . in spite of Reason, when Mrs W reaches the Continent she will be but a woman."

MW arrived in Paris in time to see the King passing to his trial, and her first experiences of the Revolution upset her positive views. "Letter on the Present Character of the French Nation" revealed her disillusion with perfectibility and her fear that vice and evil provoked action. In time, however, she managed to achieve a more balanced view. Her history of the early Revolution, written in 1792–93, *An His-*

torical and Moral View of the Origin and Progress of the French Revolution (1794), condemns many of the events of the Revolution, while holding to its underlying principles. MW became friends with the liberal faction of the Revolution, the Girondists; she met HELEN MARIA WILLIAMS, whose work she admired, and renewed friendship with Paine. In this circle she encountered an American author and commercial speculator, Gilbert Imlay, who soon succeeded Fuseli in her affections. In the difficult and lonely months that followed she grew obsessively fond of Imlay, whose love waned as her dependence grew. When foreigners were ordered from Paris, she moved to a small village outside and met Imlay at intervals. To prevent her imprisonment as an Englishwoman, he registered her as his wife. When Imlay left Paris for Le Havre, MW followed him; there in 1794 Fanny Imlay was born. MW's love letters to Imlay, published posthumously, chart the disintegration of the affair and show MW aware of her own and Imlay's weaknesses. Early in 1795, she returned to England where Imlay was staying. Learning of his infidelity, she attempted suicide, failed, and agreed to go with her baby and nursemaid as Imlay's business representative to Scandinavia. She set off mournfully, "I never forget . . . the misery." Her journey through Scandinavia is well described in her *Letters Written during a Short Residence in Sweden, Norway, and Denmark* (1796), which, along with the private letters to Imlay, describes her views on Scandinavia and traces her emotional odyssey. Denied the meeting she had been promised by Imlay on her return and informed of further infidelities, she threw herself into the Thames in late 1795. She was rescued unconscious. Her feelings for Imlay remained strong, although she composed many letters of parting, the final known one being in 1796 when she wrote, "I part with you in peace."

Determining to make a new life, MW reasserted herself as an author and began reviewing again. She renewed acquaintance with other writers, including MARY HAYS, at whose house she remet Godwin, now the successful author of *Political Justice*. Of the relationship, Godwin wrote in his *Memoirs*, "There was . . . no period of throes and resolute explanation attendant on the tale. It was friendship melting into love." Although it had its difficulties, the relationship with Godwin was calm after the obsessive passion of the past years and, with his encouragement, MW began her last novel, *The Wrongs of Woman, or Maria*, a work which, in describing the legal oppression of the middle-class woman and the total oppression of the lower, is in many ways a sequel to her earlier feminist work. When MW became pregnant, she and Godwin were married, an act ridiculed by those remembering Godwin's opposition to marriage and condemned by those who now realized MW's earlier unmarried state and who heard of their unconventional plan of living separately. In 1797 MW gave birth to a daughter, who would become Mary Shelley; eleven days later she died. In the following year, Godwin published his frank *Memoirs* of his wife, describing her affair with Imlay, an action which much shocked contemporaries; at the same time, he issued her *Posthumous Works*, which included the letters to Imlay, an autobiographical fictional fragment, "The Cave of Fancy," and the unfinished *Wrongs of Woman*. By this time conservative reaction in England had modified the earlier, often favorable opinion of MW, and she was much attacked as an unsexed woman and a licentious corrupter of female morals, whose books aimed, in the words of the *Anti-Jacobin Review*, at the propagation of whores.

MW's works are almost all concerned with education. *Thoughts* showed her early dissatisfied with the status of women, although her Christian emphasis urged acceptance of much she later condemned. "I wish them to be taught to think," she wrote of girls. *Original Stories* reiterates her Lockean view, that the years of childhood are extremely important for the creation of character; the girls she describes are taught the virtues, especially of benevolence and patience, through stories and exemplary situations. Her two *Vindications* show a shift from emphasis on female submission to one on reason as the basis of morality. *The Rights of Men* argues against "the demon of property" that creates privilege and injustice and against primogeniture. This work, in MW's digressive and often exaggerated style, has powerful rhetorical moments: "Why is our fancy to be appalled by terrific perspectives of a hell beyond the grave?—Hell stalks abroad;—the lash resounds on the slave's naked sides; and the sick wretch, who can no longer earn the sour bread of unremitting labour, steals to a ditch to bid the world a long good night— or, neglected in some ostentatious hospital, breathes his last amidst the laugh of mer-

cenary attendants. / Such misery demands more than tears." *A Vindication of the Rights of Woman*, her most famous work, aims, like her first book, to make women think, but it goes far beyond it in passionate argument for women's rights and for the opportunity to prove themselves intellectually equal to men. "It is time to effect a revolution in female manners—time to restore to them their lost dignity." MW's history, *The French Revolution*, represents a struggle to align ideology and impression; concerning only the early events of 1789, it was written in the violent Jacobin period of 1793 and 1794 and shows MW trying to subsume the distasteful aspects into a general view of final good. The disintegrating relationship with the trader Imlay may have influenced its fulminations against brutalizing commerce. *Letters Written . . . in Sweden*, perhaps her most successful work in its mingling of personal and political, describes the influence of governmental systems on the three Scandinavian countries and records MW's own response to scenery, her sadness, and her love for her daughter: "I feel more than a mother's fondness and anxiety, when I reflect on the dependent and oppressed state of her sex. I dread lest she should be forced to sacrifice her heart to her principles, or principles to her heart." The novels are shot through with autobiography: *Mary, A Fiction* presents an idealized view of MW as benevolent and sensitive child and reveals too her sexual fears and longings. *The Wrongs of Woman*, in the character of Maria, takes stock of the mistakes of the Imlay affair but goes beyond autobiography in its sympathetic depiction of the lower-class servant and prostitute, Jemima.

Throughout her life MW was a prolific letter writer, and her two series of letters to Imlay and Godwin have been edited as separate books. The former, ringing the changes of joy, loneliness, and misery, much moved Godwin, who called the letters "offspring of a glowing imagination, and a heart, penetrated with the passion it essays to describe." The letters to Godwin are milder but add a note of happy domesticity: "A husband is a convenient part of the furniture of a house." By the end of her life, MW was aware of the exposed position her unconventional acts had given her but sure of the feminist propositions she had been struggling to advance through most of her writing career. "All the world is a stage, thought I," she wrote in her last published work, "and few are there in it who do not play the part they have learnt by rote; and those who do not, seem marks set up to be pelted at by fortune; or rather as signposts, which point out the road to others." J.T.

WOOD, Sally [Sarah] (1759–1855), American novelist, was born at the home of her maternal grandfather, Judge Jonathan Sayward, in York, Maine (then in Mass.), while her father, Nathaniel Barrell, member of a successful merchant family of Portsmouth, was serving as a lieutenant in the British army in Quebec. SW was the eldest of 11 children and lived with her grandfather until she married Richard Keating, one of her grandfather's clerks, in 1778. They had two daughters before Keating's death in 1783; a son was born four months later. During the next 21 years SW turned to writing as a means of financial support, and she published four novels under pseudonyms. She was very defensive of her employment as a writer, and in the preface of her second book stated "that not one social, or domestic duty, have ever been sacrificed or postponed by her pen." Her privileged upbringing had given her the social background necessary for the accurate portrayal of the culture and milieu found in her books. In 1804 SW married Gen. Abiel Wood, a wealthy widower of Wiscasset, Maine. He died in 1811, leaving her in affluence. At this time she moved to Portland to be nearer her son, Capt. Richard Keating. There in 1827 her final publication was made. In Portland, "Madam Wood," as she was known in social circles, was regarded as a celebrity because of her literary efforts. In 1830 she moved to New York to live with her son, who drowned in 1833. After his death she returned to Maine and lived with her widowed granddaughter in Kennebunk, where she died at 95.

During her 21 years of widowhood SW wrote four novels. Her first, *Julia, and the Illuminated Baron* (1800), was "founded on recent facts, which have transpired in the course of the late revolution of moral principles in France." The second, *Dorval; or, the Speculator* (1801), was a sentimental tale intended to illuminate "the evils which have arisen from speculation, and which have fallen upon the virtuous and the good as well as the wicked." *Amelia; or, the Influence of Virtue, an Old Man's Story* (1802) and *Ferdinand and Elmira: a Russian Story* (1804) followed. *Tales of the Night* (1827) was her last published work.

This book, containing two narratives, relies heavily upon improbable sentimental plots, as did her four previous books. The first narrative, "Storms and Sunshine; or the House on the Hill," involves the return to prosperity of a family which underwent sudden financial disaster. The second, "The Hermitage," portrays the happy reunion of two lovers after an intervening period of separation and unhappy marriage. In the preface to this book, SW stated that this was to be the first of two volumes, yet no second volume ever appeared. It is alleged that she attempted to destroy her manuscripts in dissatisfaction with her own work after reading a novel by Walter Scott. SW's works have been compared with those of ANN RADCLIFFE and may be characterized as sentimental morality tales, based on overworked and improbable plots with little originality or literary distinction. Her overt moralizing tends toward didacticism: "Love has a variety of attributes: it teaches cunning to the artless, and instills deception in to the frankest bosoms." Nonetheless, her situation as a writer is significant as an early example of a common pattern: she first wrote out of financial necessity, owing to the exclusion of women from other professions, and she rigorously defended writing as an occupation for women. She insisted on cultivating native literary talents rather than relying upon European sources: "If a small share of [our wasted] time were attached to the pen, I am certain no further author would agree with Abbe Raynal, 'That America had produced but few persons of genius.' Envy would be banished from society; and while a woman was drawing a picture of virtue and amiableness from imagination, she would imperceptibly follow the example and copy the portrait." G.D.G.

WOODFIN, Mrs. A. (fl. 1756–65), novelist, operated a school in Bullen Court in the Stand around 1763. Whether she chose to give up writing in favor of her school (as one reviewer suggested she do) is uncertain, but her last book was published in 1765. Contemporary reviewers commented on the mystery of her origins and background. *Monthly Review* (October 1756) was noncommittal in its reaction to AW's first novel, *Northern Memoirs, or the History of a Scotch Family* (1756), published anonymously: "If it affords no indications of genius, it shews no want of invention; and if the incidents are not very affecting, they are more natural and probable, than those with which most of our late adventure-books have been stuffed." *Critical Review* (December 1756) considered the work "natural, pleasing, and in some measure affecting. [It has] more merit than the common run of such pieces." Praise for AW's later novels was less forthcoming; she was often referred to as a "mediocre" novelist. AW's fiction is interesting as an indication of contemporary literary fashions. For example, the theme of incest is crucial to the plot of *History of Sally Sable* (1765), a theme probably traceable to the work of Prévost. Marivaux was also an influence. AW deals with a variety of social issues: recurring topics include the treatment of orphans, religious conversion, poverty, and adultery. A characteristic of her work is that men who have done wrong usually meet unpleasant ends, whereas women experience moral and social regeneration. AW's other novels are *The History of Miss Harriet Watson* (1762); *The Auction* (1763?), in which her characters discuss a current production of Aaron Hill's drama, "Zara"; and *The Discovery, or the History of Miss Marian Middleton* (1764).   P.D.L.

WOOLLEY [Wolley, or Woolly], Hannah (1623?–?; fl. 1670), writer of works on domestic science, was orphaned by both parents at an early age; her maiden name is unknown. Although she claims to have had scant education, she became sole mistress at 15 of a small school, where she taught for two years. A gentlewoman of the neighborhood then took her into the household as governess to the family's only daughter. Already having acquired some knowledge of "Physick and Chirurgery" from her mother and elder sisters, a smattering of Italian, and some skill at singing and dancing, she now learned much about domestic crafts, household management, and manners, and was introduced at court. After the death of her first patroness, she became governess in another family and soon became in turn her lady's waiting woman, stewardess, and secretary. By this time she had learned French and was reading widely in poetry, plays, and romances. In 1647 she married a schoolmaster named Woolley and lived happily with him at Newport, Essex, for about seven years and then at Hackney, near London, managing the domestic affairs of his boarding school. Widowed by Woolley, to whom she had borne four sons, in 1666 she married Francis Challinor (or Chaloner), a widower of 45, who also died a few years laters. By 1674

she was making and selling medicines at the London home of her son Richard Woolley and operating there a registry and training school for servants.

Beginning probably in her first widowhood, HW wrote and published several books of recipes, among them *The Cook's Guide* (1661) and *The Ladies' Directory* (1662). In 1671 she published her most successful work, *The Queen-like Closet*, a book of recipes and domestic advice that ran through five editions. This and *The Gentlewoman's Companion*, a combined cookbook and treatise on social behavior that was published in 1675 in an unsatisfactory editon and later revised and retitled *The Ladies' Guide*, are her two most significant works. The *Gentlewoman's Companion* is valuable for the insights it provides into female life during the Restoration. HW's aim was to prepare young women of good family for the possible reality of supporting themselves as domestic servants. She opens the work lamenting that female education is neglected, condemning "the great negligence of Parents, in letting the fertile Ground of their Daughters lie fallow, yet send[ing] the barren Noddles of their sons to the University." The book is a manual of advice urging women not to rebel against parents and husbands, but to become useful in the skills of domestic management, without which they "render themselves insignificant." Replete with advice about the duties and deportment appropriate to various sorts of domestic position, and containing pages of menus, recipes, and formulas for home remedies, some borrowed from other books but most of them her own, it is laced with autobiographical anecdotes that give the instruction credibility. In her books, HW proffers hope for oppressed women that study, hard work, and integrity can make them self-sufficient.   D.W.M.

WRIGHT, Mehetabel [Hetty] (1697–1750), poet, was the clever and pretty daughter of a remarkable mother, SUSANNA WESLEY. She received the same education as her famous brothers. By the age of six she read the Bible in Greek; at 27 she eloped with a lawyer, only to return the next day. Her father made her marry a drunken plumber, William Wright, "a man in no desirable rank of life, of coarse mind and manners, inferior to herself in education and in intellect, and every way unworthy of a woman whose equal in all things it would have been difficult to find." Although she was dutiful and affectionate to the "miserable creature whom she had made her husband, the brutal profligacy of his conduct almost broke her heart," wrote Robert Southey. Children miscarried or died, probably becaue of the lead boiling constantly at the back of the house. Her brothers visited her occasionally and eventually converted her to Methodism. MW gained a considerable reputation for her poems, some of which were printed in the *Gentleman's Magazine* (March and Dec. 1736), in Fawkes and Woty's *Poetical Calendar* (1763), and in the *Arminian Magazine*, 1778. Dr. Adam Clarke printed ten in his *Memoirs*: see also *The Bards of Epworth: or Poetic Gems from the Wesley Cabinet* (1856). Her longest and most accomplished poem, *Eupolis, a Hymn to the Creator*, John Wesley claimed to be her father's. The *DNB* is firm that it is hers because it is largely in her hand, and because of its "superiority to Wesley's other verse." MW receives scant mention in the Wesley biographies, but Southey and Quiller-Couch stand indignant champions of the woman who is a perfect example of Virginia Woolf's "Shakespeare's sister." Her poems, "tho' of a melancholy cast," as John Duncombe says (*The Feminiad,* 1754), "are wrote in a genuine spirit of poetry." She ends "A Mother's Address to her Dying Infant" thus: "Drooping Sweetness! verdant Flow'r! / Blooming, withering in an hour! / E're thy gentle Breast sustains / Latest, fiercest, mortal Pains, / Hear a Suppliant! Let me be / Partner in thy Destiny!" J.H.

WRIGHT, Susanna (1697–1784), American poet, was born into the Quaker family of John Wright and Patience Gibson. She seems to have received a good education in England before emigrating to America, since she knew French, Italian, Latin, and natural philosophy. By 1714 the family was living in Chester, Penna., where her father was a shopkeeper. Her mother died in 1722, and SW became responsible for the seven younger children. By 1728 they were in Wright's Ferry, on the Pennsylvania frontier. After 1745 SW lived with her brother and family in an estate nearby, willed to her for life by Samuel Blunston, a man to whom she had not been married but who is said to have courted her. SW had an active and curious mind and was famous for her witty replies. She experimented with medicinal herbs and the cultivation of silkworms, and was interested in the cause of the Indian tribes. She read widely and corresponded with Benjamin Franklin, as well as with ELIZABETH GRAEME FERGUSON, DEBORAH NORRIS LOGAN, and HANNAH GRIFFITTS, with whom she formed a poetic network. Her occasional pieces circulated among friends, but only two MS poems seem to have survived. Always a Quaker, she gave her life and feelings religious interpretation. An anonymous biographical sketch of SW in "Some Account of the Early Poets and Poetry of Pennsylvania" is probably by Logan; the poems and letters are in the Historical Society of Pennsylvania. SW's 1737 poem "On the Death of a Young Girl" in ballad stanza is a competent elegy on a child, called "the poppet" and "the small machine," in which death is given inevitability by the natural imagery: "Flowers on thy breast, and round thy head, / With thee their sweets resign, / Nipp'd from their tender stalks, and dead, / Their fate resembles thine." The second work is a birthday poem of 1761, which sees "a vision all the past, / A bubble on the water's shining face." It is a melancholy poem, asserting the sad events of SW's life, the death of her brother, of "a darling child, all lovely, all admir'd," and of a sister "who long causeless anguish knew." With such sadness, she feels that, however many years she may live, "The starting tear stands ready to descend." Her only comfort is in "The Savior, friend of man." J.T.

Y

YEARSLEY, Ann [Cromartie] (1752–1806), poet and novelist known as "Lactilla" or "the poetical milkwoman," was born in Clifton, near Bristol, to working-class parents. Following her mother's calling, she delivered milk from door to door and acquired only the most rudimentary education. AY married in 1774 and bore six children in rapid succession. During the summer of 1784 she aroused the zealous and energetic compassion of HANNAH MORE, whose cook brought to her attention the pathetic plight of the milkwoman whose family had been rescued from veritable starvation earlier that year. More read some of AY's verses, presented her with a few basic texts on grammar and spelling and, by her own estimation, spent the better part of 13 months and more than 1,000 pages editing AY's poetry and obtaining subscriptions. The first edition of *Poems on Several Occasions* (1784) brought in £350, and subsequent editions carried the total to £600. More and ELIZABETH MONTAGU invested the money and appointed themselves joint trustees. An acrimonious quarrel ensued, carried on in print as well as in private, in which AY accused her patron of ruining her poems and demanded the right to control her own money. More finally acceded, comforting herself that, although she had been the victim of an ingrate, AY's conduct should not harden her heart against others in want. AY opened an unsuccessful circulating library at Bristol Hot Wells, published three more volumes of poetry, an unfinished historical novel, an unsuccessful tragedy, and several occasional poems. Despite her limited education, her poetry is highly derivative, remarkable primarily for its sustained note of self-pity, as AY gloried in the role assigned by her erstwhile Bluestocking patrons, "Lactilla" the natural genius deprived of cultivation by cruel circumstances. She refers to herself in a dedicatory letter to the Earl of Bristol as "unadorned by art, unaccomplished by science" and complacently describes her poems as having been written "in the short intervals of a life of labour, and under every disadvantage which can possibly result from a confined education." She died in obscurity in Melksham, Wilts.

Although she wrote a novel (*The Royal Captives: A Fragment of Secret History,* 4 vols., 1795) and a play (*Earl Goodwin,* performed 1789, published 1791), AY's reputation must rest on her poetry. Most of the works in *Poems on Several Occasions* (1784), *Poems on Various Subjects* (1787), and *The Rural Lyre* (1796) are occasional, commemorative, or meditative lyrics, replete with the formulaic personifications, apostrophes, and conventional figures of inferior 18th-century verse and occasionally enriched by a lugubrious sprinkling of classical allusions. Sometimes the syntax defies sense. She wrote her best poetry in simple metrical and stanzaic forms, usually in a narrative where the sequence of events imposed some structural discipline. Occasionally she demonstrates a sensitive ear: "and here I'll stand / Till Time shall roll his thousand worlds, in rage, / Down vast Eternity: in that loud hour, / When Nature throws her dark foundations up / To meet the liquid skies."

Given the circumstances of her life, it is not surprising that AY dwelt much upon death and the vanity of human wishes. She prayed in verse for resignation to God's will, and most of her elegies offer consolation based on belief in the soul's union with God and loved ones on a conventional "happier shore." Important personages, such as the Dowager Duchess of Portland, ascend to heaven amid much pomp and circumstance, while lesser mortals must rest content with the assurance that they share a universal mortality. AY frequently hoped for spiritual serenity achieved through faith and contemplation, but her own restless thoughts and speculations on the nature of consciousness frightened her. The preoccupation with death is accompanied by a pervasive tone of melancholy, and one volume is even entitled *Stanzas of Woe* (1790). But life offered some consolations to AY. She asserted the value of friendship above all earthly things, and many of her poems extol its glories. This preoccupation probably derived from the quarrel with Hannah More and the disillusion the poet claims to have suffered. Friendship is the "social angel" and must not be confused with the relationship between dependent and superior which instills only a sense of obligation. Friendship at its best brings poetic inspiration. AY vehemently defended herself against charges of ingratitude, and decried the "crafty lip" that would profane friendship with "guilty blandishments." AY also found happiness, if not great poetry, in motherhood: "Delicious toil! raptures that never cloy! / A mother only can define her joy." Her concept of woman's proper role was conventional; it is the mother's duty to nurse her child and to satisfy its quest for knowledge: "No! whilst our heroes from their homes retire / We'll nurse the infant, and lament the fire." In a relatively successful poem, "On Jephthah's Vow," she conveys a strong mixture of revulsion and sympathy for the father who exchanged his daughter's life for victory in battle. The conventional attitude toward parenthood, however, was not matched by a glorification of marriage. In "Lucy, A Tale for the Ladies" she argues that the world conspires against marriage for love. Women are thus subject to tyrannical husbands—"Hard lesson—yet, dear girl, 'tis true / For marriage rights are very few."—but men also suffer from the superficial preferences of women. AY descanted upon public events. Her politics appear to be both conservative and humanitarian. In the ode on "The Genius of England" she exhorts "Women and men, my family of Britons / Deface not Order!" In the "Bristol Elegy" she sentimentally mourns the murder by soldiers of some 200 people demonstrating against the reimposition of bridge tolls. In her "Poem on the Inhumanity of the Slave Trade" (1788) she humanizes diatribe with narrative. The villains here are the "crafty merchants," and the argument turns on the evils of slavery as a disruption of domestic ties. The poem concludes with an invocation to "social love! true soul of *order*," the matrix of justice and humanity. This "social love" is basically the power of the sympathetic imagination to "touch the soul of man; / Subdue him; / make a fellow-creature's woe / His own by heart-felt sympathy." AY also wrote topical poems entitled "Reflections on the Death of Louis XVI" (1793) and "An Elegy on Marie Antoinette" (1795).

Her contemporaries assessed AY as a "natural" poet, and their judgment is usually tempered by compassion. Before they quarreled, More praised her perfect ear and freedom from incongruous metaphors, although she acknowledged problems of redundancy and obscurity. Horace Walpole extolled "the dignity of her thoughts and the chastity of her style" but wisely suggested she stay away from blank verse. Joseph Cottle, who helped AY out of financial difficulties in 1793, found in her a "sound masculine understanding" and "the unequivocal marks of genius." Southey's praise was more moderate: "Ann Yearsley, though gifted with voice, had no strain of her own whereby to be remembered, but she was no mocking bird."   J.R.

YOUNG, Mary Julia (?–1821), novelist and poet, was a relative of the poet Edward Young and daughter of Sir William Young, Bart. She began her writing career with poetry, apparently while quite young; her first published volumes are signed simply "By a Young Lady." MJY married the Rev. George Sewell, rector of Byfleet, Surrey, where they lived in the abbey house until he died in 1801. As a widow she seems to have retired to Chertsey, the place given on her title pages after 1801 and where she died. It was apparently from Byfleet that she began writing novels; 11 were published, all under her maiden name. As Mrs. George Sewell she turned again to poetry after the death of her husband. Three volumes of *Poems and Essays* appeared between 1803 and 1808. Each is prefaced by a long list of notable subscribers, headed by the Duchess of York; from her seat at Oatlands Park, the Duchess was an active supporter of the arts in Surrey and seems to have given special encouragement to MJY. Indeed, the author prefaces the third volume of *Poems* with "the most animated tribute of thanks" to the Duchess, who patronized her work "in a manner so peculiarly benevolent as the warmest and most sanguine expectation could never have aspired to!"

MJY's earliest works, those "By a Young Lady," are romantic narrative poems: "Horatio and Amanda" (1777), "Innocence" (1790), and "Genius and Fancy" (1791). By 1793 when she wrote "Adelaide and Antoine," also a romantic narrative poem, she was signing her work. These lines from the last are characteristic: "There—true religion's temple stands, / At various altars millions bend; / O'er all—her heav'nly radiance beams, / O'er all—her fost'ring arms extend." Such a style also marks her later poetic work, *Poems and Essays,* of which the *Monthly Review* kindly remarked, "If there be nothing peculiarly striking nor animated in these poems, they possess a softness and sensibility which, without fascinating the reader's imagination, conciliate it and win his approbation." The reviewers did find, however, that the "frequent repetition of the interjection 'oh!'—'oh! thou' fatigues the ear." The bulk of MJY's published works are conventional popular novels, many published by the Minerva Press; they are often subtitled "a pathetic tale," "a mysterious tale," or "a romantic story." Titles include *The East Indian* (1799), *Ragamount Castle* (1789), *Lindorf and Caroline* (1803), *Moss Cliff Abbey* (1803), *Right and Wrong* (1803), *The Mother and Daughter* (1804), *Donatan* (1805), *A Summer at Brighton* (1807), *A Summer at Weymouth* (1808), *The Heir of Drumiondra* (1810), and *Lenora* (?). MJY also attempted nonfiction. In *Voltairiana* (1805), she selected and translated short pieces, letters, quotations, and memorabilia of Voltaire, and in *Memoirs of Mrs. Crouch* (1806) she chronicled the life of a contemporary actress. Biography, however, proved not to be her forte; *MR* found the latter work "scarcely superior to a series of playbills and newspaper stage criticisms."   G. B.-K.

YOUNG, Sarah (fl. 1757–90), religious biographer, was born, probably into a well-to-do family, in Bristol, where she lived most of her life. In 1757, when she was apparently in her teens or early twenties, she met Rebecca Scudamore, the wife of Counsellor Scudamore of Bristol, who introduced her into society. On a vacation to Weymouth with Mrs. Scudamore in 1759, SY was "entirely won over to the side of religion" by the example of Mrs. Scudamore's devotion to prayer and Christ. Upon returning to Bristol, SY and Mrs. Scudamore found their former fashionable world unacceptable, and shortly afterward SY departed for Oxfordshire, intent on living a more ascetic life. She felt she had failed at this during her six years in Oxfordshire, and in 1765 returned to Bristol. Forsaking worldly friendships and even the company of Mrs. Scudamore, she spent the next two years in retirement, reading William Law's *Spirit of Prayer* and *Spirit of Love* and trying to rejuvenate her religious life. In 1767, SY and Mrs. Scudamore met again. By this time they were firmly grounded in their Christian faith and, as SY states, "they became of one heart and of one mind." They decided to become active members of the Church of England and to do charitable work in Bristol. In 1771, Counsellor Scudamore asked his wife to leave his household; Mrs. Scudamore moved in with SY and lived with her for a year. In 1772, Mrs. Scudamore moved to Kingsdown, but she remained close to SY until her own death in 1790. Shortly afterward, SY decided that something should be written about Mrs. Scudamore's "exemplary and uncommon" life. In 1790 she published *Some Particulars, Relating To The Life and Death, of Rebecca Scudamore* in Bristol. This is probably the only work SY ever published, a brief mixture of the biographical, autobiographical, devotional and epistolary, focusing on Mrs. Scudamore as a model of the Christian life: "She also recommended my appropriating two hours everyday, at such seasons as were most convenient, for waiting upon God in silent prayer; also to read the scriptures, and other books, that might inculcate, promote, and tend to the keeping of God in all my thoughts."   J.G.

Index

Anna Seward

Mary Delany

Anna Maria Van Schurman

Anne Finch,
Countess of Winchilsea

Clara Reeve

Elizabeth Griffith

Elizabeth Hamilton

Priscilla Wakefield

Eliza Haywood